The Politics of Globalization

A Reader

The Politics of Globalization

A Reader

Mark Kesselman
Columbia University

Houghton Mifflin Company Boston New York

For Rob Borsellino, brother-in-law,
brother, soul-mate, inspiration

Publisher: Charles Hartford
Sponsoring Editor: Katherine Meisenheimer
Senior Development Editor: Jeffrey Greene
Editorial Assistant: Kristen Craib
Project Editor: Nan Lewis-Schulz
Editorial Assistant: Brett Pasinella
Senior Art and Design Coordinator: Jill Haber
Executive Marketing Manager: Nicola Poser
Marketing Associate: Kathleen Mellon

Typographical errors in the original published versions of readings have been corrected in the versions excerpted here.

Cover image: Cover photograph © by Suril Malhotra for Reuters/CORBIS

Printed in the U.S.A.

Library of Congress Control Number: 2006922673

ISBN: 0-618-39599-7

123456789-EB-10 09 08 07 06

Contents

PREFACE

Until a few years ago, it would have been difficult locating sufficient material to include in an anthology of readings on globalization. The dilemma is now the opposite: how to limit the number of excellent readings in *The Politics of Globalization* (hereafter: PG) to keep the book to a manageable length.

Readings in PG vary from the detached and scholarly to the passionate and politically engaged. By roaming widely, this reader aims to convey the richness of reflections on globalization. Included are many of the best-known and most influential scholarly discussions about globalization, although the constraints of space have required difficult choices. Also included are selections from lesser-known sources, to highlight important issues that have not received adequate attention. Whatever their differences, all the readings are well-written and should be accessible to students new to the topic of globalization as well as instructive for students at all levels.

The volume presents strong defenses of globalization, in its present form, as well as compelling analyses identifying problems that it generates. Although supporters of neoliberal globalization have a privileged place in major media outlets and (to a lesser extent) college courses, critics are often portrayed as ignorant and irresponsible. Yet we believe that many criticisms of globalization as it is now organized are amply justified. With that said, some readers of PG may agree with one reviewer of PG that we have been overly generous to defenders of globalization, whereas other readers may agree with another reviewer, who suggested that PG contains too few selections critical of globalization!

Organization of PG

Part One presents an introduction to the topic of globalization.

- **Chapter 1** opens the book with a general Introduction that surveys the meanings of globalization and analyzes some of the important questions to be pursued in greater depth throughout the volume.
- **Chapter 2** presents readings that situate globalization historically and theoretically. Selections by Marx and Polanyi highlight possible parallels between globalization in the current period with the "great transformation" of nineteenth-century England described by Polanyi. Further, as Marx correctly understood, capitalism is inherently global and deeply transformative. Other readings in Chapter 2 qualify these claims by warning that the current era of globalization is both limited in extent (Wade) and reversible rather than a permanent condition (Ferguson).

Part Two examines economic features of globalization.

- ♦ **Chapter 3** provides selections that describe diverse aspects of economic globalization.
- ♦ **Chapter 4** highlights debates about the distributional aspects of globalization.
- ♦ **Chapter 5** samples sharply conflicting views of whether globalization involves benefits or costs for those who perform the work of globalized production.

Part Three focuses on the relationship of states to globalization.

- ♦ **Chapter 6** surveys different views on the relationship of national states to globalization. A first wave of studies (represented in PG by the selection by Susan Strange) contended that states have been eclipsed by globalization. Soon, however, more complex understandings were developed (as illustrated by other selections in Chapter 6).
- ♦ **Chapter 7** shifts the focus to global governance. Is there a global state? If so, what are its institutions? In particular, several selections analyze the role of international financial institutions (IFIs) in the new world order.
- ♦ **Chapter 8** shifts the focus by considering the possibility that the global state is an imperial nation—the United States. The selections included here analyze whether the United States is an imperial power and, if it is, how secure its rule can be.

Part Four turns from a focus on globalization from above—the subject of most selections in the first three parts of PG—to globalization from below.

- ♦ **Chapter 9** studies national and transnational challenges to neoliberal globalization.
- ♦ **Chapter 10** includes selections analyzing the globalization of culture as well as migration—that is, the flow of people across national borders.
- ♦ **Chapter 11** concludes PG by surveying proposals for reforming globalization.

Most studies and anthologies of globalization analyze particular aspects of globalization, for example, the global factory, finance, governance, culture, human rights, and resistance movements. PG surveys these topics—and others. The aim of providing a broad overview is to highlight the spacious scope and contentious nature of the topic. We hope the material presented here will enable instructors to encourage students to undertake more in-depth analyses of particular facets of globalization.

Acknowledgments

I am enormously grateful for the generous help that I have received when preparing *The Politics of Globalization*. Incisive comments on the manuscript were provided by the following reviewers:

Stephen Crowley, *Oberlin College*
Carrie Liu Currier, *Texas Christian University*
Louis DeSipio, *University of California, Irvine*
Miguel Glatzer, *University of Massachusetts–Dartmouth*
Soo Yeon Kim, *University of Maryland*
Scott B. Martin, *New School University/Princeton University*
Phillip Mikesell, *Wabash College*
Stephen D. Morris, *University of South Alabama*
John Scherpereel, *James Madison University*
Leonard Schoppa, *University of Virginia*
Matthew B. Sparke, *University of Washington*

The manuscript was developed and produced by the first-rate staff at Houghton Mifflin, including Katherine Meisenheimer, sponsoring editor; Jeff Greene, senior development editor; Nan Lewis-Schulz, project editor; Kristen Craib, editorial assistant; and Nicola Poser, executive marketing manager. Leslie Kauffman, development editor at LEAP Publishing Services, provided excellent advice and helpful replies to queries at all hours of the days, nights, and weekends. Most of all, thanks to Amrita Basu, for ensuring that globalization begins at home.

Mark Kesselman

PART ONE

INTRODUCTION

CHAPTER 1

Globalization as Contested Terrain

It is hard to pick up a newspaper or watch a television newscast nowadays without encountering the term *globalization.* Yet this situation is very recent. One study tabulated the frequency of the term *globalization* in articles published in a leading German newspaper. Whereas in 1993, the term appeared a total of 34 times, in 2001 it appeared 1,136 times—an increase of over 3,000 percent in less than a decade![1]

Within the scholarly world, too, attention to globalization has soared in the last few years. In 2004, *Globalizations*, a scholarly journal devoted to articles about globalization, began publication. Several book publishers have recently created series devoted entirely to studies of globalization. Until a few years ago, it would have been difficult locating sufficient material to include in an anthology of readings. The dilemma is now the opposite: how to limit the number of excellent readings in *Politics of Globalization* (hereafter, PG) to ensure that the book is of manageable length. College courses on globalization were unknown a decade ago; nowadays, they are routinely offered in departments of anthropology, history, political science, economics and sociology.

The fact that there has been a dramatic increase in the **salience or use** of the term *globalization* does not in itself prove that the **phenomenon** of globalization (however we define it) has accelerated at a comparable rate. Nor is there any consensus about its extent, meaning, and significance. Several selections in PG highlight that the phenomenon has deep historical roots; others claim that globalization is of quite recent origin; while yet others deny the importance of globalization

[1]Cited in World Commission on the Social Dimension of Globalization, *A Fair Globalization: Creating Opportunities for All* (Geneva, Switzerland: ILO, 2004), p. 24, footnote 8.

altogether because, they assert, the bulk of activities in the world remain rooted in local or national settings that have few connections to globalization. To complicate matters even further, *New York Times* journalist Thomas Friedman discovered that, even in a remote village in a poor country like China, there were strong connections to the outside world and people were keenly aware of this![2]

Nor is the question of how recent, widespread, or influential is globalization the only hotly contested issue in this field. Here are a few others that will be discussed in this Introduction and that help structure the organization of PG and selection of readings:

- What, in fact, is globalization? Like any concept used in scholarly analysis, one needs to specify what is included and what is excluded from the term.
- What drives globalization, and how influential is it?
- What are the normative implications or distributional impact of globalization? Which groups are the winners, which are the losers, in the era of globalization?
- To what extent is there resistance to globalization, and how successful is it?
- What proposals have been advanced for reforming globalization?

There are a host of other questions that can be asked about globalization. But the ones just identified are among the most frequently asked and important, and they will be the focus of the remainder of this Introduction.

What Is Globalization? What Is Its Opposite? When Did It Originate?

Political sociologist Charles Tilly suggests that "globalization means an increase in the geographic range of locally consequential social interactions, especially when that increase stretches a significant proportion of all interactions across international or intercontinental limits."[3]

Tilly's definition provides a useful point of departure. It calls attention to the fact that interactions involving globalization coexist with interactions that do not have an international or international character. A related but somewhat different point suggested by this definition is that globalization is not an "either-or" but a "more-or-less" phenomenon involving an increase in the frequency or ratio of long-distance interactions relative to local interactions. Although there may have been in the past or may be today places in which the frequency of long-distance (global) interactions was (is) nonexistent or minimal, it may also be the case, especially in the present era, that—to adapt the famous poem by John Donne—no place is a (completely isolated) island.

---

[2]Thomas L. Friedman, *The Lexus and the Olive Tree: Understanding Globalization* (New York: Farrar, Straus and Giroux, 1999), ch. 4.

[3]Charles Tilly, "Globalization Threatens Labor's Rights," *International Labor and Working-Class History* 47 (Spring 1995): 1–2.

Although the definition proposed by Tilly helps launch our analysis of globalization, it raises more questions than it answers. What kinds of transactions does he have in mind? How should they be measured? Are some more important than others? After all, a letter from a family member to a relative in a distant country doesn't have the same impact or significance as a communication between two heads of state. Do those who interact have equal power or is one participant more powerful—and what difference does this make? Should one distinguish various kinds of interaction, for example, those involving production processes stretching across national borders (the global factory or office place) from interactions involving culture, human rights, social protest, and political governance—to enumerate but a few of the varied forms of interactions? Are these forms not only distinct but unrelated? Or are they different elements of an integrated whole? To illustrate the challenge for those who see globalization as a unified whole, what, if anything, does the global distribution of American—or Indian—films have in common with the vast increase in cross-border financial transactions (the sale of currencies and government bonds) or the outsourcing of computer manufacture to China? And do these developments have any common elements with the bombing of the Madrid train station in 2004 or the London tube (subway) in 2005?

Even if the different elements of globalization are related, some may conflict with others. For example, some analysts have identified a possible conflict between the global diffusion of human rights and the global diffusion of production practices, which may involve exploitative labor practices.

In brief, the concept—as well as the phenomenon—of globalization is vast, vague, and contested. The editors of *Globalizations* explained why the title of the journal highlighted diverse kinds of globalization: "The move from the singular to the plural [in the title of the journal] is deliberate and implies skepticism of the idea that there can ever be a single theory or interpretation of globalization."[4] Yet the fact that globalization has multiple features and that scholars interpret the concept in different ways does not preclude rigorous analysis of globalization. Indeed, this goal animates *Politics of Globalization*.

Tilly's definition might be considered an invitation to analyze which transnational activities should be included in what he calls "locally consequential social interactions" as well as to prioritize the importance of various interactions. It invites us to be sensitive to the need to identify both the kinds of activities whose influence stretches across national borders *and also* how these activities have an impact on people's lives.

Yet the definition remains broad and abstract. One of the important tasks in understanding globalization is to decide which transnational interactions to highlight. Also note a tension or tradeoff involving what to designate as consequential: if everything that occurs in the contemporary world is considered to reflect globalization, the term becomes hopelessly stretched. If everything is globalization, why

[4]"Aims and Scope," brochure announcing publication of *Globalizations,* Routledge, undated.

use the term at all? Yet an opposite danger is to define globalization so narrowly that one neglects features that, in fact, may be highly influential.

One might note that there is a tendency toward a scholarly division of labor in the way that globalization is studied. Economists tend to focus on the activities of transnational corporations, technological change, international trade and investment, and financial flows across borders; political scientists often focus on the role of states in facilitating or hindering transnational activities, as well as the role of international organizations such as the United Nations or International Monetary Fund; and sociologists and anthropologists tend to analyze the diffusion of culture and forms of popular resistance to economic and political globalization.

Is one focus more valid than the others? One answer is that the appropriate focus is determined by the questions studied. If one wants to learn how people's lives have been changed by globalization, it makes sense to study the local level. But to understand the decisions and processes that drive globalization, it is probably more fruitful to study the overall (macro) level of states, international organizations, and transnational corporations. However, the various levels do not exist in isolation. Macrolevel decisions about organizing production and trade play a key role in people's everyday lives. And, vice versa, the ways that people organize (or fail to organize) in their local communities influence decisions at the top.

The discussion thus far has treated globalization as a quite ahistorical phenomenon. But Tilly's definition, which focuses on changes in long-distance interactions, can sensitize us to the extent of globalization across time and space. Consider the issue of historical variations in globalization. If one charted the extent of globalization in the past two centuries, the result would not be a steady increase from a less globalized past to a densely globalized present. As Wade and Ferguson describe in their selections in Chapter 2 of PG, the nineteenth and early twentieth centuries were a period of relatively great globalization, involving investment and trade among major industrialized powers and the exchange of raw materials and manufactured products between the colonial powers and their territorial possessions. Globalization was facilitated by technological innovations such as underwater telephone cable and steamships that facilitated transoceanic voyages. Political factors were also important, notably the Pax Britannica, that is, the international peace and stability that resulted from British dominance. (At its high point, one quarter of the world's population was incorporated within the British empire.)

This early era of globalization did not last forever. It came to a halt with the outbreak of World War I in 1914, when, first military hostilities, and then the Great Depression of the 1930s followed by World War II in 1938–1945, severely limited globalization. During these decades, globalization was replaced by autarky, that is, the delinking of national economies resulting from a steep decline in international trade and investment. As we describe below, a new era of globalization can be identified as beginning in the 1980s.

In similar fashion, globalization is not constant across space. The selection by Sen in Chapter 2 highlights the importance of the fact that many regions and civilizations have contributed to globalization. Contrary to what is commonly claimed, globalization is not exclusively a product of western technology or culture.

In brief, globalization varies extensively in character, time, and space. PG is a response to this fascinating challenge and opportunity.

Globalization and Capitalism Can one identify a central tendency within globalization in the present period? While readings in PG provide varying answers to this question, we claim that the essence of globalization in the recent period involves the expansion of capitalism on a global scale. What, then, is capitalism, and how and why does globalization involve capitalist expansion?

One can distinguish between fundamental, invariant features of a capitalist organization of production and features that may vary extensively from period to period and place to place. Core features, many of which are analyzed in the selection by Polanyi in Chapter 2, include:

- Production is not carried on for immediate consumption by the producer but is intended for exchange (sale) in the market.
- Markets are arenas in which buyers and sellers voluntarily meet to exchange money for commodities on the basis of a mutually agreed-upon price.
- Goods are exchanged through sales in the market by producers to consumers. A sale involves a voluntary contract or agreement between producers and consumers/purchasers to exchange a commodity at a selling price (measured in money) specified by the producer. Producers seek to reap the maximum possible gain (profit); consumers seek to purchase goods at the lowest possible price.
- Production is organized privately, rather than by public authorities (the state), and decentralized among producers, organized in firms, who compete with each other in the marketplace.
- The firm is divided between those who own and manage the firm, and those who receive a wage or salary to perform productive work.
- The core elements of capitalism therefore comprise decentralized, privately organized, market-based production for profit, with production occurring by wage labor.

Although these elements are found in all capitalist economies, actually existing capitalist societies have varied enormously. The reason is that the core elements can be combined with a highly variable mix of technological, institutional, social, political, and cultural features.

Public (or state) policies are a key element affecting the variable character of capitalism in a given society. Broadly speaking, one can distinguish public policies on the basis of the extent to which they replace market-based outcomes with politically determined ones. Take the issue of employment and unemployment. At one extreme, there may be no public assistance for those out of work; at another extreme, there may be welfare state programs involving a guaranteed minimum income to all members of the society, whether they are employed or not, as well as unemployment insurance for those who lose their jobs. Somewhere between the two, there may be programs of workfare, in which there is public assistance to those without jobs—on condition that assistance end after a limited period and those receiving it actively seek jobs. Is one or the other of these approaches more valid? The issue has generated intense political debate.

In the early period of capitalism, most countries subscribed to the theory of *laissez-faire* (the French term meaning "let act," and that is what is meant in English by free enterprise). Markets operated freely and states played a quite minimum role: they enforced law and order, protected property rights, and left most economic decisions to the play of market forces. However, the result was economic instability and the Great Depression of the 1930s, with economic stagnation and massive levels of unemployment. Searching for a way to end the economic crisis, British economist John Maynard Keynes proposed that the state should considerably expand its scope. Since markets alone could not be relied on to promote economic growth, full employment, and social equity, the state should sponsor an extensive safety net of welfare measures designed to cushion wage earners from market dislocations and promote social equity. Keynes also proposed that states should engage in what was dubbed countercyclical demand management: state spending and interest-rate manipulation to counter market instability. The goal of the new policy orientation was to use state management to promote the goals of economic growth, full employment, and social equity that markets could not achieve alone.

President Franklin Delano Roosevelt, elected in 1932, turned to Keynesianism to fight the Depression. Rightly or wrongly, Keynesianism was given credit for helping end the Depression and helping fuel the decades-long boom that followed World War II. (Some economists contend that it was the onset of World War II, not Keynesianism, that produced the powerful boost of demand that helped end the Depression.)

Just as Keynesianism became popular during the good times after World War II, it became the target of widespread criticism when the postwar boom turned sour in the 1970s and was replaced by a period of stagflation—a combination of inflation and economic slowdown or stagnation. Increasingly numerous critics charged that Keynesian policies were to blame. Thanks to Keynesianism, the state had become overextended, and it thereby discouraged risk-taking and innovation, and promoted wasteful public spending.

The revolt against Keynesianism helped produce the election of Ronald Reagan as president in 1980. In his first inaugural address in 1981, he proclaimed, "Government is not the solution to our problem." A new approach, variously dubbed supply-side economics, neoliberalism, or the Washington Consensus (once it became the new reigning orthodoxy) sought to reverse the policies recommended by Keynes and his liberal supporters. Reagan's reelection in 1984, followed by the election in 1988 of George H. W. Bush, Reagan's former vice president, signaled the defeat of Keynesianism. It was later sealed by George W. Bush's election in 2000 and reelection in 2004. The core policies of the Washington Consensus include:

- Dismantling regulations passed in the postwar years that restricted business activity in the name of social and environmental goals.
- Reducing spending on social welfare, both to reduce government expenditures and to encourage citizens forcibly to seek private employment rather than rely on public support.
- Reducing corporate and personal income taxes.
- Privatizing a host of services, products, and functions that were formerly provided by government, including telecommunications, water, education, prisons, transportation, and so on.
- Reducing tariff and nontariff barriers to international trade, investment, and other forms of capital mobility (such as currency exchanges).
- Liberalizing international capital mobility, that is, reducing restrictions on inward and outward flows of capital.

Neoliberal economic policies have powerfully fueled the development of globalization. The present era of globalization can be considered as originating in the 1980s, thanks to the adoption of neoliberal economic reforms, first in the United States and Britain, and then by governments around the world. Until that point, tariffs, import quotas, capital controls, and other restrictions on international capital mobility were powerful deterrents to globalization. The adoption of the Washington Consensus has facilitated the enormous expansion of global capitalism in the present era.

One important mechanism for diffusing neoliberal reforms and thereby promoting globalization to poor countries in the global South was what was called structural adjustment policies. When countries face financial crises and apply to international financial institutions for assistance, a condition for receiving aid was (and is) that they adopt the neoliberal policies comprising the Washington Consensus. (See the selection by Forero in Chapter 9.) The result is to enable transnational corporations (TNCs) to invest and trade more freely. Because neoliberal policies have often imposed particular hardships on the poor, since they have often involved cuts in social spending and the privatization of public services, they have become the target of widespread popular opposition. One of the principal aims of antiglobalization protests has been to scrap the neoliberal policies of the Washington Consensus and to reverse this key feature of globalization.

In brief, in the present era, globalization can be regarded as involving the spatial and functional expansion of capitalism on a global scale. By *spatial* it is meant that capitalism is becoming dominant in regions of the world in which capitalist (that is, market-organized) social and economic relations have been marginal until recently. An illustration of this is the extraordinary expansion of markets within the past decade in China and India—nearly half the world's population! (This illustration can also be extended to include other countries in Asia, as well as other less economically developed areas of the world.)

The *functional* expansion of capitalism involves the extension of market-based relations to new areas of social life. For example, in the United States, the "leisure" industry, comprising restaurants, tourism, and entertainment, is now the second-largest economic sector. Computer and video games, tourism, and dating services are commodities and activities that either did not exist until quite recently or, as in the case of tourism, existed on a relatively small scale. More generally, capitalism dominates people's lives throughout the world on a scale unimaginable even a decade or two ago.

What Drives Globalization, and How Influential Is It?

This issue involves trying to sort out causes and consequences. Is globalization a **cause** of outcomes in varied spheres, such as production, public policies, and collective identities? An **outcome** of changes in these and other spheres? Or, alternatively, a **description** of processes that may (or may not) be related, in such varied spheres as technology, migration, currency movements, production processes, ideas, communication, and culture?

Consider recent, immensely important developments in communications, including the Internet, mobile telephones, fiber-optic cables, broadband Internet, satellite TV, video conferencing, and high-speed laptop computers. These technological innovations powerfully **contribute** to (and **promote** or **cause**) globalization by enabling people throughout the world to communicate by the flick of a keystroke—on condition that all systems are up and running (which, as we all know to our intense frustration, is not always the case!). But they are also a **result** of globalization, in that innovations like those enumerated above have been made possible by transnational cooperation and coordination among scientists, engineers, support staff, and production workers throughout the world.

The changes culminating in globalization have not just happened. They have been made to happen. Who—what set of agents?—has made globalization happen? As with much else concerning globalization, the answer is bound to be controversial. To simplify, one can identify four clusters of organized actors. The first are the transnational corporations that are powerful engines promoting global economic integration. TNCs have headquarters in one country, but their finances, production facilities, subcontractors, and consumer markets are scattered far and wide. From the very beginning of capitalist development, TNCs played an essential role in locating raw materials, workers, and customers around the world. But, as many selections in PG will describe, the rapid growth of TNCs in number and importance is a hallmark of the present phase of capitalist development. In brief, no TNCs, no globalization.

States are a second important ingredient of globalization. Although some scholars claim that states have declined in importance in the era of globalization, this claim is contested by others. In any event, most agree that states retain the ability to sabotage globalization, if they so choose. This occurred in an earlier era of globalization, which was brought to a crashing halt by World War I.

When discussing states, beware of the juridical fiction in international law that specifies all sovereign states are equal. To paraphrase George Orwell, in his satirical novel *Animal Farm*, some states are more equal than others! Nowadays, one state is far more equal than all the others: the United States. What is its role in promoting globalization? The answer is: a lot. It was the United States that was mainly responsible for writing the rules of the global economic game after World War II. It was the United States that played the major role in creating the international financial institutions that have helped organize and regulate globalization. It is the United States that, since the end of the Cold War in 1989, has dominated what is often described as a unipolar world. (As you will see in Chapter 8, some dispute this claim.) In the present era, then, some analysts consider that American dominance and globalization may be considered different terms for the same phenomenon. The less appealing description for this situation is imperialism, and Chapter 8 samples widely differing views on whether the United States should be considered an imperial power.

The third powerful force promoting globalization has been international organizations, such as the International Monetary Fund (IMF), World Bank, and World Trade Organization (WTO). These organizations, usually composed of member governments or states, write the rules of the international game that regulates globalization. These rules specify what governments and transnational corporations can and cannot do. In some respects, they are a supergovernment whose policies give concrete meaning to globalization.

A fourth set of actors are the vast numbers of people and groups in the world who may be considered members of civil society, that is, ordinary citizens organized into associations and organizations. They may favor globalization when a TNC provides jobs by subcontracting production. But they may oppose globalization when their government contracts with a TNC to manage the supply of water—and water rates soar sky-high. When studying what drives globalization, do not forget that power resides at multiple levels and among diverse sets of actors.

Let us turn the question around and ask: not who causes globalization, but how influential is it? Opinions vary from those who claim, as one observer puts it, that "Globalization has become the defining process of the present age" to those who join a political economist who warns that "reports of the death of the national economy are greatly exaggerated."[5]

What is the balance between globalization and . . . its absence? Note that an answer partly hinges, as we suggested above, on how we define globalization. For example, some scholars assert that there is a distinction—and an opposition—between globalization and regionalization. Those who defend this position note that a large share of transnational economic activity is concentrated within a few regions of the world: Western Europe, North America, and East Asia are the usual sus-

[5]The first claim is by Martin Khor, *Rethinking Globalization: Critical Issues and Policy Choices* (London: Zed Press, 2001); the second, the title of an article by Robert Wade included in ch. 2 of PG: "Globalization and Its Limits: Reports of the Death of the National Economy Are Greatly Exaggerated," ch. 2 in Suzanne Berger and Ronald Dore, eds., *National Diversity and Global Capitalism* (Ithaca: Cornell University Press, 1996).

pects. In this view, it is misleading to classify, as evidence of a global economy, the intense economic interchanges among member countries who belong to the European Union (EU), or among the three countries belonging to the North American Free Trade Association (NAFTA), or among East Asian countries linked to the Japanese economy.

Yet, one might reply, the fact that crossborder activity does not reach around the world is no reason to deny that it forms part of the mosaic of the global economy. Whatever term one uses, it is surely relevant to chart the patterns of crossborder or transnational flows and to note that they are "lumpy"—that is, regionally concentrated—and that entire regions and continents (preeminently, Africa) occupy a very small space on a map that charts globalized economic activity.

What Are the Normative Implications and Distributional Impact of Globalization?

Who wins and loses from globalization? How desirable is globalization? Some analysts regard globalization as the highest phase of humankind's development, a powerful spur to progress and therefore a goal to be promoted by all possible means. Other analysts regard globalization as a deadly peril—to be eliminated by all possible means! Is the truth somewhere in the middle? Not necessarily. As King Solomon's ruse to establish who was the mother of a disputed baby reminds us, some compromises may be the worst possible alternative!

To reframe this issue: Is globalization a win-win pattern in which everyone without exception benefits from globalization? Conversely, might it be lose-lose to the entire world? In this camp are those concerned with the environmental impact of globalization, including the possibility that it contributes to global warming, an increase in regions experiencing drought, and the depletion of vital resources, including petroleum, fresh water, and forests. At another level of analysis, does globalization benefit some individuals, groups, regions, and nations while harming others? Which ones? (Are women the particular beneficiaries or victims of globalization? One can find scholarly literature defending both claims.) Yet another position is that while some groups benefit more than others, everyone is at least somewhat better off than before. In brief, is there a way to determine whether, as one economist puts it, globalization has gone "too far"?[6] Or whether it has not gone far enough?

To consider a concrete example: What is its impact on the nature of work and of workers? Does it promote an upgrading of skill, thanks to the technological changes associated with globalization? Or, by outsourcing and offshoring low-skilled jobs to low-wage countries, does it simply obscure the fact that nothing much has changed except the geographic dispersion of production? Again, evi-

---

[6]Dani Rodrick, *Has Globalisation Gone Too Far?* (Washington, D.C.: Institute for International Economics, 1997).

dence can be produced on both sides of the divide. A related issue—what is the impact of globalization on wages and salaries? To what extent is it related to the stagnation of lower-income wage workers in the industrialized countries and the soaring incomes of top corporate executives?

What is the impact of globalized production on women? For example, do women in poor countries achieve greater social and economic independence when they are hired to fill jobs in the multinational sector, in firms that are subcontractors for transnational clothing manufacturers? Or are they harmed as a result of low wages and sexual harassment? (Selections in Chapter 5 explore the question.)

What is the impact of globalized production on the possibilities and likelihood of union organizing and of corporate protection of workers' rights? Does it empower workers or weaken their leverage? Or does it increase workers' collective position in some places but decrease it elsewhere? How effective are the corporate codes of conduct, such as those developed by Nike or Levi Strauss, created in response to pressure exerted by consumer movements?

To What Extent Is There Resistance to Globalization, and How Successful Is It?

Because globalization is the product of human actions, because it can vary extensively in time and place, and because it affects our lives so deeply, it is not surprising that people try to shape its character. Most analyses of globalization focus on what might be described as "globalization from above," that is, the process by which influential individuals in transnational corporations, governments, and international organizations shape globalization. However, our understanding of globalization would be incomplete if we did not also study what can be described as globalization from below: the ways that people organize collectively in an attempt to influence the character of globalization. And such attempts occur aplenty, with highly variable results. It is useful to study popular movements concerned with globalization both because they may succeed and because, even when they fail, it is useful to understand how and why.

What Proposals Have Been Advanced for Reforming Globalization? What Is the Future of Globalization?

Proposals to extend or limit globalization are endless. The future of globalization in part hinges on which, if any, are adopted. At one extreme, some proposed reforms involve further reductions in barriers limiting international trade and investment. (See the selection by Moore in Chapter 11.) One example is the proposal to create the Central America Free Trade Agreement (CAFTA), a treaty linking the United States and the five states of Central America in an arrangement patterned on the North America Free Trade Agreement (NAFTA). CAFTA would create a free-trade area among member countries, allowing goods from one member country to freely enter the markets of all the others. There was such strong popular resistance to this initiative in 2005 that political leaders have shelved the plan, at least for now.

At the other extreme, some critics of globalization advocate abolishing existing international financial institutions and agreements. (See the selections by Cavanagh and Mander, and Bello in Chapter 11.) They stress the immense damage that globalization inspired by neoliberal economic theory has caused and the undemocratic way that globalization is organized.

Proposals that lie between these extremes target certain aspects of present-day globalization for reform. For example, a selection in Chapter 11 by Joseph Stiglitz describes ways to make the decision-making process of international financial institutions more transparent and accountable.

The variety of proposals to extend, limit, or reform globalization suggests that the future of globalization is quite open and in part depends on the kinds of reforms that may be adopted. The future of globalization also depends on developments in other spheres. Technological innovations may further facilitate transcontinental social interactions, to recall Tilly's definition of globalization. Conversely, a major international economic crisis or war could vastly reduce international interactions. If so, it would not be the first time, as the selection by Ferguson notes in Chapter 2. In analyzing the possible future of globalization, it is instructive to analyze the past.

To conclude the discussion of globalization, the future will be heavily influenced by citizen attitudes and actions—including those of the readers of PG! Consider this an invitation to develop your own informed position on the issues surveyed in PG.

Organization of *Politics of Globalization*

PG samples diverse topics, orientations, and assessments of the "great transformation" involving globalization in the present era. (See the selection by the economic historian Karl Polanyi in Chapter 2 for an analysis of the capitalist revolution in eighteenth- and nineteenth-century Britain that Polanyi described as the first "great transformation.")

The readings in Chapter 2 that conclude Part One situate globalization historically and theoretically. Selections by Marx and Polanyi highlight possible parallels between globalization in the current period with the first "great transformation" described by Polanyi. Further, as Marx correctly understood, capitalism is inherently global and deeply transformative. Other readings in Chapter 2 qualify these claims by warning that globalization is both limited in extent (Wade) and reversible rather than a permanent condition (Ferguson).

Part Two examines economic features of globalization. Chapter 3 provides selections that describe diverse aspects of economic globalization. Chapter 4 highlights debates about the distributional aspects of globalization. Chapter 5 samples the sharply conflicting views of whether globalization involves benefits or costs for those who perform the work of globalized production.

The focus of Part Three is the relationship of states to globalization. Chapter 6 surveys different views on the relationship of national states to globalization. A first wave of studies (represented in PG by the selection by Susan Strange) contended that states have been eclipsed by globalization. Soon, however, more complex understandings were developed (as illustrated by other selections in Chapter 6). Chapter 7 shifts the focus to global governance. If there is a global state, what are its constituent institutions? In particular, several selections analyze the role of international financial institutions (IFIs) in the new world order. Chapter 8 shifts the focus by considering the possibility that the global state is an imperial state—the United States. The selections included here analyze whether the United States is an imperial power and, if it is, how secure is its rule.

Part Four turns from a focus on globalization from above—the subject of the first three parts of PG—to globalization from below. Chapter 9 studies national and transnational challenges to neoliberal globalization. Chapter 10 includes selections analyzing the globalization of culture and the topic of migration—that is, the flow of people across national borders. PG concludes by surveying in Chapter 11 proposals for reforming globalization.

The selections in PG are as diverse in their approach and style as in their content. Readings vary from the detached and scholarly to the passionate and politically engaged. By roaming so widely, we aim to convey the extraordinarily rich character of reflections on globalization. We have included some of the best-known specialists on globalization and many of the most influential scholarly articles. But the constraints of space have required difficult choices. We have also included selections from lesser-known sources to highlight important issues that have not received adequate attention. If the readings in PG convince you of the complexity, importance, and constantly evolving character of globalization—as well as the value of further reflection about the topic—they will have accomplished their purpose.

CHAPTER 2

Great Transformations and Double Movements: *Déjà Vu* All Over Again?

We borrow the title of this chapter from two sources. The concepts of double movements and great transformations are drawn from economic historian Karl Polanyi's landmark study of Britain, *The Great Transformation: The Political and Economic Origins of Our Time*. (A selection is included in this chapter.) Polanyi analyzed the character of the great transformation in Britain in the late eighteenth and early nineteenth century, a transformation from a primarily agrarian precapitalist society to an industrialized, urban capitalist society. Although he focused on changes in one society two centuries ago, Polanyi's analysis is pertinent for the study of globalization in our own era, for a new wave of capitalist transformation is now occurring that is integrating formerly peripheral regions of the world into the global economy.

The term *double movement* is also borrowed from Polanyi. The phrase refers to the fact that the great transformation—capitalist revolution—did not command universal support. Instead, Polanyi notes, the great transformation engendered a movement to protect society against the upheaval caused by capitalist revolution. The goal of the double movement was to prevent the worth of the elements constituting the natural and social world from being measured solely by the price that they fetched in the market.

The selections in this chapter provide widely varying understandings of the extent of globalization in the present era and the character of that transformation. The first two selections in this chapter provide classic analyses of "the great transformation" involved in capitalist revolution. They also implicitly pose a question that we borrow from the great folk philosopher, former Yankees baseball star Yogi Berra. To what extent is the current era of globalization a case of *déjà vu* all over again, that is, the appearance of something new, which in fact is a repetition of the past? That is, applying this insight to globalization, might the present great transformation involving global capitalist revolution be the latest wave of global capitalist expansion?

The other readings in this section provide texture and nuance to the initial claims. Amartya Sen questions a commonly held view that globalization is synonymous with Westernization; on the contrary, he argues, globalization is a rich and complex product of sources that are themselves global in origin. Robert Wade warns us not to overestimate the extent of globalization. Niall Ferguson describes an earlier period of globalization, reminds us that it was sharply reversed, and suggests that present-day globalization too may eventually implode.

Taken together, the selections in this chapter provide several suggestions about the character of globalization. First, they demonstrate that globalization is historically rooted and contingent, that is, that it occurs in a particular historical context (or, rather, contexts: globalization occurs in successive **waves**). Second, the selections suggest that globalization is contingent, that is, it is not inevitable but the product of decisions—and that it is reversible, in that decisions at a future point can produce "deglobalization." (Indeed, Walden Bello, in a selection in Chapter 11, advocates just such a course.) These selections invite us to be sensitive to the specific features of globalization in the current era, to what has shaped globalization, and to how globalization might change in the future.

ARTICLE 2.1

"The Manifesto of the Communist Party" *(excerpts)*

Karl Marx and Frederick Engels

Karl Marx and Frederick Engels were theoreticians and critics of capitalism in the early years of its development in the mid-nineteenth century. They foresaw that capitalism would be a profoundly revolutionary force transforming the world—in their view, both for better and very much for worse. They wrote "The Communist Manifesto" in 1848 to provide an analysis and program for the International Workingmans' Association, the communist movement in Western Europe. (It was later called the First International and was followed by other international organizations of communist and socialist movements.) The Manifesto argues that capitalism produces both monumental achievements that in some respects exceed those of all other world civilizations—yet it also produces monumental inequality and misery.

We open PG with a passage from the Manifesto that explains why they believed that capitalism is inherently a global phenomenon and, in turn, how capitalism promotes globalization. Although Marx and Engels could not have anticipated Wal-Mart, if they were writing today they would doubtless point to the world's largest company as an excellent illustration of many of their arguments! Headquartered in a small town in Arkansas (Bentonville), Wal-Mart is extraordinarily integrated into the global economy. First, many of the products sold in Wal-Mart are produced in less-developed regions and countries, notably China. This enables Wal-Mart suppliers to pay wages that are a fraction of those in affluent countries. Second, Wal-Mart employs many immigrants in its stores, which enables it to reap additional savings. Its sales force hails from countries around the world. They are located at the bottom of the U.S. class structure, and are willing to work for the low wages that Wal-Mart pays. Third, although in its early years Wal-Mart operated stores exclusively in the United States, the company's retailing operation has gone global in recent years. Wal-Mart operates stores in scores of countries around the world. Wal-Mart (and other large corporations) might be regarded as the "battering ram" that Marx and Engels claimed promotes capitalist revolution throughout the world. Wal-Mart has revolutionized the way that goods are produced and marketed. It has changed the organization of the economy (eliminating countless small and medium-size retailers), employment patterns, and consumer tastes.

Do you agree with the analysis presented by Marx and Engel? Can or should one separate their analysis from their critique? What are the possibilities, and the pros and cons, of doing so?

Bourgeois and Proletarians

The history of all hitherto existing society is the history of class struggles.

Freeman and slave, patrician and plebeian, lord and serf, guild-master and journeyman, in a word, oppressor and oppressed, stood in constant opposition to one another, carried on an uninterrupted, now hidden, now open fight, a fight that each time ended, either in a revolutionary reconstitution of society at large, or in the common ruin of the contending classes.

In the earlier epochs of history, we find almost everywhere a complicated arrangement of society into various orders, a manifold gradation of social rank. In ancient Rome we have patricians, knights, plebeians, slaves; in the Middle Ages, feudal lords, vassals, guild-masters, journeymen, apprentices, serfs; in almost all of these classes, again, subordinate gradations.

The modern bourgeois society that has sprouted from the ruins of feudal society has not done away with class antagonisms. It has but established new classes, new conditions of oppression, new forms of struggle in place of the old ones.

Our epoch, the epoch of the bourgeoisie, possesses, however, this distinct feature: it has simplified class antagonisms. Society as a whole is more and more splitting up into two great hostile camps, into two great classes directly facing each other—Bourgeoisie and Proletariat.

From the serfs of the Middle Ages sprang the chartered burghers of the earliest towns. From these burgesses the first elements of the bourgeoisie were developed.

The discovery of America, the rounding of the Cape, opened up fresh ground for the rising bourgeoisie. The East-Indian and Chinese markets, the colonisation of America, trade with the colonies, the increase in the means of exchange and in commodities generally, gave to commerce, to navigation, to industry, an impulse never before known, and thereby, to the revolutionary element in the tottering feudal society, a rapid development.

The feudal system of industry, in which industrial production was monopolised by closed guilds, now no longer sufficed for the growing wants of the new markets. The manufacturing system took its place. The guild-masters were pushed on one side by the manufacturing middle class; division of labour between the different corporate guilds vanished in the face of division of labour in each single workshop.

Meantime the markets kept ever growing, the demand ever rising. Even manufacture no longer sufficed. Thereupon, steam and machinery revolutionised industrial production. The place of manufacture was taken by the giant, Modern Industry; the place of the industrial middle class by industrial millionaires, the leaders of the whole industrial armies, the modern bourgeois.

Marx/Engels, *Selected Works,* Volume One, Progress Publishers, Moscow, USSR, 1969, pp. 98–137.

Modern industry has established the world market, for which the discovery of America paved the way. This market has given an immense development to commerce, to navigation, to communication by land. This development has, in its turn, reacted on the extension of industry; and in proportion as industry, commerce, navigation, railways extended, in the same proportion the bourgeoisie developed, increased its capital, and pushed into the background every class handed down from the Middle Ages.

We see, therefore, how the modern bourgeoisie is itself the product of a long course of development, of a series of revolutions in the modes of production and of exchange.

Each step in the development of the bourgeoisie was accompanied by a corresponding political advance of that class. An oppressed class under the sway of the feudal nobility, an armed and self-governing association in the medieval commune: here independent urban republic (as in Italy and Germany); there taxable "third estate" of the monarchy (as in France); afterwards, in the period of manufacturing proper, serving either the semi-feudal or the absolute monarchy as a counterpoise against the nobility, and, in fact, cornerstone of the great monarchies in general, the bourgeoisie has at last, since the establishment of Modern Industry and of the world market, conquered for itself, in the modern representative State, exclusive political sway. The executive of the modern state is but a committee for managing the common affairs of the whole bourgeoisie.

The bourgeoisie, historically, has played a most revolutionary part.

The bourgeoisie, wherever it has got the upper hand, has put an end to all feudal, patriarchal, idyllic relations. It has pitilessly torn asunder the motley feudal ties that bound man to his "natural superiors," and has left remaining no other nexus between man and man than naked self-interest, than callous "cash payment." It has drowned the most heavenly ecstasies of religious fervour, of chivalrous enthusiasm, of philistine sentimentalism, in the icy water of egotistical calculation. It has resolved personal worth into exchange value, and in place of the numberless indefeasible chartered freedoms, has set up that single, unconscionable freedom—Free Trade. In one word, for exploitation, veiled by religious and political illusions, it has substituted naked, shameless, direct, brutal exploitation.

The bourgeoisie has stripped of its halo every occupation hitherto honoured and looked up to with reverent awe. It has converted the physician, the lawyer, the priest, the poet, the man of science, into its paid wage labourers.

The bourgeoisie has torn away from the family its sentimental veil, and has reduced the family relation to a mere money relation.

The bourgeoisie has disclosed how it came to pass that the brutal display of vigour in the Middle Ages, which reactionaries so much admire, found its fitting complement in the most slothful indolence. It has been the first to show what man's activity can bring about. It has accomplished wonders far surpassing Egyptian pyramids, Roman aqueducts, and Gothic cathedrals; it has conducted expeditions that put in the shade all former Exoduses of nations and crusades.

The bourgeoisie cannot exist without constantly revolutionising the instruments of production, and thereby the relations of production, and with them the whole relations of society. Conservation of the old modes of production in unaltered form, was, on the contrary, the first condition of existence for all earlier industrial classes. Constant revolutionising of production, uninterrupted disturbance of all social conditions, everlasting uncertainty and agitation distinguish the bourgeois epoch from all earlier ones. All fixed, fast-frozen relations, with their train of ancient and venerable prejudices and opinions, are swept away, all new-formed ones become antiquated before they can ossify. All that is solid melts into air, all that is holy is profaned, and man is at last compelled to face with sober senses his real conditions of life, and his relations with his kind.

The need of a constantly expanding market for its products chases the bourgeoisie over the entire surface of the globe. It must nestle everywhere, settle everywhere, establish connexions everywhere.

The bourgeoisie has through its exploitation of the world market given a cosmopolitan character to production and consumption in every country. To the great chagrin of Reactionists, it has drawn from under the feet of industry the national ground on which it stood. All old-established national industries have been destroyed or are daily being destroyed. They are dislodged by new industries, whose introduction becomes a life and death question for all civilised nations, by industries that no longer work up indigenous raw material, but raw material drawn from the remotest zones; industries whose products are consumed, not only at home, but in every quarter of the globe. In place of the old wants, satisfied by the production of the country, we find new wants, requiring for their satisfaction the products of distant lands and climes. In place of the old local and national seclusion and self-sufficiency, we have intercourse in every direction, universal inter-dependence of nations. And as in material, so also in intellectual production. The intellectual creations of individual nations become common property. National one-sidedness and narrow-mindedness become more and more impossible, and from the numerous national and local literatures, there arises a world literature.

The bourgeoisie, by the rapid improvement of all instruments of production, by the immensely facilitated means of communication, draws all, even the most barbarian, nations into civilisation. The cheap prices of commodities are the heavy artillery with which it batters down all Chinese walls, with which it forces the barbarians' intensely obstinate hatred of foreigners to capitulate. It compels all nations, on pain of extinction, to adopt the bourgeois mode of production; it compels them to introduce what it calls civilisation into their midst, i.e., to become bourgeois themselves. In one word, it creates a world after its own image.

The bourgeoisie has subjected the country to the rule of the towns. It has created enormous cities, has greatly increased the urban population as compared with the rural, and has thus rescued a considerable part of the population from the idiocy of rural life. Just as it has made the country dependent on the towns, so it has made barbarian and semi-barbarian countries dependent on the civilised ones, nations of peasants on nations of bourgeois, the East on the West.

The bourgeoisie keeps more and more doing away with the scattered state of the population, of the means of production, and of property. It has agglomerated population, centralised the means of production, and has concentrated property in a few hands. The necessary consequence of this was political centralisation. Independent, or but loosely connected provinces, with separate interests, laws, governments, and systems of taxation, became lumped together into one nation, with one government, one code of laws, one national class-interest, one frontier, and one customs-tariff.

The bourgeoisie, during its rule of scarce one hundred years, has created more massive and more colossal productive forces than have all preceding generations together. Subjection of Nature's forces to man, machinery, application of chemistry to industry and agriculture, steam-navigation, railways, electric telegraphs, clearing of whole continents for cultivation, canalisation or rivers, whole populations conjured out of the ground—what earlier century had even a presentiment that such productive forces slumbered in the lap of social labour? . . .

The Great Transformation: The Political and Economic Origins of Our Time

Karl Polanyi

Economic historian Karl Polanyi claims that for a capitalist economic system to develop and function, people must think about themselves and the natural and social world in a distinctive—and unnatural—fashion. In this selection, he describes (and laments) the changes needed for a system of self-regulating market-based production (that is, capitalism) to develop. Polanyi asserts that market-based production requires separating the economy from the remainder of social and political life, and allowing markets to function without outside interference. Such a system also requires treating people and nature as commodities, that is, artifacts produced for sale on the market. This situation is based on a false assumption, since the existence of people and nature predate the market and they are not produced by market mechanisms. But, he observes, a capitalist system requires that they be treated as "fictional commodities" that can be exchanged at market-determined prices. Yet treating people as commodities, as factors of production, is pernicious. Furthermore, the result of allowing markets to function freely produces social dislocations and economic instability. However, he notes in a suggestive aside, society often organizes to protect itself against the destructive effects of market-based production. He characterizes this development as the double movement. He does not analyze how to understand the extent, character, and impact of the double movement. Can you help?

We include this selection at the beginning of PG because economic globalization, as it now exists, involves the transformation of many regions of the world in the way that Polanyi describes for nineteenth-century England.

Do you agree with Polanyi's radical critique? Can one reap the benefits of market-based production without incurring the costs that Polanyi identifies? If so, how? What kinds of double movements can one observe in the contemporary period? What are their goals? How successful are they?

The Self-Regulating Market and the Fictitious Commodities: Labor, Land, and Money

[N]ever before our own time were markets more than accessories of economic life. As a rule, the economic system was absorbed in the social system, and whatever principle of behavior predominated in the economy, the presence of the market pattern was found to be compatible with it. The principle of barter or exchange, which underlies this pattern, revealed no tendency to expand at the expense of the rest. Where markets were most highly developed, as under the mercantile system, they throve under the control of a centralized administration which fostered autarchy both in the households of the peasantry and in respect to national life. Regulation and markets, in effect, grew up together. The self-regulating market was unknown; indeed the emergence of the idea of self-regulation was a complete reversal of the trend of development. It is in the light of these facts that the extraordinary assumptions underlying a market economy can alone be fully comprehended.

A market economy is an economic system controlled, regulated, and directed by markets alone; order in the production and distribution of goods is entrusted to this self-regulating mechanism. An economy of this kind derives from the expectation that human beings behave in such a way as to achieve maximum money gains. It assumes markets in which the supply of goods (including services) available at a definite price will equal the demand at that price. It assumes the presence of money, which functions as purchasing power in the hands of its owners. Production will then be controlled by prices, for the profits of those who direct production will depend upon them; the distribution of the goods also will depend upon prices, for prices form incomes, and it is with the help of these incomes that the goods produced are distributed amongst the members of society. Under these assumptions order in the production and distribution of goods is ensured by prices alone.

Karl Polanyi, *The Great Transformation: The Political and Economic Origins of Our Time* (Boston: Beacon Press, 1957 [first published, 1944]). Reprinted by permission of Kari Polanyi Levitt.

Self-regulation implies that all production is for sale on the market and that all incomes derive from such sales. Accordingly, there are markets for all elements of industry, not only for goods (always including services) but also for labor, land, and money, their prices being called respectively commodity prices, wages, rent, and interest. The very terms indicate that prices form incomes: interest is the price for the use of money and forms the income of those who are in the position to provide it; rent is the price for the use of land and forms the income of those who supply it; wages are the price for the use of labor power, and form the income of those who sell it; commodity prices, finally, contribute to the incomes of those who sell their entrepreneurial services, the income called profit being actually the difference between two sets of prices, the price of the goods produced and their costs, *i.e.*, the price of the goods necessary to produce them. If these conditions are fulfilled, all incomes will derive from sales on the market, and incomes will be just sufficient to buy all the goods produced.

A further group of assumptions follows in respect to the state and its policy. Nothing must be allowed to inhibit the formation of markets, nor must incomes be permitted to be formed otherwise than through sales. Neither must there be any interference with the adjustment of prices to changed market conditions—whether the prices are those of goods, labor, land, or money. Hence there must not only be markets for all elements of industry, but no measure or policy must be countenanced that would influence the action of these markets. Neither price, nor supply, nor demand must be fixed or regulated; only such policies and measures are in order which help to ensure the self-regulation of the market by creating conditions which make the market the only organizing power in the economic sphere.

To realize fully what this means, let us turn for a moment to the mercantile system and the national markets which it did so much to develop. Under feudalism and the gild system land and labor formed part of the social organization itself (money had yet hardly developed into a major element of industry). Land, the pivotal element in the feudal order, was the basis of the military, judicial, administrative, and political system; its status and function were determined by legal and customary rules. Whether its possession was transferable or not, and if so, to whom and under what restrictions; what the rights of property entailed; to what uses some types of land might be put—all these questions were removed from the organization of buying and selling, and subjected to an entirely different set of institutional regulations.

The same was true of the organization of labor. Under the gild system, as under every other economic system in previous history, the motives and circumstances of productive activities were embedded in the general organization of society. The relations of master, journeyman, and apprentice; the terms of the craft; the number of apprentices; the wages of the workers were all regulated by the custom and rule of the gild and the town. What the mercantile system did was merely to unify these conditions either through statute as in England, or through the "nationalization" of the gilds as in France. As to land, its feudal status was abolished only in so far as it was linked with provincial privileges; for the rest, land remained *extra commercium*, in England as in France. Up to the time of the Great Revolution of 1789, landed estate remained the source of social privilege in France, and even after that time in England Common Law on land was essentially medieval. Mercantilism, with all its tendency towards commercialization, never attacked the safeguards which protected these two basic elements of production—labor and land—from becoming the objects of commerce. In England the "nationalization" of labor legislation through the Statute of Artificers (1563) and the Poor Law (1601), removed labor from the danger zone, and the anti-enclosure policy of the Tudors and early Stuarts was one consistent protest against the principle of the gainful use of landed property.

That mercantilism, however emphatically it insisted on commercialization as a national policy, thought of markets in a way exactly contrary to market economy, is best shown by its vast extension of state intervention in industry. On this point there was no difference between mercantilists and feudalists, between crowned planners and vested interests, between centralizing bureaucrats and conservative particularists. They disagreed only on the methods of regulation: gilds, towns, and provinces appealed to the force of custom and tradition, while the new state authority favored statute and ordinance. But they were all equally averse to the idea of commercializing labor and land—the precondition of market economy. Craft gilds and feudal privileges were abolished in France only in 1790; in England the Statute of Artificers was repealed only in 1813–14, the Elizabethan Poor Law in 1834. Not before the last decade of the eighteenth century was, in either country, the establishment of a free labor market even discussed; and the idea of the self-regulation of economic life was utterly beyond the horizon of the age. The mercantilist was concerned with the development of the resources of the country, including full employment, through trade and commerce; the traditional organization of land and labor he took for granted. He was in this respect as far removed from modern concepts as he was in the realm of politics, where his belief in the absolute powers of an enlightened despot was tempered by no intimations of democracy. And just as the transition to a democratic system and representative politics involved a complete reversal of the trend of the age, the change from regulated to self-regulating markets at the end of the eighteenth century represented a complete transformation in the structure of society.

A self-regulating market demands nothing less than the institutional separation of society into an economic and political sphere. Such a dichotomy is, in effect, merely the restatement, from the point of view of society as a whole, of the existence of a self-regulating market. It might be argued that the separateness of the two spheres obtains in every type of society at all times. Such an inference, however, would be based on a fallacy. True, no society can exist without a system of some kind which ensures order in the production and distribution of goods. But that does not imply the existence of separate economic institutions; normally, the economic order is merely a function of the social, in which it is contained. Neither under tribal, nor feudal, nor mercantile conditions was there, as we have shown, a separate economic system in society. Nineteenth century society, in which economic activity was isolated and imputed to a distinctive economic motive, was, indeed, a singular departure.

Such an institutional pattern could not function unless society was somehow subordinated to its requirements. A market economy can exist only in a market society. . . . A market economy must comprise all elements of industry, including labor, land, and money. (In a market economy the last also is an essential element of industrial life and its inclusion in the market mechanism has, as we will see, far-reaching institutional consequences.) But labor and land are no other than the human beings themselves of which every society consists and the natural surroundings in which it exists. To include them in the market mechanism means to subordinate the substance of society itself to the laws of the market.

We are now in the position to develop in a more concrete form the institutional nature of a market economy, and the perils to society which it involves. We will, first, describe the methods by which the market mechanism is enabled to control and direct the actual elements of industrial life; second, we will try to gauge the nature of the effects of such a mechanism on the society which is subjected to its action.

It is with the help of the commodity concept that the mechanism of the market is geared to the various elements of industrial life. Commodities are here empirically defined as objects produced for sale on the market; markets, again, are empirically defined as actual contacts between buyers and sellers. Accordingly, every element of industry is regarded as having been produced for sale, as then and then only will it be subject to the supply-and-demand mechanism interacting with price. In practice this means that there must be markets for every element of industry; that in these markets each of these elements is organized into a supply and a demand group; and that each element has a price which interacts with demand and supply. These markets—and they are numberless—are interconnected and form One Big Market.

The crucial point is this: labor, land, and money are essential elements of industry; they also must be organized in markets; in fact, these markets form an absolutely vital part of the economic system. But labor, land, and money are obviously *not* commodities; the postulate that anything that is bought and sold must have been produced for sale is emphatically untrue in regard to them. In other words, according to the empirical definition of a commodity they are not commodities. Labor is only another name for a human activity which goes with life itself, which in its turn is not produced for sale but for entirely different reasons, nor can that activity be detached from the rest of life, be stored or mobilized; land is only another name for nature, which is not produced by man; actual money, finally, is merely a token of purchasing power which, as a rule, is not produced at all, but comes into being through the mechanism of banking or state finance. None of them is produced for sale. The commodity description of labor, land, and money is entirely fictitious.

Nevertheless, it is with the help of this fiction that the actual markets for labor, land, and money are organized;[1] they are being actually bought and sold on the market; their demand and supply are real magnitudes; and any measures or policies that would inhibit the formation of such markets would *ipso facto* endanger the self-regulation of the system. The commodity fiction, therefore, supplies a vital organizing principle in regard to the whole of society affecting almost all its institutions in the most varied way, namely, the principle according to which no arrangement or behavior should be allowed to exist that might prevent the actual functioning of the market mechanism on the lines of the commodity fiction.

Now, in regard to labor, land, and money such a postulate cannot be upheld. To allow the market mechanism to be sole director of the fate of human beings and their natural environment, indeed, even of the amount and use of purchasing power, would result in the demolition of society. For the alleged commodity "labor power" cannot be shoved about, used indiscriminately, or even left unused, without affecting also the human individual who happens to be the bearer of this peculiar commodity. In disposing of a man's labor power the system would, incidentally, dispose of the physical, psychological, and moral entity "man" attached to that tag. Robbed of the protective covering of cultural institutions, human beings would perish from the effects of social exposure; they would die as the victims of acute social dislocation through vice, perversion, crime, and starvation. Nature would be reduced to its elements, neighborhoods and landscapes defiled, rivers polluted, military safety jeopardized, the power to produce food and raw materials destroyed. Finally, the market administration of purchasing power would periodically liquidate business enterprise, for shortages and surfeits of money would prove as disastrous to business as floods and droughts in primitive society. Undoubtedly, labor, land, and money markets *are* essential to a market economy. But no society could stand the effects of such a system of crude fictions even for the shortest stretch of time unless its human and natural substance as well as its business organization was protected against the ravages of this satanic mill.

The extreme artificiality of market economy is rooted in the fact that the process of production itself is here organized in the form of buying and selling. No other way of organizing production for the market is possible in a commercial society. During the late Middle Ages industrial production for export was organized by wealthy burgesses, and carried on under their direct supervision in the home town. Later, in the mercantile society, production was organized by merchants and was not restricted any more to the towns; this was the age of "putting out" when domestic industry was provided with raw materials by the merchant capitalist, who controlled the process of production as a purely commercial enterprise. It was then that industrial production was definitely and on a large scale put under the organizing leadership of the merchant. He knew the market, the volume as well as the quality of the demand; and he could vouch also for the supplies which, incidentally, consisted merely of wool, woad, and, sometimes, the looms or the knitting frames used by the cottage industry. If supplies failed it was the cottager who was worst hit, for his employment was gone for the time; but no expensive plant was involved and the merchant incurred no serious risk in shouldering the responsibility for production. For centuries this system grew in power and scope until in a country like England the wool industry, the national staple, covered large sectors of the country where production was organized by the clothier. He who bought and sold, incidentally, provided for production—no separate motive was required. The creation of goods involved neither the reciprocating attitudes of mutual aid; nor the concern of the householder for those whose needs are left to his care; nor the craftsman's pride in the exercise of his trade; nor the satisfaction of public praise—nothing but the plain motive of gain so familiar to the man whose profession is buying and selling. Up to the end of the eighteenth century, industrial production in Western Europe was a mere accessory to commerce.

As long as the machine was an inexpensive and unspecific tool there was no change in this position. The mere fact that the cottager could produce larger amounts than before within the same time might induce him to use machines to increase earnings, but this fact in itself did not necessarily affect the organization of production. Whether the cheap machinery was owned by the worker or by the merchant made some difference in the social position of the parties and almost certainly made a difference in the earnings of the worker, who was better off as long as he owned his tools; but it did not force the merchant to become an industrial capitalist, or to restrict himself to lending his money to such persons as were. The vent of goods rarely gave out; the greater difficulty continued to be on the side of supply of raw materials, which was sometimes unavoidably interrupted. But, even in such cases, the loss to the merchant who owned the machines was not substantial. It was not the coming of the machine as such but the invention of elaborate and therefore specific machinery and plant which completely changed the relationship of the merchant to production. Although the new productive organization was introduced by the merchant—a fact which determined the whole course of the transformation—the use of elaborate machinery and plant involved the development of the factory system and therewith a decisive shift in the relative importance of commerce and industry in favor of the latter. Industrial production ceased to be an accessory of commerce organized by the merchant as a buying and selling proposition; it now involved long-term investment with corresponding risks. Unless the continuance of production was reasonably assured, such a risk was not bearable.

But the more complicated industrial production became, the more numerous were the elements of industry the supply of which had to be safeguarded. Three of these, of course, were of outstanding importance: labor, land, and money. In a commercial society their supply could be organized in one way only: by being made available for purchase. Hence, they would have to be organized for sale on the market—in other words, as commodities. The extension of the market mechanism to the elements of industry—labor, land, and money—was the inevitable consequence of the introduction of the factory system in a commercial society. The elements of industry had to be on sale.

This was synonymous with the demand for a market system. We know that profits are ensured under such a system only if self-regulation is safeguarded through interdependent competitive markets. As the development of the factory system had been organized as part of a process of buying and selling, therefore labor, land, and money had to be transformed into commodities in order to keep production going. They could, of course, not be really transformed into commodities, as actually they were not produced for sale on the market. But the fiction of their being so produced became the organizing principle of society. Of the three, one stands out: labor is the technical term used for human beings, in so far as they are not employers but employed; it follows that henceforth the organization of labor would change concurrently with the organization of the market system. But as the organization of labor is only another word for the forms of life of the common people, this means that the development of the market system would be accompanied by a change in the organization of society itself. All along the line, human society had become an accessory of the economic system.

We recall our parallel between the ravages of the enclosures in English history and the social catastrophe which followed the Industrial Revolution. Improvements, we said, are, as a rule, bought at the price of social dislocation. If the rate of dislocation is too great, the community must succumb in the process. The Tudors and early Stuarts saved England from the fate of Spain by regulating the course of change so that it became bearable and its effects could be canalized into less destructive avenues. But nothing saved the common people of England from the impact of the Industrial Revolution. A blind faith in spontaneous progress had taken hold of people's minds, and with the fanaticism of sectarians the most enlightened pressed forward for boundless and unregulated change in society. The effects on the lives of the people were awful beyond description. Indeed, human society would have been annihilated but for protective countermoves which blunted the action of this self-destructive mechanism.

Social history in the nineteenth century was thus the result of a double movement: the extension of the market organization in respect to genuine commodities was accompanied by its restriction in respect to fictitious ones. While on the one hand markets spread all over the face of the globe and the amount of goods involved grew to unbelievable proportions, on the other hand a network of measures and policies was integrated into powerful institutions designed to check the action of the market relative to labor, land, and money. While the organization of world commodity markets, world capital markets, and world currency markets under the aegis of the gold standard gave an unparalleled momentum to the mechanism of markets, a deep-seated movement sprang into being to resist the pernicious effects of a market-controlled economy. Society protected itself against the perils inherent in a self-regulating market system—this was the one comprehensive feature in the history of the age.

Note

1. Marx's assertion of the fetish character of the value of commodities refers to the exchange value of genuine commodities and has nothing in common with the fictitious commodities mentioned in the text.

ARTICLE 2.3

How to Judge Globalism

Amartya Sen

In this selection, Nobel prize-winner Amartya Sen recommends viewing current-day globalization from a broader historical and geographic perspective than is typically the case. In fact, globalization is "neither new nor necessarily Western." In Sen's view, globalization is a genuinely global heritage. When we closely analyze the origins and character of many important elements of globalization—for example, science and technology—we discover that they have been enriched by the contributions of many peoples, regions, and cultures. He concludes that recognizing the complex origins of globalization not only corrects the historical record but enables us better to assess the strengths and weaknesses of globalization. Other chapters in PG include discussions evaluating the merits of globalization.

How and why is your evaluation of globalization changed if you regard it from a longer time frame and as a product of both Western and non-Western influences?

Globalization is often seen as global Westernization. On this point, there is substantial agreement among many proponents and opponents. Those who take an upbeat view of globalization see it as a marvelous contribution of Western civilization to the world. There is a nicely stylized history in which the great developments happened in Europe: First came the Renaissance, then the Enlightenment and the Industrial Revolution, and these led to a massive increase in living standards in the West. And now the great achievements of the West are spreading to the world. In this view, globalization is not only good, it is also a gift from the West to the world. The champions of this reading of history tend to feel upset not just because this great benefaction is seen as a curse but also because it is undervalued and castigated by an ungrateful world.

From the opposite perspective, Western dominance—sometimes seen as a continuation of Western imperialism—is the devil of the piece. In this view, contemporary capitalism, driven and led by greedy and grabby Western countries in Europe and North America, has established rules of trade and business relations that do not serve the interests of the poorer people in the world. The celebration

---

Reprinted with permission from Amartya Sen, "How to Judge Globalism," THE AMERICAN PROSPECT, Volume 13, Number 1: January 01, 2002. The American Prospect, 11 Beacon Street, Suite 1120, Boston, MA 02108.

of various non-Western identities—defined by religion (as in Islamic fundamentalism), region (as in the championing of Asian values), or culture (as in the glorification of Confucian ethics)—can add fuel to the fire of confrontation with the West.

Is globalization really a new Western curse? It is, in fact, neither new nor necessarily Western; and it is not a curse. Over thousands of years, globalization has contributed to the progress of the world through travel, trade, migration, spread of cultural influences, and dissemination of knowledge and understanding (including that of science and technology). These global interrelations have often been very productive in the advancement of different countries. They have not necessarily taken the form of increased Western influence. Indeed, the active agents of globalization have often been located far from the West.

To illustrate, consider the world at the beginning of the last millennium rather than at its end. Around 1000 A.D., global reach of science, technology, and mathematics was changing the nature of the old world, but the dissemination then was, to a great extent, in the opposite direction of what we see today. The high technology in the world of 1000 A.D. included paper, the printing press, the crossbow, gunpowder, the iron-chain suspension bridge, the kite, the magnetic compass, the wheelbarrow, and the rotary fan. A millennium ago, these items were used extensively in China—and were practically unknown elsewhere. Globalization spread them across the world, including Europe.

A similar movement occurred in the Eastern influence on Western mathematics. The decimal system emerged and became well developed in India between the second and sixth centuries; it was used by Arab mathematicians soon thereafter. These mathematical innovations reached Europe mainly in the last quarter of the tenth century and began having an impact in the early years of the last millennium, playing an important part in the scientific revolution that helped to transform Europe. The agents of globalization are neither European nor exclusively Western, nor are they necessarily linked to Western dominance. Indeed, Europe would have been a lot poorer—economically, culturally, and scientifically—had it resisted the globalization of mathematics, science, and technology at that time. And today, the same principle applies, though in the reverse direction (from West to East). To reject the globalization of science and technology because it represents Western influence and imperialism would not only amount to overlooking global contributions—drawn from many different parts of the world—that lie solidly behind so-called Western science and technology, but would also be quite a daft practical decision, given the extent to which the whole world can benefit from the process.

A Global Heritage

In resisting the diagnosis of globalization as a phenomenon of quintessentially Western origin, we have to be suspicious not only of the anti-Western rhetoric but also of the pro-Western chauvinism in many contemporary writings. Certainly, the Renaissance, the Enlightenment, and the Industrial Revolution were great achievements—and they occurred mainly in Europe and, later, in America. Yet many of these developments drew on the experience of the rest of the world, rather than being confined within the boundaries of a discrete Western civilization.

Our global civilization is a world heritage—not just a collection of disparate local cultures. When a modern mathematician in Boston invokes an algorithm to solve a difficult computational problem, she may not be aware that she is helping to commemorate the Arab mathematician Mohammad Ibn Musa-al-Khwarizmi, who flourished in the first half of the ninth century. (The word *algorithm* is derived from the name al-Khwarizmi.) There is a chain of intellectual relations that link Western mathematics and science to a collection of distinctly non-Western practitioners, of whom al-Khwarizmi was one. (The term *algebra* is derived from the title of his famous book *Al-Jabr wa-al-Muqabilah.*) Indeed, al-Khwarizmi is one of many non-Western contributors whose works influenced the European Renaissance and, later, the Enlightenment and the Industrial Revolution. The West must get full credit for the remarkable achievements that occurred in Europe and Europeanized America, but the idea of an immaculate Western conception is an imaginative fantasy.

Not only is the progress of global science and technology not an exclusively West-led phenomenon, but there were major global developments in which the West was not even involved. The printing of the world's first book was a marvelously globalized event. The technology of printing was, of course, entirely an achievement of the Chinese. But the content came from elsewhere. The first printed book was an Indian Sanskrit treatise, translated into Chinese by a half-Turk. The book, *Vajracchedika Prajnaparamitasutra* (sometimes referred to as "The Diamond Sutra"), is an old treatise on Buddhism; it was translated into Chinese from Sanskrit in the fifth century by Kumarajiva, a half-Indian and half-Turkish scholar who lived in a part of eastern Turkistan called Kucha but later migrated to China. It was printed four centuries later, in 868 A.D. All this involving China, Turkey, and India is globalization, all right, but the West is not even in sight.

Global Interdependences and Movements

The misdiagnosis that globalization of ideas and practices has to be resisted because it entails dreaded Westernization has played quite a regressive part in the colonial and postcolonial world. This assumption incites parochial tendencies and undermines the possibility of objectivity in science and knowledge. It is not only counterproductive in itself; given the global interactions throughout history, it can also cause non-Western societies to shoot themselves in the foot—even in their precious cultural foot.

Consider the resistance in India to the use of Western ideas and concepts in science and mathematics. In the nineteenth century, this debate fitted into a broader controversy about Western education versus indigenous Indian education. The "Westernizers," such as the redoubtable Thomas Babington Macaulay, saw no merit whatsoever in Indian tradition. "I have never found one among them [advocates of Indian tradition] who could deny that a single shelf of a good European library was worth the whole native literature of India and Arabia," he declared. Partly in retaliation, the advocates of native education resisted Western imports altogether. Both sides, however, accepted too readily the foundational dichotomy between two disparate civilizations.

European mathematics, with its use of such concepts as sine, was viewed as a purely "Western" import into India. In fact, the fifth-century Indian mathematician Aryabhata had discussed the concept of sine in his classic work on astronomy and mathematics in 499 A.D., calling it by its Sanskrit name, *jya-ardha* (literally, "half-chord"). This word, first shortened to *jya* in Sanskrit, eventually became the Arabic *jiba* and, later, *jaib*, which means "a cove or a bay." In his history of mathematics, Howard Eves explains that around 1150 A.D., Gherardo of Cremona, in his translations from the Arabic, rendered *jaib* as the Latin *sinus*, the corresponding word for a cove or a bay. And this is the source of the modern word *sine*. The concept had traveled full circle—from India, and then back.

To see globalization as merely Western imperialism of ideas and beliefs (as the rhetoric often suggests) would be a serious and costly error, in the same way that any European resistance to Eastern influence would have been at the beginning of the last millennium. Of course, there are issues related to globalization that do connect with imperialism (the history of conquests, colonialism, and alien rule remains relevant today in many ways), and a postcolonial understanding of the world has its merits. But it would be a great mistake to see globalization primarily as a feature of imperialism. It is much bigger—much greater—than that.

The issue of the distribution of economic gains and losses from globalization remains an entirely separate question, and it must be addressed as a further—and extremely relevant—issue. There is extensive evidence that the global economy has brought prosperity to many different areas of the globe. Pervasive poverty dominated the world a few centuries ago; there were only a few rare pockets of affluence. In overcoming that penury, extensive economic interrelations and modern technology have been and remain influential. What has happened in Europe, America, Japan, and East Asia has important messages for all other regions, and we cannot go very far into understanding the nature of globalization today without first acknowledging the positive fruits of global economic contacts.

Indeed, we cannot reverse the economic predicament of the poor across the world by withholding from them the great advantages of contemporary technology, the well-established efficiency of international trade and exchange, and the social as well as economic merits of living in an open society. Rather, the main issue is how to make good use of the remarkable benefits of economic intercourse and technological progress in a way that pays adequate attention to the interests of the deprived and the underdog. That is, I would argue, the constructive question that emerges from the so-called antiglobalization movements.

Are the Poor Getting Poorer?

The principal challenge relates to inequality—international as well as intranational. The troubling inequalities include disparities in affluence and also gross asymmetries in political, social, and economic opportunities and power.

A crucial question concerns the sharing of the potential gains from globalization—between rich and poor countries and among different groups within a country. It is not sufficient to understand that the poor of the world need globalization as much as the rich do; it is also important to make sure that they actually get what they need. This may require extensive institutional reform, even as globalization is defended.

There is also a need for more clarity in formulating the distributional questions. For example, it is often argued that the rich are getting richer and the poor poorer. But this is by no means uniformly so, even though there are cases in which this has happened. Much depends on the region or the group chosen and what indicators of economic prosperity are used. But the attempt to base the castigation of economic globalization on this rather thin ice produces a peculiarly fragile critique.

On the other side, the apologists of globalization point to their belief that the poor who participate in trade and exchange are mostly getting richer. Ergo—the argument runs—globalization is not unfair to the poor: they too benefit. If the central relevance of this question is accepted, then the whole debate turns on determining which side is correct in this empirical dispute. But is this the right battleground in the first place? I would argue that it is not.

Global Justice and the Bargaining Problem

Even if the poor were to get just a little richer, this would not necessarily imply that the poor were getting a fair share of the potentially vast benefits of global economic interrelations. It is not adequate to ask whether international inequality is getting marginally larger or smaller. In order to rebel against the appalling poverty and the staggering inequalities that characterize the contemporary world—or to protest against the unfair sharing of benefits of global cooperation—it is not necessary to show that the massive inequality or distributional unfairness is also getting marginally larger. This is a separate issue altogether.

When there are gains from cooperation, there can be many possible arrangements. As the game theorist and mathematician John Nash discussed more than half a century ago (in "The Bargaining Problem," published in *Econometrica* in 1950, which was cited, among other writings, by the Royal Swedish Academy of Sciences when Nash was awarded the Nobel Prize in economics), the central issue in general is not whether a particular arrangement is better for everyone than no cooperation at all would be, but whether that is a fair division of the benefits. One cannot rebut the criticism that a distributional arrangement is unfair simply by noting that all the parties are better off than they would be in the absence of cooperation; the real exercise is the choice *between* these alternatives.

An Analogy with the Family

By analogy, to argue that a particularly unequal and sexist family arrangement is unfair, one does not have to show that women would have done comparatively better had there been no families at all, but only that the sharing of the benefits is seriously unequal in that particular arrangement. Before the issue of gender justice became an explicitly recognized concern (as it has in recent decades), there were attempts to dismiss the issue of unfair arrangements within the family by suggesting that women did not need to live in families if they found the arrangements so unjust. It was also argued that since women as well as men benefit from living in families, the existing arrangements could not be unfair. But even when it is accepted that both men and women may typically gain from living in a family, the question of distributional fairness remains. Many different family arrangements—when compared with the absence of any family system—would satisfy the condition of being beneficial to both men and women. The real issue concerns how fairly benefits associated with these respective arrangements are distributed.

Likewise, one cannot rebut the charge that the global system is unfair by showing that even the poor gain something from global contacts and are not necessarily made poorer. That answer may or may not be wrong, but the question certainly is. The critical issue is not whether the poor are getting marginally poorer or richer. Nor is it whether they are better off than they would be had they excluded themselves from globalized interactions.

Again, the real issue is the distribution of globalization's benefits. Indeed, this is why many of the antiglobalization protesters, who seek a better deal for the underdogs of the world economy, are not—contrary to their own rhetoric and to the views attributed to them by others—really "antiglobalization." It is also why there is no real contradiction in the fact that the so-called antiglobalization protests have become among the most globalized events in the contemporary world.

Altering Global Arrangements

However, can those less-well-off groups get a better deal from globalized economic and social relations without dispensing with the market economy itself? They certainly can. The use of the market economy is consistent with many different ownership patterns, resource availabilities, social opportunities, and rules of operation (such as patent laws and antitrust regulations). And depending on these conditions, the market economy would generate different prices, terms of trade, income distribution, and, more generally, diverse overall outcomes. The arrangements for social security and other public interventions can make further modifications to the outcomes of the market processes, and together they can yield varying levels of inequality and poverty.

The central question is not whether to use the market economy. That shallow question is easy to answer, because it is hard to achieve economic prosperity without making extensive use of the opportunities of exchange and specialization that market relations offer. Even though the operation of a given market economy can be significantly defective, there is no way of dispensing with the institution of markets in general as a powerful engine of economic progress.

But this recognition does not end the discussion about globalized market relations. The market economy does not work by itself in global relations—indeed, it cannot operate alone even within a given country. It is not only the case that a market-inclusive system can generate very distinct results depending on various enabling conditions (such as how physical resources are distributed, how human resources are developed, what rules of business relations prevail, what social-security arrangements are in place, and so on). These enabling conditions themselves depend critically on economic, social, and political institutions that operate nationally and globally.

The crucial role of the markets does not make the other institutions insignificant, even in terms of the results that the market economy can produce. As has been amply established in empirical studies, market outcomes are massively influenced by public policies in education, epidemiology, land reform, microcredit facilities, appropriate legal protections, et cetera; and in each of these fields, there is work to be done through public action that can radically alter the outcome of local and global economic relations.

Institutions and Inequality

Globalization has much to offer; but even as we defend it, we must also, without any contradiction, see the legitimacy of many questions that the antiglobalization protesters ask. There may be a misdiagnosis about where the main problems lie (they do not lie in globalization, as such), but the ethical and human concerns that yield these questions call for serious reassessments of the adequacy of the national and global institutional arrangements that characterize the contemporary world and shape globalized economic and social relations.

Global capitalism is much more concerned with expanding the domain of market relations than with, say, establishing democracy, expanding elementary education, or enhancing the social opportunities of society's underdogs. Since globalization of markets is, on its own, a very inadequate approach to world prosperity, there is a need to go beyond the priorities that find expression in the chosen focus of global capitalism. As George Soros has pointed out, international business concerns often have a strong preference for working in orderly and highly organized autocracies rather than in activist and less-regimented democracies, and this can be a regressive influence on equitable development. Further, multinational firms can exert their influence on the priorities of public expenditure in less secure third-world countries by giving preference to the safety and convenience of the managerial classes and of privileged workers over the removal of widespread illiteracy, medical deprivation, and other adversities of the poor. These possibilities do not, of course, impose any insurmountable barrier to development, but it is important to make sure that the surmountable barriers are actually surmounted.

Omissions and Commissions

The injustices that characterize the world are closely related to various omissions that need to be addressed, particularly in institutional arrangements. I have tried to identify some of the main problems in my book *Development as Freedom* (Knopf, 1999). Global policies have a role here in helping the development of national institutions (for example, through defending democracy and supporting schooling and health facilities), but there is also a need to re-examine the adequacy of global institutional arrangements themselves. The distribution of the benefits in the global economy depends, among other things, on a variety of global institutional arrangements, including those for fair trade, medical initiatives, educational exchanges, facilities for technological dissemination, ecological and environmental restraints, and fair treatment of accumulated debts that were often incurred by irresponsible military rulers of the past.

In addition to the momentous omissions that need to be rectified, there are also serious problems of commission that must be addressed for even elementary global ethics. These include not only inefficient and inequitable trade restrictions that repress exports from poor countries, but also patent laws that inhibit the use of lifesaving drugs—for diseases like AIDS—and that give inadequate incentive for medical research aimed at developing nonrepeating medicines (such as vaccines). These issues have been much discussed on their own, but we must also note how they fit into a general pattern of unhelpful arrangements that undermine what globalization could offer.

Another—somewhat less discussed—global "commission" that causes intense misery as well as lasting deprivation relates to the involvement of the world powers in globalized arms trade. This is a field in which a new global initiative is urgently required, going beyond the need—the very important need—to curb terrorism, on which the focus is so heavily concentrated right now. Local wars and military conflicts, which have very destructive consequences (not least on the economic prospects of poor countries), draw not only on regional tensions but also on global trade in arms and weapons. The world establishment is firmly entrenched in this business: the Permanent Members of the Security Council of the United Nations were together responsible for 81 percent of world arms exports from 1996 through 2000. Indeed, the world leaders who express deep frustration at the "irresponsibility" of antiglobalization protesters lead the countries that make the most money in this terrible trade. The G-8 countries sold 87 percent of the total supply of arms exported in the entire world. The U.S. share alone has just gone up to almost 50 percent of the total sales in the world. Furthermore, as much as 68 percent of the American arms exports went to developing countries.

The arms are used with bloody results—and with devastating effects on the economy, the polity, and the society. In some ways, this is a continuation of the unhelpful role of world powers in the genesis and flowering of political militarism in Africa from the 1960s to the 1980s, when the Cold War was fought over Africa. During these decades, when military overlords—Mobuto Sese Seko or Jonas Savimbi or whoever—busted social and political arrangements (and, ultimately, economic order as well) in Africa, they could rely on support either from the United States and its allies or from the Soviet Union, depending on their military alliances. The world powers bear an awesome responsibility for helping in the subversion of democracy in Africa and for all the far-reaching negative consequences of that subversion. The pursuit of arms "pushing" gives them a continuing role in the escalation of military conflicts today—in Africa and elsewhere. The U.S. refusal to agree to a joint crackdown even on illicit sales of small arms (as proposed by UN Secretary-General Kofi Annan) illustrates the difficulties involved.

Fair Sharing of Global Opportunities

To conclude, the confounding of globalization with Westernization is not only ahistorical, it also distracts attention from the many potential benefits of global integration. Globalization is a historical process that has offered an abundance of opportunities and rewards in the past and continues to do so today. The very existence of potentially large benefits makes the question of fairness in sharing the benefits of globalization so critically important.

The central issue of contention is not globalization itself, nor is it the use of the market as an institution, but the inequity in the overall balance of institutional arrangements—which produces very unequal sharing of the benefits of globalization. The question is not just whether the poor, too, gain something from globalization, but whether they get a fair share and a fair opportunity. There is an urgent need for reforming institutional arrangements—in addition to national ones—in order to overcome both the errors of omission and those of commission that tend to give the poor across the world such limited opportunities. Globalization deserves a reasoned defense, but it also needs reform.

Globalization and Its Limits *Reports of the Death of the National Economy Are Greatly Exaggerated*

Robert Wade

Political economist Robert Wade borrows the title of his essay from a famous story told about novelist Mark Twain. When a newspaper falsely published Twain's obituary, he replied that reports of his death were greatly exaggerated! Wade argues that globalization in the current era is not unprecedented: for example, the proportion of cross-border economic flows a century ago were comparable to or even greater than those of the present period (although, note, the total size of the global economy was far smaller). More significant yet, Wade argues, most production and consumption nowadays, even in the most economically advanced economies, remains securely confined to national borders. (Although Wade's article was published a decade ago, the picture has not much changed in subsequent years.) In brief, reports of the death of the national economy are grossly exaggerated!

Although Wade rightly stresses that globalization was not born yesterday, might he underestimate both what is new about globalization and the importance of its impact? Even if the bulk of goods, jobs, and capital remain at home, can you think of possible reasons why the impact of transnational flows might be greater than their relative size in national economies?

"Globalization" is the buzz word. We are now in a "globalized" era characterized by an unprecedentedly high level of integration of national economies, it is said. This integration is itself a reflection of the greatly increased mobility of finance, physical capital, and even labor across the entire world.[1] Because of this mobility, "firms all over the world [now face] a common market for products and factors."[2] In these conditions government attempts to shape the national economy's evolution are about as effective as pushing on a piece of string.

I urge skepticism. The world economy is more inter-national than global. In the bigger national economies, more than 80 percent of production is for domestic consumption and more than 80 percent of investment by domestic investors. Companies are rooted in national home bases with national regulatory regimes. Populations are much less mobile across borders than are goods, finance, or ideas. These points suggest more scope for government actions to boost the productivity of firms operating within their territory than is commonly thought and than is implied in the statement that "governments today should do [à propos direct support to industry] what they find most difficult to do: nothing!"[3]

First I present some evidence in favor of the globalization picture and then show how the picture changes when further evidence is introduced. Indeed, I stress throughout the paper the hazards of mounting exalted generalizations about the nature of the world economy or the economic significance of nation-states, so mixed is the evidence and so disputable the meaning of any piece of it.

Globalization of Production and Finance: Evidence in Favor

If we take the textbook model of national economies as sets of immobile factors of production (capital, labor, and land) and of "uninational" firms connected across borders only through the sale and purchase of mobile goods and services, then the current world economy is obviously more interconnected than that. Or to take another standard, it is certainly more interconnected today than in 1960. At the micro level a higher proportion of firms now have operations in many more countries than before; a higher percentage of total value added is produced by firms outside their home country; and any one firm faces more foreign-based competitors, both at home and abroad. At the macro level national economies are much more integrated through trade and foreign direct investment than in 1960. National borders are consequently more permeable, what happens in one country's markets is affected more by what happens in other countries', international competition has therefore become more intense, uncertainty has increased, and the "global" dimension of national economic policymaking has become more important.

For example, interconnectedness through trade has vastly increased since 1960. Among the OECD economies (the richest 24 industrial economies), the ratio of exports to GDP roughly doubled from 1960 to 1990, rising from 9.5 percent in 1960 to 20.5 percent in 1990.[4] At the world level, trade has consistently grown faster than output, implying rising interconnectedness. From 1965 to 1990 world merchandise trade grew at an average of one and a half times the rate of growth of world GDP.[5] So an increasing proportion of production from each national economy is for foreign markets, which raises the importance of foreign markets relative to domestic markets and so makes a country's relative income more dependent on the ability of its firms to compete against imports in domestic markets and against other producers in foreign markets.

Interconnectedness through foreign direct investment (FDI) has grown even faster than through trade over the 1980s. Measured FDI flows grew three times faster than trade flows and almost four times faster than output. Between 1983 and 1990 they averaged 27 percent a year, quadrupling over the decade.[6] In addition to FDI, joint ventures, nonequity corporate alliances, and subcontracting between firms located in different countries blossomed during the 1980s.[7] Many firms are now involved in complex international networks covering all areas of their operations (research, production, and marketing), as they were not in 1960. Even German and Japanese firms have begun to shift production out of their home bases, having been unusually concentrated at home until the 1980s.

Most large industrial and financial corporations are now multinational in the sense of holding some of their productive assets abroad, and this is a real change from 1960. In the United Kingdom, for example, 20 percent of the country's largest multinational corporations (MNCs) had foreign subsidiaries in more than 20 countries in 1963; only seven years later, in 1970, the figure had jumped to 70 percent, where it has subsequently remained.[8] On a world scale, more than a third of the employment and nearly a third of the sales of the world's sixty-eight largest manufacturing corporations in the mid-1980s was accounted for by their foreign subsidiaries. One estimate says that all MNCs now control a *third* of the world's private sector productive assets.[9] In terms of their domestic sales and income they control more than 30 percent of private GNP in Germany, France, Italy, the United Kingdom, Netherlands, Belgium, Switzerland, Canada, Australia and more than 20 percent for Japan and the United States. These figures have been rising since the mid-eighties.[10]

These trends have made for at least two basic changes in the nature and intensity of competition. On the one hand, competition is intensified by market interpenetration. In the United States, for example, the biggest U.S. firms typically faced two to five main competitors in 1960, almost all of them other U.S.-based firms playing by the same rules. Today, the firm may have ten or more serious competitors, half of them foreign, playing by different rules. On the other hand, competition is reduced by the growing importance of *intrafirm* trade. Intrafirm trade involving U.S.-based MNCs amounts to about 30 percent of U.S. exports and 18 percent of U.S. imports, whereas intrafirm trade of all MNCs, whether U.S.-based or not, accounts for about 40 percent of U.S. imports and 30 to 36 percent of U.S. exports.[11]

Given the increased multinationalization of firms' operations, we can agree with Robert Reich that the legal entity of a "U.S. corporation" (or British, or German) does not have the same consequences for American employment and economic growth as it did in the 1950s and 1960s.[12]

But the most dramatic multinationalization of all has come in finance. The stock of international bank lending (cross-border lending plus domestic lending denominated in foreign currency) rose in just ten years from 4 percent of OECD GDP in 1980 to 44 percent in 1990.[13] World turnover in foreign exchange, or currency trading, grew by over a third in just three and a half years between April 1989 and September 1992, at which time it was running at $900 billion each day. Yes, day. Altogether, liquid capital is ricocheting across the foreign exchanges in amounts more than thirty times greater than and quite independently of trade flows. In consequence governments have much less discretion about long-term interest rates than they did in 1960, when there were exchange controls, when lending by banks and other financial institutions was regulated, and when international borrowing and lending were tiny.

The development since the mid-1980s of markets in "financial derivative" contracts, which now in some sense implicate a large part of world finance, adds a new dimension of uncertainty and instability to world finance. Derivatives have proven very difficult to regulate, partly because little is known publicly about what the contracts look like. The IMF is on record as saying that we may only know the risk characteristics of derivatives once an economic downturn begins.[14] In terms of the ability of governments to manage finance, derivatives make the power of private financial property still more absolute, because they are so difficult to regulate.

Technology, too, has become highly internationalized in the sense that companies are exploiting their technological innovations internationally. This is clear from figures on the extent to which firms protect their innovations by taking out patents in foreign markets, so as to reap benefits from trading the disembodied innovation or the exports that embody it. The share of the patents in advanced countries that have a foreign origin is large: 45 percent of the patents granted in 1990 in the United States came from abroad (in the sense that the inventor's address was outside the United States), and 45 percent of the patent applications at the European Patent Office came from outside Europe. (Japan is the big exception, where foreign patents account for only 12 percent.)[15] If we compare the proportion of foreign patents (45 percent) with the degree of import penetration (around 20 percent), we see that the internationalization of the exploitation of technology is substantially higher even than the internationalization of trade for the OECD economies.

These integrating developments are caused in large part—so goes the standard view, which I qualify below—by . . . an astonishing cheapening and speeding of transport and telecommunications (inventions in microelectronics, new industrial materials, and lasers). . . .

Globalization: The Qualifications

However, using two eyes rather than one we find evidence that the world economy is less internationalized, less integrated than this account suggests.

Trade

The share of trade in GDP is still quite small in all but the smallest countries. Exports account for 12 percent of GDP or less for the United States, Japan, and single-unit Europe,[16] and the Asian and Latin American averages are well below 10 percent. *This means that 90 percent or more of these economies consists of production for the domestic market and that 90 percent of consumption is produced at home.*

What is more, the current level of integration of national economies through trade is apparently not much higher than the level reached by 1913, after which trade integration plummeted, beginning to recover only after World War II.[17]

World trade growth has been slowing over the 1980s and 1990s relative to output growth (the ratio fell from 1.65 in 1965–80 to 1.34 in 1980–90).[18] This slowdown is partly a function of the world economic slowdown of the 1970s and 1980s. (The average growth of GDP per head in the industrialized world fell from 3.6 percent a year in 1950–73 to 2 percent in 1973–89.)[19] But a long-term structural change is also involved, namely, the steep fall in manufacturing's share of OECD GDP (from 29 percent in the 1960s to 23 percent in the 1980s) and the rise in the share of less trade-intensive services. So we should not assume that trade integration will go on increasing as the world economy grows faster, because faster growth will accelerate the shift from manufacturing to services.

Nor should we assume that intrafirm trade, hailed by many as a major new development, will go on increasing. Analysts have tended to exaggerate the significance of intrafirm trade in the world economy by extrapolating from the United States, which has the most (perhaps only) reliable statistics on it. But this is misleading because the United States has the highest share of intrafirm trade in total trade, insofar as we can judge. And note that the share of intrafirm trade in total U.S. trade showed no significant increase between 1977 and 1989, holding steady at around a third.[20] Overall, intrafirm trade is important but not dominant, and probably not rising as a share of total trade.[21]

Moreover, the trade figures show trends that are far from consistent with the picture of global economic integration. World trade is highly concentrated among the northern countries, and the concentration is rising; the rest of the world has a small and falling share. The North's share of world trade rose from 81 percent in 1970 to 84 percent in 1989. (*North* refers to "developed market economies" [virtually the same coverage as OECD], *South* to "developing countries and territories" plus "socialist countries of Asia" in the World Bank's World Development Report classifications. *South* includes the "newly industrialized countries" [NICs].) North–South trade has fallen as a proportion of the total. The share of northern imports coming from the non-oil-exporting South, excluding the four East Asian NICs, fell from 7.1 percent in 1970 to 6.2 percent in 1990.[22]

Trade by the United States with low-wage countries (those where wages are less than one-half the U.S. levels) equals only 3 percent of its GDP. This is not much higher than the equivalent figure in 1960, when Japan and some European countries were counted as low-wage countries by the same definition.

The "marginalization" of the South as a whole over the 1970s and 1980s is due largely to the *negative* growth of primary product exports for the world as a whole and a sharp decline of the share of the South within that falling total. This development reflects both the fall in oil prices over the 1980s and a wider fall in the terms of trade for all primary product exports. Since 1980 average commodity prices have dropped by more than one-half in real terms.[23]

True, exports of manufactures from the South to the North have grown very fast over the 1970s, 1980s, and 1990s, at almost 15 percent a year from 1960 to 1990 (in constant 1980 U.S. dollars). The share of manufactures in the South's exports to the North rose from 16 percent to 53 percent between 1970 and 1989, with the increase concentrated in the 1980s, or from 23 percent of *non-fuel* exports to 71 percent between 1970 and 1989.[24] Fast-rising flows of southern manufactured exports to the North do represent a new, more globalized pattern in world trade. But this fast growth started from a very low base; and by 1989 manufactured exports from the South still accounted for only *16 percent* of world manufactured exports.[25] Indeed, several economists have argued that imports from the South cannot be a significant cause of unemployment in the North precisely because the share of the South in northern imports is too small.[26]

Moreover, the South experienced an adverse trend in its terms of trade even in manufactured exports: during the 1980s the prices of manufactured exports from the South rose slightly, but the prices of manufactured exports from the North rose four times faster.[27]

Future growth of manufactured exports from the South is in question because almost half of the South's manufactured exports go to just one market, the United States; yet, the United States has "only" 23 percent of world GNP. If and when the United States cures its balance-of-payments deficit, its imports will go down and its exports up. Perhaps the South's manufactured exports will be diverted elsewhere, or perhaps North–South trade integration will further decline.

The NICs account for a very small proportion of the North–South trade. The proportion of northern imports from the four Asian NICs increased from 2.2 percent in 1970 to 5.5 percent in 1990. But the share from the three Latin American NICs (Mexico, Brazil, Argentina) fell from 2.6 percent in 1970 to 2.1 percent in 1990. The NICs' share of world industrial output also remains small. The share of the East Asian four plus Mexico and Brazil rose from 2.7 percent in 1970 to 5.8 percent in 1989.[28] This change is small compared to shifts in earlier periods and hardly supports the idea of a globalizing transformation in world trade.

Moreover, North–South trade is strongly regionalized. Latin America trades predominantly with North America. Eastern Europe, Africa, and the Middle East trade predominantly with Western Europe. East and Southeast Asian countries have the biggest share of their trade with North America, the second biggest share with Japan.

In terms of trade policy, we see contrary movements, with trade barriers rising in the North and coming down in the South. Although northern tariffs have come down from an OECD average of 25 percent in 1950 to about 5 percent in 1990, their place has been taken by an assortment of nontariff barriers. Of the twenty-four OECD economies, only four of them on balance reduced obstacles to trade over the 1980s (the four being those that had the highest barriers to begin with: Japan, Australia, New Zealand, and Turkey). The other twenty, led by the United States, have been raising new barriers in the form of quotas, "voluntary" trade restraints, and managed trade.[29] By the mid-1980s nontariff barriers covered over a quarter of all industrialized country imports.[30] A good part of intra-OECD foreign direct investment flows is intended to hop over trade barriers to OECD markets. And a good part of foreign direct investment from OECD countries to the South is intended to capture unutilized quotas for access to OECD markets. Both flows suggest that many companies guess that trade restrictions to OECD markets will continue.

On the other hand, many southern countries over the 1980s have liberalized their trade regimes, lowering direct controls on imports and reducing the degree of overvaluation of the exchange rate. Tariffs and import controls undoubtedly remain much higher in the South than in the North, but the direction of change is sharply different.

The point to emphasize here is that in the North *national borders continue to be control points where governments can affect the quantity and price of cross-border merchandise transactions*, nowadays less through tariffs than through a whole panoply of nontariff barriers. In the South this remains true in much of Asia and Latin America (though not in most of Africa, where the state is imploding).

Overall, the trade data on both flows and policies do not support any simple idea that the world economy is operating in a new, more internationalized, or less nationally or regionally segmented, way.

Foreign Direct Investment

. . . [D]espite fast growth over the 1980s, outgoing FDI is still quite small in the major northern economies as a proportion of net domestic business investment. The typical order of magnitude is between 5 and 15 percent over the 1980s. The United Kingdom, with 65 percent, is quite exceptional. Incoming FDI is also quite small for the major northern economies relative to their net domestic business investment, between one-half of 1 percent (Japan) and 14 percent (the United States).[31] *So domestic investment by domestic capital easily dominates both direct investment overseas and foreign investment at home.*

The globalization image shows investment capital racing away from the North as companies take the whole world as their oyster. This too turns out to be largely untrue. World FDI flows are highly concentrated within the northern countries, and their share is rising (as with trade). *Two-thirds* of inward FDI flows worldwide in the 1980s have been into the United States and the EU (not including intra-EU flows). The biggest recipient by far is the United States, which alone got 46 percent of world inflows in 1985–89; the EU got just 19 percent, and Japan accepted virtually none.[32]

The South's share of the world FDI stock fell by a third between the late 1960s and the late 1980s.[33] And during the great FDI boom of the 1980s the South's share of world inflows fell from 25 percent to 19 percent. Yet this occurred at a time when dwindling access to bank finance raised developing country dependence on FDI. Even East and Southeast Asia lost a share of FDI flows from the North; and the share is now surprisingly small. In 1989–91 only 6 percent of U.S.

outgoing FDI went to Asia; 4 percent of the EU's; and 13 percent of Japan's.[34] The South's small share of world FDI stock is heavily concentrated in just six countries: the four East Asian "tigers" (South Korea, Taiwan, Hong Kong, Singapore), plus Mexico and Brazil. (So in talking about the South's integration through FDI we should disaggregate at least to two categories, these six countries on the one hand, the rest of the South on the other.) In the 1990s, however, the share of the South in world FDI flows has risen dramatically, to over a third in 1992–93. But the world total has fallen sharply since the 1980s; and most of the South's inflows have continued to be in Asia.[35]

North–South FDI patterns show the same regional clustering as for trade. That is, the dominant foreign investor in Latin America is the United States; in Eastern Europe and North Africa, Western Europe; in East and Southeast Asia, Japan followed by the United States (but there is some evidence that U.S. firms are reducing their share of foreign investment in Asia and increasing it in Latin America). With the partial exception of the United States in Asia we see rather little FDI crossover from the United States, Japan, or Europe to the low-wage region of one of the other two (e.g., EU investment in Asia or Japanese investment in Latin America). Japanese firms in northern Mexico and Hong Kong textilers in Mauritius seem to be more exceptions than harbingers. This is surprising in relation to standard FDI theories, which give little attention to spatial proximity in location decisions.

An important new development in FDI flows in the late 1980s is the emergence of the East Asian tigers as sources of outgoing FDI. In China and Southeast Asia the four are beginning to be major foreign investors, to the point where Korea and Taiwan have been the source of the biggest flows to several Southeast Asian countries in several recent years. Yet even in the case of these new FDI sources, half or more of their outgoing FDI is to North America or Europe. They fit with the bigger pattern of outgoing FDI going mostly to already rich countries.

Another parallel with the trade story (in addition to regionalization) is that countries of the South are liberalizing their FDI regimes at breakneck speed, led by Eastern Europe and the former Soviet republics. But so also—and here the FDI story departs from the trade story—are countries of the North. In the single year of 1991 at least 34 countries, rich and poor alike, made a total of 82 major changes to their FDI laws. Eighty of those changes made the rules less restrictive.[36]

Overall, what is striking is how *few* jobs have been lost in the North and gained in the South by MNCs seeking to exploit labor cost differentials. It is true that since the mid-1980s or so a labor force of some 1,200 million people has become accessible in developing countries, at an average cost of less than $2 an hour, when the North employs 350 million people at an average hourly wage of $18. But an analysis of the impact of MNCs on world employment by the United Nations Conference on Trade and Development (UNCTAD) suggests that MNC location decisions are driven mainly by the search for natural resources, markets, good infrastructure, and an educated, committed work force. Cheaper labor as such is not a major factor. Electronics assembly turns out not to be the norm.[37]. . .

Finance Capital

There is no doubt that the world market for standardized financial assets such as currencies, government bonds and commodity, currency and interest futures has become highly integrated over the 1980s. The governmental barriers to finance capital roaming across the OECD world have been largely eliminated. This development is fueling concern that more fully integrated financial markets may raise the risk of systemic failure, through the failure of one firm passing rapidly around the world or through fraud being easier to perpetuate on a world scale. But even in finance there are qualifications.

First, the number of financial products that are sold in highly integrated world markets—integrated enough to be called global—is quite limited: currencies, government bonds, and futures are the main ones. Stock markets are far from being fully integrated, because few companies have a sufficiently global reputation for trading in their stock to be active outside the home market. Financial regulations, tax systems, accounting practices, corporate ownership rules are all mainly national, with some increase in efforts to harmonize rules and practices between national authorities, supplemented by some regional rules in Europe and a limited amount of global cooperation and global rules (e.g., Bank of International Settlement capital adequacy standards).[38]

Second, domestic saving and investment rates remain highly correlated among the OECD countries. This aspect has been interpreted to mean that domestic investment is strongly constrained by domestic saving, rather than being easily financed from other countries' saving; and therefore that even financial capital is not very mobile even within the OECD world. In the 1970s about 75 percent of the variance in investment share among the OECD countries was accounted for by variation in saving; in the 1980s the figure was 60 percent. By contrast, among U.S. states, which constitute as fully integrated a real-world capital market as it is possible to get, the saving–investment correlation is essentially zero. . . .

Third, the differences in the price of borrowed funds between different national markets remain substantial, even between the three major economies, the United States, Japan, and Germany.[39] All studies agree on this. But some find that the size of the real interest rate differential is declining, and others find no evidence of a decline.[40] The differences in the price of *equity* capital in different national markets are bigger again than the differences in the price of loan capital.[41] So the overall price of capital (loan capital and equity capital) is even more unequal across national borders than differences in real interest rates would suggest.

All this suggests that there is "a major mystery in the world's capital markets. Among major countries where there was no country risk, the predicted equalization of capital costs did not occur in the 1980s, despite the existence of what everyone took to be a world capital market,"[42] all this despite a huge increase in net capital flows, especially from Japan.

Two qualifications are in order. First, for all the evidence that capital is not fully mobile and that the overall cost of capital is not equalized, it is equally striking that the cost of capital does not vary between countries by anything close to the variation on many other variables. Real interest rates differ within the North and between North and South by no more than about five times; real wages, years of schooling, number of scientists in the labor force, and so on, differ by ten to fifty times. For all the less than full mobility of financial capital across national boundaries, labor of most types is much less mobile again.[43]

Second, the differences in real interest rates between countries today are probably not so different from the differences forty and even 100 years ago. Indeed, a recent study concludes that "every available descriptor of financial markets in the late nineteenth and early twentieth centuries suggests that they were more fully integrated than they were before or have been since"[44]—despite the huge improvements in communications.

We have been considering evidence that runs counter to the notion of the world economy as highly and unprecedentedly integrated. Cross-border market exchanges are certainly much greater as a proportion of total market exchanges in 1990 than in 1960. But exports equal to 5 to 10 percent of GDP for the United States, Japan, and single-unit Europe and foreign ownership of domestic capital plus domestic ownership of foreign capital equal to 5 to 10 percent of domestic capital stock (averages for the late 1980s) hardly count as overwhelming internationalization of production. Production and investment remain very largely nationally owned and oriented (or regionally, in the case of Europe). . . .

The picture that emerges from evidence of this sort shows resources as relatively immobile across national economic borders (or regional borders in the case of the EU). Ironically, some of the reasons for the continuing immobility have to do with the greater ease of mobility. The lower costs of closing great distances mean that the competitive position of nations and firms is today less determined by differential access to raw materials, markets, or investment than it has been at any time prior to, say, 1960. At least in skill- and innovation-intensive activities competitive advantage is now far more affected by factors such as physical infrastructure, a committed, flexible work force, and by the growth of unique characteristics in supplier–user and other support relationships that can—not being open to all—generate more innovation, higher productivity, and quasi-monopolistic rents. These new factors in competitive advantage raise the advantages of immobility and colocation in the production of skill- and innovation-intensive goods and services.

Governments can do a lot to enhance the advantages of immobility and proximity, through public policies for education, infrastructure, business networks, and targeted industrial support. The overwhelming bulk of a nation's resources that are not mobile, including physical capital and the high value-added functions of even the biggest of the home-based MNCs, give governments leverage to work with. The interest of firms in social and physical infrastructure and in a skilled and committed work force may check the temptation for governments to cut social and labor standards in the hope of securing extra jobs. On the other hand, the privatization drive that has swept through both North and South over the

1980s and 1990s may have facilitated just this response, as both states and labor unions lose the ability to exercise social control over resource allocation. The point is that the picture is mixed.

Even in the case of international finance, apparently the most technology-driven liberalization of all, we may be on the verge of a reassertion of international regulations and national controls. There is now a growing reaction against some of the consequences of financial liberalization for the "real" (national) economy, including instability and loss of policy autonomy and growing political support for at least mild measures to reduce international capital mobility (such as a small transactions tax on spot foreign exchange transactions). During a financial crisis proponents of greater control will gain ground in the face of the need to defend the balance of payments. Spain, Portugal, and Ireland did in fact impose or tighten capital controls during the European financial crisis of 1992. And crisis apart, U.S. and U.K. financiers, who led the drive to financial deregulation worldwide, may begin to see some collective reregulation as a way to lessen the competitive pressures from upstart financial centers.[45]

In the states of the South we may see a reassertion of the role of the state and even a deliberate step toward disintegration from the world economy for another, more distress-driven reason. The catch-up of southern economies is about moving up the ladder of skill-intensive activities. But the North has a comparative advantage in skill-intensive activities, first, because skilled people are less scarce and therefore less expensive than unskilled people compared to the South, and second, because externalities and economies of scale mean that skills are not only cheaper but also more productive, because skilled people have a greater envelope of skilled activities (people, firms, industries) to interact with. Many countries of the South that have fast-rising populations will find it difficult to raise the ratio of skilled to unskilled people as fast as the ladder itself is rising. It is at least possible that the difficulties of competing in international markets will strengthen the hand of political forces that seek to pursue more autarchic, state-led policies. This would then be another way in which, in the South as well as in the North, reports of the death of the national economy are greatly exaggerated.

Notes

1. "The Stateless Corporation," *Business Week,* 14 May 1990. See also Robert Reich, *The Work of Nations* (New York: Knopf, 1991); Kenichi Ohmae, *The Borderless World* (New York: Harper, 1993); Paul Kennedy, "Preparing for the 21st Century: Winners and Losers," *New York Review of Books,* 11 February 1993. For arguments from a left-wing perspective that also accept the reality of full-blown globalization as the dominant process in the world economy, see Manfred Bienefeld, "Capitalism and the nation-state in the dog days of the twentieth century," *Socialist Register* 30 (1994): 94–129; and "On Transformational Growth: Edward J. Nell Interviewed by Steven Pressman," *Journal of Political Economy* 6 (1994): 107–32. David Gordon gives an alternative view from the left in "The Global Economy: New Edifice or Crumbling Foundations?," *New Left Review* 68 (1988): 24–64.
2. Richard Nelson and Gavin Wright, "The Rise and Fall of American Technological Leadership: The Postwar Era in Historical Perspective," *Journal of Economic Literature* vol. 30, no. 4 (December 1992).

3. Richard Brown and DeAnne Julius, "Is Manufacturing Still Special in the New World Order?," first prize 1993 Amex Bank Review awards, summarized in *The Amex Bank Review* 20, no. 9 (1993).
4. *OECD National Accounts (Main Aggregates), 1960–1990*, vol. 1 (Paris: OECD, 1992), using 1985 exchange rates and prices.
5. World Bank, *World Development Report, 1992* (Washington, D.C.: World Bank, 1992), World Tables, tables 2 and 14.
6. Nominal flows in U.S. dollars. United Nations, *World Investment Report* (New York: United Nations, 1992), p. 1.
7. David Levy, "International Production and Sourcing: Trends and Issues," *STI Review*, no. 13 (December 1993).
8. Grazia Ietto-Gillies, "Transnational Companies and U.K. Competitiveness: Does Ownership Matter?," table 9.5, in Kirsty Hughes, ed., *The Future of U.K. Competitiveness and the Role of Industrial Policy* (London: Policy Studies Institute, 1993). The figure for 1990 was 72 percent. The number of firms was 44 in 1963, 46 in 1970, and 63 in 1990.
9. *World Investment Report 1993: Transnational Corporations and Integrated International Production* (New York: United Nations Publications, 1993).
10. The figure is calculated by adding the value added of foreign-based MNCs in the home economy to that of the foreign output of home-based MNCs. John Dunning, "The Global Economy and the National Governance of Economies: A Plea for a Fundamental Re-think," mimeo, 1992, p. 9.
11. David Levy, "International Production and Sourcing: Trends and Issues," *STI Review*, December 1993: 13–59, table 4, figures for 1985 and 1988. Also see United Nations Centre on Transnational Corporations (UNCTC), *World Investment Report: The Triad in Foreign Direct Investment* (New York: United Nations, 1990). Figures are for 1985.
12. Robert Reich, *The Work of Nations* (New York: Knopf, 1991).
13. "Free Fall?" *The Economist*, 4–10 January 1992, p. 9.
14. IMF, "International Capital Markets: Developments and Prospects," *World Economic and Financial Surveys*, April 1989.
15. Daniele Archibugi and Jonathan Michie, "The Globalization of Technology: Myths and Realities," *Research Papers in Management Studies No. 18* (Cambridge: Cambridge University, 1992–93). The U.S. figures refer to patents granted (because patents are only published once granted); the European patents refer to patent applications (because it is the applications that are published).
16. Andrew Glyn and Bob Sutcliffe, "Global but Leaderless? The New Capitalist Order," *The Socialist Register* 28 (1992), figure 1. The earlier figure for exports to GDP was higher because it includes intra-European trade.
17. To what extent does this finding reflect the dominance in 1913 of an island economy, Britain—with an island's high dependence on trade—and the subsequent precipitous fall in Britain's share of world GDP? To what extent does it reflect a bias in the trade and income statistics in the early period—accurate trade data, undercounted income?
18. World Bank, *World Development Report, 1992* (Washington, D.C.: World Bank, 1992), World Tables, tables 2 and 14.
19. World Bank, *World Development Report, 1991* (New York: Oxford University Press, 1991), p. 14.
20. OECD, "Globalisation of Industrial Activities: Background Synthesis Report," *Directorate for Science, Technology, and Industry*, 26 November 1993, p. 16.
21. See Sheila Page, *How Developing Countries Trade* (London: Routledge, 1994), chap. 6.
22. UNCTAD, "Handbook of International Trade and Development Statistics, 1990" (New York: United Nations, 1991), table A1 3.4.
23. World Bank, "Global Economic Prospects and the Developing Countries," summarized in "Poor Relations," *The Economist*, 16 April 1994, p. 118.

24. The figures are derived from UNCTAD's "Handbook of Trade and Development Statistics" by Adrian Wood, presented in *North–South Trade, Employment and Inequality: Changing Fortunes in a Skill-driven World* (Oxford, Clarendon, 1993), chap. 1, table 1.
25. The statistics on which these direction of trade conclusions rest are in *current* exchange rates. This biases downward the *volume* of trade flows from the South, because less developed countries as a group have experienced a large depreciation of their exchange rates relative to the North since the 1960s (between 1960 and 1984, of 20 to 40 percent for low-income countries and up to 25 percent for middle-income oil-importing countries, with these figures probably having doubled by 1992). The depreciation is spread fairly evenly among geographic regions and low- and middle-income categories (except for the oil exporters in certain periods). Correcting for this effect is a difficult operation that has not been done for the sorts of disaggregations dealt with here. But in the judgment of Adrian Wood, who has wrestled with this issue at length, making the correction would not change the broad conclusions drawn. See Adrian Wood, "Global Trends in Real Exchange Rates, 1960–84," *World Development* 19, no. 4 (1991): 317–32.
26. Richard Freeman, "Is Globalization Impoverishing Low Skill American Workers?," (unpublished paper), Economics Department, Harvard University, 1993.
27. Keith Griffin and Azizur Rahman Khan, "Globalization and the Developing World: An Essay on the International Dimensions of Development in the Post–Cold War Era," *Human Development Report Occasional Papers* (United Nations Development Programme/Human Development Report Office, 1992), p. 20.
28. "World" includes the "socialist" economies (USSR, Hungary, etc.). Argentina is excluded because 1970 data were not available. UNCTAD "Handbook, 1991" tables 6.1, 6.3, 6.4. The four Asian NICs produced 0.74 percent of world industrial production in 1970, 2.54 percent in 1989. The European NICs (Ireland, Portugal, Spain, Greece, Yugoslavia) produced 2.72 percent in 1970, 3.15 percent in 1989.
29. C. Fred Bergsten, "The World Economy after the Cold War," *California Management Review,* Winter 1992: 62.
30. J. Nogues, A. Olechowski, and L. A. Winters, "The Extent of Nontariff Barriers to Industrial Countries' Imports," *World Bank Economic Review* 1 (1986): 181–99.
31. Glyn and Sutcliffe, "Global but Leaderless?," table 2.
32. United Nations, *World Investment Report, 1992* (New York: United Nations, 1992), p. 20.
33. Griffin and Khan, "Globalization and the Developing World," p. 23.
34. Ibid.
35. Report to UNCTAD's Commission on Transnational Corporations, summarized in *Financial Times,* 4 May 1994, p. 7.
36. "Asian Adventures," *The Economist,* 30 May–5 June 1992, p. 17. Is the direction really so unidirectional? What about increasing use of local content requirements and export requirements?
37. UNCTAD, *World Investment Report* (Geneva, UNCTAD, 1994).
38. "Globalisation, Regional Blocs, and Local Finance," *Amex Bank Review* 20, no. 2 (1993): 2–7.
39. See, for example, "Fear of Finance," *The Economist,* Special Survey, 19 September 1992, p. 22.
40. J. Frankel, "Measuring International Capital Mobility: A Review," *American Economic Review* 82, no. 2 (1992): 197–202, finds convergence. B. Kasman and C. Pigott, "Interest Rate Divergences among the Major Industrial Countries," *Federal Reserve Bank of New York Quarterly Review,* Autumn, 1988: 28–44, do not.
41. Lester Thurow, *Head to Head: The Coming Economic Battle among Japan, Europe, and America* (New York: Morrow, 1992), p. 43.
42. Ibid.
43. I am indebted to Adrian Wood for this point.
44. Robert Zevin, "Are World Financial Markets More Open? If So, Why and With What Effects?," in T. Banuri and J. Schor, eds., *Financial Openness and National Autonomy* (Oxford: Oxford University Press, 1992), pp. 51–52. He uses indicators such as co-movement between interest rates and share prices

in different national financial markets; international assets and liabilities relative to domestic assets and income; and proportions of foreign securities traded on national markets.

45. Eric Helleiner, "Post-globalization: Is the Financial Liberalization Trend Likely to Be Reversed?," in D. Drache and Robert Boyer, eds., *The Future of Nations and the Limits of Markets* (Montreal: McGill-Queen's University Press, forthcoming).

Sinking Globalization

Niall Ferguson

Historian Niall Ferguson documents extensive parallels between an earlier period of globalization, in the late nineteenth and early twentieth centuries, and the present era. In both cases, there have been extensive international trade and unregulated movements of capital (including financial flows, such as currency exchange and stock trading, and direct investments in manufacturing and services). Both eras have been marked by extensive technological innovation. Ferguson reminds us that the first era of globalization ended with a crash, or rather, multiple crashes: hostility among major powers culminating in World War I, revolutionary upheavals, and a stock market crash in 1914 so severe that it resulted in the closing of major stock markets for months. The important similarities in the character of globalization in the two eras suggests the possibility that present-day globalization could end as disastrously as the earlier period. Although Ferguson does not predict that such a scenario is certain, he identifies a number of signs that might be a harbinger of worse to come. However, there is a witticism that it's easier to predict the past than the future. Stay tuned.

Torpedoed

[On May 7, 1915,] the German submarine U-20 sank the Cunard liner *Lusitania* off the southern coast of Ireland. Nearly 1,200 people, including 128 Americans, lost their lives. Usually remembered for the damage it did to the image of imperial Germany in the United States, the sinking of the *Lusitania* also symbolized the end of the first age of globalization.

Niall Ferguson, "Sinking Globalization," *Foreign Affairs* 84, no. 2 (March/April 2005): 64–77.

From around 1870 until World War I, the world economy thrived in ways that look familiar today. The mobility of commodities, capital, and labor reached record levels; the sea-lanes and telegraphs across the Atlantic had never been busier, as capital and migrants traveled west and raw materials and manufactures traveled east. In relation to output, exports of both merchandise and capital reached volumes not seen again until the 1980s. Total emigration from Europe between 1880 and 1910 was in excess of 25 million. People spoke euphorically of "the annihilation of distance."

Then, between 1914 and 1918, a horrendous war stopped all of this, sinking globalization. Nearly 13 million tons of shipping were sent to the bottom of the ocean by German submarine attacks. International trade, investment, and migration all collapsed. Moreover, the attempt to resuscitate the world economy after the war's end failed. The global economy effectively disintegrated with the onset of the Great Depression and, after that, with an even bigger world war, in which astonishingly high proportions of production went toward perpetrating destruction.

It may seem excessively pessimistic to worry that this scenario could somehow repeat itself—that our age of globalization could collapse just as our grandparents' did. But it is worth bearing in mind that, despite numerous warnings issued in the early twentieth century about the catastrophic consequences of a war among the European great powers, many people—not least investors, a generally well-informed class—were taken completely by surprise by the outbreak of World War I. The possibility is as real today as it was in 1915 that globalization, like the *Lusitania*, could be sunk.

Back to the Future

The last age of globalization resembled the current one in numerous ways. It was characterized by relatively free trade, limited restrictions on migration, and hardly any regulation of capital flows. Inflation was low. A wave of technological innovation was revolutionizing the communications and energy sectors; the world first discovered the joys of the telephone, the radio, the internal combustion engine, and paved roads. The U.S. economy was the biggest in the world, and the development of its massive internal market had become the principal source of business innovation. China was opening up, raising all kinds of expectations in the West, and Russia was growing rapidly.

World War I wrecked all of this. Global markets were disrupted and disconnected, first by economic warfare, then by postwar protectionism. Prices went haywire: a number of major economies (Germany's among them) suffered from both hyperinflation and steep deflation in the space of a decade. The technological advances of the 1900s petered out: innovation hit a plateau, and stagnating consumption discouraged the development of even existing technologies such as the automobile. After faltering during the war, overheating in the 1920s, and languishing throughout the 1930s in the doldrums of depression, the U.S. economy ceased to be the most dynamic in the world. China succumbed to civil war and foreign invasion, defaulting on its debts and disappointing optimists in the West. Russia suffered revolution, civil war, tyranny, and foreign invasion. Both these giants responded to the crisis by donning the constricting armor of state socialism. They were not alone. By the end of the 1940s, most states in the world, including those that retained political freedoms, had imposed restrictions on trade, migration, and investment as a matter of course. Some achieved autarky, the ideal of a deglobalized society. Consciously or unconsciously, all governments applied in peacetime the economic restrictions that had first been imposed between 1914 and 1918.

The end of globalization after 1914 was not unforeseeable. . . . Yet most investors were completely caught off guard when the crisis came. Not until the last week of July 1914 was there a desperate dash for liquidity; it happened so suddenly and on such a large scale that the world's major stock markets, New York's included, closed down for the rest of the year. As *The Economist* put it at the time, investors and financial institutions "saw in a flash the meaning of war." The Dow Jones Industrial Average fell by about 25 percent between January 1910 and December 1913 and remained flat through the first half of 1914. European bond markets, which had held up throughout the diplomatic crises of the 1900s, crashed only at the 11th hour, as the lights went out all over Europe.

Some economic historians detect the origins of the deglobalization that followed World War I in the prewar decades. They point, variously, to rising tariffs and restrictions on migration, a slight uptick in inflation starting around 1896, and the chronic vulnerability of the U.S. economy to banking crises. To this list, it might be added that the risk of further Russian and Chinese revolutions should have been fairly apparent after those of 1905 and 1911, respectively.

The trouble is that none of these problems can be said to have caused the great conflagration that was World War I. To be sure, the prewar world was marked by all kinds of economic rivalries—not least between British and German manufacturers—but these did not suffice to cause a disaster. On the contrary, businessmen on both sides agreed that a major war would be an economic calamity. The point seemed so obvious that war came to be seen by some optimistic commentators as all but impossible—a "great illusion," in the famous phrase of the author Norman Angell. Even when the war broke out, many people optimistically clung to the illusion that it would soon be over. Economist John Maynard Keynes said that it "could not last more than a year." . . .

Parallel Universe

There are obvious economic parallels between the first age of globalization and the current one. Today, as in the period before 1914, protectionism periodically challenges the free-trade orthodoxy. By the standards of the pre-1914 United Kingdom, in fact, the major economies are already shamelessly protectionist when it comes to agriculture. Then, the United Kingdom imposed no tariffs on imported agri-

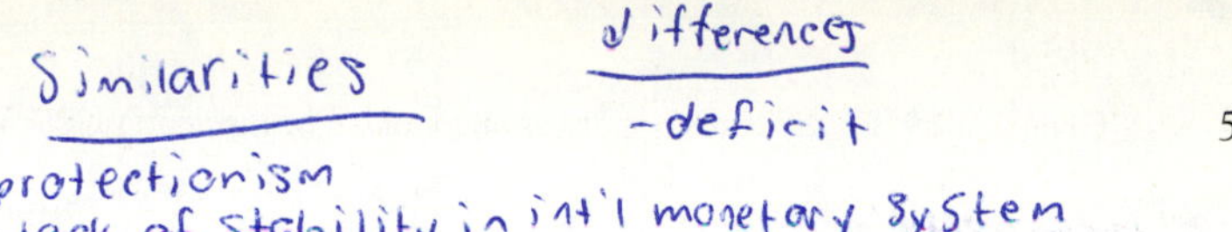

cultural goods, whereas now the United States, the European Union, and Japan all use tariffs and subsidies to protect their farmers from foreign competition.

Today, no one can be sure how stable the international monetary system is, but one thing is certain: it is no more stable than the system that preceded World War I. . . .

Today, technological innovation shows no sign of slackening. From nanocomputers the size of a pinhead to scramjets that can cross the Atlantic in an hour, there seems no limit to human ingenuity, given sufficient funding of research and development. That is the good news. The bad news is that now technology also helps the enemies of globalization. Before 1914, terrorists had to pursue their bloody trade with Browning revolvers and primitive bombs. These days, an entire city could be obliterated with a single nuclear device.

Today, as before 1914, the U.S. economy is the world's biggest, but it is now much more important as a market for the rest of the world than it was then. Although the United States may enjoy great influence as the "consumer of first resort," this role depends on the willingness of foreigners to fund a widening current account deficit. A rising proportion of Americans may consider themselves to have been "saved" in the Evangelical sense, but they are less good at saving in the economic sense. The personal savings rate among Americans stood at just 0.2 percent of disposable personal income in September 2004, compared with 7.7 percent less than 15 years ago. Whether to finance domestic investment (in the late 1990s) or government borrowing (after 2000), the United States has come to rely increasingly on foreign lending. As the current account deficit has widened (it is now approaching 6 percent of GDP), U.S. net overseas liabilities have risen steeply to around 25 percent of GDP. Half of the publicly held federal debt is now in foreign hands; at the end of August 2004, the combined U.S. Treasury holdings of China, Hong Kong, Japan, Singapore, South Korea, and Taiwan were $1.1 trillion, up by 22 percent from the end of 2003. A large proportion of this increase is a result of immense purchases by eastern Asian monetary authorities, designed to prevent their currencies from appreciating relative to the dollar.

This deficit is the biggest difference between globalization past and globalization present. A hundred years ago, the global hegemon—the United Kingdom—was a net exporter of capital, channeling a high proportion of its savings overseas to finance the construction of infrastructure such as railways and ports in the Americas, Asia, Australasia, and Africa. Today, its successor as an Anglophone empire plays the diametrically opposite role—as the world's debtor rather than the world's creditor, absorbing around three-quarters of the rest of the world's surplus savings. . . .

A sharp depreciation of the dollar relative to Asian currencies might not worry the majority of Americans, whose liabilities are all dollar-denominated. But its effect on Asia would be profound. Asian holders of dollar assets would suffer heavy capital losses in terms of their own currencies, and Asian exporters would lose some of their competitive advantage in the U.S. market. According to Michael Mussa of the Institute for International Economics, lowering the U.S. deficit to 2 percent of GDP over the next few years would require a further 20 percent decline in the dollar. The economists Maurice Obstfeld and Kenneth Rogoff estimate that the fall could be as much as 40 percent. And the University of California at Berkeley's Brad DeLong has pointed out that,

> [i]f the private market—which knows that with high probability the dollar is going down someday—decides that that someday has come and that the dollar is going down *now*, then all the Asian central banks in the world cannot stop it [emphasis in original].

That day may be fast approaching. In the words of Federal Reserve Board Chairman Alan Greenspan . . . , "the desire of investors to add dollar claims to their portfolios" must have a limit; a "continued financing even of today's current account deficits . . . doubtless will, at some future point, increase shares of dollar claims in investor portfolios to levels that imply an unacceptable amount of concentration risk." . . .

Another cause for concern is the fragility of China's financial system. This Asian miracle is unlikely to avoid the kind of crisis that marked the Asian miracles of the past. To get a sense of the dangers, consider China's Soviet-style domestic banking system and its puny domestic stock market: how can such rapid growth in manufacturing possibly be sustained with such inadequate financial institutions?

Pre-1914 globalization was remarkably susceptible to the international transmission of crises—what economists call "contagion." So is globalization nowadays. As Andrew Large of the Bank of England [has] pointed out . . . , the "search for yield" in an environment of low interest rates is encouraging investors, banks, and hedge funds to converge on similar trading strategies, raising "the prospect of oneway markets developing and market liquidity evaporating in response to a shock."

Ghosts from the Past

As the economic parallels with 1914 suggest, today's globalization shows at least some signs of reversibility. The risks increase when one considers the present political situation, which has the same . . . flaws as the pre-1914 international order: imperial overstretch, great-power rivalry, an unstable alliance system, rogue regimes sponsoring terror, and the rise of a revolutionary terrorist organization hostile to capitalism.

The United States—an empire in all but name—is manifestly overstretched. Not only is its current account deficit large and growing larger, but the fiscal deficit that lurks behind it also is set to surge as the baby boomers retire and start to claim Social Security and Medicare benefits. The Congressional Budget Office (CBO) projects that over the next four decades, Social Security, Medicaid, and Medicare spending will rise to consume at least an additional 12 percent of GDP per year. The CBO also estimates that the transition costs of President George W. Bush's planned Social Security reform, if enacted, could create a budget shortfall of up to two percent of GDP a year for ten years. Add that to the fiscal consequences of making the president's first-term tax cuts permanent, and it becomes hard to imagine how the country will manage to stem the rising tide of red ink.

The U.S. empire also suffers from a personnel deficit: 500,000 troops is the maximum number that Washington can deploy overseas, and this number is simply not sufficient to win all the small wars the United States currently has (or might have) to wage. Of the 137,000 American troops currently in Iraq, 43 percent are drawn from the reserves or the National Guard. Even just to maintain the U.S. presence in Iraq, the Army is extending tours of duty and retaining personnel due to be discharged. Such measures seem certain to hurt re-enlistment rates.

Above all, the U.S. empire suffers from an attention deficit. Iraq is not a very big war. . . . Yet the Iraq war has become very unpopular very quickly, after relatively few casualties. According to several polls, fewer than half of American voters now support it. And virtually no one seems to want to face the fact that the U.S. presence in Iraq—and the low-intensity conflict that goes with imperial policing—may have to endure for ten years or more if that country is to stand any chance of economic and political stabilization.

Then there is the second problem: great-power rivalry. It is true that the Chinese have no obvious incentive to pick a fight with the United States. But China's ambitions with respect to Taiwan are not about to disappear just because Beijing owns a stack of U.S. Treasury bonds. On the contrary, in the event of an economic crisis, China might be sorely tempted to play the nationalist card by threatening to take over its errant province. Would the United States really be willing to fight China over Taiwan, as it has pledged in the past to do? And what would happen if the Chinese authorities flexed their new financial muscles by dumping U.S. bonds on the world market? To the historian, Taiwan looks somewhat like the Belgium of old: a seemingly inconsequential country over which empires end up fighting to the death. And one should not forget Asia's most dangerous rogue regime, North Korea, which is a little like pre-1914 Serbia with nuclear weapons.

As for Europe, one must not underestimate the extent to which the recent diplomatic "widening of the Atlantic" reflects profound changes in Europe, rather than an alteration in U.S. foreign policy. The combination of economic sclerosis and social senescence means that Europe is bound to stagnate, if not decline. Meanwhile, Muslim immigration and the prospect of Turkey's accession to the European Union are changing the very character of Europe. And the division between Americans and Europeans on Middle Eastern questions is only going to get wider—for example, if the United States dismisses the European attempt to contain Iran's nuclear ambitions by diplomatic means and presses instead for military countermeasures.

These rivalries are one reason the world today also has an unstable alliance system (problem number three). NATO's purpose is no longer clear. Is it just an irrelevant club for the winners of the Cold War, which former Soviet satellites are encouraged to join for primarily symbolic reasons? Have divisions over Iraq rendered it obsolete? To say the least, "coalitions of the willing" are a poor substitute.

None of these problems would necessarily be fatal were it not for the fourth and fifth parallels between 1914 and today: the existence of rogue regimes sponsoring terror—Iran and Syria top the list—and of revolutionary terrorist organizations. It is a big mistake to think of al Qaeda as "Islamo-fascist" (as the journalist Christopher Hitchens and many others called the group after the September 11, 2001, attacks). Al Qaeda's members are much more like "Islamo-Bolshevists," committed to revolution and a reordering of the world along anti-capitalist lines.

Like the Bolsheviks in 1914, these Islamist extremists are part of an underground sect, struggling to land more than the occasional big punch on the enemy. But what if they were to get control of a wealthy state, the way Lenin, Trotsky, and company did in 1917? How would the world look if there were an October Revolution in Saudi Arabia? True, some recent survey data suggest that ordinary Saudis are relatively moderate people by the standards of the Arab world. And high oil prices mean more shopping and fewer disgruntled youths. On the other hand, after what happened in Tehran in 1979, no one can rule out a second Islamist revolution. The Saudi royal family does not look like the kind of regime that will still be in business ten years from now. The only monarchies that survive in modern times are those that give power away.

But is Osama bin Laden really a modern-day Lenin? The comparison is less far-fetched than it seems ("Hereditary Nobleman Vladimir Ulyanov" also came from a wealthy family). In a proclamation to the world before the recent U.S. presidential election, bin Laden declared that his "policy [was] bleeding America to the point of bankruptcy." As he explained, "al Qaeda spent $500,000 on the [September 11 attacks], while America, in the incident and its aftermath, lost—according to the lowest estimate—more than $500 billion. Meaning that every dollar of al Qaeda defeated a million dollars, by the permission of Allah." . . .

Apocalypse When?

A doomsday scenario is plausible. But is it probable? The difficult thing—indeed the nearly impossible thing—is to predict a cataclysm. Doing so was the challenge investors faced in the first age of globalization. They knew there could be a world war. They knew such a war would have devastating financial consequences (although few anticipated how destructive it would be). But they had no way of knowing when exactly it would happen.

The same problem exists today. We all know that another, bigger September 11 is quite likely; it is, indeed, bin Laden's stated objective. We all know—or should know—that a crisis over Taiwan would send huge shockwaves through the international system; it could even lead to a great-power war. We all know that revolutionary regime change in Saudi Arabia would shake the world even more than the 1917 Bolshevik coup in Russia. We all know that the detonation of a nuclear device in London would dwarf the assassination of Archduke Ferdinand as an act of terrorism.

But what exactly can we do about such contingencies, if, as with the Asian tsunami, we cannot say even approximately when they might occur? The opportunity cost of liquidating our portfolios and inhabiting a subterranean bunker looks too high, even if Armageddon could come tomorrow. In that sense, we seem no better prepared for the worst-case scenario than were the beneficiaries of the last age of globalization, 90 years ago. Like the passengers who boarded the *Lusitania*, all we know is that we may conceivably sink. Still we sail.

PART TWO

The Economics of Globalization

CHAPTER 3

The Character of Economic Globalization

The selections in this chapter provide a sample of the sharply diverging analyses of the major features of economic globalization. They demonstrate the sharply contrasting perspectives on this issue.

One might summarize the debate about economic globalization as follows. In one camp are those, like Friedman and Wolf in this chapter, and Dollar and Kraay, Bhagwati, and Moore in later chapters, who regard economic globalization as involving a substantial increase in the quality of economic performance. In their view, to oppose economic globalization is similar to the position of the English Luddites in the early nineteenth century. Responding to the social, economic, and technological changes involved in the industrial revolution, these workers—so named because they supported the mythical figure Ned Ludd—smashed the machines that threatened their livelihood in the weaving industry. The supporters of economic globalization believe that opposing globalization means opposing progress. Globalization produces giant increases in economic efficiency. It involves economies of scale that enable producers to lower costs of production by producing for larger markets. It enables countries that pursue appropriate economic policies to improve their position in the world economy by attracting foreign investments and exporting their products and services. It involves mutual gains from trade that enable producers throughout the world to specialize and reap benefits from doing what they do best. It involves gains for consumers as a result of the lower prices deriving from increased competition and productivity.

Given these immense benefits, what's not to like? Plenty, reply the strong critics of globalization—those in the second camp identified here. Critics of economic globalization, at least neoliberal globalization, are represented in this chapter by Stiglitz, Milanovic, and Shiva. (Note that we oversimplify: both supporters and critics of globalization may differ among themselves in important respects.) Critics ask: Do you call this progress? Whereas supporters of globalization perceive benefits, opponents catalog a host of costs deriving from globalization. Stiglitz highlights the undemocratic character of the international framework regulating globalization. Milanovic compares the present period with preceding decades and finds that economic growth was more rapid in the years *before* full-blown globalization. The selection by Amartya Sen in Chapter 2 highlights that globalization has promoted increasing global inequalities. (This last issue is so important that we devote the next chapter to the question.)

Is there a middle position in this debate? And if there is, does the fact that it is the middle position make it right? Some supporters and critics claim that there isn't a feasible middle course: they argue that if you're not on the side of the solution (that is, either supporting or opposing economic globalization), you're part of the problem. However, the selection by Stiglitz, in this chapter, and that by Sen, in Chapter 2, as well as several in Chapter 11, illustrate that one can be a strong supporter of economic globalization at the same time that one can identify shortcomings in the way that it is presently organized. Those in the middle camp focus on reforms that can address the problems identified by critics, while preserving the benefits identified by supporters.

If nothing else, this section suggests how complex is the debate about economic globalization and how important the stakes. In reading these selections, try to identify the specific points of agreement and disagreement. To what extent do supporters and critics talk past each other, that is, ignore points made by the other side; to what extent do they clash head-on—and where they do really address each other, who has the better of the argument and why? Finally, begin developing your own position on the fundamental issue at the center of this debate: the costs and benefits of economic globalization. Warning: don't reach closure too quickly. Other selections in PG may persuade you to alter your position. So much the better! To repeat: the issues are complicated and the stakes high.

The Lexus and the Olive Tree *Understanding Globalization*

Thomas L. Friedman

Thomas Friedman is an influential columnist for the *New York Times.* In this selection, he argues that globalization is a product of technological change and financial liberalization. The result is to unleash a force of enormous power, for good and ill. Friedman believes that governments have little choice but to adopt globalization-friendly policies, what he terms the Golden Straitjacket. Governments who reduce barriers to trade and respect economic fundamentals in their economic policies, such as maintaining a balanced budget, will be handsomely rewarded. Governments that defy the commands of neoliberal economic theory risk the wrath of what he calls the Electronic Herd, that is, international investors, who can punish a country by withdrawing capital from a country at the flick of a computer keystroke.

In Friedman's view, governments have little autonomy in a globalized world. Is he correct? Or might governments have greater possibility for policy innovation? (See Chapter 6 for other views on this question.) If not, where does this leave democracy?

. . . During the nineteenth and early twentieth centuries, when the Industrial Revolution and global finance capitalism roared through Europe and America, many people were shocked by their Darwinian brutality and "dark Satanic mills." They destroyed old orders and hierarchies, produced huge income gaps and put everyone under pressure, but they also produced sharply rising standards of living for those who could make a go of it. This experience triggered a great deal of debate and revolutionary theorizing, as people tried to find ways to cushion workers from the cruelest aspects of free-market capitalism in that day. As Karl Marx and Friedrich Engels described this era in the *Communist Manifesto:* "Constant revolutionizing of production, uninterrupted disturbance of all social conditions, everlasting uncertainty and agitation distinguish the bourgeois epoch from all earlier ones. All fixed, fast-frozen relations, with their train of ancient and venerable prejudices and opinions, are swept away, all new formed ones become antiquated before they can ossify. All that is solid melts into air, all that is holy is profaned, and man is at last compelled to face with sober senses, his real conditions of life, and his relations with his kind."

Eventually, people came along who declared that they could take these destabilizing, brutalizing swings out of the free market, and create a world that would never be dependent on unfettered bourgeois capitalists. They would have the government centrally plan and fund everything, and distribute to each worker according to his needs and expect from each worker a contribution according to his abilities. The names of these revolutionary thinkers were Engels, Marx, Lenin and Mussolini, among others. The centrally planned, nondemocratic alternatives they offered—communism, socialism and fascism—helped to abort the first era of globalization as they were tested out on the world stage from 1917 to 1989.

There is only one thing to say about those alternatives: *They didn't work.* And the people who rendered that judgment were the people who lived under them. So with the collapse of communism in Europe, in the Soviet Union and in China—and all the walls that protected these systems—those people who are unhappy with the Darwinian brutality of free-market capitalism don't have any ready ideological alternative now. When it comes to the question of which system today is the most effective at generating rising standards of living, the historical debate is over. The answer is free-market capitalism. Other systems may be able to distribute and divide income more efficiently and equitably, but none can generate income to distribute as efficiently as free-market capitalism. And more and more people now know that. So, ideologically speaking, there is no more mint chocolate chip, there is no more strawberry swirl, and there is no more lemon-lime. Today there is only free-market vanilla and North Korea. There can be different brands of free-market vanilla and you can adjust your society to it by going faster or slower. But, in the end, if you want higher standards of living in a world without walls, the free market is the only ideological alternative left. One road. Different speeds. But one road.

When your country recognizes this fact, when it recognizes the rules of the free market in today's global economy, and decides to abide by them, it puts on what I call "the Golden Straitjacket." The Golden Straitjacket is the defining political-economic garment of this globalization era. The Cold War had the Mao suit, the Nehru jacket, the Russian fur. Globalization has only the Golden Straitjacket. If your country has not been fitted for one, it will be soon.

The Golden Straitjacket first began to be stitched together and popularized by Margaret Thatcher in England, beginning in 1979. It was soon reinforced by Ronald Reagan in the United States in the 1980s, giving the straitjacket, and its rules, some real critical mass. It became a global fashion with the end of the Cold War, once the three democratizations blew away all the alternative fashions and all the walls that protected them.

The Thatcherite-Reaganite revolutions came about because popular majorities in these two major Western economies concluded that the old government-directed economic approaches simply were not providing sufficient levels of growth. Thatcher and Reagan combined to strip huge chunks of economic decisionmaking power from the state, from the advocates of the Great Society and from traditional Keynesian economics, and hand them over to the free market.

To fit into the Golden Straitjacket a country must either adopt, or be seen as moving toward, the following golden rules: making the private sector the primary engine of its economic growth, maintaining a low rate of inflation and price stability, shrinking the size of its state bureaucracy, maintaining as close to a balanced budget as possible, if not a surplus, eliminating and lowering tariffs on imported goods, removing restrictions on foreign investment, getting rid of quotas and domestic monopolies, increasing exports, privatizing state-owned industries and utilities, deregulating capital markets, making its currency convertible, opening its industries, stock, and bond markets to direct foreign ownership and investment, deregulating its economy to promote as much domestic competition as possible, eliminating government corruption, subsidies and kickbacks as much as possible, opening its banking and telecommunications systems to private ownership and competition, and allowing its citizens to choose from an array of competing pension options and foreign-run pension and mutual funds. When you stitch all of these pieces together you have the Golden Straitjacket.

Unfortunately, this Golden Straitjacket is pretty much "one size fits all." So it pinches certain groups, squeezes others and keeps a society under pressure to constantly streamline its economic institutions and upgrade its performance. It leaves people behind quicker than ever if they shuck it off, and it helps them catch up quicker than ever if they wear it right. It is not always pretty or gentle or comfortable. But it's here and it's the only model on the rack this historical season.

As your country puts on the Golden Straitjacket, two things tend to happen: your economy grows and your politics shrinks. That is, on the economic front the Golden Straitjacket usually fosters more growth and higher average incomes—through more trade, foreign investment, privatization and more efficient use of resources under the pressure of global competition. But on the political front, the Golden Straitjacket narrows the political and economic policy choices of those in power to relatively tight parameters. That is why it is increasingly difficult these days to find any real differences between ruling and opposition parties in those countries that have put on the Golden Straitjacket. Once your country puts on the Golden Straitjacket, its political choices get reduced to Pepsi or Coke—to slight nuances of taste, slight nuances of policy, slight alterations in design to account for local traditions, some loosening here or there, but never any major deviation from the core golden rules. Governments—be they led by Democrats or Republicans, Conservatives or Laborites, Gaullists or Socialists, Christian Democrats or Social Democrats—which deviate too far from the core rules will see their investors stampede away, interest rates rise and stock market valuations fall. The only way to get more room to maneuver in the Golden Straitjacket is by growing it, and the only way to grow it is by keeping it on tight. That's its one virtue: the tighter you wear it, the more gold it produces and the more padding you can then put into it for your society[.]

No wonder so much of the political debate in developed countries today has been reduced to arguments over minor tailoring changes in the Golden

Straitjacket, not radical alterations. In the 1996 American presidential elections, Bill Clinton was essentially arguing, "Sure, we're in this Golden Straitjacket, but I have a way we can put a little more padding in the elbows and grow the middle a bit." And Republican presidential contender Bob Dole said in effect, "No, no, you can't loosen the middle at all. Keep it on tight and we'll put a little more padding in the elbows." And in the 1997 British election campaign Tony Blair vowed in essence that if he won, "We'll keep it on as tight as the Tories, but we'll add some padding to the shoulders and the chest," while his opponent, Conservative John Major, seemed to retort, "Don't you dare touch a thread on that jacket. Margaret Thatcher designed it to be snug and by God that's the way it should stay." No wonder that Paddy Ashdown, the leader of Britain's Liberal Party, looked at Tony Blair and John Major during the 1997 British election and declared that there was not a whit of difference between them. Ashdown declared that Blair and Major were engaged in "synchronized swimming."

With the fall of the Cold War walls, and the rise of the Golden Straitjacket, I see a lot of synchronized swimming when I travel the world these days. Before the 1998 German elections, in which Social Democrat Gerhard Schroeder defeated Christian Democrat Helmut Kohl, the Associated Press quoted Karl-Josef Meiers of the German Society for Foreign Affairs as saying of the two German candidates: "You can forget the labels right and left. They're all sitting in the same boat." Korea's Lee Hong Koo learned firsthand about life in the Golden Straitjacket when he served as his country's Prime Minister in the mid-1990s. "In the old days we used to say 'History dictated this or that,'" Lee remarked to me one day. "Now we say that 'market forces' dictated this and you have to live within [those forces]. It took us time to understand what had happened. We didn't realize that the victory of the Cold War was a victory for market forces above politics. The big decisions today are whether you have a democracy or not and whether you have an open economy or not. Those are the big choices. But once you've made those big choices, politics becomes just political engineering to implement decisions in the narrow space allowed you within this system." Lee was raised in Korea's long-dominant Grand National Party. But after Korea's economic meltdown in 1997–98, when the country found it had to put on the Golden Straitjacket much more snugly if it was to continue to thrive and attract foreign investment, the Korean public spurned the veteran, old-style Korean politicians and elected longtime liberal human rights advocate Kim Dae Jung as President, from the opposition National Congress for New Politics. But Kim asked Lee to go to Washington to be his ambassador anyway. As Lee told me: "It would have been unthinkable in the past that someone like myself, who was a presidential candidate from my party and former Prime Minister and party chairman, would go to Washington as an ambassador from another party, like President Kim's. But now, with what Korea has to do to get out of this economic crisis, the differences between me and Mr. Kim are insignificant. We don't have a lot of choices." How do you say "same boat" or "synchronized swimming" in Korean?

Manmohan Singh was India's Finance Minister when his country decided in 1991 to abandon decades of statist, quasi-socialist economics and don the Golden

Straitjacket. Sitting in his office in the Indian Parliament in the summer of 1998, he spoke to me of the loss of control he felt once India embarked on this route: "We learned that there were advantages to having access to international capital markets, [but] the government's ability to deliver and control shrank the more it opened to the world. If you are operating in a globalized economy, perceptions of other participants matter much more—whether they are right or wrong. Then you have to take those perceptions and make them an important input into your decisionmaking. . . . We have a world where our fates are linked, but [India's specific] concerns and aspirations don't get taken into account. It brings a lot more anxiety. If you are operating an exchange rate policy, or monetary policy, your policies become an adjunct of what Alan Greenspan does. It reduces your degree of freedom, even in fiscal policies. In a world in which capital is internationally mobile, you cannot adopt rates of taxation that are far from the rates that prevail in other countries and when labor is mobile you also can't be out of line with others' wages. It has reduced the amount of maneuverability. . . . I have a friend from a neighboring country who also became a Finance Minister. The day he got his job I called to congratulate him. He said, 'Don't congratulate me. I am only half a minister. The other half is in Washington.'"

Not every country puts on the Golden Straitjacket all the way—some just go partway or a little at a time (India, Egypt). Some put it on and take it off (Malaysia, Russia). Some try to tailor it to their specific culture and wear a few of the buttons unfastened (Germany, Japan and France). Some think they can resist its pinch altogether because they have a natural resource such as oil (Iran, Saudi Arabia). And some are so poor and isolated, with a government able to force people to accept being poor, that they can get away with dressing their people not in a Golden Straitjacket, but in a plain old straitjacket (North Korea, Sudan, Afghanistan).

But over time, this Golden Straitjacket is becoming harder and harder for countries to avoid. Whenever I make this point in lectures, particularly to non-Americans, I get some version of the following reaction: "Don't tell us we have to put on a straitjacket and plug into the global markets. We have our own culture, our own values, and we will do it our own way at our own pace. Your thesis is way too deterministic. Why can't we all just get together and agree on a different, less restrictive model?"

To which I answer the following: "I am not saying that you will *have to* put on the straitjacket. And if your culture and social traditions are opposed to the values embodied in that jacket, I certainly sympathize with that. But I am saying this: Today's global market system, the Fast World and the Golden Straitjacket were produced by large historical forces that have fundamentally reshaped how we communicate, how we invest and how we see the world. If you want to resist these changes, that is your business. And it should be your business. But if you think that you can resist these changes without paying an increasingly steep price, or without building an increasingly high wall, then you are deluding yourself."

Here's why: The democratizations of finance, technology and information didn't just blow away all the walls protecting alternative systems—from Mao's

Little Red Book to the *Communist Manifesto* to the welfare states of Western Europe to the crony capitalism of Southeast Asia. These three democratizations also gave birth to a new power source in the world—what I call the "Electronic Herd."

The Electronic Herd is made up of all the faceless stock, bond and currency traders sitting behind computer screens all over the globe, moving their money around with the click of a mouse from mutual funds to pension funds to emerging market funds, or trading from their basements on the Internet. And it consists of the big multinational corporations who now spread their factories around the world, constantly shifting them to the most efficient, low-cost producers.

This herd has grown exponentially thanks to the democratizations of finance, technology and information—so much so that today it is beginning to replace governments as the primary source of capital for both companies and countries to grow. In order to thrive in today's globalization system a country not only has to put on the Golden Straitjacket, it also has to plug into this Electronic Herd. The Electronic Herd loves the Golden Straitjacket, because it embodies all the liberal, free-market rules the herd wants to see in a country. Those countries that put on the Golden Straitjacket and keep it on are rewarded by the herd with investment capital to grow. Those that don't put it on are disciplined by the herd—either by the herd avoiding that country or withdrawing its money from that country.

Moody's Investors Service and Standard & Poor's are the bloodhounds for the Electronic Herd. These credit-rating agencies prowl the world, constantly sniffing over countries. They are supposed to bark loudly when they see a country slipping out of the Golden Straitjacket (although sometimes Moody's and S&P also lose the scent or get caught up in euphorias, as in Southeast Asia, and don't bark until it's too late).

This interaction among the Electronic Herd, nation-states and the Golden Straitjacket is at the center of today's globalization system. I first realized this in February 1995, on the eve of President Clinton's inaugural visit to Canada. I was covering the White House at the time, and in preparation for the President's trip I was keeping an eye out for articles in the *Financial Times* and other papers to see what the Canadians might be talking about in advance of their first visit from "the Man from Hope." I was intrigued to find that they weren't talking about the U.S. President at all. Instead, they were talking about the visit that had just been made to Canada by the "the Man from Moody's." Canada's Parliament at the time was debating the country's budget. A team from Moody's had just come to Ottawa and read the riot act to the Canadian Finance Ministry and legislators. The Moody's team told them that if they did not get their deficit-to-GDP ratio more in line with international norms and expectations, Moody's would downgrade their triple-A credit rating, and therefore Canada and every Canadian company would have to pay higher interest rates to borrow abroad. To underscore that point Canada's Finance Ministry issued a statement declaring: "The sheer magnitude of Canada's foreign debt in relation to the size of the economy means that Canada has become excessively vulnerable to the volatile sentiments of global financial markets. We have suffered a tangible loss of economic sovereignty." For those

Canadians who might not have gotten the point, Finance Minister Paul Martin put it more bluntly: "We are in hock up to our eyeballs." No, the Canadians were not the least bit interested in the Man from Hope. It was the Man from Moody's, and the Electronic Herd, who had their undivided attention.

Where did this herd come from and how did it become a force so formidable that it could intimidate and enrich nation-states every bit as much as a superpower could?

The Electronic Herd

In September 1997, Malaysia's Prime Minister, Dr. Mahathir Mohamad, used the World Bank meeting in Hong Kong to denounce the evils of globalization, after Malaysia's stocks and currency were ravaged by global and local investors. Mahathir blasted "morons" who trade in currencies, and he accused the "Great Powers" and financiers such as George Soros of forcing Asians to open their domestic markets to global speculators and manipulating their currencies to destroy them as competitors. He compared today's global capital markets to "a jungle of ferocious beasts," and implied that they were directed by a Jewish cabal. Listening to Mahathir's rant, I tried to imagine what U.S. Treasury Secretary Robert Rubin, who was in the audience, would have said to the Malaysian leader had he really been able to speak his mind. I think it would have been something like this:

"Ah, excuse me, Mahathir, but what planet are you living on? You talk about participating in globalization as if it were a choice you had. Globalization isn't a choice. It's a reality. There is just one global market today, and the only way you can grow at the speed your people want to grow is by tapping into the global stock and bond markets, by seeking out multinationals to invest in your country and by selling into the global trading system what your factories produce. And the most basic truth about globalization is this: *No one is in charge*—not George Soros, not 'Great Powers' and not I. I didn't start globalization. I can't stop it and neither can you—except at a huge cost to your society and its prospects for growth. You keep looking for someone to complain to, someone to take the heat off your markets, someone to blame. Well, guess what, Mahathir, there's no one on the other end of the phone! I know that's hard to accept. It's like telling people there's no God. We all want to believe that someone is in charge and responsible. But the global marketplace today is an Electronic Herd of often anonymous stock, bond, currency and multinational investors, connected by screens and networks. And, Mahathir, don't you play dumb with me. We both know your Central Bank lost $3 billion speculating on the British pound in the early 1990s—so don't give me that innocence crap. The Electronic Herd cuts no one any slack. *No one.* It does not recognize anyone's unique circumstances. The herd knows only its own rules. But the rules of the herd are pretty consistent—they're the rules of the Golden Straitjacket. Now, the herd feeds in 180 countries, Mahathir, so it doesn't have time to look at you in detail all the time. It makes snap judgments about whether you are living by its rules, and it rewards most lavishly those countries that are transparent about what they are doing. The herd hates surprises. For years Malaysia seemed to be living by those rules, and it attracted massive amounts of direct investment and portfolio investment, which enabled you to raise your per capita income from $350 to $5,000 in a couple of decades. But when you started to break the rules by overborrowing and then overbuilding, well, the herd sold you out. Did you really need to build the two tallest office buildings in the world? Have you rented even half their office space? I hear not. So the herd stampeded you and left you as road-kill. The KLCI Index, your Dow Jones, fell 48 percent in 1997, and your currency hit a twenty-six-year low. But when that happens you don't ask the herd for mercy, you don't denounce the herd as a 'Jewish conspiracy,' you just get up, dust yourself off, put your Golden Straitjacket on a little tighter and get back with the flow of the herd. Sure, this is unfair. In some ways the herd lured you into this problem: It kept offering you all this cheap money and you took it and then overbuilt your dams, your factory capacity and your office towers. But that's what's really scary, Mahathir: *The herd is not infallible*. It makes mistakes, too. It overreacts and it overshoots. But if your fundamentals are basically sound, the herd will eventually recognize this and come back. The herd is never stupid for too long. In the end, it always responds to good governance and good economic management. Hey, America had similar fluctuations when it was an emerging market, with our railroad busts and booms. You just have to manage them and build in as many shock absorbers as possible. I track the herd's movements all day on the Bloomberg screen next to my desk. Democracies vote about a government's policies once every two or four years. But the Electronic Herd votes every minute of every hour of every day. Anytime you want to know, the herd will tell you exactly how you look in a Golden Straitjacket and whether it fits well or not. I know you think that I'm the all-powerful U.S. Treasury Secretary. But, Mahathir, I live just like you—in terror of the Electronic Herd. Those idiots in the media keep putting me on the front page, as if I'm actually in charge, and I'm sitting here terrified that if our Congress refuses to grant the President authority to expand free trade, or busts the budget ceiling, the herd is going to turn against me and trample the dollar and the Dow. So let me tell you a little secret, Mahathir—and don't tell anyone else. I don't even keep a phone on my desk anymore, because I know better than anyone: *There's nobody to call*."

Like it or not, my imaginary Treasury Secretary is basically talking the truth. Countries cannot thrive in today's world without plugging into the Electronic Herd, and they cannot survive unless they learn how to get the best out of this herd without being overwhelmed or shocked by its inevitable surges. The Electronic Herd is just like a high-voltage wire that comes into your house. In normal times it can warm you, light your home and provide many of your energy needs. But if you don't have the right electricity regulators and surge protectors, and there is a sudden power surge or drop, it can shock you, fry you to a crisp and leave you for dead.

The Electronic Herd today consists of two basic groups. One group I call the "short-horn cattle." This includes all those people involved in the buying and selling of stocks, bonds and currencies around the world, and who can and often do move their money around on a very short-term basis. The short-horn cattle are currency traders, major mutual and pension funds, hedge funds, insurance companies, bank trading rooms and individual investors. They include everyone from Merrill Lynch to Crédit Suisse, to Fuji Bank, to the Charles Schwab Web site, where anyone with a PC and a modem can trade online from his living room.

The other group I call the "long-horn cattle." These are the multinationals—the General Electrics, the General Motorses, the IBMs, the Intels, the Siemenses—which are increasingly involved in foreign direct investment, building factories around the world, or striking long-term production deals or alliances with factories around the world to make or assemble their products. I call them the long-horn cattle because they have to make longer-term commitments when they invest in a country. But even they now move in and out, like a herd, with surprising speed.

Though the Electronic Herd was born and nursed in the Cold War era, its members could never gather the critical mass, speed or reach in that overly regulated, walled-up system. Most countries maintained capital controls (at least until the 1970s), so capital could not move across borders the way it can in today's globalization system. This made it much harder to get a global herd together. In the relatively closed economies of the pre-1970s Cold War system, a government's own monetary policy completely dominated the setting of its own interest rates and a government's own fiscal policy was far and away the dominant instrument for stimulating growth. Also during the Cold War, the U.S. and Soviet governments could easily justify the high taxes needed for fiscal policy by invoking the Cold War: "We need your tax dollars to fight the enemy, put a man on the moon, and build a new highway system so we can move our army around faster." At the same time, many developing countries could muddle through by milking one of the superpowers—namely, the United States, the Soviet Union or China—or international lending institutions—to fund a dam, support an army or build a highway. And because the citizens of these developing countries were not nearly as aware as they are today of how everyone else in the world was living, they were ready to tolerate lower living standards that come from having a relatively closed economy.

But with the gradual lifting of capital controls in the 1970s, the democratizations of finance, technology and information, the end of the Cold War system and the fall of walls everywhere, there suddenly emerged a vast global plain where investor herds from many different countries could roam freely. It was on this wide-open plain, later expanded into Cyberspace, that the Electronic Herd could really graze, grow, multiply and eventually gather into powerful Supermarkets.

The Supermarkets are the megamarkets of Tokyo, Frankfurt, Sydney, Singapore, Shanghai, Hong Kong, Bombay, São Paulo, Paris, Zurich, Chicago, London, and Wall Street. They are where the biggest members of the Electronic Herd come together, exchange information, execute their trades, and issue stocks and bonds for different companies for the herd to feed upon. According to University of Chicago globalization expert Saskia Sassen, by the end of 1997 twenty-five Supermarkets controlled 83 percent of the world's equities under institutional management and accounted for roughly half of global market capitalization—around $20.9 trillion (*Foreign Affairs*, January 1999).

This Electronic Herd—and the Supermarkets where it gathers to feed and procreate—have become important international actors in the globalization system. While they cannot go to war or invade a country, like nation-states, they are able to shape the behavior of nation-states in many areas. And that is why I have argued that while the Cold War system was a system based on a balance between states, the globalization system is based on a balance between states and states, and between states and the Electronic Herd and Supermarkets.

Ever since the invention of the transatlantic cable, in the pre-World War I era of globalization, some sort of Electronic Herd has been at work, but during the Cold War system it was never as important as it is today. What is new about today's herd is not so much a difference in kind as a difference in degree. Because of globalization, today's Electronic Herd—both its short-horn cattle and its long-horn cattle—combines size, speed and diversity to a degree never seen before in history. A mouse has a tail and a Tyrannosaurus Rex has a tail. They are both called "tails," but when one swings it has a very different effect on the world around it than the other. The Electronic Herd in the first era of globalization was like the tail of a mouse. Today's Electronic Herd is like the tail of a Tyrannosaurus Rex, and when it swings it reshapes the world around it in some fundamental ways. . . .

The way in which leaders, individuals, investors and companies are all learning to adjust to this new system of globalization is really the hallmark of the late twentieth century. There is just one more thing I have to say about it, though: You ain't seen nothin' yet.

As I have tried to explain, the democratizations of technology, finance and information—which have changed how we communicate, how we invest and how we look at the world—gave birth to all the key elements in today's globalization system. They are what blew away the walls. They are what created the networks which enable each of us now to reach around the world and become Super-empowered individuals. They are what created the links and the space for the Electronic Herd and the Supermarkets to really emerge. They are what blew away all the old ideologies, other than free-market capitalism. They are what created the incredible new efficiencies that every business either has to adapt to or die. They are what lowered the barriers to entry into virtually every business. They are what is forcing people to change from thinking locally first and then globally, to thinking globally first and then locally.

It is because of the Internet that I say you ain't seen nothin' yet. The rise of the Internet, which came in the last stages of the democratizations of technology, finance and information, certainly contributed to this new era of globalization. But as the Internet proliferates, it is going to become the turbocharged engine that drives globalization forward. The Internet will ensure that how we communicate, how we invest and how we look at the world will be increasingly global. Because from the moment you log onto the Internet you can communicate with anyone globally practically for free, from the moment you log onto the Internet you can invest in any market globally practically for free and from the moment you start a business that has an Internet Web site, wherever you are in the world, you will have to think globally—in terms of both who your competitors might be and who your customers might be. . . .

Are you ready?

ARTICLE 3.2

It's a Flat World After All

Thomas L. Friedman

Thomas Friedman supplements the description of globalization in *The Lexus and the Olive Tree* (see the previous selection) with a summary of recent innovations in information technology (IT) that have taken global integration to a new level. In this selection, Friedman claims that the world is becoming flat; that is, the traditional hierarchies of power and knowledge among countries and companies are being replaced by a level playing field in which individual talent is what counts. How can Friedman's view be reconciled with selections in this chapter and the next that document the existence of steep inequalities in our globalized world?

In 1492 Christopher Columbus set sail for India, going west. He had the Nina, the Pinta and the Santa Maria. He never did find India, but he called the people he met "Indians" and came home and reported to his king and queen: "The world is round." I set off for India 512 years later. I knew just which direction I was going. I went east. I had Lufthansa business class, and I came home and reported only to my wife and only in a whisper: "The world is flat."

And therein lies a tale of technology and geoeconomics that is fundamentally reshaping our lives—much, much more quickly than many people realize. It all happened while we were sleeping, or rather while we were focused on 9/11, the

---

It's a Flat World After All by Thomas L. Friedman appeared in The New York Times Magazine, April 3, 2005 and was adapted by the author from his book, THE WORLD IS FLAT by Thomas L. Friedman.

dot-com bust and Enron—which even prompted some to wonder whether globalization was over. Actually, just the opposite was true, which is why it's time to wake up and prepare ourselves for this flat world, because others already are, and there is no time to waste.

I wish I could say I saw it all coming. Alas, I encountered the flattening of the world quite by accident. It was in late February of last year, and I was visiting the Indian high-tech capital, Bangalore, working on a documentary for the Discovery Times channel about outsourcing. In short order, I interviewed Indian entrepreneurs who wanted to prepare my taxes from Bangalore, read my X-rays from Bangalore, trace my lost luggage from Bangalore and write my new software from Bangalore. The longer I was there, the more upset I became—upset at the realization that while I had been off covering the 9/11 wars, globalization had entered a whole new phase, and I had missed it. I guess the eureka moment came on a visit to the campus of Infosys Technologies, one of the crown jewels of the Indian outsourcing and software industry. Nandan Nilekani, the Infosys C.E.O., was showing me his global video-conference room, pointing with pride to a wall-size flat-screen TV, which he said was the biggest in Asia. Infosys, he explained, could hold a virtual meeting of the key players from its entire global supply chain for any project at any time on that supersize screen. So its American designers could be on the screen speaking with their Indian software writers and their Asian manufacturers all at once. That's what globalization is all about today, Nilekani said. Above the screen there were eight clocks that pretty well summed up the Infosys workday: 24/7/365. The clocks were labeled U.S. West, U.S. East, G.M.T., India, Singapore, Hong Kong, Japan, Australia.

"Outsourcing is just one dimension of a much more fundamental thing happening today in the world," Nilekani explained. "What happened over the last years is that there was a massive investment in technology, especially in the bubble era, when hundreds of millions of dollars were invested in putting broadband connectivity around the world, undersea cables, all those things." At the same time, he added, computers became cheaper and dispersed all over the world, and there was an explosion of e-mail software, search engines like Google and proprietary software that can chop up any piece of work and send one part to Boston, one part to Bangalore and one part to Beijing, making it easy for anyone to do remote development. When all of these things suddenly came together around 2000, Nilekani said, they "created a platform where intellectual work, intellectual capital, could be delivered from anywhere. It could be disaggregated, delivered, distributed, produced and put back together again—and this gave a whole new degree of freedom to the way we do work, especially work of an intellectual nature. And what you are seeing in Bangalore today is really the culmination of all these things coming together."

At one point, summing up the implications of all this, Nilekani uttered a phrase that rang in my ear. He said to me, "Tom, the playing field is being leveled." He meant that countries like India were now able to compete equally for global knowledge work as never before—and that America had better get ready for this. As I left the Infosys campus that evening and bounced along the potholed road back to Bangalore, I kept chewing on that phrase: "The playing field is being leveled."

"What Nandan is saying," I thought, "is that the playing field is being flattened. Flattened? Flattened? My God, he's telling me the world is flat!"

Here I was in Bangalore—more than 500 years after Columbus sailed over the horizon, looking for a shorter route to India using the rudimentary navigational technologies of his day, and returned safely to prove definitively that the world was round—and one of India's smartest engineers, trained at his country's top technical institute and backed by the most modern technologies of his day, was telling me that the world was flat, as flat as that screen on which he can host a meeting of his whole global supply chain. Even more interesting, he was citing this development as a new milestone in human progress and a great opportunity for India and the world—the fact that we had made our world flat!

This has been building for a long time. Globalization 1.0 (1492 to 1800) shrank the world from a size large to a size medium, and the dynamic force in that era was countries globalizing for resources and imperial conquest. Globalization 2.0 (1800 to 2000) shrank the world from a size medium to a size small, and it was spearheaded by companies globalizing for markets and labor. Globalization 3.0 (which started around 2000) is shrinking the world from a size small to a size tiny and flattening the playing field at the same time. And while the dynamic force in Globalization 1.0 was countries globalizing and the dynamic force in Globalization 2.0 was companies globalizing, the dynamic force in Globalization 3.0—the thing that gives it its unique character—is individuals and small groups globalizing. Individuals must, and can, now ask: where do I fit into the global competition and opportunities of the day, and how can I, on my own, collaborate with others globally? But Globalization 3.0 not only differs from the previous eras in how it is shrinking and flattening the world and in how it is empowering individuals. It is also different in that Globalization 1.0 and 2.0 were driven primarily by European and American companies and countries. But going forward, this will be less and less true. Globalization 3.0 is not only going to be driven more by individuals but also by a much more diverse—non-Western, non-white—group of individuals. In Globalization 3.0, you are going to see every color of the human rainbow take part.

"Today, the most profound thing to me is the fact that a 14-year-old in Romania or Bangalore or the Soviet Union or Vietnam has all the information, all the tools, all the software easily available to apply knowledge however they want," said Marc Andreessen, a co-founder of Netscape and creator of the first commercial Internet browser. "That is why I am sure the next Napster is going to come out of left field. As bioscience becomes more computational and less about wet labs and as all the genomic data becomes easily available on the Internet, at some point you will be able to design vaccines on your laptop."

Andreessen is touching on the most exciting part of Globalization 3.0 and the flattening of the world: the fact that we are now in the process of connecting all the knowledge pools in the world together. We've tasted some of the downsides of that in the way that Osama bin Laden has connected terrorist knowledge pools together through his Qaeda network, not to mention the work of teenage hackers spinning off more and more lethal computer viruses that affect us all. But the upside is that by connecting all these knowledge pools we are on the cusp of an incredible new era of innovation, an era that will be driven from left field and right field, from West and East and from North and South. Only 30 years ago, if you had a choice of being born a B student in Boston or a genius in Bangalore or Beijing, you probably would have chosen Boston, because a genius in Beijing or Bangalore could not really take advantage of his or her talent. They could not plug and play globally. Not anymore. Not when the world is flat, and anyone with smarts, access to Google and a cheap wireless laptop can join the innovation fray.

When the world is flat, you can innovate without having to emigrate. This is going to get interesting. We are about to see creative destruction on steroids.

How did the world get flattened, and how did it happen so fast? It was a result of 10 events and forces that all came together during the 1990's and converged right around the year 2000. Let me go through them briefly. The first event was 11/9. That's right—not 9/11, but 11/9. Nov. 9, 1989, is the day the Berlin Wall came down, which was critically important because it allowed us to think of the world as a single space. "The Berlin Wall was not only a symbol of keeping people inside Germany; it was a way of preventing a kind of global view of our future," the Nobel Prize-winning economist Amartya Sen said. And the wall went down just as the windows went up—the breakthrough Microsoft Windows 3.0 operating system, which helped to flatten the playing field even more by creating a global computer interface, shipped six months after the wall fell.

The second key date was 8/9. Aug. 9, 1995, is the day Netscape went public, which did two important things. First, it brought the Internet alive by giving us the browser to display images and data stored on Web sites. Second, the Netscape stock offering triggered the dot-com boom, which triggered the dot-com bubble, which triggered the massive overinvestment of billions of dollars in fiber-optic telecommunications cable. That overinvestment, by companies like Global Crossing, resulted in the willy-nilly creation of a global undersea-underground fiber network, which in turn drove down the cost of transmitting voices, data and images to practically zero, which in turn accidentally made Boston, Bangalore and Beijing next-door neighbors overnight. In sum, what the Netscape revolution did was bring people-to-people connectivity to a whole new level. Suddenly more people could connect with more other people from more different places in more different ways than ever before.

No country accidentally benefited more from the Netscape moment than India. "India had no resources and no infrastructure," said Dinakar Singh, one of the most respected hedge fund managers on Wall Street, whose parents earned doctoral degrees in biochemistry from the University of Delhi before emigrating to America. "It produced people with quality and by quantity. But many of them rotted on the docks of India like vegetables. Only a relative few could get on ships and get out. Not anymore, because we built this ocean crosser, called fiber-optic cable. For decades you had to leave India to be a professional. Now you can plug into the world from India. You don't have to go to Yale and go to work for Goldman Sachs." India could never have afforded to pay for the bandwidth to connect brainy India with high-tech America, so American shareholders paid for it. Yes, crazy overinvestment can be good. The overinvestment in railroads turned out to be a great boon for the American economy. "But the railroad overinvestment was confined to your own country and so, too, were the benefits," Singh said. In the case of the digital railroads, "it was the foreigners who benefited." India got a free ride.

The first time this became apparent was when thousands of Indian engineers were enlisted to fix the Y2K—the year 2000—computer bugs for companies from all over the world. (Y2K should be a national holiday in India. Call it "Indian Interdependence Day," says Michael Mandelbaum, a foreign-policy analyst at Johns Hopkins.) The fact that the Y2K work could be outsourced to Indians was made possible by the first two flatteners, along with a third, which I call "workflow." Workflow is shorthand for all the software applications, standards and electronic transmission pipes, like middleware, that connected all those computers and fiber-optic cable. To put it another way, if the Netscape moment connected people to people like never before, what the workflow revolution did was connect applications to applications so that people all over the world could work together in manipulating and shaping words, data and images on computers like never before.

Indeed, this breakthrough in people-to-people and application-to-application connectivity produced, in short order, six more flatteners—six new ways in which individuals and companies could collaborate on work and share knowledge. One was "outsourcing." When my software applications could connect seamlessly with all of your applications, it meant that all kinds of work—from accounting to software-writing—could be digitized, disaggregated and shifted to any place in the world where it could be done better and cheaper. The second was "offshoring." I send my whole factory from Canton, Ohio, to Canton, China. The third was "open-sourcing." I write the next operating system, Linux, using engineers collaborating together online and working for free. The fourth was "insourcing." I let a company like UPS come inside my company and take over my whole logistics operation—everything from filling my orders online to delivering my goods to repairing them for customers when they break. (People have no idea what UPS really does today. You'd be amazed!). The fifth was "supply-chaining." This is Wal-Mart's specialty. I create a global supply chain down to the last atom of efficiency so that if I sell an item in Arkansas, another is immediately made in China. (If Wal-Mart were a country, it would be China's eighth-largest trading partner.) The last new form of collaboration I call "informing"—this is Google, Yahoo and MSN Search, which now allow anyone to collaborate with, and mine, unlimited data all by themselves.

So the first three flatteners created the new platform for collaboration, and the next six are the new forms of collaboration that flattened the world even more. The 10th flattener I call "the steroids," and these are wireless access and voice over Internet protocol (VoIP). What the steroids do is turbocharge all these new forms of collaboration, so you can now do any one of them, from anywhere, with any device.

ARTICLE 3.3

Why Globalization Works

Martin Wolf

Martin Wolf is a journalist at the *Financial Times* of London, a respected economics newspaper. He asserts that, even for countries not well-placed in international economic competition, the gains from international trade and investment exceed those that would occur if a country were delinked from the international economy, that is, did not participate in international trade or investment (the term used to describe this situation is *autarky*). Wolf suggests that one can measure the value of globalization by comparing the extent of benefits that a country obtains from international economic integration versus what it would obtain from autarky. When this calculation is performed, globalization wins hands down! However, Wolf warns, participating in the global economy does not guarantee that a country will reap benefits. To do so, one must take into account "the quality of the state and the policies it follows." In this selection, Wolf recommends the policies to adopt and avoid.

Are you persuaded by Wolf's argument that the gains of globalization always outweigh the costs? Recall Wolf's argument when you read the selection later in this chapter by Vandana Shiva, who provides evidence of how destructive globalization can be.

Wolf makes another claim in this selection: that the low wages paid workers in poor countries like China do not automatically translate into job losses in affluent countries. For, he contends that what counts is the *productivity* of labor—that is, the value of what workers produce relative to their wages and other costs of production. By this measure, the superior skills and equipment that most workers in affluent countries possess enable them to outproduce—and therefore outcompete—workers in low-wage countries like China.

Wolf's argument is based on two important assumptions: (a) that workers in affluent countries will obtain superior training and skill, and (b) that they will be provided with superior equipment and technology. To the extent that these assumptions are becoming questionable, as Friedman asserts in preceding selections, the fault lines of inequality may run less between countries in different regions of the world than between individuals with different levels of skill and access to technology, wherever they are located around the globe.

Trade[1]

Any analysis of trade starts from the assumption that movement of capital and labour is prevented. A country is a jurisdiction with a circumscribed pool of labour, capital and land. The argument for trade is that it increases opportunities for owners of these factors of production to engage in mutually beneficial transactions. It is an extension across frontiers of the division of labour. We need merely ask what our standard of living would be if we had to grow our own food, make our own clothes and shoes, build our own houses, make our own furniture, write our own books and newspapers, build our own vehicles or be our own doctors and dentists. But opportunities for the division of labour do not cease within a single national jurisdiction.

As Douglas Irwin of Dartmouth University argues, John Stuart Mill, one of the intellectual giants of the nineteenth century, divided the gains from trade into three categories. These were direct advantages, indirect advantages and intellectual and moral advantages.[2]

In the first category come the standard static gains from trade—exploitation of economies of scale and comparative advantage. David Ricardo propounded the latter idea, perhaps the cleverest in economics. The Nobel-laureate Paul Samuelson was once asked to name "one proposition in all of the social sciences which is both true and non-trivial."[3] His answer was comparative advantage. It is true and cannot be trivial, because author after author fails to understand the theory's most powerful implication.[4] Specialization makes sense, argued Ricardo, even if one country is more efficient at everything than its trading partners. Countries should specialize at what they are *relatively* most efficient at doing. Countries do not compete in trade, as companies do.[5] Rather, industries compete inside countries for the services of factors of production. Opening a country to trade moves output in the direction of activities that offer domestic factors of production the highest returns. The shrinking import-competing industry is not competing with imports from foreigners, but with what its own domestic export industry can pay.

Trade in accordance with comparative advantage is similar to a productivity increase. Instead of making a particular good, an economy can obtain more of it, indirectly, by exporting something else. These gains can be large. A classic example was the opening of Japan in 1858, under American pressure. Before opening, the prices of silk and tea were much higher in the world than in Japan, while the prices of cotton and woollen goods were far lower. After opening, Japan exported silk and tea and imported cotton and woollen goods. This is estimated to have increased Japan's real income by 65 per cent without considering the long-run productivity and growth impact of its joining the world economy.[6]

In the second indirect category come the dynamic gains from trade. Trade promotes competition and productivity growth. Companies innovate in response to

---

Martin Wolf, *Why Globalization Works* (New Haven: Yale University Press, 2004): 80–89, 175–180, 335–337, 349.

competitive pressure. Widening the market to include more competitors increases this pressure.

Trade is also a conduit for foreign technology, via imports of capital and intermediate goods that embody significant innovations. Professor Irwin observes that even in the United States between a quarter and a half of growth in so-called "total factor productivity," the part of productivity growth not explained by capital accumulation and improved skills, is attributable to new technology embodied in capital equipment. No developing country would have access to the world's advanced technologies without trade. This, as I discovered when I worked on India in the 1970s, was one of the reasons why its productivity growth was so low, even though it was operating far below the level of the world's best practice. Its imports were too restricted by the government to allow producers access to the world's best machinery.

It is virtually impossible to prove the correlation between trade liberalization and growth, beyond doubt. But as Professors Peter Lindert of the University of California, Davis and Jeffrey Williamson of Harvard state, there are *no* examples of countries that have risen in the ranks of global living standards while being less open to trade and capital in the 1990s than in the 1960s. "There are," they continue, "no anti-global victories to report for the postwar" developing world.[7] As one Indian observer has remarked of his own country's policies, "by suppressing economic liberty for forty years, we destroyed growth and the future of two generations."[8]

The third set of benefits are, claimed Mill, intellectual and moral. To the extent that trade facilitates growth, for example, as it has done in the most successful post-war developing countries, it has made a powerful contribution to the arrival of democracy. One of the most encouraging developments of the past two decades is that South Korea, Taiwan and Chile, all of which began their rapid outward-looking development under dictatorships, have now become stable and vibrant democracies. Even in China, market reforms, including trade liberalization, have brought an enormous reduction in the repressiveness of the political regime, compared to its totalitarian apogee under a Maoist dictatorship much admired by western leftists.

The bottom line then is that liberal trade is beneficial. The obstacles to it, largely created by governments, need to be reduced.

Capital

Recently, people have tended to argue for capital controls on the view that capital mobility has proved problematic for national economic management.[9] Against this should be set the strong arguments in favour of capital mobility. The most important of these is personal freedom. Controlling the ability of people to export their capital has been among the first steps of despotic or economically destructive regimes. It also imposes a constraint on the malfeasance of governments, particularly on the overt or covert theft of their people's savings or the all-too-frequent abuse of the financial system. From this point of view, freedom of movement of capital is even more important than that to buy and sell goods.

There are also efficiency reasons for being in favour of capital mobility, which allows shifting of consumption between periods, higher returns and risk-spreading. In particular, countries with surplus savings (such as today's Japan) or companies with a large stock of valuable knowledge (such as many of today's leading multinational companies) should be able to deploy what they own abroad, to mutual advantage. Placing a part of one's capital abroad is also a way to diversify risks. Since one is always heavily exposed to the country one lives and works in, it makes sense to diversify that risk away. Thus the suppliers and recipients of finance should both gain.[10]

. . . [T]he investible resources of the world are locked into already rich countries, with much the largest cross-border flow to the United States from other rich countries (especially Japan). Movement of capital from rich countries to poorer ones has been not only modest, but crisis-prone.[11] In 2000, for example, the gross dollar savings of the high-income developed countries were $5,600 billion. If a mere 10 per cent of these gross savings were to flow to the developing world, this would amount to $560 billion a year. But the highest net flow of long-term capital to developing countries in the 1990s was only $341 billion in 1997, just before the Asian crisis.[12] More than a decade ago, the Nobel-laureate Robert Lucas noted this low level of capital flow to developing countries, which is contrary to standard assumptions about where returns would be highest.[13]

Again, the multinational companies possess vast knowledge and experience in virtually every area of economic activity. In particular, . . . it is inside these institutions that much of the economically useful knowledge of the advanced countries is developed, retained and applied. It is in the interests of countries around the world, but especially of developing countries, to gain access to that knowledge via foreign direct investment. Now, many developing countries recognize that foreign direct investment brings benefits that foreign borrowing does not. The direct investor is locked in and cannot flee the country whenever trouble strikes. If investors make reasonable profits, they will consider themselves long-term participants in the host country's economy and often bring in more capital. Last and most important, direct investment brings substantial additional benefits that spill over into the domestic economy, including transfer of technology and managerial skills.[14] In many developing countries, multinational corporations have been the most important way to train nationals in modern management and technology. Some of these benefits, notably the last, are not restricted to developing country recipients. Ireland and the United Kingdom are two relatively advanced economies to have gained hugely from inward direct investment.[15]

One explanation for the modest flows of capital to developing countries is the shortage of complementary human skills. Another explanation would be external economies in the use of that capital: people are more productive if they work with other productive people. . . .

In emerging market economies, difficulties over the design of the exchange rate and monetary regimes interact with the fragility of financial arrangements, to create a host of obstacles to stable and sizeable capital flows. First, ignorance of financial and economic conditions in foreign countries is greater than at home. This applies particularly to emerging-market economies. Second, confidence in the probity of the governments and legal systems of countries abroad is low. Third, important elements of the legal and regulatory systems malfunction or do not exist. Fourth, banking institutions often have comprehensive guarantees, while being used by governments or owners for their own purposes, which makes them fundamentally unsound.[16] Fifth, financial and accounting information is often lacking altogether, or is totally unreliable. Sixth, foreigners may expect to be discriminated against during a financial crisis, especially when the state or well-connected domestic interest is insolvent. Seventh, the government may have a long history of financial profligacy and default and so a poor reputation. Finally, when there is cross-border lending in a currency other than the borrower's, which is normal in lending to emerging markets, there is the additional foreign currency risk. All these problems are relatively small if, say, American banks lend in the United Kingdom. They are large if they lend to, say, Argentina. Their net effect is to make finance expensive, small in size and, worst of all, unstable.

The low level of foreign direct investment in many emerging market economies is explained by not dissimilar factors. Confidence in the probity and effectiveness of the governmental and legal systems is often very low. The economy is likely to be unstable, as may be the politics. The risk of nationalization or some other form of expropriation may well loom. The market may be modest in size, while the inputs needed to use the country as an export platform could well be lacking. It is not surprising, for all these reasons, that foreign direct investment in Africa is so low, to take just one example. It is also unsurprising that the profit requirements on investments there are so high.

Yet none of these difficulties, real though they are, is sufficient reason for giving up on the aim of greater net capital flows to poorer countries. These should be treated as constraints to be lifted, not ones to be accepted. For if they are treated as binding and reinforced with capital controls, the world's poorest people will find it still more difficult to escape their plight.

People and Geography

Traditional economic theory suggests that if trade is free and, still more, if capital flows freely, people should not need to move to gain higher incomes. Trade and capital mobility should equalize returns to labour across the world. Unfortunately, the assumptions underlying these orthodox models have turned out to be very far from true. We see the surplus capital of some rich countries pouring into the richest country in the world. In terms of purchasing power, a bus driver in Germany receives thirteen times one in Kenya, though his skills are much the same.[17] Workers with given skills earn vastly more in rich countries than in poor ones. Yet the rich countries that pay these higher wages for the same skills do not offer lower returns on capital than poor ones. If anything, the reverse is the case. Apparently capital-scarce countries have dismally low returns on capital, while apparently capital-abundant ones offer high returns. Similarly, free trade does not equalize wages, because productive efficiency diverges immensely across countries.

This paradoxical situation has two powerful—and disturbing—implications. The first is that the simplest thing we can do to alleviate mass human poverty is to allow people to move freely or their labour services to be traded freely, though perhaps temporarily. This is not a cause critics of globalization have embraced. That is not surprising, since it would kill support for their cause in high-income countries. Yet the U.S. could fit in another billion people. There is even much empty space in Europe, too. This is not a recommendation. It is an observation of human hypocrisy.

The second implication is that there is no end of geography. Geography combined with jurisdiction matters more today than ever before in history. The quality of one's life depends even more on where one is born than on the class into which one is born. This means, in turn, that free trade and capital movement, albeit beneficial, will not, on their own, equalize global incomes. The big question then is why the productive possibilities of different jurisdictions differ to such an extent. Beyond the financial failings already mentioned above, there are three additional reasons.

The first is that richer countries can invest far more in the skills of their people. A large supply of human skills not only raises returns to capital and unskilled labour, but allows all productive processes to be run more efficiently, for it is the skilled who understand how things need to be done.

The second reason is that there are increasing returns to activities in specific locations.[18] Agglomerations of skill raise returns on all those skills. But skill also begets knowledge, which begets more knowledge, which then begets more skill. These increasing returns are location specific. We are indeed social animals: our incomes depend on the skills of those around us.

The last reason is that different jurisdictions differ in their ability to offer the requirements of productive market activity—property-rights protection, an honest and effective bureaucracy, judicial independence, good-quality infrastructure, decent health and education services, and so forth.[19] This is the hand of history at work: some places may have started from a poor resource endowment or geographical isolation; they may then have suffered predatory forms of colonization; they may be afflicted by cultural handicaps; and they may have made serious policy errors.[20] Quite possibly, they may have experienced all these things. This unhappy past may then have cumulated over time into a vicious circle of poor government, low growth, low skill formation and so back to poor growth.

The notion of such poverty traps can be overdone. Few imagined four decades ago that South Korea would be among the most successful developing countries. But history matters and so, therefore, does geography.

This is not the end of the story of human mobility. Assume the increasing-returns story is right. Then skilled people in poor countries will earn less than they could in rich ones. They will want to move and, given their skills, may well be allowed to do so. Assume also that skilled people raise the wages of the unskilled where they live. Then free movement of skilled people from poor countries benefits rich countries and the skilled migrants, but harms the poor they leave behind. This is a reverse-aid programme. It is also one in which the rich countries are deeply engaged at present. The British National Health Service, for example, could not function without imports of skilled staff from developing countries. . . .

Fear of Pauper Labour and the Myth of De-Industrialization

The scholarly debate on the impact of imports on the distribution of labour incomes in high-income countries . . . has more simplistic counterparts in the popular debate. The "pauper labour" argument is back. How can workers in high-income countries compete with Chinese workers? How can they find jobs when the ones they have go abroad? How is the world going to avoid a glut of manufacturing capacity, with deflation and mass unemployment? Happily, the answer to all these questions is: easily.

Start then with those overwhelmingly competitive Chinese workers. It is true that, on average, a worker in Chinese manufacturing cost only $730, annually, between 1995 and 1999, while a German worker cost $35,000, an American one $29,000 and a British one $24,000. Is it then not perfectly evident that German, American and British wages will be driven down to Chinese levels?[21] It is not merely not obvious; it is untrue. Chinese labour is cheap because it is unproductive (see Figure 1).[22] If an American worker produces $81,000 of value added annually, a German worker $80,000 and a British worker $55,000, while a Chinese worker produces only $2,900, it is not at all difficult for the workers of the high-income countries to compete, even if their wages are vastly higher. . . .

Why are workers in high-income countries so much more productive than those in China (or other developing countries)? One explanation is that they have far more capital at their command than a Chinese worker. In 2000, Chinese gross capital formation per person was only about 4 per cent of U.S. levels, at market exchange rates.[23] Moreover, because of China's rapid growth, its relative rates of investment were even lower just a few years ago. By comparison with high-income countries, therefore, China has very little capital to spread around. A second explanation is that Americans and Europeans are far better educated, on average, than Chinese. A third explanation is the Chinese people's lack of experience with sophisticated modern management and manufacturing. A final explanation is the different composition of Chinese manufacturing. China specializes in relatively labour-intensive manufacturing, which makes value added per worker lower than in high-income countries. By exporting the products of its cheap but relatively unskilled labour, China gains access to the physical and

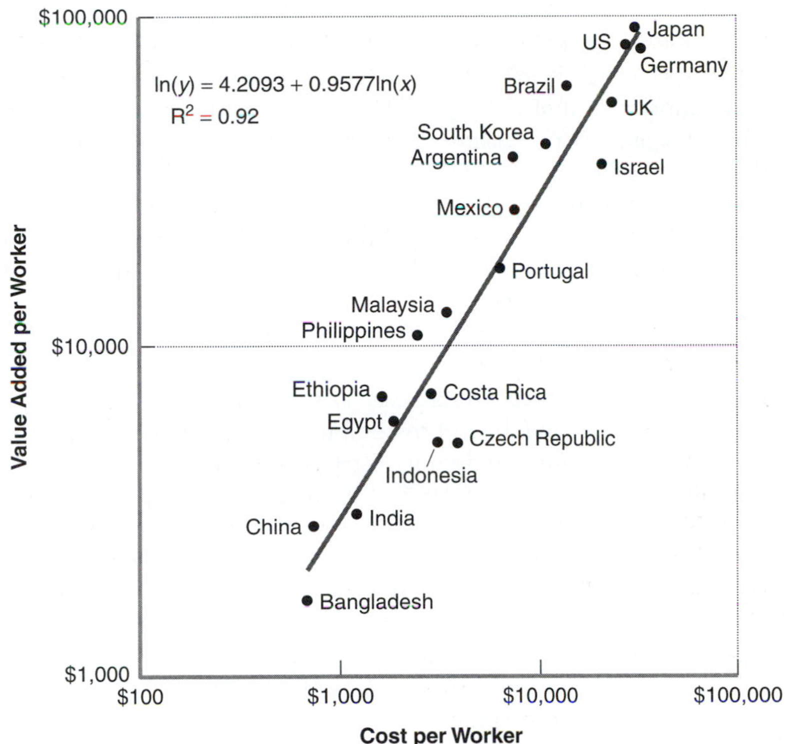

Figure 1 Labour cost and productivity per worker in manufacturing (1995–9 average)
SOURCE: World Bank, *World Development Indicators 2002* (Washington DC: World Bank, 2002), own calculations.

human capital, and know-how, of high-income countries, embodied in their exports. China does not make Boeing aircraft and the U.S., by now, makes relatively few garments.

In future, the efficiency of Chinese workers and managers and the capital at their disposal will rise rapidly, generating correspondingly swift increases in productivity.[24] That will not make China invincibly competitive, because, in a competitive economy, wages will rise as well. They have done just that in other rapidly growing east Asian countries, such as South Korea. Today, South Korea's wages are fifteen times as high as China's. Fifty years ago, they would have been much the same. In time, China's wages and so its costs will also rise, together with its productivity. As they do so, its comparative advantage will also change. Today, South Korea has largely left garment manufacture behind. In time, so will China.

At this stage, a sophisticated critic would argue that China is different from South Korea. It has an enormous potential supply of labour, whose wages, in a competitive economy, will be determined not by rising productivity in manufacturing, but by low productivity back home in rural areas. If the latter rises slowly, as it is quite likely to do, then wages in Chinese industry must also rise slowly, if the labour market remains competitive. Since underlying productive efficiency is bound to grow in Chinese manufacturing, will this not make China invincibly competitive after all?

The answer, again, is no. Assume that the real wage does not rise at all, but "total factor productivity"—the output that can be produced by a unit of capital and labour—does continue to increase. It will then become profitable to take advantage of this productivity increase through rapidly increasing employment of still cheap labour.[25] Increases in productivity per worker will then remain low, but the growth in industrial employment will be rapid. This is exactly as it ought to be in a country so early in its industrialization. Then, when the supply of labour begins to tighten, wages and labour productivity will both explode upwards. That also happened to South Korea after a decade or two of rapid growth.[26]

The same will happen in China, provided it is allowed to do so. If, however, the movement of labour into modern industry is controlled or wages are pushed up prematurely (as is, in fact, happening), China will end up with a dualistic economy instead, with higher wages for a relatively privileged few, but a smaller modern economy and a lower overall standard of living than would be desirable. Given the controls on labour mobility in China, that is quite likely to happen. These are also one of the reasons for the widening income gap between the people of the coastal provinces and the rest of the country. Either way, one can be confident that the relationship between real wages and productivity per worker will hold: either real wages *and* productivity per worker will rise slowly for a long time, or real wages will rise rapidly *and* so will productivity per worker.

If developing countries are not so overwhelmingly competitive in manufacturing, why have "good" manufacturing jobs for unskilled or semi-skilled workers in high-income countries shrunk over the past three decades? Between 1970 and 2000, the U.S. lost 2.5 million jobs in manufacturing, while the share of manufacturing in total employment fell from 26.4 per cent to 14.7 per cent. In the U.K., the reduction in employment in manufacturing was 3.5 million between 1970 and 1998, while the share of manufacturing in employment fell from 34.7 to 18.6 per cent. The U.K. was extreme. But similar patterns can be seen elsewhere: 39.5 per cent of West Germany's workers were in manufacturing in 1970, an extraordinarily high share. By 1999, this had fallen to 24.1 per cent.[27]

To understand why absolute numbers employed and, still more, the share of employment in manufacturing fell in high-income countries over the past two or three decades, one has to go back to underlying causes. Logically, employment depends on output and productivity trends. If growth of labour productivity is higher than the growth of output, employment must shrink. If growth of productivity is sufficiently higher in manufacturing than in the rest of the economy, the employment share in manufacturing will fall, even if the employment level does not. Output, in turn, will depend on the growth in demand and changes in the trade balance. If the deterioration in the trade balance is big enough, positive trends in demand for manufactures can be consistent with a reduction in output.

What then are the facts? Paul Krugman, a well-known U.S. trade economist, calculates that the increase in the U.S. trade deficit in manufactures may have accounted for just a quarter of the decline of the share of manufacturing in U.S. GDP, from 25.0 per cent in 1970 to 15.9 per cent in 2000. In 2001, the U.S. ran a trade deficit in manufactures of $300 billion (approximately 3 per cent of GDP), of which $165 billion was with developing countries. The European Union, however, ran an overall surplus in manufactures of $120 billion and a surplus with developing countries of $50 billion. In the U.S., therefore, trade created a modest gap between growth in demand for manufactures and in domestic output. But this is not true for the EU as a whole, where a negative impact of trade in manufactures with developing countries on jobs in manufacturing can only have come via differences in the labour intensity of what was exported and imported. In other words, balanced trade with developing countries will tend to raise productivity in manufacturing, since labour-intensive manufacturing will shrink and capital-intensive manufacturing rise. That is beneficial in itself, since it raises potential incomes, just as any other productivity increase does. The only requirement is a labour market capable of reallocating workers.

Now turn to output and productivity. Between 1973 and 1995, labour productivity in U.S. manufacturing rose at 2.5 per cent a year, while it grew at only 1.5 per cent a year in the business sector as a whole. Similar gaps exist in every other high-income country. Inevitably, therefore, employment in manufacturing had to shrink, relative to that in the business sector as a whole, if output merely rose at the same rate in the two sectors. But people in high-income countries also tend to spend a declining share of their incomes on manufactures and an increasing share on services.[28] The combination of sluggish growth in demand for manufactures with rapid rises in productivity guarantees a steep fall in the share of employment in manufacturing in the years ahead, *regardless of what happens to trade balances*.

Consider the following simple example: an economy with an initial share of manufacturing in employment of 15 per cent; productivity growth at 2.5 per cent a year in manufacturing and 1.5 per cent a year in the rest of the economy; growth in demand for manufactures at 2 per cent a year (in real terms) and in demand for the rest of economic output (overwhelmingly services) at 2.5 per cent a year; and balanced trade in both manufactures and services. Then, after twenty-five years, the share of manufacturing in employment will be 11 per cent; after fifty years, it will be 8 per cent; after a hundred years, it will be 4 per cent. Manufacturing is, in short, the new agriculture.

To think this will be a disaster shows one is prey to the "lump of labour fallacy"—the view that there exists a fixed number of jobs in an economy. Nobody with any knowledge of economic history could believe such a thing. Two hundred years ago, the share of the population engaged in agriculture in today's high-income countries was about three-quarters. Today it is 2 or 3 per cent in populations that have also increased many times over. Are all the people not required in the fields now unemployed? The answer is: of course not. They do a host of jobs, most of them far more amusing and less arduous than their ancestors could even have imagined in 1800. The same will be true in future.

So far, then, the notion of an insuperable tide of hyper-competitive production laying waste the jobs, industries and economic activity of the high-income countries can be seen as hysteria. But this leaves aside one last possible meaning to the notion of competition among countries. When a developing country, such as China, sends goods to the U.S. or the EU, in line with its comparative advantage, the terms of trade—and so real incomes—of the importing countries improve. This means that the prices of their imports fall in relation to exports. That, in turn, means that the importing country can buy more with what it produces. It is better off. That, indeed, is why China's entry into world markets is beneficial for the high-income countries that make the sophisticated goods and services the Chinese wish to buy. Trade is not a zero-sum game. It is mutually enriching. . . .

Notes

1. Excellent recent discussions of the underlying arguments for liberal trade are contained in Jagdish N. Bhagwati, *Free Trade Today* (Princeton: Princeton University Press, 2002). Professor Bhagwati is the world's leading trade economist. Also excellent are Douglas A. Irwin, *Free Trade under Fire* (Princeton: Princeton University Press, 2002) and *Against the Tide: An Intellectual History of Free Trade* (Princeton: Princeton University Press, 1996). Much of the discussion below draws on these sources. Also helpful is W. Max Corden, *Trade Policy and Economic Welfare* (Oxford: Clarendon Press, 1974, second edition 1997).
2. Irwin, *Free Trade under Fire*, pp. 29–48.
3. Retold in Irwin, *Free Trade under Fire*, p. 25, note 5.
4. . . . [A]mong the distinguished authors whose analysis of the consequences of globalization is vitiated by this error is John Gray in his *False Dawn: The Delusions of Global Capitalism* (London: Granta, 1998).
5. The economist who has argued most powerfully that countries do not compete like companies is Paul Krugman. See 'Competitiveness: A Dangerous Obsession', *Foreign Affairs 73* (March–April 1994), pp. 28–44 and 'Ricardo's Difficult Idea: Why Intellectuals Don't Understand Comparative Advantage', in Gary Cook (ed.), *The Economics and Politics of International Trade*, Volume 2 of *Freedom and Trade* (London: Routledge, 1998).
6. Irwin, *Free Trade under Fire*, p. 30.
7. Peter H. Lindert and Jeffrey G. Williamson, 'Does Globalization Make the World More Unequal?', paper presented at the National Bureau of Economic Research conference on Globalization in Historical Perspective, Santa Barbara, California, 3–6 May 2001, p. 25.
8. Guchuran Das, *India Unbound* (New York: Alfred A. Knopf, 2001), p. 175.
9. Even Jagdish Bhagwati, a staunch free-trader, has taken this position. See Jagdish N. Bhagwati, 'The Capital Myth', *Foreign Affairs*, Vol. 77 (May–June, 1998), pp. 7–12.
10. A discussion of many of the issues is contained in Forrest Capie, *Capital Controls: A 'Cure' Worse than the Problem* (London: Institute of Economic Affairs, 2002).
11. On crises, see *Finance for Growth: Policy Choices in a Volatile World* (Washington DC: World Bank, 2001), chapter 2.
12. Data are from *Global Development Finance: Financing the Poorest Countries, Analysis and Summary Tables 2002* (Washington DC: World Bank, 2002).
13. Robert E. Lucas, 'Why doesn't Capital Flow from Rich to Poor Countries?' *American Economic Review*, 80 (May 1990), pp. 92–6.

14. See Edward M. Graham, *Fighting the Wrong Enemy: Antiglobal Activists and Multinational Enterprises* (Washington DC: Institute for International Economics, 2000), p. 172.
15. The positive impact of inward foreign direct investment on British manufacturing is one of the themes of Geoffrey Owen's book, *From Empire to Europe: the Decline and Revival of British Industry since the Second World War* (London: HarperCollins, 1999).
16. An interesting analysis of the Asian financial crisis of 1997–8 that stresses moral hazard created by government guarantees is contained in Giancarlo Corsetti, Paolo Pesenti and Nouriel Roubini, 'Paper Tigers? A Model of the Asian Crisis', National Bureau of Economic Research, Working Paper 6783, www.nber.org, November 1998.
17. World Bank, *World Development Report 1995: Workers in an Integrating World* (Oxford: Oxford University Press, for the World Bank, 1995), pp. 10–14.
18. The increasing-return story is well told by William Easterly in *The Elusive Quest for Growth: Economists' Adventures and Misadventures in the Tropics* (Cambridge, Massachusetts: MIT Press, 2001), chapter 8.
19. This is the core of the late Mancur Olson's theory of why economies diverge to such a large extent. See his article 'Big Bills Left on the Sidewalk: Why Some Countries are Rich and Others Poor', *Journal of Economic Perspectives*, Vol. 10 (Spring 1996), pp. 3–24.
20. Daron Acemoglu, Simon Johnson and James A. Robinson, in 'Reversal of Fortune: Geography and Institutions in the Making of the Modern World Income Distribution', National Bureau of Economic Research Working Paper 8460, 2001, and *Quarterly Journal of Economics*, Vol. 117, argue that the rich places of today were poor in 1500 and vice versa, because European colonizers imposed extractive institutions on the rich places they seized (such as India and Mexico) and wealth-generating institutions on the poor ones (such as North America). The theory is neat. But many of the rich countries of 1500 already had efficient wealth-extracting institutions imposed by already established élites. All the colonizers needed to do was take them over. That was certainly true in India. The difference may be that in rich agrarian societies extractive systems were well in place and have survived in the hands of local politicians to this day. But in sparsely settled places, institutions that generated wealth had to be created. It is probably no accident that all those institutions were introduced by the British.
21. World Bank, *World Development Indicators 2002* (Washington DC: World Bank, 2002).
22. If one relates the cost of labour to that of value added per worker for a mixed sample of twenty high-income and developing countries, one obtains an R2 of 0.94 and an elasticity of the cost of labour with respect to value added per worker of 0.92 (see equation on Figure 1).
23. This would be considerably higher using a standard PPP conversion, as much as 25 per cent of U.S. levels. But equipment used in manufacturing is unlikely to be much cheaper in China than in the U.S., though construction will be. On balance, however, conversions at market exchange rates probably give a better picture of investment per person than PPP conversions.
24. More precisely, the marginal product of labour will rise over time as total factor productivity and the capital stock per worker rises. In a competitive labour market, employers cannot avoid paying the marginal product, whether they wish to or not.
25. Technically, factor substitution will offset higher total factor productivity, to keep labour-intensity and the marginal product of labour low.
26. First, there is growth on the extensive margin, with use of the additional capital to add new workers to the active labour force of the modern sector and, second, there is growth on the intensive margin, with rising capital per worker and so wages.
27. Philippe Legrain, *Open World: The Truth about Globalization* (London: Abacus, 2002), pp. 38–9.
28. Gary Burtless, Robert Z. Lawrence, Robert E. Litan and Robert J. Shapiro present a lucid analysis of the link between demand, trade, productivity and employment in manufacturing in *Globaphobia: Confronting Fears about Open Trade* (Washington DC: Brookings Institution, 1998), chapter 3, especially pp. 48–56. The book traces the actual share of manufacturing in total US employment between 1964 and 1992 and a hypothetical share, with no trade deficit. The two lines diverge very little. See *ibid.*, Figures 3–7.

Globalism's Discontents

Joseph E. Stiglitz

In this selection, Joseph Stiglitz, who has served as chair of the Council of Economic Advisers and chief economist of the World Bank, and who is a Nobel prize winner in Economics, claims that economic globalization can produce great benefits. However, for this to occur, states must provide their citizens with adequate social safety nets, such as social assistance for those dislocated by economic change. States must also impose capital controls, that is, regulate the flow of foreign capital, to reduce the risk of instability and economic and financial crisis. Unfortunately, Stiglitz warns, these measures run counter to prevailing economic theory and the policies of many states and the International Monetary Fund (IMF), a powerful international financial institution. Stiglitz does not analyze that opposition to these policies has developed around the world. Do you think it has been infuential?

Few subjects have polarized people throughout the world as much as globalization. Some see it as the way of the future, bringing unprecedented prosperity to everyone, everywhere. Others, symbolized by the Seattle protestors of December 1999, fault globalization as the source of untold problems, from the destruction of native cultures to increasing poverty and immiseration. In this article, I want to sort out the different meanings of globalization. In many countries, globalization has brought huge benefits to a few with few benefits to the many. But in the case of a few countries, it has brought enormous benefit to the many. Why have there been these huge differences in experiences? The answer is that globalization has meant different things in different places.

The countries that have managed globalization on their own, such as those in East Asia, have, by and large, ensured that they reaped huge benefits and that those benefits were equitably shared; they were able substantially to control the terms on which they engaged with the global economy. By contrast, the countries that have, by and large, had globalization managed for them by the International Monetary Fund and other international economic institutions have not done so well. The problem is thus not with globalization but with how it has been managed.

Reprinted with permission from Joseph E. Stiglitz, "Globalism's Discontents," THE AMERICAN PROSPECT, Volume 13, Number 1: January 2002. The American Prospect, 11 Beacon Street, Suite 1120, Boston, MA 02108.

The international financial institutions have pushed a particular ideology—market fundamentalism—that is both bad economics and bad politics; it is based on premises concerning how markets work that do not hold even for developed countries, much less for developing countries. The IMF has pushed these economics policies without a broader vision of society or the role of economics within society. And it has pushed these policies in ways that have undermined emerging democracies.

More generally, globalization itself has been governed in ways that are undemocratic and have been disadvantageous to developing countries, especially the poor within those countries. The Seattle protestors pointed to the absence of democracy and of transparency, the governance of the international economic institutions by and for special corporate and financial interests, and the absence of countervailing democratic checks to ensure that these informal and public institutions serve a general interest. In these complaints, there is more than a grain of truth.

Beneficial Globalization

Of the countries of the world, those in East Asia have grown the fastest and done most to reduce poverty. And they have done so, emphatically, via "globalization." Their growth has been based on exports—by taking advantage of the global market for exports and by closing the technology gap. It was not just gaps in capital and other resources that separated the developed from the less-developed countries, but differences in knowledge. East Asian countries took advantage of the "globalization of knowledge" to reduce these disparities. But while some of the countries in the region grew by opening themselves up to multinational companies, others, such as Korea and Taiwan, grew by creating their own enterprises. Here is the key distinction: Each of the most successful globalizing countries determined its own pace of change; each made sure as it grew that the benefits were shared equitably; each rejected the basic tenets of the "Washington Consensus," which argued for a minimalist role for government and rapid privatization and liberalization.

In East Asia, government took an active role in managing the economy. The steel industry that the Korean government created was among the most efficient in the world—performing far better than its private-sector rivals in the United States (which, though private, are constantly turning to the government for protection and for subsidies). Financial markets were highly regulated. My research shows that those regulations promoted growth. It was only when these countries stripped away the regulations, under pressure from the U.S. Treasury and the IMF, that they encountered problems.

During the 1960s, 1970s, and 1980s, the East Asian economies not only grew rapidly but were remarkably stable. Two of the countries most touched by the 1997–1998 economic crisis had had in the preceding three decades not a single year of negative growth; two had only one year—a better performance than the United States or the other wealthy nations that make up the Organization for Economic Cooperation and Development (OECD). The single most important factor leading to the troubles that several of the East Asian countries encountered in the late 1990s—the East Asian crisis—was the rapid liberalization of financial and capital markets. In short, the countries of East Asia benefited from globalization because they made globalization work for them; it was when they succumbed to the pressures from the outside that they ran into problems that were beyond their own capacity to manage well.

Globalization can yield immense benefits. Elsewhere in the developing world, globalization of knowledge has brought improved health, with life spans increasing at a rapid pace. How can one put a price on these benefits of globalization? Globalization has brought still other benefits: Today there is the beginning of a globalized civil society that has begun to succeed with such reforms as the [Land] Mine Ban Treaty and debt forgiveness for the poorest highly indebted countries (the Jubilee movement). The globalization protest movement itself would not have been possible without globalization.

The Darker Side of Globalization

How then could a trend with the power to have so many benefits have produced such opposition? Simply because it has not only failed to live up to its potential but frequently has had very adverse effects. But this forces us to ask, why has it had such adverse effects? The answer can be seen by looking at each of the economic elements of globalization as pursued by the international financial institutions and especially by the IMF.

The most adverse effects have arisen from the liberalization of financial and capital markets—which has posed risks to developing countries without commensurate rewards. The liberalization has left them prey to hot money pouring into the country, an influx that has fueled speculative real-estate booms; just as suddenly, as investor sentiment changes, the money is pulled out, leaving in its wake economic devastation. Early on, the IMF said that these countries were being rightly punished for pursuing bad economic policies. But as the crisis spread from country to country, even those that the IMF had given high marks found themselves ravaged.

The IMF often speaks about the importance of the discipline provided by capital markets. In doing so, it exhibits a certain paternalism, a new form of the old colonial mentality: "We in the establishment, we in the North who run our capital markets, know best. Do what we tell you to do, and you will prosper." The arrogance is offensive, but the objection is more than just to style. The position is highly undemocratic: There is an implied assumption that democracy by itself does not provide sufficient discipline. But if one is to have an external disciplinarian, one should choose a good disciplinarian who knows what is good for growth, who shares one's values. One doesn't want an arbitrary and capricious taskmaster who one moment praises you for your virtues and the next screams at you for being rotten to the core. But capital markets are just such a fickle taskmaster; even ardent advocates talk about their bouts of irrational exuberance followed by equally irrational pessimism.

Lessons of Crisis

Nowhere was the fickleness more evident than in the last global financial crisis. Historically, most of the disturbances in capital flows into and out of a country are not the result of factors inside the country. Major disturbances arise, rather, from influences outside the country. When Argentina suddenly faced high interest rates in 1998, it wasn't because of what Argentina did but because of what happened in Russia. Argentina cannot be blamed for Russia's crisis.

Small developing countries find it virtually impossible to withstand this volatility. I have described capital-market liberalization with a simple metaphor: Small countries are like small boats. Liberalizing capital markets is like setting them loose on a rough sea. Even if the boats are well captained, even if the boats are sound, they are likely to be hit broadside by a big wave and capsize. But the IMF pushed for the boats to set forth into the roughest parts of the sea before they were seaworthy, with untrained captains and crews, and without life vests. No wonder matters turned out so badly!

To see why it is important to choose a disciplinarian who shares one's values, consider a world in which there were free mobility of skilled labor. Skilled labor would then provide discipline. Today, a country that does not treat capital well will find capital quickly withdrawing; in a world of free labor mobility if a country did not treat skilled labor well, it too would withdraw. Workers would worry about the quality of their children's education and their family's health care, the quality of their environment and of their own wages and working conditions. They would say to the government: If you fail to provide these essentials, we will move elsewhere. That is a far cry from the kind of discipline that free-flowing capital provides.

The liberalization of capital markets has not brought growth: How can one build factories or create jobs with money that can come in and out of a country overnight? And it gets worse: Prudential behavior requires countries to set aside reserves equal to the amount of short-term lending; so if a firm in a poor country borrows $100 million at, say, 20 percent interest rates short-term from a bank in the United States, the government must set aside a corresponding amount. The reserves are typically held in U.S. Treasury bills—a safe, liquid asset. In effect, the country is borrowing $100 million from the United States and lending $100 million to the United States. But when it borrows, it pays a high interest rate, 20 percent; when it lends, it receives a low interest rate, around 4 percent. This may be great for the United States, but it can hardly help the growth of the poor country. There is also a high opportunity cost of the reserves; the money could have been much better spent on building rural roads or constructing schools or health clinics. But instead, the country is, in effect, forced to lend money to the United States.

Thailand illustrates the true ironies of such policies: There, the free market led to investments in empty office buildings, starving other sectors—such as education and transportation—of badly needed resources. Until the IMF and the U.S. Treasury came along, Thailand had restricted bank lending for speculative real estate. The Thais had seen the record: Such lending is an essential part of the boom-bust cycle that has characterized capitalism for 200 years. It wanted to be sure that the scarce capital went to create jobs. But the IMF nixed this intervention in the free market. If the free market said, "Build empty office buildings," so be it! The market knew better than any government bureaucrat who mistakenly might have thought it wiser to build schools or factories.

The Costs of Volatility

Capital-market liberalization is inevitably accompanied by huge volatility, and this volatility impedes growth and increases poverty. It increases the risks of investing in the country, and thus investors demand a risk premium in the form of higher-than-normal profits. Not only is growth not enhanced but poverty is increased through several channels. The high volatility increases the likelihood of recessions—and the poor always bear the brunt of such downturns. Even in developed countries, safety nets are weak or nonexistent among the self-employed and in the rural sector. But these are the dominant sectors in developing countries. Without adequate safety nets, the recessions that follow from capital-market liberalization lead to impoverishment. In the name of imposing budget discipline and reassuring investors, the IMF invariably demands expenditure reductions, which almost inevitably result in cuts in outlays for safety nets that are already threadbare. Matters are even worse—for under the doctrines of the "discipline of the capital markets," if countries try to tax capital, capital flees. Thus, the IMF doctrines inevitably lead to an increase in tax burdens on the poor and the middle classes. Thus, while IMF bailouts enable the rich to take their money out of the country at more favorable terms (at the overvalued exchange rates), the burden of repaying the loans lies with the workers who remain behind.

The reason that I emphasize capital-market liberalization is that the case against it—and against the IMF's stance in pushing it—is so compelling. It illustrates what can go wrong with globalization. Even economists like Jagdish Bhagwati, strong advocates of free trade, see the folly in liberalizing capital markets. Belatedly, so too has the IMF—at least in its official rhetoric, though less so in its policy stances—but too late for all those countries that have suffered so much from following the IMF's prescriptions.

But while the case for trade liberalization—when properly done—is quite compelling, the way it has been pushed by the IMF has been far more problematic. The basic logic is simple: Trade liberalization is supposed to result in resources moving from inefficient protected sectors to more efficient export sectors. The problem is not only that job destruction comes before the job creation—so that unemployment and poverty result—but that the IMF's "structural adjustment programs" (designed in ways that allegedly would reassure global investors) make job creation almost impossible. For these programs are often accompanied by high interest rates that are often justified by a single-minded focus on inflation. Sometimes that concern is deserved; often, though, it is carried to an extreme. In the United States, we worry that small increases in the interest rate will discourage investment. The IMF has pushed for far higher interest rates in countries with a far less hospitable investment environment. The high interest rates mean that new jobs and enterprises are not created. What happens is that trade liberalization, rather than moving workers from low-productivity jobs to high-productivity ones, moves them from low-productivity jobs to unemployment. Rather than enhanced growth, the effect is increased poverty. To make matters even worse, the unfair trade-liberalization agenda forces poor countries to compete with highly subsidized American and European agriculture.

The Governance of Globalization

As the market economy has matured within countries, there has been increasing recognition of the importance of having rules to govern it. One hundred fifty years ago, in many parts of the world, there was a domestic process that was in some ways analogous to globalization. In the United States, government promoted the formation of the national economy, the building of the railroads, and the development of the telegraph—all of which reduced transportation and communication costs within the United States. As that process occurred, the democratically elected national government provided oversight: supervising and regulating, balancing interests, tempering crises, and limiting adverse consequences of this very large change in economic structure. So, for instance, in 1863 the U.S. government established the first financial banking regulatory authority—the Office of the Comptroller of Currency—because it was important to have strong national banks, and that requires strong regulation.

The United States, among the least statist of the industrial democracies, adopted other policies. Agriculture, the central industry of the United States in the mid-nineteenth century, was supported by the 1862 Morrill Act, which established research, extension, and teaching programs. That system worked extremely well and is widely credited with playing a central role in the enormous increases in agricultural productivity over the last century and a half. We established an industrial policy for other fledgling industries, including radio and civil aviation. The beginning of the telecommunications industry, with the first telegraph line between Baltimore and Washington, D.C., was funded by the federal government. And it is a tradition that has continued, with the U.S. government's founding of the Internet.

By contrast, in the current process of globalization we have a system of what I call global governance without global government. International institutions like the World Trade Organization, the IMF, the World Bank, and others provide an ad hoc system of global governance, but it is a far cry from global government and lacks democratic accountability. Although it is perhaps better than not having any system of global governance, the system is structured not to serve general interests or assure equitable results. This not only raises issues of whether broader values are given short shrift; it does not even promote growth as much as an alternative might.

Governance Through Ideology

Consider the contrast between how economic decisions are made inside the United States and how they are made in the international economic institutions. In this country, economic decisions within the administration are undertaken largely by the National Economic Council, which includes the secretary of labor, the secretary of commerce, the chairman of the Council of Economic Advisers, the treasury secretary, the assistant attorney general for antitrust, and the U.S. trade representative. The Treasury is only one vote and often gets voted down. All of these officials, of course, are part of an administration that must face Congress and the democratic electorate. But in the international arena, only the voices of the financial community are heard. The IMF reports to the ministers of finance and the governors of the central banks, and one of the important items on its agenda is to make these central banks more independent—and less democratically accountable. It might make little difference if the IMF dealt only with matters of concern to the financial community, such as the clearance of checks; but in fact, its policies affect every aspect of life. It forces countries to have tight monetary and fiscal policies: It evaluates the trade-off between inflation and unemployment, and in that trade-off it always puts far more weight on inflation than on jobs.

The problem with having the rules of the game dictated by the IMF—and thus by the financial community—is not just a question of values (though that is important) but also a question of ideology. The financial community's view of the world predominates—even when there is little evidence in its support. Indeed, beliefs on key issues are held so strongly that theoretical and empirical support of the positions is viewed as hardly necessary.

Recall again the IMF's position on liberalizing capital markets. As noted, the IMF pushed a set of policies that exposed countries to serious risk. One might have thought, given the evidence of the costs, that the IMF could offer plenty of evidence that the policies also did some good. In fact, there was no such evidence; the evidence that was available suggested that there was little if any positive effect on growth. Ideology enabled IMF officials not only to ignore the absence of benefits but also to overlook the evidence of the huge costs imposed on countries.

An Unfair Trade Agenda

The trade-liberalization agenda has been set by the North, or more accurately, by special interests in the North. Consequently, a disproportionate part of the gains has accrued to the advanced industrial countries, and in some cases the less-developed countries have actually been worse off. After the last round of trade negotiations, the Uruguay Round that ended in 1994, the World Bank calculated the gains and losses to each of the regions of the world. The United States and Europe gained enormously. But sub-Saharan Africa, the poorest region of the world, lost by about 2 percent because of terms-of-trade effects: The trade negotiations opened their markets to manufactured goods produced by the industrialized countries but did not open up the markets of Europe and the United States to the agricultural goods in which poor countries often have a comparative advantage. Nor did the trade agreements eliminate the subsidies to agriculture that make it so hard for the developing countries to compete.

The U.S. negotiations with China over its membership in the WTO displayed a double standard bordering on the surreal. The U.S. trade representative, the chief negotiator for the United States, began by insisting that China was a developed country. Under WTO rules, developing countries are allowed longer transition periods in which state subsidies and other departures from the WTO strictures are permitted. China certainly wishes it were a developed country, with Western-style per capita incomes. And since China has a lot of "capitas," it's possible to multiply a huge number of people by very small average incomes and conclude that the People's Republic is a big economy. But China is not only a developing economy; it is a low-income developing country. Yet the United States insisted that China be treated like a developed country! China went along with the fiction; the negotiations dragged on so long that China got some extra time to adjust. But the true hypocrisy was shown when U.S. negotiators asked, in effect, for developing-country status for the United States to get extra time to shelter the American textile industry.

Trade negotiations in the service industries also illustrate the unlevel nature of the playing field. Which service industries did the United States say were very important? Financial services—industries in which Wall Street has a comparative advantage. Construction industries and maritime services were not on the agenda, because the developing countries would have a comparative advantage in these sectors.

Consider also intellectual-property rights, which are important if innovators are to have incentives to innovate (though many of the corporate advocates of intellectual property exaggerate its importance and fail to note that much of the most important research, as in basic science and mathematics, is not patentable). Intellectual-property rights, such as patents and trademarks, need to balance the interests of producers with those of users—not only users in developing countries, but researchers in developed countries. If we underprice the profitability of innovation to the inventor, we deter invention. If we overprice its cost to the research community and the end user, we retard its diffusion and beneficial effects on living standards.

In the final stages of the Uruguay negotiations, both the White House Office of Science and Technology Policy and the Council of Economic Advisers worried that we had not got the balance right—that the agreement put producers' interests over users'. We worried that, with this imbalance, the rate of progress and innovation might actually be impeded. After all, knowledge is the most important input into research, and overly strong intellectual-property rights can, in effect, increase the price of this input. We were also concerned about the consequences of denying lifesaving medicines to the poor. This issue subsequently gained international attention in the context of the provision of AIDS medicines in South Africa. The international outrage forced the drug companies to back down—and it appears that, going forward, the most adverse consequences will be circumscribed. But it is worth noting that initially, even the Democratic U.S. administration supported the pharmaceutical companies.

What we were not fully aware of was another danger—what has come to be called "biopiracy," which involves international drug companies patenting traditional medicines. Not only do they seek to make money from "resources" and knowledge that rightfully belong to the developing countries, but in doing so they squelch domestic firms who long provided these traditional medicines. While it is not clear whether these patents would hold up in court if they were effectively challenged, it is clear that the less-developed countries may not have the legal and financial resources required to mount such a challenge. The issue has become the source of enormous emotional, and potentially economic, concern throughout the developing world. This fall, while I was in Ecuador visiting a village in the high Andes, the Indian mayor railed against how globalization had led to biopiracy.

Globalization and September 11

September 11 brought home a still darker side of globalization—it provided a global arena for terrorists. But the ensuing events and discussions highlighted broader aspects of the globalization debate. It made clear how untenable American unilateralist positions were. President Bush, who had unilaterally rejected the international agreement to address one of the long-term global risks perceived by countries around the world—global warming, in which the United States is the largest culprit—called for a global alliance against terrorism. The administration realized that success would require concerted action by all.

One of the ways to fight terrorists, Washington soon discovered, was to cut off their sources of funding. Ever since the East Asian crisis, global attention had focused on the secretive offshore banking centers. Discussions following that crisis focused on the importance of good information—transparency, or openness—but this was intended for the developing countries. As international discussions turned to the lack of transparency shown by IMF and the offshore banking centers, the U.S. Treasury changed its tune. It is not because these secretive banking havens provide better services than those provided by banks in New York or London that billions have been put there; the secrecy serves a variety of nefarious purposes—including avoiding taxation and money laundering. These institutions could be shut down overnight—or forced to comply with international norms—if the United States and the other leading countries wanted. They continue to exist because they serve the interests of the financial community and the wealthy. Their continuing existence is no accident. Indeed, the OECD drafted an agreement to limit their scope—and before September 11, the Bush administration unilaterally walked away from this agreement too. How foolish this looks now in retrospect! Had it been embraced, we would have been further along the road to controlling the flow of money into the hands of the terrorists.

There is one more aspect to the aftermath of September 11 worth noting here. The United States was already in recession, but the attack made matters worse. It used to be said that when the United States sneezed, Mexico caught a cold. With globalization, when the United States sneezes, much of the rest of the world risks catching pneumonia. And the United States now has a bad case of the flu. With globalization, mismanaged macroeconomic policy in the United States—the failure to design an effective stimulus package—has global consequences. But around the world, anger at the traditional IMF policies is growing. The developing countries are saying to the industrialized nations: "When you face a slowdown, you follow the precepts that we are all taught in our economic courses: You adopt expansionary monetary and fiscal policies. But when we face a slowdown, you insist on contractionary policies. For you, deficits are okay; for us, they are impermissible—even if we can raise the funds through 'selling forward,' say, some natural resources." A heightened sense of inequity prevails, partly because the consequences of maintaining contractionary policies are so great.

Global Social Justice

Today, in much of the developing world, globalization is being questioned. For instance, in Latin America, after a short burst of growth in the early 1990s, stagnation and recession have set in. The growth was not sustained—some might say, was not sustainable. Indeed, at this juncture, the growth record of the so-called post-reform era looks no better, and in some countries much worse, than in the widely criticized import-substitution period of the 1950s and 1960s when Latin countries tried to industrialize by discouraging imports. Indeed, reform critics point out that the burst of growth in the early 1990s was little more than a "catch-up" that did not even make up for the lost decade of the 1980s.

Throughout the region, people are asking: "Has reform failed or has globalization failed?" The distinction is perhaps artificial, for globalization was at the center of the reforms. Even in those countries that have managed to grow, such as Mexico, the benefits have accrued largely to the upper 30 percent and have been even more concentrated in the top 10 percent. Those at the bottom have gained little; many are even worse off. The reforms have exposed countries to greater risk, and the risks have been borne disproportionately by those least able to cope with them. Just as in many countries where the pacing and sequencing of reforms has resulted in job destruction outmatching job creation, so too has the exposure to risk outmatched the ability to create institutions for coping with risk, including effective safety nets.

In this bleak landscape, there are some positive signs. Those in the North have become more aware of the inequities of the global economic architecture. The agreement at Doha to hold a new round of trade negotiations—the "Development Round"—promises to rectify some of the imbalances of the past. There has been a marked change in the rhetoric of the international economic institutions—at least they talk about poverty. At the World Bank, there have been some real reforms; there has been some progress in translating the rhetoric into reality—in ensuring that the voices of the poor are heard and the concerns of the developing countries are listened to. But elsewhere, there is often a gap between the rhetoric and the reality. Serious reforms in governance, in who makes decisions and how they are made, are not on the table. If one of the problems at the IMF has been that the ideology, interests, and perspectives of the financial community in the advanced industrialized countries have been given disproportionate weight (in matters whose effects go well beyond finance), then the prospects for success in the current discussions of reform, in which the same parties continue to predominate, are bleak. They are more likely to result in slight changes in the shape of the table, not changes in who is at the table or what is on the agenda.

September 11 has resulted in a global alliance against terrorism. What we now need is not just an alliance against evil, but an alliance for something positive—a global alliance for reducing poverty and for creating a better environment, an alliance for creating a global society with more social justice.

ARTICLE 3.5

The Two Faces of Globalization *Against Globalization as We Know It**

Branko Milanovic

Branko Milanovic, an economist at the World Bank, questions whether globalization is as beneficial and cost-free as some supporters claim. In his view, it does produce substantial benefits but it is doubled-edged—and the balance between costs and benefits varies depending on the particular situation of different people, countries, and regions. Milanovic also questions whether globalization generates superior economic growth. When one compares the present era with the three decades following World War II, a period when there was relatively less economic globalization than presently, it turns out that globalization has delivered much slower growth in every region of the world. Milanovic further argues that the economic success stories in the current period, above all, China, have prospered by violating the economic orthodoxy that prescribes minimum state regulation. Moreover, he concludes, the international framework regulating economic globalization is unfair. "[T]he rules [governing globalization] are far from being even-handed

*The paper represents author's own views only; the views should not be attributed to the World Bank or its affiliated organization.

as between the poor and the rich countries. They are slanted in favor of those who wield power."

The issues that Milanovic analyzes are the focus of other selections in this chapter and throughout PG: how to assess the character of globalization, what policies should regulate globalization, and the distributional impact (that is, the costs and benefits) of globalization. When you read the selection by Dollar and Kraay in Chapter 4, evaluate the validity of Milanovic's criticism of their position.

The Mainstream View

The mainstream view of globalization, at least among the people who "matter" in the countries that "matter"—the vast majority of economists, many political scientists, and political commentators—is that globalization is a benign force leading us ultimately to the era of converging world incomes (as poor countries such as China open up to the world and see their incomes rise), converging institutions as democracy becomes a universal norm, and cultural richness as people of different background interact more frequently. The most famous, or notorious, reflection of that Pollyannaish view of the world was the early announcement by Fukuyama (1989) of the "end of history." Although the ethnic warfare since then has not disproved Fukuyama's (or rather Hegel's) view, since none of the ethnic warriors had an alternative civilizational blueprint—a point which is implied in Hegel's hypothesis—the more recent debates about globalization as well as the role of Islam—a society *with* an alternative blueprint—do show that the end of history is not around the corner.

It is only a slight caricaturization of this naïve view to state that its proponents regard globalization as a *deus ex machina* for many of the problems, such as poverty, illiteracy or inequality that beset the developing world. The only thing that a country needs to do is to open up its borders, reduce tariff rates, attract foreign capital, and in a few generations if not less, the poor will become rich, the illiterate will learn how to read and write, and inequality will vanish as the poor countries catch up with the rich. This is the view conveyed implicitly and subliminally by many serious papers and publications as, for example, in the Dollar and Kraay (2000) often-repeated statement that "the poor and the rich gain one-for-one from openness,"[1] or in Sala-i-Martin's (2002) derisive statements about inequality and globalization. While, of course, the authors are careful enough not to explicitly make such statements (e.g., Dollar & Kraay do acknowledge that gains "one-for-one" are expressed in percentage terms, so that a poor person

---

whose income is one-hundredth of that of a rich person will also gain one-hundredth of the rich person's gain),[2] they do leave their statement sufficiently ambiguous, thus allowing more explicit and wrong Pollyannaish views of globalization to find currency in the mainstream popular magazines and newspapers. There the heavy guns of the globalization debate are not embarrassed by the finer points of relative *vs.* absolute gains, or with percentages or logarithms: they simply state that globalization is good for everyone. For example, *The Economist* (2000, p. 82) in a review of the Dollar and Kraay article writes: "Growth really does help the poor: in fact, it raises their incomes by about as much as it raises incomes of everybody else." This is deemed insufficient to carry the (misleading) message. In the next paragraph, they continue: "On average, incomes of the poor rise one-for-one with incomes overall."

Moreover, the past too is harnessed to support this dominant view of globalization. The period 1870–1913, the heyday of imperialism and colonialism, is made to appear as the period of universal growth, and catch-up of poor countries as, for example, in Lindert and Williamson (2001, p. 1) who somewhat incredibly write: "globalization probably mitigated the steep rise in income gaps between nations. The nations that gained the most from globalization are those poor ones that changed their policies to exploit it. . . ."

Thus, globalization is regarded as a benign and automatic force that, once certain preconditions are set in place ("sound" macropolicies, protection of property rights *etc.*), will inexorably lead countries and individuals to a state of economic bliss. We show here that this view of globalization is based on one serious methodological error: a systematic ignorance of the double-sided nature of globalization, that is, systematic ignorance of its malignant side. We show, first, how this methodological error leads to the misreading of the 19th century economic history; second, we argue that the Pollyannaish view of globalization severely distorts the lessons of the most recent period, 1980–2000, and third, we show how a more accurate and realistic reading of globalization requires, in many respects, different policies from the ones suggested by the naïve (or self-interested?) globalization cheerleaders.

The Two Faces of Globalization

In contrast to the view of globalization as a purely benign force which we have briefly sketched above are two other views. One, the Left view, regards globalization as a malignant force that leads to child labor in the South and takes away middle-class jobs in the North. For the Left, to be anti-globalization is a very difficult task since the Left is, by definition, internationalist. But what the Left resents is that today's globalization is led by a triumphant, and often, unbridled capitalism. Unbridled capitalism does produce the effects of which the Left complains: destruction of environment, obliteration of indigenous cultures (e.g., how many Mayas still speak Mayan?), and exploitation of the weak.

The conservative, and often xenophobic, Right also agrees that globalization is a malignant force. That view is more prevalent in Europe, with its history of xenophobia, than in the United States.[3] In Europe, globalization engenders not only fear of losing jobs to the poor masses in the South, but of losing cultural homogeneity that many European countries have acquired through a long process of obliteration of local cultures (where are the French Bretons today?) and three centuries of capitalist development. Their homogeneity is threatened, moreover, by the people of different color, culture, and way of life. Silvio Berlusconi's recent quip about Islam, Fallaci's (2002) diatribes against Muslim immigrants, and Heider's, Le Pen's and Fortuyn's political support is all part and parcel of the fear engendered by a more globalized society.

Can these two views, the dominant one, and the critical too, be correct? Yes, they can because globalization being such a huge and multifaceted process presents different faces to different people. Depending on where we live, whether we are rich or poor, where we stand ideologically, we are bound to see the process differently. But this is nothing new. Globalization as it played out from the mid-19th century to 1914 was also a contradictory force, with both its benign and malignant features. Thus, we believe, today too, as in the past, globalization has two faces: the benign one, based on voluntary exchanges and free circulation of people, capital, goods and ideas; and the other face, based on coercion and brute force. . . .

Misinterpreting the Recent Economic Record

Consider Tables 1 and 2. Let us then suppose that we show them to a Martian visitor endowed with elementary arithmetic knowledge and tell him three things: first, that more growth (higher income) is better than lower growth (and lower income); second, that WENAO is the richest region and that we would ideally like to see differences between the rich and poor regions decrease; and third, that there are two periods of globalization. The first period (1960–78) comprises "import substitution" in Latin America and most of Asia, and Africa; Communism in Eastern Europe/FSU, China, Vietnam; and "welfare state" in the rich countries. The second period is the era "structural adjustment" in Latin America and Africa, "transition to market economy" in Eastern Europe/FSU, and "retrenchment of welfare state" in the rich world. Then we ask him to choose which period he thinks was better.

His decision should not be too difficult. He would first observe that whether he looks at the world mean unweighted GDP per capita only (so that each country counts the same) or at the population-weighted world GDP per capita, growth rate was between two and three times greater in the first period. Then, he will notice that whatever region he selects, and whatever concept of growth he uses,

Table 1
Unweighted regional GDP per capita levels and growth rates, 1960–98[a]

	GDP per capita (in 1995 international prices)			Growth rate of GDP per capita (%, p.a.)	
	Year 1960	Year 1978	Year 1998	1960–78	1978–98
Africa	1,514	2,147	2,432	2.0	0.6
Asia	1,971	5,944	7,050	6.3	0.9
Latin America	3,458	5,338	6,329	2.4	0.9
E. Europe/FSU	2,093	5,277	4,851	5.3	−0.4
WENAO [West Europe–North Atlantic]	8,257	14,243	20,990	3.1	2.0
World	3,277	5,972	7,456	3.4	1.1

Source: Own calculations using the data from World Bank SIMA (Statistical Information Management and Analysis) database, countries' statistical yearbooks, Maddison (2001) and Penn World Tables.
[a]Each country is one observation.

growth rate is always higher in the first period than in the second. That would provide him with some additional confidence that the first period was better.

He might then remember our instruction that we would also like regional incomes to converge. Yet there too, he will notice that according to unweighted GDP per capita, in the first period, two out of four poorer regions grew faster than WENAO, while in the second, all of them grew slower than WENAO. If he wanted to confirm that finding by looking at what happened to an average citizen of each region, he would notice again that in the first period, average per capita incomes in East-

Table 2
Population-weighted regional GDP per capita levels and growth rates, 1960–98[a]

	GDP per capita (in 1995 international prices)			Growth rate of GDP per capita (%, p.a.)	
	Year 1960	Year 1978	Year 1998	1960–1978	1978–1998
Africa	1,539	2,007	2,033	1.5	0.1
Asia	963	1,945	3,967	4.0	3.6
Latin America	3,297	5,460	6,353	2.8	0.8
E. Europe/FSU	2,206	5,361	4,290	5.1	−1.1
WENAO	9,792	16,438	22,594	2.9	1.6
World	3,058	4,940	6,498	2.7	1.4

Source: Own calculations using the data from World Bank SIMA (Statistical Information Management and Analysis) database, countries' statistical yearbooks, Maddison (2001) and Penn World Tables.
[a]Each country is one observation, but each observation is weighted by country's population.

ern Europe/FSU and in Asia grew faster, and in Latin America about the same, as in WENAO. But in the second period, average incomes in Africa, Latin America and Eastern Europe/FSU were about stagnant or mildly declining (with per capita growth rates ranging from −1 to +0.8 p.a.), while WENAO grew by 1.6% p.a., and Asia, mostly thanks to China, by 3.6% p.a. Thus, he would conclude that, by the regional convergence criterion, the first period was better.

In addition, we might provide our Martian visitor with some further statistics. Consider Figure 1 which shows the average GDP per capita growth rates of all countries in the world (save the rich WENAO) during 1960–78 and 1978–98. Out of 124 countries, 95 grew faster in the first period. Notice not only that most of the dots are to the right of the 45-degree line, but also that there is a large number of the dots in the Southeastern quadrant. These are countries whose growth rates have switched from being positive—and often highly so—in the first period, to being negative in the second.[4]

Then, our Martian visitor would come back to us, and naïvely announce that he has definitely concluded that the first period was better since most countries grew

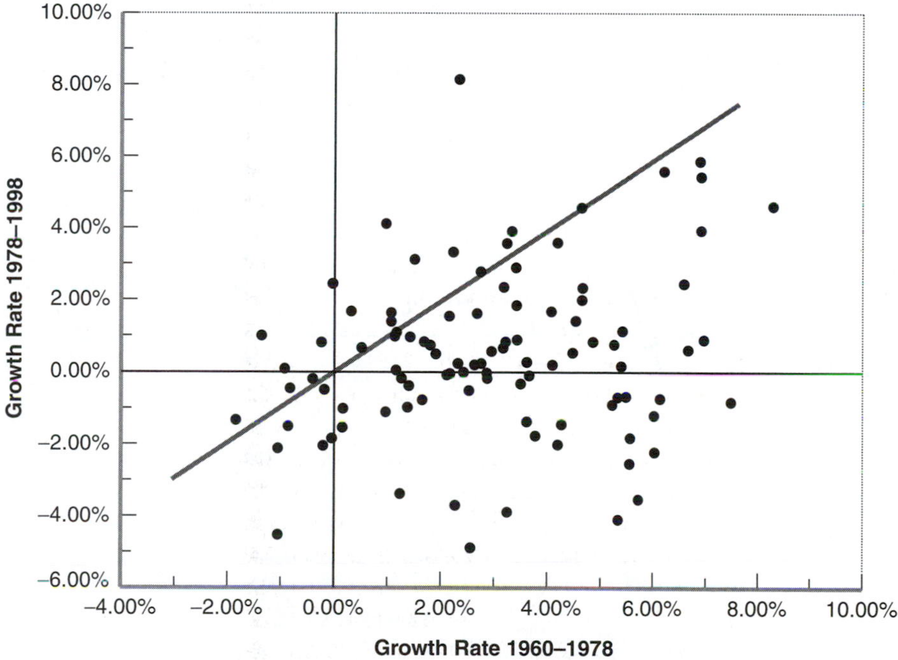

Figure 1 Average real GDP per capita growth rates in 1960–78 and 1978–98 (124 non-WENAO countries)

SOURCE: World Bank SIMA (Statistical Information Management and Analysis) database, countries' statistical yearbooks, Maddison (2001) and Penn World Tables.

faster then, and most of the poorer regions tended to catch up with the rich world. He would think that the test was rather easy and that he had done pretty well.[5]

Unfortunately, our Martian is not a good economist. Our mainstream economist would have to convince him that the *second* period—the period of structural adjustment and globalization—was actually better. It would be a hard sell, but it could be done. First, our economist would concede the fact that there was a divergence in countries' performance since the end of the 1970s and that poor countries have tended to grow slower (or even to decline) than the rich countries. As shown in Figure 2, the Gini coefficient of the GDPs per capita of all countries in the world, after being roughly stable during 1960–78, has inexorably risen since 1978, from a Gini of about 46 to a Gini of 54 today—a huge increase of almost 20%.

The economist will claim however, that the divergence in incomes is due to some "bad" countries which, unwilling to globalize, have chosen the wrong policies. So, he would like to expunge the world of these "bad" countries and to show that there was indeed a convergence in incomes among countries that adopted "good" policies and globalized.

This approach, the "weeding" of the "bad" from the "good" countries was adopted by Dollar and Kraay (1999) and by the recent World Bank report on glob-

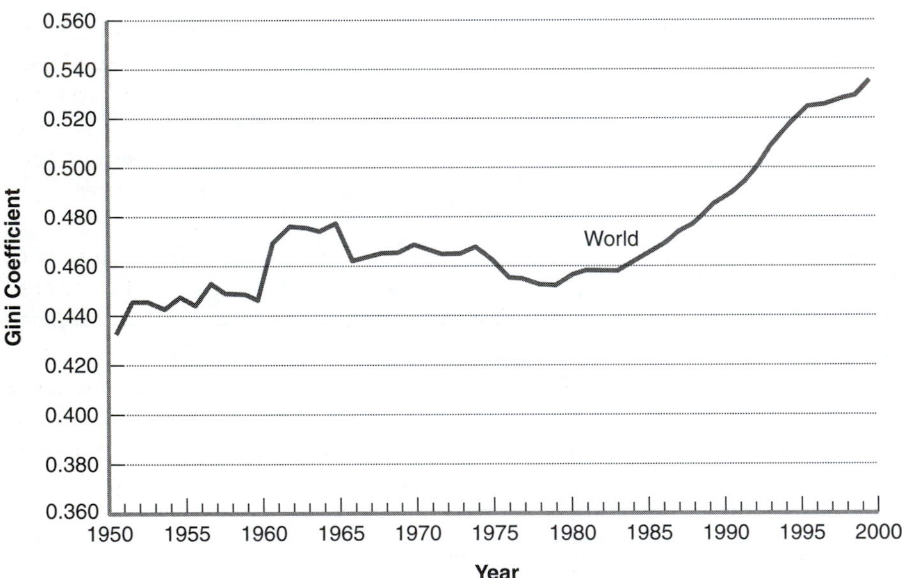

Figure 2 Gini coefficient: Unweighted inter-national inequality, 1950–98
144 countries included. All current countries (e.g., Russia, Bangladesh, Serbia, etc.) projected backward in order to avoid spurious Gini increase due to a greater number of observations/countries. Each country/year is one observation.
SOURCE: Milanovic (2002).

alization (World Bank, 2002). These studies select countries that are globalizers using the ratio of exports and imports over GDP (that is, trade openness) and then show how highly open countries' GDP per capita has either tended to catch up with rich countries' GDP per capita, or how their growth rates have gradually accelerated from decade to decade as openness ostensibly progressed. We shall show in detail, largely following Rodrik (2000), what is wrong with this selection criterion. But before we move to that, consider the prelude. Since the catch-up is defined in terms of mean *population*—weighted income of the "globalizers," and since China is among these, and since China has had such a remarkable growth record over the last two decades, the authors should not have even bothered to include other countries. All that is needed to obtain the desired conclusions is that China's growth accelerate (as shown in World Bank, 2002, Figure 1.12).[6]

Because China is a favorite example of the "openness is good for you" school, it is worth considering in somewhat greater detail. Now, one may find it rather strange that the key proof of beneficence of global capitalism is provided by one of the few remaining Communist countries. Of course, the partisans of "real" globalization argue that China is a Communist country in name only, and that what matters is its integration with world economy and *de facto* introduction of markets. Yet, the fact that a Communist country's record is wheeled out to defend capitalism is not merely a *boutade*. Almost one-third of China's industrial output is still produced by state-owned enterprises, and almost 20% of total GDP, a fraction higher than in any country in the world save for North Korea, Cuba, and a few former Soviet republics—a level of state involvement unlikely to be endorsed by mainstream economists.[7] Second, one of the preconditions for China's growth was arguably the set of policies that is also anathema to today's mainstream view: nationalization, widespread and free education at all levels, impediments to the free circulation of labor which kept lots of people from migrating into cities, land reform and abolishment of large landholdings—all hardly a favorite policy prescription for a developing country. Finally, little noticed is a paradox pointed out by Weitzman and Xu (1997) that, by far, the most dynamic sector of the Chinese economy is that of Township and Village Enterprises (TVEs) whose property rights are the very example of nontransparency: a TVE is legally owned by a "community," village or a township, is run by managers, or capitalists, and seeks private capital but pays no dividends. In effect, TVE is all that an efficient enterprise should *not* be. Yet it is this sector that shows the most significant progress. Thus, China, on these grounds alone, can hardly be taken as an example of success of the current mainstream economic policy prescriptions.

The very process of "selecting" the good globalizers based on trade ratios is flawed, as argued by Rodrik (2000). He points to several technical and data-selection problems in the Dollar and Kraay analysis, of which two seem most important. First globalizers are selected based on a combination of an outcome indicator (trade over GDP) over which policy-makers have no control and another which they do control (level of tariff rates).[8] There is an additional problem with this selection criterion. As Birdsall and Hamoudi (2002) show, most of "nonglobalizers" were *unwilling* nonglobalizers in the sense that their trade/GDP ratios had declined because their exports were heavily dependent on natural resources and primary commodities whose terms of trade declined in the 1980s. Consequently, countries' export revenues dropped, and they in turn had to curtail imports, reducing trade/GDP ratios on both accounts. In addition, they ran into balance of payments problems that required contractionary policies, and it is therefore not surprising that there was a positive correlation between openness and growth. Birdsall and Hamoudi (2002, p. 5) write: "Dollar and Kraay have not isolated the benefits of 'participating in the global trading system', but rather the 'curse' of primary commodity dependence." Second in both India and China, which, as mentioned, are used as the prime examples of "good" globalizers, the main trade reforms took place after the onset of faster growth. The Chinese case is, as Rodrik (2000) writes, well known: high growth began in the early 1980s, while trade liberalization followed more than a decade later. Throughout the 1980s and until 1995, the average weighted tariff rate in China was about 40% (Figure 3)—a rate twice as high as the average for developing countries, and more than four times the average of industrialized countries.[9] It was only in 1996 that the average tariff decreased to 26%, and has since decreased further to a level of about 16%.

Rodrik (2000) shows that the same pattern holds for India: while growth accelerated in the early 1980s, trade reform did not start until 1991–93. There, too, growth and expansion of trade took place under the protection of an even higher tariff wall than in China: in the 1980s, the weighted tariffs averaged 80–90%, and gradually came down, to the still very high level of about 40% (Figure 3). Dollar and Kraay (1999) have clearly fallen prey to one of (what Bairoch & Kozul-Wright, 1996 call) the enduring myths of economic theory, namely that "liberalization [is] an important driving force behind rising trade." On the contrary, trade often increased the most during the mild protectionist phases, since the latter saw acceleration in growth, and it is growth that generally leads to trade—not *vice versa* (Bairoch, 1997, p. 310; Yotopolos, 1996).

How hazardous the *Globalization, growth and poverty* report's (World Bank, 2002) conclusions are can be observed from the two figures in Figure 3 which chart China's and India's per capita growth rates and their average weighted tariff rates over 1980–99. Notice that in the India graph, it is very difficult to see any correlation between the two: the growth rate oscillates around 4% annually no matter what happens to the tariff rate. The China graph is not much different, except that there, if anything, we notice a correlation between the slowdown in growth rate in the last five years and a reduction in tariff rates—a relationship that is exactly the opposite of the one the World Bank report claims to have found. We cannot put much store by this finding: it obviously covers a very short period, and the rate of growth responds to a myriad of factors other than tariff rates. But the figures illustrate the perils of a monocausal approach to the evidence.

The authors of World Bank (2002) are aware that their preferred causality, low tariff rates $\Rightarrow$ high export and import growth $\Rightarrow$ high GDP growth cannot be proven.[10] They are aware also that both China and India grew behind very high protective walls. How then do they deal with these issues? With respect to the first point, they do so in a rather peculiar manner, as throughout the report there are scattered statements denying that causality can be inferred from or proven by their numbers. But these statements are often ignored, and there are a number of precisely such—causal—statements.[11] The second point is elegantly circumvented by showing the *change* in average tariff rates among the "globalizers" and "nonglobalizers" (World Bank, 2002, p. 36). But since we saw that China and India had particularly high tariff rates, it is not surprising that they reduced them more than say, Barbados or Belize which started the 1980s with tariff rates of 15%.

Our conclusion regarding the most recent period of globalization is twofold.

- The last two decades, which witnessed expansion of globalization, are, in terms of overall growth and income convergence between poor and rich countries, vastly less successful than the preceding two decades.
- The attempt to explain divergence of incomes by "eliminating" the countries with "bad" policies and focusing solely on those with "good" policies is flawed because the successful countries, and China in particular, did not follow the orthodox economic advice. One can be pretty confident that if China had exactly the same policies, but a miserable record of economic growth, those who hail it now would flaunt it as an example of how harmful to growth are state ownership, undefined property rights in TVEs, and high tariff barriers.

The Two Narratives and the Need for "Readjustment of Adjustment"

We can illustrate the difference between the dominant focus on the benign aspect of globalization alone from a more even-handed presentation of globalization's two sides: the benign and the malignant. Consider the following two historical narratives of the same set of events.

The dominant narrative goes approximately as follows. Toward the end of the 18th century, there was Industrial Revolution that spread from Europe slowly and unevenly, to the rest of the world. At the end of the Napoleonic wars, the world entered a period of almost uninterrupted peace lasting 100 years. During that period global capitalism appeared: it spread to the rest of the globe, connecting Europe with the Americas, Asia, Africa. The leading countries of the period grew the fastest, their incomes converged as trade blossomed, people freely migrated to better places, and capital flowed wherever it wanted. Then, suddenly, the calamity of WW I struck, the world was inflamed, Communism and Fascism emerged, nationalism and protectionism became rampant, trade declined, countries' incomes diverged, until another, worse, calamity of the WW II struck. For a period after the war, global capitalism could not get a free rein because large parts of the globe fell under the Communist sway. It is only in the 1980s, as China

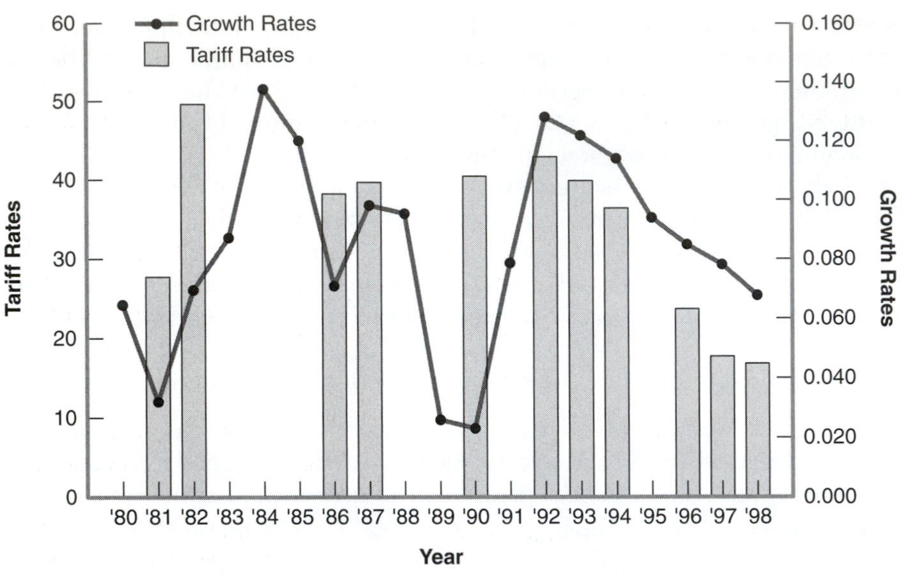

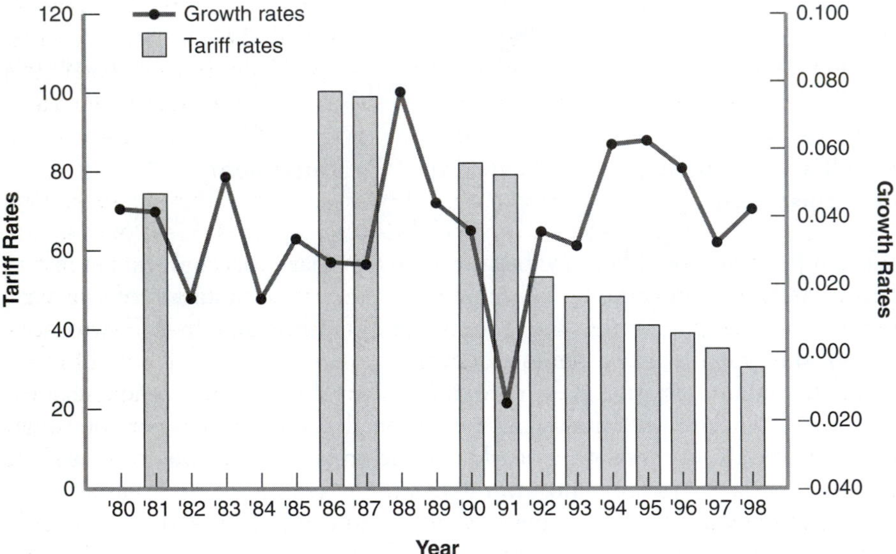

Figure 3 China's (above) and India's (below) real annual GDP per capita growth rate, and average weighted tariffs

Tariff rates are bars (levels shown on the left axis), growth rates (in fractiles) are lines (levels shown on the right axis).

SOURCE: Growth rates from World Bank SIMA database; tariff rates from Francis Ng (World Bank).

liberalized and the Soviet empire broke up and abandoned Communism, that globalization, with its attendant growth for most, if not all, could resurge. "Happy days are here again," but we must not forget that the ogres of nationalism and protectionism lurk behind the corner. So give freedom to capital, let profit be your guide, and growth is guaranteed to all.

This is, with some poetic embellishment, the most common view of events of the last two centuries, perhaps (one might surmise) because the people who subscribe to that narrative have tended to experience only the benign side of globalization. The objective of that narrative is not to stimulate discussion, but to stifle it, similarly to the dominant narratives used in the Communist countries where too the main purpose of the accepted view of history was to generate the acquiescence to the dogma. The point is well made by Said (2002):

> In this day, and almost universally, phrases such as "the free market," "privatization," "less government" and others like them have become the orthodoxy of globalization, its counterfeit universals. They are staples of the dominant discourse, designed to create consent and tacit approval. . . . The main goal of this dominant discourse is to fashion the merciless logic of corporate profit-making and political power into a normal state of affairs.

It is relatively easy to explode this rosy story of the world, told by the first narrative. One needs only to ask three simple questions: (a) where are conquest, colonialism, and slavery in this narrative? (b) how does the narrative explain the outbreak of WW I? and (c) why did capitalism suddenly become more tamed and civilized ("social market economy") after the end of WW II? To answer these questions, consider the following narrative of the same events.

After the technological and social revolutions occurred in Europe, its Northwestern part became the most advanced region of the world. It set out, at first timidly and often out of adventurism, then more seriously to conquer the rest of the world. As Europe conquered other countries, the winners established rules that were economically advantageous to themselves, developed further the already-existing slave trade, and by flooding markets of their colonies (devoid of independent commercial and economic policy) with their own manufactures, contributed to colonies' deindustrialization. All the while, gross coercion, wars, and even genocides went on in the colonies—perhaps not much noticed in Europe. So, the days of universal peace were quite far from being truly so.

European powers bent on conquest were, at the same time, in a struggle with each other. Their imperialism begot the Great War. . . . After a truce of 20 years, the Second WW erupted—a straight continuation of WW I. Fascism was defeated but Communism came out stronger and spread to cover one-third of world's population. Under Communist threat from the outside, and under pressure of growing social-democratic and Communist movements at home, the capitalist regimes, already enfeebled by the Great Depression, conceded to dramatic and far-reaching social reforms. The nature of wild capitalism of the 19th century changed dramatically with the introduction of unemployment benefits and pensions, paid vacations, 40-h working week, guaranteed and free education, health care for all, trade unions, and protection of workers' rights. In the Third World countries that became liberated, dreams of industrialization and catching-up could be realistically entertained as countries grew quickly and import-substitution became the dominant approach to development. But then under the shock of rising petroleum prices, high interest rates, and large debts, Third World growth sputtered. In the West, the ideological pendulum swung against the welfare state. The social-democratic movement weakened, the collapse of Communism eliminated the external threat, and made global capitalism again, as in the 1870s, entirely free to pursue unhindered its objectives of profit maximization—without much regard for social consequences.

To question the profit objective is not to denigrate its importance, much less to argue that it should not be an important, perhaps the most important, criterion. But it should not be the sole criterion. It needs to be tempered by other considerations, akin to the way that national capitalisms after WW II were "civilized" by the role of the state and strong social-democratic parties. The erection of "financial viability" as the only acceptable norm will not lead to imperialist wars as it did in 1914, but will exacerbate the negative effects of global capitalism which we already see, and which have grown in importance during the last decade or so—precisely the period during which the earlier constraints on the free play of capital were weakened or abandoned.[12] Let me mention a few of these effects: very high and/or increasing spatial and interpersonal inequality, blatant theft of public resources masquerading under the name of privatization and cheered on by most economists and international organizations, growth of slums, deteriorating labor conditions, return of the long-forgotten diseases such as tuberculosis, declines in education enrollment rates, dramatically increased mortality in most of the former Soviet republics and Africa, deforestation, growth of worldwide networks of mafias and drug cartels, even modern-day slavery through development of piracy and abduction of women and children for prostitution.[13] Capitalism left to itself will always produce these effects. If people want to sell themselves, why should not they? If parents do not want to send children to school, why not allow them the choice? If university education is no longer free, perhaps a child from a poor family can borrow to pay for it? If people do not have money to pay for a cure or a drug, what else can be done to ensure cost recovery?

While overt colonialism is a thing of the past, the rules are far from being even-handed as between the poor and the rich countries. They are slanted in favor of those who wield power. Khor (2001) gives some examples from the multilateral trading system: the well-known example of intellectual property rights,[14] differential treatment of subsidies (subsidies for R&D are exempt from counteraction while the subsidies used by developing countries, for industrial upgrading, are not), standards that are being set without effective participation by the less-developed countries (LDCs), and the high costs of raising and pursuing a trade dispute. We can compare the last point to the problem that Jewish survivors in Eastern Europe faced in trying to get the money impounded by the Swiss banks: how is a grand-mother surviving on $100 a month, and not speaking English or French, going to sue a Swiss bank?

. . . Continued misinterpretation of the disastrous results brought to most of Africa, Latin America, and Eastern Europe by about two decades of unabashedly free market policies will not prompt a review of these policies, and will, on the contrary, allow their continuation with probably equally bad results.[15] It is therefore incumbent on us to examine the actual results, and not the ideology of what these policies *should* have brought had they worked as originally intended. We must thus address some uncomfortable issues. Let me mention but three.

(i) How to explain that after sustained involvement and many structural adjustment loans, and as many IMF's Stand-bys, African GDP per capita has not budged from its level of 20 years ago? Moreover, in 24 African countries, GDP per capita is less than in 1975, and in 12 countries even below its 1960's level.[16]

(ii) How to explain the recurrence of Latin crises, in countries such as Argentina, that months prior to the outbreak of the crisis are being praised as model reformers?[17]

(iii) How to explain that the best "pupils" among the transition countries (Moldova, Georgia, Kyrghyz Republic, Armenia) after setting out in 1991 with no debt at all, and following all the prescriptions of the IFIs, find themselves 10 years later with their GDPs halved and in need of debt-forgiveness?

Something is clearly wrong.[18] Maintaining that globalization as we know it is the way to go and that, if the Washington consensus policies have not borne fruit so far, they will surely do so in the future, is to replace empiricism with ideology. Unfortunately, it has been done before, but the consequences were not very good.

Notes

1. In effect, the very first sentence of the abstract reads: "Income of the poor rises one-for-one with overall growth."
2. In another of their papers, Dollar and Kraay (2002) do make a point that for (a) countries cursed by "poor geography" (e.g., Mali or Chad) or (b) those with inefficient or exploitative institutions, trade liberalization alone cannot be expected to bear much fruit.
3. As Anderson (2002) rightly points out, to the European antonym: internationalism *vs.* nationalism, the United States, somewhat uniquely, presented a different one: internationalism *vs.* isolationism. Hence specifically European xenophobia rooted in ethnicity and "blood and soil" was never much of an ideology in the United States.
4. All the current countries are projected backward using their past republican/provincial growth rates. This therefore represents probably the most detailed country growth database (see Milanovic, 2002). The main building blocks for the database were World Bank SIMA, countries' statistical yearbooks,

Penn World Tables, and Maddison (2001). All GDPs per capita are expressed in 1995 international dollars.

5. The first, to my knowledge, to have noticed and discussed, with a great wealth of detail and econometrics, the discrepancy between the "improved" policies in LDCs during the last two decades, and more than disappointing results (worse than in the previous two decades) is Easterly (2001a,b).
6. This is incidently the wrong way to formulate the convergence question. Convergence is always defined in terms of *countries*. If we were interested in whether the world were becoming a more equal place, the proper way would be to study distribution of income among all *citizens* of the world. The criterion used in World Bank (2002) is neither, and is moreover the only one capable of producing the desired results.
7. These numbers refer to 1998 and include only the value added of industrial and construction sector State-owned enterprises (SOEs). They do not include mixed-ownership sector or TVEs. Calculated from the *Statistical Yearbook of China* (1999), pp. 55, 432, 473.
8. As Rodrik (2000, p. 1) writes: "Saying that 'participation in world trade is good for a country' is as meaningful as saying that 'upgrading of technological capabilities is good for growth' (and equally helpful to policy makers)."
9. Based on World Bank calculations by Francis Ng (downloadable from <www.worldbank.org/research/trade>).
10. The choice of this particular causality is all the more intriguing since there is no reason whatsoever why high exports (themselves a component of GDP) or imports should be bad for growth. I do not know if anyone has ever made such a claim. At issue is precisely the low tariffs $\Longrightarrow$ high growth causality, which would be very hard to prove.
11. I do not know how to interpret otherwise statements such as: "As they reformed and integrated with the world market, the 'more globalized' countries started to grow rapidly, accelerating steadily from 2.9% in the 1970s to 5% throughout the 1990s" (World Bank, 2002, p. 36), or the statement approvingly taken from Lindert and Williamson (2001), "We infer that this is because freer trade stimulates growth in Third world economies today, regardless of its effects before 1940" (World Bank, 2002, p. 37). Or as Dollar and Kraay (2001) write: "We provide evidence that, contrary to popular beliefs, increased trade has strongly encouraged growth and poverty reduction and has contributed to narrowing the gaps between rich and poor worldwide."
12. Gunter Grass (2002) puts it as follows: "In the fifties, sixties, and even in the seventies, a relatively successful attempt to civilize capitalism was made across Europe. If one assumes that socialism and capitalism are both indigenous, wayward children of the Enlightment, they can be regarded as having imposed certain checks on each other. Even capitalism was obliged to accept certain responsibilities. In Germany this was called the social market economy. . . . The consensus broke down in the early eighties. And since the collapse of the Communist hierarchies, capitalism—recast as neoliberalism—has felt it could run riot, as if out of control. There is no longer a counterweight to it. Today even the few remaining responsible capitalists are raising a warning finger . . . and see neoliberalism repeating the mistakes of communism—issuing articles of faith that deny that there is any alternative to the free market and claiming infallibility."
13. Kanbur (2001) writes of the spread of "obnoxious goods."
14. That poor countries have no money and expertise to enforce even the rules that may favor them is well known. I have recently noticed that there is such a thing as French feta cheese. But I remember how Armenian cognac, known to all under such a name, had to change its appellation because "cognac" is a registered trademark.
15. For a review of these policies see Easterly (2001a,b).
16. Meanwhile, from a much higher level, US GDP per capita has increased by a third since 1975, and has doubled since 1960.
17. Including in the World Bank report on globalization, issued a month before the Argentine crisis, where Argentina proudly belongs to the group of "well-known" reformers (World Bank, 2002, p. 35). It has been demoted from that august group though in Dollar and Kraay (2002) published in February 2002. By then the crisis was all too obvious. Note that that in 1999 and 2000, The Heritage Index of Economic Freedom, an ultra right-wing think-tank, scored Argentina's economic policies

about the same as Chile's, that poster-child of the neoconservatives. Even in 2001, Argentina was scored only marginally worse (2.25 *vs*. Chile's 2), yet much better than 3.25 given to Brazil.

18. The typical excuse that the policies were right but were badly implemented is wrong and is a very lame excuse indeed. It reminds me of the constant litany under Communism, that the Communist ideas were very good, but were either poorly implemented, or people were too wicked for such beautiful ideas. (I saw through that when I was less than 20. I am surprised that many smart people do not see through similar excuses today; but then it is true that, at 20, I did not have a stake in *not* seeing the truth.) A policy that does not take into account the actual situation and people as they are is inadequate. Furthermore, it is not true, even on IFI's reckoning, that the governments always failed to fully implement the programs. Even when they did implement them, the results—as in the transition countries—were often relentlessly bad.

References

Anderson, P. (2002). Internationalism: a breviary. *New Left Review*, March–April, downloaded from <http://www.newleftreview.net/index.shtml>.

Bairoch, P. (1989). The paradoxes of economic history: economic laws and history. *European Economic Review*, *33*, 225–249.

Bairoch, P. (1997). *Victoires and déboires* (3 vols.). Paris: Gallimard.

Bairoch, P., & Kozul-Wright, R. (1996). Globalization myths: some historical reflections on integration, industrialization and growth in the world economy. United Nations Conference on trade and development, Discussion paper no. 113.

Birdsall, N., & Hamoudi, A. (2002). Commodity dependence, trade and growth: When "Openness" is not Enough. Center for Global Development Working Paper No. 7; Available: <http://www.cgdev.org/rp/publications.html>.

Dollar, D., & Kraay, A. (1999). Trade, growth and poverty. Policy research working paper no. 2199, World Bank, Washington DC.

Dollar, D., & Kraay, A. (2000). Growth is *good* for the poor. Policy research working paper no. 2587. *Journal of Economic Growth*, *7*(3), 195–225.

Dollar, D., & Kraay, A. (2001). Trade, growth and poverty. Finance and Development, 38, (3). Downloaded from http://www.imf.org/external/pubs/ft/fandd/2001/09/dollar.htm.

Dollar, D., & Kraay, A. (2002). Spreading the wealth. *Foreign Affairs* (January/February).

Easterly, B. (2001a). The lost decades: developing countries' stagnation in spite of policy reforms, 1980–1998. Mimeo. Downloaded from <http://www.worldbank.org/research/growth/pdfiles/lost%20decades_joeg.pdf>.

Easterly, B. (2001b). *The elusive quest for economic growth: Economists' adventures and misadventures in the tropics*. Cambridge and London: MIT Press.

Fallaci, O. (2002). La rabbia e l'orgoglio. *Corriere della Sera*, September 29.

Fukuyama, F. (1989). The end of history. *National Interest*, Summer.

Grass, G. (2002). The "progressive" restoration: a discussion with Pierre Bourdieu. *New Left Review*, March–April. Downloaded from <http://www.new-leftreview.net/index.shtml>.

Kanbur, R. (2001). On obnoxious markets. Downloaded from <http://www.people.cornell.edu/pages/sk145/papers.htm>.

Khor, M. (2001). The multilateral trading system: a development perspective. Mimeo, *World Network*, December.

Lindert, P., & Williamson, J. (2001). Does globalization make the world more unequal. National Bureau of Economic Research, Working paper 8228. Cambridge MA: NBER.

Maddison, A. (2001). *World economy: a millennial perspective*. Paris: OECD Development Centre Studies.

Milanovic, B. (2002). Worlds apart: the twentieth century's promise that failed. Manuscript, downloadable from <http://www.worldbank.org/research/inequality/>.

Odenheimer, M. (2002). Where Stalin has admirers, and Maoists fight on. *Washington Post*, April 7.
Rodrik, D. (2000). Comments on "Trade, growth and poverty" by D. Dollar and A. Kraay. Mimeo, October. Downloadable from <http://ksghome.harvard.edu/~.drodrik.academic.ksg/>.
Said, E. W. (2002). The public role of writers and intellectuals. The 15th Jan Patocka Memorial Lecture, October 24, delivered at IWM Institute, Vienna.
Sala-i-Martin, X. (2002). The disturbing "rise" in global income inequality. Mimeo, March.
The Economist (2000). Growth is good. May 27, 82.
Weitzman, M., & Xu, C. (1997). Chinese Township–village enterprises as vaguely defined cooperatives. In: J. Roemer (Ed.), *Property relations, incentives and welfare*. Proceedings of a Conference held in Barcelona, Spain, by the International Economic Association, June 1994, London: MacMillan Press.
World Bank (2002). *Globalization, growth and poverty: building an inclusive world economy*. Policy Research Report. Washington, DC: World Bank.
Yotopolos, P. (1996). *Exchange rate parity for trade and development*. Cambridge: Cambridge University Press.

ARTICLE 3.6

Stolen Harvest *The Hijacking of the Global Food Supply*

Vandana Shiva

Vandana Shiva, an Indian physicist and environmental activist, is highly critical of how transnational corporations (TNCs) have exploited the people and resources of poor countries. In this selection, she identifies two major problems. First, by using their greater financial resources to gain control over the land and water of poor countries, TNCs force small farmers off the land without a corresponding gain in efficiency or benefits to the people and regions affected. Quite the contrary, for the shift to commercial, export-oriented agriculture from small-scale subsistence farming produces extensive harm to people and the environment. Second, the international legal regime that protects intellectual property rights via patents granted TNCs causes great harm to poor people and poor regions of the world. The result? A handful of TNCs headquartered in the West are in the process of hijacking the global food supply and causing immense social and economic dislocations in the poor countries around the world.

Does Shiva exaggerate the harm caused by TNCs? Does she ignore possible benefits when poor countries become integrated into the global economy? Are there any remedies to the problems she identifies?

The Corporate Hijacking of Food and Agriculture

. . . As farmers are transformed from producers into consumers of corporate-patented agricultural products, as markets are destroyed locally and nationally but expanded globally, the myth of "free trade" and the global economy becomes a means for the rich to rob the poor of their right to food and even their right to life. For the vast majority of the world's people—70 percent—earn their livelihoods by producing food. The majority of these farmers are women. In contrast, in the industrialized countries, only 2 percent of the population are farmers.

Food Security Is in the Seed

For centuries Third World farmers have evolved crops and given us the diversity of plants that provide us nutrition. Indian farmers evolved 200,000 varieties of rice through their innovation and breeding. They bred rice varieties such as Basmati. They bred red rice and brown rice and black rice. They bred rice that grew 18 feet tall in the Gangetic floodwaters, and saline-resistant rice that could be grown in the coastal water. And this innovation by farmers has not stopped. Farmers involved in our movement, Navdanya, dedicated to conserving native seed diversity, are still breeding new varieties.

The seed, for the farmer, is not merely the source of future plants and food; it is the storage place of culture and history. Seed is the first link in the food chain. Seed is the ultimate symbol of food security.

Free exchange of seed among farmers has been the basis of maintaining biodiversity as well as food security. This exchange is based on cooperation and reciprocity. A farmer who wants to exchange seed generally gives an equal quantity of seed from his field in return for the seed he gets.

Free exchange among farmers goes beyond mere exchange of seeds; it involves exchanges of ideas and knowledge, of culture and heritage. It is an accumulation of tradition, of knowledge of how to work the seed. Farmers learn about the plants they want to grow in the future by watching them grow in other farmers' fields.

Paddy, or rice, has religious significance in most parts of the country and is an essential component of most religious festivals. The *Akti* festival in Chattisgarh, where a diversity of *indica* rices are grown, reinforces the many principles of biodiversity conservation. In Southern India, rice grain is considered auspicious, or *akshanta*. It is mixed with *kumkum* and turmeric and given as a blessing. The priest is given rice, often along with coconut, as an indication of religious regard. Other agricultural varieties whose seeds, leaves, or flowers form an essential component of religious ceremonies include coconut, betel, arecanut, wheat, finger

---

Vandana Shiva, *Stolen Harvest: The Hijacking of the Global Food Supply* (Cambridge: South End Press, 2000). Reprinted by permission of South End Press.

and little millets, horsegram, blackgram, chickpea, pigeon pea, sesame, sugarcane, jackfruit seed, cardamom, ginger, bananas, and gooseberry.

New seeds are first worshipped, and only then are they planted. New crops are worshipped before being consumed. Festivals held before sowing seeds as well as harvest festivals, celebrated in the fields, symbolize people's intimacy with nature. For the farmer, the field is the mother; worshipping the field is a sign of gratitude toward the earth, which, as mother, feeds the millions of life forms that are her children.

But new intellectual-property-rights regimes, which are being universalized through the Trade Related Intellectual Property Rights Agreement of the World Trade Organization (WTO), allow corporations to usurp the knowledge of the seed and monopolize it by claiming it as their private property. Over time, this results in corporate monopolies over the seed itself.

Corporations like RiceTec of the United States are claiming patents on Basmati rice. Soybean, which evolved in East Asia, has been patented by Calgene, which is now owned by Monsanto. Calgene also owns patents on mustard, a crop of Indian origin. Centuries of collective innovation by farmers and peasants are being hijacked as corporations claim intellectual-property rights on these and other seeds and plants.

"Free Trade" or "Forced Trade"

Today, ten corporations control 32 percent of the commercial-seed market, valued at $23 billion, and 100 percent of the market for genetically engineered, or transgenic, seeds.[1] These corporations also control the global agrochemical and pesticide market. Just five corporations control the global trade in grain. In late 1998, Cargill, the largest of these five companies, bought Continental, the second largest, making it the single biggest factor in the grain trade. Monoliths such as Cargill and Monsanto were both actively involved in shaping international trade agreements, in particular the Uruguay Round of the General Agreement on Trade and Tarriffs, which led to the establishment of the WTO.

This monopolistic control over agricultural production, along with structural adjustment policies that brutally favor exports, results in floods of exports of foods from the United States and Europe to the Third World. As a result of the North American Free Trade Agreement (NAFTA), the proportion of Mexico's food supply that is imported has increased from 20 percent in 1992 to 43 percent in 1996. After 18 months of NAFTA, 2.2 million Mexicans have lost their jobs, and 40 million have fallen into extreme poverty. One out of two peasants is not getting enough to eat. As Victor Suares has stated, "Eating more cheaply on imports is not eating at all for the poor in Mexico."[2]

In the Philippines, sugar imports have destroyed the economy. In Kerala, India, the prosperous rubber plantations were rendered unviable due to rubber imports. The local $350 million rubber economy was wiped out, with a multiplier effect of $3.5 billion on the economy of Kerala. In Kenya, maize imports brought prices crashing for local farmers who could not even recover their costs of production.

Trade liberalization of agriculture was introduced in India in 1991 as part of a World Bank/International Monetary Fund (IMF) structural adjustment package. While the hectares of land under cotton cultivation had been decreasing in the 1970s and 1980s, in the first six years of World Bank/IMF-mandated reforms, the land under cotton cultivation increased by 1.7 million hectares. Cotton started to displace food crops. Aggressive corporate advertising campaigns, including promotional films shown in villages on "video vans," were launched to sell new, hybrid seeds to farmers. Even gods, goddesses, and saints were not spared: in Punjab, Monsanto sells its products using the image of Guru Nanak, the founder of the Sikh religion. Corporate, hybrid seeds began to replace local farmers' varieties.

The new hybrid seeds, being vulnerable to pests, required more pesticides. Extremely poor farmers bought both seeds and chemicals on credit from the same company. When the crops failed due to heavy pest incidence or large-scale seed failure, many peasants committed suicide by consuming the same pesticides that had gotten them into debt in the first place. In the district of Warangal, nearly 400 cotton farmers committed suicide due to crop failure in 1997, and dozens more committed suicide in 1998.

Under this pressure to cultivate cash crops, many states in India have allowed private corporations to acquire hundreds of acres of land. The state of Maharashtra has exempted horticulture projects from its land-ceiling legislation. Madhya Pradesh is offering land to private industry on long-term leases, which, according to industry, should last for at least 40 years. In Andhra Pradesh and Tamil Nadu, private corporations are today allowed to acquire over 300 acres of land for raising shrimp for exports. A large percentage of agricultural production on these lands will go toward supplying the burgeoning food-processing industry, in which mainly transnational corporations are involved. Meanwhile, the United States has taken India to the WTO dispute panel to contest its restrictions on food imports.

In certain instances, markets are captured by other means. In August 1998, the mustard-oil supply in Delhi was mysteriously adulterated. The adulteration was restricted to Delhi but not to any specific brand, indicating that it was not the work of a particular trader or business house. More than 50 people died. The government banned all local processing of oil and announced free imports of soybean oil. Millions of people extracting oil on tiny, ecological, cold-press mills lost their livelihoods. Prices of indigenous oilseed collapsed to less than one-third their previous levels. In Sira, in the state of Karnataka, police officers shot farmers protesting the fall in prices of oilseeds.

Imported soybeans' takeover of the Indian market is a clear example of the imperialism on which globalization is built. One crop exported from a single country by one or two corporations replaced hundreds of foods and food producers, destroying biological and cultural diversity, and economic and political democracy. Small mills are now unable to serve small farmers and poor consumers with low-cost, healthy, and culturally appropriate edible oils. Farmers are robbed of their freedom to choose what they grow, and consumers are being robbed of their freedom to choose what they eat.

Creating Hunger with Monocultures

Global chemical corporations, recently reshaped into "life sciences" corporations, declare that without them and their patented products, the world cannot be fed.

As Monsanto advertised in its $1.6 million European advertising campaign:

> Worrying about starving future generations won't feed them. Food biotechnology will. The world's population is growing rapidly, adding the equivalent of a China to the globe every ten years. To feed these billion more mouths, we can try extending our farming land or squeezing greater harvests out of existing cultivation. With the planet set to double in numbers around 2030, this heavy dependency on land can only become heavier. Soil erosion and mineral depletion will exhaust the ground. Lands such as rainforests will be forced into cultivation. Fertilizer, insecticide, and herbicide use will increase globally. At Monsanto, we now believe food biotechnology is a better way forward.[3]

But food is necessary for all living species. That is why the *Taittreya Upanishad* calls on humans to feed all beings in their zone of influence.

Industrial agriculture has not produced more food. It has destroyed diverse sources of food, and it has stolen food from other species to bring larger quantities of specific commodities to the market, using huge quantities of fossil fuels and water and toxic chemicals in the process.

It is often said that the so-called miracle varieties of the Green Revolution in modern industrial agriculture prevented famine because they had higher yields. However, these higher yields disappear in the context of total yields of crops on farms. Green Revolution varieties produced more grain by diverting production away from straw. This "partitioning" was achieved through dwarfing the plants, which also enabled them to withstand high doses of chemical fertilizer.

However, less straw means less fodder for cattle and less organic matter for the soil to feed the millions of soil organisms that make and rejuvenate soil. The higher yields of wheat or maize were thus achieved by stealing food from farm animals and soil organisms. Since cattle and earthworms are our partners in food production, stealing food from them makes it impossible to maintain food production over time, and means that the partial yield increases were not sustainable.

The increase in yields of wheat and maize under industrial agriculture were also achieved at the cost of yields of other foods a small farm provides. Beans, legumes, fruits, and vegetables all disappeared both from farms and from the calculus of yields. More grain from two or three commodities arrived on national and international markets, but less food was eaten by farm families in the Third World.

The gain in "yields" of industrially produced crops is thus based on a theft of food from other species and the rural poor in the Third World. That is why, as more grain is produced and traded globally, more people go hungry in the Third

World. Global markets have more commodities for trading because food has been robbed from nature and the poor.

Productivity in traditional farming practices has always been high if it is remembered that very few external inputs are required. While the Green Revolution has been promoted as having increased productivity in the absolute sense, when resource use is taken into account, it has been found to be counterproductive and inefficient.

Perhaps one of the most fallacious myths propagated by Green Revolution advocates is the assertion that high-yielding varieties have reduced the acreage under cultivation, therefore preserving millions of hectares of biodiversity. But in India, instead of more land being released for conservation, industrial breeding actually increases pressure on the land, since each acre of a monoculture provides a single output, and the displaced outputs have to be grown on additional acres, or "shadow" acres.[4]

A study comparing traditional polycultures with industrial monocultures shows that a polyculture system can produce 100 units of food from 5 units of inputs, whereas an industrial system requires 300 units of input to produce the same 100 units. The 295 units of wasted inputs could have provided 5,900 units of additional food. Thus the industrial system leads to a decline of 5,900 units of food. This is a recipe for starving people, not for feeding them.[5]

Wasting resources creates hunger. By wasting resources through one-dimensional monocultures maintained with intensive external inputs, the new biotechnologies create food insecurity and starvation.

The Insecurity of Imports

As cash crops such as cotton increase, staple-food production goes down, leading to rising prices of staples and declining consumption by the poor. The hungry starve as scarce land and water are diverted to provide luxuries for rich consumers in Northern countries. Flowers, fruits, shrimp, and meat are among the export commodities being promoted in all Third World countries.

When trade liberalization policies were introduced in 1991 in India, the agriculture secretary stated that "food security is not food in the *godowns* but dollars in the pocket." It is repeatedly argued that food security does not depend on food "self-sufficiency" (food grown locally for local consumption), but on food "self-reliance" (buying your food from international markets). According to the received ideology of free trade, the earnings from exports of farmed shrimp, flowers, and meat will finance imports of food. Hence any shortfall created by the diversion of productive capacity from growing food for domestic consumption to growing luxury items for consumption by rich Northern consumers would be more than made up.

However, it is neither efficient nor sustainable to grow shrimp, flowers, and meat for export in countries such as India. In the case of flower exports, India spent Rs.1.4 billion as foreign exchange for promoting floriculture exports and earned a mere Rs.320 million.[6] In other words, India can buy only one-fourth of the food it could have grown with export earnings from floriculture.[7] Our food security has therefore declined by 75 percent, and our foreign exchange drain increased by more than Rs.1 billion.

In the case of meat exports, for every dollar earned, India is destroying 15 dollars' worth of ecological functions performed by farm animals for sustainable agriculture. Before the Green Revolution, the byproducts of India's culturally sophisticated and ecologically sound livestock economy, such as the hides of cattle, were exported, rather than the ecological capital, that is, the cattle themselves. Today, the domination of the export logic in agriculture is leading to the export of our ecological capital, which we have conserved over centuries. Giant slaughterhouses and factory farming are replacing India's traditional livestock economy. When cows are slaughtered and their meat is exported, with it are exported the renewable energy and fertilizer that cattle provide to the small farms of small peasants. These multiple functions of cattle in farming systems have been protected in India through the metaphor of the sacred cow. Government agencies cleverly disguise the slaughter of cows, which would outrage many Indians, by calling it "buffalo meat."

In the case of shrimp exports, for every acre of an industrial shrimp farm, 200 acres of productive ecosystems are destroyed. For every dollar earned as foreign exchange from exports, six to ten dollars' worth of destruction takes place in the local economy. The harvest of shrimp from aquaculture farms is a harvest stolen from fishing and farming communities in the coastal regions of the Third World. The profits from exports of shrimp to U.S., Japanese, and European markets show up in national and global economic growth figures. However, the destruction of local food consumption, ground-water resources, fisheries, agriculture, and livelihoods associated with traditional occupations in each of these sectors does not alter the global economic value of shrimp exports; such destruction is only experienced locally.

In India, intensive shrimp cultivation has turned fertile coastal tracts into graveyards, destroying both fisheries and agriculture. In Tamil Nadu and Andhra Pradesh, women from fishing and farming communities are resisting shrimp cultivation through *satyagraha*. Shrimp cultivation destroys 15 jobs for each job it creates. It destroys $5 of ecological and economic capital for every dollar earned through exports. Even these profits flow for only three to five years, after which the industry must move on to new sites. Intensive shrimp farming is a non-sustainable activity, described by United Nations agencies as a "rape and run" industry.

Since the World Bank is advising all countries to shift from "food first" to "export first" policies, these countries all compete with each other, and the prices of these luxury commodities collapse. Trade liberalization and economic reform also include devaluation of currencies. Thus exports earn less, and imports cost more. Since the Third World is being told to stop growing food and instead to buy food in international markets by exporting cash crops, the process of globalization leads to a situation in which agricultural societies of the South become increasingly dependent on food imports, but do not have the foreign exchange to pay for imported food. Indonesia and Russia provide examples of countries that have moved rapidly from food-sufficiency to hunger because of the creation of dependency on imports and the devaluation of their currencies.

Stealing Nature's Harvest

Global corporations are not just stealing the harvest of farmers. They are stealing nature's harvest through genetic engineering and patents on life forms.

Genetically engineered crops manufactured by corporations pose serious ecological risks. Crops such as Monsanto's Roundup Ready soybeans, designed to be resistant to herbicides, lead to the destruction of biodiversity and increased use of agrochemicals. They can also create highly invasive "superweeds" by transferring the genes for herbicide resistance to weeds. Crops designed to be pesticide factories, genetically engineered to produce toxins and venom with genes from bacteria, scorpions, snakes, and wasps, can threaten non-pest species and can contribute to the emergence of resistance in pests and hence the creation of "superpests." In every application of genetic engineering, food is being stolen from other species for the maximization of corporate profits.

To secure patents on life forms and living resources, corporations must claim seeds and plants to be their "inventions" and hence their property. Thus corporations like Cargill and Monsanto see nature's web of life and cycles of renewal as "theft" of their property. During the debate about the entry of Cargill into India in 1992, the Cargill chief executive stated, "We bring Indian farmers smart technologies, which prevent bees from usurping the pollen."[8] During the United Nations Biosafety Negotiations, Monsanto circulated literature that claimed that "weeds steal the sunshine."[9] A worldview that defines pollination as "theft by bees" and claims that diverse plants "steal" sunshine is one aimed at stealing nature's harvest, by replacing open, pollinated varieties with hybrids and sterile seeds, and destroying biodiverse flora with herbicides such as Monsanto's Roundup.

This is a worldview based on scarcity. A worldview of abundance is the worldview of women in India who leave food for ants on their doorstep, even as they create the most beautiful art in *kolams*, *mandalas*, and *rangoli* with rice flour. Abundance is the worldview of peasant women who weave beautiful designs of paddy to hang up for birds when the birds do not find grain in the fields. This view of abundance recognizes that, in giving food to other beings and species, we maintain conditions for our own food security. It is the recognition in the *Isho Upanishad* that the universe is the creation of the Supreme Power meant for the benefits of (all) creation. Each individual life form must learn to enjoy its benefits by farming a part of the system in close relation with other species. Let not any one species encroach upon others' rights.[10] The *Isho Upanishad* also says,

> a selfish man over-utilizing the resources of nature to satisfy his own ever-increasing needs is nothing but a thief, because using resources beyond one's needs would result in the utilization of resources over which others have a right.[11]

In the ecological worldview, when we consume more than we need or exploit nature on principles of greed, we are engaging in theft. In the anti-life view of agribusiness corporations, nature renewing and maintaining herself is a thief. Such a worldview replaces abundance with scarcity, fertility with sterility. It makes theft from nature a market imperative, and hides it in the calculus of efficiency and productivity.

Food Democracy

What we are seeing is the emergence of food totalitarianism, in which a handful of corporations control the entire food chain and destroy alternatives so that people do not have access to diverse, safe foods produced ecologically. Local markets are being deliberately destroyed to establish monopolies over seed and food systems. The destruction of the edible-oil market in India and the many ways through which farmers are prevented from having their own seed supply are small instances of an overall trend in which trade rules, property rights, and new technologies are used to destroy people-friendly and environment-friendly alternatives and to impose anti-people, anti-nature food systems globally.

The notion of rights has been turned on its head under globalization and free trade. The right to produce for oneself or consume according to cultural priorities and safety concerns has been rendered illegal according to the new trade rules. The right of corporations to force-feed citizens of the world with culturally inappropriate and hazardous foods has been made absolute. The right to food, the right to safety, the right to culture are all being treated as trade barriers that need to be dismantled.

This food totalitarianism can only be stopped through major citizen mobilization for democratization of the food system. This mobilization is starting to gain momentum in Europe, Japan, India, Brazil, and other parts of the world.

We have to reclaim our right to save seed and to biodiversity. We have to reclaim our right to nutrition and food safety. We have to reclaim our right to protect the earth and her diverse species. We have to stop this corporate theft from the poor and from nature. Food democracy is the new agenda for democracy and human rights. It is the new agenda for ecological sustainability and social justice.

Notes

1. These companies are DuPont/Pioneer (U.S.), Monsanto (U.S.), Novartis (Switzerland), Groupe Limagrain (France), Advanta (U.K. and Netherlands), Guipo Pulsar/Semins/ELM (Mexico), Sakata (Japan), KWS HG (Germany), and Taki (Japan).
2. Victor Suares, Paper presented at International Conference on Globalization, Food Security, and Sustainable Agriculture, July 30–31, 1996.

3. "Monsanto: Peddling 'Life Sciences' or 'Death Sciences'?" New Delhi: RFSTE, 1998.
4. ASSINSEL (International Association of Plant Breeders), "Feeding the 8 Billion and Preserving the Planet," Nyon, Switzerland: ASSINSEL.
5. Francesca Bray, "Agriculture for Developing Nations," *Scientific American*, July 1994, pp. 33–35.
6. *Business India*, March 1998.
7. T.N. Prakash and Tejaswini, "Floriculture and Food Security Issues: The Case of Rose Cultivation in Bangalore," in *Globalization and Food Security: Proceedings of Conference on Globalization and Agriculture*, ed. Vandana Shiva, New Delhi, August 1996.
8. Interview with John Hamilton, *Sunday Observer*, May 9, 1993.
9. Hendrik Verfaillie, speech delivered at the Forum on Nature and Human Society, National Academy of Sciences, Washington, DC, October 30, 1997.
10. Vandana Shiva, "Globalization, Gandhi, and Swadeshi: What is Economic Freedom? Whose Economic Freedom?" New Delhi: RFSTE, 1998.
11. Vandana Shiva, "Globalization, Gandhi, and Swadeshi."

CHAPTER 4

The Impact of Globalization on Poverty and Inequality

Among the most hotly contested issues regarding globalization is its impact on poverty and inequality. As suggested by the selections in this chapter (and by selections in other chapters) there is a deep chasm—or, rather, several chasms—that separate participants on these issues. Consider responses to this question: has globalization reduced poverty? On the one hand, several selections in this chapter answer the question with a resounding "yes." They provide abundant evidence to back up their claim involving national income statistics, growth rates, and household surveys. A widely cited finding is that the number of those who are extremely poor, with income below $1 per day, dropped dramatically in the current era of globalization. Dollar and Kraay, Wolf, and Bhagwati in this chapter, and Moore in Chapter 11, the returns are in and the controversy is over: for this group, empirical evidence conclusively demonstrates that globalization is the best tool to fight poverty. Although those who seek to limit globalization may do so because they believe that they are helping the poor, they are simply wrong. According to proglobalization poverty fighters, since those who remain mired in poverty are likely to be located in countries, sectors, and regions poorly integrated into the global economy, the obvious solution is to proceed full speed ahead with globalization. Opposing globalization means opposing the opportunity for poor people to obtain its benefits.

Not so fast, reply opponents of globalization. First, critics like Wade (in this chapter) challenge the methods used to assess gains made by the poor. For example, the case for globalization often rests on calculating the growth of a country's national income following its integration in the global economy. Yet this measure fails to take account of the *distribution* of income—and rising income *inequality* can offset increases in overall national *income*. In other words, the size of the national income pie may increase at the same time that the size of the slices of pie received by the poor can shrink.

A second criticism of the globalization-reduces-poverty position is that, for globalization to produce its beneficent effects, a country must be lucky enough to occupy a sufficiently favorable position at the outset to benefit from participation in the global economy. Among the preconditions that have been suggested are appropriate political institutions, geographic situation, and social infrastructure (such as a well-educated population). Otherwise, as the selection by Sachs describes in Chapter 11, countries may be caught in a poverty trap that globalization cannot alleviate. Indeed, in such cases globalization may worsen the situation, for example, by saddling a country with debt repayments and internationally imposed requirements to pursue destructive policies.

The third criticism of the claim that globalization is a tool to fight poverty extends this last point. It claims that the measures involved in promoting globalization can *cause* people to become poor. Shiva describes the process by which the replacement of subsistence farming and fishing by export-oriented agribusiness and aquaculture impoverishes local communities. Even if, in some distant future, globalization might hypothetically increase income, recall the warning delivered by British economist John Maynard Keynes during the Great Depression of the 1930s in response to the argument that, in the long run, markets would solve the problem of economic dislocation: "The only problem with the long-run effect is that in the long run, we're all dead!"

As you will see, the debate about the impact of globalization on poverty is heated, and the stakes are high. A different question, also addressed by selections in this chapter, is the effect of globalization on inequalities within and among countries. Broadly speaking, there are three positions: globalization invariably increases inequalities, globalization invariably reduces inequalities, and globalization has variable effects depending on the policies pursued by national governments and international financial institutions (IFIs). A related debate is whether inequality matters. For Dollar and Kraay, and Bhagwati, in this chapter, whether inequality is increasing matters less than the question of whether incomes are rising. Indeed, the selection by Wolf in this chapter develops an extreme version of this argument. For Wolf contends that an increase in the absolute gap between rich and poor can be considered positively beneficial for the poor since it often indicates that growth is occurring. He describes the paradox as follows: if the income of rich and poor countries increases at the same rate—or even if poor countries grow somewhat faster than rich ones—the absolute income gap between rich and poor countries (and therefore economic inequality) will increase. (Wolf's selection in this chapter describes how and why.)

The debate over what can be called the distributional impact of globalization—who wins and loses from globalization—is among the most vibrant and important in the entire field. The selections in this chapter, as well as others in PG that address the issues of poverty and inequality, underline just how important—and yet how difficult—is clear thinking on these vital matters. It is a hard job sorting out the conflicting evidence and arguments. But it's an effort worth making. Your assessment of the impact of globalization on poverty and inequality will probably influence your overall position on the character and desirability of globalization. Because the issue is so complex and involves so many aspects, a large number of selections in PG bear on this question. Give the various participants a respectful—yet constructively critical—hearing. Begin to develop your position right away. But reserve final judgment on where you stand (and why) until you have read further in PG.

Spreading the Wealth

David Dollar and Aart Kraay

David Dollar and Aart Kraay are economists at the Development Group of the World Bank, an international financial institution to which most countries of the world belong. The Bank's mission is to alleviate poverty in the world by providing development assistance and policy advice. (See the selection by Cammack in Chapter 7 for a critique of the Bank's policies.) Dollar and Kraay contend that globalization, in the form of free trade and capital mobility, has fueled economic growth, which in turn has significantly promoted equality and reduced poverty for countries integrated into the world economy. They pay particular attention to China and India, the two largest countries in the world (which together account for nearly 40 percent of the world's population), which they claim are recent and major beneficiaries of globalization. According to Dollar and Kraay, since becoming more closely integrated into the global economy and reducing barriers to trade and foreign investment, the economies of China and India have soared, and the number of poor citizens has shrunk. Dollar and Kraay warn that globalization will not automatically have beneficial effects. Three conditions are necessary: wealthy countries must refrain from erecting tariff and nontariff barriers to trade, developing countries must adopt appropriate institutions and policies, and migration must be permitted to ease population pressures on poor countries.

Read this article in conjunction with the responses by critics that follow, as well as the next selection, by Wade. These analysts charge that Dollar and Kraay have manipulated statistics to bolster their case and have ignored counterevidence. Which side presents the stronger case and why?

A Rising Tide

One of the main claims of the antiglobalization movement is that globalization is widening the gap between the haves and the have-nots. It benefits the rich and does little for the poor, perhaps even making their lot harder. As union leader Jay Mazur put it . . . , "globalization has dramatically increased inequality between and within nations" ("Labor's New Internationalism," *Foreign Affairs*, January/

February 2000). The problem with this new conventional wisdom is that the best evidence available shows the exact opposite to be true. So far, the current wave of globalization, which started around 1980, has actually promoted economic equality and reduced poverty.

Global economic integration has complex effects on income, culture, society, and the environment. But in the debate over globalization's merits, its impact on poverty is particularly important. If international trade and investment primarily benefit the rich, many people will feel that restricting trade to protect jobs, culture, or the environment is worth the costs. But if restricting trade imposes further hardship on poor people in the developing world, many of the same people will think otherwise.

Three facts bear on this question. First, a long-term global trend toward greater inequality prevailed for at least 200 years; it peaked around 1975. But since then, it has stabilized and possibly even reversed. The chief reason for the change has been the accelerated growth of two large and initially poor countries: China and India.

Second, a strong correlation links increased participation in international trade and investment on the one hand and faster growth on the other. The developing world can be divided into a "globalizing" group of countries that have seen rapid increases in trade and foreign investment over the last two decades—well above the rates for rich countries—and a "nonglobalizing" group that trades even less of its income today than it did 20 years ago. The aggregate annual per capita growth rate of the globalizing group accelerated steadily from one percent in the 1960s to five percent in the 1990s. During that latter decade, in contrast, rich countries grew at two percent and nonglobalizers at only one percent. Economists are cautious about drawing conclusions concerning causality, but they largely agree that openness to foreign trade and investment (along with complementary reforms) explains the faster growth of the globalizers.

Third, and contrary to popular perception, globalization has not resulted in higher inequality within economies. Inequality has indeed gone up in some countries (such as China) and down in others (such as the Philippines). But those changes are not systematically linked to globalization measures such as trade and investment flows, tariff rates, and the presence of capital controls. Instead, shifts in inequality stem more from domestic education, taxes, and social policies. In general, higher growth rates in globalizing developing countries have translated into higher incomes for the poor. Even with its increased inequality, for example, China has seen the most spectacular reduction of poverty in world history—which was supported by opening its economy to foreign trade and investment.

Although globalization can be a powerful force for poverty reduction, its beneficial results are not inevitable. If policymakers hope to tap the full potential of economic integration and sustain its benefits, they must address three critical challenges. A growing protectionist movement in rich countries that aims to limit integration with poor ones must be stopped in its tracks. Developing countries need to acquire the kinds of institutions and policies that will allow them to prosper under globalization, both of which may be different from place to place. And more migration, both domestic and international, must be permitted when geography limits the potential for development.

The Great Divide

Over the past 200 years, different local economies around the world have become more integrated while the growth rate of the global economy has accelerated dramatically. Although it is impossible to prove causal linkage between the two developments—since there are no other world economies to be tested against—evidence suggests the arrows run in both directions. As Adam Smith argued, a larger market permits a finer division of labor, which in turn facilitates innovation and learning by doing. Some of that innovation involves transportation and communications technologies that lower costs and increase integration. So it is easy to see how integration and innovation can be mutually supportive.

Different locations have become more integrated because of increased flows of goods, capital, and knowledge. From 1820 to 1914, international trade increased faster than the global economy. Trade rose from about 2 percent of world income in 1820 to 18 percent in 1914. The globalization of trade took a step backward during the protectionist period of the Great Depression and World War II, and by 1950 trade (in relation to income) was lower than it had been in 1914. But thanks to a series of multilateral trade liberalizations under the General Agreement on Tariffs and Trade (GATT), trade dramatically expanded among industrialized countries between 1960 and 1980. Most developing countries remained largely isolated from this trade because of their own inward-focused policies, but the success of such notable exceptions as Taiwan and South Korea eventually helped encourage other developing economies to open themselves up to foreign trade and investment.

International capital flows, measured as foreign ownership of assets relative to world income, also grew during the first wave of globalization and declined during the Great Depression and World War II; they did not return to 1914 levels until 1980. But since then, such flows have increased markedly and changed their nature as well. One hundred years ago, foreign capital typically financed public infrastructure projects (such as canals and railroads) or direct investment related to natural resources. Today, in contrast, the bulk of capital flows to developing countries is direct investments tied to manufacturing and services.

The change in the nature of capital flows is clearly related to concurrent advances in economic integration, such as cheaper and faster transportation and revolutionary changes in telecommunications. Since 1920, seagoing freight charges have declined by about two-thirds and air travel costs by 84 percent; the cost of a three-minute call from New York City to London has dropped by 99 percent. Today, production in widely differing locations can be integrated in ways that simply were not possible before.

Another aspect of integration has been the movement of people. Yet here the trend is reversed: there is much more international travel than in the past but much less permanent migration. Between 1870 and 1910, about ten percent of the world's population relocated permanently from one country to another; over the past 25 years, only one to two percent have done so.

As economic integration has progressed, the annual growth rate of the world economy has accelerated, from 1 percent in the mid-nineteenth century to 3.5 percent in 1960–2000. Sustained over many years, such a jump in growth makes a huge difference in real living standards. It now takes only two to three years, for example, for the world economy to produce the same amount of goods and services that it did during the entire nineteenth century. Such a comparison is arguably a serious understatement of the true difference, since most of what is consumed today—airline travel, cars, televisions, synthetic fibers, life-extending drugs—did not exist 200 years ago. For any of these goods or services, therefore, the growth rate of output since 1820 is infinite. Human productivity has increased almost unimaginably.

All this tremendous growth in wealth was distributed very unequally up to about 1975, but since then growing equality has taken hold. One good measure of inequality among individuals worldwide is the mean log deviation—a measure of the gap between the income of any randomly selected person and a general average. It takes into account the fact that income distributions everywhere are skewed in favor of the rich, so that the typical person is poorer than the group average; the more skewed the distribution, the larger the gap. Per capita income in the world today, for example, is around $5,000, whereas a randomly selected person would most likely be living on close to $1,000—80 percent less. That gap translates into a mean log deviation of 0.8.

Taking this approach, an estimate of the world distribution of income among individuals shows rising inequality between 1820 and 1975. In that period, the gap between the typical person and world per capita income increased from about 40 percent to about 80 percent. Since changes in income inequality within countries were small, the increase in inequality was driven mostly by differences in growth rates across countries. Areas that were already relatively rich in 1820 (notably, Europe and the United States) grew faster than poor areas (notably, China and India). Global inequality peaked sometime in the 1970s, but it then stabilized and even began to decline, largely because growth in China and India began to accelerate.

Another way of looking at global inequality is to examine what is happening to the extreme poor—those people living on less than $1 per day. Although the percentage of the world's population living in poverty has declined over time, the absolute number rose fairly steadily until 1980. During the Great Depression and World War II, the number of poor increased particularly sharply, and it declined somewhat immediately thereafter. The world economy grew strongly between 1960 and 1980, but the number of poor rose because growth did not occur in the places where the worst-off live. But since then, the most rapid growth has occurred in poor locations. Consequently the number of poor has declined by 200 million since 1980. Again, this trend is explained primarily by the rapid income growth in China and India, which together in 1980 accounted for about one-third of the world's population and more than 60 percent of the world's extreme poor.

Upward Bound

The shift in the trend in global inequality coincides with the shift in the economic strategies of several large developing countries. Following World War II, most developing regions chose strategies that focused inward and discouraged integration with the global economy. But these approaches were not particularly successful, and throughout the 1960s and 1970s developing countries on the whole grew less rapidly than industrialized ones. The oil shocks and U.S. inflation of the 1970s created severe problems for them, contributing to negative growth, high inflation, and debt crises over the next several years. Faced with these disappointing results, several developing countries began to alter their strategies starting in the 1980s.

For example, China had an extremely closed economy until the mid-1970s. Although Beijing's initial economic reform focused on agriculture, a key part of its approach since the 1980s has involved opening up foreign trade and investment, including a drop in its tariff rates by two-thirds and its nontariff barriers by even more. These reforms have led to unprecedented economic growth in the country's coastal provinces and more moderate growth in the interior. From 1978 to 1994 the Chinese economy grew annually by 9 percent, while exports grew by 14 percent and imports by 13 percent. Of course, China and other globalizing developing countries have pursued a wide range of reforms, not just economic openness. Beijing has strengthened property rights through land reform and moved from a planned economy toward a market-oriented one, and these measures have contributed to its integration as well as to its growth.

Other developing countries have also opened up as a part of broader reform programs. During the 1990s, India liberalized foreign trade and investment with good results; its annual per capita income growth now tops four percent. It too has pursued a broad agenda of reform and has moved away from a highly regulated, planned system. Meanwhile, Uganda and Vietnam are the best examples of very low-income countries that have increased their participation in trade and investment and prospered as a result. And in the western hemisphere, Mexico is noteworthy both for signing its free-trade agreement with the United States and Canada in 1993 and for its rapid growth since then, especially in the northern regions near the U.S. border.

These cases illustrate how openness to foreign trade and investment, coupled with complementary reforms, typically leads to faster growth. India, China, Vietnam, Uganda, and Mexico are not isolated examples; in general, countries that have become more open have grown faster. The best way to illustrate this trend is to rank developing countries in order of their increases in trade relative to national income over the past 20 years. The top third of this list can be thought of as the "globalizing" camp, and the bottom two-thirds as the "nonglobalizing" camp. The globalizers have increased their trade relative to income by 104 percent over the past two decades, compared to 71 percent for rich countries. The nonglobalizers, meanwhile, actually trade less today than they did 20 years ago. The globalizers have also cut their import tariffs by 22 percentage points on average, compared to only 11 percentage points for the nonglobalizers.

How have the globalizers fared in terms of growth? Their average annual growth rates accelerated from 1 percent in the 1960s to 3 percent in the 1970s, 4 percent in the 1980s, and 5 percent in the 1990s. Rich countries' annual growth rates, by comparison, slowed to about 2 percent in the 1990s, and the nonglobalizers saw their growth rates decline from 3 percent in the 1970s to 1 percent in the 1980s and 1990s.

The same pattern can be observed on a local level. Within both China and India, the locations that are integrating with the global economy are growing much more rapidly than the disconnected regions. Indian states, for example, vary significantly in the quality of their investment climates as measured by government efficiency, corruption, and infrastructure. Those states with better investment climates have integrated themselves more closely with outside markets and have experienced more investment (domestic and foreign) than their less-integrated counterparts. Moreover, states that were initially poor and then created good investment climates had stronger poverty reduction in the 1990s than those not integrating with the global economy. Such internal comparisons are important because, by holding national trade and macroeconomic policies constant, they reveal how important it is to complement trade liberalization with institutional reform so that integration can actually occur.

The accelerated growth rates of globalizing countries such as China, India, and Vietnam are consistent with cross-country comparisons that find openness going hand in hand with faster growth. The most that these studies can establish is that more trade and investment is highly correlated with higher growth, so one needs to be careful about drawing conclusions about causality. Still, the overall evidence from individual cases and cross-country correlation is persuasive. As economists Peter Lindert and Jeffrey Williamson have written, "even though no one study can establish that openness to trade has unambiguously helped the representative Third World economy, the preponderance of evidence supports this conclusion." They go on to note that "there are no anti-global victories to report for the postwar Third World."

Contrary to the claims of the antiglobalization movement, therefore, greater openness to international trade and investment has in fact helped narrow the gap between rich and poor countries rather than widen it. During the 1990s, the economies of the globalizers, with a combined population of about 3 billion, grew more than twice as fast as the rich countries. The nonglobalizers, in contrast, grew only half as fast and nowadays lag further and further behind. Much of the discussion of global inequality assumes that there is growing divergence between the developing world and the rich world, but this is simply not true. The most important development in global inequality in recent decades is the growing divergence within the developing world, and it is directly related to whether countries take advantage of the economic benefits that globalization can offer.

The Path out of Poverty

The antiglobalization movement also claims that economic integration is worsening inequality within countries as well as between them. Until the mid-1980s, there was insufficient evidence to support strong conclusions on this important topic. But now more and more developing countries have begun to conduct household income and consumption surveys of reasonable quality. (In low-income countries, these surveys typically track what households actually consume because so much of their real income is self-produced and not part of the money economy.) Good surveys now exist for 137 countries, and many go back far enough to measure changes in inequality over time.

One way of looking at inequality within countries is to focus on what happens to the bottom 20 percent of households as globalization and growth proceed apace. Across all countries, incomes of the poor grow at around the same rate as GDP. Of course, there is a great deal of variation around that average relationship. In some countries, income distribution has shifted in favor of the poor; in others, against them. But these shifts cannot be explained by any globalization-related variable. So it simply cannot be said that inequality necessarily rises with more trade, more foreign investment, and lower tariffs. For many globalizers, the overall change in distribution was small, and in some cases (such as the Philippines and Malaysia) it was even in favor of the poor. What changes in inequality do reflect are country-specific policies on education, taxes, and social protection.

It is important not to misunderstand this finding. China is an important example of a country that has had a large increase in inequality in the past decade, when the income of the bottom 20 percent has risen much less rapidly than per capita income. This trend may be related to greater openness, although domestic liberalization is a more likely cause. China started out in the 1970s with a highly equal distribution of income, and part of its reform has deliberately aimed at increasing the returns on education, which financially reward the better schooled. But the Chinese case is not typical; inequality has not increased in most of the developing countries that have opened up to foreign trade and investment. Furthermore, income distribution in China may have become more unequal, but the income of the poor in China has still risen rapidly. In fact, the country's progress in reducing poverty has been one of the most dramatic successes in history.

Because increased trade usually accompanies more rapid growth and does not systematically change household-income distribution, it generally is associated with improved well-being of the poor. Vietnam nicely illustrates this finding. As the nation has opened up, it has experienced a large increase in per capita income and no significant change in inequality. Thus the income of the poor has risen dramatically, and the number of Vietnamese living in absolute poverty dropped sharply from 75 percent of the population in 1988 to 37 percent in 1998. Of the poorest 5 percent of households in 1992, 98 percent were better off six years later. And the improved well-being is not just a matter of income. Child labor has declined, and school enrollment has increased. It should be no surprise that the vast majority of poor households in Vietnam benefited immediately from a more liberalized trading system, since the country's opening has resulted in exports of rice (produced by most of the poor farmers) and labor-intensive products such as footwear. But the experience of China and Vietnam is not unique. India and Uganda also enjoyed rapid poverty reduction as they grew along with their integration into the global economy.

The Open Societies

These findings have important implications for developing countries, for rich countries such as the United States, and for those who care about global poverty. All parties should recognize that the most recent wave of globalization has been a powerful force for equality and poverty reduction, and they should commit themselves to seeing that it continues despite the obstacles lying ahead.

It is not inevitable that globalization will proceed. In 1910, many believed globalization was unstoppable; they soon received a rude shock. History is not likely to repeat itself in the same way, but it is worth noting that antiglobalization sentiments are on the rise. A growing number of political leaders in the developing world realize that an open trading system is very much in their countries' interest. They would do well to heed Mexican President Vicente Fox, who said recently,

> We are convinced that globalization is good and it's good when you do your homework, . . . keep your fundamentals in line on the economy, build up high levels of education, respect the rule of law. . . . When you do your part, we are convinced that you get the benefit.

But today the narrow interests opposed to further integration—especially those in the rich countries—appear to be much more energetic than their opponents. In Quebec City last spring and in Genoa last summer, a group of democratically elected leaders gathered to discuss how to pursue economic integration and improve the lives of their peoples. Antiglobalization demonstrators were quite effective in disrupting the meetings and drawing media attention to themselves. Leaders in developed and developing countries alike must make the proglobalization case more directly and effectively or risk having their opponents dominate the discussion and stall the process.

In addition, industrialized countries still raise protectionist measures against agricultural and labor-intensive products. Reducing those barriers would help developing countries significantly. The poorer areas of the world would benefit from further openings of their own markets as well, since 70 percent of the tariff barriers that developing countries face are from other developing countries.

If globalization proceeds, its potential to be an equalizing force will depend on whether poor countries manage to integrate themselves into the global economic system. True integration requires not just trade liberalization but wide-ranging institutional reform. Many of the nonglobalizing developing countries, such as Myanmar, Nigeria, Ukraine, and Pakistan, offer an unattractive investment climate. Even if they decide to open themselves up to trade, not much is likely to happen unless other reforms are also pursued. It is not easy to predict the reform paths of these countries; some of the relative successes in recent years, such as China, India, Uganda, and Vietnam, have come as quite a surprise. But as long as a location has weak institutions and policies, people living there are going to fall further behind the rest of the world.

Through their trade policies, rich countries can make it easier for those developing countries that do choose to open up and join the global trading club. But in recent years, the rich countries have been doing just the opposite. Gatt was originally built around agreements concerning trade practices. Now, institutional harmonization, such as agreement on policies toward intellectual property rights, is a requirement for joining the WTO. Any sort of regulation of labor and environmental standards made under the threat of WTO sanctions would take this requirement for harmonization much further. Such measures would be neoprotectionist in effect, because they would thwart the integration of developing countries into the world economy and discourage trade between poor countries and rich ones. . . .

A final potential obstacle to successful and equitable globalization relates to geography. There is no inherent reason why coastal China should be poor; the same goes for southern India, northern Mexico, and Vietnam. All of these locations are near important markets or trade routes but were long held back by misguided policies. Now, with appropriate reforms, they are starting to grow rapidly and take their natural place in the world. But the same cannot be said for Mali, Chad, or other countries or regions cursed with "poor geography"—i.e., distance from markets, inherently high transport costs, and challenging health and agricultural problems. It would be naive to think that trade and investment alone can alleviate poverty in all locations. In fact, for those locations with poor geography, trade liberalization is less important than developing proper health care systems or providing basic infrastructure—or letting people move elsewhere.

Migration from poor locations is the missing factor in the current wave of globalization that could make a large contribution to reducing poverty. Each year, 83 million people are added to the world's population, 82 million of them in the developing world. In Europe and Japan, moreover, the population is aging and the labor force is set to shrink. Migration of relatively unskilled workers from South to North would thus offer clear economic benefits to both. Most migration from South to North is economically motivated, and it raises the living standard of the migrant while benefiting the sending country in three ways. First, it reduces the South's labor force and thus raises wages for those who remain behind. Second, migrants send remittances of hard currency back home. Finally, migration bolsters transnational trade and investment networks. In the case of Mexico, for example, ten percent of its citizens live and work in the United States, taking pressure off its own labor market and raising wages there. India gets six times as much in remittances from its workers overseas as it gets in foreign aid.

Unlike trade, however, migration remains highly restricted and controversial. Some critics perceive a disruptive impact on society and culture and fear downward pressure on wages and rising unemployment in the richer countries. Yet anti-immigration lobbies ignore the fact that geographical economic disparities are so strong that illegal immigration is growing rapidly anyway, despite restrictive policies. In a perverse irony, some of the worst abuses of globalization occur because there is not enough of it in key economic areas such as labor flows. Human traffic, for example, has become a highly lucrative, unregulated business in which illegal migrants are easy prey for exploitation.

Realistically, none of the industrialized countries is going to adopt open migration. But they should reconsider their migration policies. Some, for example, have a strong bias in their immigration rules toward highly skilled workers, which in fact spurs a "brain drain" from the developing world. Such policies do little to stop the flow of unskilled workers and instead push many of these people into the illegal category. If rich countries would legally accept more unskilled workers, they could address their own looming labor shortages, improve living standards in developing countries, and reduce illegal human traffic and its abuses.

In sum, the integration of poor economies with richer ones over the past two decades has provided many opportunities for poor people to improve their lives. Examples of the beneficiaries of globalization can be found among Mexican migrants, Chinese factory workers, Vietnamese peasants, and Ugandan farmers. Many of the better-off in developing and rich countries alike also benefit. After all the rhetoric about globalization is stripped away, many of the policy questions come down to whether the rich world will make integrating with the world economy easy for those poor communities that want to do so. The world's poor have a large stake in how the rich countries answer.

The following selections discuss the claims of Dollar and Kraay, who then provide a reply to their critics.

Is Inequality Decreasing? Debating the Wealth and Poverty of Nations

James K. Galbraith: *"By the Numbers"*

In "Spreading the Wealth" (*Foreign Affairs*, January/February 2002), David Dollar and Aart Kraay make the provocative claim that global inequality has declined since 1975, mainly due to rapid growth in India and China, and that "globalizing" countries have performed far better in per capita growth than "nonglobalizers."

It is extraordinary that India, China, and Vietnam should be offered as three of the five major examples of globalizing success stories. India's relative success began in the 1980s, partly because strict capital controls and long-term official development assistance helped protect it from the debt crisis that occurred in Latin America and elsewhere. China grew at first on the strength of agricultural reform and then through a program of industrialization financed mainly by internal savings; it has to this day not liberalized its capital account. Vietnam and China remain under the control of their communist parties; these are not "Washington consensus" countries by any means.

Missing from Dollar and Kraay's list of successes are the true globalizers of recent times, including Argentina, until just a few months ago the leading neoliberal poster child, or Russia, now attempting to recover from the collapse that followed shock globalization. So too are the erstwhile "Asian tigers" who liberalized in the early 1990s and failed before the end of the decade. Nor are these examples isolated. World growth rates were systematically higher under the structured international financial regime of Bretton Woods from 1945 to 1971 than they became in the era of deregulation after 1980.

Dollar and Kraay assert that there is no general pattern of rising inequality under globalization. However, the source on which they base this assertion, the World Bank's inequality data set, is riddled with gaps and implausible measurements. According to these measures, for instance, inequality declined in Canada from 1971 to 1991 and in Mexico from 1975 to 1994, Spain is one of the most egalitarian countries in Europe, and India and Indonesia have general measures of inequality similar to that of Norway.

My own work, in contrast, shows a clear and severe global pattern of rising inequality in industrial pay, beginning in the early 1980s. This is based on the United Nations data that permit about 3,000 data points to be estimated, roughly five times as many as in the published editions of the World Bank data set (and more than three times as many as in a forthcoming edition).

Rising inequality after 1980 is the rule in this data, with limited exceptions mainly in Scandinavia and in Southeast Asia before 1997. The patterns strongly suggest that forces of globalization, including high global interest rates, debt crises, and shock liberalizations, are associated with rising inequality in pay structures. Pay is, of course, the major component of income, and if pay inequalities are rising, it is a good bet that broader income and social inequalities are rising too.

Joe W. Pitts III: *"Inequality Is No Myth"*

David Dollar and Aart Kraay's argument that globalization is a "powerful force for equality" is strange in light of widely accepted empirical evidence that inequality within and between countries has increased over the last 200 years. Although they claim that inequality has leveled off or started to decrease in the last two decades, the evidence on this topic remains unclear. To make their case, Dollar and Kraay rather arbitrarily classify a certain group of nations as "globalizers" and point to a decrease in inequality. However, as Harvard economist Dani Rodrik and others have pointed out, using more objective criteria (such as tariffs) for selecting the globalizers suggests that economic growth peaked in the 1960s and 1970s. Indeed, the latest World Bank report on globalization, of which Dollar was a principal author, backed away from the claim that the most globalized countries were those that had adopted the most protrade policies.

Even if Dollar and Kraay had not made faulty assumptions in choosing their globalizers, their breathtaking conclusion that "greater openness to international trade and investment has . . . helped narrow the gap between rich and poor countries rather than widen it" confuses correlation with causation. When average national income is examined, the fact that China and India have had higher growth and relatively fewer poor people distorts the picture because of the size of those two countries. In addition, higher growth in these nations preceded more open trade. Almost everywhere else, growth has slowed or (as in sub-Saharan Africa) reversed. Moreover, as illustrated by rising inequality within China and India, just because growth also raises the incomes of the poor does not mean that it reduces inequality, since the poor start from a radically lower position than the rich. Indeed, if incomes of both the rich and poor increase at a similar rate, inequality is increased, not reduced. Another study published in January by another World Bank economist, Branko Milanovic, evaluates household survey data, which is arguably a more relevant measure of inequality. This work shows that global inequality (as measured between individuals, with the world as one "nation") actually increased, at least in the five-year period examined (1988–93).

Inequality is no myth. According to well-known statistics produced by the World Health Organization and the UN Development Program, the net worth of the world's richest 200 individuals exceeds that of the world's poorest 2.5 billion people. And if, as Dollar and Kraay acknowledge, 82 million of the 83 million people added to the world each year are in poor countries, global equality will not be easily advanced.

Globalization and progrowth policies do reduce poverty. But as competitive systems that produce winners and losers, they do not necessarily reduce the inequality that is increasingly visible in a globalized world. Policies such as greater and more effective foreign aid; investment in developing countries' education, infrastructure, and technological capacity; enhanced access to rich-country markets; and international financial reforms are also vital in achieving a more stable, just, and sustainable system.

Andrew Wells-Dang: *"Having It Both Ways"*

David Dollar and Aart Kraay's claim that "globalization . . . has actually promoted economic equality and reduced poverty" is based on a selective use of data and dubious assumptions about causality. Indeed, their evidence remains far short of convincing.

To defend their views, Dollar and Kraay play fast and loose with the economics of inequality. The "mean log deviation" measure they use to claim a global reduction in inequality since 1975 is not a particularly good indicator. All it measures is the relative difference in distribution among the rich compared to the poor. To take an extreme example, a society with half of its members earning $50,000 and half earning $500 would have a mean log deviation of zero. Surely this is not what Dollar and Kraay mean by perfect equality.

The authors then proceed to confuse the issue of inequality with poverty reduction. It is indisputable that absolute poverty has declined dramatically in countries such as China and Vietnam following market reforms, and that millions of people are better off as a result. Nevertheless, relative inequality has risen just as dramatically, creating a host of social problems.

Dollar and Kraay admit from the outset that China and India have a huge effect on global aggregate statistics. In fact, the skew comes primarily from China, as India resembles other developing economies much more than China does. For this reason, other economists, such as the authors of the UN Human Development Report, routinely exclude China from aggregate data covering developing nations. Dollar and Kraay, however, include China in their statistics when it suits their purposes—for instance, to show rising global economic growth in the 1990s. Since China had the highest growth rates in the world during the past decade, emerged unscathed by the Asian financial crisis, and contains nearly 25 percent of the world's population, including it obscures what was actually a quite average decade for most developing countries.

When addressing inequality within nations, however, Dollar and Kraay treat China as an exception, noting that "some countries" experience higher inequality with growth and other countries do not. If they were to aggregate this data as they do in other sections of their article, they would likely find that rapid growth tends to increase inequality worldwide. Conversely, if they were to disaggregate links between globalization and growth, they would find that some countries with liberal trade and investment policies grow rapidly, whereas others do not. If China is excluded, the evidence of a correlation becomes substantially weaker.

Finally, as Dollar and Kraay admit, "one needs to be careful about drawing conclusions about causality." Unfortunately, they are not particularly careful. All positive changes, such as economic growth and reduced inequality, are said to be "promoted" and "supported by" globalization, while poverty and increased inequality are the fault of "domestic education, taxes, and social policies." One cannot have it both ways. Trade and investment policies are determined by governments just as social policies are, and governments deserve credit for their economic successes as much as they deserve criticism for their failings. Increased international integration might be as much a result of growth as its cause. If Dollar and Kraay were to take a more comprehensive look at their data, they would see a more complicated picture, in which global trade and investment produce some positive and some negative effects, with neither caused solely by reduced poverty or increased inequality.

Dollar and Kraay Reply

Is global inequality rising or falling? We argued in our article that inequality rose dramatically over the two centuries prior to 1980. Since then, inequality has stabilized, and it has even declined somewhat during the recent era of globalization. We are neither the first nor the only ones to make this point. Our observation on the long historical trend in inequality is based on work by economists Francois Bourguignon and Christian Morrison (forthcoming in the *American Economic Review*). Recent work by Xavier Sala-i-Martin at Columbia University shows a sharp reduction in all measures of global inequality between 1980 and 1998.

The authors of the three letters disagree, with Pitts even going so far as to claim that there is "widely accepted empirical evidence that inequality within and between countries has increased over the last 200 years." How can there be so much disagreement over such a basic and important fact? We offer three explanations.

First, there may be confusion over concepts. We reiterate that by "global inequality" we refer to the distribution of income across individuals around the world. This reflects both differences in average per capita incomes across countries and income inequalities within countries. Many poor countries have grown more slowly than rich countries in the past 20 years, and within some (although certainly not all) countries, inequality has increased. But global inequality has fallen precisely because populous poor countries (notably China and India, but also Vietnam and Bangladesh) have seen sharp accelerations in their growth rates. This acceleration in growth has helped nearly half the inhabitants of the developing world narrow the income gulf between themselves and the rich world. Large countries therefore figure prominently in measures of global inequality, rather than "[distorting] the picture" as suggested by Pitts.

Second, the data used to measure inequality matter. There is only one comprehensive source of data on income inequality within countries: representative household surveys carried out by countries' statistical agencies. Although such data certainly have flaws, they are the best we have, and so we use them. Moving from comprehensive measures to narrow measures such as intersectoral pay differences in industry (as advocated by Galbraith in his letter) seems inappropriate for our purposes. In most developing countries, only a small fraction of income consists of wages in the formal manufacturing sector, and most poor people work in agriculture and the informal sector. So it seems unlikely that trends in manufacturing-wage inequality will provide a reliable picture of overall inequality trends, which are often dominated by rural-urban and regional income gaps (as is the case in China, for example).

Third, some of the "facts" offered by the authors of the responses are simply wrong. Wells-Dang asserts that "relative inequality has risen . . . dramatically" in Vietnam. This statement is not true. A comparison of data from the only two comprehensive household surveys in the 1990s shows that there has been very little change in the Gini index of inequality, from .33 in 1993 to .35 in 1998. Wells-Dang is also incorrect to suggest that a country in which half the population earns $50,000 and the other half earns $500 would show zero inequality according to the mean log deviation measure of inequality we use. The correct figure is 1.6, which is roughly twice as high as the global inequality we measure.

Finally, what is the role of globalization in all of this? Our point is not (as Pitts suggests) that trade, or even growth for reasons other than trade, lowers inequality within countries. In fact, our research shows that countries that grow faster or trade more are as likely to see inequality decrease as increase. Our point is simply that countries that have become more globalized, in the sense of becoming more open to trade and direct foreign investment, have grown faster. This observation is supported by a large body of cross-country and case-study evidence that has tried carefully to separate out the effects of trade from other factors driving growth. Merely observing that growth in China accelerated in the late 1970s and early 1980s before trade took off does not reverse the conclusions of this research, as Galbraith and Pitts suggest. If anything, it does the opposite. A more careful reading of China's reforms clearly shows that most of the initial acceleration in growth after 1978 was driven by the one-time gains from the dismantling of communal agriculture, and that reforms in state enterprises had at best disappointing effects on performance. It is hard to imagine that China would have been able to sustain as high a growth rate over the next two decades without the benefits of further integration with the world economy.

In short, some of the countries that have become more integrated with the world economy in the past two decades have also been among the poorest and most populous in the world. The acceleration of growth in these countries has been an important force in ending a 200-year-long pattern of rising global inequality.

The Disturbing Rise of Poverty and Inequality *Is It All a "Big Lie"?*

Robert Hunter Wade

Political economist Robert Hunter Wade believes that the defenders of globalization wrongly claim that globalization has reduced poverty and inequality. In fact, by some measures, the numbers of people living in absolute poverty may have increased since 1980. And the statistics on global inequality are even more clear: globalization has been associated with rising levels of inequality among people and regions of the world.

Wade argues that supporters of globalization often misuse statistics to support their argument. For example, he questions classifying countries like China and

India as highly globalized, since the bulk of economic activity occurs within their own borders. Further, he contends, the sharp increase in China and India's economic growth *predates* the rise in their foreign trade. Conversely, he questions the decision to classify many poor countries as nonglobalized when in fact much of their gross domestic product derives from the export of raw materials. Further, like Stiglitz and Milanovic in Chapter 3, Wade argues that countries which have benefited the most from globalization first engaged in extensive economic regulation and state promotion and protection of their home industries before reducing tariffs and other barriers to foreign trade. Finally, Wade contends that the major benefits of globalization are reaped not by poor countries but by affluent nations, and especially by TNCs based in these countries. In brief, for Wade, the essence of globalization is that the rich get richer and the poor get poorer.

Can you explain the drastically different accounts of the impact of globalization on poverty and inequality presented by Wade, Milanovic, Stiglitz, and Shiva on the one hand, and Friedman, Dollar and Kraay, and Wolf on the other? Can the contending positions be reconciled? Which side develops more persuasive arguments and provides superior empirical data to support its position?

Globalization

What is the evidence that globalization—rising integration of poorer countries into the world economy, as seen in rising trade/GDP, foreign direct investment/GDP, and the like—is the world's most powerful means of reducing poverty and inequality?

Clearly the proposition is not well supported at the world level if we agree that globalization has been rising while income inequality and poverty have not been falling. But it might still be possible to argue that globalization explains differences between countries: that more globalized countries have a better record of economic growth, poverty reduction and inequality reduction than less globalized ones.

This is what World Bank studies claim. One of the best known, *Globalization, Growth and Poverty*,[1] distinguishes "newly globalizing" or "more globalized" countries from "nonglobalizing" or "less globalized" countries. It measures globalizing by *changes* in the ratio of trade to GDP between 1977 and 1997. Ranking developing countries by the change, it calls the top third the globalizing or more globalized countries, and the remaining two-thirds are called less globalized countries or weak globalizers. The globalizing countries are then found to have had faster economic growth, no increase in inequality, and faster reduction of poverty than the weak globalizers. "Thus, globalization clearly can be a force for poverty reduction."

Robert Hunter Wade, The Disturbing Rise of Poverty and Inequality: Is It All a "Big Lie"?, ch. 1 in David Held and Mathias Koenig-Archibugi, eds., *Taming Globalization: Frontiers of Governance* (Cambridge: Polity, 2003): 30–46. Reprinted by permission of Robert Hunter Wade.

The argument is undermined by the use of "change in trade/GDP" as the measure of globalization.[2] The list of "globalizers" includes China and India, as well as countries like Nepal, Côte d'Ivoire, Rwanda, Haiti, and Argentina. As the cases of China and India suggest, it is quite possible that "more globalized" countries are less open in terms of *levels* of integration than "less globalized" countries; and also less open in terms of trade policy than "less globalized" countries. A country with very high trade/GDP and very free trade could still be categorized as a weak globalizer. It turns out that the globalizing countries are mainly ones that initially had very *low* trade/GDP in 1977. Many of them still had relatively low trade/GDP at the *end* of the period, in 1997—and this does not just reflect the fact that larger economies tend to have lower ratios of trade/GDP. To call them globalizers, and countries with much higher ratios of trade/GDP nonglobalizers, is an audacious use of language.

Excluding countries with high but not rising levels of trade to GDP from the category of more globalized excludes many very poor countries dependent on a few natural resource commodity exports, which have had very poor economic growth. The structure of their economy and the low skill endowment of the population make them very dependent on trade. If they were included as globalized their poor economic performance would cast doubt on the proposition that the more globalized countries have the best performance.

The inclusion of China and India as globalizers—with their good economic performance over the past one or two decades attributed in large part to their globalization—guarantees that the globalized will show better performance than the nonglobalized. But two big facts question the Bank's argument. First, China and India experienced a sharp increase in the trend rate of growth about a decade prior to their liberalizing trade and investment reforms. Second, they have achieved their relatively fast rise in trade/GDP with policies far from the liberal trade and investment policies advocated by the globalists. They remain highly protected economies. The World Bank would be the first to denounce their current trade policies and internal market-restricting policies as inhibiting to growth and efficiency if they had not been growing fast.

Their experience—and that of Japan, South Korea and Taiwan earlier—shows that countries do not have to adopt liberal trade policies in order to reap benefits from trade, to grow fast, and to grow an industrial structure able to produce an increasing proportion of national consumption.[3] They all experienced relatively fast growth behind protective barriers, and fast growth fueled rapid trade expansion increasingly focused on capital goods and intermediate goods. As they became richer they tended to liberalize their trade—providing the basis for the common misunderstanding that trade liberalization fueled their growth. For all the Bank study's qualifications (such as "We label the top third 'more globalized' [that is, bigger increase in trade/GDP] without in any sense implying that they adopted pro-trade policies. The rise in trade may have been due to other policies or even to pure chance"), it concludes that trade liberalization has been the driving force of the increase in developing countries' trade. "The result of this trade liberalization in the developing world has been a large increase in both imports and exports." On this questionable proposition the Bank rests its case for trade liberalization as a central element in its core development recipe for all countries.

The Bank's argument about the benign effects of globalization on growth, poverty and income distribution does not survive scrutiny. The argument is also questioned by a recent cross-country study of the relationship between openness and income equality. This study finds that among the subset of countries with low and middle levels of average income (below roughly $5,000 per capita in purchasing power terms, or below that of Chile and the Czech Republic), higher levels of trade openness are associated with *more* inequality, while among higher-income countries more openness goes with more equality.[4]

Why Is Globalization Probably Not Reducing Poverty and Inequality?

If the number of people in absolute poverty is probably not falling and probably higher than the World Bank says, and if income inequality by several plausible measures (especially those that measure polarization) is not falling and probably rising, why? Not because of the failure of industrialization in developing countries. If we take the share of GDP in manufacturing in developing countries as a group and developed countries as a group, we find a remarkable convergence—developing countries now have a *bigger* share of GDP in manufacturing than developed. But each additional increment of manufacturing in developing countries is yielding less income over time. This is quite contrary to the understandings of the "modernization" champions of the 1950s to 1980s, ancestors of today's globalists. They thought that (market-friendly) industrialization would be the vehicle to carry developing countries to the living standards of the developed world. The failure of this prediction may help to explain why industrialization as such is given little attention in today's development agenda. It has virtually disappeared from the concerns of the World Bank, which has switched its notion of development from production and economic growth to human needs and capabilities.

If failure to industrialize is not the culprit, what other factors might explain widening inequality? What is causing a shift in the distribution of world population toward the extremes of the world income distribution and a shift in the distribution of world income toward the top end of the distribution? At the bottom end, population is growing several times faster in the low-income zone than in the rich zone, raising the share of world population living in countries in the low-income zone. Also at the bottom end, the terms of trade facing developing countries—the prices of their exports, especially primary commodities, over the prices of their imports from developed countries—have fallen sharply over the past two decades, depressing the share of world income going to the low-income zone.[5] The harnessing of China's vast reservoirs of labor has particularly depressed the terms of trade for developing country manufactures.

Regional, Not Global, Focus of Multinational Corporations

At the top end, we see that—contrary to the common idea of markets and firms becoming increasingly global—most of the Fortune 500 biggest multinational corporations depend for most of their sales on their home region, whether North America, the European Union, or East Asia (the "Triad").[6] Less than a dozen are "global" in their sales, even in the restricted sense of having 20 percent or more of total sales (from parents and subsidiaries) in each of these three regions. They sell a negligible proportion of total sales in developing countries outside of East Asia. Moreover, their focus on just one of the three Triad regions intensified in the second half of the 1990s as compared with the first half. The foreign operations of the multinationals became less profitable than their home-based operations in the second half of the 1990s, having been more profitable in the first half of the 1990s. Multinational corporations are "regionalizing," not "globalizing."

Spatial Clustering of High Value-Added Activities

Underlying the observed patterns of location, trade and prices is a general property of modern economic growth related to spatial clustering. We know that some kinds of economic activities and production methods are more lucrative than others, have stronger unpriced spillover benefits, and more positive effects on growth and productivity; and that countries and regions with higher proportions of such activities enjoy higher levels of real incomes. We also know that in free market conditions (not as a result of market "imperfections") the high value-added activities—in manufacturing and in services—cluster in the high-cost, high-wage zone of the world economy. German skilled workers cost about 15 times as much to employ as Chinese skilled workers; yet Germany remains a powerful center of manufacturing.

When it comes to the higher value-added activities, in other words, locations are "sticky," for several reasons. First, costs per unit of output, especially labor costs, may not be lower in the lower wage zone, because lower wages may be more than offset by lower productivity. In any case, the cost of employing people has fallen to a small proportion of total costs in automated assembly operations, often 10 percent or less. As the technology content of many engineering products, including vehicle parts and aircraft, becomes increasingly sophisticated, this raises the premium on the company keeping highly skilled workers to develop and manufacture these products—by paying them highly.

Second, many forms of higher value-added activities are subject both to increasing returns to scale and to linkage or network effects (which lower transactions costs for firms located in physical or social proximity). In the presence of increasing returns to scale and linkages much of the liberal argument about the virtues of private property, competition and specialization based on comparative advantage in spreading the benefits of economic growth "evenly" loses force. On the contrary, we expect tendencies towards divergence, polarization, twin peaks.[7]

Increasing returns and network effects may show up inside firms. The "capability" of a firm relative to that of rivals (the maximum quality level it can achieve, and its cost of production) depends not only on the sum of the skills of its workforce, but also on the *collective* or firm-level knowledge and social organization of its employees; and much of this knowledge and social organization is essentially *tacit*, transferred mainly through face-to-face relationships—not able to be transferred easily from place to place in the form of (technical and organizational) blueprints or embodied in machinery.[8] If a firm were to move to a lower wage zone and some of its employees were not mobile, the costs to the firm's capacity, including the loss of tacit knowledge, might outweigh the advantages of relocation.

Manufacturing firms in the OECD countries are engaged in dense input-output linkages with other firms. (About two-thirds of manufacturing output in the OECD is sold by one firm to another firm.) The presence of a dense and spatially concentrated network of input-output linkages provides spillover benefits to firms in the network. So does the presence of well-functioning factor markets and a supply of formally educated people able to gain technology-specific (and partly tacit) knowledge at low cost. And as noted, tacit knowledge, whose economic value typically increases even as the ratio of tacit to codified knowledge falls with computerization, is transferred more easily within networks underpinned by social relationships, cultural similarity, and the disposition to trust. These network effects compound the tendency for any one firm not to move to a low-wage zone, or to move only its *low* value-added, assembly activities by outsourcing or establishing subsidiaries while keeping other activities that depend on varied inputs, tacit knowledge and social contacts in the core.

All the more so because for many products and services, quality and value added go up not continuously but in steps. (Ballbearings below a quality threshold are useless.) Getting to higher steps may require big investments, critical masses, targeted assistance from public entities, and long-term supply contracts with multinational corporations seeking local suppliers. "Normal" market processes can keep producers and countries stuck at low steps.

In some of the biggest manufacturing sectors—including electronics and vehicles—parent companies based in the high-income zone have formed increasingly concentrated vertical production networks through which they obtain the major share of value added by their control of proprietary technology, branding and marketing. They have put an increasing proportion of routine manufacturing operations in lower tier suppliers in the low-income zone, often locally owned companies; and then used their market power and intense competition among the lower tier suppliers to extract more value added from them. When global recession comes the lower tier suppliers are first to suffer, especially those locked into Japanese production hierarchies.

This is not the end of the story. At the next round the greater wealth and variety of economic activities in the high-wage zone—not to mention fiscal redistribution, a legal system that supports limited liability, and a socially more homogeneous population—mean that it can more readily absorb the Schumpeterian shocks from innovation and bankruptcies, as activity shifts from products and processes with more intense competition to those with less competition closer to the innovation end. There is less resistance to the "creative destruction" of market processes, even though organizing people to pursue common objectives, including resistance, tends to be easier than in the low-wage zone. Enron may go bankrupt but there are plenty more companies to take on its business and employ its employees.

These effects—plus limited labor movement from the low-wage zone to the high-wage zone when international borders intervene—help to explain a stably "divided world" in which high wages remain high in one zone while low wages elsewhere stay low, even as the industrialization gap has been eliminated. The important point is that well-functioning free markets in a highly economically interdependent or globalized world produce, "spontaneously," a stable equilibrium division of activities between the high-wage zone and the low-wage zone—one that is hardly desirable for the low-wage zone. Or to connect the argument to the empirical findings on openness and inequality reported earlier, one might hypothesize that in low-income developing countries higher levels of trade to GDP raise the income share of the rich, who have education and control over critical trade-related services, while shrinking the share of the bulk of the population with minimal or no education; and the consumption preferences of the rich lock the low-income countries into dependence on imports of consumption goods from the high-income countries, restricting the replacement of imports by local production that is the key to expanding prosperity. Oligopolistic industrial organization in the high-income zone reinforces the inequalities by supporting markup pricing, and prompting declining terms of trade for the low-wage zone.

Even about East Asia we should not get too optimistic. Only a minuscule portion of world R&D work is done in (non-Japan) East Asia; virtually all of it continues to be done in the developed countries of North America, Western Europe and Japan. Even Singapore, that looks to be an Asian center of research and development, does not do "real" R&D; its R&D labs mostly concentrate on adapting products developed in North America and Europe for the regional market and listening in on what competitors are doing.[9] So much for the much heralded "globalization of R&D." China still relies heavily on foreign investment for its higher tech manufactured output; and foreign investment is still mainly seeking low-cost labor, tax breaks and implied promises of protection, as distinct from rapidly rising skills. Its export competitiveness remains concentrated in labor-intensive products of foreign-owned factories. Even its information technology engineering complex around Shanghai depends heavily on Taiwanese and other foreign know-how. Japanese alarm bells have been ringing at graphs showing Japan's personal computer exports to the U.S. falling as China's rise; but the figures conceal the fact that the computers are assembled in China using high value-added technology from Japan and elsewhere. Some of the technology is spilling into the heads of the millions of Chinese employees, almost certainly more than is occurring in other developing countries. But added to doubts about the accuracy of China's growth statistics, these qualifications should caution us about a scenario of declining world income inequality that rests on China's continued fast growth and transformation.

In short, the benign effects of free markets in spreading benefits around the world, as celebrated in the liberal argument, may be offset by tendencies toward increasing returns and spatially concentrated networks, seen in the agglomeration of high value-added activities in the high-income zone. These tendencies can maintain a stable division between a high value-added, high-wage zone and a low value-added, low-wage zone—even as ratios of manufacturing to GDP, total trade/GDP, and manufacturing exports/total exports rise in the latter.

There are other basic drivers as well. They include the transformations of capitalism from assembly lines to information manipulation, from manufacturing to finance, that place higher premiums on skills and education and penalize those without. They include the international monetary system in place since the breakdown of the Bretton Woods system in the early 1970s, which among other things put pressure on the more successful developing countries—those that have liberalized their capital account—to limit their growth rates so as to limit the risk of crisis triggered by sudden capital flight. And the drivers include the withdrawal of support by international financial institutions such as the World Bank and the International Monetary Fund for industrial policies aimed at creating import-replacing industries and ones that might challenge those of the West. What is clear is that open, well-functioning markets need not produce convergence between parts of the low-income zone and the high-income zone, and can produce divergence, polarization; which underlines the need for nonmarket measures of intervention if sizable fractions of the world's population are to catch up in living standards over the next half century or so.

Conclusions

The globalists set up a Manichean dichotomy between pro-globalist and anti-globalist positions. My conclusions constitute a third way. I agree with the globalizers that economic growth is essential to raise the living standards of the world's poorer people (as are changes in our measures of economic growth to weigh environmental quality and public services properly). I agree that more open markets in the West for labor-intensive and land-intensive exports from developing countries would help, and that more foreign direct investment from the West, more technology transfer, is generally to be welcomed. Attempts at national self-sufficiency are foolish, though few countries apart from North Korea are trying and nobody is claiming that China would be better off if it had remained as closed as before 1978. Protectionist business associations and trade unions in the wealthiest countries, who claim that any threat to jobs must be because of "unfair competition" from elsewhere, are generally to be resisted.

I part company from the globalists in my reading of the trends in poverty and income distribution. On poverty I say that we must be agnostic, because our current statistics are too deficient to yield a confident answer (though it is quite plausible that the *proportion* of the world's population in extreme poverty has fallen in the past two decades). My weaker conclusion is that the numbers are probably higher than the World Bank says, and have probably been rising over the past two decades. On income distribution I say that world inequality is increasing when incomes are measured in current exchange rates (and this is more relevant than PPP incomes for judging the relative impacts of one part of the world on others, including the participation or marginalization of developing countries in international rule-making fora, and the ability to borrow and repay loans). Income inequality is increasing too when PPP-adjusted inequality is measured in terms of ratios of richer to poorer, which better captures the idea of polarization. All the several other combinations of measures yield more ambiguous trend results, more contingent on things like the time period and the countries included in the sample. But several recent independent studies, using different methodologies, different samples, different time periods, do find that world income inequality has risen since the early 1980s. It is simply disingenuous to keep repeating that world income distribution has become more equal as undeniable fact. Taken as a whole the evidence allows no such confidence.

Finally, absolute income gaps between the West and the rest are widening, even in the case of countries growing relatively fast like China and India, and are likely to go on widening for another half century at least. No one disputes this, but globalists tend to focus on relative incomes only. I suggested several kinds of negative effects likely to follow from widening absolute income gaps even when relative income gaps are falling.

I also part company with the globalists by giving higher priority to reductions not only in world poverty but also in world income inequality. This cannot be a direct objective of public policy, which has to focus on inequalities within nation-states or (via trade rules, aid, etc.) inequalities among states. But it can be taken as a higher level objective and built into our measures of world development. We should not accept the commonly heard assertion that widening world income inequality is not a negative provided that "real" indicators like life expectancy are improving and the proportion living in extreme poverty is going down.

I disagree with the globalist proposition that globalization is the driver of the allegedly positive poverty and inequality results. The point is not that "globalization" cannot be precisely defined for these purposes; it is that the definitions used in the globalists' studies do not stand scrutiny. In particular, the main World Bank studies, by defining globalization in terms of *increases* in trade/GDP or foreign direct investment/GDP and ignoring the level, manage to include China and India as "globalizers" or "open economies" and many highly open, trade-dependent, badly performing African countries as "nonglobalizers." Having constructed a definition of a globalized country that puts China and India into this category, the Bank does not go on to emphasize that the economic policies of the best-performing "globalizers"—China in particular—are far from the core economic policy package that it has recommended over the past two decades.

At the very least, analysts have to separate out the effect of country size on trade/GDP levels from other factors determining trade/GDP, including trade policies; and make a clear distinction between statements about (1) levels of trade, (2) changes in levels, (3) restrictiveness or openness of trade policy, and (4) changes in restrictiveness of policy. These distinctions are fudged in common globalist assertions that "openness is a necessary—though not sufficient—part of modern economic growth," or assertions that the World Bank studies referred to earlier demonstrate that "more open" economies perform better than "less open."

If global inequality is widening by plausible measures and the number of people in extreme poverty probably not falling, we cannot conclude that globalization—or the spread of free-market relations—is moving the world in the right direction, with Africa's poverty as a special case in need of international attention. The balance of probability is that—like global warming—the world is moving in the wrong direction in terms of poverty and income inequality, which strengthens the case for applying the precautionary principle and revisiting development prescriptions and the design of the international economic regime. . . .

Notes

1. *Globalization, Growth, and Poverty: Building an Inclusive World Economy,* World Bank Policy Research Report (Oxford: World Bank and Oxford University Press, 2002).
2. In this section I draw on the arguments of Dani Rodrik, *The New Global Economy and the Developing Countries: Making Openness Work,* Overseas Development Council (Washington DC: Johns Hopkins University Press, 1999); "Trading in Illusions," *Foreign Policy,* 123 (Mar./Apr. 2001).
3. Robert Wade, *Governing the Market* (Princeton: Princeton University Press, 1990).
4. Branko Milanovic, "Can We Discern the Effect of Globalization on Income Distribution? Evidence from Household Budget Surveys," World Bank Policy Research Working Paper 2876, Apr. 2002, at http://econ.worldbank.org. Milanovic finds that in countries below the average income of about $PPP5,000 higher levels of openness (imports plus exports/GDP) are associated with lower income shares of the bottom 80 percent of the population.
5. *Globalization and Development,* Economic Commission for Latin America and the Caribbean (ECLAC), Apr. 2002, Box 2.1, p. 38.
6. Michael Gestrin, Rory Knight and Alan M. Rugman, "The Templeton Global Performance Index," Templeton College, University of Oxford, 1999, 2000 and 2001, at www.templeton.ox.ac.uk.
7. This is the non-neoclassical realm of analysts such as Alfred Marshall, Allyn A. Young, Nicholas Kaldor, Gunnar Myrdal, Albert Hirschman, Arthur Lewis, Paul Krugman, and Jane Jacobs; and also Karl Marx, whose defining features of capitalism included "the centralization of capital" and "the entanglement of all peoples in the net of the world-market."
8. I draw on John Sutton, "Rich Trades, Scarce Capabilities: Industrial Development Revisited," Keynes Lecture, British Academy, Oct. 2000. Also, Ralph Gomory and William Baumol, "Toward a Theory of Industrial Policy-Retainable Industries," C. V. Starr Center for Applied Economics, New York University, RR 92–54, Dec. 1992; Michael Porter, "Clusters and the New Economics of Competition," *Harvard Business Review,* 76, no. 6 (1998), pp. 77–90; Masahisa Fujita, Paul Krugman, and Anthony Venables, *The Spatial Economy: Cities, Regions, and International Trade* (Cambridge, Mass.: MIT Press, 1999).
9. Alice H. Amsden, Ted Tschang and Akira Goto, "A New Classification of R&D Characteristics for International Comparison (with a Singapore Case Study)," Asian Development Bank Institute, Tokyo, Dec. 2001.

Why Globalization Works

Martin Wolf

Financial Times journalist Martin Wolf challenges the position of Robert Hunter Wade (preceding selection) and others who contend that globalization does not reduce poverty and inequality. He asserts that World Bank statistics demonstrate that the average incomes of people in developing countries with the highest rates of increases in international trade rose much faster than the incomes of people in developing countries where international trade rose more slowly. He classifies China and India, the two most populous countries in the world (with about 40 percent of the world's population) in the globalizing category. (Recall that Wade questions this classification.) As a result, Wolf contends, economic inequality among the world's population has diminished, even though the absolute gap between the rich and poor has increased.

Wolf observes that the particular mix of policies varies from one success story to another. But "[t]hey [all] chose, however haltingly, the path of economic liberalization and international integration." Wolf also asks what might prevent countries from pursuing progrowth policies and economic integration. One handicap, paradoxically, is what has been called the resource curse, that is, countries with abundant natural resources, such as timber or petroleum, are tempted to live off the revenue from exporting these resources. The result is that they fail to develop productive capacity and have stagnant economies. Other handicaps include predatory states (that is, corrupt states that, because they misappropriate whatever their citizens produce, discourage productive activity); geographic location in the tropics, where diseases like malaria are rampant; and poorly developed political institutions (that are often a legacy of exploitative colonial powers). To what extent and how can these handicaps be overcome? (The selection by Sachs, in Chapter 11, addresses this issue.)

. . . Globalization has not increased inequality. It has reduced it, just as it has reduced the incidence of poverty. How can this be, critics will demand? Are absolute and proportional gaps in living standards between the world's richest and poorest countries not rising all the time? Yes is the answer. And is inequality not rising in most of the world's big countries? Yes, is

---

Martin Wolf, *Why Globalization Works* (New Haven: Yale University Press, 2004): 142–150, 342–345.

again the answer. So how can global inequality be falling? To adapt Bill Clinton's campaign slogan, it is the growth, stupid. Rapid economic growth in poor countries with half the world's population has powerful effects on the only sort of inequality which matters, that among individuals. It has similarly dramatic effects on world poverty. The rise of Asia is transforming the world, very much for the better. It is the "Asian drama" of our times, to plagiarize the title of a celebrated work by a Nobel-laureate economist, the late Gunnar Myrdal.

What, the reader may ask, has this progress to do with international economic integration? In its analysis of globalization, published in 2002, the World Bank divided seventy-three developing countries, with aggregate population, in 1997, of 4 billion (80 per cent of all people in developing countries), into two groups: the third that had increased ratios of trade to GDP, since 1980, by the largest amount and the rest.[1] The former group, with an aggregate population of 2.9 billion, managed a remarkable combined increase of 104 per cent in the ratio of trade to GDP. Over the same period, the increase in the trade ratio of the high-income countries was 71 per cent, while the 'less globalized' two-thirds of countries in the sample of developing countries experienced a decline in their trade ratios.

The average incomes per head of these twenty-four globalizing countries rose by 67 per cent (a compound rate of 3.1 per cent a year) between 1980 and 1997. In contrast, the other forty-nine countries managed a rise of only 10 per cent (a compound rate of 0.5 per cent a year) in incomes per head over this period. As Table 1 shows, these more globalized countries did not have particularly high levels of

Table 1

Characteristics of more globalized and less globalized developing economies (population-weighted average)

Socioeconomic characteristics	More globalized (24)	Less globalized (49)
Population, 1997 (billions)	2.9	1.1
Per-capita GDP, 1980	$1,488	$1,947
Per-capita GDP, 1997	$2,485	$2,133
Compound annual growth rate of GDP per head, 1980–1997	3.1%	0.5%
Rule of law index, 1997 (world average = 0)	−0.04	−0.48
Average years primary schooling, 1980	2.4	2.5
Average years primary schooling, 1997	3.8	3.1
Average years secondary schooling, 1980	0.8	0.7
Average years secondary schooling, 1997	1.3	1.3
Average years tertiary schooling, 1980	0.08	0.09
Average years tertiary schooling, 1997	0.18	0.22

Source: World Bank, *Globalization, Growth & Poverty: Building an Inclusive World Economy* (Washington DC: World Bank, 2002), Table 1.1.

education in 1980. At that time, they were also a little poorer, as a group, than the rest. Subsequently, the new globalizers, as the World Bank calls them, cut their import tariffs by 34 percentage points, on average, against 11 percentage points for the other group. They also achieved a better reading on the rule of law than the others. The World Bank's conclusion is that, "as they reformed and integrated with the world market, the 'more globalized' developing countries started to grow rapidly, accelerating steadily from 2.9 per cent in the 1970s to 5 per cent in the 1990s."[2]

While what the Bank says is both true and important, it should be observed that its notion of a group of twenty-four countries is something of a fiction. China and India contain, between them, 75 per cent of the group's combined population. With Brazil, Bangladesh, Mexico, the Philippines and Thailand, one has 92 per cent of the group's population. Moreover, Asian countries dominate: they make up 85 per cent of the population of this group of globalizing countries.

What then do we learn from the success of the countries picked out as globalizers by the World Bank? We can say, with confidence, that the notion that international economic integration necessarily makes the rich richer and the poor poorer is nonsense. Here is a wide range of countries that increased their integration with the world economy and prospered, in some cases dramatically so. A subtler question . . . is precisely what policies relatively successful developing countries have followed. Critics are right to argue that success has not required adoption of the full range of so-called "neo-liberal" policies—privatization, free trade and capital-account liberalization. But, in insisting upon this point, critics are wilfully mistaking individual policy trees for the market-oriented forest. What the successful countries all share is a move towards the market economy, one in which private property rights, free enterprise and competition increasingly took the place of state ownership, planning and protection. They chose, however haltingly, the path of economic liberalization and international integration. This is the heart of the matter. All else is commentary.

If one compares the China of today with the China of Mao Zedong or the India of today with the India of Indira Gandhi, the contrasts are overwhelming. Market forces have been allowed to operate in ways that would have been not just unthinkable but criminal a quarter of a century ago. Under Mao, economic freedom had been virtually eliminated. Under the Indian control system, no significant company was allowed to produce, invest or import without government permission. From this starting-point, much of the most important liberalization was, necessarily and rightly, internal. Given where it was in the 1970s, liberalizing agriculture alone started China on the path towards rapid development. Similarly, eliminating the more absurd controls on industry permitted an acceleration in Indian economic growth. In both cases then these initial reforms and the abundance of cheap and hard-working labour guaranteed accelerated growth.

Yet in neither case can the contribution of economic integration be ignored. This is spectacularly true of China. The volume of China's exports grew at 13 per cent a year between 1980 and 1990 and then at 11 per cent between 1990 and 1999. Between 1990 and 2000 the ratio of trade in goods to Chinese GDP, at market prices, jumped from 33 to 44 per cent, an extraordinarily high ratio for such a large economy. The ratio of merchandise trade to output of goods in the economy rose from 47 per cent to 66 per cent over the same period.[3] In 2001, China's gross merchandise exports of $266 billion amounted to 4.3 per cent of the world total, up from a mere 0.7 per cent in 1977.[4] By that year, China was the world's sixth largest merchandise exporter (including intra-European Union trade in the total), just behind the UK, but already ahead of Canada and Italy. Meanwhile, private capital flows into China jumped from 3 per cent of GDP in 1990 to 13 per cent in 2000. By 2001, the stock of inward foreign direct investment in China was $395 billion, 6 per cent of the world's total, up from $25 billion in 1990. In 2000, inward direct investment financed 11 per cent of the giant's gross fixed capital formation, while foreign affiliates generated 31 per cent of China's manufacturing sales and, more astonishingly, 50 per cent of its exports.[5] It is possible to argue that China's dramatic economic growth somehow had nothing to do with its headlong rush into the global market economy. But it would be absurd to do so.

India's integration was much less spectacular. So, not coincidentally, was its growth. Yet here, too, the change was palpable. India's volume of merchandise exports fell in the 1980s, which contributed mightily to the foreign exchange crisis that brought to an end its overwhelmingly inward-looking liberalization of the 1980s. But export volume rose at 5.3 per cent a year between 1990 and 1999, after external liberalization had begun. India's share in world merchandise exports had fallen from 2.1 per cent in 1951 to a low of 0.4 per cent in 1980. But by 2001 this share was modestly back up, to 0.7 per cent, putting it in thirtieth place globally. Between 1990 and 2000, the share of trade in goods also rose from 13 to 20 per cent of GDP. India did achieve a significant success in exports of commercial services (particularly software). By 2001, its exports of such services were $20 billion, almost half as much as its $44 billion in merchandise exports. Its share in world exports of commercial services was 1.4 per cent, double its share in exports of goods, while its rank in the world was nineteenth, though even here it was behind China's exports of $33 billion (2.3 per cent of the world total). India also lagged in openness to inward direct investment, which only reached $3.4 billion in 2001. But even this was close to revolutionary in a country that had, for decades, discouraged all inward FDI. In 1990, the total stock of inward FDI was a mere $1.7 billion. By 2001, it had reached $22 billion. The 1990s were, in all, India's most economically successful post-independence decade. They were also the decade in which the country liberalized both internal and external transactions and increased its integration into the global economy. An accident? Hardly.

Now consider an even more fascinating example in the Bank's list of globalizing economies—Bangladesh, certainly the poorest sizeable country in the world in the 1970s and, as I remember well, almost universally deemed a hopeless case. Even this country has benefited from international economic integration. The GDP per head of Bangladesh rose at 2.3 per cent a year between 1975 and 2001, generating a 60 per cent rise in real income per head over more than a quarter of a century. Between 1990 and 2001, GDP per head grew considerably faster, at 3.1 per cent a year, as the economy opened. In 1975, Bangladesh's real GDP per head (measured at purchasing power parity) was roughly half that of sub-Saharan Africa.

By 2000, its real GDP per head was close to the average level of sub-Saharan Africa. In the 1980s, Bangladesh's volume of merchandise exports barely rose. In the 1990s, it rose at a remarkable 15 per cent a year. Between 1990 and 2000, the ratio of exports to GDP jumped from 18 to 32 per cent. The volume of trade also grew 6 percentage points a year faster than GDP in the decade. Bangladesh did not suddenly become a magnet for foreign direct investment. That is hardly surprising, since it has been ranked bottom of seventy-five countries in the cost of corruption.[6] But the stock of inward direct investment did reach $1.1 billion by 2001, up from $150 million in 1990. Even for Bangladesh, international economic integration has paid off. It is only a start. But it is, at least, that.

If a successful move to the market, including increasing integration in the world economy, explains the success stories of the past two decades, what explains the failures, that is, those which have failed to take advantage of the opportunities for global economic integration? Failure to develop has involved a complex interplay of institutions, endowments and policies.

Emphasis on institutions and their evolution has, quite properly, become a dominant focus of analysts of development. It is discovered, not surprisingly, that poor performers have corrupt, predatory or brutal governments or, sometimes even worse, no government at all, but rather civil war among competing warlords.[7] The failure of the state to provide almost any of the services desperately needed for development is at the root of the African disaster. This reflects both the artificiality of the states and the weak—if not non-existent—sense of moral responsibility of Africa's "big men." Mobutu's Zaire was perhaps the most catastrophic example. But he was also one of many. Today, Robert Mugabe's destruction of once-prosperous Zimbabwe is almost equally horrifying.[8] An even more depressing case is that of sub-Sahara's giant, Nigeria. Today, Nigeria's GDP per head, at PPP, is the same as it was in 1970, despite three decades of abundant oil revenues, all of which has been wasted in foolish public spending and capital flight. The proportion of Nigeria's population in extreme poverty (real incomes of less than a dollar a day, at PPP) has doubled over this period. The élite has been predatory in the extreme: in 2000, the top 2 per cent had the same income as the bottom 55 per cent.[9] Much of Nigeria's wealth has been squirrelled away abroad. Alas, Nigeria is merely an extreme case. It is estimated that about 40 per cent of Africa's private wealth was held overseas by 1990. But bad governments have also failed to provide the infrastructure on which development depends. As a result, African countries trade even less with one another and the rest of the world than would be predicted from their adverse locations.[10]

The second obstacle to development is a country's natural endowments. There is much evidence that location in the tropics is a handicap, though whether this is only via the impact on the evolution of countries' institutions, or independently, remains controversial. The probability is that it is a bit of both. Debilitating diseases have long been rife in the tropics. But it is also true that colonial regimes tended to create predatory institutions in their tropical possessions.[11] Distance from the sea is also a handicap and particularly being landlocked. The disadvantages faced by the landlocked—a natural form of protection against foreign trade—also underline the costs of nonglobalization.[12]

Endowments enter into development in another way, as resources. Natural resources, especially mineral wealth, seem to be an obstacle, not a spur, to economic development. This "resource curse" has many dimensions: resources tend to corrupt politics, turning it into a race to seize the incomes produced by resources, often generating debilitating civil wars; they generate unstable terms of trade, because prices of natural resources or agricultural commodities fluctuate widely; and they produce a high real exchange rate that, among other things, hinders development of internationally competitive manufacturing.[13]

Data on real GDP per head show that developing countries with few natural resources grew two to three times faster between 1960 and 1990 than countries with abundant natural resources. The World Bank demonstrates that no fewer than forty-five countries experienced "unsustained growth" over the past four decades: they matched their 1999 level of real income per head in a previous decade, many as far back as the 1960s. All but six of these countries possess "point-source natural resources"—oil or minerals. Nigeria is one example of a country ruined by an abundance of oil. Angola is another: its GDP per head is lower today than it was in 1960.[14] So much, by the way, for the view that what countries need for successful development is more aid. If foreign resources were all that was needed to make a country rich, Angola and Nigeria would not be in the state they are in.[15]

Even where natural resources do not generate corrupt, rent-seeking societies, they can be an obstacle to sustained development. In the post-war era, the most successful route to development seems to have been via the export of labour-intensive manufactures, the route on which China has followed Hong Kong, Singapore, Taiwan and South Korea. The success of developing countries with exports of manufactures has been astonishing: in 1980 only 25 per cent of the merchandise exports of developing countries were manufactures. By 1998, this had risen to 80 per cent. The old view in which developing countries exported commodities in return for manufactures is entirely outmoded. Today, they are just as likely to export manufactures (and services, too, since their share in total exports of developing countries has risen to 17 per cent, from 9 per cent in the early 1980s) in return for commodities.[16]

The path of manufactures offers a number of significant advantages. World markets for manufactures, while not free, have been relatively open and dynamic. Markets for agricultural commodities have either been slow-growing and price-insensitive (as for the classic tropical commodities—cocoa, tea and coffee), highly protected in the world's most important markets (as for temperate agricultural commodities), or both (as for sugar). Manufactures also offer a natural ladder up the chain of comparative advantage. A country that has specialized in natural-resource exports will find it hard to shift into competitive manufactures as it must break into world markets after having already achieved quite high real wages and, correspondingly, must do so at relatively high levels of productivity. Since there is learning-by-doing (and other spillovers) in manufacturing, achieving this transition to exports of manufactures can be tricky at relatively high wages. The transition can be thwarted altogether by policies of blanket protection used, as they were in Argentina and other resource-rich countries, to spread resource rents to a politically influential working class. The task is not hopeless: the U.S. itself is an example of such a transition, successfully completed a century or so ago. More recently, Chile has had great success with a path based on commodity exports.

A final aspect of resources is human resources, both latent and overt. Under latent resources are the underlying cultural and behavioural assumptions of a society—its software, so to speak. Under overt human resources is the level of education achieved by the population. It cannot be altogether an accident that the most successful region of the world, after Europe and the British offshoots in the New World, is east Asia, long home to sophisticated agrarian states, with established bureaucratic cultures and developed mercantile traditions. From this point of view, sub-Saharan Africa has been doubly handicapped, long isolated from Eurasia, still enveloped in tribal traditions and lacking a sizeable number of highly educated people at the time of independence, when many mistakes were made.

Finally, there are policies. If all that mattered were endowments and institutions, one would never have seen sudden take-offs by some countries in response to policy changes. But the rapid growth of South Korea and Taiwan in the 1960s only followed a move to realistic exchange rates and export promotion. The mistakes repeatedly made by other countries have included overvalued real exchange rates, often used to suppress the inflationary consequences of fiscal imprudence (as in Zimbabwe today), creation of corrupt and incompetent public sector monopolies in vital areas, such as electric power generation and distribution or marketing of export commodities; and high and variable protection against imports, often via corruption-fuelling controls. How much these mistakes matter tends to depend on a country's comparative advantage. If a country possesses a supply of very cheap and highly motivated labour, as China does today, it seems easier to survive mistakes (and institutional failings) that would cripple an Argentina or a Mexico. Nevertheless, it was only after a series of reforms that China began to integrate into the world economy. Countries without China's human resources must try even harder to get policy right.

Growth and Inequality

Now what does the performance of those who have succeeded in growing through economic integration mean for inequality? Inequality is a measure of relative incomes. If the average real incomes of poor countries containing at least half of the world's population have been rising faster than those of the relatively rich, inequality among countries, weighted by population, will have fallen. This will be true even if the ratio of the incomes of the world's richest to the world's poorest countries and the absolute gaps in average incomes per head between rich countries and almost all developing countries have risen (as they have).

These two points may need a little explanation. First, compare, say, the U.S. with China. Between 1980 and 2000, according to the World Bank, Chinese average real incomes rose by about 440 per cent. Over the same period, U.S. average real incomes per head rose by about 60 per cent. The ratio of Chinese real incomes per head, at purchasing power parity, to those of the U.S. rose, accordingly, from just over 3 per cent in 1980 to just under 12 per cent in 2000. This is a big reduction in relative inequality. But the absolute gap in real incomes between China and the U.S. rose from $20,600 to $30,200 per head (at PPP). The reason is simple: since China's standard of living was, initially, about a thirtieth of that of the U.S., the absolute gap could have remained constant only if China's growth had been thirty times faster than that of the U.S. That would have been impossible. If China continues to grow faster than the U.S., however, absolute gaps will ultimately fall, as happened with Japan in the 1960s and 1970s.

Second, while the *ratio* of the average incomes per head in the richest country to those in the world's least successful countries is rising all the time, the *proportion* of the world's population living in the world's poorest countries has, happily, been falling. Thirty years ago, China and India were among the world's poorest countries. Today, the poorest seems to be Sierra Leone, a country with a population of only 5 million. China's average real income per head is now some ten times higher than Sierra Leone's. The largest very poor country today is Nigeria, with a population of 127 million in 2000 and a real income, at PPP, just a fortieth of that of the U.S. (and a fifth of China's). Again, this means that rising ratios between the average incomes of the world's richest and poorest countries are consistent with declining inequality among countries, weighted by their populations. Moreover, it is also perfectly possible for inequality to have risen in every single country in the world . . . while global inequality has fallen. Unless the increase in inequality among individuals within countries offsets the reduction in population-weighted inequality among countries, not only inequality among (population-weighted) countries, but also inequality among individuals will have declined.

Andrea Boltho of Oxford University and Gianni Toniolo of Rome University have computed population-weighted inequality among forty-nine countries that contain 80 per cent of the world's population, back to 1900. . . .[17] They conclude that inequality among countries, weighted in this way, reached its maximum in 1980, at a value of 0.54, but has fallen by 9 per cent since then, to 0.50, a level not seen since some six decades ago. This decline in inequality among countries, weighted by their population size, is exactly what one would expect. . . .

Notes

1. World Bank, *Globalization, Growth & Poverty: Building an Inclusive World Economy* (Washington DC: 2002), Table 1.1, p. 34.
2. *Ibid.*, p. 36.
3. These data are from World Bank, *World Development Indicators 2002* (Washington DC: World Bank, 2002).
4. World Trade Organization, *International Trade Statistics 2002* (Geneva: WTO, 2002), and T.N. Srinivasan, *Eight Lectures on India's Economic Reforms* (New York: Oxford University Press, 2000), p. 73, for the data on China in the 1970s and a comparison between China and India.
5. United Nations Conference on Trade and Development, *World Investment Report 2002: Transnational Corporations and Export Competitiveness* (New York: United Nations, 2002).
6. World Economic Forum, *The Global Competitiveness Report 2001–02* (New York: Oxford University Press, 2002).

7. See, on the role of government, particularly chapter 5, Martin Wolf, *Why Globalization Works*.
8. See, on this, Johan Norberg's splendid tract, *In Defence of Global Capitalism* (Timbro, 2001), pp. 102 and, more generally, 98–113.
9. See, for example, Xavier Sala-I-Martin and Arvind Subramanian, "Addressing the Natural Resource Curse: An Illustration from Nigeria," May 2003, mimeo.
10. See World Bank, *Globalization, Growth & Poverty*, pp. 38–40.
11. See, on this debate, Daron Acemoglu, Simon Johnson and James A. Robinson, 'Reversal of Fortune: Geography and Institutions in the Making of the Modern World Income Distribution', National Bureau of Economic Research Working Paper 8460, 2001, and *Quarterly Journal of Economics*, Vol. 117; William Easterly and Ross Levine, 'Tropics, Germs and Crops: How Endowments Influence Economic Development', National Bureau of Economic Research Working Paper 9106, August 2002; and Jeffrey D. Sachs, 'Institutions Don't Rule: Direct Effects of Geography on Per Capita Income', National Bureau of Economic Research Working Paper 9490, February 2003. The first of these papers emphasizes the role of colonial history in explaining the poverty of previously wealthy tropical countries. The second argues that location affects development only through institutions. The third argues against the second the case of malaria, a tropical disease with a directly negative impact on development.
12. A study that brought out the benefits of trade by focusing on natural barriers of distance is: Jeffrey Frankel and David Romer, 'Does Trade Cause Growth?', *American Economic Review*, June 1999.
13. See, on the resource curse, specifically, Alan Gelb and associates, *Oil Windfalls: Blessing or Curse?* (New York: Oxford University Press, for the World Bank, 1989), Jeffrey Sachs and Andrew Warner, 'Natural Resource Abundance and Economic Growth' Harvard Institute for International Development (November 1997), Ricardo Hausmann and Roberto Rigobon, 'An Alternative Interpretation of the "Resource Curse": Theory and Policy Implications', National Bureau of Economic Research Working Paper 9424, December 2002, and Sala-I-Martin and Subramanian, 'Addressing the Natural Resource Curse'. On the argument that natural resources generate civil wars, see Paul Collier and A. Höffler, 'Greed and Grievance in African Civil Wars', *Quarterly Journal of Economics* (forthcoming).
14. See, on the role of resources in development, World Bank, *World Development Report 2003: Sustainable Development in a Dynamic World: Transforming Institutions, Growth and Quality of Life* (New York: Oxford University Press, for the World Bank, 2003), pp. 148–56.
15. The great critic of foreign aid was, of course, the late Peter (Lord) Bauer. See, for example, 'Foreign Aid: Abiding Issues', in *From Subsistence to Exchange and Other Essays* (Princeton: Princeton University Press, for the Cato Institute, 2000), chapter V.
16. See World Bank, *Globalization, Growth & Poverty*, pp. 32–3.
17. Data come from Angus Maddison, *Monitoring the World Economy, 1820–1992* (Paris: Development Centre of the Organization for Economic Co-operation and Development, 1995 and 1998) and the International Monetary Fund's *World Economic Outlook*. See Andrea Boltho and Gianni Toniolo, 'The Assessment: The Twentieth Century—Achievements, Failures, Lessons', *Oxford Review of Economic Policy*, Vol. 15, No. 4 (Winter 1999), pp. 1–17, Table 4.

ARTICLE 4.4

In Defense of Globalization

Jagdish Bhagwati

Economist Jagdish Bhagwati is among the most distinguished and spirited supporters of globalization. In this selection, he challenges the argument that globalization tends to increase economic inequalities. Bhagwati maintains that what counts is not the impact of globalization on inequality but its impact on poverty reduction. Those in need are not harmed by increased inequality, whereas they are deeply benefited by an improvement in their own situation—even if it is part of changes that produce greater economic inequalities. If one applies this commonsense standard, he claims that the statistics are crystal clear. Bhagwati's position is supported by Dollar and Kraay, in their selection in this chapter—and challenged by Sen (Chapter 2), Milanovic (Chapter 3), and Wade (Chapter 4).

What are the strengths and weaknesses of the two sides? What is your position?

Exploitation of Workers?

If any conviction strongly unites the critics of multinationals today, . . . it is that they exploit the workers in the poor countries. At first blush this sounds very strange, since firms that create job opportunities should be applauded, no matter that their motivation in investing abroad is to make profits, not to do good. . . .

So why are the critics agitated? Much of their ire has been aroused by their assumption that the multinationals, so rich and with such deep pockets, pay such low wages. Then there is also the related assertion, including by the leaders of the anti-sweatshop movement on U.S. campuses, that multinationals run sweatshops in the poor countries. Sweatshops are accused of paying "unfair" or "inadequate" or "low" wages, often of not paying a "living wage." More often, they are condemned for violating "labor rights."

Wages and Exploitation

That multinationals exploit workers in the poor countries by paying low wages is the most frequent and least persuasive charge. The typical critique asserts that if a Liz Claiborne jacket sells for $190 in New York while the female worker abroad who sews it gets only 90 cents an hour, it is obviously exploitation.[1]

But there is surely no necessary relationship between the price of a specific product and the wage paid by a company that can be interpreted in this accusatory fashion. Just for starters, for every jacket that succeeds, there are probably nine that do not. So the effective price of jacket one must consider is a tenth of the successful jacket: only $19, not $190. Then again, owing to distribution costs, and in the case of apparel tariff duties, the price of a jacket almost doubles between landing in New York and finding its way to Lord & Taylor's display hangers.

But that is not all. Consider the diamond polishing industry in the town of Surat, India, which has witnessed rising prosperity ever since Surat has become a rival to Antwerp in this business. If the final price of the diamond in Paris is a million dollars, even a wage payment of $10 an hour and total wage payment to the worker of $1,000 will appear minuscule as a fraction of the final price. But so what?

Again, I have heard people argue that wages in Jakarta or Phnom Penh are a pittance compared to Michael Jordan's multimillion-dollar advertising remuneration by Nike. But it is inappropriate to compare a company's advertising budget with the wage rate or even the wage bill: it proves nothing, certainly not exploitation under any plausible and persuasive definition.

A possible question of interest may be whether Nike and other multinationals are earning huge monopoly profits while paying their workers only a competitive wage, and whether these firms should share these "excess" profits with their workers. But, as it happens, nearly all multinationals such as Liz Claiborne and Nike are in fiercely competitive environments. A recent study of the profits performance of 214 companies in the 1999 Fortune Global 500 list showed a rather sorry performance—about 8.3 percent on foreign assets, and even a decline to 6.6 percent in 1998.[2] Where is the beef that might be shared with workers?

So let me turn to the question of low wages. Are the multinationals paying their workers wages that are *below* what these workers get in alternative occupations in what are really poor countries with low wages? This is virtually implied by the critics. We must ask if this is really true or whether the multinationals are actually paying higher wages than the workers would get elsewhere—say, from local firms in the industry or in alternative jobs.

If the wages received are actually *higher* than those available in alternative jobs, even if low according to the critics (and reflective of the poverty in the poor countries), surely it seems odd to say that the multinationals are exploiting the workers they are hiring! Now, if there were slavery elsewhere and the workers were being whipped daily, as the Romans did with the galley slaves, then the fact that multinationals were whipping them only every other day would hardly turn away the critics! But wages are another matter, obviously. So what are the facts on wage payments?

As it happens, several empirical studies do find that multinationals pay what economists now call a "wage premium": they pay an average wage that exceeds the going rate, mostly up to 10 percent and exceeding it in some cases, with affiliates of U.S. multinationals sometimes paying a premium that ranges from 40 to 100 percent.[3] The University of Michigan economist Linda Lim has reviewed much of the available evidence from a number of studies in Bangladeshi export processing zones, in Mexico, in Shanghai, in Indonesia, and in Vietnam, and reports that they overwhelmingly confirm the existence of such a premium.[4]

In one of the careful and convincing studies, the economist Paul Glewwe, using Vietnamese household data for 1997–98, was able to isolate and focus on the incomes of workers employed in foreign-owned firms, joint ventures, and wholly Vietnamese-owned enterprises. About half of the Vietnamese workers in the study worked in precisely the foreign-owned textile or leather firms that so often come in for criticism. Contrary to the steady refrain from the critics—some of whom man websites continually directed at Nike, for instance—Glewwe found that "workers in foreign-owned enterprises fare better, making an average of 42 cents per hour," almost twice that of the average wage earner. Glewwe concludes:

> Overall, the evidence shows that these workers [in foreign-owned enterprises] are better off than the average Vietnamese worker. . . . The data also show that people who obtained employment in foreign-owned enterprises and joint ventures in Vietnam in the 1990s experience increases in household income (as measured by per capita consumption expenditures) that exceeded the average increases for all Vietnamese households. This appears to contradict the claims that foreign-owned enterprises in poor countries such as Vietnam are "sweatshops." On the other hand, it is clear that the wages paid by these enterprises . . . are a fraction of wages paid in the U.S. and other wealthy countries. Yet Vietnam is so poor that it is better for a Vietnamese person to obtain this kind of employment than almost any other kind available in Vietnam.[5]

In fact, econometric studies have tried to explain why this premium exists by controlling for scale, worker quality, age of the establishment, and other differences among the firms being compared; the premium, while diminished, still persists. There is also some evidence that this irreducible premium reflects higher productivity in firms under foreign ownership.[6]

What about subcontracting by multinationals? There does not appear to be any significant evidence, that these subcontractors pay less than the going wage in domestic firms and in alternative jobs. It is likely, however, that the wages paid are closer to these alternatives; the wage premium is possibly negligible, if it obtains at all, in subcontracted work.

In both cases, whether there is direct employment at a wage premium by the multinationals or subcontracted employment at a negligible premium, these are only direct or proximate effects. By adding to the demand for labor in the host countries, multinationals are also overwhelmingly likely to improve wages all around, thus improving the incomes of the workers in these countries.

Labor Rights

But if the wage argument against multinationals must be dismissed, there is still the accusation that these corporations violate labor rights. One view is that local labor laws are violated on safety and other working conditions. Another is that the conditions at work violate not domestic laws in the host countries but customary international law. Both critiques raise difficulties.

At the outset, it is highly unlikely that multinational firms would violate domestic regulatory laws, which generally are not particularly demanding. Since the laws are often not burdensome in poor countries, it is hard to find evidence that violations are taking place in an egregious, even substantial fashion. Ironically, sweatshops exist in the New York garment district (*not* in Guatemala, mind you), where the laws *are* demanding and simultaneously the ability of the affected workers to invoke them is impaired, as in the case of illegal immigrant workers.

Moreover, sweatshops are typically small-scale workshops, not multinationals. If the subcontractors who supply parts to the multinationals, for example, are tiny enterprises, it is possible that they, like local entrepreneurs, violate legislation from time to time. But since the problem lies with lack of effective enforcement in the host country, do we hold multinationals accountable for anything that they buy from these countries, even if it is not produced directly by the multinationals? That is tantamount to saying that the multinationals must effectively boycott anything that is produced and sold by countries where labor laws are not enforced effectively. But then why impose this obligation only on the multinationals? Surely it should apply equally to all citizens and legal entities in countries whose multinationals are being asked to indulge in the boycott of the offending country. This means going to the ILO to invoke Article 35 (which permits serious censure) or, better still, to the United Nations to invoke Article 7 on embargos. Short of that, the demands on the multinationals are incoherent.

Second, the insistence that local laws be enforced raises two questions. First, what is effective enforcement? What resources must be spent? The expenditure by the United States itself on enforcement against violations of OSHA and labor regulations has been minuscule; does that mean that multinationals investing in the United States must cease operation in this country? More important, the demand that local laws be enforced flies in the face of political practice in many democratic countries. It is important to see why.

Typically, one encounters two dominant practices in regard to social legislation: either there are no laws or there are many excessively generous ones. The lack-of-enforcement critique applies naturally to the latter situation. But then we must ask why the legislation is not enforced. The most likely reason is that there was no intention to enforce the legislation in the first place. Often extraordinarily expensive provisions are mandated simply because the enforcement is going to be negligible. Thus, as a wit once said, progressive taxes are enacted to please the Democrats and the loopholes are put in to please the Republicans. In the same spirit, countries such as India have some of the most progressive, and expensive, legislation on the books concerning even minimum wages, but with no real intention to enforce it precisely because the cost of such mandates would be forbidding. So the generosity of these provisions in the face of acutely limited resources is simply meant to produce a good feeling—the legislators mean well, but beyond that, alas. . . . In fact, why not offer yet more generous benefits to the workers? I recall the Nobel laureate Robert Solow, a famous wit, being told that Harvard's highest salary was $150,000 but that no one was being paid it. In that case, he replied, why not say that the highest salary was $250,000?

Indeed, legislation may often be dated, and people may have changed their minds about its advisability, but the political battle to drop or modify it would be too expensive, so the legislation remains but is ignored. Thus, New Hampshire reportedly still has anti-adultery statutes on the books, but they are dead like a skunk in deep snow.

Often, however, it is not the violation of domestic law that is at issue. It is rather that the practice of multinationals, even when in conformity to local legislation, does not meet the demands of customary international law. When asked to explain customary international law, the activists refer to ILO conventions on workers, the covenants on civil and political rights at the United Nations, and other norms established at international agencies and conferences, whether universally adopted or not. This route to condemning multinationals is predictably quite problematic, however.

For one thing, the domestic regulation may be less demanding than these international norms for good reasons, in both economics and ethics. Take the case of working hours, which can be quite long in the EPZs and suggest exploitation that violates what an activist may consider to be human rights norms. But Nicholas Kristof and Sheryl WuDunn of the *New York Times* . . . have pointed out in an essay in the *New York Times Magazine*, provocatively titled "Two Cheers for Sweatshops," that the young women who work long hours are often doing so voluntarily. Why? Because many want to make as quickly as possible the money they planned to earn and then return to their homes. And, like many of us who work long hours, they are not being exploited; they drive themselves.[7] . . .

Indeed, even the restraints put on union rights in export processing zones, which are considered violations of customary international law, need to be reassessed, and possibly condoned rather than criticized, when this is done in democratic poor countries. Even governments that will not tolerate draconian mistreatment of union activists and have legislation protective and supportive of union rights such as the ability to organize will put some restraints in place in EPZs. Why? Because when unions assert rights but object to obligations, as when one cannot discipline or fire workers who hold down two jobs and collect pay while working elsewhere—a common practice in parts of India, for example—and one cannot reform them, it is tempting to think of carving out little EPZs where unions do not exist, just as the free-traders who cannot reduce trade barriers due to political obstacles then think of EPZs, where free trade obtains. As Saburo Okita, one of Japan's leading internationalists and an architect of Japan's postwar recovery, once told me when he was looking at India's self-imposed economic follies, if only India could take half a dozen small areas the size of Hong Kong and turn them into EPZs that followed the outward-oriented Hong Kong polices, while the bulk of India continued to wallow in its inward-looking inefficiencies; it would only take a couple of decades for these EPZs to overtake the rest of India!

In short, it is really the wish to escape unions, because in the country's experience they act only to enjoy rights and accept no obligations, that drives these governments to say, "Let the EPZs have no unions, for the only kind we will get are those that do harm rather than good." This is certainly not the same as saying,

"We do not want unions, and we will even break them brutally!" As it happens, India, which also has gone in for EPZs, has maintained union rights but with one proviso: that wild-cat strikes are not allowed in the EPZs, the rationale being that export industries are "essential" industries, an exception that is allowed even in the rich Western nations, including the United States.

What worries me also is that customary international law is often quite broadly stated (e.g., gender discrimination, which can be defined in several ways, is not permissible), much like domestic constitutions and unlike legislation and executive orders (e.g., that red mercury is not to be discharged into lakes, rivers, and oceans), which are much more narrowly stated and hence clear to follow. How is the multinational then to follow "laws" that are not legislated but are norms, and which can be interpreted in so many different ways that whether you conform to them depends on who does the interpretation?

Thus today nations have agreed to, and many have ratified, conventions dealing with so-called core labor rights. These are contained in the ILO Declaration of Fundamental Principles and Rights at Work:

- Freedom of association and the effective recognition of the right to collective bargaining
- The elimination of all forms of forced or compulsory labor
- The effective abolition of child labor
- The elimination of discrimination in respect of employment and occupation

But once one gets down to brass tacks, difficulties arise. Take the simple injunction about the freedom of association—that is, the right to unionize. How is one to cope with the fact that this right has several nuances and dimensions (and that virtually all countries could be found in violation of it in some way)? Central to this right is the ability to strike; a union without an effective right to strike is almost like a paper tiger. But . . . for half a century the Taft-Hartley law's provisions have allowed the hiring of replacement workers and discouraged sympathetic strikes, and this has badly crippled U.S. unions' ability to strike. [A] Human Rights Watch report concluded, therefore, that "millions of workers" in the United States were denied the "freedom of association."[8] Human Rights Watch and I consider this quite a reasonable interpretation of the violation of the core agreement to respect the right to unionize, but will this interpretation be accepted or rejected for the purpose of enforcement and litigation?[9] And who will bring action against what must be all corporations in the United States, because they are all acting under these legal provisions that are judged to violate this core right agreed at the ILO?

A similar problem can be shown to arise in the case of gender discrimination, yet another core labor right. There is no society today that is free from gender discrimination in some form. Besides . . . even something narrower, such as pay discrimination, can be diversely defined. So how does a broad statement of these core rights, interpreted as customary international law for the purpose at hand, work?

My view is that we do need to assert these broad aspirational objectives but that, for purposes of assessing whether corporations in the poor countries are to be condemned (and even litigated against, as is beginning to happen in U.S. courts), we need to arrive at much narrower and more realistic agreements on specific practices.[10] For instance, on the right to unionize, we could reach agreement today on outlawing the killing of union leaders, but not on whether replacement workers can be hired or whether the firing of workers is allowed for economic or disciplinary reasons. Agreement could be reached, I suspect, on minimum safety provisions (e.g., the issuance of goggles to foundry workers working near blast furnaces, and enforcement of the use), though not on rich-country, OSHA standards that are very expensive for poor countries. In short, just as there is virtual agreement that torture in the shape of pulling someone's fingernails out is unacceptable (there is less on whether torture through the use of isolation and significant deprivation of sleep should be permissible), it should be possible to find areas of agreement on narrowly specific practices that may be proscribed. We could then move to bring in yet others. In short, start narrow and go broad. If you start broad and seek to use NGOs and courts to object to narrowly specific practices, you are likely to create a world of subjective interpretations and unpredictable outcomes. It will produce chaos and, in fact, imperil the flow of international investment by adding serious uncertainty and risk of expensive litigation by zealous activists peddling their preferred interpretation of the core right that they allege to have been violated by the multinational defendant.

The argument that customary international law, interpreted broadly, should be used to say that multinationals are exploiting workers in the poor countries is therefore open to serious criticism. The anti-Nike and other campaigns, which allege that these multinationals do not pay a living wage or do not have OSHA standards in their factories, are little more than assertions of what these specific critics would like a corporation to do, even when customary international law and norms are invoked to justify such accusations. It is perfectly possible and proper for others, equally motivated to do good, to say that these demands will harm rather than help the workers in these poor countries by raising the cost of production and thus making the inward flow of investment and jobs less likely. If so, these critics are themselves in unwitting violation of perhaps the most important core value: that globalization, and multinationals, should help the working class, not harm it! . . .

Notes

1. This precise estimate, and the inference of exploitation, were the central contention, in a letter to the editor in the *Financial Times* (written in response to my defense of Nike in an op-ed piece in the same newspaper) by Eileen Applebaum, who held a senior professional position on the staff of the Economic Policy Institute, a liberal-left think tank in Washington D.C. See Eileen Applebaum, "Unsuitable Wages Comparison," *Financial Times*, May 5, 2000.
2. The study was conducted at Templeton College, Oxford University.

3. See Edward M. Graham, *Fighting the Wrong Enemy: Antiglobal Activists and Multinational Enterprises* (Washington, D.C.: Institute for International Economics, 2000).
4. Linda Lim, *The Globalization Debate: Issues and Challenges* (Geneva: International Labor Organization, 2001). In addition, there are several econometric studies of the reasons for the wage premium, which also produce further evidence of a wage premium in Mexico, Venezuela, and Indonesia, by economists such as Robert Feenstra, Gordon Hanson, and Ann Harrison. These econometric studies are reviewed in Drusilla Brown, Alan Deardorff, and Robert Stern, "The Effects of Multinational Enterprises on Wages and Working Conditions in Developing Countries," March 11, 2002, available at http://www.econ.kuleuven.ac.be/ew/academic/intecon/home/WorkingGroupSeminars/Files/Deardorff.pdf.
5. Paul Glewwe, "Are Foreign-Owned Businesses in Viet Nam Really Sweatshops?" University of Minnesota, 1999.
6. For Venezuela, see Brian Aiken and Ann Harrison, "Does Proximity to Foreign Firms Induce Technology Spillover?" PRD Working Paper, World Bank, Washington, D.C., 1993; and for Morocco, see M. Haddad and Ann Harrison, "Are There Positive Spillovers from Direct Foreign Investment? Evidence from Panel Data for Morocco," *Journal of Development Economics*, October 1993. Brown, Deardorff, and Stern, "The Effects of Multinational Enterprises," discuss further evidence.
7. September 24, 2000. The article is adapted from their latest book, *Thunder from the East: Portrait of a Rising Asia* (New York: Alfred A. Knopf, 2000).
8. *Unfair Advantage: Workers' Freedom of Association in the United States Under International Human Rights Standards*, Human Rights Watch, August 2000.
9. As it happens, the AFL-CIO has argued plausibly that massive direct violations of the right to organize are widespread in the United States as well, with employers often firing workers who attempt to form unions, for instance. For the disturbing documentation of this reality, see David Moberg, "Labor Fights for Rights," *The Nation*, September 15, 2003, 24–28.
10. The growing numbers of such lawsuits (under the 1789 Alien Torts Act) against U.S. corporations in U.S. courts by plaintiffs, mostly workers, who were employed elsewhere than in the United States, is being listed at http://www.worldmonitors.com. I am indebted to Elliot J. Schrage for providing this reference.

CHAPTER 5

Workers and Work in the Global Economy

Analyzing workers and work in the global economy is high on the list of issues relating to globalization, for a key feature of globalization involves decentralizing production of goods and services around the world at the same time that the different segments are integrated in global commodity chains organized by transnational corporations (TNCs). The reorganization of work and production is occurring at breakneck speed. The process generates intense hopes—and fears—among those who have already been affected and/or believe that they will be affected by the globalization of production. For example, in 2004, *The Economist,* a respected magazine analyzing economic trends, published a lengthy survey on outsourcing, that is, delegating the production of goods and services to other (often low-wage) countries.[1] The survey reported that, whereas in 2002 about 100,000 Indians living in India had jobs in the Information Technology (IT) sector, that number would triple by 2006 and would nearly triple again—to over one million—by 2009.[2] Not all jobs can be outsourced. Some products are highly time-sensitive and need to be located adjacent to customers. Transportation costs for some goods give local markets an edge, although less so since the development of containerized shipping. Many personal services (haircutting, food service) must be performed "on location," that is, locally. But to suggest that many products and jobs cannot be outsourced merely indicates the limits to the process. What is the value and impact of the outsourcing that does occur?

There are clear benefits to outsourcing for companies that recruit workers at low wages and for workers who obtain outsourced jobs that would otherwise be scarce. Those who stress the benefits of outsourcing, including Bhagwati in Chapter 4 and Kristof and WuDunn in this chapter, do not claim that globalization necessarily produces pleasant, high-wage jobs, although it does produce some jobs

---

[1] "A Survey of Outsourcing," *The Economist* 373, no. 8401, (November 13–19, 2004).

[2] Ibid., p. 10.

of this kind. What they do claim is that even relatively unappealing jobs may be superior to the alternatives that exist in the absence of globalization. For, so runs the argument, in countries and regions not integrated in the global economy, jobs are likely either to be less abundant—that is, employment levels are lower—or to be even less attractive than the entry-level jobs offered by the offshore subcontractors of transnational corporations.

The selections in PG by Millen and Holtz, D'Mello, and Shiva provide a very different story—one in which wages are low; monotony, stress, and occupational hazards are common; and there is a yawning chasm between those who direct production and those at the bottom of the hierarchy who do the actual work of producing.

It may appear difficult to decide which position is valid. First, jobs in both the multinational and domestic sectors vary so much that it is hard to make an overall comparison. Highly paid currency traders, lawyers, and corporate executives in New York and London are part of the globalized sector; so too are the low-paid workers in the footwear industry described in the selection below by D'Mello. Second, the world does not provide a laboratory setting for controlled experiment. Comparison often involves questionable assumptions that cannot be tested. For example, Dollar and Kraay in Chapter 4 argue that the majority of Africans are worse off than other people in the world because Africa is less integrated in the global economy. But Milanovic (Chapter 3) and Wade (Chapter 4) claim that Dollar and Kraay's argument reverses the causal sequence: Africa's difficult situation is in part a product of factors such as unfavorable climate that has nothing to do with globalization and indeed helps produce Africa's lower degree of global integration and its economic problems. And third, comparison may involve multiple dimensions, which makes it difficult to apply a common standard. For example, are the higher wages that transnational corporations may offer adequate compensation for increased risks to workers' health and safety? One possible reply is that workers themselves are the best judge: if they choose to take such jobs, that decides the question. But this response assumes that workers are offered a genuine choice—that is, that other jobs are available. And this may be a questionable assumption.

The selections in this chapter remind us to connect macroanalyses of the global economy to people's everyday lives. But doing so is easier said than done. As you read the selections in this chapter, think about how to relate the issues discussed here to those analyzed in other selections in this book.

ARTICLE 5.1

Dying for Growth, Part I *Transnational Corporations and the Health of the Poor*

Joyce V. Millen and Timothy H. Holtz

This selection enumerates a disturbing list of problems associated with globalized production processes. In the global production or commodity chains organized by transnational corporations, the production of goods and services is often farmed out or outsourced to local subcontractors in poor countries. In order to land contracts to supply TNCs, subcontractors are tempted to violate labor laws, pay low wages, and work their employees to the hilt. Exploitation is facilitated when plants are located in export processing zones (EPZs), such as the *maquiladoras* in Mexico and Latin America. Firms in EPZs are exempt from local labor laws, such as prohibitions on firing union organizers. In EPZs, wages may be low, working conditions hazardous, and sexual harassment common (most workers in the EPZs are women). This selection highlights that globalized production may not only cause harm to workers; lax environmental regulation in poor countries affects all citizens of these countries and threatens the survival of the entire planet.

Millen and Holtz's account, as well as those by Shiva in Chapter 3, and D'Mello in this chapter, support Millen's argument. Yet selections in previous chapters by Friedman, Bhagwati, and Wolf, as well as that by Kristof and WuDunn, present dramatically different accounts of workers and work in the global economy. Can the conflicting perspectives be reconciled? What is your position and why?

Manufacturers Without Factories

Retailers such as Wal-Mart, Sears Roebuck, JCPenney, Nike, Reebok, Liz Claiborne, and The Limited design and market their brand-name products, but often no longer make them. These "manufacturers without factories" have separated the physical production of goods from the design and marketing stages of the production process.[1] Such companies avoid "troublesome legislation" by paying middlemen to do the manufacturing for them. When corporate retailers (buyers who put their labels on products) decide to contract out cutting, sewing, and pressing,

---

Joyce V. Millen and Timothy H. Holtz, "Dying for Growth, Part I: Transnational Corporations and the Health of the Poor," in Jim Yong Kim et al, eds., *Dying for Growth: Global Inequality and the Health of the Poor* (Monroe, ME: Common Courage Press, 2000): 187-201. Reprinted by permission of Common Courage Press.

they seek bids from local manufacturers—bids that are competitive with the lowest prices on the international labor market. In poor countries, the bids often presuppose the use of child labor, significantly lower health and safety standards, and sweatshop working conditions, for all of which the contracted agent, *but not the company,* is usually held accountable.

The subcontracting arrangement ensures the lowest possible costs for the production of a company's product. It also enables the parent company to avoid responsibility for improving working conditions and paying benefits to those who supply the company with its goods and services.[2] It is the means by which large companies obtain extremely cheap labor without compromising their own corporate image and name. Even though parent TNCs often pressure their subcontracting companies to cut costs—where ever and how ever possible—the subcontracting system enables parent firms to turn a blind eye to both the actual production process and the working conditions of the workers making their products. As John Fread, an Adidas spokesperson, describes it: "We do not own any factories. We license our ball-making through Molten (a Japanese sporting goods company). They in turn do the actual factory-sourcing and production. It's all subcontracted out."[3] Despite the often deplorable working conditions in their facilities and the low wages they offer, most subcontractors have little difficulty finding workers because of the very competitive labor market described previously.

Export Processing or Free Trade Zones[4]

Another way TNCs avoid national regulatory measures is by setting up their operations, or those of their subcontractors, in *export processing zones* (EPZs). In these zones, millions of people in Mexico, El Salvador, Haiti, Honduras, Mauritius, Sri Lanka, Indonesia, Vietnam, and other countries work for meager wages in unhealthy and dangerous conditions, producing goods for export.[5] In fact, export activities in many poor countries today are based largely on the labor-intensive assembly of manufactured goods in such EPZs or free trade zones.

Countries create these zones to attract export-oriented manufacturing investment by setting aside a physical area in the country where investors are given a range of incentives. The zones are usually located on the outskirts of large cities, and often on the banks of large rivers. Most EPZs offer foreign companies a combination of tax exemptions, near complete profit repatriation, waivers of industry regulations, special exchange systems, strict assurances against expropriation, and lax social, environmental, and labor regulations. Often, labor unions are forbidden to organize in EPZs.

The first EPZs, created in the early 1970s, were promoted as a means of attracting foreign investment to "underdeveloped" areas.[6] By the mid-1990s, over 200 EPZs employed over 2 million workers in more than 50 countries. Around 80 percent of the workforce in EPZs are women, the majority of whom are single and between the ages of 18 and 25.[7]

Conventional wisdom tells us that governments create EPZs to attract TNCs, which in turn supply needed foreign currency and jobs to the local economy. However, these jobs often do not provide laborers with enough salary to adequately feed themselves and their families. In Haiti, for example, a market basket survey among EPZs showed that wages were not sufficient to meet workers' immediate needs for food, clothing, minimal shelter, and cooking fuel. According to the study's authors, the salaries allowed only enough money for workers to purchase carbohydrates, which can stave off hunger but prevent neither protein malnutrition nor diseases due to vitamin deficiency. Without resources to purchase protein, fruits, and vegetables, workers could not maintain their health.[8] The same authors reported similar findings in Mexico and Indonesia.[9]

According to sources as varied as the National Labor Committee, the popular press, the business press, the U.S. Agency for International Development, and academic journals, workers employed in these zones suffer many types of abuse. Working hours in EPZs are 25 percent longer than elsewhere, and in some cases reach up to 90 hours per week. Wages paid women are from 20 to 50 percent lower than those paid to men.[10] Mandatory production quotas set above achievable limits are common, forcing employees to work overtime without extra compensation. In many plants, ventilation is poor, and drinking water is not available. Workers in many plants report being denied legally permitted leave and being fired for taking it. According to one observer in Haiti, "Many [workers] face a real risk of starvation if they lose their jobs, and are therefore compelled to do whatever their boss asks of them, which for many women involves sexual favors."[11] In El Salvador and Guatemala, women workers report being beaten, sexually harassed, and cursed at by supervisors.[12] Workers in the zones complain of sheer exhaustion. As one fifteen-year-old seamstress in a Guatemala City EPZ explains:

> The starting bell for work rings at 6:15 and I can feel pretty tired the first hour, but I have to work fast anyway—we have quotas. When the bell finally rings at 6:30 p.m. [over 12 hours later], you are ready to go home—but it is not always possible. If there is more work, the owners tell you they need people to stay for the night shift. If not enough people say yes, the supervisor sits in front of the doors and no one can leave. They let you rest a few minutes, and work starts again at 7:00 p.m. When the bell rings at 3 a.m., they pass out cardboard from old boxes. I look for my friends, and we put out cardboards next to each other and sleep under the tables. Then you go back to work whether you are tired or not. This happens two or three times a week. Do you think I would do this if we didn't need the money? I liked school. I would like to be a bilingual secretary, sit in front of a computer, answer telephones and say, "Just a moment, please, I'll see if he is in."[13]

According to the National Labor Committee, many girls and women who work in foreign-owned manufacturing plants in Honduras are forced to take birth control injections or pills so they won't get pregnant and cost the company money.[14] According to Human Rights Watch, many female workers in the Mexican EPZ factories known as *maquiladoras* undergo mandatory pregnancy tests and are summarily fired if they test positive.[15] And in Saipan, which is part of the

U.S. commonwealth of Northern Mariana Islands, pregnant apparel workers in U.S.-based TNCs have reported being forced to have abortions so they would "remain productive."[16]

Witnessing the labor and environmental conditions in EPZs, an outraged writer reported: "Part of the 'incentive' package that a government offers to companies when it creates Free Trade Zones is the right to despoil the environment, the right to flout basic standards of social welfare, and the right to poison workers."[17] Furthermore, he contends, EPZs "illustrate the social, ecological, and human consequences of almost total deregulation, which we now seek to achieve globally as a means of maximizing world trade."[18]

Despite the difficulties faced by TNC employees who toil in EPZ factories, however, workers have no recourse to improve their situation. Labor unions in most zones are either tightly controlled or entirely forbidden. Naturally, under such conditions, labor unrest has occurred repeatedly with violent consequences.

Union Busting

In TNC-owned or controlled factories across the developing world, worker activism has been crushed: workers have been harassed, detained, attacked by police and hired thugs, and even assassinated by death squads. In Sri Lanka, when 7,000 workers from Colombo's free trade zone marched peacefully to deliver a grievance to their prime minister, they were met by a police blockade, fired upon, and attacked with truncheons. Several workers suffered gunshot wounds and many more were beaten.[19]

An extreme example of brutal suppression waged against workers who attempt to organize occurred in Mexico in 1987. In the midst of a two-month labor strike, Ford Motor Company unilaterally nullified its union contract, fired 3,400 of its workers, and cut wages by 45 percent. When in response workers at a Ford Motor Company plant rallied around dissident labor leaders and tried to organize a union independent of the state-sponsored Confederation of Mexican Trade Unions (CMT), "gunmen hired by the official government-dominated union shot workers at random in the factory."[20] In 1997, the International Confederation of Free Trade Unions (ICFTU) concluded its annual report with a telling statement on the potential for workers to organize in EPZs: "Anti-union repression is an integral part of the export processing zone concept. Potential investors see the absence of trade unions as a major advantage of the zones, and their preference for women workers is a deliberate part of their anti-union policy."[21]

In July 1998, Mexican workers at an automotive parts production facility, Echlin, Inc., were intimidated and threatened with dismissal, beating, and rape if they voted to join a branch of an independent union. Fifty workers accused of being union activists were summarily fired and forced to accept "voluntary departure." Although an arbitration board ordered the company to reinstate the workers, the latter were fired again after they returned to work.[22]

Another visible and ongoing labor dispute in Mexico is at the Han Young *maquiladora* plant in Tijuana; the plant makes parts for the Korean automotive TNC, Hyundai. Since the beginning of 1998, workers at the plant have been organizing a new union, independent from the CMT. Despite the new union's victory in two elections, the Hyundai company refuses to recognize it. The second election was necessary after the Tijuana arbitration board refused to register the union, and workers from the plant went on a hunger strike. The conflict between the workers and the TNC captivated the press, but despite the public attention, the corporation continued to harass, fire, and attempt to bribe workers not to vote for the new union.

Though the data are not presented in terms of transnational versus national corporations, the 1998 Annual Survey of Violations of Trade Union Rights compiled by the ICFTU illustrates the difficulty faced by would-be union organizers throughout the world. The report counts 4,210 cases of trade-union worker harassment and 2,330 arrests or detentions of workers involved in union-related activities in 1998 alone. In the same year, the ICFTU reported 299 documented murders of trade unionists; in virtually all cases, the perpetrators were not punished.[23]

Winners or Losers?

> The direct labor cost to assemble a $90 pair of Nike sneakers [in Indonesia] is approximately $1.20, which means that the workers' wages amount to just 1.3 percent of the retail price. If Nike was to raise Indonesian workers' wages by 50 percent, the labor costs to assemble the same $90 pair of sneakers would be just $1.80, still only two percent of the sneakers' retail price.[24]

It is not so simple to calculate who most benefits—the companies or the nation-states—when TNCs set up operations in poor or less industrialized countries. Often, when local, state, or national governments go out of their way to offer appealing incentives to TNCs,[25] they operate under the premise that their community or state will necessarily gain in the exchange either financially or in terms of skills, technology transfers, and linkages to domestic industry. In fact, government elites often rationalize the exploitative behavior of their foreign investors and frequently turn a blind eye to labor abuses, because they believe a net gain will accrue to the country or to themselves.[26] However, the elites' assumption does not always hold true. Especially in EPZs, where foreign companies rely on imported materials and make few linkages with domestic sectors, the actual benefits to a host country may be minimal. In a World Bank discussion paper, the authors suggest that "poorer countries will always be at a disadvantage if the relative attractiveness of fiscal incentive packages in different countries determines investment locations."[27] And as a report written by the secretariat of the WTO argues:

> The more intense the competition among potential hosts, the greater is the proportion of potential gains which is transferred to the TNCs. . . . If a country offers $185 million in incentives to obtain an FDI [the investment of a foreign company or *foreign direct*

> *investment*] project that brings $135 million in total benefits, the country as a whole is $50 million worse off with the FDI. . . . Such incentives are nothing more than a transfer of income from these countries to the investing firms.[28]

With the new rules of international trade under the tutelage of the WTO, EPZs no longer exist solely within delineated boundaries; they have, in fact, begun to "encompass the entire globe."[29] Where historical and geographical circumstances are favorable, and where governments are able to regulate TNC entry and operations, these zones can help fuel developing economies. The "Asian Tiger" economies before the 1997 economic crash were able to advance economically by taking advantage of protectionist policies and pursuing an export-oriented strategy at a time when most other nations were still looking inward. Their success may not be repeatable, however, as today most developing nations are forced into a global competition for foreign investment. The greater the competition to attract foreign firms, the more elaborate and "generous" the incentive structures governments offer to TNCs. In Cameroon, for example, foreign investors receive a 100 percent tax exemption for ten years, followed by a 15 percent tax ceiling thereafter, and free repatriation of profits. In Cameroon's industrial free zone TNCs also receive flexibility in hiring and firing workers, and an exemption from the nation's standard wage classification scheme.[30] In other words, they are officially permitted to pay their workers less than the minimum wage.

For workers who come from rural areas and for various reasons are unable to return to their land, and for those who have no other means of earning a living, work in TNC facilities represents survival, and not only for themselves.[31] On their meager salaries, workers in less industrialized and poor countries often support several, and sometimes many, unemployed members of their extended families. When a person's life and the lives of family members depend upon continued employment in a factory, field, or mine, such a worker will tend to silence complaints and accept all manner of hardships just to keep the job.[32]

What if a government chooses to protect its workforce from exploitative working conditions? Transnational corporations may opt to pick up and move elsewhere, to wherever conditions are more "favorable." Ultimately, protected workers lose their jobs. And if a country does not compete for TNCs' foreign investment using the same low standards as its neighbors, it risks "falling out" of the global economy. But with such standards, workers are left unprotected from labor abuse and may have little or no job security. The current rules of the global economy that allow TNCs to move rapidly from one country to another, coupled with surpluses of people in desperate need of employment, leave workers in a no-win situation.

TNCs and the Environment

Every morning in the southern Peruvian town of Ilo, Pedro and his youngest son Jaime wake up coughing and wheezing. Often they do not sleep through the night because they are awakened by their labored breathing. Pedro never experienced health problems be-

fore coming to work in the copper smelters of Ilo, six years ago. He worries now because he has seen several fellow workers die from lung cancer and other respiratory complications.

But what troubles Pedro most is his ailing child. When his wife took eight-year-old Jaime to the local medical clinic, the doctor gave the boy cough medicine and vitamins. But the remedies did little, and Jaime's cough is often so bad he is forced to stay home from school. Many of Jaime's young friends complain of similar symptoms.

Pedro suspects that if he could afford to quit his job and move to where the air is clean, he and his son would be spared their chronic breathing difficulties. Yet he knows he is among the few in Peru who are fully employed, and he is in no position to give up this privilege.

In Ilo the dark, acrid smoke from the copper smelters is so ubiquitous motorists must use their headlights during the day to see the road. Among the residents of the town severe respiratory ailments are common, and few escape the chronic coughing and wheezing that arise from continuous exposure to the toxic dust.[33]

Pedro and his son Jaime are but two among hundreds of town dwellers whose health suffers from the careless industrial practices of the TNC operating in their backyard. Every day in the town of Ilo, 2,000 tons of sulfur dioxide are spewed into the air from the smelters of American-owned Southern Peru Copper, the largest mining company in Peru. This level of emissions is well over ten times the legal limit for similar plants operating in the United States.[34] Farmers in valleys outside the town center complain that the air pollution has affected their alfalfa, maize, rice, sugar, and olive crops. The smoke causes native vegetation to wilt and often die. According to company data, the air quality around the smelter is routinely 20 times worse than the maximum levels recommended by the U.S. Environmental Protection Agency (EPA). Peruvian environmental experts report that the actual emissions could be as much as 100 times greater than those permitted in the United States.[35] The double standard typifies the ability and willingness of a TNC to take advantage of differences in social and environmental standards existing between wealthy and poor countries.[36]

Whether through normal production processes or through accidents such as chemical spills, fires, and explosions, many TNC activities have a detrimental impact on the environment and people's health. While domestically based corporations also cause environmental damage and health problems, agricultural and industrial TNCs are the major users of hazardous materials and generate a significant source of pollution worldwide.[37] TNCs and their subcontractors use increasingly large quantities of dangerous raw materials in advanced and complex production systems that are beyond the technical reach of most national corporations. Enormous quantities of explosive, toxic, and radioactive materials are stored, transported, utilized, and disposed of by TNCs.[38] Transnational corporations dominate oil extraction and refining—as well as the extraction, refining, and marketing of gas and coal. They have virtually exclusive control of the production and use of ozone-destroying chlorofluorocarbons (CFCs) and related compounds. Large global corporations manufacture most of the world's chlorine, which is at the base of many of the most toxic chemicals known, such as PCBs, DDT, and dioxins. Transnational corporations also account for about 90 percent of worldwide sales of hazardous pesticides.[39] And despite international laws banning such practices, TNCs continue to transport and dump tons of hazardous waste in poor countries.[40]

Occupational health and environmental laws are usually more lax in developing countries than in wealthier nations, where strong political support for protective regulations is more common. Even when poor countries have environmental laws, monitoring and enforcement are expensive and often inadequate.[41] Conducting business transnationally allows corporations to take advantage of this situation and, in foreign subsidiaries, to carry out activities that would be illegal in the parent companies' home countries. Compared with national firms, whose historic ties to local areas may lead to good neighborly commitments, TNCs have little social accountability to the communities in which their subsidiaries operate. Thus, where legal accountability is lacking, community pressure weak, and local consumer advocacy undeveloped, TNCs have little incentive to regulate their environmental practices.

Transnational corporations tend to locate near low-income areas where people are not well-organized politically. When they locate in populated areas such as poor towns in Bangladesh or India, their arrival can exacerbate already overcrowded, substandard living conditions. In less populated areas, TNCs tend to invite the spread and growth of urban squatter settlements, as in many parts of southeast Asia and Central and South America. In communities along the U.S.-Mexico border, where hundreds of TNCs are in operation, higher than average rates of hepatitis A, dysentery, and shigellosis have been observed.[42] Transnational corporations in the agricultural, timber, and extracting businesses naturally locate where arable land or other natural resources are most abundant. Through deforestation, contamination, or erosion, their activities often devastate rural lands and disrupt local subsistence patterns.[43] Perhaps no case better illustrates this pattern than the environmental degradation provoked by more than 40 years of oil extraction in the Niger River Delta by TNCs such as Royal Dutch Shell. . . .

At the Worksite: In Plants and Factories

In almost every corner of the globe, workers employed by TNCs—as well as by national firms—are at risk for job-related health problems. Occupational risks to these employees include toxic exposures to lead, mercury, and other metals; increased chance of developing occupational respiratory diseases such as asthma and byssinosis; exposure to excessive noise levels; and physical injuries resulting from industrial accidents.[44] Specific cases of work-related injuries and diseases illustrate the problems that can occur in TNC factory operations.

Twenty years ago, Pennwalt Incorporated, a U.S. transnational chemical firm in Nicaragua, was found to be releasing mercury effluent into Lake Managua. When workers in the Pennwalt plants were examined, 37 percent of them were identified as suffering from symptoms of mercury poisoning such as tremors, memory deficits, and numbness. Levels of airborne mercury in the plants were measured at six times the legal limit set by the U.S. Occupational Safety and Health Administration (OSHA).[45]

Bayer, the Swiss transnational known for its aspirin, is a major manufacturer of industrial chromates. Since 1936, lung cancer from occupational chromate exposure has been well documented in the public health literature. Nonetheless, until recently, Bayer continued to ignore the dangerous, substandard working conditions in its overseas chromate manufacturing facilities. In both Mexican and South African Bayer plants during the 1980s, clinicians found that nearly 50 percent of the workers had perforated nasal septa, a classic sign of exposure to high levels of chromate. Bayer finally closed its South African plant in 1990, in the face of public outcry over the discovery of increasing cases of lung cancer among its employees. To date, Bayer has refused to offer compensation to any of these cancer victims.[46]

With heightened public awareness of the harmful effects of asbestos in their home countries, Western transnationals are moving the manufacture of asbestos products overseas, causing heated debates between public health experts and industry groups.[47] In some poor countries, asbestos is now a major cause of disability, ill health, and death among miners and construction and asbestos workers.[48] Similarly, the processes of lead smelting and refining and the recycling and production of lead-containing products such as batteries, paints, dyes, and gasoline, are now being shifted by TNCs from wealthy to poor nations. The latter are often unprepared to handle the occupational and environmental hazards created by lead.[49] In Indonesia, workers producing Union Carbide batteries suffer from severe kidney disease.[50] And in TNC textile plants around the world, workers continue to use banned benzidine dyes, despite research clearly linking these chemicals to bladder cancer.[51]

In Bhopal, India, workers at the Bharat Zinc waste processing plant toil under deplorable working conditions. In this plant, used car batteries from Europe and zinc ash from the U.S. transnational Ruby Metals are processed to extract zinc. Despite the dangers of inhaling the toxic metal dust being generated, workers are not provided with masks or gloves. After processing, the residual material, containing toxic levels of zinc, lead, aluminum, and copper, is dumped in an open area behind the factory. The lead waste is of particular concern because it can cause metabolic, neurologic, and neuropsychiatric disorders after acute and chronic exposure. Environmental lead exposure is strongly correlated with poor mental development in children, which is the reason for strict regulations on the use of lead paint in the United States. According to Greenpeace calculations, 450 tons of lead are dumped each year by the Bharat Zinc plant into the open, where it readily contaminates the air, water, and soil of the local community.[52] These are but a few examples of occupational hazards faced by TNC workers.[53]

Agricultural Production

With export-led growth now being promoted in most developing nations and monetary devaluations changing the terms of trade, large-scale agricultural production for export expanded considerably in the 1980s and 1990s. Throughout

Latin America, Africa, and south Asia, small farmers continue to lose their land to large-scale, mostly transnational agribusinesses and commercial fisheries. The quick returns most TNCs seek on their investments often lead to environmentally unsound practices. In India, Bangladesh, Thailand, Malaysia, Ecuador, and Mexico, for example, commercial projects produce tiger prawns and other "exotics" such as eels for export to rich countries. These commercial aquaculture schemes have been ecologically disastrous to coastal zones, damaging fragile mangrove and wetland systems and polluting sea water. They also tend to deplete groundwater and poison the farmlands of surrounding villages, ruining previously rich agricultural land for generations to come.[54] Because farmers are rarely compensated sufficiently for their losses and have no other sources of support, one net result of agro-industrial growth in developing countries has been greatly increased landlessness and rural impoverishment. The disruption of traditional subsistence agriculture in many parts of the world has been accompanied by massive migrations of displaced farmers into urban squatter settlements and slums.[55]

Major changes in farming methods occur when native crop plants are replaced with imported species not well adapted to regional soils and climates. Moreover, produce intended for export markets must be in near-perfect shape to satisfy Western consumers. In order to carry out large-scale production of export-quality fruits and vegetables, agricultural TNCs tend to use enormous quantities of pesticides and herbicides. Most of these compounds are themselves produced by transnational agro-chemical corporations operating aggressive marketing campaigns in developing countries. Many of the most commonly used pesticides in poor countries are banned from the wealthy countries that export them because of demonstrated toxicities.[56] In fact, 25 percent of all pesticides exported from the United States in the late 1980s were chemicals that were unregistered, banned, canceled, or withdrawn in the United States.[57] The wide use of these toxins, especially in poor countries, leads to significant occupational and environmental health risks for farm workers and their families.[58]

Particular problems occur in developing nations lacking regulations and guidelines for pesticide use and disposal, and technical resources for monitoring.[59] Surveys suggest that TNC agribusiness laborers often receive little training in the risks of exposure and the appropriate techniques for safe handling of these toxins.[60] Pesticides are often handled without protective gear or may even be applied by hand. In poorer areas where literacy is low and little information about pesticides' dangers is available, farmers have been known to take small quantities of the toxic substances home from the farm areas where they work to spray on their beds and even in their children's hair to kill bed bugs and other annoying pests.[61] In the Philippines, women agricultural laborers suffer sustained exposure to toxic pesticides. They work eight to ten hours in the rice fields, "planting, uprooting the seedlings, transplanting, weeding, and picking up golden snails. They inhale pesticide residues, transport pesticide-laden seedlings on their heads, and transplant with their hands pesticide-laden seedlings into the pesticide-laden mud in which they soak all day up to their buttocks."[62]

The pesticides chlordane and heptachlor were banned from use in the United States long before manufacturers exported more than 5 million pounds to 25 countries from 1987 to 1989.[63] Dichlorodiphenyl trichloroethane (DDT), dibromochloropropane (DBCP), and the methylmercuric fungicides were also widely sold by TNCs in poor countries long after being banned in the United States. Male agricultural workers using DBCP have shown significantly increased rates of sterility or reduced fertility.[64] Several pesticides have also been associated with elevated risk for spontaneous abortions and fertility problems in women.[65] Known carcinogenic pesticides such as aldrin, hexachlorobenzene, lindane, and benzenehexachloride (BHC) are still widely manufactured by TNCs and sold in the developing world.[66]

Growing public awareness about the health risks of persistent exposure to certain pesticides has led researchers and farmers to develop alternative methods for crop protection. The use of integrated pest management and biological control programs is expanding rapidly in parts of Western Europe, the United States, and elsewhere. In a study conducted in Israel, reduced pesticide use and alternative pest control programs have resulted in improved yields of cotton per unit area of cultivated land, indicating that alternative methods *can* be economically sustainable.[67] As demand for organic produce increases and chemical pesticide use is reduced in wealthier countries, transnational chemical manufacturers are likely to continue shifting their production facilities to poor areas, and expanding their markets to consumers in poor countries.[68]

A controversial subject currently receiving considerable public attention is agricultural biotechnology.[69] Since the late 1970s, plant biologists have been working to develop new crop varieties through the technology known as genetic modification. Genetic modification goes beyond traditional techniques of hybridization and selective breeding, by employing direct genetic manipulation to custom-tailor crops through the insertion of desirable genes from one organism into the genetic material of another organism. In less than a decade, this technology has exploded. The total area of land planted with genetically modified crops went from zero acres in 1990 to an estimated 100 million acres by the end of 1999—an area larger than three times the size of England. The majority of land cultivated with genetically modified crops is in the United States,[70] and large TNCs, such as Monsanto, DuPont, and Novartis, are conducting the preponderance of new research and development in the field. With so much invested in the new technologies, the agricultural TNCs are also aggressively campaigning to frame the parameters of a rapidly intensifying international debate concerning the safety of genetically modified crops and foods.[71]

The potential positive and negative effects of genetic modification farming in poor countries are still unclear. The development of new crop plants capable of higher yields and more resistant to drought and other environmental conditions could help boost the worldwide food supply considerably. Similarly, crops modified to improve the nutritional value of foods could help prevent certain diseases and alleviate much malnutrition in the world. These are not, however, the sort of crop modifications most companies are developing. Rather, TNCs are genetically modifying crops to further enhance commercial interests and sell more seeds; they create seeds with sterile progeny, crops with resistance to insect pests or commercial herbicides, potatoes with better starch content for improved french fries, and other produce with delayed ripening to prolong transportability. Occasionally, though not necessarily intentionally, companies' commercial interests overlap with efforts to resolve the wider, aforementioned health and social problems.

Despite the fact that genetically modified products are being grown and sold in countries around the world (including the United States, Argentina, Australia, Canada, China, and Mexico) the potential risks associated with genetic modification technology are not well understood and have been only minimally evaluated.[72] The European Union is adopting rigorous regulations for the production, release, and marketing of genetically modified crops, but a striking lack of consumer attention and public oversight is more common in the rest of the world. There are two basic categories of concern: the risks posed to individuals who consume genetically modified foods, and the potential impact of releasing such plants into the environment. Vulnerable consumers of genetically modified foods could risk severe health consequences if food allergens are introduced into crop plants or if genes with antibiotic resistance transfer to pathogenic microorganisms. With respect to environmental consequences, it is almost impossible to predict potential outcomes without further testing under controlled conditions. However, it is clear that the widespread use of genetically modified insect- and herbicide-resistant crop varieties could have profound long-term effects on both local and global biodiversity. Loss of biodiversity is of particular concern to poor communities in Asia, Africa, and Latin America, where most of the global centers of crop origin and diversification are located. A further loss of plant biodiversity, critical for sustainable agriculture, could endanger already precarious food supplies. Beyond these concerns, farmers in poor countries are likely to incur additional social and economic costs. One new genetic modification technology, for example, causes seed sterility after a single generation. When farmers plant this "terminator" seed, the plant grows, but its seeds cannot be used in the next planting cycle. By forcing farmers to purchase seeds annually, this process severely disadvantages those farmers who traditionally stored seeds for future use.[73]

Now that TNCs have obtained greater ease of entry into developing countries and expanded international property rights protections as a result of GATT/WTO policies, agricultural biotechnology TNCs are bringing genetic modification experiments to poor countries. Until these countries develop relevant precautions and safety regulations, this practice could prove hazardous: "There is a well-justified concern that the new biotechnologies will develop food products which would displace the traditional export [crops] of the [poor countries of the] South."[74] As farmers everywhere become increasingly dependent on the products of biotechnology firms, the TNCs are beginning to assert far-reaching monopoly rights over seed stocks, while showing little inclination to shoulder the economic or social responsibility that ought to be associated with such large-scale environmental experiments.[75] The TNCs are globalizing the corporatization of agriculture and, in the process, changing forever humanity's relationship to agriculture and food.

Environmental Exposures

Even more troubling than occupational hazards are the risks associated with environmental pollutants—because they can affect many more people at once.[76] Once they are released into the environment, toxic materials from industrial emissions or agricultural runoff can infiltrate local water sources and contaminate air and soil.[77] When this occurs, not only workers but entire communities are put at risk as they breathe the air, drink the water, and eat produce grown in the soil of a polluted environment. Unlike toxins confined within the workplace, toxins in the environment may affect any and all vulnerable members of a community, such as children and pregnant women, and may lead to increased birth defects and developmental problems in growing children.[78]

The most insidious environmental pollutants are toxins that remain stable in the environment or are taken up into the food chain. Such pollutants continue to exert their poisonous effects for years. In one study, children living near a former copper smelter in Montana were found to have elevated levels of arsenic—a toxin associated with a variety of cancers—*12 years after operations had ceased.*[79] Mercury is another toxin that persists in the environment, putting communities at risk for neurologic damage many years after industrial and mining operations have closed down. One recent study revealed elevated blood levels of mercury in a Native American population living near a cinnabar mine in California; the mine has been closed since 1957.[80]

On the U.S.-Mexican border, TNCs (mainly U.S.-owned) take advantage of the world's largest export processing zone. The *maquiladoras* in this region import most of their raw material from the United States and are supposed to repatriate the waste for disposal. But, according to the EPA, only a tiny percentage is actually returned north. An Arizona-based environmental group, the Border Ecology Project, found that the *maquiladoras* were unable to account for 95 percent of the waste they generated between 1969 and 1989. Not surprisingly, the U.S. National Toxics Campaign detected high levels of pollutants outside the plants and in the communities where the *maquiladoras* operate. In drainage water, one such pollutant, the industrial solvent xylene, was measured at concentrations of 6,000 times the U.S. drinking water standard. Moreover, tests conducted by an EPA-certified laboratory "reveal[ed] levels of xylene up to 50,000 times what is allowed in the United States, and of methylene chloride up to 215,000 times the U.S. standard."[81] The same study found that in 17 out of 23 sites studied, *maquiladoras* contained high concentrations of toxic discharges such as lead, chromium, mercury, nickel, and other metals. Severe health problems caused by exposure to these pollutants and observed in populations living near the plants include anencephaly (babies born without a brain), other severe physical deformities, and mental defects. . . .

Over a span of almost 30 years, national and transnational oil companies—U.S.-based Texaco chief among them—have extracted over 2 billion barrels of crude oil from the Ecuadorian Amazon. This region is known as one of the most biodiverse zones on earth. It is home to over 500,000 indigenous people and settlers. In the course of oil extraction, the oil companies have released billions of gallons of untreated toxic wastes and oil directly into the environment. After visiting the region, Robert Kennedy, Jr. reported:

> We met with the center's chief clinician and with the representatives of fourteen communities accounting for about 40,000 people from the Aguarico River basin. Each of them told the same story. Sick and deformed children, adults and children affected with skin rashes, headaches, dysentery and respiratory ailments, cattle dead with their stomachs rotted out, crops destroyed, animals gone from the forest and fish from the rivers and streams.[82]

Despite epidemiological reports linking the widespread oil contamination in the region to a substantial increase in the occurrence of miscarriages, birth defects, child diseases, and other health problems, the Ecuadorian government continues, under the advisement of the World Bank and IMF, to offer attractive incentives to private petroleum-extracting TNCs. The business concessions undermine efforts to monitor and regulate oil-extracting activities in the region, exacerbating the socioeconomic and health problems faced by the affected communities. Furthermore, most of the benefits derived from oil development in Ecuador have gone to a small segment of the population. Very little profit has been reinvested to help improve life quality among the poor communities in the Amazon region where the oil is extracted.[83]

Mining

Perhaps no industry is more destructive to the environment and more damaging to the long-term health of local populations than mineral extraction, and TNCs conduct the vast majority of mineral extraction in the world. Recent technological advances enable companies to mine deeper into the earth at a faster pace for less money. Though mining is not usually counted among the leading threats to people or the environment, its cumulative impact on ecosystems and the livelihood of farmers may be more destructive than the international timber trade or agribusiness.[84]

Through erosion, siltation, deforestation, and desertification, mining destroys rivers, mountains, forests, and agricultural lands. The most severe human consequences of mining operations affect mine workers and those living in close proximity to the mines, including subsistence farmers and indigenous groups. Mining firms appropriate land from local communities for their extracting operations and often cause massive displacements of people, especially in poor countries.[85] For laborers, mining has long been one of the world's most hazardous sectors. According to the International Labour Organization (ILO): "Mine workers are continually exposed to risks such as extremes of noise, vibration, heat and cold, repetitive task strain and harmful chemicals, radioactive materials, dangerous gases and dust inhalation. Worse still, they often face combinations of many of these risks at the same time."[86] Some of the more common health problems associated with large-scale mining operations include various cancers; brain damage; respiratory illnesses such as tuberculosis, silicosis, and asbestosis; skin diseases; gastrointestinal disorders; and reproductive problems such as frequent miscarriages and congenital defects.[87]

Health and environmental problems associated with mining have become more severe today, especially in poor countries implementing SAPs and adopting strict, export-led development strategies. By the end of 1995, for example, 35 African countries had radically rewritten their mining codes, incorporating incentives for foreign investors that include reduced taxation, import tax exemptions for equipment, and liberal immigration laws for expatriates.[88] The incentive measures in the mining sector appear to have worked; TNCs are now spending more money than ever before on mineral extraction in poor countries. Sixty percent of Africa's foreign direct investment in 1997 went to the mineral extraction sector. Exploration in West Africa doubled between 1993 and 1995, and several new mines have been opened. In Latin America spending on the exploration of metals went from $200 million in 1991 to $1.7 billion in 1997. And in the Philippines, over 25 percent of the country is now open to foreign-owned exploration and extraction concessions, due to the government's adoption of new investment regimes and mining laws.[89]

While, in theory, the foreign investment from TNC mining operations *could* benefit local economies and bring improved living standards to local people in poor countries, in practice, it rarely does so. This is in part because governments often deliberately relax the enforcement of social and environmental regulations as an additional incentive for investors.[90] According to a paper written for an international conference on mining in Ghana in 1997: "Presently, the benefits from mining tend to stay with the TNCs, while the negative consequences like pollution of water and soil, which may threaten the livelihood of surrounding communities, stay within the country."[91] With respect to job creation, some analysts contend that mining actually hurts employment because of the increasingly mechanized nature of the work and the massive displacements of people in mining areas. Furthermore, the clean-up costs from mines are externalized and left to future generations, rather than being paid by the TNCs responsible for the environmental degradation.[92] According to an international observer of the mining industry: "The economic model is clearly one of extraction and export to core countries—not one of enrichment for producing nations."[93]

Notes

1. Gereffi and Hempel, 1996.
2. Barten and Fustukian, 1994; Cameron and Mackenzie, 1994.
3. Schanberg and Dorigny, 1996.
4. The terms are used synonymously.
5. For examples, see Cavanagh, Gershman, Baker, *et al.*, 1992; Henwood, 1996; Gereffi and Hempel, 1996; Ratnapriya, 1995; Clifford, Shari, and Himelstein, 1996; Herbert, 1996a; Herbert, 1996b; Zimmerman, 1995; Harris and McKay, 1996.

6. Goldsmith, 1996.
7. Gereffi and Hempel, 1996.
8. Rosenbaum, Charkoudian, and Wrinn, 1996.
9. Rosenbaum, 1994.
10. Gereffi and Hempel, 1996.
11. Verhoogen, 1996, p. 10.
12. Verhoogen, 1996.
13. From an interview by Mary Jo McConahay with Myra Esperanza Mejia, which appeared in "In Their Own Words," *Boston Globe*, June 15, 1997.
14. National Labor Committee, 1995.
15. Human Rights Watch at www.hrw.org.
16. Steven Greenhouse, "18 Major Retailers and Apparel Makers Are Accused of Using Sweatshops," *New York Times*, January 14, 1999.
17. Goldsmith, 1996, p. 269.
18. Goldsmith, 1996, p. 267.
19. Ratnapriya, 1995, p. 32.
20. Korten, 1995, p. 129.
21. ICFTU, 1997.
22. ICFTU, 1997.
23. ICFTU, 1997.
24. National Labor Committee Statement, "Raising Wages a Penny an Hour," March 29, 1999. Available at www.nlcnet.org.
25. This is distinct from decisions made as a result of bribes offered by TNCs to governmental elites.
26. Political, business, and social elites in poor countries can benefit from TNCs in many ways, including stock ownership, partnership agreements, and consultative or executive positions within the companies (Lippman, 1992, p. 392).
27. Low and Subramanian, 1995.
28. WTO, 1996.
29. Goldsmith, 1996.
30. Weissman, 1996, p. 13.
31. The same is true for workers in national facilities.
32. It is often assumed that people in poor countries choose to migrate to urban centers and work in free processing zones in order to improve their living standards and increase their degree of personal freedom. However, workers in many regions migrate because they have little choice: either they have been forced off their land by (often transnational) agribusiness, or they were pushed to abandon their farms when their crops could no longer compete in markets flooded with cheaper foreign foods.
33. Calvin Sims, "In Peru, A Fight for Fresh Air: U.S.-Owned Smelter Makes Residents Ill and Angry," *New York Times*, December 12, 1995.
34. Calvin Sims, "In Peru, A Fight for Fresh Air: U.S.-Owned Smelter Makes Residents Ill and Angry," *New York Times*, December 12, 1995.
35. The EPA standards recommend that the average amount of sulphur dioxide in the air should not exceed 30 parts per billion. Daily levels should not exceed 140 parts per billion more than once a year. The company numbers show that in 1995, levels of sulphur dioxide in Ilo exceeded 300 parts per billion on 20 days in the month of May alone.
36. It is important to note that the phrase "double standard" is not meant to endorse the standards TNCs practice in their home countries, which may also be harmful. In the United States, for example, innumerable cases of corporate negligence, deception, abuse, and labor and environmental exploitation have been reported.
37. Dunning, 1993, p. 539.
38. Cairncross, Hardoy, and Satterthwaite, 1990.
39. Jeb Greer and Kavaljit Singh. "A Brief History of TNCs." Available on Corporate Watch website, www.corpwatch.org.
40. Cairncross, Hardoy, and Satterthwaite, 1990.
41. LaDou, 1997, p. 315.

42. Warner, 1991. Air pollution from border factories, large-scale farming, and automobiles is on the rise on both sides of the border, raising concerns about exposure to particulates, sulfur dioxides, and acid aerosols. Especially among the poor of the region, whose living conditions are already substandard, these pollutants are expected to further increase overall morbidity and mortality by decreasing lung function and elevating childhood and adult asthma rates.
43. The activities of transnational forestry corporations continue to contribute to the loss of biodiversity, and to diminish global ecological sustainability. Forestry TNCs have displaced thousands of indigenous communities in Central and South America, Africa, and Asia. Two factors are fueling these processes. Many new free trade agreements contain energy and resource codes designed to facilitate the rapid development and export of natural resources, such as minerals and trees. Also, the export-led growth strategy promoted by the World Bank, IMF, and other IFIs leads poor countries with resource-based economies to lower their existing environmental protections and open their doors to forestry TNCs. Several groups have focused considerable attention on this topic. For more information, contact the Rainforest Action Network, Resource Conservation Alliance, and Greenpeace.
44. Jeyaratnam, 1992; Cullen, Cherniak, and Rosenstock, 1990.
45. Hassan, Velasquez, Belmat, *et al.*, 1981.
46. Castleman, 1995.
47. Bates, 1994, p. 36.
48. LaDou, 1997, p. 320. Despite the severe occupational and environmental hazards posed by asbestos, the asbestos industry continues to promote their products in poor countries, where demand for low-cost building materials is high and information about the dangers of asbestos is often low.
49. LaDou, 1997, pp. 320–321.
50. Castleman, 1995.
51. Averill and Samuels, 1992.
52. Leonard and Rispens, 1996.
53. For a thorough overview of recent work on U.S. and international issues in occupational health and safety, see Levenstein and Wooding, 1997.
54. Khor, 1998, p. 6. See *Third World Resurgence*, 59, July 1995, in which eight articles are dedicated to exploring the damaging social and environmental effects of aquaculture.
55. Christiani, Durvasula, and Myers, 1990, p. 397.
56. Forget, 1991.
57. From "Pesticides: Export of Unregistered Pesticides is not Adequately Monitored by the EPA," General Accounting Office of the U.S. Congress, April 1989. Cited in "Unregistered Pesticides: Rejected Toxics Escape Export Controls," Greenpeace International and Pesticide Action Network-FRG. October 1990, p. 2.
58. Levy, 1995.
59. El Sebae, 1993.
60. Wesseling, McConnell, Partanen, *et al.*, 1997.
61. Joyce Millen, interview transcripts with farmers in Senegal, The Gambia, Togo, Burkina Faso, and Ghana, 1987–1989. According to Judith Achieng ("Pesticides Pose Risk to African Farmers," *Inter Press Service*, Feb. 16, 1998), "The organization, which acts as a watchdog for pesticide poisoning in East Africa—Kenya, Uganda, and Tanzania—claims the rising trend of poisoning cases in the region is a result of manufacturers cashing in on farmers' ignorance of the health effects of exposure to dangerous pesticides."
62. B. See, "Pesticides and Cordillera Women: The Right to Health and Sustainable Development," undated, p. 6.
63. Levy, 1995.
64. Thrupp, 1991.
65. Sharara, Seifer, and Flaws, 1998.
66. Moses, 1992.
67. Richter and Safi, 1997.
68. Organochlorine pesticides are no longer in use in most industrialized nations because of their low biodegradability and their tendency to accumulate in biologic tissues (Al-Saleh 1994).

69. See, for example, Michael Pollan, "Playing God in the Garden," *New York Times Magazine*, October 25, 1998, pp. 44–92; Mark Arax and Jeanne Brokaw, "No Way Around Roundup: Monsanto's Bioengineered Seeds Are Designed to Require More of the Company's Herbicide," *Mother Jones*, Jan/Feb, 1997, p. 40–42. For detailed information on GM technology and a review of current scientific findings, see Union of Concerned Scientists on Agriculture, Biotechnology and the World Food Supply (www.ucsusa.org/agriculture).
70. *Economist*, June 19, 1999, page 19.
71. Since the mid 1990s, efforts have been underway to set global standards for the safe transfer, handling, and use of living modified organisms (LMOs). An international biosafety working group comprising officials from about 100 countries has met several times to develop protocols for the protection of biodiversity, environmental safety, and public health. The meetings have been contentious, and progress in developing universally acceptable protocols slow—due largely to the opposition of the biotechnology industry, represented in the meetings by delegates of wealthy countries, where the industry is strongest.
72. "The Need for Greater Regulation and Control of Genetic Engineering." Penang, Malaysia: Third World Network, 1995.
73. See "Terminator Seeds," *Multinational Monitor*, November, 1998. For a review of current scientific findings, see Union of Concerned Scientists on Agriculture, Biotechnology, and the World Food Supply (www.ucsusa.org/agriculture).
74. Khor, 1998, p. 7.
75. In letters to *Nature* (329, April 23, 1998, p. 751), for example, several scientists make the case for assessing the socioeconomic impact of genetically modified organisms prior to their transboundary movement. A journalist for India's *The Hindu* explains: "This one-sided system in which seed companies have all the rights and bear no social or environmental responsibility, and farmers and citizens have no rights but bear all the risks and costs, can neither protect biodiversity nor provide food security" ("Sowing the Seeds of Conflict," March 23, 1997).
76. The risks associated with environmental toxins can be difficult to measure because routes of exposure may be uncertain. Moreover, because risk analysis traditionally involves the evaluation of one potential hazard at a time, it tends to underestimate the risks populations face when exposed to several hazardous materials simultaneously (Brickey, 1995).
77. Averill and Samuels, 1992.
78. Upton, 1990. Polychlorinated biphenyls from industrial sources and organochlorine pesticides used in agriculture have been found in breast milk of women in many areas throughout the world as a result of the women eating fish taken from contaminated waters.
79. Hwang, Bornschein, Grote, *et al.*, 1997.
80. Harnly, Seidel, Rojas, *et al.*, 1997.
81. Goldsmith, 1996, p. 269.
82. Cited in Center for Economic and Social Rights (CESR), "Rights Violations in the Ecuadorian Amazon: The Human Consequences of Oil Development," March 1994, p. 9.
83. Center for Economic and Social Rights (CESR), "Rights Violations in the Ecuadorian Amazon: The Human Consequences of Oil Development," March, 1994.
84. Kennedy, 1998.
85. Tauli-Corpuz, 1998.
86. Panos Briefing Paper, 19, May 1996. See also *Africa Agenda*, 15, 1997, which is devoted to the topic of mining in Africa.
87. Tauli-Corpuz, 1998. Workers in gold and silver mines throughout the world face a high risk of chronic overexposure to mercury, which in miners can be absorbed through the lungs, skin, or digestive track. Chronic exposure to mercury deleteriously affects the brain, the central nervous system, the kidneys, and the reproductive system.
88. Abugre, 1998.
89. Kennedy, 1998.
90. Abugre, 1998.
91. Machipisa, 1998.
92. Abugre, 1998.
93. Kennedy, 1998.

References

Abugre, Charles. 1998. "Mining Boon: A Gain for Africa?" *Third World Resurgence* 93: 20–23.

Al-Saleh, I.A. 1994. "Pesticides: A Review Article." *Journal of Environmental Pathology, Toxicology and Oncology* 13(3): 151–161.

Averill, Elizabeth and Sheldon W. Samuels. 1992. "International Occupational and Environmental Health." In *Environmental and Occupational Medicine*. 2nd ed. W.N. Rom, ed. Boston: Little, Brown, and Co. Pp. 1357–1364.

Barten, F., and S. Fustukian. 1994. *The Occupational Health Needs of Workers: The Need for a New International Approach (Testimony)*. London: Permanent Peoples' Tribunal on Industrial and Environmental Hazards and Human Rights.

Bates, David. 1994. *Environmental Health Risks and Public Policy: Decision Making in Free Societies*. Seattle: University of Washington Press.

Brickey, C. 1995. "Relevance of Risk Assessment to Exposed Communities." *Environmental Health Perspectives* 103(Supplement 1): 89–91.

Cairncross, S., J.E. Hardoy, and D. Satterthwaite, eds. 1990. *The Poor Die Young: Housing and Health in Third World Cities*. London: Earthscan Publications.

Cameron, J. and R. Mackenzie. 1994. *Implementation of Rights in Relation to Industrial Hazards (Evidence)*. London: Permanent Peoples' Tribunal on Industrial and Environmental Hazards and Human Rights.

Castleman, Barry I. 1995. "The Migration of Industrial Hazards." *International Journal of Occupational and Environmental Health* 1(2): 85–96.

Cavanagh, John, John Gershman, Karen Baker, et al., eds. 1992. *Trading Freedom: How Free Trade Affects Our Lives, Work, and Environment*. San Francisco: The Institute for Food and Development Policy.

Christiani, D.C., R. Durvasula, and J. Myers. 1990. "Occupational Health in Developing Countries Review of Research Needs." *American Journal of Industrial Medicine* 17: 393–401.

Clifford, Mark L., Michael Shari, and Linda Himelstein. 1996. "Pangs of Conscience: Sweatshops Haunt U.S. Consumers." *Business Week*, July 29, pp. 46–47.

Cullen, Mark R., Martin G. Cherniak, and Linda Rosenstock. 1990. "Occupational Medicine." *New England Journal of Medicine* 322(9): 594–601, 675–683.

Dunning, J.H. 1993. *Multinational Enterprises and the Global Economy*. Workingham, England: Addison-Wesley Publishing Company.

El Sebae, A.H. 1993. "Special Problems Experienced with Pesticide Use in Developing Countries." *Regulatory Toxicology and Pharmacology* 17: 287–291.

Forget, G. 1991. "Pesticides and the Third World." *Journal of Toxicology and Environmental Health* 32: 11–31.

Gereffi, G. and L. Hempel. 1996. "Latin America in the Global Economy: Running Faster to Stay in Place." *NACLA Report on the Americas* 29(4): 18–27.

Goldsmith, Alexander. 1996. "Seeds of Exploitation: Free Trade Zones in the Global Economy." In *The Case Against the Global Economy*. Jerry Mander and Edward Goldsmith, eds. Pp. 267–272.

Harnly, M., S. Seidel, P. Rojas, et al. 1997. "Biological Monitoring for Mercury within a Community with Soil and Fish Contamination." *Environmental Health Perspectives* 105(4): 424–429.

Harris, John F. and Peter McKay. 1996. "Companies Agree to Meet on 'Sweatshops.' " *Washington Post*, August 3.

Hassan, Amin, Eliana Velasquez, Roberto Belmar, *et al.* 1981. "Mercury Poisoning in Nicaragua: A Case Study of the Export of Environmental and Occupational Health Hazards by a Multinational Corporation." *International Journal of Health Services* 11(2): 221–226.

Henwood, Doug. 1996. "The Free Flow of Money." *NACLA Report on the Americas* 19(4): 11–17.

———. 1997 *Wall Street*. London and New York: Verso.

Herbert, B. 1996a. "From Sweatshops to Aerobics." *New York Times*, June 24.

———. 1996b. "Nike's Bad Neighborhood." *New York Times*, June 14.

Hwang, Y.H., R.L. Bornschein, J. Grote, *et al.* 1997. "Environmental Arsenic Exposure of Children around a Former Copper Smelter Site." *Environmental Research* 72: 72–81.

ICFTU (International Confederation of Free Trade Unions). 1997. *Annual Survey, 1997*. Brussels: International Confederation of Free Trade Unions.

———. 1998. *Annual Survey, 1998*. Brussels: International Confederation of Free Trade Unions.

Jeyaratnam, Jerry, ed. 1992. *Occupational Health in Developing Countries*. Oxford: Oxford University Press.

Kennedy, Danny. 1998. "Mining, Murder and Mayhem: The Impact of the Mining Industry in the South." *Third World Resurgence* 93: 15–19.

Khor, Martin. 1998. "Developing Countries—Problems with Current Agricultural AID Policy." *IFG News* 3: 6.

Korten, David C. 1995. *When Corporations Rule the World*. West Hartford, CT: Kumarian Press, Inc.

LaDou, Joseph. 1997. "Global Migration of Hazardous Industries." In *International Perspectives on Environment, Development, and Health: Toward a Sustainable World*. Gurinder S. Shahi, Barry S. Levy, Al Binger, *et al.*, eds. New York: Springer Publishing Company. Pp. 313–324.

Leonard, Ann and Jan Rispens. 1996. "Exposing the Recycling Hoax: Bharat Zinc and the Politics of the International Waste Trade." *Multinational Monitor*, January/February, pp. 30–34.

Levenstein, Charles and John Wooding, eds. 1997. *Work, Health, and Environment: Old Problems, New Solutions*. New York: Guilford Press.

Levy, Barry S. 1995. "Occupational Health Policy Issues in Developing Countries: The Experience of Kenya." *International Journal of Occupational and Environmental Health* 1(2): 79–85.

Lippman, Matthew. 1992. "Multinational Corporations and Human Rights." In *Human Rights and the World Community: Issues and Action*. Richard Pierre Claude and Burns H. Weston, eds. Philadelphia: University of Pennsylvania Press. Pp. 392–400.

Low, P. and A. Subramanian. 1995. *TRIMS in the Uruguay Round: An Unfinished Business?* Discussion Paper 307. Washington, D.C.: World Bank.

Machipisa, Lewis. 1998. "Mining Companies Wreak Havoc in Africa." *Third World Resurgence* 93: 24–25.

Moses, Marion. 1992. "Pesticides." In *Public Health and Preventive Medicine*. John M. Last and Robert B. Wallace, eds. Norwalk, CT: Appleton and Lange. Pp. 479–489.

National Labor Committee. 1995. *Zoned for Slavery: The Child Behind the Label*. Video. New York: Crowing Rooster Arts.

Ratnapriya, S. 1995. "Busting Labor in Sri Lanka." *Multinational Monitor*, January/February, pp. 32–34.

Richter, E.D. and J. Safi. 1997. "Pesticide Use, Exposure, and Risk: A Joint Israeli-Palestinian Perspective." *Environmental Research* 73: 211–218.

Rosenbaum, Ruth. 1994. *Market Basket Survey: A Comparison of the Buying Power of Maquiladora Workers in Mexico and the United Auto Worker Assembly Workers in General Motors Plants in the United States*. Newton Center, MA: Research and Report Service for Ethical and Socially Responsible Investing. F.L. Putnam Securities, Inc.

Rosenbaum, Ruth, L. Charkoudian, and K. Wrinn. 1996. *In Whose Interest? Using the Purchasing Power Index to Analyze Plans, Programs, and Policies of Industrialization and Development in Haiti*. Hartford: The Center for Research, Education, and Action, Inc.

Schanberg, Sydney and Marie Dorigny. 1996. "Six Cents an Hour." *Life*, June, pp. 38–48.

Tauli-Corpuz, Victoria. 1998. "The Globalization of Mining and Its Impact and Challenges for Women." *Third World Resurgence* 93: 29–32.

Thrupp, L.A. 1991. "Sterilization of Workers from Pesticide Exposure: The Causes and Consequences of DBCP-Induced Damage in Costa Rica and Beyond." *International Journal of Health Services* 21(4): 731–757.

Upton, Arthur C., ed. 1990. "Environmental Medicine: Introduction and Overview." *Medical Clinics of North America* 74(2): 235–535.

Verhoogen, E. 1996. "The U.S.-Haiti Connection: Rich Companies, Poor Workers." *Multinational Monitor*, April, pp. 7–10.

Warner, David C. 1991. "Health Issues at the U.S.-Mexican Border." *Journal of the American Medical Association* 265(2): 242–247.

Weissman, Robert. 1996. "Waiting to Export: Africa Embraces Export Processing Zones." *Multinational Monitor*, July/August, pp. 12–16.

Wesseling, C.R., R. McConnell, T. Partanen, *et al.* 1997. "Agricultural Pesticide Use in Developing Countries: Health Effects and Research Needs." *International Journal of Health Services* 27(2): 273–308.

WTO (World Trade Organization). 1996. *Trade and Foreign Direct Investment*. Geneva: World Trade Organization.
Zimmerman, R. 1995. "Nike Laces Up Vietnam Factories." *Business Journal*, May 5.

ARTICLE 5.2

Reebok and the Global Footwear Sweatshop

Bernard D'Mello

Bernard D'Mello notes an important characteristic of Reebok shoe production, a feature that Millen and Holtz, in the previous selection, term "manufacturing without factories": Reebok designs and purchases from subcontractors the shoes that it markets under its brand name. The arrangement provides Reebok with important benefits: it can shop around the world for the lowest cost and most reliable suppliers, maximize flexibility in response to changes in market conditions, and fend off possible criticisms concerning violations of labor standards in the plants manufacturing Reeboks by alleging that it does not own the factory responsible for the violations.

D'Mello's article focuses on a case study of one Reebok subcontractor, the Phoenix International plant located near New Delhi, India. He found an extensive pattern of abuse of workers at the plant, including forcing workers to work overtime, paying wages below the legally mandated minimum, sexual harassment, and beating workers for mistakes. Although workers temporarily checked these abuses by organizing a strike, Reebok responded by ending its supply contract with Phoenix and moving elsewhere. Is this kind of defeat inevitable? Several selections in Chapter 9 focus on movements that challenge neoliberal globalization.

The Indian power elite decided in July 1991 to embrace a package of policies, coupled with an ideological framework, that has since taken India on the path toward free trade, access to transnational capital, privatization, elimination of government regulations, and a reduction in provisions for social welfare. In 1992, Lou Pannacione, vice president of Reebok Technical Services for the Far East, recommended India as a sourcing base as "an alternative to China."

Bernard D'Mello, "Reebok and the Global Footwear Sweatshop," *Monthly Review* 54 no. 9 (February 2003): 26–40.

Liberals expected that Reebok, given its vast global commodity chain and international marketing network, would not only create employment in India by subcontracting the manufacture of shoes and apparel, but also help improve industry labor practices and standards. After all, Reebok's monitoring of the implementation of its "Human Rights Production Standards" at the subcontractor level could be expected to entail decent work in these factories.* But what in fact happened is that there were violations of Reebok's "Human Rights Production Standards" across the board at their key subcontractor's plant. And the evidence suggests that Reebok was aware of these violations but persisted for quite some time with the manufacture of its athletic shoes at this plant.

The Movement Against Sweatshops

The use of the term "sweatshops" perhaps conjures up images of the conditions under which industrial laborers toiled in nineteenth century England. William Blake's "Satanic mills" were horrifying. The workday was long, the pay was abysmally low, and the conditions of work were unhealthy and unsafe. In 1889, the British government finally set up a Select Committee of the House of Lords on the Sweating System. With the massive migrations from Europe to the United States in the late nineteenth century, the sweatshop system was transplanted to U.S. cities on the East Coast. Public opinion, set in motion by muckraking journalism and the early socialist movement in the United States, forced the adoption in the first decades of the twentieth century of legislation aimed at eliminating sweatshops. By the end of the twentieth century all developed nation states had, with significant exceptions, eliminated sweatshop conditions by means of regulations setting minimal standards for hours and conditions of work.

Clean, bright, and inviting shopping arcades or malls are ubiquitous today in developed market economies, and in the more developed metropolitan areas in emerging economies. One cannot miss the big swoosh of Nike, and all the other

---

*Reebok's "Human Rights Production Standards" first sets out "A Commitment to Human Rights" as follows:

> Reebok's devotion to human rights worldwide is a hallmark of our corporate culture. As a corporation in an ever more global economy, we will not be indifferent to the standards of our business partners around the world. We believe that the incorporation of internationally recognized human rights standards into our business practice improves worker morale and results in a higher quality working environment and higher quality products. In developing this policy, we have sought to use standards that are fair, that are appropriate to diverse cultures and that encourage workers to take pride in their work.

Particular standards are then set out under the following headings: "Application of Standards"; "Non-Retaliation Policy"; "Non-Discrimination"; "Working Hours/Overtime"; "Forced or Compulsory Labor"; "Fair Wages"; "Child Labor"; "Freedom of Association"; and, "Safe and Healthy Work Environment."

brand names and logos—Benetton, the Body Shop, and the Gap, among others. But in the sprawling backyards of the emerging markets, where much of the clothing on sale in the malls is produced, one cannot but be reminded of William Blake's "Satanic mills." The contrast poses several problems for the corporate bosses of the malls and brands: but above all a potential *sales* problem. In the mental space of our times, Reebok, Adidas, or Nike athletic footwear is not a commodity but an "image," "identity," "attitude," "experience," and "lifestyle." Branded athletic footwear fits well into the social ambience created by popular TV, shopping malls, fast-food chains, and freeways, theme parks, and sports entertainment. It also does its bit toward what Herbert Marcuse called "repressive desublimation." The impression is created that if one gains a satisfying consumer "lifestyle," "image," "identity," and so on, via the consumption of products embodying these "experiences," this is equivalent to gaining political freedom and economic liberty. Image management is critical to the sales effort. Behind this phantasmagoria of dreams of affluence there is a bitter economic reality, whose image must not appear. To give an example of a prohibited image: the stitching of one of those "produced with no child labor" labels by a child worker in a sweatshop. . . .

The Globalization of Footwear Production

International subcontracting is widely practiced in the footwear industry, a process that has been underway at a significant level since 1980. According to the International Labor Organization (ILO), production is "worldwide and connected through various arrangements and strategic decisions to serve the world market." The industry is "global in so far as trade, which is expanding more rapidly than the average of the manufacturing sector, is highly influenced by the changing characteristics of international competitiveness and *the relocation strategies implemented by the global companies*" (emphasis added). The "geographical distribution of world employment is affected by the rapid changes in production and trade. The footwear industry can be regarded, accordingly, as a '*one-world employer.*'"

In 1980, world footwear output was $42 billion. By 1995, output was 44 percent higher than in 1980, at around $60.5 billion. What is remarkable is the growth of Asian output by 424 percent, during the period 1980–1995, compared to the growth of output in the Americas of only 16 percent and in Europe of only 10 percent during the same period. Available employment figures are those of organized sector employment alone, and are thus gross underestimates. All the same, Indonesia was the largest footwear employer after China in 1995. Brazil, the Russian Federation, Romania, and Italy followed. By 1998 India became the fourth largest employer of labor in footwear manufacturing.

Women workers have been the first to be affected by technological change, as machines have replaced low-skilled jobs. With modernization the developing working patterns include extra working hours, shift work and working over weekends, allowing the machines to run almost continuously, perhaps compensating for the higher investment costs of the machinery. Women's wages are lower than that of men, even in Europe where equal pay for equal work has been on the agenda for some time. The principal employer countries for women in the footwear industry are Indonesia, Mexico, Italy, Portugal, the United States, and the Republic of Korea. Employment data for China, which is probably the biggest employer, was not separately available for female workers in the footwear industry.

The footwear industry is labor intensive and likely to remain so for some time, and so labor costs tend to be important in production costs. Labor costs are of course contingent upon wage levels, including various social benefits. Western European countries have the highest labor costs in the footwear industry, followed by the United States at about nine dollars per hour, and then the newly industrializing countries, like South Korea at six dollars per hour. The lowest hourly labor costs among the reporting countries are in Bangladesh, the Philippines, and Trinidad and Tobago, where labor costs are below one dollar per hour. It is said that the most labor-intensive parts of footwear production follow the same relocation pattern as that of clothing production—creating employment in the lowest wage countries, providing livelihoods that are insecure and unstable, but where the alternatives are even worse. These low levels of wages are not merely explainable by the level of education and productivity of the workers; the structures of underdevelopment are perhaps the main determinants. That is where India comes in, where workers are paid roughly less than twenty-five cents an hour (1998). Further, average weekly hours worked are among the highest in Asia.

The trend toward labor flexibility (that is, the absence of stable and secure employment) dominates the industry. Fashions change rapidly, demand is seasonal, and these affect the entire production process. For instance, in the United States demand peaks for footwear are in the first and third quarters. In line with this seasonal pattern of demand, firms adapt their production methods and systems of organizing the workflow and managing inventories. They apply various labor flexibility strategies inherently incompatible with labor legislation. The multinationals and other large firms have virtually withdrawn from those activities that require the most flexibility, handing these activities over to subcontractors.

In the export-oriented clothing enterprises, hiring, especially of women workers, may be on the basis of a verbal agreement with the employer. There is generally an absence of organized trade union representation. Jobs can be lost at a moment's notice. Where the large trading companies tend to switch their orders for production there tends to be a very high insecurity of employment with verbal contracts. Temporary workers, seasonal workers or daily contract workers paid piece rates may constitute the bulk of the labor force. Labor laws are frequently totally disregarded, and the situation of the workers is often highly insecure.

Extreme forms of discrimination against women in the industries include corporal punishment and sexual harassment. According to the ILO, threats to close the plant and move elsewhere are "an underhand form of harassment, since it does not involve any particular act that can be legally challenged. Only in the case of actual closure of an enterprise and collective lay-off are employees likely to have means of redress, depending on legislation in force." It should be added that in countries like India these workers might not have the staying power to engage in litigation that goes on for many years on end.

Subcontractors compete via the low road, to lower costs per unit of output in a number of ways. These ways can be easily identified in terms of a violation of the core labor conventions of the ILO. International subcontracting uses workers in the periphery and semiperiphery of the world economy to produce for developed markets. The average wage rate is low in such countries, and if the labor process is organized to derive a high average labor productivity there, then labor costs per unit can be lowered considerably. The quasimonopoly power of each of the three primary brands allows them to maintain high mark-up prices in the developed countries. This taken together with the super-exploitation of labor that goes on in modern sweatshops in the periphery and semi-periphery of the world economy, and the immense market power of these brands and multinationals vis-à-vis the subcontractors, means that the business is highly profitable for the athletic footwear transnationals.

Reebok in the International Division of Footwear Labor

Reebok International is a marketing organization, and not a production organization. Its vast profits depend on international political and economic relations of a particular sort. For instance, the annual threats of adverse action against Chinese imports into the United States, prior to the admission of China to the World Trade Organization in 2001, were noted in each Reebok annual report as posing a potentially negative financial impact. Overall, in the 1990s, China and Indonesia were the primary sources of supply of Reebok footwear. Out of the total number of units of footwear produced for the Reebok supply chain in 2000, China contributed 48 percent and Indonesia 28 percent. A disruption of supplies from China, which the U.S. Congress threatened annually throughout the 1990s, could have adversely affected Reebok's bottom line. In this context, what role was India to have in Reebok's changing global supplier base? Reebok was developing India as a supply base for the middle segment of the footwear market in Africa, the Middle East, and Central and South Asia, and as a fallback in the event of an interruption in Chinese supplies.

Why Locate in India? Price and Costs Do Matter

India has a vast pool of surplus labor living in abject poverty. The wage rate at which India's poor are obliged to offer their labor services is so low that India can possibly emerge cost and price competitive in a whole range of relatively labor intensive manufactured goods. This despite the fact that the technology used in the process of production may be inferior to that used in other countries. From a social perspective, the cost and price competitiveness may not reflect the strength of the Indian economy but rather the weakness, because it is predicated upon the relative poverty of the Indian people. This pool of surplus labor is actually obliged to make what may be called a distress sale of its labor power, which then gets reflected in the cost of production calculus. Now given the structure of input-output relations in the production structure, it may be very difficult to distinguish between cost competitiveness resulting from the distress sale of labor services and that coming from superior technology used. But corporations such as Nike and Reebok can potentially combine the advantages of their superior technology with that of low wages in India, if they transfer that technology to their longer-term manufacturing subcontractors.

Let us take the leather industry. At the end of the 1980s only about 4.2–4.3 percent (about 60,000 workers) of the 1.4 million workers in this industry worked in factories, that is, in those productive units that come within the purview of the Factories Act of 1948. Import dependence for the manufacture of leather shoes is quite high. There are around thirty imported components, including the soles, that go into the manufacture of good quality shoes in India. Yet given the wages that India's poor are forced to accept, there is good reason to concentrate the most labor-intensive part of the process of manufacture in India. When Rockport, a Reebok subsidiary, announced that it was ready to organize in India the manufacture of Rockport shoes, the company's country manager, Manish Davar stated: "It makes economic sense to import the soles, uppers, etc. and assemble the product in India."

Marketing Rules at Reebok India

Reebok entered the Indian market by setting up a subsidiary, but with a minority stake (20 percent) held by the Phoenix group, an existing Indian shoe manufacturer that became Reebok's primary subcontractor, joint-venture partner, and minority partner. Reebok could also use Phoenix's manufacturing plant as a development base for trial runs of adapted Reebok global products. For instance, the Reebok sandal was made as an all leather sandal, with some cost reduction by changing the sock liner from hexalite to Argentine leather, and replacing ethyl vinyl acetate with micro rubber. And Phoenix also ventured in the dedicated Infiniti chain of concept stores, with management expertise provided by Reebok. Reebok, however, later realized that in India, as its sales manager put it: "[Indian consumers] don't necessarily link the brand image with the outlet's image." Reebok also adapted its advertising strategy too—positioning the products as making "fitness" statements rather than "sports" statements.

The Reebok brand was launched in India in October 1995, ahead of the two biggest rivals in the market worldwide—Nike and Adidas. Reebok International was the first among the big three that identified India as a huge emerging market and a sourcing base for global exports. Under the joint-venture agreement with Phoenix, Reebok was to conduct some marketing and trading, while Phoenix was to manufacture and share in the marketing. An entire retail chain infrastructure of fifty-five stores was to be created by Phoenix under the agreement. But problems started when after setting up ten stores, Phoenix ran out of steam and resources and decided to focus on manufacturing, and the retailing and marketing of their own brands. Reebok had to change its marketing strategy. It started identifying individual partners to run franchised stores in every city and location and began to appoint distributors for each state to distribute its low-price products in multi-brand footwear and apparel stores. Reebok was successful. Its Indian managing director stated, "[t]he brand is number one in India with a 50 percent market share, and has created one of the largest chains of sports fashion stores with exclusive franchised outlets in over fifty cities in India as well as a distribution network to supply 1500 multi-brand footwear and apparel shops. The distribution penetration is almost double that of its nearest rivals and includes the most expensive locations in the country." Retail sales turnover more than tripled in the first few years, from 250 million rupees in 1996, to around 900 million rupees in 1999. In a short period Reebok India has become the market leader; it has even found it necessary to launch an offensive against counterfeiting of its products.

Most of Reebok India's investments seem to have gone into the creation of a marketing infrastructure. It has created "an international and uniform retail ambience" in eighty-eight exclusive stores. In order to build "authenticity and brand equity, the Company has fulfilled contracts worth $1.5 million since its inception, sponsoring the best teams, events and sports stars. . . ." Reebok has also spent heavily on "memorable advertising campaigns, using Indian sports icons on TV, the Press and Outdoor media. . . ." The management takes credit for building "a lean but talented pool of good Indian managers (total strength—45), drawn from India's best companies such as HLL, Pepsi, Titan, ITC, etc. and is *totally run by Indians*" (emphasis added). Indeed, Reebok India's first CEO—Muktesh Pant—moved as vice president of global brand marketing to Reebok International's headquarters in Stoughton, Massachusetts. But it is time we entered the underside of this heartwarming globalization success story, the hidden abode of production.

Reebok's "Commitment" to Labor Welfare and Work Conditions

Reebok claims that its "sourcing in India is audited by Reebok International's manager—South Asia for Human Rights, Mr. Zia Ahad." We will take a look over Ahad's shoulder at Phoenix, given the choice of the latter as a long-term strategic partner with an equity stake in Reebok India. Phoenix was chosen as Reebok's "first sourcing base in India for the local market."

Reebok is essentially a non-manufacturing marketing company, and hence the cost of goods sold reflects in part the contractual value of subcontracting and payments to vendors. In the first several years of Reebok India, these numbers were rising as a percent of the net sales. These yearly figures are as follows:

1995	1996	1997	1998
57.9	58.3	60.4	65.5

The above figures suggest that Reebok India had a motive to put pressure on its subcontractors. This brings us to labor standards and rights at the subcontractor level.

The Phoenix plant we focus on is located at A-37, Sector 60, Noida, in the backyard of India's capital city of New Delhi. Its workers were locked out on July 8, 2000, and the plant closed on October 23, 2000, "without proper notice to the authorities," according to Uday Chandra Jha of the Noida district committee of the Center of Indian Trade Unions (CITU). Based on the workers' experiences, as some of them related these to us, we attempt to throw some light on the impact, if any, of Reebok International's "Human Rights Production Standards" at its strategic subcontractor's works in India.

An Independent Union—Not Reebok—Safeguarded Human Rights in the Workplace

Mr. Avadh Kishore was a worker in the stitching department of the Phoenix works at Sector 60, Noida, before the closure on October 23, 2000. He is the general secretary of the Phoenix International Workers Union, which is affiliated with the Leather and Garment Workers Union of the CITU, the trade union wing of the Communist Party of India (Marxist). We first met him on March 6, 2001 at a general meeting of the Phoenix workers held at a park in Noida. He had invited us to meet the workers at this venue when we first made contact with him during a casual visit to the union office of the district committee of the CITU at the Gautam Buddha Nagar. At the Phoenix workers' general meeting we met Bhiku Prasad, a more experienced leather worker, around thirty-five years of age, who had worked earlier for Bata. We also met a very bright young man, Manoj Kumar, a worker in the lasting department of the Phoenix works, as well as Ram Babu and Rajesh Kumar, among others. We later made appointments to meet these workers on March 9 for more detailed discussions.

Avadh Kishore first knew of "the Phoenix group as having eight manufacturing units at Noida in 1987–1988. It had a bad reputation in respect of violations of labor laws and resort to unfair labor practices." The Phoenix International plant at Sector 60 "was started around 1994." According to Kishore, and this was seconded by Uday Chandra Jha of CITU, Reebok shoes began to be produced at the Sector 60 plant of Phoenix International during 1994 and continued into the spring of 1997. Out of a total of eight production lines, generally four were Reebok lines. The number of workers employed was around 2000. These workers got absorbed on a permanent basis only on June 2, 1997, after a struggle and the formation of the Phoenix International Workers Union. Before this date, only around 200 workers were permanent, the rest were casual or contract, even day-to-day workers. The number of female workers was "around 735."

The "compensation paid to most of the workers before the formation of the union was below the minimum wage, which was around 60 rupees per day in 1996." Was Reebok aware of the violation of the Minimum Wages Act? It seems hard to conclude that it was not. The workers were mostly between nineteen and thirty-five years of age, and had some education. Illiterate workers were few, mostly in the age group thirty-five years and above. According to Bhikhu Prasad: "These were more experienced workers in leather and footwear work, and as such, illiteracy was not a handicap as far as performance on the job was concerned." The point stressed by most of the workers we interviewed was that the "implementation of the minimum wage provision by the management came only after June 2, 1997, when the union was recognized." Before this date there were a few workers "who could be called child workers." When the issue of permanency came up, the management dismissed these workers. According to Kishore, "women workers did not get paid maternity leave when there was no union." Indeed, "there were no rules regarding leave during this time."

In the words of Bhiku Prasad, "Before the formation of the union in 1997, overtime work was compulsory." Indeed, "overtime was beyond reasonable limits and at times, quite unplanned. More important, workers were not paid for the overtime worked. After the formation of the union in 1997, the management practice of compulsory and unplanned overtime continued, but, at least, we were paid the usual double of the wage rate for the hours of overtime worked."

Discipline and Punish, at Times Brutally

According to Avadh Kishore, Ajay Kalsi—the Phoenix boss and a member of the Board of Directors of Reebok India until his resignation on January 15, 1999—"used to humiliate and even personally beat workers (including women) for mistakes that led to quality problems or waste." That corporal punishments were meted out to workers, including women, was the common complaint of the workers whom we met at the general meeting of the union members on March 6, 2001. A specific form of punishment was "being made to stand in the hot sun, especially in the summer months for an hour." In fact, the workers were especially provoked in May 1997, when on a particular day practically all the workers on a stitching line were disciplined and punished in this manner. There were repeats of this episode on May 26 and 27. The workers bore these punishments and humiliations because they were threatened with dismissal. In fact, it was after these repeated episodes of hot sun punishments that the workers resolved that enough was enough and the union got a boost. However, after the formation of the union the workers found that they were being punished with suspensions or threatened suspensions.

Among the incidents of May 1997, the workers singled out one as simply unbearable, and they said it precipitated the formation of the union. While the hot sun punishment meted out to male and female workers alike was tolerated, when the same punishment was meted out to a pregnant woman the workers struck work to demonstrate their opposition to such barbaric practices. On May 28, the workers demonstrated at the district magistrate's office, followed by a strike notice by the union, which brought the management to the negotiating table, perhaps for the first time at this factory. An agreement with the management on June 2 led to the regularization of the workers.

It may be noted that the Reebok lines were discontinued around the time of the workers struggle for union recognition and regularization of jobs. According to the workers whom we talked to in a group, and this was also later confirmed by Avadh Kishore and Uday Chandra Jha separately: "Before the establishment of the union we used to fear answering the questions posed by Reebok personnel about wages, etc. But after the union was formed we openly began to answer such questions posed by Reebok personnel without fear of being victimized." Yet, according to the workers: "Reebok persons who supervised the Reebok lines surely knew about the various violations of the Factories Act in regard to the basic minimum requirements of health, safety and welfare of the workers. Even proper ventilation was lacking. It is difficult to believe that the Reebok persons didn't know of the unpaid extra working hours, the lack of rest intervals, the arbitrary fines imposed, etc. How could they (Reebok personnel) have not known that the management was cheating us on our wages, making short payments, unauthorized deductions, non-maintenance of registers, etc, and all kinds of unfair labor practices?"

Sexual Harassment of Women Workers

Before the workers organized themselves into a union, it was not uncommon for women workers to be subjected to physical molestation and sexual harassment by supervisory and managerial personnel. Workers at the general meeting alleged that once the owner and boss, Ajay Kalsi, even went to the extent of grabbing the breasts of a woman worker and trying to sweep her off her feet! Otherwise, verbal abuse and use of foul language was the usual practice of some supervisory personnel. All this was happening when Reebok shoes were being manufactured at the plant. A request for leave was usually turned down with abusive language by a supervisor, Narendra Pal, and also by the personnel manager, Girish Mohan.

On the basis of what we learned, it appears that Reebok production at the Sector 60 plant of Phoenix International continued through a three-year period during which abusive and illegal practices were standard. Reebok production ceased only around the time that the workers organized and conditions were publicized, and to some degree improved. In short, the reality would appear to be almost the exact opposite of what Reebok's image protection program has sought to project.

Did Corporate Social Responsibility Get Lost Along the Way?

In this situation should Reebok International have insisted on its subcontractors complying with the legal minimum? According to Jha: "It seems that Reebok was concerned about the violations of labor standards because it was perhaps paying Phoenix, as part of the contract value, on the basis of the assumption that labor laws will be adhered to. But it is too far fetched to expect that Reebok could have obliged Phoenix to adhere to labor standards in the absence of a union such as ours." Jha thinks of the struggle ahead, for in his view, "it is only through united struggles that workers have won rights." But he is also worried about the failure of such struggles and the ultimate loss of livelihood of the workers, already without wages for more than a year, when we last met them in July 2001. Jha is convinced that "the Phoenix management wants a return to the status quo, a carte blanche to violate labor laws." And, again according to Jha, "both Reebok and Phoenix are more concerned about their exotic sales outlets, not the livelihoods and lives of the workers who make the shoes. They simply move the whole operation to a location where a trade union such as ours is not in control." Jha reiterated: "Reebok orders or not, it is workers' and union struggles that ultimately secured some of the rights of the workers, for instance, a minimum wage, overtime payments, and the right to challenge the Phoenix management's whole host of unfair labor practices."

The workers are now being badly punished for their assertion of their rights. Around 2000 workers of this factory at Sector 60, Noida, have been out of work for more than a year. According to Jha: "The factory at Sector 60 has been illegally closed following the union's winning of worker rights through struggles. The entire administration, from the district magistrate down to the deputy labor commissioner and the police, and the bourgeoisie of Noida, are behind Ajay Kalsi, the Phoenix boss, to crush the union and restore the status quo, which would mean the workers' forced surrender of their rights. What other alternative do we have but to continue the struggle?" The Phoenix workers have been evoking the public conscience with creative forms of protest, including a *jail bharo andolan* (courting mass arrests), much in the tradition of Gandhi's tactics to stir the conscience of the British colonialist rulers.

How long will these workers hold out without a regular job and wage? As of January 2003, after organizing various forms of mass action, but failing to pressure the Phoenix management to accept its terms, the union is pursuing the workers' claims in the Allahabad High Court. Under the circumstances a number of workers have accepted individual settlements offered by the Phoenix management and moved on to whatever means of livelihood they could find. The workers, besides lacking the resources to pursue their legal claims effectively, know from bitter experience how the judicial system deliberately and callously discriminates against them.

Conclusion

Athletic shoe manufacturing subcontractors like Phoenix are part of buyer-driven global commodity chains controlled by transnational corporations like Reebok International. If we disaggregate the total value-added in the chains, the sum of the value added per unit in the production process is but a fraction of the value added per unit in the marketing, sales, and distribution of the branded product. The difference between final sales price and the socially necessary unit cost of producing and distributing the product is the surplus per unit sold, in the classical political economy sense of the term. A very significant part of this surplus per unit sold is accounted for by the huge compensation of owner managers and corporate officers and the huge payments for legal, financial, and advertising services. Yet, the pressure to show ever-increasing earnings translates above all into pressure on the cost of supplies, i.e. pressure on the third world subcontractors and their employees. The investment in publicity that makes claims regarding the auditing of subcontractors is the most cost effective means by which to deal with the danger of growing public awareness of working conditions in subcontractor factories. The reality, as in the case of Reebok and Phoenix, is likely to remain as brutal as before.

In conclusion, we would prefer to focus on the workers who make the shoes rather than the problems of Reebok's financial officers. We have seen in the case of the Phoenix workers the degrading ways and conditions in which they have earned a meager living and how this seems to have affected their lives and their class consciousness. The system of labor that they are exposed to made them more aware of four dimensions of *alienation:* (1) They have little choice in deciding what to do and how to utilize their productive capacities; (2) They have no say in who benefits from the use of the athletic shoes that they produce and in what manner; (3) They even found themselves divided, especially when they found that Reebok and Phoenix were shifting the subcontract order fulfillment to factories where there were no effective trade unions; and, (4) When we met them after they were out of work for more than a year, they seemed tragically to be losing a sense of their potential as a collective of human beings. Reebok and Phoenix's appropriation of the surplus of their labor seemed to them the source of this domination over them and over the "entire administration, from the district magistrate down to the deputy labor commissioner and the police."

What they learned, and we learned, through following their struggles, was that rights had been gained by the workers themselves through struggle, which had little to do with the claimed paternalism of Reebok. But soon they realized, and in turn we realized, that these rights can be lost, and were therefore not secure, as long as power remains in the hands of capital—the Reeboks and the Phoenixes.

ARTICLE 5.3

Two Cheers for Sweatshops

Nicholas D. Kristof and Sheryl WuDunn

Kristof and WuDunn are aware of the hardships faced by workers (often young women) in poor countries who toil long hours in sweatshops and factories for low wages. In this respect, they join critics like D'Mello (see selection in this chapter).

However, Kristof and WuDunn claim, these criticisms fade when confronted by two questions: Are preferable jobs available? Can these demanding jobs be a first step in escaping from poverty?

Who gets the better of the argument—D'Mello or Kristof and WuDunn—and why?

It was breakfast time, and the food stand in the village in northeastern Thailand was crowded. Maesubin Sisoipha, the middle-aged woman cooking the food, was friendly, her portions large and the price right. For the equivalent of about 5 cents, she offered a huge green mango leaf filled with rice, fish paste and fried beetles. It was a hearty breakfast, if one didn't mind the odd antenna left sticking in one's teeth.

One of the half-dozen men and women sitting on a bench eating was a sinewy, bare-chested laborer in his late 30's named Mongkol Latlakorn. It was a hot, lazy day, and so we started chatting idly about the food and, eventually, our families. Mongkol mentioned that his daughter, Darin, was 15, and his voice softened as he spoke of her. She was beautiful and smart, and her father's hopes rested on her.

"Is she in school?" we asked.

"Oh, no," Mongkol said, his eyes sparkling with amusement. "She's working in a factory in Bangkok. She's making clothing for export to America." He explained that she was paid $2 a day for a nine-hour shift, six days a week.

"It's dangerous work," Mongkol added. "Twice the needles went right through her hands. But the managers bandaged up her hands, and both times she got better again and went back to work."

"How terrible," we murmured sympathetically.

Mongkol looked up, puzzled. "It's good pay," he said. "I hope she can keep that job. There's all this talk about factories closing now, and she said there are rumors that her factory might close. I hope that doesn't happen. I don't know what she would do then."

He was not, of course, indifferent to his daughter's suffering; he simply had a different perspective from ours—not only when it came to food but also when it came to what constituted desirable work.

Nothing captures the difference in mind-set between East and West more than attitudes toward sweatshops. Nike and other American companies have been hammered in the Western press over the last decade for producing shoes, toys and other products in grim little factories with dismal conditions. Protests against sweatshops and the dark forces of globalization that they seem to represent have become common at meetings of the World Bank and the World Trade Organization and, this month, at a World Economic Forum in Australia, livening up

---

Nicholas D. Kristof and Sheryl WuDunn, "Two Cheers for Sweatshops," *The New York Times Magazine,* September 24, 2000: 70–71.

the scene for Olympic athletes arriving for the competition. Yet sweatshops that seem brutal from the vantage point of an American sitting in his living room can appear tantalizing to a Thai laborer getting by on beetles.

Fourteen years ago, we moved to Asia and began reporting there. Like most Westerners, we arrived in the region outraged at sweatshops. In time, though, we came to accept the view supported by most Asians: that the campaign against sweatshops risks harming the very people it is intended to help. For beneath their grime, sweatshops are a clear sign of the industrial revolution that is beginning to reshape Asia.

This is not to praise sweatshops. Some managers are brutal in the way they house workers in firetraps, expose children to dangerous chemicals, deny bathroom breaks, demand sexual favors, force people to work double shifts or dismiss anyone who tries to organize a union. Agitation for improved safety conditions can be helpful, just as it was in 19th-century Europe. But Asian workers would be aghast at the idea of American consumers boycotting certain toys or clothing in protest. The simplest way to help the poorest Asians would be to buy more from sweatshops, not less.

On our first extended trip to China, in 1987, we traveled to the Pearl River delta in the south of the country. There we visited several factories, including one in the boomtown of Dongguan, where about 100 female workers sat at workbenches stitching together bits of leather to make purses for a Hong Kong company. We chatted with several women as their fingers flew over their work and asked about their hours.

"I start at about 6:30, after breakfast, and go until about 7 P.M.," explained one shy teenage girl. "We break for lunch, and I take half an hour off then."

"You do this six days a week?"

"Oh, no. Every day."

"Seven days a week?"

"Yes." She laughed at our surprise. "But then I take a week or two off at Chinese New Year to go back to my village."

The others we talked to all seemed to regard it as a plus that the factory allowed them to work long hours. Indeed, some had sought out this factory precisely because it offered them the chance to earn more.

"It's actually pretty annoying how hard they want to work," said the factory manager, a Hong Kong man. "It means we have to worry about security and have a supervisor around almost constantly."

It sounded pretty dreadful, and it was. We and other journalists wrote about the problems of child labor and oppressive conditions in both China and South Korea. But, looking back, our worries were excessive. Those sweatshops tended to generate the wealth to solve the problems they created. If Americans had reacted to the horror stories in the 1980's by curbing imports of those sweatshop products, then neither southern China nor South Korea would have registered as much progress as they have today.

The truth is, those grim factories in Dongguan and the rest of southern China contributed to a remarkable explosion of wealth. In the years since our first conversations there, we've returned many times to Dongguan and the surrounding towns and seen the transformation. Wages have risen from about $50 a month to $250 a month or more today. Factory conditions have improved as businesses have scrambled to attract and keep the best laborers. A private housing market has emerged, and video arcades and computer schools have opened to cater to workers with rising incomes. A hint of a middle class has appeared—as has China's closest thing to a Western-style independent newspaper, *Southern Weekend*.

Partly because of these tens of thousands of sweatshops, China's economy has become one of the hottest in the world. Indeed, if China's 30 provinces were counted as individual countries, then the 20 fastest-growing countries in the world between 1978 and 1995 would all have been Chinese. When Britain launched the Industrial Revolution in the late 18th century, it took 58 years for per capita output to double. In China, per capita output has been doubling every 10 years.

In fact, the most vibrant parts of Asia are nearly all in what might be called the Sweatshop Belt, from China and South Korea to Malaysia, Indonesia and even Bangladesh and India. Today these sweatshop countries control about one-quarter of the global economy. As the industrial revolution spreads through China and India, there are good reasons to think that Asia will continue to pick up speed. Some World Bank forecasts show Asia's share of global gross domestic product rising to 55 to 60 percent by about 2025—roughly the West's share at its peak half a century ago. The sweatshops have helped lay the groundwork for a historic economic realignment that is putting Asia back on its feet. Countries are rebounding from the economic crisis of 1997–98 and the sweatshops—seen by Westerners as evidence of moribund economies—actually reflect an industrial revolution that is raising living standards in the East.

Of course, it may sound silly to say that sweatshops offer a route to prosperity, when wages in the poorest countries are sometimes less than $1 a day. Still, for an impoverished Indonesian or Bangladeshi woman with a handful of kids who would otherwise drop out of school and risk dying of mundane diseases like diarrhea, $1 or $2 a day can be a life-transforming wage.

This was made abundantly clear in Cambodia, when we met a 40-year-old woman named Nhem Yen, who told us why she moved to an area with particularly lethal malaria. "We needed to eat," she said. "And here there is wood, so we thought we could cut it and sell it."

But then Nhem Yen's daughter and son-in-law both died of malaria, leaving her with two grandchildren and five children of her own. With just one mosquito net, she had to choose which children would sleep protected and which would sleep exposed.

In Cambodia, a large mosquito net costs $5. If there had been a sweatshop in the area, however harsh or dangerous, Nhem Yen would have leapt at the chance to work in it, to earn enough to buy a net big enough to cover all her children.

For all the misery they can engender, sweatshops at least offer a precarious escape from the poverty that is the developing world's greatest problem. Over the past 50 years, countries like India resisted foreign exploitation, while countries that started at a similar economic level—like Taiwan and South Korea—accepted sweatshops as the price of development. Today there can be no doubt about which approach worked better. Taiwan and South Korea are modern countries with low rates of infant mortality and high levels of education; in contrast, every year 3.1 million Indian children die before the age of 5, mostly from diseases of poverty like diarrhea.

The effect of American pressure on sweatshops is complicated. While it clearly improves conditions at factories that produce branded merchandise for companies like Nike, it also raises labor costs across the board. That encourages less well established companies to mechanize and to reduce the number of employees needed. The upshot is to help people who currently have jobs in Nike plants but to risk jobs for others. The only thing a country like Cambodia has to offer is terribly cheap wages; if companies are scolded for paying those wages, they will shift their manufacturing to marginally richer areas like Malaysia or Mexico.

Sweatshop monitors do have a useful role. They can compel factories to improve safety. They can also call attention to the impact of sweatshops on the environment. The greatest downside of industrialization is not exploitation of workers but toxic air and water. In Asia each year, three million people die from the effects of pollution. The factories springing up throughout the region are far more likely to kill people through the chemicals they expel than through terrible working conditions.

By focusing on these issues, by working closely with organizations and news media in foreign countries, sweatshops can be improved. But refusing to buy sweatshop products risks making Americans feel good while harming those we are trying to help. As a Chinese proverb goes, "First comes the bitterness, then there is sweetness and wealth and honor for 10,000 years."

Falling Fortunes of the Wage Earner *Average Pay Dipped Last Year for First Time in Nearly a Decade*

Steven Greenhouse

In this selection, *New York Times* reporter Steven Greenhouse tries to explain why, despite substantial increases in productivity—output per worker—in recent years, the wages of most American workers have stagnated or diminished (after taking inflation into account). He asks whether this disturbing development is temporary or part of a longer-run trend. To the extent that it is part of a longer-run trend, various aspects of globalization are a significant part of the explanation: the direct impact of offshore outsourcing of jobs to lower-wage countries, the threat of outsourcing as a downward pressure on wages, technological changes that displace jobs, and global supply chains, as exemplified by Wal-Mart's, that put American-based companies and workers into competition with suppliers worldwide. (He identifies other factors not connected to globalization, including increased health care and pension costs.) Greenhouse doesn't attempt to quantify what proportion of the trend is a direct or indirect effect of globalization. Further, since recent changes are often intertwined, it is difficult to isolate the impact of globalization. He also alludes to another facet of the recent changes: a tendency for income inequality to increase between a minority who reap handsome benefits and the large majority of American wage earners—the focus of the article—who do not. Do you think this change is related to globalization?

Do you regard the changes that Greenhouse describes as temporary or permanent? How important a role does globalization play in the trend he identifies? Are there possible reforms that might safeguard the living standards of Americans presently paying the costs of globalization?

Beginning in the mid-1990's, pay increases for most workers slowly but steadily outpaced the rate of inflation, improving the living standards for nearly all Americans. But an unexpected reversal last year in those gains has set off a vigorous debate among economists over whether the decline is just a temporary dip or portends a deeper shift that may cause the pay of average Americans to lag for years to come.

Even though the economy added 2.2 million jobs in 2004 and produced strong growth in corporate profits, wages for the average worker fell for the year, after adjusting for inflation—the first such drop in nearly a decade.

"Pay increases are not rebounding, even though the factors normally associated with higher pay have rebounded," said Peter LeBlanc of Sibson Consulting, a division of Segal, a human resources consulting firm.

The problem is not with the jobs themselves. Most economists dismiss as overblown the widespread fear that the number of jobs will shrink in the United States because of foreign competition from China, India and other developing nations. But at the same time many of these economists argue that the increasing exposure of the American economy to globalization, along with other forces—including soaring health insurance costs that leave less money for raises—is putting pressure on wages that could leave millions of workers worse off.

"We're in for a long period where inflation-adjusted wages will be under acute pressure," said Stephen S. Roach of Morgan Stanley. "That's a most unusual

---

Steven Greenhouse, "Falling Fortunes of the Wage Earner: Average Pay Dipped Last Year for the First Time in Nearly a Decade."

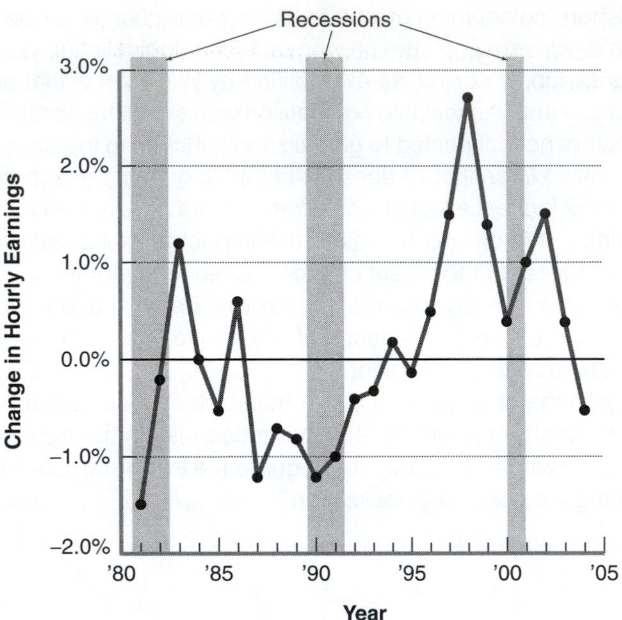

Figure 1 Slipping Pay
Change in hourly earnings of production or nonsupervisory workers on private nonfarm payrolls, adjusted for inflation.
SOURCE: Bureau of Labor Statistics

development in a period of high productivity growth. Normally, real wages track productivity."

But some economists are more optimistic, saying that the wage sluggishness is temporary and that real wages have slipped only because a sudden spike in oil prices has briefly left workers behind the curve. These economists assert that wage stagnation will end soon, as normal growth brings a tighter labor market.

"What we're seeing now is not atypical; employers can't pay the wage bill to keep up with the oil price increase," said Allan H. Meltzer, an economist at Carnegie Mellon University. "I think the long-term trend will be that wages will right themselves and look like productivity growth on average."

The most commonly used yardstick of wages—the Bureau of Labor Statistics' measure of nonsupervisory private-sector workers, covering 80 percent of the labor force—fell 0.5 percent last year, after inflation. Real wages for these workers are now lower, on average, than two years ago. A broader measure, the employment cost index, which includes supervisors, managers and most government workers, dropped 0.9 percent.

At a Sprint call center in North Carolina, 180 customer service representatives are well aware of how such forces are squeezing them. Their jobs have not migrated overseas, but the employees just concluded their most bruising battle ever over wages.

The Sprint workers in Fayetteville emerged from negotiations that lasted months with a contract that left them with a pay freeze for last year and no definite increase for 2005. While the best performers are promised 2 percent merit raises, even those are likely to lag inflation.

"It's like their wages are in a severe coma," said Rocky Barnes, president of the union local. "Sprint said they had to restrain wages because the company's performance wasn't so good, but we think a lot of it has to do with offshoring."

Sandra J. Price, a Sprint vice president, took issue with union leaders. She said Sprint sought the freeze not because of low-wage competition overseas, but because benefit costs were soaring and the company felt the call center's compensation was generous for the area.

Whatever the explanation for Sprint's action, many economists, liberal and conservative, are perplexed by two unusual trends. Wage growth has trailed far behind productivity growth over the last four years, and the share of national income going to employee compensation is low by historic standards.

Mr. Roach of Morgan Stanley said wages were being held down by foreign competition; corporations that are moving jobs offshore; the uncertainty of businesses over demand; and management's ability to substitute computers and other devices to replace workers.

"These factors aren't going to go away," he said. "The competitive pressures for companies to hold the line on labor costs are intense, and the alternatives they have—technological substitution and offshoring labor—are growing."

The overall wage figures hide a split, with an elite group getting relatively large gains. In a study of census data, the Economic Policy Institute, a liberal research group, found that for the bottom 95 percent of workers, after-inflation wages were flat or down in 2004, but for the top 5 percent, wages rose by an average of 1 percent, with some gaining much more.

The upper-income group enjoyed strong pay increases largely because of bonuses, stock options and other inducements and because of robust demand in certain fields, like law and investment banking.

J. Bradford DeLong, an economist at the University of California, Berkeley, said that current wage patterns, while perhaps only temporary, did not conform to traditional economic explanations.

"You'd think that with the unemployment rate near 5 percent and productivity growth so strong, employers would be anxious to raise payrolls and would have plenty of headroom to raise wages," he said. "But they're not."

Since 2001, when the recovery began, productivity growth has averaged 4.1 percent a year; overall compensation—wages and benefits—has risen about one-third as fast, by 1.5 percent a year on average. By contrast, over the previous seven business cycles, productivity rose by 2.5 percent a year on average while compensation rose roughly three-fourths as fast, by 1.8 percent a year.

"The question is not whether corporations are seeking higher profits; the question is how come they're getting them to such a degree at the expense of compensation," said Jared Bernstein, an economist with the Economic Policy Institute. "I'm struck at how successful they've been at restraining labor costs."

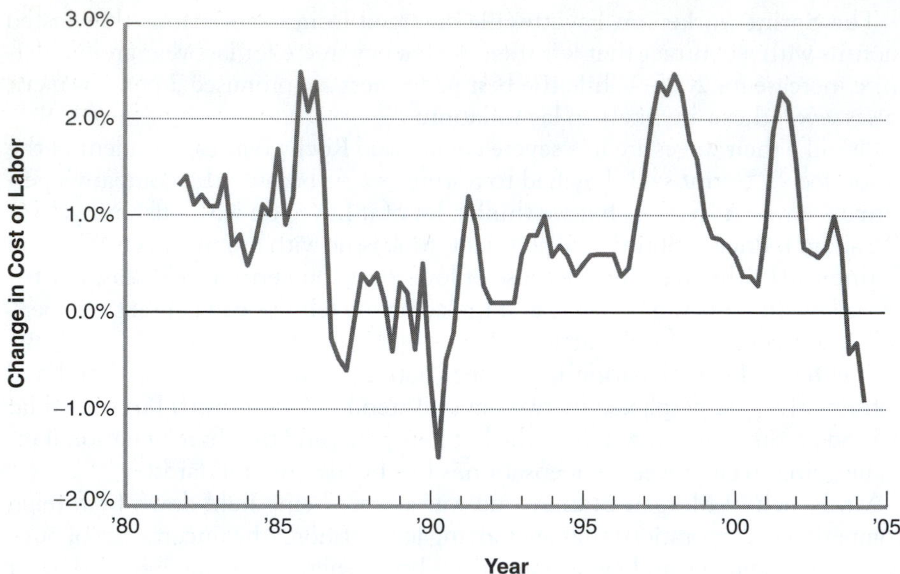

Figure 2 Cheaper Labor
Employee compensation fell in the last three quarters of 2004.

Labor unions' declining bargaining power has given corporations a stronger hand to hold down wages, he argued, but more recent trends, including the emergence of Wal-Mart Stores as a central force in the economy, now play crucial roles, too.

Laurie Piazza, a Safeway cashier in Santa Clara, Calif., said she reluctantly voted to approve a pay freeze in the first two years of her union's three-year contract because Safeway insisted that it needed to hold down costs to compete with Wal-Mart. Her take-home pay will fall $20 a week because the contract reduces the premium for working on Sundays to 33 percent of regular pay, from 50 percent.

"We tried to get weekly pay increases, but the company wouldn't do it," said Ms. Piazza, who earns $19 an hour after 18 years on the job. "I think Wal-Mart has a lot to do with this. They're setting the model."

With Wal-Mart moving aggressively into California with supercenters, Safeway officials say they need to clamp down on what they consider high labor costs to meet the challenge.

Last year's double-digit rise in health costs helped squeeze wages as well; many companies also required employees to cover more of the premiums out of their own pay.

"Benefit costs are rising fairly substantially, and that may explain the tendency to hold down wages," said Sylvester J. Schieber of Watson Wyatt, a human resources consulting firm. "If you throw an extra 10 percent into your health plan, that can suck 1 percent out of your budget for compensation."

Many executives say they are offering raises that do not exceed inflation. Pitney Bowes, which provides mail and document-management systems, plans to offer merit raises averaging 3 percent this year, about equal to the expected inflation rate, compared with recent merit raises, also in line with inflation, averaging 2 percent to 2.5 percent.

"The past couple of years we've maintained a moderation of our wages," said Johnna G. Torsone, the company's chief human resources officer, who noted that the company has had to greatly increase spending on health and pensions.

While agreeing that these factors are important, Richard B. Freeman, a Harvard economist, predicted that new competition in the form of millions of skilled Chinese, Indian and other Asian workers entering the global labor market will increasingly pull down American wages.

"Globalization is going to make it harder for American workers to have the wage increases and the benefits that we might have expected," he said.

Facing intense foreign competition, Delphi, the auto parts manufacturer, has decided against any merit raises this year for its salaried workers. And at its air bag and door panel factory in Vandalia, Ohio, it persuaded unionized workers to accept a three-year pay freeze, warning that the plant would be closed otherwise.

"The majority of workers felt they had to agree to this," said Earl Shepard of the United Steelworkers local in Vandalia. "People here say the big problem is competition from Asia."

Lindsey C. Williams, a Delphi spokesman, said the company was seeking to keep the Vandalia factory "viable" and was working with the union.

Many economists say the nation may be returning to a period like 1973 to 1996, when inflation-adjusted wages stagnated or rose glacially. That era was a reversal from the golden years of 1947 to 1973, when wages marched steadily upward.

From 1996 to 2001, wages grew strongly again because of an unusually low jobless rate, caused in part by the high-technology boom. In the late 1990's, the tight labor market pressured companies to give sizable raises to attract and retain workers even as a surge in productivity helped business afford them without substantially cutting into profits.

Thomas A. Kochan, an economist at the Massachusetts Institute of Technology, said wages could once again rise, but only if there was especially robust economic growth.

"To produce real wage gains now, it takes sustaining a very tight labor market," he said. "Without that, we're going to continue to see what we're seeing now: abysmal growth in real wages."

PART THREE

States and Globalization

CHAPTER 6

National States and Globalization

Among the most hotly contested issues in the study of globalization is the relation of states to globalization. The selection by Susan Strange that opens this chapter forcefully develops a position held by many scholars. The title of Strange's book, *The Retreat of the State*, says it best: states have been forced to retreat in face of the superior power of globalization. For Strange and others in this camp, states have lost the capacity to control movements within and across their borders. Again, concepts like retreat or decline best describe this development. As a result, according to this view, states can no longer be relied upon—or feared—as in the past.

Yet, from very different perspectives, Linda Weiss and Saskia Sassen challenge the retreat-of-the-state position. For Weiss, states are neither being "hollowed out" nor transformed. Nor have they lost the capacity to steer economic development. Instead, basing her analysis on the Korean state, Weiss demonstrates that states can retain the capacity to promote economic development if they make marginal adjustments in their orientation.

The selection by Sassen suggests another possible weakness in the state-decline approach. Sassen asserts that states have now assumed a new function that powerfully promotes economic globalization. Traditionally, a bedrock difference existed between corporations headquartered in a country as opposed to domestic subsidiaries of foreign firms or foreign-based corporations that exported goods to that country. A dense array of state laws and regulations distinguished between domestic and foreign firms and granted differential—and more favorable—treatment to a country's domestic firms. For example, tax laws and government procurement policies provided domestic firms important advantages. This differential treatment of domestic firms hinders economic integration and the construction of global markets.

Sassen suggests that states have now altered their stance and seek to eliminate differential treatment of domestic and foreign firms, what she calls the denationalization of the state. Yet accomplishing this goal is no easy matter, since locally based business firms and their employees typically oppose losing their former advantages.

When you read these selections, ask whether and how the contending positions might be reconciled. Further, might there be other possible relationships of states to globalization? Another issue to ponder: many analyses discuss the role of states in general and fail to distinguish among kinds of states. Yet, to paraphrase George Orwell's observation in *Animal Farm,* although all states are equal, some are more equal than others! That is, although international law may specify that states are equal by virtue of possessing sovereignty, this is often a legal fiction. On just about every issue that counts, states vary enormously in power. One cannot equate the capacity of the United States government to exercise control over its economic fate with that of virtually any other country in the world. (Note, however, that several selections in Chapter 8 claim that the United States is far from being all-powerful.)

As has been the case with other issues in PG, the selections in this chapter demonstrate that there are no ready-made answers explaining the state's relationship to globalization. However, the fact that there is a scholarly debate about the relationship of the state to globalization does not mean that anything goes: although you are free to develop your own position, you must defend that position with persuasive theoretical and empirical evidence!

The Retreat of the State *The Diffusion of Power in the World Economy*

Susan Strange

Political economist Susan Strange devoted her career to studying the role of states in the international economy. In many books and articles, she made distinguished contributions to our understanding of how states develop international economic policy. In this selection from a book written shortly before her death, she claims that the international political economy has been fundamentally transformed by globalization and that it is time for scholars to catch up with the new realities. In particular, technological changes and the liberalization of international trade, production, and finance have dealt a decisive blow to the formerly unchallenged position of states in the international arena and to the academic understanding that assumes the primacy of states. She notes that this situation involves multiple paradoxes. First, states do continue to intervene—indeed, increasingly so—in citizens' everyday lives. (The book was published before September 11, 2001; events since then give greater force to her argument.) But, she contends, increased intervention does not signify increased power. Second, while state power is declining, the number of groups seeking their own state in the modern world is increasing. Finally, it might appear that the basic argument is contradicted by the example of East Asian states—Japan, Korea, and Taiwan—states that were especially energetic in sponsoring national economic growth. However, she concludes, those states were success stories in the period beginning after World War II and extending through the Cold War. In the period since then, even these states have been pressured to adopt hands-off economic policies of a kind pursued recently by states in Western Europe and North America. (For a different view of the changing role of East Asian states, see the selection by Weiss in this chapter.)

Selections in this chapter by Sassen and Weiss challenge Strange's argument, while the selection by van Creveld is consistent with Strange's position. Assess the strengths and weaknesses of the contending approaches, and provide your own approach to the question of how to understand the character and power of states in the current era of globalization.

. . . The argument put forward [here] is that the impersonal forces of world markets, integrated over the postwar period more by private enterprise in finance, industry and trade than by the cooperative decisions of governments, are now more powerful than the states to whom ultimate political authority over society and economy is supposed to belong.

Where states were once the masters of markets, now it is the markets which, on many crucial issues, are the masters over the governments of states. And the declining authority of states is reflected in a growing diffusion of authority to other institutions and associations, and to local and regional bodies, and in a growing asymmetry between the larger states with structural power and weaker ones without it.

There are, to be sure, some striking paradoxes about this reversal of the state-market balance of power. One, which disguises from many people the overall decline of state power, is that the *intervention* of state authority and of the agencies of the state in the daily lives of the citizen appears to be growing. Where once it was left to the individual to look for work, to buy goods or services with caution in case they were unsafe or not what they seemed to be, to build or to pull down houses, to manage family relationships and so on, now governments pass laws, set up inspectorates and planning authorities, provide employment services, enforce customer protection against unclean water, unsafe food, faulty buildings or transport systems. The impression is conveyed that less and less of daily life is immune from the activities and decisions of government bureaucracies.

That is not necessarily inconsistent with my contention that state *power* is declining. It is less effective on those basic matters that the market, left to itself, has never been able to provide—security against violence, stable money for trade and investment, a clear system of law and the means to enforce it, and a sufficiency of public goods like drains, water supplies, infrastructures for transport and communications. Little wonder that it is less respected and lacks its erstwhile legitimacy. The need for a political authority of some kind, legitimated either by coercive force or by popular consent, or more often by a combination of the two, is the fundamental reason for the state's existence. But many states are coming to be deficient in these fundamentals. Their deficiency is not made good by greater activity in marginal matters, matters that are optional for society, and which are not absolutely necessary for the functioning of the market and the maintenance of social order. Trivialising government does not make its authority more respected; often, the contrary is true.

The second paradox is that while the governments of established states, most notably in North America and western Europe, are suffering this progressive loss of real authority, the queue of societies that want to have their own state is lengthening. This is true not only of ethnic groups that were forcibly suppressed by the single-party government of the former Soviet Union. It is true of literally hundreds of minorities and aboriginal peoples in every part of the world—in Canada and Australia, in India and Africa, even in the old so-called nation-states of Europe. Many—perhaps the majority—are suppressed by force, like the Kurds or the Basques. Others—like the Scots or the Corsicans—are just not strong enough or angry enough to offer a serious challenge to the existing state. Still others such as the native Americans, the Aboriginals, the Samis or the Flemish are pacified by resource transfers or by half-measures that go some way to meet their perceived

---

Susan Strange, *The Retreat of the State: The Diffusion of Power in the World Economy* (New York: Cambridge University Press, 1996): 4–11.

need for an independent identity. Only a few, such as the Greenlanders, the Slovaks or Slovenes or the unwanted, unviable Pacific island-states, have succeeded in getting what they wanted—statehood. But once achieved, it does not seem to give them any real control over the kind of society or the nature of their economy that they might have preferred. In short, the desire for ethnic or cultural autonomy is universal; the political means to satisfy that desire within an integrated world market economy is not. Many, perhaps most, societies have to be content with the mere appearance of autonomy, with a facade of statehood. The struggle for independence has often proved a pyrrhic victory.

The final paradox which can be brought as evidence against my basic contention about the hollowness of state authority at the end of this century is that this is a western, or even an Anglo-Saxon phenomenon, and is refuted by the Asian experience of the state. The Asian state, it is argued, has in fact been the means to achieve economic growth, industrialisation, a modernised infrastructure and rising living standards for the people. Singapore might be the prime example of a strong state achieving economic success. But Japan, Korea, Taiwan are all states which have had strong governments, governments which have successfully used the means to restrict and control foreign trade and foreign investment, and to allocate credit and to guide corporate development in the private sector. Is it not premature—just another instance of Eurocentrism therefore—to assume the declining authority of the state?

There are two answers to this third paradox. One is that all these Asian states were exceptionally fortunate. They profited in three ways from their geographical position on the western frontier of the United States during the Cold War. Their strategic importance in the 1950s and after was such that they could count on generous military and economic aid from the Americans, aid which was combined with their exceptionally high domestic savings and low patterns of consumption. The combination gave a head start to rapid economic development. Secondly, and also for strategic reasons, they could be—almost had to be—exempted from the pressure to conform to the norms of the open liberal economy. They were allowed, first formally and then informally, to limit foreign imports and also to restrict the entry of the foreign firms that might have proved too strong competitors for their local enterprises. At the same time, they were given relatively open access first to the large, rich U.S. market for manufactures, and later, under some protest, to the European one. And thirdly, the technology necessary to their industrialisation was available to be bought on the market, either in the form of patents, or in the person of technical advisors from Europe and America or through corporate alliances which brought them the technology without the loss of managerial control.

Now, I would argue, these special dispensations are on the way out, and not only because the Cold War is over. The Asian governments will be under increasing pressure from Washington to adopt more liberal non-discriminatory policies on trade and investment. And they will also be under pressure from within to liberalise and to allow more competition, including foreign competition, for the benefit of consumers and of other producers. In short, the exceptionalism of the Asian state during the Cold War has already been substantially eroded, and will continue to be so. As it has been at other times, and in other places, there will be contests for control over the institutions and agencies of government in most of the Asian countries. There will be contests between factions of political parties, between vested interests both in the private sectors and in the public sector. There will be power struggles between branches of the state bureaucracy. Both the unity and the authority of government is bound to suffer.

The Neglected Factor—Technology

My argument . . . depends a good deal on the accelerating pace of technological change as a prime cause of the shift in the state-market balance of power. Since social scientists are, not, by definition, natural scientists, they have a strong tendency to overlook the importance of technology which rests, ultimately, on advances in physics, in chemistry and related sciences like nuclear physics or industrial chemistry. In the last 100 years, there has been more rapid technological change than ever before in human history. On this the scientists themselves are generally agreed. It took hundreds—in some places, thousands—of years to domesticate animals so that horses could be used for transport and oxen (later heavy horses) could be used to replace manpower to plough and sow ground for the production of crops in agriculture. It has taken less than 100 years for the car and truck to replace the horse and for aircraft to partly take over from road and rail transport. The electric telegraph as a means of communication was invented in the 1840s and remained the dominant system in Europe until the 1920s. But in the next eighty years, the telegraph gave way to the telephone, the telephone gave way to radio, radio to television and cables to satellites and optic fibres linking computers to other computers. No one under the age of thirty or thirty-five today needs convincing that, just in their own lifetime, the pace of technological change has been getting faster and faster. The technically unsophisticated worlds of business, government and education of even the 1960s would be unrecognisable to them. No fax, no personal computers, no accessible copiers, no mobile phones, no video shops, no DNA tests, no cable TV, no satellite networks connecting distant markets, twenty-four hours a day. The world in which their grandparents grew up in the 1930 or 1940s is as alien to them as that of the Middle Ages. There is no reason to suppose that technological change in products and processes, driven by profit, will not continue to accelerate in future.

This simple, everyday, commonsense fact of modern life is important because it goes a long way to explaining both political and economic change. It illuminates the changes both in the power of states and in the power of markets. Its dynamism, in fact, is basic to my argument, because it is a continuing factor, not a once-for-all change.

For the sake of clarity, consider first the military aspects of technical change, and then the civilian aspects—although in reality each spills over into the other. In what are known as strategic studies circles, no one doubts that the development of the atom bomb in the middle of the twentieth century, and later of nuclear weapons carried by intercontinental missiles, has brought about a major change in the nature of warfare between states. Mutual assured destruction was a powerful reason for having nuclear weapons—but equally it was a good reason for not using them. After the paradoxical long peace of the Cold War, two things began to change. The expectation that, sooner or later, nuclear war would destroy life on the planet began to moderate. And confidence began to wane that the state could, by a defensive strategy, prevent this happening. Either it would or it wouldn't, and governments could do little to alter the probabilities. Thus, technology had undermined one of the primary reasons for the existence of the state—its capacity to repel attack by others, its responsibility for what Adam Smith called "the defence of the realm."

At the same time technology has had its effect on civilian life. Medical technology has made human life both longer and more comfortable. Electrical technology has liberated millions of women from the drudgery that imprisoned previous generations in the day-long labour of preparing food, keeping the family's clothes clean and mended, and houses clean and warm. As washing machines, vacuum cleaners, dishwashers, central heating and refrigerators and freezers spread down the income levels, more people had more to lose from inter-state conflict. Comfort bred conservatism in politics. Moreover, the new wealth was being acquired by the Germans and the Japanese who had actually been defeated in World War II. Acquiring territory was no longer seen as a means to increase wealth. Losing territory did not mean the state became poorer or weaker. Gaining market shares in the world outside the territorial borders of the state, however, did enable formerly poor countries like Japan, Taiwan or Hong Kong to earn the foreign exchange with which to buy capital goods, foreign technology and the necessary resources of energy and raw materials. As John Stopford and I have argued, competition for world market shares has replaced competition for territory, or for control over the natural resources of territory, as the "name of the game" between states (Stopford and Strange, 1991; Strange in Rizopoulos (ed.), 1990). In this new game, the search for allies among other states goes on, but not for their added military capabilities. It is for the added bargaining power conferred by a larger economic area.

Moreover, the search for allies is not confined to other states or intergovernmental organisations. It is supplemented by a search for allies among foreign-owned firms. These firms may be persuaded, in exchange for access to the national market, to raise the finance, apply their technology, provide the management and the access to export markets—in short, to take all the steps necessary to locate production of goods or services within the territory of the host state. In most developing or ex-socialist countries, the prospect of new jobs and extra export earnings brought by such investments have become powerful reasons for a change of attitude toward the so-called "multinationals."

The Second Neglect—Finance

Not the least of the TNC's attractions to host states is its ability to raise finance both for the investment itself and—even more important—for the development of new technology. Another key part of the argument . . . is that, besides the accelerating pace of technological change, there has been an escalation in the capital cost of most technological innovations—in agriculture, in manufacturing and the provision of services, and in new products and in new processes. In all of these, the input of capital has risen while the relative input of labour has fallen. It is this increased cost which has raised the stakes, as it were, in the game of staying up with the competition. This is so whether we look at competition from other firms who are also striving for larger market shares, or whether we look at governments trying to make sure that the economies for whose performance they are held responsible stay up with the competition in wealth-creation coming from other economies. Thus, to the extent that a government can benefit from a TNC's past and future investments without itself bearing the main cost of it, there are strong reasons for forging such alliances.

But the escalating costs of technological change are also important for a more fundamental reason, and not just because it explains the changing policies of host states to TNCs. It has to do with change in the world system. The cost of new technology in the production structure has added to the salience of money in the international political economy. It is no exaggeration to say that, with a few notable exceptions, scholars in international relations for the past half-century have grossly neglected the political aspects of credit-creation, and of changes in the global financial structure.[1] In much theorising about international relations or even international political economy there is no mention at all of the financial structure (as distinct from the international monetary order governing the exchange relations of national currencies). Briefly, the escalating capital costs of new technologies could not have been covered at all without, firstly, some very fundamental changes in the volume and nature of credit created by the capitalist market economy; and secondly, without the added mobility that in recent years has characterised that created credit. The *supply* of capital to finance technological innovation (and for other purposes) has been as important in the international political economy as the *demand* from the innovators for more money to produce ever more sophisticated products by ever more capital-intensive processes of production.

These supply and demand changes take place, and take effect, in the market. And it is markets, rather than state-state relations that many leading texts in international political economy tend to overlook. Much more emphasis is put on international monetary relations between governments and their national currencies. To the extent that attention is paid at all to the institutions creating and marketing credit in the world economy, they are held to be important chiefly for the increased volatility they may cause to exchange rates, or to the impact they may have on the ability of governments to borrow abroad to finance development or the shortfall between revenue and spending, or between export earnings and import bills.

More significant in the long run, however, when it comes to evolving better theories to explain change in the international political economy is the accompanying neglect of the three-way connections between the supply side of international finance (credit), the demand side from firms, and the political intervention of governments as regulators of banking and financial markets and as borrowers or lenders, at home and abroad. There are theories to explain each of the three, but no unifying theory to explain their mutual connections. . . .

Note

1. The notable exceptions include Cerny, 1993; Porter, 1994; Veseth 1990; Wachtel, 1986; Frieden, 1987; Moffitt, 1983; Calleo, 1982. . . .

References

Calleo, D. 1982, *The Imperious Economy*. Cambridge MA: Harvard University Press.

Cerny, Philip 1989, *The Changing Architecture of Politics: Structure, Agency, and the Future of the State*. London: Sage.

Frieden, Jeffry 1987, *Banking on the World: The Politics of American International Finance*. New York: Harper & Row.

Moffitt, M. 1984, *The World's Money: International Banking from Bretton Woods to the Brink of Insolvency*. London: Joseph.

Porter, Michael 1990, *The Competitive Advantage of Nations*. New York: Free Press.

Rizopoulus, N. 1990, *Sea-Changes: American Foreign Policy in a World Transformed*. New York: Council on Foreign Relations.

Stopford, John and Strange, Susan 1991, *Rival States, Rival Firms Competition for World Market Shares*. Cambridge: Cambridge University Press.

Veseth, Michael 1990, *Mountains of Debt—Crisis and Change in Renaissance Florence, Victorian Britain and Post-war America*. Oxford: Oxford University Press.

Wachtel, Howard 1986, *The Money Mandarins: The Making of a New Supranational Economic Order*. New York: Pantheon Books.

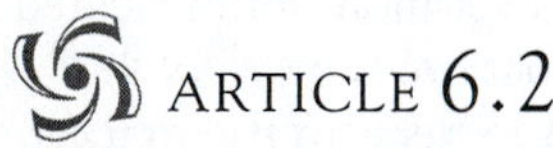

ARTICLE 6.2

The Fate of the State

Martin van Creveld

Martin van Creveld argues that, although states have been the dominant political institutions for several centuries, they are now losing power in key domains: military affairs, control over domestic economic and social matters, the technologies of communication (for example, the Internet), and the maintenance of public order. Van Creveld questions whether the results of declining state power are positive or negative. Good question to ponder! However, before concluding that the positions developed by van Creveld and Strange (in the preceding selection) are correct, consider challenges to this position by Sassen and Weiss, which follow. They seek to show why, in their view, states continue to play a central role in world politics.

The State, which since the Treaty of Westphalia (1648) has been the most important and most characteristic of all modern institutions, is dying. Wherever we look, existing states are either combining into larger communities or falling apart; wherever we look, organizations that are not states are taking their place. On the international level, we are moving away from a system of separate, sovereign, states toward less distinct, more hierarchical, and in many ways more complex structures. Inside their borders, it seems that many states will soon no longer be able to protect the political, military, economic, social, and cultural life of their citizens. These developments may lead to upheavals as profound as those that took humanity out of the Middle Ages and into the Modern World. Whether the direction of change is desirable, as some hope, or undesirable, as others fear, remains to be seen.

In this article the state of the state will be discussed under five headings. Part I looks at the state's declining ability to fight other states. Part II outlines the rise and fall of the welfare state. Part III examines the effects of modern technology, economics, and the media. Part IV focuses on the state's ability to maintain public order. Finally, Part V is an attempt to tie all the threads together and to see where we are headed.

Part I. The Declining Ability to Fight

The principal function of the state, as that of all previous forms of government, has always been to fight other states, whether defensively in an attempt to defend its interests or offensively to extend them. Usually a state that was unable to do this was doomed to disappear. The best it could hope for was to lead a sort of shadowy existence under the protection of some other state, as Lebanon, for example, does under Syrian tutelage; even that existence was likely to be temporary.

Conversely, the need to fight other states has played a critical role in the development of the state's most important institutions. This includes the government bureaucracy, whose original function was to levy taxes for the purpose of waging war; the note-issuing state bank, an early 18th-century invention designed specifically to help pay for Britain's military effort during the wars against Louis XIV; and of course the regular armed forces. In most states, the latter continued to take up the lion's share of expenditure until well into the 19th century.

Driven largely by the need to fight other states, the power of the state expanded from 1700 on. The number of bureaucrats (the word itself is an 18th-

---

Martin van Creveld, "The Fate of the State," *Parameters,* Spring 1996: 4–17. Reprinted by permission of Artellus, Ltd.

century neologism) multiplied, and the amount of statistical information at their disposal increased, as did the share of GDP that was extracted by government. Technology drove war, and war, technology. International competition intensified until, during the second half of the 19th century, it reached the point where much of the world had been turned into an armed camp. Each of the so-called great powers was looking anxiously over its shoulder at all the rest to see which one was the most threatening, and which one, being less so for the moment, could be drawn into an alliance.

Most important of all, the French Revolution led to the nationalization of the masses and, with that, to a drastic change in the role of the state in the popular consciousness. Hobbes, Locke, and many of their 18th-century successors saw the state simply as an instrument for maintaining public order and permitting a civilized life; to quote a rhyme by Alexander Pope: "Over government fools contest/What is best administered is best." Now it became an end unto itself, an earthly god in whose honor festivals were celebrated, monuments erected, and hymns composed and sung. It was a vengeful god who, according to his greatest prophet, Georg Hegel, fed on blood and periodically demanded the sacrifice of hundreds of thousands if not millions—for their own highest good, needless to say. In retrospect, nothing in the history of the modern state is more astonishing than the willingness, occasionally even eagerness, of people to fight for it and lay down their lives for it.

The climax of these developments was reached during the years of total war between 1914 and 1945. Acting in the name of the need to protect or extend something known as the national interest, states conscripted their populations and fought each other on an unprecedented scale and with an unprecedented ferocity. Nor was it merely a question of soldiers killing each other in the field. At the grand strategic level, both 1914–18 and 1939–45 were conducted by attrition; this gave states time to mobilize not only troops but civilians (including women and children) as well, putting them to work in fields and factories. . . .

Thanks to the unprecedented mobilization of demographic, economic, industrial, technological, and scientific resources, the two world wars together, and each separately, dwarfed all the armed conflicts that had taken place in the past. More important to our purpose, mobilization warfare accelerated—if it did not create—technological progress. All through World War II in particular, tens of thousands of scientists were engaged in research and development, producing devices that ranged from radar to the electronic computer and from the jet engine to the first ballistic missiles. The climax arrived on 6 August 1945 when the first atomic bomb exploded over Hiroshima, killing an estimated 75,000 people.

At first, nuclear weapons were thought to have put unprecedented military power in the hands of the state; after a few years, though, it began to be realized that they did not so much serve the objectives of war as put an end to it. As the power of nuclear weapons grew—from 20,000 kilotons in 1945 to 58 megatons in 1961—and their numbers increased, wherever they made their appearance large-scale interstate war came to a halt. First the superpowers; then their close allies in NATO and the Warsaw Pact; then the U.S.S.R. and China; then China and India; then India and Pakistan; then Israel and its Arab neighbors. Much as they hated each other, they each in turn saw themselves with their horns locked and unable to fight each other in earnest.

Without exception, what large-scale interstate wars have taken place since 1945 have been waged either between or against third- and fourth-rate military powers. . . . Since 1945 no two first-rate states, meaning such as were armed with nuclear weapons, have fought each other; by some accounts they have not even come close to fighting each other.

Even more striking than the marginalization of the belligerents was the declining scale on which war was waged. Though the world's population has almost tripled since 1945, and though its ability to produce goods and services has increased many times over, both the size of armed forces and the number of the major weapon systems with which they are provided now amount to only a fraction of what they were in 1945. For example, the forces mobilized by the coalition in the Gulf were just one-seventh of the size of those deployed by Germany for its invasion of Russia in 1941. In most places the shrinking process is still under way. Not a day passes without some new cuts being announced. And in the face of the potential for nuclear destruction, there is not much chance of the mass forces of World War II being rebuilt in any kind of foreseeable future.

Part II. The Rise and Fall of the Welfare State

As the state lost its ability to expand at its neighbors' expense—a handicap confirmed by the Charter of the United Nations, which, as the most subscribed-to document in history, prohibits using force to annex territory—it turned its energies inward. It lies in the nature of a bureaucratic construct that it should seek to control and regulate everything; in so doing it created the welfare state.

The beginning of the story is in the period 1789 to 1830. First came the French Revolution, which, exported across the length and width of Europe, broke up the ancient feudal and ecclesiastic institutions; by atomizing society, it put the state in a much stronger position than ever before. Next came the industrial revolution. Starting in Britain, it brought with it economic freedom, unbridled capitalism (including its worst manifestations—a total lack of planning, widespread poverty, and inhumane exploitation), and the invisible hand. The influence of such figures as Adam Smith and Friedrich List caused one nation after another to dismantle internal and external economic controls and switch to free trade; with the Manchester School firmly in control, during the first half of the century the motto was *laissez faire*.

After 1850 or so, the prevailing mood began to change. One reason for this was a number of inquiries, some of them official, that were launched into the state of the working class and that brought to light the often shocking conditions in which working people lived. Another was the military competition mentioned in the previous section; with the most important states increasingly dependent on mass armies consisting of conscripts and reservists, their rulers felt they could no longer afford to neglect the populations that provided those armies. Finally there was the steady, if often stormy, movement toward democratization and the rise in many countries of socialist parties. The former made it necessary, in the words of one English parliamentarian, "to educate our masters." The latter attracted a growing number of voters and openly threatened violent revolution unless something was done to improve the lot of the masses.

Be the exact reasons what they may, the first Factory Acts were passed in Britain during the 1840s over howls of protests by the owners and their spokesmen. The laws' purpose was to put limits on working hours—initially those of women and children—and to institute at least some safety controls. Imitated by many countries, originally the new laws only applied to a few industries considered particularly dangerous, such as mining. Later they were extended to others such as textile and metalworking plants. Among the last to be reached were agriculture, domestic service, and small-scale light industry, particularly in the form of sweatshops. These were affected, to the extent that they were affected at all, only during the early years of the 20th century.

Once the state had begun to supervise the conditions of labor—including the establishment of labor exchanges, another early 20th-century development—it soon sought to do the same for education and public health. The pioneer in the former field was Prussia; following beginnings made in the reign of Frederick the Great, something like universal—although, as yet, not free—elementary education was achieved in the years after 1815 when Prussia became a much-imitated model and educators from all over the world flocked to see how it was done. In the rest of Europe the real push was provided by the war of 1870–71. The French in particular looked for an explanation; unable to agree on the causes of the defeat, in the end they pointed a finger at the schoolmaster. Around 1900 the "utopian vision"—the phrase used by the British Fabian socialist Beatrice Webb—of universal elementary education had been achieved in all the most advanced countries.

Advances in public health were made necessary by urban growth and were initially decentralized. In Britain, Germany, and to a growing extent the United States, laws were enacted that entrusted the task of providing better sanitation, better disease controls, to local authorities and municipalities; they also took over from the church and private charitable organizations by providing at least some hospitals for the indigenous ill. In the most advanced countries, ministries of health were established during the first two decades after 1900. Their task was to supervise those countries' entire health systems, including both medical practice and training; in addition, many of them also provided various programs, such as inoculation and prenatal care, that were compulsory, free, or both.

Like state-run education, state-run welfare was originally a German invention. The 1880s found Bismarck worried about the progress of the Social Democratic Party. This caused him to institute the so-called "Revolution from above" and the world's first schemes for unemployment, accident, sickness, and old age insurance.

Between 1890 and 1914 his example was followed by others through much of Western Europe and Scandinavia. Seen from this point of view, the Bolshevik Revolution of 1917 was anything but an anomaly; instead it was simply an attempt to grab one particularly backward country by the neck, institute universal welfare at a single stroke, and extend state control to the point where civil society itself almost ceased to exist. Only the United States, with its tradition of free enterprise and rugged individualism, resisted the trend and, as a result, found itself lagging behind. In the land of the dollar it took the Great Depression and 13 million unemployed to make first the New Deal and then social security during the 1930s.

Still, what really made the modern welfare state was World War II. As had already been the case during World War I, governments took responsibility for running many aspects of their citizens' lives, including even the number of inches of hot water they were allowed to put in their tubs; but this time they did so with no intention of giving up their power after the war had ended. In one developed country after another, extensive health programs covering the entire population—as under the British National Health System which served as the model for many others—were established. To this were added a vast variety of ancillary programs, such as free or subsidized meals for children and the elderly, cheap housing, vocational training and retraining, and education. The latter often led to free education up to, and in some instances including, the university level.

These developments led to a huge increase in the number of bureaucrats per population and per square mile. By the end of the 1950s the number of ministries, which during the state's formative years in the 17th and 18th centuries had usually stood at four, had risen to something nearer 20 in most countries. . . .

To pay for these programs and these ministries, it became necessary to raise taxes—particularly direct ones—until, in countries such as Britain and Sweden, marginal rates of income tax could reach 90 percent and more. Taxation, though, was only part of the solution. The nationalization of industry had been demanded by socialist parties ever since the time of the *Communist Manifesto*. The way ahead had been shown in Britain by the creation of the Electricity Board in 1926; next, France during the premiership of Léon Blum (1936–37) nationalized its arms industry. Following World War II, in one European country after another entire sectors of the economy were taken out of private hands and put into those of the state. The exact identity of the industries in question varied. Often they included mass transportation such as sea, air, and rail; telecommunications, energy, banking, insurance, mining (particularly for coal and oil), and critical branches of manufacturing such as steel, shipbuilding, aviation, and military equipment. Initially it was hoped that the profits of these industries would be made to work for the community at large rather than for their shareholders alone. In practice it did not take long before many of them, run on electoral principles rather than business ones, turned into albatrosses that were grossly overstaffed, incurred enormous losses, demanded vast subsidies, and hung like chains around the state's neck.

In retrospect, the turning point in the history of nationalization and the welfare state came during the second half of the 1970s. Until then the trend toward greater state control had been increasing steadily. Even in the United States, always a latecomer in such matters, "big government" made its debut during the 1950s; in the 1960s the Kennedy and Johnson administrations declared "war on poverty" and presided over a vast expansion of various social programs. Then, in one country after another a reaction set in. It was motivated partly by the immense losses attributable to many nationalized industries; partly by the drastic increase in unemployment—and consequently in the cost of insuring against it—brought about by the oil crisis; and partly by the desire to cut the burden of taxes, which was regarded as stifling economic enterprise. On top of all this the welfare state had become a victim of its own success. The more it sought to help disadvantaged groups such as the aged or single parents, the larger the number of those who claimed the benefit of its services and the greater also the addition to the national debt.

By this time the naïve belief in the virtues of an "impartial" state bureaucracy that had inspired political scientists from Hegel to Max Weber was long since dead. Instead of representing rationality, bureaucracy was coming to be seen as its antithesis; instead of being an instrument of social progress, it was now perceived as an obstacle to change of any kind. During the late 1970s there emerged a number of political leaders such as Margaret Thatcher and Ronald Reagan whose goal, loudly professed, was to roll back the power of the state. "Standing on one's own feet" and "getting government off our backs" became the rallying cries under which some of the most important states set out to dismantle themselves; even though, in many places, progress—if that is the correct term—was greater in words than in deeds.

All through the 1980s the movement back to the 19th century gathered momentum. Late in the decade it was given a tremendous boost by the collapse of the U.S.S.R. For 70 years, communism had provided an alternative model in which the state, for all its manifold and perceived shortcomings, claimed to have eliminated the worst forms of poverty and promised security from the cradle to the grave; now the system's sudden demise left East Bloc states naked and their respective civil societies poorer than ever. Not only was laissez faire capitalism able to reemerge as the only way toward a better future, but it no longer felt obliged to apologize for its seamier sides, such as gross inequality, ever-present insecurity for both employers and employees, and the colossal waste resulting from the business cycle on the one hand and unplanned development on the other. To the contrary, many of the advocates of the new supply-side economics regarded those features as potentially useful tools toward the all-important goals of low inflation and steady economic growth.

As the last years of the century approached, not even those countries that were loudest in their praise of capitalism had made significant progress in reducing their bureaucracies, much less in cutting taxes as a percentage of GDP. On the other hand, in virtually all countries some of the juicier morsels of the economy had been sold off and others deregulated, to say nothing of the cuts that, with or without the aid of inflation, were effected in the real value of numerous social programs including, not least, the quality of education. The homeless people appearing on the streets of cities everywhere offered visible proof of the fact that the post–World War II trend toward a narrowing of social gaps had been reversed; it became a matter of policy for the state to take more and more but give less and less. No wonder that loyalty to it—as manifested most clearly in the willingness to do conscript service and fight if necessary—declined. In the United States under the Carter Administration, even the attempt to register young males for an eventual call-up met with opposition.

Part III. Modern Technology, Economics, and the Media

Meanwhile, and often going almost unnoticed, technology also had performed an about-face. The role played by print in the establishment of the state cannot be overestimated; after all, where would any government be without forms? Next, the telegraph and the railways enabled states to bring their populations under control and to cast their networks over entire countries, even continents. Nor were rulers satisfied when the time it took to travel from the capital to the provinces (for example, from Paris to Bordeaux or Toulouse) was reduced from weeks to days or hours. The role of technologies such as telephones, teleprinters, computers (first put to use in calculating the results of the U.S. census), highways, and other systems of transportation and communication was even greater than that of their predecessors. Without them it would have been impossible for the state to contemplate the task that it had undertaken since the beginning of the 19th century: to impose its control over every part of society from the highest to the lowest and almost regardless of distance and geographical location.

From the beginning, though, much of modern technology bore a Janus face. On the one hand it gave governments the tools with which to dominate their countries and populations as never before. On the other it tended to transcend national borders, crossing them and turning them into obstacles to domination. This was because, unlike its pre-1800 predecessors, much of modern technology can operate only when, and to the extent that, it is grouped into systems. A plough, a hammer, a musket, or a ship can do its job even in the absence of others of its kind; but an individual railway station—or a telegraph apparatus, or a telephone—is simply useless on its own. In such systems what matters is the network of tracks, or wires, or switchboards, that connects each unit with countless others. Even more crucial is the central directing hand which, sorting out routes and priorities, enables them to communicate with each other at will, in an orderly manner and without mutual interference.

As the history of both telegraphs and railways shows, most of the early technological systems were launched by private entrepreneurs. However, in most countries the demand for economic efficiency or military effectiveness soon caused them to be taken over by governments. Either this was done by way of outright ownership, through nationalization and the establishment of a state monopoly, or else by means of regulations designed to ensure that they would be available in wartime. Still, there were limits to the extent that governments could control this technology without at the same time reducing its cost-effectiveness. A railway net designed exclusively for meeting the needs of a single country—such as the broadgauged one constructed by Imperial Russia and later passed to the USSR—provided some protection against invasion but also acted as a barrier to Russian trade with other countries. The same applies to various attempts to build autonomous electricity grids, highway systems, or telephone networks, to say nothing of fax machines and computers.

In theory each state was free to exercise its sovereignty and build its own networks, ignoring those of its neighbors and refusing to integrate with them. In practice it could do so only by incurring a tremendous technological and economic cost. The current plight of North Korea is a perfect case in point; the price of isolation was inefficiency and an inability to maximize the benefits of precisely those technologies that have developed most rapidly since 1945—communication (including data processing) and transportation. Conversely, in order to enjoy those benefits, states had to integrate their networks with those of their neighbors. What is more, it was necessary for them to join the international bodies whose task was to regulate the new technologies on behalf of all. The first such body was the International Railway Committee, which traces its origins to the 1860s. A century later they numbered in the hundreds, and the only way for any state to avoid becoming entangled in their coils was to doom itself to something like a pre-industrial existence.

These technological developments brought about a decisive change in the nature of the global economy. The interwar period had been characterized by attempts to build self-contained empires; now, the most successful states were those which, like Germany and Japan and South Korea, were most integrated into the world market. By and large the more one exported and imported—in other words, maximized one's comparative advantage—the greater one's economic success. As more and more stock exchanges were opened to foreign investors and capital, a greater and greater percentage of a state's assets, and those of its citizens, was likely to be located beyond its borders. Conversely, inside those borders more and more wealth was likely to be controlled by persons and corporations based elsewhere. During the 1980s economic statistics began to recognize the change by separating GNP from GDP. Generally the gap between the two provided a good index for the economic performance of any particular country; for example, 40 percent of all Japanese goods are now being produced outside Japan.

Another blow to state control implicit in the shift toward a global economy was that governments gradually lost their grip over their own currencies. If a nation was to participate in international trade, its currency had to be convertible, as free as possible from administrative controls. But freedom from administrative controls put it at the mercy of the international market. Gone were the days when, as during the period 1914–39, most governments tried to create closed monetary systems and lay down the value of their currencies by fiat. Gone, too, were the

Bretton Woods agreements which lasted from 1944 to 1971 and which pegged the various currencies to a U.S. dollar which was itself pegged to gold. Governments did not lose all influence over their currencies; they still controlled the money supply as well as interest rates. Nevertheless, the values of these currencies became subject to wild fluctuations that were often beyond the power of central banks, or even combinations of central banks, to regulate. Their inability to do so put a premium on hedging, on holding at least some of one's assets in foreign currency. The merry-go-round leading to less and less government control continued.

Finally, the unprecedented development of electronic information services seems to mark another step toward the coming collapse of the state. Traditionally no state has ever been able to completely control the thoughts of all its citizens; to the credit of the more liberally-minded among them, it must be added that they never even tried. Though the invention of print greatly increased the amount of information that could be produced, the ability to move that information across international borders remained limited by the need to physically transport paper, as well as by language barriers. The first of these problems was solved by the invention of radio. The introduction of television, which relies on pictures instead of words, to a large extent eliminated the second. During the 1980s cable and satellite TV, as well as videotape, became widely available and capable of providing near-instant coverage of events on a global scale. With the advent of computer networks and the consequent democratization of access to information, the battle between freedom and control was irretrievably lost by the latter, much to the regret of numerous governments. . . .

Part IV. Maintaining Public Order

As governments surrender or lose their hold over many aspects of the media, the economy, and technology, and as public ownership as well as welfare programs stagnate or retreat, one of the principal functions still remaining to the state is to protect its own integrity against internal disorder. Thus the question that must be asked is whether they have been successful in this task; is it being mastered, and can they be expected to accomplish it in the future?

So far this article has concentrated on the developed countries. However, at this point it is useful to invert the order, starting our survey with undeveloped ones. It is a characteristic of many traditional societies that the right to resort to violence, instead of being monopolized by an all-powerful state, is diffused in the hands of family heads, tribal chieftains, feudal noblemen, and the like, each of whom is responsible for policing his own subjects and for fighting off challenges by the rest. Conversely, the extent to which so-called Third World countries have succeeded in demolishing other organizations and concentrating violence in their own hands is one very good index of their progress toward modernization.

To look at many developing countries today, that progress has been either slow or nonexistent. . . . In much of sub-Saharan Africa the state has already collapsed, often before it was able to properly establish itself. Angola, Burundi, Ethiopia, Liberia, Nigeria, Rwanda, Somalia, the Sudan, and Zaire all have been torn by civil war or, at the very least, disorder on a scale that approximates it. On the Mediterranean littoral the position of Egypt and Algeria is scarcely better, confronted as those states are by the formidable challenge of Islamic fundamentalism, which in recent years has led to the deaths of thousands and which shows no sign of abating. Meanwhile, in the southern extremity of the continent, it is touch and go whether South Africa will be able to make progress toward a peaceful multiracial society or be torn apart by the war of all against all.

From Japan to Taiwan, South Korea, and Singapore, some Asian states have been enormously successful in maintaining internal order and protecting the lives and property of their residents. Not so others such as Afghanistan, Burma, Cambodia, India, Iran, Iraq, the Philippines, Sri Lanka, Turkey, and most recently, Pakistan; all of these are now confronted with a loss of control that ranges from riots and clashes between opposing gangs to full-scale civil war. China, too, is not immune. It is true that the coastal regions are making unprecedented economic progress; however, Beijing does not seem to be capable of dealing either with the 30-year-old Tibetan uprising or with the challenge of Muslim separatists in the undeveloped far west of the country. Against this background much of the Chinese leaders' opposition to liberalization may be attributed to the fear—which is certainly not unfounded—that the outcome may be anarchy of the kind that all but destroyed China between 1911 and 1949.

Finally, in Latin America the ability of the state to guarantee internal law and order has, given the lack of a proper technological infrastructure and the immense gaps between rich and poor, always been in doubt. While some parts of the continent, such as Chile, are making good progress toward modernization many others are clearly lagging behind and may be becoming less orderly rather than more. To adduce just two examples that have made headlines during the last few months, the government of Mexico has lost control over the southern part of the country, whereas that of Brazil is even now using the army in an attempt to reconquer its own former capital of Rio de Janeiro. In still other places it is the druglords who exercise de facto power. In countries where repeated assassinations of public officials take place, there can be no expectation for the rule of law or the kind of stability necessary for economic growth.

What makes these facts all the more disturbing is that, so far from remaining limited to Third World countries, the disorder seems to be spreading. The chaos that overtook Armenia, Azerbaijan, Chechnya, Georgia, Moldavia, Tajikistan, and Yugoslavia following the collapse of communist rule is well known; current conditions in these countries resemble those of the Hundred Years' War (1337–1453) more than they do anything that we would expect from a well-ordered modern state. Nor, to judge by the experience of Spain in the Basque country and of Britain in Northern Ireland (to say nothing of the recent Tokyo poison gas attack and the Oklahoma City bombing), does it appear that First World countries are in principle immune to threats of this kind. Many of them are challenged by organizations which, whatever their goals, are capable of commanding fanatical loyalties and unleashing them against the state; these organizations, incidentally, often take better care of their members than the state does.

Attempting to deal with nongovernmental organizations resorting to violence, many modern states have found themselves in a quandary. On the one hand their most important weapons and weapon systems—including not just nuclear ones but most conventional ones as well—are clearly too powerful and indiscriminate to be of much use against those groups. On the other hand, should they use the terrorists' own methods against them, there exists the clear danger that they will turn into terrorists themselves. Under these circumstances many First World governments have chosen to diddle. They counter the challenge without much resolution and pretend that since the number of casualties is often smaller than that which results from ordinary motor traffic, the problem is merely a nuisance. Others have given way and decentralized, as Spain did in the case of Catalonia; or else they are even now preparing to share control over some of their provinces with others, as are the British in Northern Ireland.

Meanwhile, from the White House to 10 Downing Street, the residences of presidents and prime ministers as well as entire government quarters have been transformed into fortresses. Private security has turned into a growth industry par excellence; in the United States alone it is said to employ 1.6 million people (as many as the number of active troops) and to cost $52 billion a year, far more than all U.S. police departments combined. Feeling themselves exposed, more and more individuals and corporations are either renting protection or setting up their own. While one does not want to exaggerate the problem, unquestionably all of this is symptomatic of the state's faltering ability to hold on to its monopoly over violence—or, in plain words, to protect its citizens' lives and property.

Part V. The Outlook

At a time when new states are being born almost daily, paradoxically the fate of the state appears sealed. The growth in numbers may itself be a sign of decay; what everybody has is worth little or nothing. Furthermore, far from safeguarding their hard-won sovereignty, most new states do not even wait until they have been properly established before they start looking for ways to integrate with their neighbors. A good example is provided by that unique political construct, the Commonwealth of Independent States. Another is the eventual Palestinian state. Its leaders are even now talking of cooperation with Israel, Jordan, and Egypt—in fact with anyone who can help them transcend the limits of their own people's small size.

Contrary to the fears of George Orwell in 1984, modern technology, in the form of nuclear weapons on the one hand and unprecedented means for communication and transportation on the other, has not resulted in the establishment of unshakable totalitarian dictatorships. Instead of thought control we have CNN and, which many regimes consider almost as dangerous, Aaron Spelling; instead of unpersons, Amnesty International. The net effect has been to make governments lose power in favor of organizations that are not sovereign and are not states.

Some of these organizations stand above the state—for example, the European Common Market, the West European Union, and, above all, the United Nations, which since the Gulf War has begun to play a role akin to that of the medieval popes in authorizing or prohibiting a state from waging international war. Others are of a completely different kind, such as international bodies, multinational corporations, the media, and various terrorist organizations some of which can barely be told apart from gangs of ordinary criminals. What they all have in common is that they either assume some of the functions of the state or manage to escape its control. All also have this in common: being either much larger than states or without geographical borders, they are better positioned to take advantage of recent developments in transportation and communications. The result is that their power seems to be growing while that of the state declines.

To sum up, the 300-year period that opened at Westphalia and during which the state was the most important organization in which people lived—first in Europe, then in other places—is coming to an end. Nobody knows the significance of the transition from a system of sovereign, territorial, legally equal states to one that takes greater cognizance of the new realities; it is likely to be eventual and, as is already the case in many places, quite possibly bloody. Still, it is worth recalling that the state's most remarkable products to date have been Hiroshima and Auschwitz; the former could never have been built by any organization but a state (and the most powerful one, at that), whereas the latter was above all an exercise in bureaucratic management. Whatever the future may bring, it cannot be much worse than the past. For those who regret and fear the passing away of the world with which we are familiar, let that be their consolation.

ARTICLE 6.3

The State and Globalization

Saskia Sassen

Contrary to claims, such as those by Strange and van Creveld in this chapter, that the state's role has declined as a result of globalization, Saskia Sassen suggests that the state is assuming an important new role, involving the passage of legislation, administrative regulations, and court decisions aiming to treat foreign-based and domestic business firms and banks equally. This represents an important change. In the past, domestically owned firms enjoyed strong advantages over foreign firms. According to Sassen, the new stance aims to "denationalize" the state. This development involves state-sponsored laws, regulations, and court decisions that reduce the different treatment of foreign-based and domestic business firms and banks. The result fosters more homogeneous space that enables companies freedom to trade, invest, and operate across national borders.

This chapter attempts to recover the ways in which the state participates in governing the global economy in a context increasingly dominated by deregulation, privatization, and the growing authority of non-state actors.[1] A key organizing proposition, derived from my previous work on global cities,[2] is the embeddedness of much of globalization in national territory, that is to say, in a geographic terrain that has been encased in an elaborate set of national laws and administrative capacities. The embeddedness of the global requires at least a partial lifting of these national encasements, and hence signals a necessary participation by the state, even when it concerns the state's own withdrawal from regulating the economy.

The question becomes one of understanding the specific type of authority/power this participation might entail for the state or, more precisely, for the particular state institutions involved. Does the weight of private, often foreign, interests in this specific work of the state become constitutive of that authority and indeed produce a hybrid that is neither fully private nor fully public? My argument is that, indeed, we are seeing the incipient formation of a type of authority and state practice that entail a partial denationalizing of what had been constructed historically as national.[3] This conceptualization introduces a twist into the analysis of private authority because it seeks to detect the presence of private agendas inside the state, that is, inside a domain represented as public. However, it differs from an older scholarly tradition on the captured state which focused on cooptation of states by private actors, because it emphasizes the privatization of norm-making capacities and the enactment of these norms in the public domain.

The purpose here is, then, to understand and specify a particular aspect of globalization and the state which is lost in what are typically rather dualized accounts of this relation; in such accounts, the spheres of influence of respectively the national and the global, or of state and non-state actors, are seen as distinct and mutually exclusive. While it may indeed be the case that most components of each of these are separate and mutually exclusive, there is a specific set of conditions or components that does not fit in this dual structure. Key among these are some components of the work of ministries of finance, central banks, and the increasingly specialized

---

Saskia Sassen, "The State and Globalization," ch. 5 in Rodney Bruce Hall and Thomas J. Biersteker, eds., *The Emergence of Private Authority in Global Governance* (Cambridge: Cambridge University Press, 2002): 91–92, 94–112.

technical regulatory agencies, such as those concerned with finance, telecommunications, and competition policy. In this regard, then, my position is not comfortably subsumed under the proposition that nothing has much changed in terms of state power, nor under the proposition of the declining significance of the state.

An important methodological assumption here is that focusing on economic globalization can help us disentangle some of these issues precisely because, in strengthening the legitimacy of claims by foreign investors and firms, it adds to and renders visible the work of accommodating their rights and contracts in what remain basically national economies. However, these dynamics can also be present when privatization and deregulation concern native firms and investors, even though in much of the world privatization and deregulation have been constituted through the entry of foreign investors and firms. . . .

One of the roles of the state vis-à-vis today's global economy has been to negotiate the intersection of national law and foreign actors—whether firms, markets, or supranational organizations. This raises a question as to whether there are particular conditions that make execution of this role in the current phase distinctive and unlike what it may have been in earlier phases of the world economy. We have, on the one hand, the existence of an enormously elaborate body of law developed mostly over the past hundred years, which secures the exclusive territorial authority of national states to an extent not seen in earlier centuries, and, on the other, the considerable institutionalizing, especially in the 1990s, of the "rights" of non-national firms, the deregulation of crossborder transactions, and the growing influence/power of some of the supranational organizations. If securing these rights, options, and powers entailed an even partial relinquishing of components of state authority as constructed over the past century, then we can posit that this sets up the conditions for a necessary engagement by national states in the process of globalization.

We need to understand more about the nature of this engagement than is represented by concepts such as deregulation. It is becoming clear that the role of the state in the process of deregulation involves the production of new types of regulations, legislative items, court decisions[4]—in brief, the production of a whole series of new "legalities."[5] The background condition here is that the state remains as the ultimate guarantor of the "rights" of global capital, i.e., the protector of contracts and property rights, and, more generally, a major legitimator of claims.[6] In this regard the state can be seen as incorporating the global project of its own shrinking role in regulating economic transactions[7] and giving it operational effectiveness and legitimacy.[8] The state here can be conceived of as representing a technical administrative capacity which cannot be replicated at this time by any other institutional arrangement; although not in all cases,[9] this is a capacity backed by military power, with global power in the case of some states. The objective for foreign firms and investors is to enjoy, transnationally, the protections traditionally exercised by the state in the national realm of the economy for national firms, notably guaranteeing property rights and contracts. How this gets done may involve a range of options. To some extent this work of guaranteeing is becoming privatized, as is signaled by the growth of international commercial arbitration,[10] and by key elements of the new privatized institutional order for governing the global economy.[11]

It is in fact some states, particularly the United States and the UK, that are producing the design for these new legalities, i.e., items derived from Anglo-American commercial law and accounting standards, and are hence imposing these on other states given the interdependencies at the heart of the current phase of globalization. This creates and imposes a set of specific constraints on the other participating states.[12] Legislative items, executive orders, adherence to new technical standards, and so on will have to be produced through the particular institutional and political structures of each of these states. In terms of research and theorization, this is a vast uncharted terrain: it would mean examining how that production takes place and gets legitimated in different countries. This signals the possibility of crossnational variations (which then would need to be established, measured, interpreted). The emergent, often imposed consensus in the community of states to further globalization is not merely a political decision: it entails specific types of work by a large number of distinct state institutions in each of these countries. Clearly, the role of the state will vary significantly depending on the power it may have both internally and internationally.

The U.S. government as the hegemonic power of this period has led/forced other states to adopt these obligations toward global capital. And, in so doing, it has contributed to strengthening the forces that can challenge or destabilize what have historically been constructed as state powers.[13] In my reading this holds both for the United States and for other countries. One way in which this becomes evident is in the fact that, while the state continues to play a crucial, though no longer exclusive, role in the production of legality around new forms of economic activity, at least some of this production of legalities is increasingly feeding the power of a new emerging structure marked by denationalization or privatization of some of its components.

A crucial part of the argument is the fact of the institutional and locational embeddedness of globalization. Specifying this embeddedness has two purposes. One is to provide the empirical specification underlying my assertion that the state is engaged, which in turn feeds the proposition about the denationalizing of particular state functions and capacities. The second purpose is to signal that, given this embeddedness, the range of ways in which the state can be involved is far broader than what it is today, when it is largely confined to furthering economic globalization. Conceivably state involvement could address a whole series of global issues, including the democratic deficit in the multilateral system governing globalization.[14]

The Locational and Institutional Embeddedness of the Global Economy

Some of the key features of economic globalization allow for a broader range of forms of state participation than is generally recognized in analyses of the declining significance of the state. There are at least two distinct issues here. One is that the current condition, marked by the ascendance of private authority, is but one possible mode of several in which the state could be articulated. The other is that this current condition still leaves room for new forms of participation by the state as well as new forms of crossborder state collaboration in the governing of the global economy.[15] Among these are forms of state participation aimed at recognizing the legitimacy of claims for greater social justice and democratic accountability in the global economy, although both would require administrative and legal innovations.[16] The effort here is then not so much to show the enormous power and authority amassed by global markets and firms, but rather to detect the particular ways in which the power and authority of the state does and could shape and reshape those particular forms of private economic power.

There are three features of the global economy I want to emphasize here. First, the geography of economic globalization is strategic rather than all-encompassing, and this is especially so when it comes to the managing, coordinating, servicing, and financing of global economic operations. The fact that it is strategic is significant for a discussion about the possibilities of regulating and governing the global economy. Second, the center of gravity of many of the transactions that we refer to in an aggregate fashion as the global economy lies in the North Atlantic region, a fact which also facilitates the development and implementation of convergent regulatory frameworks and technical standards, and enables a convergence around "Western" standards. If the geography of globalization were a diffuse condition at the planetary scale, and one involving equally powerful countries and regions with a much broader range of differences than those evident in the North Atlantic, the question of its regulation might well be radically different. Third, the strategic geography of globalization is partly embedded in national territories, i.e., global cities and Silicon Valleys. The combination of these three characteristics suggests that states may have more options to participate in governing the global economy than much of the focus on the loss of regulatory authority allows us to recognize.

There are sites in this strategic geography where the density of economic transactions and the intensity of regulatory efforts come together in complex, often novel configurations. Two of these are the focus of this section. They are foreign direct investment, which mostly consists of crossborder mergers and acquisitions, and the global capital market, undoubtedly the dominant force in the global economy today. Along with trade, they are at the heart of the structural changes constitutive of globalization and the efforts to regulate it. These two processes also make evident the enormous weight of the North Atlantic region in the global economy.

Both foreign direct investment and the global capital market bring up specific organizational and regulatory issues.[17] There is an enormous increase in the complexity of management, coordination, servicing, and financing for firms operating worldwide networks of factories, service outlets, and/or offices, and for firms operating in crossborder financial markets. For reasons I discuss later, this has brought about a sharp growth in control and command functions, and their concentration in a crossborder network of major financial and business centers. This in turn contributes to the formation of a strategic geography for the management of globalization. Nowhere is this as evident as in the structure of the global capital market and the network of financial centers within which it is located. Elsewhere I examine this institutional order as the site of a new type of private authority.[18]

Each of these also is at the heart of a variety of regulatory initiatives. The growth of foreign direct investment has brought with it a renewed concern with questions of extraterritoriality and competition policy, including the regulation of crossborder mergers. The growth of the global capital market has brought with it specific efforts to develop the elements of an architecture for its governance: international securities regulation, new international standards for accounting and financial reporting, various European Union provisions. Each has tended to be ensconced in fairly distinct regulatory frameworks: foreign direct investment in antitrust law, and global finance in national regulatory frameworks for banking and finance.[19]

Further, while this strategic geography of globalization is partly embedded in national territories, this does not necessarily entail that existing national regulatory frameworks can regulate those functions. Regulatory functions have shifted increasingly toward a set of emerging or newly invigorated crossborder regulatory networks and the development of a whole array of standards to organize world trade and global finance. Specialized, often semi-autonomous regulatory agencies, and the specialized crossborder networks they are forming, are taking over functions once enclosed in national legal frameworks, and standards are replacing rules in international law. The question for research and theory is whether this mode of regulation is sufficient, and whether state participation may not emerge again as a more significant factor for the ultimate workability of some of these new regulatory regimes.

Finally, the empirical patterns of foreign direct investment and global finance show to what extent their centers of gravity lie in the North Atlantic region. The northern trans-Atlantic economic system (specifically the links among the European Union, the United States, and Canada) represents the major concentration of processes of economic globalization in the world today. This holds whether one looks at foreign direct investment flows generally, at crossborder mergers and acquisitions in particular, at overall financial flows, or at the new strategic alliances among financial centers. At the turn of the millennium this region accounts for two-thirds of worldwide stock market capitalization, 60 percent of inward foreign investment stock and 76 percent of outward stock, 60 percent of worldwide sales in mergers and acquisitions, and 80 percent of purchases in M&As. There are other major regions in the global economy: Japan, South East Asia, Latin America. But except for some of the absolute levels of capital resources in Japan, they are dwarfed by the size of the northern trans-Atlantic system. . . .

. . . We are seeing the consolidation of a transnational economy that has its center of gravity in the North Atlantic system both in terms of the intensity and value of transactions, and in terms of the emerging system of rules and standards.

This system is articulated with a growing network of sites for investment, trade, and financial transactions in the rest of the world. It is through this incorporation in a hierarchical global network, which has its center in the North Atlantic, that the relations with their zones of influence is now constituted. Thus, while the United States is still a dominant force in Latin America, several European countries have become major investors there, on a scale far surpassing past trends. And while several European Union countries have become leaders in investment in Central and Eastern Europe, U.S. firms are playing a role they have never before played.

What we are seeing today is a new grid of economic transactions superimposed on the old geoeconomic patterns. The latter persist to variable extents, but they are increasingly submerged under this new crossborder grid which amounts to a new, though partial geoeconomics. In my own research I have found that these new configurations are particularly evident in the organization of global finance and, to a lesser extent, in direct foreign investment, especially crossborder mergers and acquisitions. . . .

Worldwide Networks and Central Command Functions

There are, clearly, strong dispersal trends contained in the patterns of foreign investment and capital flows generally: the offshoring of factories, the expansion of global networks of affiliates and subsidiaries, the formation of global financial markets with a growing number of participating countries. What is excluded from this account is the other half of the story. This worldwide geographic dispersal of factories and service outlets takes place as part of highly integrated corporate structures with strong tendencies toward concentration in control and profit appropriation. The North Atlantic system is the site for most of the strategic management and coordination functions of the new global economic system.

Elsewhere I have shown that, when the geographic dispersal of factories, offices, and service outlets through crossborder investment takes place as part of such integrated corporate systems, there is also a growth in central functions; we can see a parallel trend with financial firms and markets.[20] One hypothesis this suggests is that the more globalized firms become, the more their central functions grow—in importance, in complexity, in number of transactions.[21] The specific forms assumed by globalization over the last decade have created particular organizational requirements. The emergence of global markets for finance and specialized services, the growth of investment as a major type of international transaction—all have contributed to the expansion in command functions and in the demand for specialized services for firms.[22]

We can make this more concrete by considering some of the staggering figures involved in this worldwide dispersal, and imagining what it entails in terms of coordination and management for parent headquarters, such as the fact that by the late 1990s there were almost half a million foreign affiliates of firms worldwide, most of them belonging to firms from North America and Western Europe.[23] There has been a greater growth in foreign sales through affiliates than through direct exports: the foreign sales through affiliates were US $11 trillion in 1999 and through worldwide exports of goods and services US $8 trillion. This has of course also fed the intrafirm share of so-called free crossborder trade. The data on foreign direct investment show clearly that the United States and the EU are the major receiving and sending areas in the world. Finally, the transnationality index of the largest transnational firms shows that many of the major firms from these two regions have over half of their assets, sales, and workforces outside their home countries.[24] Together these types of evidence provide a fairly comprehensive picture of this combination of dispersal and the growth of central functions.

The globalization of a firm's operations brings with it a massive task of coordination and management. Much of this has been going on for a long time but has accelerated over the decades. Further, this dispersal does not proceed under a single organizational form—rather, behind these general figures lie many different organizational forms, hierarchies of control, degrees of autonomy. The globally integrated network of financial centers is yet another form of this combination of dispersal and the growing complexity of central management and coordination.

Of importance to the analysis here is the dynamic that connects the dispersal of economic activities with the growth of central functions. In terms of sovereignty and globalization, this means that an interpretation of the impact of globalization as creating a space economy that extends beyond the regulatory capacity of a single state is only half the story; the other half is that these central functions are disproprotionately concentrated in the national territories of the highly developed countries.

By central functions I do not only mean top-level headquarters; I am referring to all the top-level financial, legal, accounting, managerial, executive, and planning functions necessary to run a corporate organization operating in more than one country, and increasingly in several countries. These central functions are partly embedded in headquarters, but also in good part in what has been called the corporate services complex, that is, the network of financial, legal, accounting, and advertising firms that handle the complexities of operating in more than one national legal system, national accounting system, advertising culture, etc., and do so under conditions of rapid innovations in all these fields. Such services have become so specialized and complex that headquarters increasingly buy them from specialized firms rather than producing them in-house. These agglomerations of firms producing central functions for the management and coordination of global economic systems are disproportionately concentrated in the highly developed countries—particularly, though not exclusively, in the kinds of cities I call global cities. Such concentrations of functions represent a strategic factor in the organization of the global economy.

One argument I am making here is that it is important to unbundle analytically the fact of strategic functions for the global economy or for global operation, and the overall corporate economy of a country. These global control and command functions are partly embedded in national corporate structures but also constitute a distinct corporate subsector. This subsector can be conceived of as part of a network that connects global cities across the globe.[25] For the purposes of certain kinds of inquiry this distinction may not matter; for the purposes of understanding the global economy, it does. And it seems to me that this distinction also matters for questions of regulation, notably regulation of crossborder activities.

If the strategic central functions—both those produced in corporate headquarters and those produced in the specialized corporate services sector—are located in a network of major financial and business centers, the question of regulating what amounts to a key part of the global economy is not the same as if the strategic management and coordination functions were as distributed geographically as are the factories, service outlets, and affiliates. However, regulation of these activities is evolving along lines of greater specialization and crossborder capabilities than most current state-centric national systems can comfortably accommodate today.

Another instance today of this negotiation between a transnational process or dynamic and a national territory is that of the global financial markets. The orders of magnitude have risen sharply, as illustrated by the US $68 trillion in the 1999 value of internationally traded derivatives, a major component of the global economy. These transactions are partly embedded in telecommunications systems that make possible the instantaneous transmission of money/information around the globe. Much attention has gone to these capacities for instantaneous transmission. But the other half of the story is the extent to which the global financial markets are located in particular cities, especially though not exclusively in the highly developed countries; indeed, the degrees of concentration are unexpectedly high.

Stock markets worldwide have become globally integrated. In addition to deregulation in the 1980s in all the major European and North American markets, the late 1980s and early 1990s saw the addition of such markets as Buenos Aires, São Paulo, Bangkok, Taipei, etc. The integration of a growing number of stock markets has contributed to raise the capital that can be mobilized through stock markets. Worldwide market value reached over US $30 trillion in 2000. This globally integrated stock market, which makes possible the circulation of publicly listed shares around the globe in seconds, is embedded in a grid of very material, physical, strategic places—that is, cities belonging to national territories.

A crucial issue for understanding the question of regulation and the role of the state in the global capital market is the ongoing embeddedness of this market in these networks of financial centers operating within national states; these are not offshore markets. The North Atlantic system contains an enormous share of the global capital market through its sharp concentration of leading financial centers.[26] Further, as the system expands through the incorporation of additional centers into this network—from Eastern Europe, Latin America, etc.—the question of regulation also pivots on the existence of dominant standards and rules, i.e. those produced by the economies of the North Atlantic.

In my reading, studies that emphasize deregulation and liberalization do not sufficiently recognize an important feature, one which matters for the analysis here: the global financial system has reached levels of complexity that require the existence of a crossborder network of financial centers to service the operations of global capital. Each actual financial center represents a massive and highly specialized concentration of resources and talent; and the network of these centers constitutes the operational architecture for the global capital market.

Denationalized State Agendas

The representation of economic globalization coming out of the two preceding sections is quite different from many of the standard accounts. For the purposes of this section it is especially two of the features of globalization as discussed above that matter. One of these is that the global economy needs to be produced, reproduced, serviced, financed. It cannot be taken simply as a given, such as the fact of more interdependence, or merely as a function of the power of multinational corporations and financial markets. There is a vast array of highly specialized functions that need to be ensured. These have become so specialized that they can no longer be contained in corporate headquarters functions. Global cities are strategic sites for the production of these specialized functions to run and coordinate the global economy. Inevitably located in national territories, these cities are the organizational and institutional location for some of the major dynamics of denationalization. While such processes of denationalization—for instance, certain aspects of financial and investment deregulation—are institutional and not geographic, the geographic location of many of the strategic institutions—financial markets and financial services firms—means these processes are embedded geographically.

The second feature, partly connected to the first, is that the global economy to a large extent materializes in national territories. Its topography is one that moves between digital space and national territories. This requires a particular set of negotiations which have the effect of leaving the geographic boundaries of the national state's territory unaltered, but do transform the institutional encasements of that geographic fact, that is, the state's territorial jurisdiction or, more abstractly, exclusive territoriality.

Precisely because global processes need to be coordinated and serviced and because many of these functions materialize to a large extent in national territories, national states have had to become deeply involved in the implementation of the global economic system. In this process states have experienced transformations of various aspects of their institutional structure. This signals that the global economy and the national state are not mutually exclusive domains. Globalization leaves national territory basically unaltered but is having pronounced effects on the exclusive territoriality of the national state—that is, its effects are not on territory as such but on the institutional encasements of the geographic fact of national territory. But alongside and, in my reading, distinct from this diminished territorial authority of the state, there is the denationalizing of specific state agendas. The work of states in producing part of the technical and legal infrastructure for economic globalization has involved both a change in the exclusivity of state authority and in the composition of the work of states. Economic globalization entails a set of practices that destabilize another set of practices, i.e., some of the practices that came to constitute national state sovereignty.

Implementing today's global economic system in the context of national territorial sovereignty required multiple policy, analytic, and narrative negotiations. These negotiations have typically been summarized or coded as "deregulation." There is much more going on in these negotiations than the concept "deregulation" captures. The encounter of a global actor—firm or market—with one or another instantiation of the national state can be thought of as a new frontier. It is not merely a dividing line between the national economy and the global economy. It is a zone of politico-economic interactions that produce new institutional forms and alter some of the old ones. Nor is it just a matter of reducing regulations. For instance, in many countries, the necessity for autonomous central banks in the current global economic system has required a thickening of regulations in order to delink central banks from the influence of the executive branch of government and from deeply "national" political agendas.

Central banks illustrate this well. These are national institutions, concerned with national matters. Yet over the last decade they have become the institutional home within the national state for monetary policies that are necessary to further the development of a global capital market and indeed, more generally, a global economic system. The new conditionality of the global economic system—the requirements that need to be met for a country to become integrated into the global capital market—contains as one key element the autonomy of central banks.[27] This facilitates the task of instituting a certain kind of monetary policy, e.g., one privileging low inflation over job growth even when a president may have preferred it the other way around, particularly at reelection time. While securing central bank autonomy has certainly eliminated a lot of corruption, it has also been the vehicle for one set of accommodations on the part of national states to the requirements of the global capital market. A parallel analysis can be made of ministries of finance (known as the Treasury in the United States and the UK) which have had to impose certain kinds of fiscal policies as part of the new conditionalities of economic globalization.

There is a set of strategic dynamics and institutional transformations at work here. They may incorporate a small number of state agencies and units within departments, a small number of legislative initiatives and of executive orders, and yet have the power to institute a new normativity at the heart of the state; this is especially so because these strategic sectors are operating in complex interactions with private, transnational, powerful actors. Much of the institutional apparatus of the state remains basically unchanged; the inertia of bureaucratic organizations, which creates its own version of path dependence, makes an enormous contribution to continuity. . . .

Further, the new types of crossborder collaborations among specialized government agencies concerned with a growing range of issues emerging from the globalization of capital markets and the new trade order are yet another aspect of this participation by the state in the implementation of a global economic system. A good example is the heightened interaction in the past three or four years among competition policy regulators from a large number of countries. This is a period of renewed concern about competition policy because economic globalization puts pressure on governments to work toward convergence given the cross-country diversity of competition laws or enforcement practices. This convergence around specific competition policy issues can coexist with ongoing, often enormous differences among these countries when it comes to laws and regulations about those components of their economies that do not intersect with globalization. There are multiple other instances of this highly specialized type of convergence: regulatory issues concerning telecommunications, finance, the Internet, etc. It is, then, a very partial type of convergence among regulators of different countries who often begin to share more with each other than they do with colleagues in their home bureaucracies.

What is of particular concern here is that today we see a sharp increase in the work of establishing convergence.[28] We can clearly identify a new phase in the past ten years. In some of these sectors there has long been an often elementary convergence, or at least coordination, of standards. For instance, central bankers have long interacted with each other across borders, but today we see an intensification in these transactions, which becomes necessary in the effort to develop and extend a global capital market. The increase of crossborder trade has brought with it a sharpened need for convergence in standards, as is evident in the vast proliferation of International Organization for Standardization (ISO) items. Another example is the institutional and legal framework necessary for the operation of the crossborder commodity chains identified by Gereffi.[29]

One outcome of these various trends is the emergence of a strategic field of operations that represents a partial disembedding of specific state operations from the broader institutional world of the state that had been geared exclusively to national agendas. It is a field of crossborder transactions among government agencies and business sectors aimed at addressing the new conditions produced and demanded by economic globalization. In positing this I am rejecting the prevalent notion in much of the literature on globalization that the realm of the national and the realm of the global are two mutually exclusive zones. My argument is rather that globalization is partly endogenous to the national, and is in this regard produced through a dynamic of denationalizing what had been constructed as the national.[30]

It is also a field of particular types of transactions: they are strategic, cut across borders, and entail specific interactions with private actors. These transactions do not entail the state as such, as in international treaties, but rather consist of the operations and policies of specific subcomponents of the state—for instance, legislative initiatives, specialized technical regulatory agencies, or some of the agendas pursued by central banks. These are transactions that cut across borders in that they concern the standards and regulations imposed on firms and markets operating globally,[31] and hence produce a certain convergence at the level of national regulations and law in the creation of the requisite conditions for globalization. The result is a mix of new or strengthened forms of private authority and partly denationalized state authority, such as the instituting of private interests into state normativity.[32]

Conclusion

. . . Economic globalization has emerged as a key dynamic in the formation of a transnational system of power which lies in good part outside the formal interstate system. One instance of this is the relocation of national public governance functions to transnational private arenas. . . . But I argue that it also lies, to a far higher degree than is usually recognized, inside particular components of national states. This second feature can be recognized in the work done by legislatures, courts, and various agencies in the executive to produce the mechanisms necessary to accommodate the rights of global capital in what are still national territories under the exclusive control of their states. Rather than interpreting this as signaling that not much has changed, or as a capturing of the state by private interests, I interpret this as a denationalizing of what had been constructed in national terms.

The much examined decrease in state regulatory capacities resulting from some of the basic policies associated with economic globalization is a far more differentiated process than notions of an overall decline in the significance of the state suggest. And it entails a more transformative dynamic inside the state than the notion of a simple loss of power suggests. There are significant policy implications to this type of reading. Up to now much of the work of the state has concerned the claims made by powerful economic actors. I would like to posit the possibility of new types of state authority, including the possibility of forms going well beyond the current modes of state action. In principle, such new modes could also involve elements of a new politics of accountability vis-à-vis global actors rather than the current orientation of state work toward furthering the rights and guarantees of global capital. The enabling condition is, precisely, the institutional and locational embeddedness of the global economy, at least partly, in national institutional orders and territories.

Notes

1. This chapter is part of my larger multiyear research project to be published as *Denationalization: Economy and Polity in a Global Digital Age* (under contract with Princeton University Press).
2. Saskia Sassen, *The Global City: New York, London, Tokyo* (Princeton, N.J.: Princeton University Press, 2001, 2nd edn. [1991]).
3. Sassen, *Denationalization*.
4. Sol Picciotto, *International Business Taxation: A Study in the Internationalization of Business Regulation* (London: Weidenfeld and Nicolson, 1992); and P. G. Cerny, *The Changing Architecture of Politics* (London: Sage, 1990).
5. I use this term to distinguish this production from "law" or "jurisprudence": Saskia Sassen, *Losing Control? Sovereignty in an Age of Globalization*, 1995 Columbia University Leonard Hastings Schoff Memorial Lectures (New York: Columbia University Press, 1996), ch. 1.
6. While well known, it is worth remembering that this guarantee of the rights of capital is embedded in a certain type of state, a certain conception of the rights of capital, and a certain type of international legal regime: it is largely embedded in the state of the most developed and most powerful countries in the world, in Western notions of contract and property rights, and in new legal regimes aimed at furthering economic globalization, e.g., the push to get countries to support copyright law.
7. Leo Panitch, "Rethinking the Role of the State in an Era of Globalization," in James Mittelman (ed.), *Globalization: Critical Reflections. International Political Economy Yearbook*, vol. 9 (Boulder, Colo.: Lynne Rienner, 1996), pp. 83–113; Stephen Gill, "Globalization, Democratization, and the Politics of Indifference," in the same volume, pp. 205–28.
8. Sassen, *Losing Control?*, chs. 1 and 2, and Sassen, *Denationalization*.
9. See Phil Williams, "Transnational Organized Crime and the State," Rodney Bruce Hall and Thomas J. Biersteker, eds., *The Emergence of Private Authority in Global Governance* (Cambridge: Cambridge University Press, 2002), ch. 8.
10. Yves Dezalay and Bryant Garth, *Dealing in Virtue: International Commercial Arbitration and the Construction of a Transnational Legal Order* (Chicago and London: University of Chicago Press, 1996).
11. A. Claire Cutler "Private International Regimes and Interfirm Cooperation," ch. 2 in Hall and Biersteker, eds., The Emergence of Private Authority in Global Governance.
12. This dominance assumes many forms and does not affect only poorer and weaker countries. France, for instance, ranks among the top providers of information services and industrial engineering services in Europe, and has a strong, though not outstanding, position in financial and insurance services. But it has found itself at an increasing disadvantage in legal and accounting services because Anglo-American law and standards dominate in international transactions. Anglo-American firms with offices in Paris do the servicing of the legal needs of firms, whether French or foreign, operating out of France (Sassen, *Global City*). Similarly, Anglo-American law is increasingly dominant in international commercial arbitration, an institution grounded in continental, particularly French and Swiss, traditions of jurisprudence (Dezalay and Garth, *Dealing in Virtue*).
13. See, in this regard, Giovanni Arrighi, *The Long Twentieth Century: Money, Power, and the Origins of Our Times* (London: Verso, 1994); Diana E. Davis (ed.), "Chaos and Governance," *Political Power and Social Theory*, 13, Part IV: Scholarly Controversy (Stamford, Conn.: JAI Press, 1999).
14. Elsewhere (*Denationalization*) I examine how these dynamics also position citizens (still largely confined to national state institutions for the full execution of their rights) vis-à-vis these types of global struggles. My argument is that state participation creates an enabling environment not only for global corporate capital but also for those seeking to subject the latter to greater accountability and public scrutiny. But unlike what has happened with global corporate capital, the necessary legal and administrative instruments and regimes have not been developed. The tradeoffs and the resources that can be mobilized are quite different in the case of citizens seeking to globalize their capacities for governing compared to those of global capital seeking to form regimes that enable and protect it.
15. Alfred C. Aman, Jr., "The Globalizing State: A Future-Oriented Perspective on the Public/Private Distinction, Federalism, and Democracy," *Vanderbilt Journal of Transnational Law*, 31 (4) (1998), 769–870.

16. I examine these two issues in greater detail in Sassen, *Denationalization*.
17. For a detailed examination of these two aspects, see Sassen, *Global City*, chs. 4, 5, and 7.
18. Sassen, *Losing Control?*, ch. 2.
19. It is quite possible that globalization may have the effect of blurring the boundaries between these two regulatory worlds.
20. Sassen, *Global City*.
21. This process of corporate integration should not be confused with vertical integration as conventionally defined. See also Gary Gereffi, "Global Production Systems and Third World Development," in Barbara Stallings (ed.), *Global Change, Regional Response: The New International Context of Development* (New York: Cambridge University Press, 1995), pp. 100–42, on commodity chains, and Michael Porter, *The Competitive Advantage of Nations* (New York: Free Press, 1990), on value-added chains, two constructs that also illustrate the difference between corporate integration at a world scale and vertical integration as conventionally defined.
22. A central proposition here, developed at length in my work (*Global City*), is that we cannot take the existence of a global economic system as a given, but rather need to examine the particular ways in which the conditions for economic globalization are produced. This requires examining not only communication capacities and the power of multinationals, but also the infrastructure of facilities and work processes necessary for the implementation of global economic systems, including the production of those inputs that constitute the capability for global control and the infrastructure of jobs involved in this production. The emphasis shifts to the *practice* of global control: the work of producing and reproducing the organization and management of a global production system and a global marketplace for finance, both under conditions of economic concentration. The recovery of place and production also implies that global processes can be studied in great empirical detail.
23. Affiliates are but one form of operating overseas and hence their number underrepresents the dispersal of a firm's operations. There are today multiple forms, ranging from new temporary partnerships to older types of subcontracting and contracting.
24. This index is an average based on ratios of the share that foreign sales, assets, and employment represent in a firm's total of each. If we consider the world's top 100 transnational corporations (TNCs) in 1997, the EU had 48 of these firms and the United States 28; many of the remaining were from Japan. Thus together the EU and the United States accounted for over two-thirds of the world's 100 largest TNCs. The United States, the UK, France, Germany, and Japan together accounted for 3/4 of these 100 firms in 1997; this has been roughly so since 1990. The average transnationality index for the EU is 56.7 percent compared to 38.5 percent for the United States (but 79.2 for Canada). Most of the US and EU TNCs in this top 100 list have very high levels of foreign assets as a percentage of total assets: for instance, 98 percent for Seagram, 97 percent for Thomson, 96 percent for Asea Brown Boveri, 91 percent for Bayer, 91 percent for Nestlé, 85 percent for Michelin, 85 percent for Unilever, 79 percent for Hoechst, 77 percent for Philips Electronics, 71 percent for Ericsson, 69 percent for Ferruzi/Montedison, 68 percent for Coca-Cola, 67 percent for Rhône-Poulenc, 62 percent for Elf Aquitaine, 59 percent for BMW, 58 percent for Exxon, 55 percent for McDonald's, 55 percent for Volkswagen Group, 51 percent for IBM, 45 percent for Renault, 43 percent for Siemens, and so on. The share of foreign in total employment is often even higher. (See Organization for Economic Co-operation and Development, *Transborder Data Flow Contracts in the Wider Framework Mechanisms for Privacy Protection in Global Networks* [Paris: OECD, 2000], for the full listing.)
25. In this sense, global cities are different from the old capitals of erstwhile empires, in that they are a function of crossborder networks rather than simply the most powerful city of an empire. There is, in my conceptualization, no such entity as a single global city as there could be a single capital of an empire; the category global city makes sense only as a component of a global network of strategic sites. The corporate subsector which contains the global control and command functions is partly both embedded in, and constitutive of this network.
26. Two major developments that can alter some of the features of the present configuration are the growth of electronic trading and the growth of the eurozone. The creation of an enormous consolidated capital market in the eurozone raises serious questions about the feasibility of maintaining the current pattern with as many international financial centers as there are member countries; some of

these markets may lose top international functions and get repositioned in complex and hierarchical divisions of labor. Second, electronic trading is leading to a distinct shift toward setting up strategic alliances among major financial centers, producing a combination of a crossborder digital market embedded in a set of specific city-based financial markets. I have examined this at greater length in Sassen, *Global City,* chs. 4, 5, and 7.

27. While we take this autonomy for granted in the United States or in most EU countries (though not all—thus France's central bank is still not considered as quite autonomous from the executive), in many countries the head of state or local oligarchies have long had undue influence on central banks. Incidentally, this influence has not necessarily always worked to the disadvantage of the disadvantaged, as is evident for instance in monetary policies that promoted employment by letting inflation rise.
28. I use the term convergence for expediency. In the larger project I posit that conceptualizing these outcomes as convergence is actually problematic and often incorrect. Rather than a dynamic whereby individual states wind up converging, what is at work is a global dynamic that gets filtered through the specifics of each "participating" state. Hence my central research concern is not so much the outcome, "convergence," but the work of producing this outcome.
29. Gereffi, "Global Production Systems."
30. Further, insofar as it is partly embedded in national settings, e.g., global cities, the state has had to reregulate specific aspects of its authority over national territory.
31. An important point, which is usually disregarded in much general commentary about the global economy, is that a firm can participate in the latter even if it operates inside a single country: the key is whether it participates in a market or a transaction that is part of the global "system." My concern in this regard has been to show that there is considerable institutional development of that which is called the global economy—it is not simply a matter of goods or money crossing borders. For a firm's operations to be part of the global economy, they need to be encased in this institutional framework. If they are not, they may constitute an informal crossborder transaction or part of the new transnational criminal economy. A simplified illustration of the point that the distinctiveness of participating in the global economy does not necessarily lie in the fact of crossing borders is, for example, a U.S.-based firm (whether U.S. or non-U.S.) that invests in a non-U.S. firm listed on the New York stock market. The point here is that there is a regime—a set of conditions and legalities—that governs the listing of foreign firms on a stock market that has been incorporated in the global system and that governs the conditions under which the investor can acquire stock in that firm. I see the key, determining issue to be whether the firms and investors involved are operating under the umbrella of this regime. This umbrella is partly constituted through national institutions and partly, perhaps increasingly so, through the new privatized institutional framework I discuss later. What comes together in this example in my reading are some of the specifications I summarize in the global city model and in the notion of denationalization. On the other hand, the following would not be an instance of firms operating in the global economic system, even though it entails actual physical crossing of borders: two individuals residing in different countries making a deal informally for one of them to bring items, also informally—without following regulations, including WTO regulations—for the second individual to sell in the second country, with both individuals using informal accounting and trust systems to guarantee enforcement of the conditions of the agreement. This is an extreme contrast; there are many cases that are more ambiguous than this.
32. As I indicated earlier, I conceptualize denationalization as multivalent. Thus, in the case of human rights, matters which had been considered the prerogative of states—security and protection of its citizens—are universalized and in that sense denationalized (see Sassen, *Denationalization*).

ARTICLE 6.4

Guiding Globalisation in East Asia *New Roles for Old Developmental States*

Linda Weiss

The title and subtitle of the selection by Weiss neatly summarizes her major claim. A large volume of scholarship beginning in the 1970s claimed that state policies were responsible for the extraordinarily successful economic performance of Japan, the Republic of Korea, Taiwan, and Singapore. The key to the East Asian economic miracle, in this view, was clever state policies that encouraged business firms to compete successfully in the international economy. (This orientation is called *export promotion.*) A later wave of scholarship claimed that globalization produced a fundamental transformation in these states' economic orientation. Their formerly interventionist approach was replaced by a more modest stance. Weiss disagrees. She suggests that, at least in the case of Korea, states have engaged in marginal adaptations but not a wholesale transformation or abandonment of their interventionist stance.

How can one distinguish transformation from adaptation? Can Weiss's analysis of Korea be applied to other capitalist states? What kinds of adaptations of state policies are effective? Why? Is there a relationship between Weiss's approach and the selections in Chapter 4 on the impact of globalization on poverty and inequality?

According to the new mantra of globalisation analysis, states are not "disappearing" or "declining" in importance. They are being "transformed." Since states are increasingly pressured from below by capital mobility and from above by supranational forms of governance such as the WTO, their traditional hold over economic actors has diminished, their control of the domestic economy has eroded, and their room for manoeuvre in the policy arena has been reduced to the margins. While meant to apply more generally, this view has become increasingly influential in the literature on East Asia's developmental

---

Linda Weiss, "Guiding Globalisation in East Asia: New Roles for Old Developmental States," in Linda Weiss, ed., *States in the Global Economy: Bringing Domestic Institutions Back In* (New York: Cambridge University Press, 2003): 245–258, 266–270.

states (DS). It is now widely anticipated that whatever remained of developmental states in the region before the financial turmoil of 1997, the pressures of financial liberalisation as well as the market-opening measures being imposed by the WTO agreements and IMF conditionalities have squeezed out developmental ambitions and eliminated the scope for coordinating economic outcomes in the domestic arena.

This claim is examined in the light of the Korean and Taiwanese experiences. As capitalist developmental states with Japan-style institutions, they are seen to be the most deviant, within the region, from the free-market model and it is the forced retreat of such developmental states from economic governance that now defines the standard view inside and outside the academy. We must ask therefore in what significant ways are developmental states affected by increasing exposure to global markets, and in what respects is state transformation real?

This chapter advances two propositions. First, globalisation impacts on the state, but not necessarily in the restrictive way anticipated by the standard view. Contrary to the idea of globalisation as constraint, the global economy does not preclude a role for national governance, but tends increasingly to demand it. As we shall see in a number of cases—ranging from the management of currency appreciation and industrial restructuring to foreign exchange and investment flows—the challenges of interdependence provide states with both the impetus for action and the room in which to act. The related proposition however is that the ways in which these enabling conditions of globalisation are likely to inform state responses and be actualised in policy outcomes will depend heavily on existing features of the domestic institutional environment. As stable constellations of norms, rules, and organisational arrangements, domestic institutions filter the effects of external pressures and condition responses to them—softening, exaggerating, or neutralising the impacts of openness, as the case may be.

In order to assess the nature and extent of domestic changes and, in particular, to see where the impact of globalisation comes into play, I discuss developments before and after the 1997 financial crisis in Taiwan and Korea—arguably postwar capitalism's two most successful examples of state-guided development, outside of Japan. As such, they offer a fruitful context for appraising globalist claims about state transformation. . . . [T]he thrust of the evidence to date does indicate that there continues to be considerable scope for state guidance in national economic management and for government–business cooperation, even—or perhaps especially—as economies restructure to meet the new conditions of economic openness. In Taiwan, the state's capacity to coordinate structural change has been enhanced by economic liberalisation; in Korea, where significant dismantling of the developmental state had occurred prior to the Asian crisis, a newly created state agency has been hastening chaebol restructuring and preparing firms to withstand the entry of foreigners; while the government–business nexus has been reconstituted in completely new ways to develop new sectors of the economy. . . .

Developmental Capitalism in . . . Korea

The concept of developmental state means more than a state that is pro-development. As originally conceived and applied to Japan, Korea, and Taiwan (and Singapore) during their high-growth periods, developmental states could be distinguished by their commitment to production-enhancing, growth-oriented priorities; their organisational arrangements (a relatively insulated pilot agency in charge of that transformative project); and institutionalised government–business cooperation (formal and informal links with organised economic actors privileging sectors or industry associations rather than simply individual firms) as the basis for policy input, negotiation, and implementation. In addition to the three fundamentals, one should note the importance of a political system which supports a shared project of economic transformation, where there is elite cohesion over core national goals, and where the economic bureaucracy is given sufficient scope to take initiatives and act effectively (see the contributors to Woo-Cumings 1999; also Weiss 1998: ch. 3).

Thus, transformative goals, a pilot agency, and institutionalised government–business cooperation form the three essential ingredients of any developmental state. In the absence of the first two criteria, the state lacks an insulated coordinating intelligence and is vulnerable to capture by special interests. In the absence of the third, the state lacks the embedded (quasi-corporatist) quality of effective policy design and implementation, and is vulnerable to information blockage and policy failure. I call this institutional set-up "governed interdependence," which in its most evolved form involves negotiated policymaking under government sponsorship.

State Transformation in Korea: The Prince Who Leaps Like a Frog

Few would argue that little has changed in the Korean political economy, either before or since the crisis. If "transformation" means a "major change in the form, appearance, character, disposition, or function,"[1] then globalists are right, in some respects at least, to speak of state "transformation" in post-authoritarian Korea. But the Korean experience of "state transformation" is not—as transformationalists would expect—a case of the proverbial "frog being transformed into a prince" (or "prince into frog," depending on one's perspective). What we find nowadays in Korea seems closer to a prince who leaps like a frog. Moreover, as already intimated, the main drivers of state "transformation" have been more often domestic than international, and have appeared well in advance of financial opening and the Asian crisis.

Ironically, the impact of the Asian crisis has not been *to disengage* the state from the economy *even further*, as many have anticipated, but rather *to bring it back in*—in a number of new and significant ways. Under the first all-civilian democratic regime of Kim Young-Sam, the Korean state abandoned what remained of its long-standing industry policy, stepped up financial liberalisation, and dismantled the core agency of its developmental state, the EPB. However, spurred on by the crisis which ravaged its economy in 1997 and keen to diversify its industrial base by encouraging high-technology start-ups the Korean government has been actively leading industry development in a number of new arenas.

Among the most important of the new state-backed initiatives is the development of a venture industry to finance high-technology start-ups (as in Germany), and the creation of a software retail market to support a Korean software industry. In spite of earlier half-hearted efforts to promote venture capital in the 1980s, only after the crisis did the industry begin to boom, inspired by the Silicon Valley experience and boosted by extensive state assistance. Under the 1997 Special Law for the Promotion of Venture Businesses, the state now offers a 10 year programme of tax incentives, exemptions from general corporate laws, R&D support, and state-sponsored funding opportunities. New regulatory measures for venture businesses (VBs) not only facilitate listing on the KOSDAQ (see, e.g., Young 2001) but also increase the availability of venture capital through the creation of joint public– private venture capital companies (Oh 2000). Thus, unlike Silicon Valley, where venture capital grew from market forces, in Korea the industry has emerged from a state initiative. Its centrepiece however is public–private cooperation—a jointly created venture investment fund of about US$900 million. Like the French . . . , the Koreans have abandoned credit activism and policy loans for large industrial corporations, but they have not abandoned financial involvement for developmentalist goals.

The VB promotion policies have begun to bear fruit. By the end of 1999, the number of mostly high-technology VBs in Korea had reached 4,800, exceeding that of Japan (4,700) and Taiwan (1,200). By August 2000, the number exceeded 8,000 and VBs accounted for 8 per cent of total manufacturing firms.

Another developmentally oriented, yet novel, aspect of the state's evolving economic role can be seen in recent moves to create a Korean software industry. The software case is especially interesting in view of the fact that, as a consequence of the pervasive practice of pirating, a consumer market has been virtually non-existent. (An estimated 65 per cent of software in use in Korea is pirated.) The involvement of the state is therefore not only essential, but also welcomed by the industry in order to help create a market for local products.

The thrust of the software industry policy is, once again, public–private partnership. Three features of this relationship deserve highlighting. First, the Ministry of Information and Communication has sponsored a consortium of thirty-seven companies, the Software Infra Network of Korea (SOFRANO), with which to interact in the policy arena and to establish a software retail business and distribution network. Second, in conjunction with SOFRANO, it has initiated an Internet PC project which will greatly expand the number of PCs in circulation with uniform specifications. The ministry's goal for the project is to supply some 9 million low-end multimedia PCs in the next three years, thus bringing more software developers to the industry. Third, it has appointed SOFRANO to operate government projects on its behalf, such as seeking out and supporting software venture companies, aiding them in commercialising and marketing their products, and marketing overseas the software developed in Korea.

Both cases—that of venture capital and especially software—underline the increasing importance of a collaborative relationship between government and business in joint pursuit of transformative projects. In this relationship, each party retains its independence, while the government remains the ultimate arbiter of the rules and goals of interaction in which information is exchanged, resources are pooled, and tasks shared. Elsewhere I have called this negotiated relationship "governed interdependence," and analysed its varied and changing forms in Asia and Europe. Governed interdependence, I have argued, forms one important pillar of the state's "transformative capacity" (Weiss 1998). . . . Whilst governed interdependence has definitely waned in regard to the traditional chaebol-subsidised credit-developmental state nexus, our sectoral evidence indicates that new forms are continuing to emerge in post-crisis Korea.

However unclear the outlines of the institutional configuration emerging from new developments such as these, the evidence to date suggests that it would be unwise to anticipate the emergence of a state expunged of developmentalist norms and habits. Whether the principal challenges to a neodevelopmental state like Korea are located in domestic or international processes, the outcomes of regulatory reforms are more likely to be consistent with pre-existing structures than to overturn them. . . .

Conclusion

The retreat, eclipse, or withering away of the developmental state and its transformation into a different kind of beast has been a widely anticipated outcome in search of a single compelling cause—"globalisation" being only the latest in a strong line-up of potential assassins. The evidence reported here gives us reason to doubt the decline and transformation thesis, at least in its current form. Neither the experience of Korea nor that of Taiwan offers support for the view that the scope for policy choice or the role for a central coordinating intelligence like the state have been whittled away under conditions of increased openness and interdependence.

At the very least, the findings reported here give us pause to consider ways in which the character of international competition and global markets may actually reaffirm, renew, or recompose state capacities. . . . [I]ncreasing openness is compatible with the strengthening of national governance. The new rules of increased market opening can be deployed to bolster developmental purpose.

The Korean and Taiwanese experiences are but two cases. And two swallows do not make a summer. Nonetheless, they are significant swallows, both increasingly exposed to the larger international economy and subject to its dictums, one recently sustaining significant damage from the impact of global flows.

Increasing openness notwithstanding, the state would appear to have ample room to move in both the financial and industrial strategy arenas. Rather than shrinking under the grip of external constraints, a more plausible conclusion would seem to be that industrial policy is constantly shifting in character and focus. In part this is because, under conditions of interdependence, upgrading the industrial economy can never be a one-off event, but has to be a continuous process, even in the developed democracies. Thus, in some respects, examples of which we have seen most recently in Korea (but which extend well beyond there), increased exposure to global markets makes the state's infrastructural and coordinating role more, not less, important.

Most important, where economic actors are well organised and under pressure from international competitors, they may end up inviting, rather than rejecting, state involvement in a shared transformative project. Indeed, rather than driving a wedge between government and business, meeting the challenges of openness may serve to strengthen public-private cooperation. . . .

While globalisation is having an impact on states, we should neither overstate its importance among the contending pressures on governing institutions, nor oversell its capacity constraining tendency. There is after all no such thing as uniformity of impact or unmediated adjustment to market pressures. All adjustments to economic openness require new laws, regulations, and policies, and this is where the character of the existing domestic regulatory and institutional context comes into play. . . . This is a less expected, but surely more plausible, outcome than the widely canvassed idea of the tightly "constrained" or extensively "transformed" state. It shows that institutions equipped with the relevant sense of purpose and capacities can guide the impact of globalisation—much as they guided the process of development in the first developmental state phase.

Note

1. A composite definition from the Oxford and Webster's Dictionaries.

References

Oh, Sekyung 2000, The Korean venture capital industry: present and future, Paper presented at the international symposium on financial reforms and venture business in Korea, The Korea Institute of Finance and Center for International Development, Harvard University.

Weiss, Linda 1998, *The Myth of the Powerless State*, Ithaca, NY: Cornell University Press.

Woo-Cumings, Meredith (ed.) 1999, *The Developmental State*, Ithaca, NY: Cornell University Press.

Young, Cheol Jeong 2001, Korea: venture businesses, venture capital and KOSDAQ, *International Financial Law Review*: 85–7. Supplement.

CHAPTER 7

Global Governance *with* Global Government?

More than thirty years ago, Robert Dahl, a distinguished political scientist, published a classic book, *Who Governs?*, that attempted to answer this question for New Haven, Connecticut.[1] Dahl did not believe that the city government of New Haven had a monopoly of power. He found that elected officials did play a key role. But so too did party leaders, interest group officials, the media, and active citizens.

In a similar manner, one might ask: Who governs the international economic system? Answering this question is much more daunting than tracing the contours of power in one middle-sized American city. Not surprisingly, given the complexity of the topic, no comparably penetrating study of the topic has yet been published. Further, as the reader will not be surprised to learn, there are sharply differing views on the question of the extent to which one can identify a set of institutions that can be considered a global government.

A first task involves theoretical clarification, of the kind that Krahmann undertakes in her selection in this chapter: How can one distinguish governance from government? How useful is it to do so?

A major focus of the selections in this chapter is the role of three international financial institutions (IFIs). One is the International Monetary Fund (IMF), which provides assistance to countries encountering economic problems. There are discussions of the IMF in many selections in PG. Two other key international economic institutions are the World Trade Organization (WTO) and the World Bank.

---

[1]Robert Dahl, *Who Governs: Democracy and Power in the American City* (New Haven: Yale University Press, 1963). Note that Dahl's approach and findings were challenged by G. William Domhoff in the provocatively entitled *Who Really Rules? New Haven and Community Power Reexamined* (Somerset, N.J.: Transaction Publishers, 1978). Domhoff used a different methodology to claim that power was much more centralized in New Haven than appeared from Dahl's study.

Do IFIs constitute an informal global government or state? One answer is that it depends on how one defines *state.* Since IFIs have no army or police force, they lack the traditional means of coercion that states exercise to enforce their writ. For this reason, Joseph Stiglitz, for example (in the selection in this chapter), considers that the most accurate description of the international order is "global governance without global government.[2]" (We have turned the phrase on its head for the title of this chapter.) Indeed, the realist school—the dominant theoretical approach within the field of international relations—rests its case that a global state does not exist, and that IFIs are dependent on national states for whatever power they exercise, on precisely this point. Moreover, realists claim, even in the era of globalization, the global arena continues to be characterized by anarchy because the basic actors within that arena continue to be individual, sovereign states. Cooperation exists among states, of course, but the presence of alliances—or even support for international institutions such as IFIs—simply signifies that states find it in their self-interest to suspend unilateral action temporarily.

If there is a global state, how democratic is it? How are its rulers selected? How accountable are they, and to whom? A term used to characterize the governmental structure of the European Union (EU), the organization in Europe that promotes the economic and political integration of member states, is the democratic deficit. The criticism is that the executive and administrative institutions of the EU have far more power than the European Parliament, the legislature elected by citizens of the member states of the EU. Granted there is truth to this criticism, but how much greater is the democratic deficit of the global state—for which there is no elected parliament at all!

In reading the selections that follow, think about how useful is the concept of the global state as a description of the organization of the international economic and financial system. What is the value of doing so? How misleading is it? Where do you come out and why?

---

[2]For a different view, similar to the claim that will be developed below, see Martin Shaw, *Theory of the Global State: Globality as an Unfinished Revolution* (Cambridge: University Press, 2000).

National, Regional, and Global Governance

One Phenomenon or Many?

Elke Krahmann

Elke Krahmann suggests that governance and government are useful concepts in analyzing the organization of political units, whether national, regional, or global. In her conceptualization, the two represent opposite ends of a continuum. They differ regarding the extent to which the units are directed by formal institutions with legal authority and political capacity to exert control. Governance involves a situation of decentralization, in which there is no central authority but, instead, informal coordination among multiple authorities. At the other extreme, government consists of a statelike authority with a monopoly of legal coercion. In any concrete situation, there can be a hybrid form, that is, a government with limited scope and, for the issues not under the jurisdiction of government, informal coordination among independent authorities, that is, governance. Another possibility is the absence of both governance *and* government, that is, what classical political theorists like Thomas Hobbes, John Locke, and Jean-Jacques Rousseau called a state of nature. As these theorists recognized, the absence of authority may invite fierce conflict among participants, or it may involve peaceful coexistence.

The distinction between governance and government can be applied to the distribution of authority at national, regional, and global levels. Thus, for example, it can illuminate the character of regional associations like the North American Free Trade Association (NAFTA) and the European Union (EU), as well as the contrast between them. NAFTA is much closer to the governance pole. It has a quite limited mandate, mainly directed to lowering tariffs among Canada, Mexico, and the United States, and lacks formal institutions to implement its directives. (It relies on member states for this purpose.) The EU has been described as a quasi-state: it consists of a dense and powerful network of authoritative institutions (the European Commission, European Central Bank, European Parliament, and European Court of Justice). Each one has jurisdiction in important issue areas, such as harmonizing economic regulations or distributing funds for specified purposes like agricultural subsidies. The EU is thus far closer to the government end of the continuum.

What difference does this distinction make? Do you agree with Krahmann that the distinction can be applied to different levels? Can you apply it to different cases within a given level, such as different countries? (For example, are some countries closer than others to the government pole?) Can informal coordination have the same effect as a unified government? In reading this and other selections in this chapter, think about how to characterize the global arena. To what extent is there governance as opposed to government? To what extent is there both governance and government? To what extent is there neither, that is, a state of nature or anarchy among the nation states and other actors, such as TNCs?

Since the 1980s, the concept of governance has increasingly been employed to describe policymaking in the national, regional, and global arenas. Definitions and uses of governance, however, are as varied as the issues and levels of analysis to which the concept is applied. They range from definitions that subsume any form of social coordination to policymaking in the absence of an overarching political authority, from descriptions of the withdrawal of the European welfare state to analyses of public sector reforms in Africa.[1] Common to these notions is the changing locus of political authority.

. . . The emergence and uses of governance across levels of analysis illustrate that, despite apparent differences, governance arrangements at the national, regional, and global levels display crucial similarities. . . .

My aim is to facilitate future substantive research by examining the possibilities for a common definition and comparative analysis. The . . . article outlines the similarities of governance at the national, regional, and global levels. . . .

National Governance

In the literature on national policymaking, which for the purposes of this article subsumes subregional and local structures and processes, the term governance has been used as a distinct concept since the 1980s. Specifically, the literature distinguishes governance from government in order to describe the emergence of policymaking arrangements that, in addition to governments, increasingly involve private actors—such as nongovernmental agencies, firms, associations, and interest groups—in the provision of public services and in social and economic regulation. With these changes in mind, Gerry Stoker concludes that governance can be defined as "a concern with governing, achieving collective action in the realm of public affairs, in conditions where it is not possible to rest on recourse to the authority of the state."[2]

Although the origins of the growing role of private actors in national public policy can be traced back to governmental reforms, the underlying causes of these reforms appear to have stemmed mainly from the international environment. Among industrialized nations, the "withdrawal" of the state from the direct pro-

---

vision of public goods in favor of private or public-private arrangements has specifically been linked to the 1970s world recession, the pressure of globalization, and the rise of the European Union as an alternative political authority in Western Europe.[3] In the third world, similar reforms appear to have been driven by demands from the International Monetary Fund (IMF) and World Bank in the early 1990s that aimed at the improvement of public sector management in developing countries.[4]

However, some authors contend that the seeds for the pressure on governments to reduce their direct role in public services were already contained within the welfare state system. They identify as one cause the tendency of state bureaucracies to extend their functions, which in time led to an organizational overload.[5] Among developing countries, this expansion of the public sector was also facilitated by structural development programs in the 1960s and 1970s.[6]

The specific nature of government failure seems to be less clear. Most authors appear to agree that the "crisis of the welfare state" among industrialized countries and the "developmentalist" state in the third world was characterized by problems such as low levels of compliance, reduced financial resources, limited effectiveness, and a perceived lack of accountability and legitimacy.[7] Yet the immediate features and the degree to which these problems were new or had increased are unclear. Recent studies that attempt to compare the efficiency of governance with government are often inconclusive.[8] Indeed, some authors argue that, among developing nations, governance mechanisms have not necessarily improved the efficiency or accountability of public services.[9]

Nevertheless, in the 1980s, a consensus emerged among advanced industrialized nations, such as Britain, the United States, and New Zealand, that existing governmental policymaking structures were unsatisfactory and needed to be replaced.[10] The blueprint for an alternative, namely governance, was provided by neoliberal and new-right ideologies. These ideologies advocated the introduction of competition and market principles into public administrative systems. The suggested reforms followed two main strategies. The first strategy sought to increase the involvement of the private sector in the provision of public services through privatization, outsourcing, coproduction, and public-private partnerships. The second strategy envisaged the remodeling of the remaining public sector according to new public management ideals.[11] The new public management model proposed the introduction of competitive tendering, performance incentives, and internal auditing within a decentralized and customer-oriented structure in order to increase accountability, transparency, and civil society participation. Redefined as good governance, these principles were subsequently adopted by the World Bank and the IMF as conditions for development aid.[12]

In sum, it can be argued that, at the national and subnational levels, the concept of governance has come to represent political systems in which authority is fragmented among a multitude of governmental and nongovernmental actors to increase efficiency and effectiveness. However, the following illustrates that these features of governance are not unique to the level of the state.

Regional Governance

In the analysis of the regional level, the term governance has primarily been used since the mid-1990s to describe the complex, multilevel decisionmaking and implementation process within the European Union (EU). Simon Hix defines the new governance within the EU as having several interrelated characteristics: "First, the process of governing is no longer conducted exclusively by the state, but involves all those activities of social, political and administrative actors that . . . guide, steer, control or manage society." Second, the relationship between state and non-state actors in this process is "polycentric and non-hierarchical" and "mutually dependent." Third, the key governance function is the regulation of social and political risk instead of redistribution.[13]

While the above definition already shows significant commonalities with the characterization of governance at the national level, the similarities are even clearer with regard to the internal and external factors that appear to have led to the emergence of governance in the EU. Internally, the reliance of the EU on governance has been associated with the lack of resources by community institutions,[14] whereas, externally, the growing role of governance mechanisms within the EU has been interpreted as a response to increasing international interdependence and the inability of governments to unilaterally deal with problems such as the free flow of goods and peoples.[15]

Of course, it can be argued that the making and implementation of EU policies has never approached the level of centralization associated with national government but has always been dispersed among a variety of national and international authorities. Moreover, the EU has traditionally more strongly relied on governance mechanisms, such as regulation, to achieve its policy aims because it has no direct role in the implementation of European policies.[16] Nevertheless, it can be argued that in the EU also, the contribution and participation of subnational and private actors has increased considerably over the past twenty years. Key factors that drove this development were the strengthening of neoliberal values in the Single European Act, the embrace of the subsidiarity principle in the Maastricht treaty, and increasing flexibility following the Intergovernmental Conference in Amsterdam.[17]

As a result, the system of governance within the EU today is characterized by six main features. First, policymaking and implementation involve a broad range of public and private actors at the national and international levels, such as regional authorities, employers, labor associations, and multinational corporations.[18] Second, policymaking is functionally differentiated according to distinct policy sectors, such as external relations, internal market, agriculture, and the environment.[19] Third, similar to national governments, the EU is increasingly relying on quasi-autonomous agencies, such as the European Court of Justice and the European Central Bank, for the implementation and supervision of its policies.[20] Fourth, since the relations among the diverse actors in the EU are increasingly based on mutual dependence, they are typically nonhierarchical.[21]

Fifth, the strengthening of neoliberal principles among the member states and EU institutions has favored a shift of emphasis from redistribution to regulation.[22] And finally, due to the shift in the EU's underlying ideology, market principles are increasingly regarded as the most suitable means of coordination.[23]

Together these findings illustrate that the notion of EU regional governance matches in many ways the use of the concept at the national and subnational levels. At its core is the fragmentation of authority and resources among multiple governmental, semigovernmental, and nongovernmental actors. In addition, the increased emphasis on devolution and market within the new public management is progressively reflected by institutions at the European level. However, the next section shows that similar developments can also be observed at the global level.

Global Governance

The application of the term governance to the global level has particularly increased since the early 1990s. Although the term global governance appears to suggest a world system or world society,[24] the concept is typically, and hence also in this article, used to describe the increasingly regulated character of transnational and international relations.[25] Most authors emphasize that global governance is concentrated in specific regions, such as the industrialized world, or in particular issue areas, such as trade and the use of the oceans.[26] Leon Gordenker and Thomas Weiss define global governance accordingly as "efforts to bring more orderly and reliable responses to social and political issues that go beyond capacities of states to address individually. Like the NGO universe, global governance implies an absence of central authority, and the need for collaboration or cooperation among governments and others who seek to encourage common practices and goals in addressing global issues."[27]

A number of explanations have been offered as to the origins of global governance. Some authors have linked the rise of global governance to the end of the Cold War and the greater willingness of governments to collaborate internationally.[28] Others point out that the quantitative and qualitative growth of international institutions, rules, and regulations has been a long-term process that started at the beginning of the twentieth century.[29] Nevertheless, there is an agreement that the process of institutionalization has accelerated. Three interrelated causes that mirror the origins of national and regional governance appear to have contributed to the progressive demand for global governance.

Most noticeable has been the growing pressure and awareness of global problems, such as environmental pollution, transnational crime, terrorism, infectious diseases, and migration, which can only be resolved through international cooperation.[30] The process of globalization—that is, the expansion of transnational contacts and international interdependence in trade, finance, technology, and security—has created or exacerbated many of these problems.[31] As governments have recognized the limitations to their resources and capabilities in dealing with global issues, globalization has also contributed to the formation of networks among governments, international organizations, and nongovernmental organizations (NGOs) that engage in global governance. Thus, like national and regional governance, the rise of global governance arrangements seems to have been fostered in part by the processes of globalization and in part by national governments themselves through their adoption of neoliberal ideas that have encouraged greater use of private actors.[32]

The characteristics of global governance arrangements vary widely. Most are concentrated around sets of states that share specific geographic, economic, and cultural similarities. However, even within these sets, governance is fragmented among governmental and nongovernmental actors at the national and international level. While states continue to play a central role in global governance, international organizations, NGOs, and multinational corporations increasingly participate in the formulation, implementation, and monitoring of international policies, rules, and regulations.[33] Moreover, in the absence of a central authority in the international system and given shifting balances of power, the relationships between governmental and nongovernmental actors at the national and international levels are becoming complex and horizontal.[34] In fact, not only has the control of governments over international and transnational affairs been curtailed by global interdependence, but their national sovereignty has also been challenged.[35]

In comparison, global governance shows a considerable resemblance to national and regional governance arrangements. Specifically, global governance is characterized by the need for greater collaboration among governments and nongovernmental actors as the result of states being faced with new and growing demands on the one hand and shrinking resources on the other. The consistency of these similarities across levels of analysis supports the proposition that governance can be understood as a general phenomenon. The next part examines how this phenomenon might be defined.

Conceptualizing Governance Across Levels of Analysis

Contrary to the profusion of definitions and meanings of the term governance, the previous sections have demonstrated that governance at the national, regional, and global levels displays many common characteristics. Core features include the fragmentation of authority and policy functions among governmental and nongovernmental actors and the preference for market solutions, as well as similar origins in the growth of global interdependence and the shift toward a neoliberal ideology. These commonalities suggest that governance, although implemented in different ways, may be understood as a universal phenomenon. Furthermore, they imply that governance may usefully be defined as a general concept that describes a specific set of policymaking arrangements across levels of analysis.

Two observations help pave the way for a general conceptualization of the phenomenon. First, the previous analysis demonstrates that the recent increase in the use of the term governance can be linked to a change in meaning. It challenges the definition of governance as a generic term synonymous with concepts such as political system or state structures, which appear to have prevailed in the academic discourse before the 1980s. The new uses of governance commonly refer to the fragmentation of political authority among governmental and nongovernmental actors at the national, regional, and global levels. They pose governance against government, which is understood as the centralization of authority within the state.

Second, the variety of institutions and modes of policymaking commonly associated with governance and government across levels of analysis suggest that both concepts are best perceived as ideal types. Even political systems described as centralized, such as the French, delegate some political authority to regional and municipal institutions. What identifies centralized and federal states as government rather than governance is the observation that political authority is predominantly divided among different government agencies rather than between governmental and nongovernmental actors. Similarly, governance arrangements incorporate a broad variety of modes that range from public-private partnerships to self-regulation. However, all of them are defined by the fragmentation of policymaking capabilities among a multitude of governmental and nongovernmental actors.

In terms of a general definition, governance can thus be understood as the structures and processes that enable governmental and nongovernmental actors to coordinate their interdependent needs and interests through the making and implementation of policies in the absence of a unifying political authority. Conversely, government is defined here as policymaking arrangements and processes that centralize political authority within the state and its agencies. . . .

Conclusion

. . . [T]his article has proposed conceiving of governance and government as two ideal-typical poles on a scale that differentiates fragmented from centralized policymaking. It is difficult to specify which or how many dimensions have to be fragmented to qualify a policymaking arrangement as governance rather than government, not least because the institutions and practices in each dimension are dynamic and constantly evolving. Separate dimensions may proceed either toward greater fragmentation or toward integration. In fact, different dimensions might display countervailing trends.

Nonetheless, the ideal-type definition of governance has several advantages. Most important, it allows governance to be understood as a general phenomenon. It not only helps to address the conceptual confusion within and across levels of analysis, but it also facilitates new research into the nature of governance. In particular, a common understanding of governance encourages the comparison between governance arrangements at the national, regional, and global levels as well as helps to determine the suitability of specific governance mechanisms across sectors and levels. Furthermore, it raises the question of whether governance failures encountered at one level might come to affect others. Indeed, a common definition of governance might help identify solutions to these problems by suggesting research into the applicability of particular compensation mechanisms across levels of analysis.

In addition, using government and governance as ideal-typical poles at either end of a continuum ranging from centralization to fragmentation permits an analysis of the transformation of political authority at the national, regional, and global levels. In particular, this definition suggests that the rise of governance in practice and as a theoretical concept across levels of analysis, which was traced in the first part of this article, can be understood as a common development. Moreover, this definition suggests a research design that compares the emergence of governance arrangements not only across sectors, but also across the national, regional, and global arenas. Such a research project could help identify which areas or levels have progressed most toward governance across the dimensions, thereby providing new insights into the spread of governance processes and mechanisms. Specifically, it would investigate why some systems have progressed more toward governance than others and thus help explain the emergence of governance itself. . . .

Notes

1. Bob Jessop, "The Changing Governance of Welfare: Recent Trends in Its Primary Functions, Scale and Modes of Coordination," Social Policy and Administration 33, no. 4 (1999): 351; Ernst-Otto Czempiel, "Governance and Democratization," in James N. Rosenau and Ernst-Otto Czempiel, eds., Governance Without Government: Order and Change in World Politics (Cambridge: Cambridge University Press, 1992), p. 250; Gerry Stoker, "Introduction," in Gerry Stoker, ed., The New Politics of British Local Governance (Basingstoke, England: Macmillan, 2000), p. 31; Daniel Davis, David Hulme, and Philip Woodhouse, "Decentralisation by Default: Local Governance and the View from the Village in The Gambia," Public Administration and Development 14, no. 3 (1994): 253–269.
2. Stoker, "Introduction," p. 3.
3. Richard Rose, "The Nature of the Challenge," in Richard Rose, ed., Challenges to Governance: Studies in Overloaded Polities (Beverly Hills: Sage, 1980), pp. 5–28, 7; Giandomenico Majone, "From the Positive to the Regulatory State: Causes and Consequences of Changes in the Mode of Governance," Journal of Public Policy 17, no. 2 (1997): 139, 142.
4. Cynthia Hewitt de Alcantara, "Uses and Abuses of the Concept of Governance," International Social Science Journal 50, no. 1 (1998): 107–108; World Bank, Governance and Development (Washington, D.C.: World Bank, 1992).
5. Peter Self, "Resource and Policy Co-ordination Under Pressure," in Rose, Challenges to Governance, p. 45; Renate Mayntz, "Governing Failures and the Problem of Governability: Some Comments on a Theoretical Paradigm," in Jan Koiman, ed., Modern Governance: New Government-Society Interactions (London: Sage, 1993), p. 10.
6. Pierre de Senarchens, "Governance and the Crisis in International Mechanisms of Regulation," International Social Science Journal 50, no. 1 (1998): 95; Ole Therkildsen, "Public Sector Reform in a Poor Aid-Dependent Country, Tanzania," Public Administration and Development 20, no. 1 (2000): 61; Rita Abrahamsen, Disciplining Democracy: Development Discourse and Good Governance in Africa (London and New York: Zed Books, 2000), pp. 50–52.
7. Mayntz, "Governing Failures and the Problem of Governability," p. 10; Jon Pierre, "Introduction: Understanding Governance," in Jon Pierre, ed., Debating Governance: Authority, Steering, and Democracy (Oxford: Oxford University Press, 2000), p. 4; Majone, "From the Positive to the

Regulatory State," p. 142; de Senarchens, "Governance and the Crisis in the International Mechanisms of Regulation," p. 95.

8. Bob Jessop, "Governance Failure," in Stoker, The New Politics of British Local Governance, pp. 11–32; John Steward and Gerry Stoker, "Fifteen Years of Local Government Restructuring 1979–94: An Evaluation," in John Steward and Gerry Stoker, eds., Local Government in the 1990s (Basingstoke, England: Macmillan, 1995), pp. 191–209; Martin Minogue, Should Flawed Models of Public Management Be Exported? Issues and Practices, Working Paper No. 15, Institute for Development Policy and Management, University of Manchester, February 2000.
9. de Alcantara, "Uses and Abuses of the Concept of Governance," pp. 108, 111–112; Peter Blunt, "Cultural Relativism, 'Good' Governance and Sustainable Human Development," Public Administration and Development 15, no. 1 (1995): 1–9; George Philip, "The Dilemmas of Good Governance: A Latin American Perspective," Government and Opposition 34, no. 2 (1999): 226–242.
10. Other governments, such as Denmark and Germany, have been more reluctant to adopt governance arrangements. See Peter Munk Christiansen, "A Prescription Rejected: Market Solutions to Problems of Public Sector Governance," Governance 11, no. 3 (1998): 273–295.
11. Majone, "From the Positive to the Regulatory State," p. 140; R. A. W. Rhodes, "Foreword: Governance and Networks," in Stoker, The New Management of British Local Governance. p. xvii; Pierre, "Introduction," p. 1.
12. Minogue, "Should Flawed Models of Public Management Be Exported?"; Kenneth Stowe, "Good Piano Won't Play Bad Music: Administrative Reform and Good Governance," Public Administration 70, no. 3 (1992): 387–394.
13. Simon Hix, "The Study of the European Union II: The 'New Governance' Agenda and Its Rival," Journal of European Public Policy 5, no. 1 (1998): 39.
14. Giandomenico Majone, "The Rise of the Regulatory State in Europe," West European Politics 17, no. 3 (1994): 87.
15. Simon J. Bulmer, "New Institutionalism and the Governance of the Single European Market," Journal of European Public Policy 5, no. 3 (1998): 366; Beate Kohler-Koch, "Catching Up with Change: The Transformation of Governance in the European Union," Journal of European Public Policy 3, no. 3 (1996): 360.
16. Ibid.
17. Bulmer, "New Institutionalism and the Governance of the Single European Market," p. 368.
18. Alberta Sbragia, "The European Union as Coxwain: Governance by Steering," in Pierre, Debating Governance, p. 220; Thomas O. Hueglin, "Government, Governance, Governmentality," in Beate Kohler-Koch and Rainer Eising, eds., The Transformation of Governance in the European Union (London: Routledge, 1999), p. 252; Hix, "The Study of the European Union II," p. 39; Lisbet Hooghe, "Introduction: Reconciling EU-wide Policy and National Diversity," in Lisbet Hooghe, ed., Cohesion Policy and European Integration: Building Multi-level Governance (Oxford: Oxford University Press, 1996), p. 16.
19. Hueglin, "Government, Governance, Governmentality," pp. 251–252; Hix, "The Study of the European Union II," p. 39.
20. Hueglin, "Government, Governance, Governmentality," p. 254; Hix, "The Study of the European Union II," p. 40.
21. Sbragia, "The European Union as Coxwain," p. 220; Hix, "The Study of the European Union II," p. 40.
22. Bulmer, "New Institutionalism and the Governance of the Single Market," p. 368; Hix, "The Study of the European Union II," p. 40.
23. Kohler-Koch, "Catching Up with Change," p. 364; Majone, "The Rise of the Regulatory State in Europe," p. 87; Hueglin, "Government, Governance, Governmentality," p. 254.
24. Marie-Josee Massicotte, "Global Governance and the Global Political Economy: Three Texts in Search of a Synthesis," Global Governance 5, no. 1 (1999): 139ff.; Mihaly Simai, The Future of Global Governance: Managing Risk and Change in the International System (Washington, D.C.: United States Institute of Peace Press, 1994).
25. Lawrence S. Finkelstein, "What Is Global Governance?" Global Governance 1, no. 3 (1995): 367–372.

26. James N. Rosenau, "Change, Complexity, and Governance in Globalizing Space," in Pierre, Debating Governance, p. 172; Dieter Senghaas, "Global Governance: How Could It Be Conceived?" Security Dialogue 24, no. 3 (1993): 248; James H. Mittelman, "Rethinking the 'New Regionalism' in the Context of Globalization," Global Governance 2, no. 2 (1996): 189.
27. Leon Gordenker and Thomas G. Weiss, "Pluralizing Global Governance: Analytical Approaches and Dimensions," in Leon Gordenker and Thomas G. Weiss, eds., NGOs, the UN, and Global Governance (Boulder: Lynne Rienner, 1996), p. 17. For similar definitions, see Finkelstein, "What Is Global Governance?" p. 368; Commission on Global Governance, Our Global Neighbourhood: The Report of the Commission on Global Governance (Oxford: Oxford University Press, 1995), pp. 2–3; Oran Young, International Governance: Protecting the Environment in a Stateless Society (Ithaca: Cornell University Press, 1994), p. 53.
28. Mittelman, "Rethinking the 'New Regionalism,' " p. 189; James N. Rosenau, "Governance in the Twenty-first Century," Global Governance 1, no. 1 (1995): 17; Martin Hewson and Timothy Sinclair, "The Emergence of Global Governance Theory," in Martin Hewson and Timothy Sinclair, eds., Approaches to Global Governance Theory (Albany: State University of New York Press, 1999), pp. 3–22.
29. Mark W. Zacher, "The Decaying Pillars of the Westphalian Temple: Implications for International Order and Governance," in Rosenau and Czempiel, Governance Without Government, p. 65.
30. James N. Rosenau, "Governance, Order and Change in World Politics," in Rosenau and Czempiel, Governance without Government, p. 3; Zacher, "The Decaying Pillars of the Westphalian Temple," p. 76ff.; Gearoid O Tuathail, Andrew Herod, and Susan M. Roberts, "Negotiating Unruly Problematics," in Andrew Herod, Gearoid O Tuathail, and Susan M. Roberts, eds., An Unruly World? Globalization, Governance and Geography (London: Routledge, 1998), p. 12.
31. Gordenker and Weiss, "Pluralizing Global Governance," p. 20; Senghaas, "Global Governance," p. 251; Nicola Yeates, "Social Politics and Policy in an Era of Globalization: Critical Reflections," Social Policy and Administration 33, no. 4 (1999): 374; Bernhard Zangl and Michael Zurn, "The Effects of Denationalisation on Security in the OECD World," Global Society 13, no. 2 (1999): 140.
32. Mittelman, "Rethinking the 'New Regionalism,' " p. 191; O Tuathail, Herod, and Roberts, "Negotiating Unruly Problematics," pp. 6–9.
33. James N. Rosenau, "Change, Complexity, and Governance in Globalizing Space," in Pierre, Debating Governance, pp. 172–173; Commission on Global Governance, Our Global Neighbourhood, pp. 2–3; O Tuathail, Herod, and Roberts, "Negotiating Unruly Problematics," p. 14.
34. Rosenau, "Change, Complexity, and Governance in Globalizing Space," p. 189; Finkelstein, "What Is Global Governance?" p. 367; Gordenker and Weiss, "Pluralizing Global Governance," p. 17.
35. Gordenker and Weiss, "Pluralizing Global Governance," p. 20.

ARTICLE 7.2

Globalization and Its Discontents

Joseph E. Stiglitz

When Joseph Stiglitz published *Globalization and Its Discontents*, from which this selection was taken, it made headlines. Stiglitz was not only a Nobel prizewinner in economics but former chair of President Clinton's Council of Economic Advisers as well as former chief economist of the World Bank, an international agency whose mandate is to alleviate poverty in the world. When an economic heavyweight voices criticisms similar to those of youthful protestors opposing economic globalization, it's bound to make headlines!

Elsewhere in the book from which this selection was excerpted, Stiglitz alludes to a phrase that has become widely adopted in characterizing the organization of the global economic system: *governance without government.* (See the selection by Krahmann in this chapter.) Governance involves coordination among decentralized authorities, including states and international financial institutions (IFIs), to make rules for the global system. Government denotes a single, relatively unified and coherent central authority that makes and enforces rules. If governance exists at the global level, who participates in developing rules? Stiglitz suggests that the key decision makers are international financial institutions. IFIs are delegated great power by national states, but they are not democratically elected or accountable. He is especially critical of the International Monetary Fund (IMF), an organization to which most nations of the world belong. Stiglitz asserts that the IMF is particularly attentive to the governments of the most powerful countries in the affluent North. And, within governments, the IMF's closest links are to finance ministers, whose primary concern is the well-being of private banks, institutions with interests that may conflict with other organizations and the broad mass of the population.

The IMF issues annual assessments of the economies and economic policies of member states. Its real muscle is felt when countries apply to the IMF for loans. In order to qualify, a country must accept conditions imposed by the IMF, such as cutting social expenditures, that is, spending on the poor, as well as liberalizing its economy by lowering tariffs and permitting free capital flows. Stiglitz claims that by imposing harsh adjustment measures, guided by neoliberal theory (what he terms the Washington Consensus), the IMF has often aggravated economic instability and lowered living standards for the most vulnerable. Further, the IMF deprives countries of their autonomy since they have little choice but to accept IMF-imposed conditions. He provides illustrations of how the IMF can be highly destructive of the well-being of nations forced to accept its advice.

Stiglitz's criticisms did not go unanswered. In the next selection, Kenneth Rogoff, former managing director of the IMF, aggressively challenges critics like Stiglitz.

The IMF has a distinct role in international assistance. It is supposed to review each recipient's macroeconomic situation and make sure that the country is living within its means. If it is not, there is inevitably trouble down the road. In the short run, a country can live beyond its means by borrowing, but eventually a day of reckoning comes, and there is a crisis. The IMF is particularly concerned about inflation. Countries whose governments spend more than they take in in taxes and foreign aid often will face inflation, especially if they finance their deficits by printing money. Of course, there are other dimensions to good macroeconomic policy besides inflation. The term *macro* refers to the *aggregate* behavior, the overall levels of growth, unemployment, and inflation, and a country can have low inflation but no growth and high unemployment. To most economists, such a country would rate as having a disastrous macroeconomic framework. To most economists, inflation is not so much an end in itself, but a means to an end: it is because *excessively* high inflation often leads to low growth, and low growth leads to high unemployment, that inflation is so frowned upon. But the IMF often seems to confuse means with ends, thereby losing sight of what is ultimately of concern. A country like Argentina can get an "A" grade, even if it has double-digit unemployment for years, so long as its budget seems in balance and its inflation seems in control! . . .

It is hard even for a moderate-sized institution like the IMF to know a great deal about every economy in the world. Some of the best IMF economists were assigned to work on the United States, but when I served as chairman of the Council of Economic Advisers, I often felt that the IMF's limited understanding of the U.S. economy had led it to make misguided policy recommendations for America. The IMF economists felt, for instance, that inflation would start rising in the United States as soon as unemployment fell below 6 percent. At the Council, our models said they were wrong, but they were not terribly interested in our input. We were right, and the IMF was wrong: unemployment in the United States fell to below 4 percent and still inflation did not increase. Based on their faulty analysis of the U.S. economy, the IMF economists came up with a misguided policy prescription: raise interest rates. Fortunately, the Fed paid no attention to the IMF recommendation. Other countries could not ignore it so easily.

But to the IMF the lack of detailed knowledge is of less moment, because it tends to take a "one-size-fits-all" approach. The problems of this approach become particularly acute when facing the challenges of the developing and transition economies. The institution does not really claim expertise in development—its original mandate is supporting global economic stability, as I have said, not reducing poverty in developing countries—yet it does not hesitate to weigh in, and weigh in heavily, on development issues. Development issues are complicated; in many ways developing countries present far greater difficulties than more developed countries. This is because in developing nations, markets are often absent, and when present, often work imperfectly. Information problems abound, and cultural mores may significantly affect economic behavior.

Unfortunately, too often the training of the macroeconomists does not prepare them well for the problems that they have to confront in developing countries. In some of the universities from which the IMF hires regularly, the core curricula involve models in which there is never any unemployment. After all, in the standard competitive model—the model that underlies the IMF's market fundamentalism—demand always equals supply. If the demand for labor equals supply, there is never any *involuntary* unemployment. Someone who is not working has evidently chosen not to work. In this interpretation, unemployment in the Great Depression, when one out of four people was out of work, would be the result of a sudden increase in the desire for more leisure. It might be of some interest to psychologists why there was this sudden change in the desire for leisure, or why those who were supposed to be enjoying this leisure seemed so unhappy, but according to the standard model these questions go beyond the scope of economics. While these models might provide some amusement within academia, they seemed particularly ill suited to understanding the problems of a country like South Africa, which has been plagued with unemployment rates in excess of 25 percent since apartheid was dismantled.

The IMF economists could not, of course, ignore the existence of unemployment. Because under market fundamentalism—in which, *by assumption*, markets work perfectly and demand must equal supply for labor as for every other good or factor—there cannot be unemployment, the problem cannot lie with markets. It must lie elsewhere—with greedy unions and politicians interfering with the workings of free markets, by demanding—and getting—excessively high wages. There is an obvious policy implication—if there is unemployment, wages should be reduced.

But even if the training of the typical IMF macroeconomist had been better suited to the problems of developing countries, it's unlikely that an IMF mission, on a three-week trip to Addis Ababa, Ethiopia's capital, or the capital of any other developing country, could really develop policies appropriate for that country. Such policies are far more likely to be crafted by highly educated, first-rate economists already in the country, deeply knowledgeable about it and working daily on solving that country's problems. Outsiders can play a role, in sharing the experiences of other countries, and in offering alternative interpretations of the economic forces at play. But the IMF did not want to take on the mere role of an adviser, competing with others who might be offering their ideas. It wanted a more central role in shaping policy. And it could do this because its position was based on an ideology—market fundamentalism—that required little, if any, consideration of a country's particular circumstances and immediate problems. IMF economists could ignore the short-term effects their policies might have on the country, content in the belief that *in the long run* the country would be better off; any adverse short-run impacts would be merely pain that was necessary as part of the process. Soaring interest rates might, today, lead to starvation, but market efficiency requires free markets, and eventually, efficiency leads to growth, and growth benefits all. Suffering and pain became part of the process of redemption, evidence that a country was on the right track. To me, sometimes pain *is* necessary, but it is not a virtue in its own right. Well-designed policies can often avoid much of the pain; and some forms of pain—the misery caused by abrupt cuts in food subsidies, for example, which leads to rioting, urban violence, and the dissolution of the social fabric—are counterproductive.

The IMF has done a good job of persuading many that its ideologically driven policies were necessary if countries are to succeed in the long run. Economists always focus on the importance of scarcity and the IMF often says it is simply the messenger of scarcity: countries cannot persistently live beyond their means. One doesn't, of course, need a sophisticated financial institution staffed by Ph.D. economists to tell a country to limit expenditures to revenues. But IMF reform programs go well beyond simply ensuring that countries live within their means.

There are alternatives to IMF-style programs, other programs that may involve a reasonable level of sacrifice, which are not based on market fundamentalism, programs that have had positive outcomes. . .

But the IMF is not particularly interested in hearing the thoughts of its "client countries" on such topics as development strategy or fiscal austerity. All too often, the Fund's approach to developing countries has had the feel of a colonial ruler. . . .

A quarter of a century ago, those in the developing countries might rightly have given some deference to the "experts" from the IMF. But just as there has been a shift in the military balance of power, there has been an even more dramatic shift in the intellectual balance of power. The developing world now has its own economists—many of them trained at the world's best academic institutions. These economists have the significant advantage of lifelong familiarity with local politics, conditions, and trends. The IMF is like so many bureaucracies; it has repeatedly sought to extend what it does, beyond the bounds of the objectives originally assigned to it. As IMF's mission creep gradually brought it outside its core area of competency in macroeconomics, into structural issues, such as privatization, labor markets, pension reforms, and so forth, and into broader areas of development strategies, the intellectual balance of power became even more tilted.

The IMF, of course, claims that it never dictates but always negotiates the terms of any loan agreement with the borrowing country. But these are one-sided negotiations in which all the power is in the hands of the IMF, largely because many countries seeking IMF help are in desperate need of funds. Although I had seen this so clearly in Ethiopia and the other developing countries with which I was involved, it was brought home again to me during my visit to South Korea in December 1997, as the East Asia crisis was unfolding. South Korea's economists knew that the policies being pushed on their country by the IMF would be disastrous. While, in retrospect, even the IMF agreed that it imposed excessive fiscal stringency, in prospect, few economists (outside the IMF) thought the policy made sense. Yet Korea's economic officials remained silent. I wondered why they had kept this silence, but did not get an answer from officials inside the government until a subsequent visit two years later, when the Korean economy had recovered. The answer was what, given past experience, I had suspected all along. Korean officials reluctantly explained that they had been scared to disagree openly. The IMF could not only cut off its own funds, but could use its bully pulpit to discourage investments from private market funds by telling private sector financial institutions of the doubts the IMF had about Korea's economy. So Korea had no choice. Even implied criticism by Korea of the IMF program could have a disastrous effect: to the IMF, it would suggest that the government didn't fully understand "IMF economics," that it had reservations, making it less likely that it would actually carry out the program. (The IMF has a special phrase for describing such situations: the country has gone "off track." There is one "right" way, and any deviation is a sign of an impending derailment.) A public announcement by the IMF that negotiations had broken off, or even been postponed, would send a highly negative signal to the markets. This signal would at best lead to higher interest rates and at worst a total cutoff from private funds. Even more serious for some of the poorest countries, which have in any case little access to private funds, is that other donors (the World Bank, the European Union, and many other countries) make access to their funds contingent on IMF approval. Recent initiatives for debt relief have effectively given the IMF even more power, because unless the IMF approves the country's economic policy, there will be no debt relief. This gives the IMF enormous leverage, as the IMF well knows.

The imbalance of power between the IMF and the "client" countries inevitably creates tension between the two, but the IMF's own behavior in negotiations exacerbates an already difficult situation. In dictating the terms of the agreements, the IMF effectively stifles any discussions within a client government—let alone more broadly within the country—about alternative economic policies. In times of crises, the IMF would defend its stance by saying there simply wasn't time. But its behavior was little different in or out of crisis. The IMF's view was simple: questions, particularly when raised vociferously and openly, would be viewed as a challenge to the inviolate orthodoxy. If accepted, they might even undermine its authority and credibility. Government leaders knew this and took the cue: they might argue in private, but not in public. The chance of modifying the Fund's views was tiny, while the chance of annoying Fund leaders and provoking them to take a tougher position on other issues was far greater. And if they were angry or annoyed, the IMF could postpone its loans—a scary prospect for a country facing a crisis. But the fact that the government officials *seemed* to go along with the IMF's recommendation did not mean that they really agreed. And the IMF knew it.

Even a casual reading of the terms of the typical agreements between the IMF and the developing countries showed the lack of trust between the Fund and its recipients. The IMF staff monitored progress, not just on the relevant indicators for sound macromanagement—inflation, growth, and unemployment—but on intermediate variables, such as the money supply, often only loosely connected to the variables of ultimate concern. Countries were put on strict targets—what would be accomplished in thirty days, in sixty days, in ninety days. In some cases the agreements stipulated what laws the country's Parliament would have to pass to meet IMF requirements or "targets"—and by when.

These requirements are referred to as "conditions," and "conditionality" is a hotly debated topic in the development world. Every loan document specifies basic conditions, of course. At a minimum, a loan agreement says the loan goes out on the condition that it will be repaid, usually with a schedule attached. Many loans impose conditions designed to increase the likelihood that they will be repaid. "Conditionality" refers to more forceful conditions, ones that often turn the loan into a policy tool. If the IMF wanted a nation to liberalize its financial markets, for instance, it might pay out the loan in installments, tying subsequent installments to verifiable steps toward liberalization. I personally believe that conditionality, at least in the manner and extent to which it has been used by the IMF, is a bad idea; there is little evidence that it leads to improved economic policy, but it does have adverse political effects because countries resent having conditions imposed on them. Some defend conditionality by saying that any banker imposes conditions on borrowers, to make it more likely that the loan will be repaid. But the conditionality imposed by the IMF and the World Bank was very different. In some cases, it even *reduced* the likelihood of repayment.

For instance, conditions that might weaken the economy in the short run, whatever their merits in the long, run the risk of exacerbating the downturn and thus making it more difficult for the country to repay the short-term IMF loans. Eliminating trade barriers, monopolies, and tax distortions may enhance long-run growth, but the disturbances to the economy, as it strives to adjust, may only deepen its downturn.

While the conditionalities could not be justified in terms of the Fund's fiduciary responsibility, they might be justified in terms of what it might have perceived as its moral responsibility, its obligation to do everything it could to strengthen the economy of the countries that had turned to it for help. But the danger was that even when well intentioned, the myriad of conditions—in some cases over a hundred, each with its own rigid timetable—detracted from the country's ability to address the central pressing problems. . . .

Sometimes, the conditions seemed little more than a simple exercise of power: in its 1997 lending agreement to Korea, the IMF insisted on moving up the date of opening Korea's markets to certain Japanese goods although this could not possibly help Korea address the problems of the crisis. To some, these actions represented "seizing the window of opportunity," using the crisis to leverage in changes that the IMF and World Bank had long been pushing; but to others, these were simply acts of pure political might, extracting a concession, of limited value, simply as a demonstration of who was running the show.

While conditionality did engender resentment, it did not succeed in engendering development. Studies at the World Bank and elsewhere showed not just that conditionality did not *ensure* that money was well spent and that countries would grow faster but that there was little evidence it worked at all. Good policies cannot be bought.

There are several reasons for the failure of conditionality. The simplest has to do with the economists' basic notion of fungibility, which simply refers to the fact that money going in for one purpose frees up other money for another use; the net impact may have nothing to do with the intended purpose. Even if conditions are imposed which ensure that this particular loan is used well, the loan frees up resources elsewhere, which may or may not be used well. A country may have two road projects, one to make it easier for the president to get to his summer villa, the other to enable a large group of farmers to bring their goods to a neighboring port. The country may have funds for only one of the two projects. The Bank may insist that its money go for the project that increases the income of the rural poor; but in providing that money, it enables the government to fund the other.

There were other reasons why the Fund's conditionality did not enhance economic growth. In some cases, they were the wrong conditions: financial market liberalization in Kenya and fiscal austerity in East Asia had adverse effects on the countries. In other cases, the way conditionality was imposed made the conditions politically unsustainable; when a new government came into power, they would be abandoned. Such conditions were seen as the intrusion by the new colonial power on the country's own sovereignty. The policies could not withstand the vicissitudes of the political process. . . .

Fiscal austerity, privatization, and market liberalization were the three pillars of Washington Consensus advice throughout the 1980s and 1990s. The Washington Consensus policies were designed to respond to the very real problems in Latin America, and made considerable sense. In the 1980s, the governments of those countries had often run huge deficits. Losses in inefficient government enterprises contributed to those deficits. Insulated from competition by protectionist measures, inefficient private firms forced customers to pay high prices. Loose monetary policy led to inflation running out of control. Countries cannot persistently run large deficits; and sustained growth is not possible with hyperinflation. Some level of fiscal discipline is required. Most countries would be better off with governments focusing on providing essential public services rather than running enterprises that would arguably perform better in the private sector, and so privatization often makes sense. When trade liberalization—the lowering of tariffs and elimination of other protectionist measures—is done in the right way and at the right pace, so that new jobs are created as inefficient jobs are destroyed, there can be significant efficiency gains.

The problem was that many of these policies became ends in themselves, rather than means to more equitable and sustainable growth. In doing so, these policies were pushed too far, too fast, and to the exclusion of other policies that were needed.

The results have been far from those intended. Fiscal austerity pushed too far, under the wrong circumstances, can induce recessions, and high interest rates may impede fledgling business enterprises. The IMF vigorously pursued privatization and liberalization, at a pace and in a manner that often imposed very real costs on countries ill-equipped to incur them. . . .

ARTICLE 7.3

The IMF Strikes Back

Kenneth Rogoff

Kenneth Rogoff was managing director of the International Monetary Fund (IMF) when he wrote this article. Rogoff claims that criticisms like those of Joseph Stiglitz (see the preceding selection) wrongly target the IMF when in fact it is the defective policies of states that create the need for IMF intervention. Thus, the IMF is the messenger unfairly blamed for announcing bad tidings that it did not create. In addition, although the IMF's prescriptions, such as reducing governmental expenditures and raising taxes, may appear harsh, they are in the interests of the countries seeking IMF assistance, for the bitter medicine of austerity policies are needed to obtain the confidence of international investors. When investors are persuaded that a country is pursuing appropriate policies and is a sound investment, they will provide the capital needed to revive ailing economies. In brief, Rogoff claims that, however unpalatable IMF prescriptions may be, countries would face even greater economic problems in their absence.

Where do you stand in this debate, and why?

Vitriol against the IMF, including personal attacks on the competence and integrity of its staff, has transcended into an art form in recent years. One best-selling author labels all new fund recruits as "thirdrate," implies that management is on the take, and discusses the IMF's role in the Asian financial crisis of the late 1990s in the same breath as Nazi Germany and the Holocaust. Even more sober and balanced critics of the institution—such as *Washington Post* writer Paul Blustein, whose excellent inside account of the Asian financial crisis, *The Chastening*, should be required reading for prospective fund economists (and their spouses)—find themselves choosing titles that invoke the devil. Really, doesn't *The Chastening* sound like a sequel to 1970s horror flicks such as *The Exorcist* or *The Omen*? Perhaps this race to the bottom is a natural outcome of market forces. After all, in a world of 24-hour business news, there is a huge return to being introduced as "the leading critic of the IMF."

Regrettably, many of the charges frequently leveled against the fund reveal deep confusion regarding its policies and intentions. Other criticisms, however, do hit at potentially fundamental weak spots in current IMF practices. Unfortunately, all the recrimination and finger pointing make it difficult to separate spurious critiques from legitimate concerns. Worse yet, some of the deeper questions that ought to be at the heart of these debates—issues such as poverty, appropriate exchange-rate systems, and whether the global financial system encourages developing countries to take on excessive debt—are too easily ignored.

Consider the four most common criticisms against the fund: First, IMF loan programs impose harsh fiscal austerity on cash-strapped countries. Second, IMF loans encourage financiers to invest recklessly, confident the fund will bail them out (the so-called moral hazard problem). Third, IMF advice to countries suffering debt or currency crises only aggravates economic conditions. And fourth, the

---

Kenneth Rogoff, The IMF Strikes Back, *Foreign Policy* 134 (January/February 2003): 38–46.

fund has irresponsibly pushed countries to open themselves up to volatile and destabilizing flows of foreign capital.

Some of these charges have important merits, even if critics (including myself in my former life as an academic economist) tend to overstate them for emphasis. Others, however, are both polemic and deeply misguided. In addressing them, I hope to clear the air for a more focused and cogent discussion on how the IMF and others can work to improve conditions in the global economy. Surely that should be our common goal.

The Austerity Myth

Over the years, no critique of the fund has carried more emotion than the "austerity" charge. Anti-fund diatribes contend that, everywhere the IMF goes, the tight macroeconomic policies it imposes on governments invariably crush the hopes and aspirations of people. (I hesitate to single out individual quotes, but they could easily fill an entire edition of *Bartlett's Quotations*.) Yet, at the risk of seeming heretical, I submit that the reality is nearly the opposite. As a rule, fund programs lighten austerity rather than create it. Yes, really.

Critics must understand that governments from developing countries don't seek IMF financial assistance when the sun is shining; they come when they have already run into deep financial difficulties, generally through some combination of bad management and bad luck. Virtually every country with an IMF program over the past 50 years, from Peru in 1954 to South Korea in 1997 to Argentina today, could be described in this fashion.

Policymakers in distressed economies know the fund will intervene where no private creditor dares tread and will make loans at rates their countries could only dream of even in the best of times. They understand that, in the short term, IMF loans allow a distressed debtor nation to tighten its belt less than it would have to otherwise. The economic policy conditions that the fund attaches to its loans are in lieu of the stricter discipline that market forces would impose in the IMF's absence. Both South Korea and Thailand, for example, were facing either outright default or a prolonged free fall in the value of their currencies in 1997—a far more damaging outcome than what actually took place.

Nevertheless, the institution provides a convenient whipping boy when politicians confront their populations with a less profligate budget. "The IMF forced us to do it!" is the familiar refrain when governments cut spending and subsidies. Never mind that the country's government—whose macroeconomic mismanagement often had more than a little to do with the crisis in the first place—generally retains considerable discretion over its range of policy options, not least in determining where budget cuts must take place.

At its heart, the austerity critique confuses correlation with causation. Blaming the IMF for the reality that every country must confront its budget constraints is like blaming the fund for gravity.

Admittedly, the IMF does insist on being repaid, so eventually borrowing countries must part with foreign exchange resources that otherwise might have gone into domestic programs. Yet repayments to the fund normally spike only after the crisis has passed, making payments more manageable for borrowing governments. The IMF's shareholders—its 184 member countries—could collectively decide to convert all the fund's loans to grants, and then recipient countries would face no costs at all. However, if IMF loans are never repaid, industrialized countries must be willing to replenish continually the organization's lending resources, or eventually no funds would be available to help deal with the next debt crisis in the developing world.

A Hazardous Critique

Of course, in so many IMF programs, borrowing countries must pay back their private creditors in addition to repaying the fund. Yet wouldn't fiscal austerity be a bit more palatable if troubled debtor nations could compel foreign private lenders to bear part of the burden? Why should taxpayers in developing countries absorb the entire blow?

That is a completely legitimate question, but let's start by getting a few facts straight. First, private investors can hardly breathe a sigh of relief when the fund becomes involved in an emerging-market financial crisis. According to the Institute of International Finance, private investors lost some $225 billion during the Asian financial crisis of the late 1990s and some $100 billion as a result of the 1998 Russian debt default. And what of the Latin American debt crisis of the 1980s, during which the IMF helped jawbone foreign banks into rolling over a substantial fraction of Latin American debts for almost five years and ultimately forced banks to accept large write-downs of 30 percent or more? Certainly, if foreign private lenders consistently lose money on loans to developing countries, flows of new money will cease. Indeed, flows into much of Latin America—again the current locus of debt problems—have been sharply down during the past couple of years.

Private creditors ought to be willing to take large write-downs of their debts in some instances, particularly when a country is so deeply in hock that it is effectively insolvent. In such circumstances, trying to force the debtor to repay in full can often be counterproductive. Not only do citizens of the debtor country suffer, but creditors often receive less than they might have if they had lessened the country's debt burden and thus given the nation the will and means to increase investment and growth. Sometimes debt restructuring does happen, as in Ecuador (1999), Pakistan (1999), and Ukraine (2000). However, such cases are the exception rather than the rule, as current international law makes bankruptcies by sovereign states extraordinarily messy and chaotic. As a result, the official lending community, typically led by the IMF, is often unwilling to force the issue and sometimes finds itself trying to keep a country afloat far beyond the point of no return. In Russia in 1998, for example, the official community threw money behind a fixed exchange-rate regime that was patently doomed. Eventually, the fund cut the cord and allowed a default, proving wrong those many private investors who thought Russia was "too nuclear to fail." But if the fund had allowed the default to take place at an earlier stage, Russia might well have come out of its subsequent downturn at least as quickly and with less official debt.

Since restructuring of debt to private creditors is relatively rare, many critics reasonably worry that IMF financing often serves as a blanket insurance policy for private lenders. Moreover, when private creditors believe they will be bailed out by the IMF, they have reason to lend more—and at lower interest rates—than is appropriate. The debtor country, in turn, is seduced into borrowing too much, resulting in more frequent and severe crises, of exactly the sort the IMF was designed to alleviate. I will be the first to admit the "moral hazard" theory of IMF lending is clever (having introduced the theory in the 1980s), and I think it is surely important in some instances. But the empirical evidence is mixed. One strike against the moral hazard argument is that most countries generally do repay the IMF, if not on time, then late but with full interest. If the IMF is consistently paid, then private lenders receive no subsidy, so there is no bailout in any simplistic sense. Of course, despite the IMF's strong repayment record in major emerging-market loan packages, there is no guarantee about the future, and it would certainly be wrong to dismiss moral hazard as unimportant.

Fiscal Follies

Even if IMF policies are not to blame for budget cutbacks in poor economies, might the fund's programs still be so poorly designed that their ill-advised conditions more than cancel out any good the international lender's resources could bring? In particular, critics charge that the IMF pushes countries to increase domestic interest rates when cuts would better serve to stimulate the economy. The IMF also stands accused of forcing crisis economies to tighten their budgets in the midst of recessions. Like the austerity argument, these critiques of basic IMF policy advice appear rather damning, especially when wrapped in rhetoric about how all economists at the IMF are third-rate thinkers so immune from outside advice that they wouldn't listen if John Maynard Keynes himself dialed them up from heaven.

Of course, it would be wonderful if governments in emerging markets could follow Keynesian "countercyclical policies"—that is, if they could stimulate their economies with lower interest rates, new public spending, or tax cuts during a recession. In its September 2002 "World Economic Outlook" report, the IMF encourages exactly such policies where feasible. (For example, the IMF has strongly urged Germany to be flexible in observing the budget constraints of the European Stability and Growth Pact, lest the government aggravate Germany's already severe economic slowdown.) Unfortunately, most emerging markets have an extremely difficult time borrowing during a downturn, and they often must tighten their belts precisely when a looser fiscal policy might otherwise be desirable. And the IMF, or anyone else for that matter, can only do so much for countries that don't pay attention to the commonsense advice of building up surpluses during boom times—such as Argentina in the 1990s—to leave room for deficits during downturns.

According to some critics, though, a simple solution is staring the IMF in the face: If those stubborn fund economists would only appreciate how successful expansionary fiscal policy can be in boosting output, they would realize countries can simply wave off a debt crisis by borrowing even more. Remember former U.S. President Ronald Reagan's economic guru, Arthur Laffer, who theorized that by cutting tax rates, the United States would enjoy so much extra growth that tax revenues would actually rise? In much the same way, some IMF critics—ranging from Nobel Prize–winning economist Joseph Stiglitz to the relief agency Oxfam—claim that by running a fiscal deficit into a debt storm, a country can grow so much that it will be able to sustain those higher debt levels. Creditors would understand this logic and happily fork over the requisite extra funds. Problem solved, case closed. Indeed, why should austerity ever be necessary?

Needless to say, Reagan's tax cuts during the 1980s did not lead to higher tax revenues but instead resulted in massive deficits. By the same token, there is no magic potion for troubled debtor countries. Lenders simply will not buy into this story.

The notion that countries should reduce interest rates—rather than raise them—to fend off debt and exchange-rate crises is even more absurd. When investors fear a country is increasingly likely to default on its debts, they will demand higher interest rates to compensate for that risk, not lower ones. And when a nation's citizens lose confidence in their own currency, they will require a large premium to accept debt denominated in that currency or to keep their deposits in domestic banks. No surprise that interest rates in virtually all countries that experienced debt crises during the last decade—from Mexico to Turkey—skyrocketed even though their currencies were allowed to float against the dollar.

The debate over how far interest rates should be allowed to rise in defending against a speculative currency attack is a legitimate one. The higher interest rates go, the more stress on the economy and the more bankruptcies and bank failures; classic cases include Mexico in 1995 and South Korea in 1998. On the other hand, since most crisis countries have substantial "liability dollarization"—that is, a lot of borrowing goes on in dollars—an excessively sharp fall in the exchange rate will also cause bankruptcies, with Indonesia in 1998 being but one example among many. Governments must strike a delicate balance in the short and medium term, as they decide how quickly to reduce interest rates from crisis levels. At the very least, critics of IMF tactics must acknowledge these difficult tradeoffs. The simplistic view that all can be solved by just adopting softer "employment friendly" policies, such as low interest rates and fiscal expansions, is dangerous as well as naive in the face of financial maelstrom.

Capital Control Freaks

Although currency crises and financial bailouts dominate media coverage of the IMF, much of the agency's routine work entails ongoing dialogue with the fund's 184 member countries. As part of the fund's surveillance efforts, IMF staffers regularly visit member states and meet with policymakers to discuss how best to achieve sustained economic growth and stable inflation rates. So, rather than judge the fund solely on how it copes with financial crises, critics should consider its ongoing advice in trying to help countries stay out of trouble. In this area, perhaps the most controversial issue is the fund's advice on liberalizing international capital movements—that is, on how fast emerging markets should pry open their often highly protected domestic financial markets.

Critics such as Columbia University economist Jagdish Bhagwati have suggested that the IMF's zeal in promoting free capital flows around the world inadvertently planted the seeds of the Asian financial crisis. In principle, had banks and companies in Asia's emerging markets not been allowed to borrow freely in foreign currency, they would not have built up huge foreign currency debts, and international creditors could not have demanded repayment just as liquidity was drying up and foreign currency was becoming very expensive. Although I was not at the IMF during the Asian crisis, my sense from reading archives and speaking with fund old-timers is that although this charge has some currency, the fund was more eclectic in its advice on this matter than most critics acknowledge. For example, in the months leading to Thailand's currency collapse in 1997, IMF reports on the Thai economy portrayed in stark terms the risks of liberalizing capital flows while keeping the domestic currency (the baht) at a fixed level against the U.S. dollar. As Blustein vividly portrays in *The Chastening,* Thai authorities didn't listen, still hoping instead that Bangkok would become a financial center like Singapore. Ultimately, the Thai baht succumbed to a massive speculative attack. Of course, in some cases—most famously South Korea and Mexico—the fund didn't warn countries forcefully enough about the dangers of opening up to international capital markets before domestic financial markets and regulators were prepared to handle the resulting volatility.

However one apportions blame for the financial crises of the past two decades, misconceptions regarding the merits and drawbacks of capital-market liberalization abound. First, it is simply wrong to conclude that countries with closed capital markets are better equipped to weather stormy financial markets. Yes, the relatively closed Chinese and Indian economies did not catch the Asian flu, or at least not a particularly bad case. But neither did Australia nor New Zealand, two countries that boast extremely open capital markets. Why? Because the latter countries' highly developed domestic financial markets were extremely well regulated. The biggest danger lurks in the middle, namely for those economies—many of which are in East Asia and Latin America—that combine weak and underdeveloped financial markets with poor regulation.

Moreover, a country needs export earnings to support foreign debt payments, and export industries do not spring up overnight. That's why the risks of running into external financing problems are higher for countries that fully liberalize their capital markets before significantly opening up to trade flows. Indeed, economies with small trading sectors can run into problems even with seemingly modest debt levels. This problem has repeatedly plagued countries in Latin America, where trade is relatively restricted by a combination of inward-looking policies and remote location.

Perhaps the best evidence in favor of open capital markets is that, despite the international financial turmoil of the last decade, most developing countries still aim to liberalize their capital markets as a long-term goal. Surprisingly few nations have turned back the clock on financial and capital—account liberalization. As domestic economies grow increasingly sophisticated, particularly regarding the depth and breadth of their financial instruments, policymakers are relentlessly seeking ways to live with open capital markets. The lessons from Europe's failed, heavy-handed attempts to regulate international capital flows in the 1970s and 1980s seem to have been increasingly absorbed in the developing world today.

Even China, long the high-growth poster child for capital-control enthusiasts, now views increased openness to capital markets as a central long-term goal. Its economic leaders understand that it's one thing to become a $1,000 per capita economy, as China is today. But to continue such stellar growth performance—and one day to reach the $20,000 to $40,000 per capita incomes of the industrialized countries—China will eventually require a worldclass capital market.

Even though a continued move toward greater capital mobility is emerging as a global norm, absolute unfettered global capital mobility is not necessarily the best long-term outcome. Temporary controls on capital outflows may be important in dealing with some modern-day financial crises, while various kinds of light-handed taxes on capital inflows may be useful for countries faced with sudden surges of inflows. Chile is the classic example of a country that appears to have successfully used market-friendly taxes on capital inflows, though a debate continues to rage over their effectiveness. One way or another, the international community must find ways to temper debt flows and at the same time encourage equity investment and foreign direct investment, such as physical investment in plants and equipment. In industrialized countries, the pain of a 20 percent stock market fall is shared automatically and fairly broadly throughout the economy. But in nations that rely on foreign debt, a sudden change in investor sentiment can breed disaster.

Nevertheless, financial authorities in developing economies should remain wary of capital controls as an easy solution. "Temporary" controls can easily become ensconced, as political forces and budget pressures make them hard to remove. Invite capital controls for lunch, and they will try to stay for dinner.

Striking a Global Bargain

Should the international community just give up on global capital mobility and encourage countries to shut their doors? Looking further ahead in the 21st century, does the world really want to adopt greater financial isolationism?

Perhaps the greatest challenge facing industrialized countries in this century is how to deal with the aging bulge in their populations. With that in mind, wouldn't it be more helpful if rich countries could find effective ways to invest in much younger developing nations, and later use the proceeds to support their own increasing number of retirees? And let's face it, the world's developing countries need funds for investment and education now, so such a trade would prove mutually beneficial—a win-win. Yes, recurring debt crises in the developing world have been sobering, but the potential benefits to financial integration are enormous. Full-scale retreat is hardly the answer.

Can the IMF help? Certainly. The fund provides a key forum for exchange of ideas and best practices. Yes, one could go ahead and eliminate the IMF, as some of the more extreme detractors wish, but that is not going to solve any fundamental problems. This increasingly globalized world will still need a global economic forum. Even today, the IMF is providing such a forum for discussion and debate over a new international bankruptcy procedure that could lessen the chaos that results when debtor countries become insolvent.

And there are many other issues where the IMF, or some similar multilateral organization, seems essential to any solution. For example, the current patchwork system of exchange rates seems too unstable to survive into the 22nd century. How will the world make the transition toward a more stable, coherent system? That is a global problem, and dealing with it requires a global perspective the IMF can help provide.

And what of poverty? Here, the IMF's sister organization, the World Bank, with its microeconomic and social focus and commensurately much larger staff, is appropriately charged with the lead role. But poor countries in the developing world still face important macroeconomic challenges. For example, if enhanced aid flows ever materialize, policymakers in emerging markets will still need to find ways to ensure that domestic production grows and thrives. Perhaps poor nations won't need the IMF's specific macroeconomic expertise—but they will need something awfully similar.

ARTICLE 7.4

The Mother of all Governments *The World Bank's Matrix for Global Governance*

Paul Cammack

The World Bank is an international agency that distributes loans and assistance to alleviate poverty in poor countries. Its funds derive from contributions by governments of wealthy countries. The Bank has come under fire for seeking to impose its development strategy on governments of poor countries. Paul Cammack analyzes the Bank's Comprehensive Development Framework, a recent initiative that sought to counter this criticism. He contends that the Bank has not fundamentally changed: even when it apparently delegates control over political, social, and economic development policies to governments receiving aid, it maintains indirect control.

How persuasive is Cammack's argument? How might he respond to counterclaims that the World Bank is not responsible for the economic and political difficulties of poor countries, and that it must ensure that its funds are spent wisely? (For a related debate, involving the role of the World Bank's sister organization, the IMF, see the selections by Rogoff and Stiglitz in this chapter.) Who should decide how World Bank assistance is directed?

> It is . . . clear to all of us that ownership is essential. Countries must be in the driver's seat and set the course. They must determine goals and the phasing, timing and sequencing of programs. Where there is not adequate capacity in the government to do this, we must support and help them to establish, own, and implement the strategy. . . . The existence of the matrix is not a clandestine attempt on the part of the Bank to dominate the international development arena, or the donor dialogue in a given country. Quite the contrary. It is a tool to have greater cooperation, transparency, and partnership. . . . The matrix is open to all. It is a step towards inclusion, transparency and to accountability. . . . Ultimately, the matrix is a tool for the governments and people of the countries we serve. It is they who must own the programs, not us, and it is they who must set the pace.
>
> (James D. Wolfensohn, "A Proposal for a Comprehensive Development Framework," World Bank, 21 January 1999, pp. 9, 23)

> **Matrix. 1.** The uterus or womb. **2.** A place or medium in which something is bred, produced or developed. **3.** An embedding or enclosing mass. **4.** A piece of metal, usually copper, by means of which the face of a type is cast, having the letter stamped on it in intaglio with a punch. **5.** A rectangular arrangement of quantities or symbols.
>
> From *The Shorter Oxford English Dictionary on Historical Principles* (Oxford: Oxford University Press, 1977)

In January 1999 the World Bank launched its "Comprehensive Development Framework" (CDF). At its heart was a matrix which mapped key policy issues and areas in relation to four actors: the international development community, governments, civil society, and the private sector. World Bank President James D. Wolfensohn was eager to assure his audience that the matrix was a tool for governments to own rather than a clandestine attempt by the Bank to dominate the international development arena. The argument of this chapter is that on the contrary the CDF is a vehicle for global governance managed and co-ordinated by the Bank:

Paul Cammack, "The Mother of all Governments: The World Bank's Matrix for Global Governance," ch. 3 in Rorden Wilkinson and Steve Hughes, eds., *A Global Governance: Critical Perspectives* (London and New York: Routledge, 2002): 36–53. Reprinted by permission of Taylor & Francis.

governments do *not* own the matrix through which it is operated, as it was devised within the Bank over a decade in accordance with its own priorities; rather, as Wolfensohn's language discloses, they are obliged to *assume* ownership of it. It is instructive, in this respect, that the definitions of "matrix" in the *Shorter Oxford English Dictionary* move from images of birth and development to ideas of enclosure, imposition, and rigid containment. The same is true of the World Bank's matrix, which is presented as developmental, but intended and employed as a means of control.

The CDF is absolutely rigid in the set of fundamental macroeconomic disciplines it imposes. It prescribes on top of these a range of economic and social policies without parallel in their scope and in the depth and intensity of intervention they represent in the affairs of supposedly sovereign states. Presented as a vehicle for incorporating social and structural policies into an agenda previously dominated by macroeconomic policy alone, it is in fact a means of *shaping* social and structural policies so that they reinforce and extend macroeconomic discipline, and *subordinating* them to imperatives of capitalist accumulation. The launching of the CDF was accompanied by the introduction of a range of new disciplinary institutions (such as the Financial Stability Forum (FSF) and the Global Corporate Governance Forum (GCGF)), and new mechanisms designed to control policies across the board down to the smallest detail (such as Poverty Reduction Strategy Papers (PRSP), Sectoral Strategy Papers (SSP), the City Development Strategy (CDS), and a revised framework for Economic and Sector Work (ESW)). In this broader context, it is a fundamental goal of the Bank's strategy to impose "country ownership" of the CDF both because it recognises that it lacks the means to enforce the strategy itself, and because the legitimation of its project *vis-à-vis* citizens around the world depends upon its adoption by national governments, which remain indispensable intermediaries in the project for global governance. A key aspect of the strategy, in this context, is that the CDF is presented as benevolent, facilitating and empowering. The Bank presents itself as the mother of development—but the reality is that it aspires to be the mother of all governments.

The Comprehensive Development Framework

In setting out the CDF in January 1999, Wolfensohn shared with his colleagues his conviction that the World Bank and its allies had "contributed significantly to the betterment of mankind and to the improvement in the lives of many in poverty."[1] He drew attention to a division of labour between the International Monetary Fund (IMF) and the World Bank (supplemented by a shared commitment to work with and support the World Trade Organisation (WTO)):

> Broadly, our sister institution [the IMF] has the responsibility for macroeconomic stabilization for our client countries and for surveillance. We have the responsibility for the structural and social aspects of development. Obviously, these are not two isolated roles and we work together very closely on a day-to-day basis. As I have said

> before, the two functions are like breathing in and breathing out. An appropriate macroeconomic framework is essential for our work, but the social, structural, and human agenda, which we share with the regional banks, members of the UN system, and other partners in development, is essential for the IMF which cannot and does not prescribe in a vacuum.[2]

Wolfensohn presented development as "a balance sheet with two sides, a coin with two sides, a duet with two parts," emphasising the need to bring the macroeconomic and the social, structural and human aspects together into an integrated framework. He identified two weaknesses in this regard—bilateral and multilateral practitioners in the development field were not working together effectively to take forward structural and social reforms alongside their macroeconomic agenda, and the governments with overall responsibility for growth and poverty alleviation did not always have "the capacity to do so, or the resources, or sometimes even the will." Hence the need for "an overarching framework—an approach agreed with the government concerned—which will allow us all to work together to meet our goals for poverty alleviation and environmental sustainability."[3]

There was nothing much wrong, in Wolfensohn's opinion, with the international architecture of the Bretton Woods system, or the macroeconomic and financial frameworks it sustained. The fault lay in the failure to integrate social and structural programmes firmly into them, and this could only be remedied by adopting a "comprehensive, holistic framework" that would allow the Bank and its allies "to think more strategically about the sequencing of policies, programs and projects, and the pacing of reforms."[4] The framework Wolfensohn offered featured ten structural, human, and physical aspects, and four specific strategies (Box 1). Its individual elements would have been familiar to readers of the *World Development Reports* published by the World Bank from 1990 onwards.[5] In pride of place came four structural requirements: for good government, the rule of law, strong financial systems, and safety nets. The first step was to build an "effective government framework," which entailed "capacity building, an open legislative and transparent regulatory system, properly trained and remunerated officials and an absolute commitment to clean government." Second, governments required "an effective system of property, contract, labor, bankruptcy, commercial codes, personal rights laws and other elements of a comprehensive legal system that is effectively, impartially and cleanly administered by a well-functioning, impartial and honest judicial and legal system." Third, they must

> establish an internationally accepted and effective supervisory system for banks, financial institutions and capital markets to ensure a well-functioning and stable financial system. Information and transparency, adequately trained practitioners and supervisors, and internationally acceptable accounting and auditing standards will be essential. Regulation and supervision must include banking, savings institutions, insurance and pension plans, leasing and investment companies. Capital markets should also be developed and strengthened as resources allow.[6]

Box 1 The comprehensive development framework

A. *Structural*

1. Good and clean government
2. An effective legal and justice system
3. A well-organised and supervised financial system
4. A social safety net and social programs

B. *Human*

5. Education and knowledge institutions
6. Health and population issues

C. *Physical*

7. Water and sewerage
8. Energy
9. Roads, transportation and telecommunications
10. Sustainable development, environmental and cultural issues

D. *Specific strategies—rural, urban, and private sector*

11. Rural strategy
12. Urban strategy
13. Private sector strategy
14. Special national considerations

Source: James D. Wolfensohn, "A Proposal for a Comprehensive Development Framework," 21 January 1999.

Fourth, "whether by informal arrangement, familial or tribal support or by government-provided programs, provision must be made for the elderly, the disadvantaged and disabled, for children, for those men and women unable to find work, and those affected by natural disasters and the aftermath of war."[7]

With this structural framework in place, governments should provide universal primary education, aligning the needs of the market to "progressive" social and cultural attitudes:

> Construction of schools, modern curricula geared to the new technological age, and the real needs of the emerging local market, and effective teacher training and supervision all contribute to successful educational programs. Adult education, literacy and lifelong learning must be combined with the fundamental recognition that education of women and girls is central to the process of development. A government must also be careful to learn lessons of practice and history from indigenous peoples and communities, so that education is not imposed from afar but benefits from relevant local, communal experience. Finally, preschool education must be given its full weight in programs.[8]

In addition, they should bring population growth under control, and provide basic health care:

> It is obviously crucial that mothers are supported and that children get adequate health care before and during school years or they will have their capacities diminished. Governments must ensure the provision of health services for adults and elderly at communal and local levels, as well as services for family health care and family planning.[9]

Next came investment in essential infrastructure—water and sewerage, energy, and roads, transport and communications—and environmental protection, echoing the 1994 and 1992 *World Development Reports* respectively.[10] In these cases the emphasis of the Reports had been on the need for governments to secure areas where the uncoordinated and unregulated activities of private capital either failed to produce investment in areas of infrastructure essential to industrial and agricultural enterprise, or threatened to destroy the physical environment within which entrepreneurial activity unfolded.

Against this background, the CDF demanded specific strategies towards rural and urban development, and the private sector. These comprised integrated solutions to rural development which avoided "a return to complex comprehensive and complicated state planning," urban strategies which addressed the concentration of population in megacities, and a range of policies to promote a vibrant private sector in recognition of its character as the "engine of growth":

> A vibrant private sector requires that crucial elements of structural policy are in place. These include trade policy, tax policies, competition and regulatory policy, and corporate governance. Conditions must be created for a climate of investor confidence—with appropriate laws, transparent regulations, and predictable taxes. Whether the issue is protection of property rights or fair and equitable labor practices, governments must give certainty to the investor about the "rules of the game." Provision of credit, guarantees, sources of funding for projects all play a part in the competitive search by governments for investment and for job creation. Nothing is more significant to economic growth than the private sector.[11] . . .

The Twenty-Eighth Imperative

The most notable feature of the framework is its imperative tone—the word "must" appears twenty-seven times, as the policies promoted by the World Bank are laid out one after another as mandatory elements of a development framework. But the exposition of the comprehensive framework is accompanied by a twenty-eighth imperative, apparently at odds with the rest:

> It is also clear to all of us that ownership is essential. Countries must be in the driver's seat and set the course. They must determine goals and the phasing, timing and sequencing of programs. Where there is not adequate capacity in the government to do this, we must support and help them to establish, own, and implement the strategy. And we must work to achieve the strategy with our colleagues in the government, in the international development community, the civil society, and the private sector.[12]

Here, then, is the contradiction at the heart of the CDF. It is defined in advance down to a level of detail, but countries are obliged to own it. And where they cannot, they must be brought to do so. In other words, the imperative that countries should "own" and drive the strategy is not a reflection of the reality of its origins or character, or a requirement arising from the countries themselves, but an imperative for the Bank. It is simply a further instruction to the "clients" of the Bank—"You must own this strategy." In this way, the twenty-eighth imperative highlights both the character and the potential fragility of the twenty-seven that accompany it, reflecting the fact that the Bank cannot succeed unless its goals are adopted, internalised and implemented by countries themselves. The instrument through which this is to be achieved is the matrix.

With the elements of the framework already identified in the *World Development Reports* and elsewhere, the CDF was actually about securing "country ownership," rather than about identifying appropriate policies. As the quotation at the head of this chapter discloses, the Bank envisaged a coordinated approach involving four actors—the international development community, the government, civil society, and the private sector—and it is this coordinated approach that the Matrix is intended to secure. Although it is presented as an instrument for countries to use for their own benefit, it turns out to be a means of providing for the monitoring of implementation in real time. The surveillance the IMF exercised over macroeconomic policy is to be matched by an equal level of surveillance by the Bank over structural and social policy.

The Matrix

The matrix was presented as a management tool to overcome the lack of coordination between participants in the search for development. Wolfensohn presented it as an enabling device, "open to all" and characterised by transparency and accountability. But the accompanying detail makes clear that its logic as a management tool is to allow the Bank to step away from day-to-day control of individual programme elements and their implementation in favour of overall strategic control, and to make country policies transparent and *accountable to the Bank and its allies* in order to facilitate that control. In short, the Bank is applying to itself the principle of strategic selectivity it applies to the role of states in its overall policy guidance. Hence its reluctance to assume the role of the coordinator of all programmes in the matrix.

The Bank's claim that "the existence of the matrix is not a clandestine attempt on the part of the Bank to dominate the international development arena" but "a tool to have greater co-operation, transparency, and partnership" ignores the fact that the "judgment of the effectiveness of programs and strategies" is to be the World Bank's judgment, and that the evaluation and accountability for which it provides a basis come down to World Bank evaluation exercised through the institutionalisation of accountability to it by country "partners."

Flexibility in operation of the matrix on the part of governments is limited to the *pace* at which countries wish to "move to a comprehensive program of coordination and measurement of performance." Its principal purpose is to allow the Bank to exercise surveillance as implementation proceeds. The matrix is a "summary management tool," to be "kept up to date in real time." It is conceived as the front end of a comprehensive tracking system, encompassing all programmes behind their relevant cell, and "kept up-to-date using modern communication and information technology, possibly with open designated websites." First,

> the governmental structure of a country must be in charge of the process of development strategy and implementation. Government should aspire to have programs under each of the 14 headings along the top of the matrix and these will be entered into the grid. Obviously, the entries will have to be made in a form of shorthand and as I just noted, annexes behind each subject heading will give fuller details. For example, an annex on Justice Systems, an annex on education, giving far more detail on each subject. Government should include not only national programs, but provincial and state, city and municipal to the extent that they are relevant.[13]

Second, despite its denials, the Bank *is* seeking to bring about strategic coordination across the international development community. After listing the IMF, UN agencies and programmes, the WTO, the European Union (EU), regional development banks, bilateral agencies and international organisations as those multilateral and bilateral participants "involved in the programmatic thrusts," Wolfensohn comments that:

> All of these participants, as well as the World Bank Group, are involved in projects and programs for development. At a time of lessening resources for overseas development assistance and budgetary restraints on agencies which reduce available human resources, each of us needs to know what the other is doing so that we can cooperate and avoid duplication of effort.[14]

Third, civil society is to be *engaged in* programmes and projects defined from outside, in order to maximise their prospects for acceptance:

> Depending on local political circumstances, civil society has a greater or lesser voice, but our experience is that by engaging civil society in projects and programs, better results are achieved both with design and implementation and usually greater effectiveness, including more local ownership. I think we all recognize more and more that local ownership is the key to success and project effectiveness.[15]

In sum, Wolfensohn concludes, "The Matrix will allow us to see quickly what is going on in a country from the point of view of structural and social development, and will also show us what is not going on." For this goal to be secured, however:

> The annexes to the matrix will play a crucial role. They might start with a general overview of the objectives of the government over the long term in each subject area. It will be crucial in each annex to set forth where the country stands in terms of achievement and where they want to go. The matrix should be read in terms of the stipulated and agreed goals. There would follow a strategy for implementation with a timeline. Thereafter, one could imagine a more detailed listing of projects achieved, projects underway, and projects planned, together with a listing of those institutions providing assistance and a detailed description of the projects planned and undertaken with their

> results. The format of the annexes should be set according to the subject and to those participating in preparing and managing it.[16]

The matrix, then, is unequivocally a management tool through which the Bank and other agencies can monitor government policy across the board and in detail, against objectives and programmes agreed with the Bank. It was proposed as the principal instrument in a strategy of comprehensive global governance spear-headed by the Bank in close liaison with the IMF, to be coordinated with other relevant multilateral and bilateral actors in the area of international development. It remained to be seen, however, whether the Bank could even begin to turn its dream of global governance into reality.

Towards a Global Architecture of Governance

Since January 1999 the World Bank has indeed been systematically putting into place the elements of a Global Architecture of Governance (GAG). It has developed an operational tool through which commitment to the CDF and use of the matrix can be secured and monitored—the Poverty Reduction Strategy Paper (PRSP)—and it has surrounded the CDF and the Poverty Reduction Strategy Papers with a range of complementary disciplinary instruments which give it increasing scope for an unprecedented level of intervention in the domestic affairs of states. As we shall see, the PRSP is structured and employed to ensure direct IMF intervention in dictating the broad framework of macroeconomic policy, while the World Bank takes the lead in ensuring that social and structural policies are systematically subordinated to it, and will induce the institutional and behavioural changes that will lock it in place. In the period since the CDF and the PRSP were proposed, the CDF itself has been trialled and evaluated; a large number of interim PRSPs and a smaller number of final PRSPs have been agreed; a number of countries have accepted the matrix as an operational tool along the lines prescribed by the Bank; a method has been devised to extend the system beyond the heavily indebted and impoverished countries who are most easily persuaded of the need to obey the joint dictates of the Bank and the Fund and assume ownership of the CDF; and an effort has been made to coordinate the elements of a larger overarching framework within which the CDF and the PRSP can take their place. The Bank has also launched a process of systematic internal reform intended to transform its ability to play the strategic role of global leadership it sees as essential if the system is to work. These developments testify to the seriousness with which the Bank has launched itself on a process of creating a Global Architecture of Governance, and of transforming itself as an institution in the process.

Poverty Reduction Strategy Papers

The PRSP is a key mechanism in the World Bank's Global Architecture of Governance. It was introduced as an instrument for operationalising the CDF in a paper on the HIPC (Heavily Indebted Poor Countries) Initiative by the Joint IMF/World

Bank Development Committee (officially the *Joint Ministerial Committee of the Board of Governors of the Bank and the Fund on the Transfer of Real Resources to the Developing Countries*) on 17 September 1999.[17] The paper reported an elaborate process of consultation with NGOs focused on the virtues of outcome-oriented poverty reduction programmes as prerequisites for debt relief, then proposed, in the form of a requirement for prior agreement of PRSPs, a mechanism which used the language and ideas of some NGO contributors to the consultation to impose and validate precisely the set of policies and priorities developed by the IMF and the World Bank in advance—a classic case of the manipulation of "participation" as part of a strategy of securing hegemony. The PRSP was to be a "tripartite document endorsed by the government, the Bank and the Fund."[18] . . . [T]he strategy was to tie social and structural policies directly to IMF-approved macroeconomic frameworks; it was to be "owned" by the government, but on the basis of content agreed and where necessary provided by the Bank and the Fund; and it was to be monitored and updated annually, and reworked completely at three-year intervals. In other words, the Bank and the Fund claimed the right to monitor and amend economic, social and structural policies across the board in heavily indebted countries; and with the CDF and its matrix supplemented by the PSRP, they were in a position to exercise it. . . .

Conclusion: The CDF as a Comprehensive Dependency Framework

The CDF has been presented by the World Bank as a means of incorporating structural and social issues into development, but on closer inspection it has turned out to be a means of tying them to a rigid IMF-prescribed macroeconomic framework and a disciplinary agenda devised and promoted by the Bank. In summary, IMF surveillance of macroeconomic policy is to be matched by Bank surveillance of social and structural policy. With this goal in mind, the Bank is now actively engaged upon extending the scope of its CDF-PSRP framework and drawing its "development partners" into the process. Four full PRSPs and thirty-two Interim PRSPs were in place by March 2001.[19] The Bank was moving (with a target date of 1 July 2002) to a point where all Country Assistance Strategies (CAS) presented by the International Development Association (IDA) to the Boards of the IMF and the World Bank would be underpinned by sector-by-sector SSPs (Sectoral Strategy Papers) and by an agreed PRSP, with the intention that "all Bank lending and nonlending activities in IDA countries will be organized under a CAS business plan responding to the PRSP."[20] The models here were Burkina Faso and Uganda, for whom the Bank Board discussed Country Assistance Strategies based on PSRPs in November 2000.

Finally, the CAS-CDF-PSRP framework was to be extended beyond the small group of low-income countries covered by the HIPC Initiative to the much larger group of World Bank–classified "Middle-Income Countries," with the intention of generalising the disciplinary framework developed in the CDF and the PRSP to all countries eligible for International Bank for Reconstruction and Development (IBRD) lending. Middle-income countries are to be asked to present a "vision of development" in the form of a "Letter of Development Strategy," incorporating a systematic and comprehensive diagnosis of its priorities. The matching CAS will identify a programme of Economic and Sector Work (ESW), so that all the Bank's "lending products" can be aligned to support medium-term reform programmes in turn underpinned by enhanced public expenditure management capacity. This comprehensive framework will in turn allow strengthened collaboration with the IMF, and a clear division of labour between the Bank itself, the Fund and the multilateral development banks.[21]

The CDF-PRSP framework, with its supporting matrix, has not been developed purely as a means of addressing debt relief and poverty reduction in a small number of low-income countries heavily dependent on World Bank and IMF support: it has been trialled with the most heavily indebted countries, prior to being extended to the remaining clients of the Bank and the Fund as a generalised means of intervention in economic and social policy and political governance. In other words, it constitutes a Global Architecture of Governance which takes a giant step beyond the International Financial Architecture already under construction. A key element of this Global Architecture of Governance is that countries should assume "ownership" of the essential disciplinary elements through which it is exercised—the CDF and its matrix, and the PRSP through which it is operationalised. As we have seen, the Chief Executives of the IMF and the World Bank have proved themselves to be aware both of the need for "country ownership," and of the reality that the set of policies they are invited to "own" have been defined in advance by the Bank and the Fund. The way to square the circle, they propose, is for the Bank and the Fund to provide technical assistance to strengthen strategy formulation and participation, and to offer, as some countries were realistic enough to request, "extra guidance on the expected core content of PRSPs and the participatory processes to be used in preparing them."[22] The Bank now proposes to supplement the CDF, the matrix and the PRSP with the provision of "sound diagnostic analysis and advice" through its enhanced Economic and Sector Work, and to focus its strategic efforts on two integrative diagnostic analyses or "core integrative assessments," a "*fiduciary assessment* . . . to analyze the country's public financial accountability arrangements, including its systems for public expenditure procurement, and financial management," and a *development policy review*—"a concise cross-cutting assessment of policy reform and institutional development priorities for growth and poverty reduction." The additional analytic products developed for each country through ESW will then "provide building blocks for the core integrative instruments described above and would aim to help countries build capacity."[23] The Bank does indeed aspire to be "the mother of all governments."

Notes

1. James D. Wolfensohn, 'A Proposal for a Comprehensive Development Framework', Memo to the Board, Management and Staff of the World Bank Group, 21 January 1999, p. 1.
2. 'Proposal for a CDF', p. 3.

3. 'Proposal for a CDF', pp. 5–6.
4. 'Proposal for a CDF', p. 8.
5. The comprehensive framework was rehearsed in the 1997 World Development Report, *The State in a Changing World,* but this largely summarized policies outlined in previous reports. For an overview of their content, and the argument that they constitute an explicit programme for the creation of an easily exploitable global proletariat, see Paul Cammack, 'Attacking the Poor', *New Left Review,* 2: 13 (January–February 2002), pp. 125–34.
6. 'Proposal for a CDF', pp. 10–11. Compare *From Plan to Market* (World Bank, 1996), especially chapters 5–7.
7. 'Proposal for a CDF', pp. 11–12.
8. 'Proposal for a CDF', pp. 13–14. Compare *Poverty* (World Bank, 1990).
9. 'Proposal for a CDF', p. 14. Compare *Investing in Health* (World Bank, 1993).
10. 'Proposal for a CDF', pp. 15–18. Compare *Development and the Environment* (World Bank, 1992), and *Infrastructure for Development* (World Bank, 1994).
11. 'Proposal for a CDF', pp. 19–20.
12. 'Proposal for a CDF', p. 9.
13. 'Proposal for a CDF', p. 24.
14. 'Proposal for a CDF', p. 25. This is an old theme, highlighted in the 1990 World Development Report. After setting out the elements of what would mature into the comprehensive development framework there, the Report commented that 'These principles . . . should be regarded as applicable to the aid community as a whole. If the aid strategy outlined here were adopted and followed consistently by bilateral donors, nongovernmental organizations, and multinational agencies, its effectiveness would be greatly increased'; and at the end of the Report it urged other institutions to follow the lead of the World Bank, denying aid to countries that were not 'serious about reducing poverty'—or in other words, unwilling to restructure their economies and societies comprehensively along the lines required by the Bank. See *Poverty* (World Bank, 1990), pp. 4, 137.
15. 'Proposal for a CDF', p. 26.
16. 'Proposal for a CDF', p. 28.
17. Development Committee, 'Heavily Indebted Poor Countries (HIPC) Initiative: Strengthening the Link between Debt Relief and Poverty Reduction', DC/99–24, 17 September 1999.
18. 'HIPC Initiative', p. 30, paragraph 74.
19. IBRD/IDA, 'Strategic Directions for FY02–FY04: Implementing the World Bank's Strategic Framework', 28 March 2001, p. 2.
20. International Monetary Fund and International Development Association, 'Poverty Reduction Strategy Papers—Progress in Implementation', paragraph 45, p. 21.
21. Development Committee, 'Supporting Country Development: Strengthening the World Bank Group's Support for Middle Income Countries', DC 2001–005, 10 April 2001.
22. A joint Memorandum from the Managing Director of the IMF and the President of the World Bank', 7 September 2000, in Development Committee, 'Heavily Indebted Poor Countries (HIPC) Initiative and Poverty Reduction Strategy Papers (PRSP): A Joint Memorandum from the Managing Director of the IMF and the President of the World Bank and Reports on Progress in Implementation', DC/2000–18, 8 September 2000, p. 6.
23. 'Supporting Country Development', p. 7.

Dying for Growth, Part II *The Political Influence of National and Transnational Corporations*

Joyce V. Millen, Evan Lyon, and Alec Irwin

This selection highlights the powerful influence wielded by transnational corporations (TNCs) over national governments and international organizations, including international financial institutions (IFIs) and the United Nations. As in the selection by Mellen and co-authors in Chapter 5, the impact of global processes on the health of the poor is highlighted. Millen, Lyon, and Irwin claim that the TNC-friendly policies of IFIs, such as the World Trade Organization (WTO), have a destructive impact on the health of the poor. In addition, the tax breaks that TNCs receive from governments reduce the revenue needed "to improve the environmental, health, economic, and social conditions of poor and vulnerable communities." However, Millen and her co-authors conclude that the power of TNCs over international organizations can be challenged. Selections in Chapters 9–11 describe some attempts.

TNCs in International Politics

Large TNCs today have expanded their exploring, processing, refining, manufacturing, and marketing to most regions of the world. The largest corporations now operate in over 100 countries. Along with their geographical expansion, large corporations have expanded their spheres of influence. Most TNCs no longer influence only the legislative efforts of individual nations. Corporate managers have found that they can more expeditiously realize their cost-cutting, market-expanding goals by also monitoring and exerting their political influence at the international level—within the deliberations of regional trade meetings, in the WTO, the World Bank, the IMF, the Organization for Economic Cooperation and Development (OECD), the Group of Eight (G-8), the United Nations, and other international organizations. Especially since the early 1980s, by increasing their involvement in these international assemblies, TNC leaders and representatives have played a decisive role in shaping the current global economic system. In fact, many analysts characterize the system as one of "corporate-driven globalization."

Joyce V. Millen, Evan Lyon, and Alec Irwin, "Dying for Growth, Part II: The Political Influence of National and Transnational Corporations," in Jim Yong Kim et al., eds., *Dying for Growth: Global Inequality and the Health of the Poor* (Monroe, ME: Common Courage Press, 2000), pp. 233–235, 237–243. Reprinted by permission of Common Courage Press.

Corporate Interests and Influence in Trade Agreements

When TNC representatives successfully press international organizations for increased freedoms on the movement of capital, technology, and goods and services, they undermine the efforts of individual governments to regulate TNCs within their borders. Thus, international corporate power limits national governments' ability to protect their citizens. In the current global trade system, which began to take shape at the beginning of the Uruguay Round of the General Agreement on Tariffs and Trade (GATT) in 1986, TNCs successfully lobbied to have a vast array of environmental, health, consumer, and worker-safety standards categorized as non-tariff barriers to trade. Because these quotas and standards ostensibly inhibit trade, they may be considered illegal under the WTO. Any WTO member country may now challenge the laws and regulations of any other country on the grounds that the laws in question impede free trade. Such complaints are addressed by unelected WTO bureaucrats in secret tribunals, and they cannot be appealed. By signing on to the WTO, 134 member nations have effectively agreed to limit their own powers, vis-à-vis the TNCs operating within their country.[1] Ralph Nader, founder of Public Citizen, and Lori Wallach, the director of the group's Global Trade Watch, explain: "The concept of nontariff barriers being illegal gives corporate interests a powerful tool to undermine safety, health, or environmental regulations they do not like." Speaking more generally about the WTO and regional trade agreements, they assert:

> Approval of these agreements has institutionalized a global economic and political situation that places every government in a virtual hostage situation, at the mercy of a global financial and commercial system run by empowered corporations. This new system is not designed to promote the health and well-being of human beings but to enhance the power of the world's largest corporations and financial institutions.[2]

Trade liberalization is the primary goal of most current regional trade agreements, such as the North American Free Trade Agreement (NAFTA). When trade is liberalized between countries of unequal size and wealth, however, the benefits of liberalization accrue largely to the TNCs of the wealthier trading partner, sometimes at the expense of poor communities in both countries. Efforts to address this extensively documented problem currently occupy the agendas of many human rights, economic justice, and environmental groups, whose members tend to witness firsthand the effects of growing trade liberalization on local communities, industry, and environment. These groups and a growing number of national-level political leaders affirm that "the benefits of trade must be widely shared by the majority of the common working people in every participating society, not just benefit the business and financial interests of an elite few."[3] To render trade fair in this way would require *increasing* social, labor, and environmental protections, not reducing them. But in regional trade negotiations, social concerns and the problems that are inherent in trade between vastly unequal partners are considered peripheral issues, if they are addressed at all. This results in part from the identity and loyalties of those officially asked to participate in trade talks. While grassroots nongovernmental organizations (NGOs), consumer groups, labor, and representatives of the communities most impacted by the agreements are rarely invited to participate in such negotiations, corporate representatives are often integrally and officially involved at virtually every stage.

Through trade advisory committees, . . . as well as through powerful trade groups, lobbying firms, and business coalitions, corporate leaders have had significant influence over debates on U.S. trade relations with China and in the planning of trade agreements such as NAFTA. The Boeing Corporation, now the United States' second largest arms contractor and largest arms exporter, with annual sales of $50 billion, retains seven lobby organizations and an entire army of *influence peddlers* to advocate for open commercial relations with China. China is a primary purchaser of Boeing's arms products, and accounts for 10 percent of the company's business. The country also offers Boeing a cheap labor pool from which the company engages increasing numbers of Chinese workers to manufacture its products—workers employed for a pittance, and often under the aegis of the People's Liberation Army. For Boeing to retain its attractive commercial ventures and labor advantages with China, it has had to become a dominant force in Sino-American trade policy. The company's legions of lobbyists press legislators and the office of the U.S. Trade Representatives to scale back pertinent trade barriers with China and resist efforts to link China's "most favored nation" trade status with human rights.[4]

The largest American business coalition, U.S. Business Roundtable, was conspicuously involved in official policy debates on NAFTA: "All but four (of 200) Roundtable members enjoyed privileged access to the NAFTA negotiation process through representation on advisory committees to the U.S. trade representative."[5] One of the aims of the pro-NAFTA Business Roundtable was to convince the negotiators and the public that the treaty would raise environmental and labor standards in the participating countries. Ironically, many of the Roundtable corporations most active in NAFTA negotiations were known for their environmental and labor abuses. Several had produced products in Mexico that were banned in the United States, or exported such products to the Mexican market. Others had been cited for violating workers' rights in Mexico and for failing to comply with worker safety standards.[6] . . . NAFTA has facilitated the continuation of such practices. Yet despite reports revealing deleterious social, health, and environmental consequences for vulnerable populations during the first half decade of NAFTA, U.S.-based TNCs are pressing the U.S. government to expand NAFTA to all of the Americas and to create a similar trade agreement with African governments. The latter proposal has been labeled by some of its critics, "NAFTA for Africa." . . .

The Influence of TNCs at the United Nations

A striking development that has the potential to substantially strengthen the influence of TNCs at the international level is the new "partnering" between the business community and the United Nations. In the recent past, as late as 1993,

TNCs and the United Nations had an antagonistic relationship. This was in part due to the existence of the now-defunct U.N. Centre on Transnational Corporations, which was charged with developing a worldwide TNC "Code of Conduct." By 1998, however, the climate between business and the United Nations had changed so radically that the U.N. secretary-general and other U.N. officials had begun to meet regularly with business leaders in gatherings sponsored by the International Chamber of Commerce (ICC), the World Business Council on Sustainable Development, and other international business organizations.

In June 1997, the chief executive officers of ten TNCs met with U.N. leaders and several senior government officials to discuss avenues for a formalization of corporate involvement in the affairs of the United Nations. The luncheon took place at the United Nations in New York City and was co-hosted by the president of the U.N. General Assembly and the executive director of the World Business Council on Sustainable Development. Two scholars and two representatives from NGOs were also invited to attend. David Korten, formerly a business school professor, was one of the academics on the panel. Reflecting on the idea of using public resources—through the United Nations—to advance unrestrained global corporate expansion, Korten wrote in a letter about the meeting: "The defining structure of fascist regimes is a corporate dominated alliance between big business and big government to support the expansion of corporate empires."[7] While Korten's reference to fascism may appear misplaced, the emerging patterns that are crystalized in the *rapprochement* of U.N. leadership and corporate powerholders suggest, at the very least, that the grounds for Korten's concern must be examined carefully.

Even the United Nations Development Programme (UNDP), the branch of the United Nations charged with addressing inequality and serving the world's poor, is now being courted by global business leaders. A proposed joint venture between the UNDP and TNCs, called the "Global Sustainable Development Facility," would give corporations unprecedented access to the UNDP's global network and the high-level government representatives with whom the UNDP collaborates. In response to this plan, NGOs from around the world drafted a letter to both the UNDP administrator and the U.N. secretary-general, calling for the UNDP to "halt its Global Sustainable Development Facility and in so doing preserve the credibility of its mission to serve the world's poor."[8]

The International Chamber of Commerce, which counts among its members such corporate giants as General Motors, Coca-Cola, Rio Tinto Zinc, Mitsubishi, Shell, Bayer, and Nestlé, has for several years lobbied for global economic deregulation within the WTO, the G-8, and the OECD. The commission is now attempting to ally itself with the United Nations. In the aftermath of a meeting sponsored by the ICC in February 1998, the ICC and U.N. Secretary-General Kofi Annan issued a joint statement to the press affirming that "broad political and economic changes have opened up new opportunities for dialogue and cooperation between the United Nations and the private sector."[9] The two groups pledged to "forge a close global partnership to secure greater business input into the world's economic decision-making and boost the private sector in the least developed countries."[10] One of the projects the ICC and the U.N. Conference for Trade and Development (UNCTAD) agreed to undertake was a jointly produced series of business investment guides to the world's poorest 48 countries.

The president of the ICC, Helmut Maucher, has explained what motivates him to organize international meetings between the United Nations and the world's largest TNCs. He seeks to "bring together the heads of international companies and the leaders of international organizations so that business experiences and expertise is channeled into the decision-making process for the global economy."[11] In a guest column for the *Financial Times*, Maucher laid out his plan for the ICC to work within the WTO and the United Nations to push for "a framework of global rules."[12] In the joint statement issued by the ICC and the U.N. secretary-general, the ICC reveals its agenda: "Business has a strong interest in multilateral cooperation, including standard-setting through the United Nations and other intergovernmental institutions and international conventions on the environment and other global and transborder issues."[13]

Some political analysts speculate that the United Nations and its branches are seeking political and economic support from corporations because the organization faces financial difficulties in light of the U.S. government's refusal to pay the $1.6 billion it owes the United Nations. John Cavanagh of the Institute for Policy Studies suggests that the U.N.'s fiscal constraints—stemming substantially from the unpaid American bill—push agencies such as the UNDP to "serve the short-term interests of corporate shareholders rather than foster the long-term goals of sustainable human development."[14] Others question the logic of encouraging TNCs—some of which have committed significant human rights, labor, or environmental abuses—to play a primary role in standard setting and in defining the rules of international development and business. Ward Morehouse of the Council on International and Public Affairs suggests, rather, that "the United Nations should be *monitoring* the human rights and environmental impacts of corporations in developing and industrialized nations, not granting special favors."[15]

One can reasonably assume that the collaboration between the United Nations and business is being driven by corporate leaders, some of whom have expressed concern at the close association between the United Nations and increasingly outspoken labor, human rights, and environmental groups. Many NGOs from around the world are, in fact, organizing to place limits on the political powers of corporations.[16] A growing number of groups are working within national and international political frameworks to design new and legally binding systems to hold TNCs accountable for their harmful impact on the environment and on the communities where they operate. The efforts of these organizations threaten the corporate world.[17] Speaking in an interview about the sway of environmental and human rights groups within the United Nations, ICC President Maucher warned: "We have to be careful that they do not get too much influence."[18] In an international meeting, the Geneva Business Dialogue, organized by the ICC, Maucher actively attempted to de-legitimate the scientific claims of environmental groups, urging U.N. and WTO representatives, national leaders, and his own business colleagues to refuse such groups' "emotional and irrational arguments."

Moreover, in his concluding remarks to the Geneva Business Dialogue, Maucher recommended to his colleagues that: "Broader efforts should now follow in order to foster rules-based freedom for business." Rules-based freedom for business meant, according to Maucher, that governments should refrain from regulation where possible, but also set and strictly implement rules that help enhance the performance of TNCs.[19] On this view, a truly rules-based freedom for corporations would require universal adoption of policies such as the controversial Multilateral Agreement on Investment (MAI), or what Maucher describes as "a truly global framework of rules for cross-border investment."[20]

TNC Political Influence and the Health of the Poor: Possibilities for Change?

Having made the case that TNCs exert significant and growing influence on national and international political processes, we conclude by returning to how this influence affects the health of poor people. The political issue differs from concerns about the health and safety of workers in TNC manufacturing plants, and about health problems in communities in the vicinity of TNC facilities. The political influence of TNCs has a less direct, yet perhaps even more pervasive, effect on health. This influence can touch virtually all aspects of poor peoples' lives: what they eat, the conditions of the land they live on, what crops they can cultivate, the air they breathe, and the water they drink.

Consider the concrete example of food. The World Trade Organization's global health and safety standards are set by the Codex Alimentarius Commission, or Codex, an intergovernmental body run jointly by the WHO and the Food and Agriculture Organization (FAO) of the United Nations. Codex is charged with setting international standards on a wide variety of products that affect health, such as pesticide residues, additives, veterinary drug residues, and labeling. The organization is highly influenced by TNCs, which tend to promote the least rigorous standards of protection. For example, Codex safety levels for at least eight widely used pesticides were up to 25 times less strict than current U.S. standards. Meanwhile, 140 of the world's largest transnational food and agrochemical companies participated in Codex meetings between 1989 and 1991. Of the 2,587 individual participants in attendance, only 26 came from public-interest groups, while 37 came from a single transnational food company—Nestlé.[21]

Transnational corporations have actively participated in defining the current economic philosophy that guides international relations and shapes government policy in most of the world's nations. This corporate-led, market-determined philosophy gives primacy to the needs of corporations as the entities best fueling economic growth, and it forces the state to retreat so that business can be free from government intervention. As local, state, national, and global governments put this philosophy into practice throughout the 1980s and 1990s, corporations were accorded business freedoms and political powers they had not enjoyed since the colonial era. During this period, corporations have been empowered to disregard the sovereignty of nations; to undermine the efforts of governments to protect their citizens; and to compromise the efforts of communities to retain their land and cultural heritage.[22] At the same time, TNCs garner public favors: they are given tax breaks and receive outright billions of dollars of public money annually. Although the public monies funneled to TNCs are intended to provide "business incentives," many of the TNCs receiving these resources require no special incentives to do business: they are already among the most financially successful corporations in the world! Often, the public monies have been withdrawn from efforts to improve the environmental, health, economic, and social conditions of poor and vulnerable communities, and redirected to the enhancement of corporate wealth.

To be fair, not all TNC executives eschew efforts to render corporations more socially and environmentally responsible. In fact, in the latter part of the 1990s corporations from diverse sectors began a publicized effort to heed the concerns of their *stakeholders*—individuals affected by a company's operation and who are not shareholders. In the wake of public attention . . . , some TNCs have improved their environmental records, and others have amended labor practices and increased wages. Executives of TNCs have also begun to take part in a dialogue about creating a "triple bottom line," or a merging of financial with social and environmental objectives. In March 1999, senior executives from leading TNCs such as I.B.M., British Telecom, Levi Strauss, and Kodak met in London to share their concerns for businesses' and societies' future. In the meeting, they examined the potential for business to take part in addressing world poverty, mounting inequality, and environmental concerns. Via this gathering and other similar meetings, many ideas have been put on the table, among them: pressing corporate executives to be more accountable to company stakeholders; incorporating quantified assessments of social and environmental performance into corporate annual reports; and enforcing ethical trading practices.

Despite the public image concerns manifest in TNCs' efforts to clean up their practices (poor public image directly impacts profits), optimists welcome what appears to be a modest sea change toward increased social contributions from the corporate world. Pessimists, on the other hand, dismiss corporate statements about social responsibility as hollow rhetoric and doubt corporations' efforts will yield substantive improvements for those most in need. As one author asks, "Is it progress if cannibals start eating their victims with cutlery instead of using their hands, if oil companies start worrying about the environment while still pumping billions of gallons of carbon dioxide into the air?"[23]

Corporations have succeeded in creating an economic and cultural landscape in which their abusive, exploitative practices appear to many as simultaneously deplorable, banal, inevitable. This sense of inevitability is the first barrier to overcome in seeking change, or even in seeking to ask whether change is genuinely desirable. If current patterns of corporate behavior are to be challenged, what would appear to be necessary, as authors like Korten have argued, is a fundamental critique of the values of a consumption-driven society, accompanied by intelligent, coordinated efforts to limit corporate power legally and politically.[24] People from "less developed" nations often observe that corruption comes in many forms. Whereas European and U.S. leaders frequently ascribe the problems plaguing poor countries to the "endemic corruption" of government officials, many Third World activists and intellectuals trace a considerable portion of their countries' difficulties to the materially and morally corrupting power of wealthy nations and corporations driven by relentless greed. The destructive effects of corporate behavior must of course be documented on a case-by-case basis.[25] . . . Yet even as we wait for more evidence to come in, we can affirm broadly that TNCs have currently succeeded in institutionalizing a particular brand of corporate influence peddling within national and international bodies. The aggressive efforts of TNCs to influence decisions in national legal systems and foreign policy regimes, U.N. programs, and the WTO (to name only a few examples) are now viewed as routine. However, destructive, immoral routines *can* be broken. Reversing this form of corruption through a moratorium on aggressive corporate lobbying within national and international bodies would constitute a significant step toward enabling countries and international organizations to design legal, regulatory, financial, and political structures that genuinely and effectively protect the poor.

Notes

1. Countries failing to comply with WTO legislation face trade sanctions, which can devastate the economies of poor countries.
2. Nader and Wallach, 1996, p. 97.
3. From a press conference introducing a new trade bill to the U.S. House of Representatives Committee on Ways and Means, Sub-Committee on Trade, Description of H.R. 434. The African Growth and Opportunity Act.
4. From the *Mother Jones* website (www.mother-jones.com/arms).
5. Korten, 1995, p. 145. The Business Roundtable, counting approximately 200 members including the CEOs of most of the largest U.S.-based TNCs, took on its current form in 1972 with the merger of three separate lobbying groups. The Roundtable's promotional literature states that members of the U.S. government "respect the fact that business leaders care enough to study issues in detail and spend time to present their views to government." The Roundtable's nominal goal is "to present government and the public with knowledgeable, timely information, and with practical, positive suggestions for action." For more about the activities of the Business Roundtable, see their website (www.brtable.org).
6. Korten, 1995.
7. David Korten, "The United Nations and the Corporate Agenda," *Corporate Watch*, June, 1997. Available at www.corpwatch.org. Korten observed: "Those of us who have been studying these issues have long known of the strong alignment of the World Trade Organization, the World Bank, and the IMF to the corporate agenda. By contrast, the United Nations has seemed a more open, democratic, and people-friendly institution. What I found so shattering was the strong evidence that the differences I have been attributing to the U.N. are largely cosmetic."
8. From "Key United Nations Agency Solicits Funds from Corporations," available at www.corpwatch.org-/trac/undp/undppress.html.
9. From "Key United Nations Agency Solicits Funds from Corporations," available at www.corpwatch.org-/trac/undp/undppress.html.
10. From "UN-Business Partnership to Boost Economic Development," ICC Statement, February 9, 1998.
11. Helmut Maucher, "Ruling by Consent," *Financial Times*, December 6, 1997.

12. Helmut Maucher, "Ruling by Consent," *Financial Times*, December 6, 1997.
13. From "Key United Nations Agency Solicits Funds from Corporations," available at www.corpwatch.org-/trac/undp/undppress.html.
14. From "Key United Nations Agency Solicits Funds from Corporations," available at www.corpwatch.org-/trac/undp/undppress.html.
15. From "Key United Nations Agency Solicits Funds from Corporations," available at www.corpwatch.org-/trac/undp/undppress.html.
16. See literature from the International Forum on Globalization. For example, Clarke, 1996a.
17. Representatives of TNCs are particularly defensive in their response to environmental groups and international efforts to improve the environment. Prior to the 1992 United Nations Conference on Environment and Development (UNCED) in Rio de Janeiro, TNCs successfully lobbied government officials to have selected items removed from the UNCED agenda. These topics included efforts to regulate TNCs' environmental practices.
18. Reported in the *Corporate Europe Observer*, May 1998.
19. "The Geneva Business Declaration," available at www.iccwbo.org/Geneva_Business_Declaration.htm.
20. As cited in "Power: The Central Issue," *Ecologist, July/August, 1992*, p. 159; Korten, 1995.
21. Korten, 1995, p. 179.
22. See, for example, Chartrand, 1995; Weissman, 1996a.
23. Roger Cowe, "Boardrooms Discover Corporate Ethics," *Guardian Weekly*, March 28, 1999, p. 27. Polish poet Stanislaw Lec provided the original form of the question: "Is it progress if a cannibal uses a fork?" The idea was adapted by Elkington (1998), on whose book Cowe's article comments.
24. Korten, 1995, pp. 293–324.
25. Victims of corporate excesses must be encouraged to expose specific TNC offenders by making public the circumstances of their work-related or environmental injuries or illnesses. Leaders involved in the standard-lowering competitive push to recruit TNCs to their local, state, or national territories must re-examine their strategies and share with the public information about the net gains and losses associated with corporate incentive packages. Are funds for corporate enrichment being diverted from social services like public health? Is the trade-off worth it?

References

Chartrand, Harry Hillman. 1995. "Intellectual Property in the Global Village." *Government Information in Canada* 1(4): 1–10.

Clarke, Tony. 1996a. *The Emergence of Corporate Rule and What to Do About It: A Set of Working Instruments for Social Movements*. San Francisco: International Forum on Globalization.

Elkington, John. 1998. *Cannibals with Forks: The Triple Bottom Line of 21st Century Business*. Gabriola Island, BC: New Society Publishers.

Huang, C.C., N.S. Chu, C.S. Lu, *et al.* 1998. "Long-Term Progression in Chronic Manganism: Ten Years of Follow-Up." *Neurology* 50(3): 698–700.

Korten, David C. 1995. *When Corporations Rule the World*. West Hartford, CT: Kumarian Press, Inc.

Nader, Ralph and Lori Wallach 1996. "GATT, NAFTA, and the Subversion of the Democratic Process." In *The Case Against the Global Economy*. Jerry Mander and Edward Goldsmith, eds. San Francisco: Sierra Club Books. pp. 92–107.

Weissman, Robert 1996a. "A Long, Strange TRIPS: The Pharmaceutical Industry's Drive to Harmonize Global Intellectual Property Rules, and the Remaining WTO Legal Alternatives Available to Third World Countries." *University of Pennsylvania Journal of International Economic Law* 17: 1069–1125.

CHAPTER 8

Imperialism

The term *imperialism* has often been used to describe European nations, including Britain, France, Belgium, the Netherlands, and Germany in the nineteenth century, that conquered territories in Africa, Asia, and South America and established formal rule over them. When the scramble for colonies among the European powers ended at the close of the nineteenth century, a sizeable proportion of the world's territory and people were colonial subjects. The imperialist tide crested during the twentieth century. After World War II, the pendulum swung in the opposite direction, and colonies throughout what came to be called the Third World gained their independence. (The Third World were those regions of the world not part of the industrialized, capitalist West—the First World—or the Soviet bloc of powers, the Second World.) In most cases, independence was achieved as a result of struggles, often violent, by anticolonial movements.

Gaining legal independence rarely resulted in the former colonies achieving political autonomy and economic development. Instead, their economies often stagnated, and their governments were corrupt. The terms *neocolonial* or *dependency* were often used in the 1960s and 1970s to describe the fact that the newly independent countries of the Third World remained under the informal domination of the First World.

Until the period following World War II, the United States had been relatively uninvolved in countries in the Third World. An important exception was South and Central America, a region that the United States claimed as a protectorate ever since the proclamation of the Monroe Doctrine in 1823. The United States traditionally considered this region an informal protectorate, and dispatched troops on countless occasions to subdue threats to U.S. dominance.

When European dominance over the Third World ended in the 1950s and 1960s, the United States moved in. As part of the global struggle with the Soviet Union, termed the cold war, the United States sought allies throughout the world. These efforts only partially succeeded in the Third World: the Soviet Union sought to check U.S. influence by arming and financing insurgent movements. In some cases, including Cuba, Mozambique, and Vietnam, radical movements gained power. In other countries, there were civil wars and stalemate.

The end of the cold war has removed the shackles that limited U.S. military intervention, enabled the United States to sponsor a more fully unified international capitalist economy (see Chapter 6), and freed American-based TNCs to intervene more fully and forcefully throughout the world. Given that the United States has no immediate political, military, economic, or ideological rival in sight, and that the United States has engaged several times recently in military operations and exerted unilateral political pressure to force other countries to do its bidding, a heated debate has developed about whether to characterize the United States as an imperialist power. Some scholars believe that the term does not accurately describe the position of the United States in the world. (See selections below by Ikenberry and Mann.) Others are highly critical of what they regard as U.S. imperialism. (See the selection below by Panitch and Gindin.) Finally, some characterize American dominance as imperialism but do not view this situation as illegitimate. (See Ferguson below.)

All agree that, even if the United States can be described as imperialist, it is imperialism of a different sort from the nineteenth-century European variety. Except for those countries conquered in battle, like Iraq, the United States does not exert control over other countries. Its enormous influence derives from the clout of American-based TNCs, U.S. dominance of international organizations, like the United Nations or IMF, that write global regulatory rules, the "soft power" deriving from the powerful influence of U.S. media, and U.S. government pressure of governments and peoples around the world.

Many questions are suggested in considering the United States as an imperialist power. As one might expect, the selections that follow differ a great deal in their responses to these questions. What difference does it make that the United States government does not exercise juridical control over other countries but exerts power in informal ways? Are the foreign operations of U.S.-based TNCs an aspect of U.S. imperialism? Are the interests of U.S.-based TNCs and the U.S. government identical? If not, where do their interests differ? Is U.S. imperialism, if such there be, secure or fragile? What forms does opposition to U.S. imperialism take, and how effective is it? Does it make sense to speak of the United States as imperialist when it runs annual trade deficits of $500 billion and its economic health requires the governments of China and other countries to purchase massive amounts of U.S. Treasury bills to finance this deficit? Finally, if the United States can be characterized as an imperial power (albeit of a different kind from past ones), how desirable is it? Historian Niall Ferguson claims, in his selection below, that what is lacking for the United States to succeed as an imperialist power is sufficient will at home. If it had the backbone of, say, Britain in the nineteenth century, he implies, the world would be a better place. Contrast this view with that of Panitch and Gindin, and Kaldor, who see the United States as all too ready to dispatch missiles and troops first and ask questions after. These critics of U.S. imperialism believe that the problem is not, as Ferguson claims, a failure of will, but on the contrary arrogant exploitation of others for the sake of the powerful and privileged in the United States.

ARTICLE 8.1

Liberal Hegemony or Empire? *American Power in the Age of Unipolarity*

G. John Ikenberry

John Ikenberry recognizes that the United States possesses unprecedented power. However, he claims that it remains constrained by a web of institutions and norms that promote a multilateral orientation. (Multilateralism involves working with other nations, going it alone is a position designated as unilateralism.) He claims that these constraints mean that while the United States is indisputably first among equals in the world, it should not be described as imperial.

What is Ikenberry's evidence for his claim? What counterevidence exists? Where does the balance lie?

. . . Governments and people around the world worry that the United States is "out of control." The rise of terrorism has made the United States feel more vulnerable—and it has responded by mobilizing its military power and searching out new enemies and threats. Divided from the world, the United States is now at war while most other countries are still at peace. Likewise, the rise of unipolarity has given the United States the opportunity to disentangle itself from the constraints of postwar commitments and obligations. The United States needs the world—partners, rules, alliances, institutions—less than other states do, and so it can recapture its sovereignty and freedom of action. Capturing the view of many unipolar worriers, one author has called the United States a "rogue nation."[1]

Indeed, the United States appears poised between two logics of global order. One logic is American hegemonic order with "liberal" characteristics. This is order built around multilateralism, alliance partnership, strategic restraint, cooperative security, and institutional and rule-based relationships. This is the order that the United States and its partners built after World War II and which has come to dominate the global system for half a century—surviving the end of the Cold War and other upheavals.[2] The other logic is American hegemonic order

G. John Ikenberry, "Liberal Hegemony or Empire? American Power in the Age of Unipolarity," ch. 3 in David Held and Mathias Koenig-Archibugi, eds., *American Power in the Twenty-First Century* (Cambridge: Polity Press, 2004): 85–102, 109–112. Reprinted by permission of G. John Ikenberry.

with "imperial" characteristics. This is order built about American unilateralism, coercive domination, and reduced commitment to shared rules of the game. In this order, American power is the provider, protector, arbiter, and final word in international order.[3]

The view that America is making a grand historic turn toward imperial rule is reflected in a growing body of scholarship that evokes images of empire. "No one can deny the extent of the American informal empire," argues Niall Ferguson, who likens today's imperium to its British precursor. "Even recent American foreign policy recalls the gunboat diplomacy of the British Empire in its Victorian heyday, when a little trouble on the periphery could be dealt with by a short, sharp 'surgical strike.' "[4] The new theorists of empire argue that multilateralism and the rule of law will give way to American power exercised more directly. It is a vision in which sovereignty becomes more absolute for America even as it becomes more conditional for countries that challenge Washington's standards of external and internal behavior.[5]

The vision of coercive-unilateral American power inspires other theorists to argue that unipolarity will eventually generate counterbalancing resistance. Other states will not want to live in a world of imperial American power with its constant risks of domination and exploitation—and so balance of power politics will inevitably emerge. Because unipolarity is prone toward the rule of power rather than the rule of law, states will respond with the only strategy available to restrain and limit unipolar power, namely counterbalancing power.[6] Unipolarity will go the way of all great historical projects of geopolitical domination. The United States has too much power for its own good.[7] The rise of the European Union is driven, at least in part, by an effort to amass power so as to resist the vagaries and humiliations of a too powerful and increasingly unpredictable America.[8] The rest of the world will pull back and find alternative centers of power to resist unipolar dangers.

I argue otherwise. Unipolarity is actually quite consistent with multilateral, rule-based order. At the very least, powerful—even unipolar—states have deep and enduring incentives to construct and operate in a world of rules and institutions. The United States will act unilaterally in many areas—as it has in the past. But it is not destined to untangle itself from the postwar order and reorganize itself as a global imperial state. The best image of what is happening today is not an American rejection of rule-based order in favor of neo-imperial rule—even though many right-wing officials and pundits in Washington do indeed wish to end America's postwar commitment to multilateral order. A better image of what is happening today is a rising America trying to renegotiate the existing rule-based order. The United States is more powerful, so it wants a better deal. It also faces a transformed international environment, so it wants a different deal. But at the end of this sequence of crisis and institutional bargaining, the resulting international order will still be organized around agreed rules and institutions—but adjusted to the new realities. The United States is not abandoning its commitment to multilateral and rule-based order and the Western order is not falling apart. The postwar order is going through a crisis of renegotiation.

In what follows, I advance the thesis that the United States' unipolar order is relatively stable. Indeed, it is best to see it as a durable, complex, and distinctive transcontinental political formation. It is a political formation—built around capitalism, democracy, and security community among the advanced industrial countries—that is bigger than the United States itself. The political order was given shape by the United States over the decades—as it still is. But it is also an order that has structures and features in which the United States itself is embedded. In this sense, the United States must adjust and accommodate itself to this order and not simply run it as an imperial state.[9] American unipolar power is a dominant reality of this order but that power is expressed within and through the institutions, markets, politics, and community of this larger order. American presidents do not always act to restrain and bind power but the larger system—at least over the long haul—biases power in that direction.

The genius of today's unipolar order is that it is based on both power and restraint. On the one hand, American power is sufficiently benign, complex, and institutionalized not to trigger a counterbalancing coalition. On the other, American power advantages are sufficiently robust, multidimensional, and rooted in global structures of modernity to last for decades. At the worst, the United States–centered international order of today is entering a new era with rising conflict among states that essentially are incapable or unwilling to go to war against each other. The United States and the other democratic great powers may not be as united or harmonious as they were during the Cold War, when an external threat created unusual amounts of cohesion. But there is a foundation of democracy, capitalism, and security community on which today's differences rest.[10]

The first section of the paper explores the complex ways that American power is manifest and experienced around the world today. The United States is powerful but—despite the best efforts of the Bush administration—it is not neo-imperial. The second section examines the four major facets of American power. Again, the conclusion is drawn that American power is robust but not neo-imperial. Finally, the last section looks at the three major sources or incentives that give the United States reasons—despite its unipolar power—to commit itself to at least a loose form of rule-based order.

The Uniqueness of American Power

America confronts the world as a complex creature. During the last century, the United States has shown the world many different faces—it is to various degrees and in different mixtures at different moments unilateral, interventionist, isolationist, militarist, hegemonic, nationalist, and unrivaled champion of democracy and international law. The world has, in return, complex views of American power. It worries about American excesses—but also the absences of U.S. power. The United States can be both too pushy and too ready to go home. The United States provides both dangers and opportunities for other states. Peoples in countries around the world can simultaneously be drawn to American culture, political ideals, or its civil society and hate its leaders or policies. American power—as manifested and experienced—is anything but simple.[11]

In characterizing American power, it is useful to make five general observations. First, it is important to note that despite the rise of American unipolar power, the other major states are not making systematic choices to pull away from and balance against the United States. This is interesting. History suggests that states do not like to live in a world of a single dominant state. Balancing is a deeply rooted reaction to concentrated state power.[12] Charles V, Louis XIV, Napoleon I, and post-Bismarck Germany—all these hegemonic aspirants were eventually brought down by coalitions of states that were determined to rebalance the distribution of power.[13] Yet this sort of dynamic has not emerged. Despite the collapse of the Soviet Union and huge shifts in the distribution of power in favor of the United States, other states have not made moves toward geopolitical balance. United States relations with Western Europe and Japan after the Cold War have remained relatively stable. Deep shifts have not surfaced. The advanced democratic countries have reaffirmed their alliance ties, contained political conflict, expanded trade and investment across the continents, and avoided a return to strategic rivalry. Indeed, despite the crisis in 2002–3 over America's invasion of Iraq, Western Europe and Japan have not articulated visions of world order based on geopolitical balancing against the United States. France has been the most resistant to American unipolar power, but it has not attempted to organize a counterbalancing coalition based on independent and opposing military power.[14]

Even more surprisingly, rather than try to balance against United States power, China and Russia have moved closer to the United States. Russia is now in a near permanent alliance with the United States, integrated into the Western security framework. Remarkably, China has also dropped its rhetoric of anti-American "hegemonism" and worked with the United States in the fight against terrorism and the diplomatic engagement of North Korea. As Michael Mastanduno has argued:

> Rather than edging away from the United States, much less balancing against it, Europe and Japan have been determined to maintain the pattern of engagement that characterized the Cold War. Neither China nor Russia, despite having differences with the United States, has sought to organize a balancing coalition against it. Rather than edging away, much less balancing against it, the other great powers have maintained a pattern of engagement with the United States. Indeed, the main security concern in Europe and Asia is not how to distance from an all-too-powerful United States, but how to prevent the United States from drifting away.[15]

Interestingly, the end of the Cold War has not eliminated the cohesion among the advanced industrial democracies. In both economic and military spheres, the United States leads its nearest rivals by a larger margin than has any other leading state in the last three centuries. Yet despite this concentration of American power, there is very little evidence that other states are actively seeking to balance against it or organize a counter-hegemonic coalition. This is a puzzle that must be answered: in a decade of sharp shifts in the distribution of power, why has there been so much stability and persistence of order among the major states?[16]

Second, the United States is a unique sort of global superpower. That is, it has a distinctive cluster of capabilities, institutions, attractions, and impulses. Indeed, American power is manifest in complex and paradoxical ways. For example, during the twentieth century, the United States was the greatest champion of rule-based order. It pushed onto the global stage a long list of international institutions and rules—the League of Nations, the United Nations, GATT, human rights norms, and so forth. But the United States has also been unusually ambivalent about actually operating itself within legal and institutional constraints. Moreover, the United States has used military force more than any other state in the last 50 years (with and without UN or NATO backing). Yet it also has an anti-imperial political culture and a strong isolationist tradition.[17]

The point here is that it is difficult for other countries to simply decide that American power is manifest in any one way. American power is sometimes menacing but at other times it helps provide global public goods and at other times it turns inward. American power is sufficiently complex and multifaceted that it is difficult for countries to simply decide to counter or work against United States power. American power is complex and because of this there are reasons for other states to have complex views of and strategies for dealing with the United States.

Third, countries and peoples "experience" American unipolar power in different ways. A threat to some is an opportunity to others. This is true across states—some states find American power more useful and easy to accommodate than others. For example, Japan finds America's security role in East Asia more useful to it than France finds America's security role in Europe. Likewise, people in particular states will see American power differently. In most states there is a range of views, and these views can be directed at American policy or more generally at America as a global power.[18]

Fourth, in this regard, it is useful to distinguish at least three levels or types of American power that are generating reactions around the world. At the most basic level, American power is manifest as the underwriter of American capitalism and globalization. This is where America gets implicated in the protests over the WTO and the IMF. In effect, the global spread of modern Western systems of politics and economics is a process in which power is being exercised. Power is manifest in two ways. One is "power through integration"—that is, power is manifest through the spread of capitalism and democracy which displaces local and non-Western social and political structures. As more and more parts of the world are absorbed into this American-dominated order, weak and vulnerable societies lose aspects of their autonomy and distinctiveness. The structures of global order act on them. The other way is "power through subordination"—that is, power is manifest as these newly integrated societies find themselves increasingly shaped and constrained by the more powerful societies at the core of the system, particularly the United States. The spread of modern, Western order creates new forms of superordinate and subordinate relations.[19]

At another level, American power is manifest as the leader of a global political and military alliance system. This is power that is evident as the United States builds on its postwar order making efforts—dating back to the 1940s—and extends and defends it today. Americans tend to see their country's global role as enlightened leadership, providing markets and security protection to Europe and East Asia in exchange for cooperation and partnership from countries in these regions. But peoples and governments in these regions can see the presence of American military and political power as intrusive and domineering. The institutional expression of American power is relatively stable over the postwar era, anchored in security and economic partnerships with key states in all geographical regions. But the circumstances in which America's extended order is perceived and experienced does change. Obviously, the end of the Cold War has altered the character of the threats that Europeans and Asians encounter, and this alters the way the United States is seen and appreciated as a security provider. Political change inside partner countries—and the turnover of generations of leaders—also alters the way American power is perceived.

It is at this level of American power, for example, that people in nations such as South Korea or Germany seek to push the United States out of their country. Some people attack or oppose the United States because it is the alliance partner that is supported by their own government. American power is challenged because that power—in some countries such as Pakistan or Saudi Arabia—helps perpetuate unwanted regimes.[20]

A final level of American power is manifest in specific policies or issues. For example, some people—such as in South Korea—oppose the United States because of specific Status of Forces Agreements in their country which protect American soldiers from local justice. Others oppose the United States because of its decisions on the use of force, such as in the recent invasion of Iraq. Governments and peoples can oppose the United States because of its new doctrine of preemption. This manifestation of American power—specific policies of specific leaders—is in constant motion. If you do not like American policy today, be patient—times will change. Germany's Chancellor Schroeder and French President Chirac may have unresolvable differences with American President Bush, but these elected leaders pass from the stage on a regular basis, and so too do views of United States power change.

Fifth, most of the great powers' responses to American unipolarity seem to be falling between the extremes of balancing and bandwagoning. States can resist without balancing and they can engage without simply acquiescing. During the

Iraq War, British Prime Minister Tony Blair pursued a strategy of getting as close as possible to the Bush administration. The strategy was to be so close to and supportive of the American exercise of power that Britain would ultimately get some voice in how policy unfolded. French President Chirac pursued a different policy, attempting to build an opposing political coalition to the Bush administration's Iraq policy. Both were attempting to deal with a difficult reality: the United States was powerful enough to go on its own. How to get some leverage over American exercise of power was the challenge. The two leaders chose different strategies. In the aftermath of the war, the effectiveness of the two strategies is being debated across Europe. How this debate unfolds will say a lot about future resort to the strategies. Again, it is useful to see the present moment as one where governments are making judgments, experimenting with strategies, learning lessons, and adapting their behavior.

Four Facets of American Power

American power advantages are multidimensional. In particular, four facets of American power reinforce unipolarity and undercut incentives to resist or balance against the United States. These facets of power are: traditional power assets; geography and historical timing; democracy and institutional restraints; and modernization and civic identity. Together these multiple dimensions of American power suggest that unipolarity is likely to persist and that the other major states are likely to continue to have incentives to engage and work with the United States—even as they devise new strategies to cope with unipolarity.[21]

Traditional Power Assets

The first facet of American power is its traditional power assets—material capabilities that allow it to pursue its objective and get other states to go along with it.[22] One aspect of material capabilities is the sheer size of the American military establishment. American military expenditures are greater than those of the next 14 countries combined—and if current trends continue, the United States' military expenditure will be equal to the rest of the world combined by 2007. The advanced technological character of much of this military power makes this power disparity even greater.

This mass of military power makes it difficult if not impossible for a group of states to develop capabilities that could balance or counter that of the United States. But other considerations further increase the difficulties of organizing a counterbalancing coalition. First, there are collective action problems. States might like to see the formation of a counter-unipolar coalition but they would prefer other states to do the work of organizing it and covering its costs. This is the problem of "buck passing"—the collective action problem that makes it less likely that a coalition will form. There is also the problem of regional blocking problems. If particular great powers do decide to amass greater military power to challenge the United States, other major states in their region are likely to be threatened by this move and challenge it. For example, if Japan were to undertake military mobilization to counter the United States, it would find a hostile East Asian neighborhood awaiting it. These considerations make counterbalancing unlikely.[23]

Other material power assets also work to America's advantage—namely, security protection, markets, and nuclear weapons. Alliance security protection that the United States has the capacity to extend to states in all four corners of the world provides a positive incentive to cooperate with the United States. This incentive is of two sorts. One is simply that American security protection reduces the resources that these countries would otherwise need to generate to cover their own protection. It is a cost-effective way to deal with the elemental problem of national security. If it means working with the United States and not offering opposition to it, the forgoing of this option of opposition is a cost that is more than compensated for by the value of the security protection itself. The second benefit of security protection, at least for some states, is that it means that these states won't need to face the regional challenges that might come if they provided for their own security. Germany and Japan are the best examples of this. By positioning themselves under the American security umbrella, Germany and Japan were able to reassure their worried neighbors that they would not become future security threats to their respective regions. The United States is able to provide it to so many countries because it has the economic and military capabilities to do so on a worldwide basis. Indeed, it might well be that economies of scale exist for a versatile and high-tech military power such as the United States.

Another aspect of American material power is its large domestic market. Both Europeans and East Asians depend mightily on access to the American market. Of course, the United States relies heavily on both regions for its own economic prosperity. But the simple point here is that East Asia and Western Europe have incentives not to resist American unipolarity in such a way as to break apart the open markets that cut across the Pacific and Atlantic.

American unipolarity is also sustained by nuclear weapons. Even if the other major powers wanted to overturn the existing order, the mechanism of great-power war is no longer available. As Robert Gilpin has noted, great-power war is precisely the mechanism of change that has been used throughout history to redraw the international order. Rising states depose the reigning—but declining—state and impose a new order.[24] But nuclear weapons make this historical dynamic profoundly problematic. On the one hand, American power is rendered more tolerable because in the age of nuclear deterrence American military power cannot now be used for conquest against other great powers. Deterrence replaces alliance counterbalancing. On the other hand, the status quo international order led by the United States is rendered less easily replaceable. War-driven change is removed as an historical process, and the United States was lucky enough to be on top when this happened.

Geography and Historical Setting

The geographic setting and historical timing of America's rise to power have also shaped the way American primacy has been manifest. The United States is the only great power that is not neighbored by other great powers. This geographical remoteness made the power ascent of the United States less threatening to the rest of the world and it reinforced the disinclination of American leaders to directly dominate or manage great-power relations. In the twentieth century, the United States became the world's preeminent power but the location and historical entry point of that power helped shape how this arrival was greeted. . . .

Because the United States is geographically remote, abandonment rather than domination has been seen as the greater risk by many states. As a result, the United States has found itself constantly courted by governments in Europe, Asia, and elsewhere. When Winston Churchill advanced ideas about postwar order he was concerned above all to find a way to tie the United States to Europe.[25] As Geir Lundestad has observed, the expanding American political order in the half-century after World War II has been in important respects an "empire by invitation."[26] The remarkable global reach of American postwar hegemony has been at least in part driven by the efforts of European and Asian governments to harness American power, render that power more predictable, and use it to overcome their own regional insecurities. The result has been a durable system of America-centered economic and security partnerships.

Finally, the historical timing of America's rise in power also left a mark. The United States came relatively late to the great power arena, after the colonial and imperial eras had run their course. This meant that the pursuit of America's strategic interests was not primarily based on territorial control but on championing more principled ways of organizing great-power relations. As a late-developing great power the United States needed openness and access to the regions of the world rather than recognition of its territorial claims. The American issuance of its Open Door policy toward China reflected this orientation. American officials were never fully consistent in wielding such principled claims about order and they were often a source of conflict with the other major states. But the overall effect of this alignment of American geostrategic interests with enlightened normative principles of order reinforced the image of the United States as a relatively noncoercive and nonimperial hegemonic power.

Democracy and Institutional Restraints

The American unipolar order is also organized around democratic polities and a complex web of intergovernmental institutions, and these features of the American system alter and mute the way in which hegemonic power is manifest. One version of this argument is the democratic peace thesis: open democratic polities are less able or willing to use power in an arbitrary and indiscriminate manner against other democracies.[27] The calculations of smaller and weaker states as they confront a democratic hegemon are altered. Fundamentally, power asymmetries are less threatening or destabilizing when they exist between democracies. American power is "institutionalized"—not entirely, of course, but more so than in the case of previous world-dominating states. This institutionalization of hegemonic strategy serves the interest of the United States by making its power more legitimate, expansive, and durable. But the price is that some restraints are indeed placed on the exercise of power.[28]

In this view, three elements matter most in making American power more stable, engaged, and restrained. First, America's mature political institutions organized around the rule of law have made it a relatively predictable and cooperative hegemon. The pluralistic and regularized way in which American foreign and security policy is made reduces surprises and allows other states to build long-term, mutually beneficial relations. The governmental separation of powers creates a shared decision-making system that opens up the process and reduces the ability of any one leader to make abrupt or aggressive moves toward other states. An active press and competitive party system also provide a service to outside states by generating information about United States policy and determining its seriousness of purpose. The messiness of democracy can frustrate American diplomats and confuse foreign observers. But over the long term, democratic institutions produce more consistent and credible policies than autocratic or authoritarian states.[29]

This open and decentralized political process works in a second way to reduce foreign worries about American power. It creates what might be called "voice opportunities"—it offers opportunities for political access and, with it, the means for foreign governments and groups to influence the way Washington's power is exercised. Foreign governments and corporations may not have elected officials in Washington but they do have representatives.[30] Looked at from the perspective of the stable functioning of America's unipolar order, this is one of the most functional aspects of the United States as a global power. By providing other states with opportunities to play the game in Washington, the United States draws them into active, ongoing partnerships that serve its long-term strategic interests.

A final element of the unipolar order that reduces the worry about power asymmetries is the web of institutions that mark the postwar order. After World War II, the United States launched history's most ambitious era of institution building. The UN, IMF, World Bank, NATO, GATT, and other institutions that emerged provided the most rule-based structure for political and economic relations in history. The United States was deeply ambivalent about making permanent security commitments to other countries or allowing its political and economic policies to be dictated by intergovernmental bodies. The Soviet threat was critical in overcoming these doubts. Networks and political relationships were built that—paradoxically—both made American power more far-reaching and durable but also more predictable and malleable.[31]

Modernization and Civic Nationalism

American power has been rendered more acceptable to the rest of the world because the United States "project" is congruent with the deeper forces of modernization. The point here is not that the United States has pushed other states to embrace its goals and purposes but that all states are operating within a transforming global system—driven by modernization, industrialization, and social mobilization. The synchronicity between the rise of the United States as a liberal global power and the system-wide imperatives of modernization creates a sort of functional "fit" between the United States and the wider world order. If the United States were attempting to project state socialist economic ideas or autocratic political values, its fit with the deep forces of modernization would be poor. Its purposes would be resisted around the world and trigger resistance to American power. But the deep congruence between the American model and the functional demands of modernization both boost the power of the United States and make its relationship with the rest of the world more harmonious.

Industrialization is a constantly evolving process and the social and political characteristics within countries that it encourages and rewards—and that promote or impede industrial advancement—change over time and as countries move through developmental stages. In this sense, the fit between a polity and modernization is never absolute or permanent.[32] Industrialism in advanced societies tends to feature highly educated workforces, rapid flows of information, and progressively more specialized and complex systems of social and industrial organization. These features of industrial society—sometimes called "late industrialism"—tend to foster a citizenry that is heterogeneous, well educated, and difficult to coerce.[33] From this perspective it is possible to see why various state socialist and authoritarian countries—including the Soviet Union—ran into trouble as the twentieth century proceeded. The old command order impeded industrial modernization while, at the same time, industrial modernization undercut the old command order. In contrast, the American polity has tended to have a relatively good fit with the demands and opportunities of industrial modernization. European and Asian forms of capitalist democracy have also exhibited features that seem in various ways to be quite congruent with the leading edge of advanced industrial development. The success of the American model is partly due to the fact that it used its postwar power to build an international order that worked to the benefit of the American style of industrial capitalism. But the success of the American model—and the enhanced global influence and appeal that the United States has experienced in recent decades—is also due to the deep congruence between the logic of modernization and the American system.

The functionality between the United States polity and wider evolutionary developments in the international system can also be traced to the American political identity, which is rooted in civic nationalism and multiculturalism. The basic distinction between civic and ethnic nationalism is useful in locating this feature. Civic nationalism is group identity that is composed of commitments to the nation's political creed. Race, religion, gender, language, or ethnicity are not relevant in defining a citizen's rights and inclusion within the polity. Shared belief in the country's principles and values embedded in the rule of law is the organizing basis for political order, and citizens are understood to be equal and rights-bearing individuals. Ethnic nationalism, in contrast, maintains that individuals' rights and participation within the polity are inherited—based on ethnic or racial ties.[34]

Because civic nationalism is shared with other Western states it tends to be a source of cohesion and cooperation. Throughout the industrial democratic world, the dominant form of political identity is based on a set of abstract and juridical rights and responsibilities, which coexist with private ethnic and religious associations. Just as warring states and nationalism tend to reinforce each other, so too do Western civic identity and cooperative political relations. Political order—domestic and international—is strengthened when there exists a substantial sense of community and shared identity. It matters that the leaders of today's advanced industrial states are not seeking to legitimate their power by making racial or imperialist appeals. Civic nationalism, rooted in shared commitment to democracy and the rule of law, provides a widely embraced identity across most of the American hegemonic order. At the same time, potentially divisive identity conflicts—rooted in antagonistic ethnic or religious or class divisions—are dampened by relegating them to secondary status within civil society.

Unipolar Power and Multilateralism

Has the rise of American unipolar power in the 1990s reduced its incentives for operating in a multilateral, rule-based order? In this view, the United States has become so powerful that it does not need to sacrifice its autonomy and freedom of action within multilateral agreements. With the end of the Cold War and the absence of serious geopolitical challengers, the United States is able to act alone without serious costs.

Multilateralism can be a tool or expedient in some circumstances but states will not want to be tangled up in institutions and rules and they will avoid or shed entanglements when they can. Power disparities make it easier for the United States to walk away from potential international agreements. Across the spectrum of economic, security, environmental, and other policy issues, the sheer size and power advantages of the United States make it easier to resist multilateral restraints. That is, the costs of non-agreement are lower for the United States than for other states—which gives it bargaining advantages if it wants them but also a greater ability to live without agreement without suffering consequences.

The shifting power differentials have also created new divergent interests between the United States and the rest of the world, which further reduces possibilities for multilateral cooperation. For example, the sheer size of the American economy—and a decade of growth unmatched by Europe, Japan, or the other advanced countries—means that United States obligations under the Kyoto Protocol would be vastly greater than those of other states. In the security realm, the United States has global interests and security threats that no other state has. Its troops are more likely to be dispatched to distant battlefields than those of the other major states—which means that it is more exposed to the legal liabilities of the ICC (International Criminal Court) than others. The United States must worry about threats to its interests in all the major regions of the world. American unipolar power makes it a unique target for terrorism. It is not surprising that Europeans and Asians make different threat assessments about terrorism and rogue states seeking weapons of mass destruction than American officials do. If multilateralism entails working within agreed rules and institutions for the use of force, this growing divergence will make such multilateral agreements less easy to achieve—and less desirable in the view of the United States. . . .

Notes

1. Clyde Prestowitz, *Rogue Nation: American Unilateralism and the Failure of Good Intentions* (New York: Basic Books, 2003).
2. I have sketched this logic of order in various writings, including Ikenberry, *After Victory: Institutions, Strategic Restraint, and the Rebuilding of Order After Major War* (Princeton: Princeton University Press, 2001).
3. Ikenberry, "America's Imperial Ambition," *Foreign Affairs*, 81, 5 (September–October 2002), pp. 44–60.
4. Niall Ferguson, *Empire: The Rise and Demise of the British World Order and the Lessons for Global Power* (New York: Basic Books 2003), p. 368.
5. See Andrew J. Bacevich, *American Empire: The Realities and Consequences of U.S. Diplomacy* (Cambridge, MA: Harvard University Press, 2002); Robert Kaplan, "Supremacy by Stealth," *Atlantic Monthly* (July–August 2003), pp. 65–84; Jack Snyder, "Imperial Temptation," *National Interest* (Spring 2003); Stephen Rosen, "An Empire, If You Can Keep It," *National Interest* (Spring 2003); "An American Empire?" Special Issue of *The Wilson Quarterly* (Summer 2002); and Andrew J. Bacevich, ed., *The Imperial Tense: Prospects and Problems of American Empire* (Chicago, IL: Ivan R. Dee, 2003).
6. This argument is developed most systematically by Kenneth N. Waltz. See Waltz, "Structural Realism after the Cold War," *International Security*, 25, 1 (Summer 2000), pp. 5–41. For an exploration of this thesis, see Ikenberry, ed., *America Unrivaled: The Future of the Balance of Power* (Ithaca, NY: Cornell University Press, 2002).
7. See Timothy Garton Ash, "The Peril of Too Much Power," *The New York Times* (9 April 2002).
8. See Charles A. Kupchan, *The End of the American Era: U.S. Foreign Policy and the Geopolitics of the Twenty-First Century* (New York: Alfred A. Knopf, 2002).
9. If I am right, the Bush administration's unilateral and neo-imperial policy extremes will be found—even by their supporters—to be politically unsustainable and functionally incompatible with America's own postwar multilateral order. American policy will change and adapt as much or more than the larger international order will change and adapt to neo-imperial thinking in Washington.
10. I develop earlier versions of this argument in Ikenberry, "American Power and the Empire of Democratic Capitalism," *Review of International Studies* (December–January 2001–2); and "America's Liberal Hegemony," *Current History* (January 1999).
11. For a collection of essays that survey European views of the United States, see R. Laurence Moore and Maurizio Vaudagna, eds, *The American Century in Europe* (Ithaca, NY: Cornell University Press, 2003).
12. See Kenneth N. Waltz, *Theory of International Politics* (Reading, MA: Addison-Wesley, 1979). For discussions of balancing under conditions of unipolarity, see Ikenberry, ed., *America Unrivaled;* Michael

Mastanduno and Ethan Kapstein, eds, *Unipolar Politics: Realism and State Strategies after the Cold War* (New York: Columbia University Press, 1999).

13. See Paul Kennedy, *The Rise and Fall of the Great Powers: Economic Change and Military Conflict from 1500 to 2000* (New York: Random House, 1987); and William R. Thompson, ed., *Great Power Rivalries* (Columbia: University of South Carolina Press, 1999).
14. Ikenberry, "The Myth of Post–Cold War Chaos," *Foreign Affairs* (May–June 1996).
15. Michael Mastanduno, "Preserving the Unipolar Moment: Realist Theories and U.S. Grand Strategy after the Cold War," *International Security*, 21, 4 (Spring 1997), pp. 49–88.
16. This puzzle is posed in Ikenberry, *After Victory*, chapter 1.
17. On American ambivalence about multilateralism, see Joseph Nye, *The Paradox of American Power: Why the World's Only Superpower Can't Go It Alone* (New York: Oxford University Press, 2002); Edward C. Luck, *Mixed Messages: American Politics and International Organization, 1919–1999* (Washington, DC: The Brookings Institution, 1999); John Gerard Ruggie, *Winning the Peace: America and World Order in the New Era* (New York: Columbia University Press, 1996).
18. For a recent survey of views of the United States, see The Pew Global Attitudes Project, "Views of a Changing World 2003: War with Iraq Further Divides Global Publics," (June 3, 2003). The full report is available at http://people-press.org/reports/display.php3?ReportID=185; and see German Marshall Fund of the United States, "Europeans See the World as Americans Do, But Critical of U.S. Foreign Policy," press release (September 4, 2002).
19. This form of power has been described most recently in Michael Hardt and Antonio Negri, *Empire* (Cambridge, MA: Harvard University Press, 2000). In a sweeping neo-Marxist vision of world order, the authors argue that globalization is not eroding sovereignty but transforming it into a system of diffuse national and supranational institutions—in other words, a new "empire."
20. The most evocative view of American hegemony that emphasizes its coercive and exploitive character is Chalmers Johnson, *Blowback: The Costs and Consequences of American Empire* (New York: Metropolitan Books, 2000).
21. This section draws on Ikenberry, "American Unipolarity: The Sources of Persistence and Decline," in Ikenberry, ed., *America Unrivaled*, pp. 287–99.
22. This dimension of American predominance is stressed by Robert Gilpin in his work on power and international order. See Gilpin, *War and Change in World Politics* (New York: Cambridge University Press, 1981).
23. This is argued in William Wohlforth, "The Stability of a Unipolar World," *International Security* (Summer 1999).
24. Gilpin, *War and Change*.
25. See Ikenberry, *After Victory*, chapter 6.
26. Geir Lundestad, "Empire by Invitation? The United States and Western Europe, 1945–1952," *The Journal of Peace Research*, 23 (September 1986), pp. 263–77.
27. See Bruce Russett and John Oneal, *Triangulating Peace: Democracy, Interdependence, and International Organizations* (New York: Norton, 2001).
28. This is the argument of Ikenberry, *After Victory*.
29. For an important statement of the "contracting advantages" of democratic states, see Charles Lipson, *Reliable Partners: How Democracies Have Made a Separate Peace* (Princeton, NJ: Princeton University Press, 2003).
30. For a discussion of "voice opportunities," see Joseph M. Grieco, "State Interests and Institutional Rule Trajectory: A Neorealist Interpretation of the Maastricht Treaty and European Economic and Monetary Union," *Security Studies*, 5, 3 (Spring 1996). The classic formulation of this logic is Albert Hirschman, *Exit, Voice, and Loyalty—Responses to Decline in Firms, Organizations, and States* (Cambridge, MA: Harvard University Press, 1970).
31. On the logic of security binding, see Paul Schroeder, "Alliances, 1815–1945: Weapons of Power and Tools of Management," in Klaus Knorr, ed., *Historical Dimensions of National Security Problems* (Lawrence, KS: University of Kansas Press, 1975), pp. 227–62. For more recent formulations, see

Daniel Deudney and G. John Ikenberry, "The Sources and Character of Liberal International Order," *Review of International Studies*, 25, 2 (1999), pp. 179–96.

32. For discussions of industrial society arguments, see Raymond Aron, *The Industrial Society: Three Essays on Ideology and Development* (New York: Clarion Books, 1996); Leon Lindberg, ed., *Politics and the Future of Industrial Society* (New York: David McKay, 1976); and Clark Kerr, *The Future of Industrial Societies: Convergence or Continuing Diversity?* (Cambridge, MA: Harvard University Press, 1983).
33. See Daniel Bell, *The Coming of Post-Industrial Society* (New York: Basic Books, 1973).
34. This distinction is made by Anthony D. Smith, *The Ethnic Origins of Nations* (Oxford: Blackwell, 1986).

ARTICLE 8.2

Global Capitalism and American Empire

Leo Panitch and Sam Gindin

Leo Panitch and Sam Gindin believe that important changes have recently occurred in American public discourse and political practice. On the one hand, a dramatic shift has occurred in the way that public intellectuals describe the position of the United States in the world. Throughout American history, opinion makers insisted that the United States should not seek to control people and territory abroad (although in fact the United States did intervene repeatedly). Recently, however, Panitch and Gindin assert, a tidal shift in America's self-conception has occurred. It has now become fashionable to proclaim that the United States is—and should be—an imperial power.

According to Panitch and Gindin, this change in ideological doctrine is closely connected to—and for many thinkers justifies—a shift in American political practice. Although the United States traditionally did intervene throughout the world to exert economic and political influence, it does so nowadays in a quite distinctive manner. Panitch and Gindin believe that the current phase of U.S. imperialism is intimately linked to globalization: the United States is now the guardian of the international capitalist economy, and in a far more open way than occurred in even the recent past. At the same time, they assert, this situation reflects the weakness, not strength, both of the international economy and the United States' own position.

Panitch and Gindin's position, inspired by Marxist theory, falls outside the scholarly mainstream. But the persuasive evidence they present to defend their position provoke you to question the character of globalization and the role of the United States in the world.

> American imperialism . . . has been made plausible and attractive in part by the insistence that it is not imperialistic.
>
> — Harold Innis, 1948[1]

The American empire is no longer concealed. In March 1999, the cover of the *New York Times Magazine* displayed a giant clenched fist painted in the stars and stripes of the U.S. flag above the words: "What The World Needs Now: For globalization to work, America can't be afraid to act like the almighty superpower that it is." Thus was featured Thomas Friedman's "Manifesto for a Fast World," which urged the United States to embrace its role as enforcer of the capitalist global order: ". . . the hidden hand of the market will never work without a hidden fist. . . . The hidden fist that keeps the world safe for Silicon Valley's technologies is called the United States Army, Air Force, Navy and Marine Corps." Four years later, in January 2003, when there was no longer any point in pretending the fist was hidden, the *Magazine* featured an essay by Michael Ignatieff entitled "The Burden": ". . . [W]hat word but 'empire' describes the awesome thing that America is becoming? . . . Being an imperial power . . . means enforcing such order as there is in the world and doing so in the American interest."[2] The words, "The American Empire (Get Used To It)," took up the whole cover of the *Magazine*.

Of course, the American state's geopolitical strategists had already taken this tack. Among those closest to the Democratic Party wing of the state, Zbigniew Brzezinski did not mince words in his 1997 book, *The Grand Chessboard: American Primacy and Its Geostrategic Imperatives*, asserting that "the three great imperatives of geo-political strategy are to prevent collusion and maintain security dependence amongst the vassals, to keep tributaries pliant, and to keep the barbarians from coming together."[3] In the same year the Republican intellectuals who eventually would write the Bush White House's National Security Strategy founded the Project for a New American Century, with the goal of making imperial statecraft the explicit guiding principle of American policy.[4] . . .

. . . The neglect of any serious political economy or pattern of historical determination that would explain the emergence and reproduction of today's American empire, and the dimensions of structural oppression and exploitation pertaining to it, is striking. It serves as a poignant reminder of why it was Marxism that made the running in theorizing imperialism for most of the twentieth century. But as a leading Indian Marxist, Prabhat Patnaik, noted in his essay "Whatever Happened to Imperialism?," by 1990 the topic had also "virtually disappeared from the pages of Marxist journals" and even Marxists looked "bemused" when the term was mentioned. The costs of this for the left were severe. The

---

First published in SOCIALIST REGISTER 2004, by permission of the Merlin Press, Suite 4, 96 Monnow Street, Monmouth, NP25 3EQ. www.merlinpress.co.uk

concept of imperialism has always been especially important as much for its emotive and mobilizing qualities as for its analytic ones. Indeed, in Patnaik's view, rather than "a theoretically self-conscious silence," the "very fact that imperialism has become so adept at 'managing' potential challenges to its hegemony made us indifferent to its ubiquitous presence."[5] Yet the left's silence on imperialism also reflected severe analytic problems in the Marxist theory of imperialism. Indeed, this was obvious by the beginning of the 1970s—the last time the concept of imperialism had much currency—amidst complaints that the Marxist treatment of imperialism "as an undifferentiated global product of a certain stage of capitalism" reflected its lack of "any serious historical or sociological dimensions."[6] As Giovanni Arrighi noted in 1978, "by the end of the 60s, what had once been the *pride* of Marxism—the theory of imperialism—had become a tower of Babel, in which not even Marxists knew any longer how to find their way."[7]

The confusion was apparent in debates in the early 1970s over the location of contemporary capitalism's contradictions. There were those who focused almost exclusively on the "third world," and saw its resistance to imperialism as the sole source of transformation.[8] Others emphasized increasing contradictions within the developed capitalist world, fostering the impression that American "hegemony" was in decline. This became the prevalent view, and by the mid-1980s the notion that "the erosion of American economic, political, and military power is unmistakable" grew into a commonplace.[9] Although very few went back to that aspect of the Marxist theory of inter-imperial rivalry that suggested a military trial of strength, an era of intense regional economic rivalry was expected. As Glyn and Sutcliffe put it, all it was safe to predict was that without a hegemonic power "the world economy will continue without a clear leader. . . ."[10]

There was indeed no little irony in the fact that so many continued to turn away from what they thought was the old-fashioned notion of imperialism, just when the ground was being laid for its renewed fashionability in the *New York Times*. Even after the 1990–91 Gulf War which, as Bruce Cumings pointed out, "had the important goal of assuring American control of . . . Middle Eastern oil," you still needed "an electron microscope to find 'imperialism' used to describe the U.S. role in the world." The Gulf War, he noted, "went forward under a virtual obliteration of critical discourse egged on by a complacent media in what can only be called an atmosphere of liberal totalism."[11] This continued through the 1990s, even while, as the recent book by the conservative Andrew Bacevich has amply documented, the Clinton Administration often outdid its Republican predecessors in unleashing military power to quell resistance to the continuing aggressive American pursuit of "an open and integrated international order based on the principles of democratic capitalism." Quoting Madeleine Albright, Clinton's Secretary of State, in 1998: "If we have to use force, it is because we are America. We are the indispensable nation," and, in 2000, Richard Haas, the State Department's Director of Policy Planning in the incoming Bush Administration, calling on Americans finally to reconceive their state's "global role from one of a traditional nation state to an imperial power," Bacevich argues that the continuing avoidance of the term imperialism could not last. It was at best an "astigmatism," and at worst "an abiding preference for averting our eyes from the unflagging self-interest and large ambitions underlying all U.S. policy."[12]

By the turn of the century, and most obviously once the authors of the Project for a New American Century were invested with power in Washington D.C., the term imperialism was finally back on even a good many liberals' lips. The popularity of Hardt and Negri's tome, *Empire,* had caught the new conjuncture even before the second war on Iraq. But their insistence (reflecting the widespread notion that the power of all nation states had withered in the era of globalization) that "*the United States does not, and indeed no nation state can today, form the center of an imperialist project*" was itself bizarrely out of sync with the times.[13] . . .

The American Republic: "Extensive Empire and Self-Government"

The central place the United States now occupies within global capitalism rests on a particular convergence of structure and history. . . . The crucial phase in the reconstruction of global capitalism—after the earlier breakdowns and before the reconstitution of the last quarter of the twentieth century—occurred during and after World War II. It was only after (and as a state-learned response to) the disasters of Depression and the Second World War that capitalist globalization obtained a new life. This depended, however, on the emergence and uneven historical evolution of a set of structures developed under the leadership of a unique *agent:* the American imperial state.

The role the United States came to play in world capitalism was not inevitable but nor was it merely accidental: it was not a matter of teleology but of capitalist history. The capacity it developed to "conjugate" its "*particular* power with the *general* task of coordination" in a manner that reflected "the particular matrix of its own social history," as Perry Anderson has recently put it, was founded on "the attractive power of U.S. models of production and culture . . . increasingly unified in the sphere of consumption." Coming together here were, on the one hand, the invention in the U.S. of the modern corporate form, "scientific management" of the labour process, and assembly-line mass production; and, on the other, Hollywood-style "narrative and visual schemas stripped to their most abstract," appealing to and aggregating waves of immigrants through the "dramatic simplification and repetition."[14] The dynamism of American capitalism and its worldwide appeal combined with the universalistic language of American liberal democratic ideology to underpin a capacity for informal empire far beyond that of nineteenth century Britain's. Moreover, by spawning the modern multinational corporation, with foreign direct investment in production and services, the American informal empire was to prove much more penetrative of other social formations.

Yet it was not only the economic and cultural formation of American capitalism, but also the formation of the American state that facilitated a new informal empire. Against Anderson's impression that the American state's constitutional structures lack the "carrying power" of its economic and cultural ones (by virtue of being "moored to eighteenth century arrangements")[15] stands Thomas Jefferson's observation in 1809 that "no constitution was ever before as well-calculated for extensive empire and self-government."[16] Hardt and Negri were right to trace the pre-figuration of what they call "Empire" today back to the American constitution's incorporation of Madisonian "network power."[17] This entailed not only checks and balances within the state apparatus, but the notion that the greater plurality of interests incorporated within an extensive and expansive state would guarantee that the masses would have no common motive or capacity to come together to check the ruling class.[18] Yet far from anticipating the sort of decentred and amorphous power that Hardt and Negri imagine characterized the U.S. historically (and characterizes "Empire" today), the constitutional framework of the new American state gave great powers to the central government to expand trade and make war. As early as 1783, what George Washington already spoke of ambitiously as "a rising empire"[19] was captured in the Federalist Paper XI image of "one great American system superior to the control of all transatlantic force or influence and able to dictate the terms of connection between the old and the new world!"[20]

The notion of empire employed here was conceived, of course, in relation to the other mercantile empires of the eighteenth century. But the state, which emerged out of the ambitions of the "expansionist colonial elite,"[21] with Northern merchants (supported by artisans and commercial farmers) and the Southern plantation-owners allying against Britain's formal mercantile empire, evinced from its beginnings a trajectory leading to capitalist development and informal empire. The initial form this took was through territorial expansion westward, largely through the extermination of the native population, and blatant exploitation not only of the black slave population but also debt-ridden subsistence farmers and, from at least the 1820s on, an emerging industrial working class. Yet the new American state could still conceive of itself as embodying republican liberty, and be widely admired for it, largely due to the link between "extensive empire and self-government" embedded in the federal constitution. . . .

The expansionist tendencies of American capitalism in the latter half of the nineteenth century (reflecting pressures from domestic commercial farmers as much as from the industrialists and financiers of the post–civil war era) were even more apt to take informal forms than had those of British capitalism, even though they were not based on a policy of free trade. The modalities were initially similar, and they began long before the Spanish-American War of 1898, which is usually seen as the start of U.S. imperial expansion. This was amply documented in a paper boldly called "An Indicator of Informal Empire" prepared for the U.S. Center for Naval Analysis: between 1869 and 1897 the U.S. Navy made no less than 5,980 ports of call to protect American commercial shipping in

Argentina, Brazil, Chile, Nicaragua, Panama, Colombia and elsewhere in Latin America.[22] Yet the establishment of colonies in Puerto Rico and the Philippines and the annexation of Hawaii "was a deviation . . . from the typical economic, political and ideological forms of domination already characteristic of American imperialism."[23] Rather, it was through American foreign direct investment and the modern corporate form—epitomized by the Singer Company establishing itself as the first multinational corporation when it jumped the Canadian tariff barrier to establish a subsidiary to produce sewing machines for prosperous Ontario wheat farmers—that the American informal empire soon took shape in a manner quite distinct from the British one.[24]

The articulation of the new informal American empire with military intervention was expressed by Theodore Roosevelt in 1904 in terms of the exercise of "international police power," in the absence of other means of international control, to the end of establishing regimes that know "how to act with reasonable efficiency and decency in social and political matters" and to ensure that each such regime "keeps order and pays its obligations": "[A] nation desirous both of securing respect for itself and of doing good to others [Teddy Roosevelt declared, in language that has now been made very familiar again] must have a force adequate for the work which it feels is allotted to it as its part of the general world duty . . . A great free people owes to itself and to all mankind not to sink into helplessness before the powers of evil."[25]

The American genius for presenting its informal empire in terms of the framework of universal rights reached its apogee under Woodrow Wilson. It also reached the apogee of hypocrisy, especially at the Paris Peace Conference, where Keynes concluded Wilson was "the greatest fraud on earth."[26] Indeed, it was not only the U.S. Congress's isolationist tendencies, but the incapacity of the American presidential, treasury and military apparatuses, that explained the failure of the United States to take responsibility for leading European reconstruction after World War One. The administrative and regulatory expansion of the American state under the impact of corporate liberalism in the Progressive era,[27] and the spread of American direct investment through the 1920s (highlighted by General Motors' purchase of Opel immediately before the Great Depression, completing the "virtual division" of the German auto industry between GM and Ford)[28] were significant developments. Yet it was only during the New Deal that the U.S. state really began to develop the modern planning capacities that would, once they were redeployed in World War II, transform and vastly extend America's informal imperialism.[29] . . .

The American Reconstruction of a Capitalist World Order

The shift of "U.S. state capacities towards realizing internationally-interventionist goals versus domestically-interventionist ones"[30] was crucial to the revival of capitalism's globalizing tendencies after World War II. This not only took place through the wartime reconstruction of the American state, but also through the more radical postwar reconstruction of all the states at the core of the old inter-imperial rivalry. And it also took place alongside—indeed it led to—the multiplication of new states out of the old colonial empires. Among the various dimensions of this new relationship between capitalism and imperialism, the most important was that *the densest imperial networks and institutional linkages, which had earlier run north-south between imperial states and their formal or informal colonies, now came to run between the U.S. and the other major capitalist states*.

What Britain's informal empire had been unable to manage (indeed hardly to even contemplate) in the nineteenth century was now accomplished by the American informal empire, which succeeded in integrating all the other capitalist powers into an effective system of coordination under its aegis. Even apart from the U.S. military occupations, the devastation of the European and Japanese economies and the weak political legitimacy of their ruling classes at the war's end created an unprecedented opportunity which the American state was now ready and willing to exploit. In these conditions, moreover, the expansion of the informal American empire after World War II was hardly a one-way (let alone solely coercive) imposition—it was often "imperialism by invitation."[31]

However important was the development of the national security state apparatus and the geostrategic planning that framed the division of the world with the USSR at Yalta,[32] no less important was the close attention the Treasury and State Department paid during the war to plans for relaunching a coordinated liberal trading regime and a rule-based financial order. This was accomplished by manipulating the debtor status of the U.S.'s main allies, assisted by the complete domination of the dollar as a world currency and the fact that 50% of world production was now accounted for by the U.S. economy. The American state had learned well the lesson of its post–World War I incapacity to combine liberal internationalist rhetoric with an institutional commitment to manage an international capitalist order. . . .

The immense managerial capacity the American state had developed . . . was nowhere more clearly confirmed than at the Bretton Woods conference in 1944. . . .

With the IMF and World Bank headquarters established at American insistence in Washington, D.C., a pattern was set for international economic management among all the leading capitalist countries that continues to this day, one in which even when European or Japanese finance ministries and central banks propose, the U.S. Treasury and Federal Reserve dispose.[33] The dense institutional linkages binding these states to the American empire were also institutionalized, of course, through the institutions of NATO, not to mention the hub-and-spokes networks binding each of the other leading capitalist states to the intelligence and security apparatuses of the U.S. as part of the strategy of containment of Communism during the Cold War. These interacted with economic networks, as well as with new propaganda, intellectual and media networks, to explain, justify and promote the new imperial reality.

Most of those who stress the American state's military and intelligence links with the coercive apparatuses of Europe and Japan tend to see the roots of this in the dynamics of the Cold War.[34] Yet as Bacevich, looking at American policy from the perspective of the collapse of the USSR, has recently said:

> To conceive of U.S. grand strategy from the late 1940's through the 1980's as "containment"—with no purpose apart from resisting the spread of Soviet power—is not wrong, but it is incomplete . . . [S]uch a cramped conception of Cold War strategy actively impedes our understanding of current U.S. policy. . . . No strategy worthy of the name is exclusively passive or defensive in orientation. . . . U.S. grand strategy during the Cold War required not only containing communism but also taking active measures to open up the world politically, culturally, and, above all, economically —which is precisely what policymakers said they intended to do.[35]. . .

Though informal imperial rule seemed to place the "third world" and the core capitalist countries on the same political and economic footing, both the legacy of the old imperialism and the vast imbalance in resources between the Marshall Plan and third world development aid reproduced global inequalities. The space was afforded the European states to develop internal economic coherence and growing domestic markets in the post-war era, and European economic integration was also explicitly encouraged by the U.S. precisely as a mechanism for the "European rescue of the nation-state," in Alan Milward's apt formulation.[36] But this contrasted with American dislike of import-substitution industrialization strategies adopted by states in the south, not to mention U.S. hostility to planned approaches to developing the kind of auto-centric economic base that the advanced capitalist states had created for themselves before they embraced a liberal international economic order. (Unlike the kind of geostrategic concerns that predominated in the American wars in Korea and Vietnam, it was opposition to economic nationalism that determined the U.S. state's involvement in the overthrow of numerous governments from Iran to Chile.) The predictable result — given limits on most of the third world's internal markets, and the implications of all the third world states competing to break into international markets—was that global inequalities increased, even though a few third world states, such as South Korea, were able to use the geostrategic space that the new empire afforded them to develop rapidly and narrow the gap.

Still, in general terms, the new informal form of imperial rule, not only in the advanced capitalist world but also in those regions of the third world where it held sway, was characterized by the penetration of borders, not their dissolution. It was not through formal empire, but rather through the reconstitution of states as integral elements of an informal American empire, that the international capitalist order was now organized and regulated. Nation states remained the primary vehicles through which (a) the social relations and institutions of class, property, currency, contract and markets were established and reproduced; and (b) the international accumulation of capital was carried out. The vast expansion of direct foreign investment worldwide, whatever the shifting regional shares of the total, meant that far from capital escaping the state, it expanded its dependence on *many* states. At the same time, capital as an effective social force within any given state now tended to include both foreign capital and domestic capital with international linkages and ambitions. Their interpenetration made the notion of distinct national bourgeoisies—let alone rivalries between them in any sense analogous to those that led to World War I—increasingly anachronistic.

A further dimension of the new relationship between capitalism and empire was thus the *internationalization of the state*, understood as a state's acceptance of responsibility for managing its domestic capitalist order in [a] way that contributes to managing the international capitalist order.[37] For the American imperial state, however, the internationalization of the state had a special quality. It entailed defining the American national interest in terms of acting not only on behalf of its own capitalist class but also on behalf of the extension and reproduction of global capitalism. . . .

The internationalization of the American state was fully encapsulated in National Security Council document NSC-68 of 1950, which (although it remained "Top Secret" until 1975) Kolko calls "the most important of all postwar policy documents." It articulated most clearly the goal of constructing a "world environment in which the American system can survive and flourish. . . . Even if there were no Soviet Union we would face the great problem . . . [that] the absence of order among nations is becoming less and less tolerable."[38]

The Reconstitution of American Empire in the Neoliberal Era

This pattern of imperial rule was established in the post-war period of reconstruction, a period that, for all of the economic dynamism of "the golden age," was inherently transitional. The very notion of "reconstruction" posed the question of what might follow once the European and Japanese economies were rebuilt and became competitive with the American, and once the benign circumstances of the post-war years were exhausted. Moreover, peasants' and workers' struggles and rising economic nationalism in the third world, and growing working class militancy in the core capitalist countries, were bound to have an impact both on capital's profits and on the institutions of the post-war institutional order.

In less than a generation, the contradictions inherent in the Bretton Woods agreement were exposed. By the time European currencies became fully convertible in 1958, almost all the premises of the 1944 agreement were already in question. The fixed exchange rates established by that agreement depended on the capital controls that most countries other than the U.S. maintained after the war.[39] Yet the very internationalization of trade and direct foreign investment that Bretton Woods promoted (along with domestic innovations and competition in mortgages, credit, investment banking and brokerage that strengthened the capacity of the financial sector within the United States) contributed to the restoration of a global financial market, the corresponding erosion of capital controls, and the vulnerability of fixed exchange rates.[40]

Serious concerns over a return to the international economic fragmentation and collapse of the interwar period were voiced by the early sixties as the American economy went from creditor to debtor status, the dollar moved from a currency in desperately short supply to one in surplus, and the dollar-gold standard, which had been embedded in Bretton Woods, began to crumble.[41] But in spite of new tensions between the U.S. and Europe and Japan, the past was not replayed. American dominance, never fundamentally challenged, would come to be reorganized on a new basis, and international integration was not rolled back but intensified. This reconstitution of the global order, like earlier developments within global capitalism, was not inevitable. What made it possible—what provided the American state the time and political space to renew its global ambitions—was that by the time of the crisis of the early seventies American ideological and material penetration of, and integration with, Europe and Japan was sufficiently strong to rule out any retreat from the international economy or any fundamental challenge to the leadership of the American state.

The United States had, of course, established itself as the military protectorate of Europe and Japan, and this was maintained while both were increasingly making their way into American markets. But the crucial factor in cementing the new imperial bond was foreign direct investment as the main form now taken by capital export and international integration in the post-war period. American corporations, in particular, were evolving into the hubs of increasingly dense host-country and cross-border networks amongst suppliers, financiers, and final markets (thereby further enhancing the liberalized trading order as a means of securing even tighter international networks of production). Even where the initial response to the growth of such American investment was hostile, this generally gave way to competition to attract that investment, and then emulation to meet "the American challenge" through counter-investments in the United States.

Unlike trade, American FDI directly affected the class structures and state formations of the other core countries.[42] Tensions and alliances that emerged within domestic capitalist classes could no longer be understood in purely "national" terms. German auto companies, for example, followed American auto companies in wanting European-wide markets; and they shared mutual concerns with the American companies inside Germany, such as over the cost of European steel. They had reason to be wary of policies that discriminated in favour of European companies but might, as a consequence, compromise the treatment of their own growing interest in markets and investments in the United States. And if instability in Latin America or other "trouble spots" threatened their own international investments, they looked primarily to the U.S. rather than their own states to defend them.

With American capital a social force within each European country, domestic capital tended to be "dis-articulated" and no longer represented by a coherent and independent national bourgeoisie.[43] The likelihood that domestic capital might challenge American dominance—as opposed to merely seeking to renegotiate the terms of American leadership—was considerably diminished. Although the West European and Japanese economies had been rebuilt in the post-war period, the nature of their integration into the global economy tended to tie the successful reproduction of their own social formations to the rules and structures of the American-led global order. However much the European and Japanese states may have wanted to renegotiate the arrangements struck in 1945, now that only 25% of world production was located in the U.S. proper, neither they nor their bourgeoisies were remotely interested in challenging the hegemony that the American informal empire had established over them. . . .

It was in this context that the internationalization of the state became particularly important. In the course of the protracted and often confused renegotiations in the 1970s of the terms that had, since the end of World War II, bound Europe and Japan to the American empire, all the nation states involved came to accept a responsibility for creating the necessary *internal* conditions for sustained *international* accumulation, such as stable prices, constraints on labour militancy, national treatment of foreign investment and no restrictions on capital outflows. . . . Nation states were thus not fading away, but adding to their responsibilities.

Not that they saw clearly what exactly needed to be done. The established structures of the post-1945 order did not, in themselves, provide a resolution to the generalized pressures on profit rates in the United States and Europe. They did not suggest how the U.S. might revive its economic base so as to consolidate its rule. Nor did they provide an answer to how tensions and instabilities would be managed in a world in which the American state was not omnipotent but rather depended, for its rule, on working through other states. The contingent nature of the new order was evidenced by the fact that a "solution" only emerged at the end of the seventies, two full decades after the first signs of trouble, almost a decade after the dollar crisis of the early seventies, and after a sustained period of false starts, confusions, and uncertain experimentation.[44]

The first and most crucial response of the Nixon administration, the dramatic end to the convertibility of the American dollar in 1971, restored the American state's economic autonomy in the face of a threatened rush to gold; and the subsequent devaluation of the American dollar did, at least temporarily, correct the American balance of trade deficit. Yet that response hardly qualified as a solution to the larger issues involved. The American state took advantage of its still dominant position to defend its own economic base, but this defensive posture could not provide a general solution to the problems facing all the developed capitalist economies, nor even create the basis for renewed U.S. economic dynamism. By the end of the seventies, with the American economy facing a flight of capital (both domestic and foreign), a Presidential report to Congress (describing itself as "the most comprehensive and detailed analysis of the competitive position of the United States") confirmed a steep decline in competitiveness—one that it advised *could* be corrected, but not without a radical reorientation in economic policy to address the persistence of domestic inflation and the need for greater access to savings so as to accelerate investment.[45] . . .

The critical "turning point" in policy orientation came in 1979 with the "Volcker shock"—the American state's self-imposed structural adjustment program. The Federal Reserve's determination to establish internal economic discipline by allowing interest rates to rise to historically unprecedented levels led to the vital restructuring of labour and industry and brought the confidence that the money markets and central bankers were looking for. Along with the more general neoliberal policies that evolved into a relatively coherent capitalist policy paradigm through the eighties, the new state-reinforced strength of finance set the stage for what came to be popularly known as "globalization"—the accelerated drive to a seamless world of capital accumulation.

The mechanisms of neoliberalism (the expansion and deepening of markets and competitive pressures) may be economic, but neoliberalism was essentially a *political* response to the democratic gains that had been previously achieved by subordinate classes and which had become, in a new context and from capital's perspective, barriers to accumulation. Neoliberalism involved not just reversing those gains, but weakening their institutional foundations—including a shift in the hierarchy of state apparatuses in the U.S. towards the Treasury and Federal Reserve at the expense of the old New Deal agencies. The U.S. was of course not the only country to introduce neoliberal policies, but once the American state itself moved in this direction, it had a new status: capitalism now operated under "a new form of social rule"[46] that promised, and largely delivered, (a) the revival of the productive base for American dominance; (b) a universal model for restoring the conditions for profits in other developed countries; and (c) the economic conditions for integrating global capitalism.

In the course of the economic restructuring that followed, American labour was further weakened, providing American capital with an even greater competitive flexibility vis-à-vis Europe. Inefficient firms were purged—a process that had been limited in the seventies. Existing firms restructured internally, outsourced processes to cheaper and more specialized suppliers, relocated to the increasingly urban southern states, and merged with other firms—all part of an accelerated reallocation of capital within the American economy. The new confidence of global investors (including Wall Street itself) in the American economy and state provided the U.S. with relatively cheap access to global savings and eventually made capital cheaper in the U.S. The available pools of venture capital enhanced investment in the development of new technologies (which also benefited from public subsidies via military procurement programs), and the new technologies were in turn integrated into management restructuring strategies and disseminated into sectors far beyond "high tech." The U.S. proportion of world production did not further decline: it continued to account for around one-fourth of the total right into the twenty-first century.

The American economy not only reversed its slide in the 1980s, but also set the standards for European and Japanese capital to do the same.[47] The renewed confidence on the part of American capital consolidated capitalism as a global project through the development of new formal and informal mechanisms of international coordination. Neoliberalism reinforced the material and ideological conditions for guaranteeing "national" treatment for foreign capital in each social formation, and for "constitutionalizing"—by way of NAFTA, European Economic and Monetary Union and the WTO—the free flow of goods and capital (the WTO was a broader version of GATT, but with more teeth).[48] The American economy's unique access to global savings through the central place of Wall Street within global money markets allowed it to import freely without compromising other objectives. This eventually brought to the American state the role, not necessarily intended, of "importer of last resort" that limited the impact of slowdowns elsewhere, while also reinforcing foreign investors' and foreign exporters' dependence on American markets and state policies. The Federal Reserve, though allegedly concerned only with domestic policies, kept a steady eye on the international context. And the Treasury, whose relative standing within the state had varied throughout the post-war era, increasingly took on the role of global macro-economic manager through the 1980s and 1990s, thereby enhancing its status at the top of the hierarchy of U.S. state apparatuses.[49]

The G-7 emerged as a forum for Ministers of Finance and Treasury officials to discuss global developments, forge consensus on issues and direction, and address in a concrete and controlled way any necessary exchange rate adjustments. The U.S. allowed the Bank for International Settlements to re-emerge as major international coordinating agency, in the context of the greater role being played by increasingly "independent" central bankers, to improve capital adequacy standards within banking systems. The IMF and the World Bank were also restructured. The IMF shifted from the "adjustment" of balance of payments problems to addressing structural economic crises in third world countries (along the lines first imposed on Britain in 1976), and increasingly became the vehicle for imposing a type of conditionality, in exchange for loans, that incorporated global capital's concerns. The World Bank supported this, although by the 1990's, it also focused its attention on capitalist state-building—what it called "effective states."[50]

The reconstitution of the American empire in this remarkably successful fashion through the last decades of the twentieth century did not mean that global capitalism had reached a new plateau of stability. Indeed it may be said that dynamic instability and contingency are systematically incorporated into the reconstituted form of empire, in good part because the intensified competition characteristic of neoliberalism and the hyper-mobility of financial liberalization aggravate the uneven development and extreme volatility inherent in the global order. Moreover, this instability is dramatically amplified by the fact that the American state can only rule this order through other states, and turning them all into "effective" states for global capitalism is no easy matter. It is the attempt by the American state to address these problems, especially vis-à-vis what it calls "rogue states" in the third world, that leads American imperialism today to present itself in an increasingly unconcealed manner.

Beyond Inter-Imperial Rivalry

We cannot understand imperialism today in terms of the unresolved crisis of the 1970s, with overaccumulation and excess competition giving rise again to inter-imperial rivalry. The differences begin with the fact that while the earlier period was characterized by the relative economic strength of Europe and Japan, the current moment underlines their relative *weakness*. Concern with the American trade deficit seems to overlap both periods, but the context and content of that concern has radically changed. Earlier, the American deficit was just emerging, was generally seen as unsustainable even in the short run, and was characterized by foreign central bankers as exporting American inflation abroad. Today, the global economy has not only come to live with American trade deficits for a period approaching a quarter of a century, but global stability has come to depend on these deficits and it is the passage to their "correction" that is the threat—this time a deflationary threat. In the earlier period, global financial markets were just emerging; the issue this raised at the time was their impact in undermining existing forms of national and international macro-management, including the international role of the American dollar. The consequent explosive development of financial markets has resulted in financial structures and flows that have now however, made "finance" itself a focal point of global macro-management—whether it be enforcing the discipline of accumulation, reallocating capital across sectors and regions, providing the investor/consumer credit to sustain even the modest levels of growth that have occurred, or supporting the capacity of the U.S. economy to attract the global savings essential to reproducing the American empire.

In this context, the extent of the theoretically unselfconscious use of the term "rivalry" to label the economic competition between the EU, Japan (or East Asia more broadly) and the United States is remarkable. The distinctive meaning the concept had in the pre–World War I context, when economic competition among European states was indeed imbricated with comparable military capacities and Lenin could assert that "imperialist wars are absolutely inevitable,"[51] is clearly lacking in the contemporary context of overwhelming American military dominance. But beyond this, the meaning it had in the past is contradicted by the distinctive economic as well as military integration that exists between the leading capitalist powers today.

The term "rivalry" inflates economic competition between states far beyond what it signifies in the real world. While the conception of a transnational capitalist class, loosened from any state moorings or about to spawn a supranational global state, is clearly exceedingly extravagant,[52] so too is any conception of a return to rival national bourgeoisies. The asymmetric power relationships that emerged out of the penetration and integration among the leading capitalist countries under the aegis of informal American empire were not dissolved in the wake of the crisis of the Golden Age and the greater trade competitiveness and capital mobility that accompanied it; rather they were refashioned and reconstituted through the era of neo-liberal globalization. None of this means, of course, that state and economic structures have become homogeneous or that there is no divergence in many policy areas, or that contradiction and conflict are absent from the imperial order. But these contradictions and conflicts are located not so much in the relationships between the advanced capitalists states as *within* these states, as they try to manage their internal processes of accumulation, legitimation and class struggle. This is no less true of the American state as it tries to manage and cope with the complexities of neo-imperial globalization. . . .

Notes

1. "Great Britain, The United States and Canada," Twenty-First Cust Foundation Lecture, University of Nottingham, May 21, 1948, in H. Innis, *Essays in Canadian Economic History,* Toronto: University of Toronto Press, 1956, p. 407.
2. The Friedman manifesto appeared in the *New York Times Magazine* on March 28, 1999, and the Ignatieff essay on January 5, 2003. Ignatieff adds: "It means laying down the rules America wants (on everything from markets to weapons of mass destruction) while exempting itself from other rules (the Kyoto protocol on climate change and the International Criminal Court) that go against its interests."
3. *The Grand Chessboard,* New York: Basic Books, 1997, p. 40.
4. See "Rebuilding America's Defenses: Strategy, Forces and Resources for a New Century," A Report of the Project for the New American Century. http://www.newamericancentury.org/publicationsreports.htm; and *The National Security Strategy of the United States of America,* Falls Village, Connecticut: Winterhouse, 2002.
5. *Monthly Review* 42(6), 1990, pp. 1–6. For two of those who insisted, from different perspectives, on the need to retain the concept of imperialism, see Susan Strange, "Towards a Theory of Transnational Empire," in E-O. Czempiel and J. Rosenau, eds., *Global Changes and Theoretical Challenges,* Lexington: Lexington Books, 1989, and Peter Gowan, "Neo-Liberal Theory and Practice for Eastern Europe," *New Left Review,* 213, 1995.
6. Gareth Stedman Jones, "The Specificity of U.S. Imperialism" *New Left Review,* 60 (first series), 1970, p. 60, n. 1.
7. Giovanni Arrighi, *The Geometry of Imperialism,* London: NLB, 1978, p. 17. What in good part lay behind the left's disenchantment with the concept of imperialism was the extent to which the words that opened Kautsky's infamous essay in 1914—the one that so attracted Lenin's ire—increasingly rang true: "First of all, we need to be clear what we understand from the term imperialism. This word is used in every which way, but the more we discuss and speak about it the more communication and understanding becomes weakened." "Der Imperialismus," *Die Neue Ziet,* Year 32, XXXII/2, Sept 11th, 1914, p. 908. Only the last part of this famous essay was translated and published in *New Left Review* in 1970.
8. Bob Rowthorn, "Imperialism in the Seventies: Unity or Rivalry," *New Left Review,* 69, 1971.
9. "In recent years no topic has occupied the attention of scholars of international relations more than that of American hegemonic decline. The erosion of American economic political and military power is unmistakable. The historically unprecedented resources and capabilities that stood behind United States early postwar diplomacy, and that led Henry Luce in the 1940s to herald an 'American century,' have given way to an equally remarkable and rapid redistribution of international power and wealth. In the guise of theories of 'hegemonic stability,' scholars have been debating the extent of hegemonic decline and its consequences." G. John Ikenberry, "Rethinking the Origins of American Hegemony," *Political Science Quarterly,* 104(3), 1989, p. 375. Among the few critics of this view, see Bruce Russett, "The Mysterious Case of Vanishing Hegemony. Or is Mark Twain Really Dead?," *International Organization,* 39(2), 1985; Stephen Gill, "American Hegemony: Its Limits and Prospects in the

Reagan Era," *Millennium*, 15(3), 1986; and Susan Strange, "The Persistent Myth of Lost Hegemony," *International Organization*, 41(4), 1987.

10. Andrew Glyn and Bob Sutcliffe, "Global But Leaderless," *Socialist Register 1992*, London: Merlin, 1992, p. 93.
11. Bruce Cumings. "Global Realm with no Limit, Global Realm with no Name," *Radical History Review*, 57, 1993, pp. 47–8. This issue of the journal was devoted to a debate on "Imperialism: A Useful Category of Analysis?"
12. Andrew L. Bacevich, *American Empire: The Realities and Consequences of U.S. Diplomacy*, Cambridge, MA: Harvard University Press, 2002, pp. x, 3, 219.
13. Michael Hardt and Antonio Negri, *Empire*, Cambridge, MA: Harvard University Press, 2000, p. xiv, emphasis in text. See our review essay, "Gems and Baubles in Empire," *Historical Materialism*, 10, 2002, pp. 17–43.
14. Perry Anderson, "Force and Consent," *New Left Review*, 17, 2002, p. 24.
15. *Ibid.*, p. 25. See also Daniel Lazare's *The Frozen Republic*, New York: Harcourt Brace, 1996 which fails to distinguish between the democratic constraints and domestic policy gridlocks that the old elitist system of checks and balances produces and the remarkable informal imperial "carrying power" of the American constitution in the sense argued here.
16. Quoted in William Appleman Williams, *Empire as a Way of Life*, New York: Oxford University Press, 1980, p. 61. . . .
17. See Hardt and Negri, *Empire*, chapter 2.5.
18. See John F. Manley, "The Significance of Class in American History and Politics," in L.C. Didd and C. Jilson, eds., *New Perspectives on American Politics*, Washington, D.C.: Congressional Quarterly Press, 1994, esp. pp. 16–19.
19. Quoted in Williams, *Empire as a Way of Life*, p. 43.
20. *The Federalist Papers*, No. 11 (Hamilton), Clinton Rossiter, ed., New York: Mentor, 1999, p. 59.
21. See Marc Engel, *A Mighty Empire: The Origins of the American Revolution*, Ithaca: Cornell University Press, 1988.
22. S.S. Roberts, "An Indicator of Informal Empire: Patterns of U.S. Navy Cruising on Overseas Stations, 1869–97," Center for Naval Analysis, Alexandria, Virginia, n.d., cited in Williams, p. 122.
23. Stedman Jones, "The Specificity," p. 63.
24. See L. Panitch, "Class and Dependency in Canadian Political Economy," *Studies in Political Economy*, 6, 1980, pp. 7–34; W. Clement, *Continental Corporate Power*, Toronto: McLelland & Stewart, 1977; and M. Wilkins, *The Emergence of Multinational Enterprise*, Cambridge, Mass: 1970. . . .
25. Quoted in G. Achcar, *The Clash of Barbarisms*, New York: Monthly Review Press, 2002, p. 96.
26. Letter to Duncan Grant, quoted in Nicholas Fraser, "More Than Economist," *Harper's Magazine*, November, 2001, p. 80. The issue here, of course, was the American state's refusal to forgive Allied war debts, with all the consequences this entailed for the imposition of heavy German reparations payments. See Michael Hudson's *Super Imperialism: The Economic Strategy of American Empire*, New York: Holt, Rinehart and Winston, 1971.
27. See R. Jeffery Lustig, *Corporate Liberalism: The Origins of American Political Theory 1890–1920*, Berkeley: University of California Press, 1982; and Stephen Skowronek, *Building a New American State: The Expansion of National Administrative Capacities 1877–1920*, New York: Cambridge University Press, 1982.
28. See Kees van der Pijl, *The Making of an Atlantic Ruling Class*, London: Verso, 1984, p. 93.
29. This was glimpsed by Charles and Mary Beard even before the war in their analysis of the passage from the old "Imperial Isolationism" to the newer "Collective Internationalism" in their *America in Midpassage*, New York: Macmillan, 1939, Volume I, Ch. X, and Vol, II, Ch. XVII.
30. Brian Waddell, "Corporate Influence and World War II: Resolving the New Deal Political Stalemate," *Journal of Political History*, 11(3), 1999, p. 2.
31. Geir Lundestad, "Empire by Invitation? The United States and Western Europe, 1945–52," *Journal of Peace Research*, 23(3), September, 1986; and see van der Pijl, *The Making*, chapter 6.
32. See Gabriel Kolko, *The Politics of War: The World and United States Foreign Policy 1943–1945*, New York: Random House, 1968.

33. The very words which senior officials at the German Bundesbank used in an interview we conducted in October, 2002.
34. Martin Shaw, *Theory of the Global State*, Cambridge, U.K.: Cambridge University Press, 2000.
35. Bacevich, *American Empire*, p. 4.
36. Alan S. Milward, *The European Rescue of the Nation-State*, London: Routledge, 2000.
37. See Robert Cox, *Production, Power and World Order*, New York: Columbia University Press, 1987, esp. p. 254. Cf. N. Poulantzas, *Classes in Contemporary Capitalism*. (London: New Left Books, 1974), p. 73.
38. Quoted in Williams, p. 189; and see Gabriel Kolko, *Century of War*, New York: The New Press, 1994, p. 397.
39. The interwar collapse of the gold standard had demonstrated that capital mobility and democratic pressures from below, which limited any "automatic" adjustment process, were incompatible with stable exchange rates.
40. On the relationship between the collapse of the gold standard, capital mobility, and the development of democratic pressures, see Barry Eichengreen, *Globalizing Capital: A History of the International Monetary System*, Princeton: Princeton University Press, 1996, Chapters 2–3. On the developments within U.S. finance itself in the 1970s, and their impact abroad, see Michael Moran, *The Politics of the Financial Services Revolution*, London: Macmillan, 1991.
41. Looking back to that period, two Vice-Presidents of Citibank observed, "it is not surprising that economists were so sure in the late 60's and early 70's that the breakdown of fixed exchange rates would further weaken economic links between countries." See H. Cleveland and R. Bhagavatula, "The Continuing World Economic Crisis," *Foreign Affairs*, 59(3), 1981, p. 600. See also Louis Pauly's observation that, at the time, "[i]nternational monetary disarray appeared quite capable of restoring the world of the 1930s." Louis B. Pauly, *Who Elected the Bankers?*, Ithaca: Cornell University Press, 1997, p. 100.
42. The "induced reproduction of American monopoly capitalism within the other metropolises . . . implies the extended reproduction within them of the political and ideological conditions for [the] development of American imperialism." N. Poulantzas, *Classes*, 1974, p. 47.
43. "It is this dis-articulation and heterogeneity of the domestic bourgeoisie that explains the weak resistance, limited to fit and starts, that European states have put up to American capital." *Ibid.*, p. 75.
44. At one time or another, policy during the seventies included import surcharges, attempts at international co-operation on exchange rates, wage and price controls, monetarism, and fiscal stimulus.
45. *Report of the President on U.S. Competitiveness*, Washington: Office of Foreign Economic Research, U.S. Department of Labour, September, 1980.
46. The term is from G. Albo and T. Fast's "Varieties of Neoliberalism" paper presented to the Conference on the Convergence of Capitalist Economies, Wake Forest, North Carolina September 27–29, 2002.
47. See S. Gindin and L. Panitch, "Rethinking Crisis," *Monthly Review*, November, 2002.
48. See Stephen Gill, *Power and Resistance in the New World Order*, London: Palgrave-Macmillan, 2003, pp. 131ff. and pp. 174ff.
49. See Leo Panitch, "The New Imperial State," *New Left Review*, 2, 2000.
50. See Leo Panitch, "'The State in a Changing World': Social-Democratizing Global Capitalism?," *Monthly Review*, October, 1998.
51. Lenin, preface to the French and German editions of *Imperialism*, p. 674.
52. Compare W. Ruigrok and R. van Tulder, *The Logic of International Restructuring*, London: Routledge, 1995 (esp. chs. 6 & 7) against W.I. Robinson, "Beyond Nation-State Paradigms," *Sociological Forum*, 13(4), 1998; and see the debate on Robinson's "Towards a Global Ruling Class?," *Science and Society*, 64(1), 2000 in the "Symposium" in 65(4) of that journal, 2001–2.

The Sorrows of Empire *Militarism, Secrecy, and the End of the Republic*

Chalmers Johnson

Political scientist Chalmers Johnson makes a claim that may seem shocking: "[S]ince 9/11, our country has undergone a transformation from republic to empire that may well prove irreversible." Johnson believes that, although the seeds of empire predate September 2001 (at that time, there were already 725 U.S. military bases outside the United States), a substantial shift of power has occurred since 9/11. Justified in the name of the "war on terrorism," the power to make and administer foreign policy has gravitated from the Department of State, the traditional center of American diplomacy, to the Pentagon (that is, the Department of Defense).

Other analysts in this chapter disagree with Johnson's argument. Panitch and Gindin assert that the United States was an empire long before 9/11. G. John Ikenberry argues that even after 9/11, it is not accurate to regard the United States as an empire. Do you agree with Chalmers Johnson that 9/11 represented a turning point? If so, do you believe that the shift is justified? Can and should it be reversed?

Prologue: The Unveiling of the American Empire

Our nation is the greatest force for good in history.

—President George W. Bush, Crawford, Texas, August 31, 2002

As distinct from other peoples on this earth, most Americans do not recognize—or do not want to recognize—that the United States dominates the world through its military power. Due to government secrecy, they are often ignorant of the fact that their government garrisons the globe. They do not realize that a vast network of American military bases on every continent except Antarctica actually constitutes a new form of empire.

Our country deploys well over half a million soldiers, spies, technicians, teachers, dependents, and civilian contractors in other nations and just under a dozen

Chalmers Johnson, *The Sorrows of Empire: Militarism, Secrecy, and the End of the Republic* (New York: Henry Holt, 2004): 1–6.

carrier task forces in all the oceans and seas of the world. We operate numerous secret bases outside our territory to monitor what the people of the world, including our own citizens, are saying, faxing, or e-mailing to one another. Our globe-girding military and intelligence installations bring profits to civilian industries, which design and manufacture weapons for the armed forces or undertake contract services to build and maintain our far-flung outposts. One task of such contractors is to keep uniformed members of the imperium housed in comfortable quarters, well fed, amused, and supplied with enjoyable, affordable vacation facilities. Whole sectors of the American economy have come to rely on the military for sales. On the eve of our second war on Iraq, for example, the Defense Department ordered 273,000 bottles of Native Tan sunblock (SPF 15), almost triple its 1999 order and undoubtedly a boon to the supplier, Control Supply Company of Tulsa, Oklahoma, and its subcontractor, Sun Fun Products of Daytona Beach, Florida.[1]

The new American empire has been a long time in the making. Its roots go back to the early nineteenth century, when the United States declared all of Latin America its sphere of influence and busily enlarged its own territory at the expense of the indigenous people of North America, as well as British, French, and Spanish colonialists, and neighboring Mexico. Much like their contemporaries in Australia, Algeria, and tsarist Russia, Americans devoted much energy to displacing the original inhabitants of the North American continent and turning over their lands to new settlers. Then, at the edge of the twentieth century, a group of self-conscious imperialists in the government—much like a similar group of conservatives who a century later would seek to implement their own expansive agendas under cover of the "war on terrorism"—used the Spanish-American War to seed military bases in Central America, various islands in the Caribbean, Hawaii, Guam, and the Philippines.

With the Second World War, our nation emerged as the richest and most powerful on earth and a self-designated successor to the British Empire. But as enthusiastic as some of our wartime leaders, particularly President Franklin D. Roosevelt, were for the task, the American people were not. They demanded that the country demobilize its armies and turn the nation's attention to full employment and domestic development. Peace did not last long, however. The Cold War and a growing conviction that vital interests, even national survival, demanded the "containment" of the Soviet Union helped turn an informal empire begun during World War II into hundreds of installations around the world for the largest military we ever maintained in peacetime.

During the almost fifty years of superpower standoff, the United States denied that its activities constituted a form of imperialism. Ours were just reactions to the menace of the "evil empire" of the USSR and its satellites. Only slowly did we Americans become aware that the role of the military was growing in our country and that the executive branch—the "imperial presidency"—was eroding the democratic underpinnings of our constitutional republic. But even at the time of the Vietnam War and the abuses of power known as Watergate, this awareness never gained sufficient traction to reverse a Cold War–driven transfer of power from the representatives of the people to the Pentagon and the various intelligence agencies, especially the Central Intelligence Agency.

By the time the Soviet Union collapsed in 1991, and with it the rationale for American containment policies, our leaders had become so accustomed to dominance over half the globe that the thought of giving it up was inconceivable. Many Americans simply concluded that they had "won" the Cold War and so deserved the imperial fruits of victory. A number of ideologists began to argue that the United States was, in fact, a "good empire" and should act accordingly in a world with only one dominant power. To demobilize and turn our resources to peaceful ends would, they argued, constitute the old-fashioned sin of "isolationism."

In the first post–Cold War decade, we mounted many actions to perpetuate and extend our global power, including wars and "humanitarian" interventions in Panama, the Persian Gulf, Somalia, Haiti, Bosnia, Colombia, and Serbia, while maintaining unchanged our Cold War deployments in East Asia and the Pacific. In the eyes of its own people, the United States remained at worst an informal empire. After all, it had no colonies and its massive military forces were deployed around the world only to maintain "stability," or guarantee "mutual security," or promote a liberal world order based on free elections and American-style "open markets."

Americans like to say that the world changed as a result of the September 11, 2001, terrorist attacks on the World Trade Center and the Pentagon. It would be more accurate to say that the attacks produced a dangerous change in the thinking of some of our leaders, who began to see our republic as a genuine empire, a new Rome, the greatest colossus in history, no longer bound by international law, the concerns of allies, or any constraints on its use of military force. The American people were still largely in the dark about why they had been attacked or why their State Department began warning them against tourism in an ever-growing list of foreign countries. ("Why do they hate us?" was a common plaint heard on talk shows, and the most common answer was "jealousy.") But a growing number finally began to grasp what most non-Americans already knew and had experienced over the previous half century—namely, that the United States was something other than what it professed to be, that it was, in fact, a military juggernaut intent on world domination.

Americans may still prefer to use euphemisms like "lone superpower," but since 9/11, our country has undergone a transformation from republic to empire that may well prove irreversible. It suddenly became "un-American" to question the Bush administration's "war on terrorism," let alone a war on Iraq, or on the whole "axis of evil," or even on the sixty or so countries that the president and his secretary of defense announced contained al-Qaeda cells and so were open targets for unilateral American intervention. The media allowed themselves to be manipulated into using sanitized expressions like "collateral damage," "regime change," "illegal combatants," and "preventive war" as if these somehow explained and justified what the Pentagon was doing. At the same time, the government was making strenuous efforts to prevent the new International Criminal Court from ever having the option of considering war crimes charges against American officials.

. . . [T]he American empire[,] as it begins openly to spread its imperial wings[,] . . . is global: as of September 2001, the Department of Defense acknowledged at least 725 American military bases existed outside the United States. Actually, there are many more, since some bases exist under leaseholds, informal agreements, or disguises of various kinds. And more have been created since the announcement was made. The landscape of this military empire is as unfamiliar and fantastic to most Americans today as Tibet or Timbuktu were to nineteenth-century Europeans. Among its recent additions are the al-Udeid air base in the desert of Qatar, where several thousand American military men and women live in air-conditioned tents, and the al-Masirah Island naval air station in the Gulf of Oman, where the only diversion is "wadi ball," a cross between volleyball and football. It includes expensive, permanent garrisons built between 1999 and 2001 in such unlikely places as Kosovo, Kyrgyzstan, and Uzbekistan. America's modern empire of bases also has its entertainment and getaway spots, much like those north Indian hill towns the administrators of the British Raj used for rest and recreation in the summer heat. The modern equivalents of Darjeeling, Kalimpong, and Srinagar are the armed forces' ski and vacation center at Garmisch in the Bavarian Alps, its resort hotel in downtown Tokyo, and the 234 military golf courses it operates worldwide, not to mention the seventy-one Learjets, thirteen Gulfstream IIIs, and seventeen Cessna Citation luxury jets used to fly admirals and generals to such spots. At a cost of $50 million apiece, each Gulfstream accommodates twelve passengers plus two pilots, one flight engineer, a communications systems operator, and a flight attendant.

Like empires of old, ours has its proconsuls, in this case high-ranking military officers who enforce extraterritorial "status of forces agreements" on host governments to ensure that American troops are not held responsible for crimes they commit against local residents. Our militarized empire is a physical reality with a distinct way of life but it is also a network of economic and political interests tied in a thousand different ways to American corporations, universities, and communities but kept separate from what passes for everyday life back in what has only recently come to be known as "the homeland." And yet even that sense of separation is disappearing—for the changing nature of the empire is changing our society as well.

For example, slowly but surely the Department of Defense is obscuring and displacing the Department of State as the primary agency for making and administering foreign policy. We now station innumerably more uniformed military officers than civilian diplomats, aid workers, or environmental specialists in foreign countries—a point not lost on the lands to which they are assigned. Our garrisons send a daily message that the United States prefers to deal with other nations through the use or threat of force rather than negotiations, commerce, or cultural interaction and through military-to-military, not civilian-to-civilian, relations. This point was made clear in a speech at the military academy at West Point on June 1, 2002, when President George W. Bush argued that the United States must be prepared to wage a "war on terror" against as many as sixty countries. "We must take that battle to the enemy, disrupt his plans and confront the worst threats before they emerge." Americans must be "ready for preemptive action when necessary to defend our liberty and to defend our lives. . . . In the world we have entered, the only path to safety is the path of action. And this nation will act."

As historian Arthur Schlesinger Jr., adviser to President John F. Kennedy, observed on the first anniversary of the 9/11 attacks, "One of the astonishing events of recent months is the presentation of preventive war as a legitimate and moral instrument of U.S. foreign policy. . . . During the Cold War, advocates of preventive war were dismissed as a crowd of loonies. . . . The policy of containment plus deterrence won the Cold War. After the collapse of the Soviet Union, everyone thanked heaven that the preventive-war loonies had never got into power in any major country. Today, alas, they appear to be in power in the United States."[2] He was referring specifically to the first Bush administration's secretary of defense, Dick Cheney—now, of course, vice president—the second Bush administration's secretary of defense, Donald Rumsfeld, and their cronies in the Pentagon. The last time civilian and uniformed militarists even approximated the domination of American political life we see today was when Secretary of Defense Robert McNamara was dictating policy toward Vietnam. . . .

Notes

1. Paul Sperry, "Defense Department Orders 273,000 Bottles of Sunblock," *WorldNetDaily*, October 9, 2002, http://www.worldnetdaily.com/news/article.asp?ARTICLE_ID=29225.
2. Arthur Schlesinger Jr., "The Immorality of Preventive War," History News Network, August 26, 2002. Also see Jimmy Carter, "The Troubling New Face of America," *Washington Post*, September 5, 2002.

ARTICLE 8.4

Beyond Militarism, Arms Races, and Arms Control

Mary Kaldor

Mary Kaldor describes a new generation of "smart weapons" that puts American military capability in another league. The result is that the United States is "the only state, in this globalized world, that still has the capacity to act unilaterally." Yet despite its military supremacy, Kaldor believes that the United States is not an imperial power. Why not? Compare her position with those of other selections in this chapter.

The New American Militarism

It could be argued that if September 11 had not happened, the American military-industrial complex might have had to invent it. Indeed, what happened on September 11 could have come out of what seemed to be the wild fantasies of "asymmetric threats" that were developed by American strategic analysts as they sought a new military role for the United States after the end of the Cold War. A reporter for the London *Observer* claimed to have found, in one of the headquarters for terrorist training in Afghanistan, a photocopy of a "terrorist cookbook," some of which circulates among the American fundamentalist right.

World military spending declined by one-third in the decade after 1989. America military spending also declined, but by less than the global average, and began to rise again after 1998. As of the year 2000, American military spending in real terms was equivalent to its spending in 1980, just before the Reagan military build-up. More importantly, what took place during the 1990s was a radical shift in the structure of U.S. military expenditure. Spending on military research and development declined less than overall military spending and has increased faster since 1998. As of 2000, U.S. military research and development (R&D) spending was 47 percent higher in real terms than in 1980.[1] Instead of ushering in a period of downsizing, disarmament and conversion (although some of that did take place at local levels in the U.S.), the end of the Cold War led to a feverish

---

technological effort to apply information technology to military purposes, known as the Revolution in Military Affairs (RMA).

Indeed, it can be argued that the cuts of the early 1990s are equivalent to the reductions that can be expected in the normal post-1945 U.S. military procurement cycle. The high points in the procurement cycle were in the early 1950s, late 1960s, early 1970s, and the early 1980s. During the downturns, military R&D is always sustained, designing and developing the systems to be procured in the next upturn. As new systems reach the more expensive development and procurement phases, this has always coincided with renewed preoccupations with threats of various kinds. The North Korean invasion of South Korea in 1950, for example, occurred at a moment when pressure to increase military spending was mounting as a result of overcapacity in the arms industry, especially the aircraft industry, and of fears about the return of mass unemployment after the end of the postwar consumer boom. NSC 68, the famous report which recommended an increase in military spending to meet the Soviet threat, was published just before the Korean invasion. A parallel can be drawn with the current situation since the systems developed under the rubric of the RMA are reaching the development and production phase, and there is overcapacity in the aerospace industry.

During the 1990s, great efforts were expended in "imagining" new "worst-case scenarios" and new post-Soviet threats. With the collapse of the Soviet military-industrial complex, strategic planners have come up with all sorts of inventive new ways of attacking America, through spreading viruses, poisoning water systems, causing the collapse of the banking system, disrupting air-traffic control or power transmission. Of particular importance has been the idea of state-sponsored terrorism and the notion of "rogue states" who sponsor terrorism and acquire long-range missiles as well as WMD (weapons of mass destruction). These new threats emanating from a collapsing Russia or from Islamic fundamentalism are known as "asymmetric" threats, as weaker states or groups develop WMD or other horrific techniques to attack U.S. vulnerabilities to compensate for conventional inferiority. Hence what happened on September 11, and the subsequent anthrax scare, seems like a confirmation of these anticipations of horror.

RMA consists of the interaction between various systems for information collection, analysis, and transmission and weapons systems—the so-called "system of systems." It has spawned a suitably sci-fi jargon—"battlespace" to replace "battlefield," connoting the three-dimensional character of contemporary battle; "dominant battlespace knowledge," "precision violence," "near-perfect mission assignment," C4I/BM (command, control, communications, computers, intelligence, and battle management); "cooperative engagement capability" (Navy); "digitalized ground forces" (Army); and (one of my favorites) "just-in-time warfare" (referring to reduced logistical requirements).[2]

The cruise missile, the target of peace-movement campaigns in the 1980s, can be described as the paradigmatic weapon of RMA. It is a "system that can be delivered by a variety of platforms (i.e. all three services can use it) and strike in a precise manner and with low collateral damage."[3] It was the cruise missile that was used in the summer of 1998 against terrorist camps in Afghanistan and an alleged chemical-weapons factory in Sudan after the bombings of the U.S. embassies in Kenya and Uganda.

Enthusiasts for RMA suggest that the introduction of information technology is akin to the introduction of the stirrup or gunpowder in its implications for warfare. Unlike these earlier innovations, however, RMA takes place within the traditional force structures inherited from the past. Earlier innovations were adopted only when force structures changed in such a way as to be capable of assimilating the new technologies. Thus the introduction of the stirrup depended on the evolution of feudal relations and the emergence of knights, while gunpowder was applied to warfare only after capitalist development made possible the use of mercenaries.

The origins of the RMA can be traced to the 1970s, when the effect of growing accuracy and lethality of munitions was observed in the wars in Vietnam and the Middle East. The so-called military reformers suggested that this implied an historic shift to the defense. The offensive maneuvers characteristic of World War II and planned in Europe for World War III were no longer possible, since tanks and aircraft were almost as vulnerable as troops had been in World War I. In particular, it was argued that this historic shift lessened the need for nuclear weapons to compensate for Soviet conventional superiority, since this could be nullified by improvements in conventional defense. The opponents of this view argued that the offense was even more important in the context of information technology, because it made possible unmanned guided offensive weapons and because of the importance of area-destruction munitions, which could destroy widely scattered defensive forces. It was the latter view that prevailed, perhaps because it left force structures undisturbed and sustained defense companies, retaining an emphasis on offensive maneuvers and delivery platforms in a more or less linear extension from the strategic bombing missions of World War II.

The consequence was what became known as "emerging technologies" in the 1980s. These were long-range strike weapons using conventional munitions that were nearly as lethal as nuclear weapons. Terms such as "deep strike," "airland battle," and the "maritime strategy" became the buzzwords of the 1980s. The idea was that the West would meet any Soviet attack by striking deep into Soviet territory. When Iraq invaded Kuwait in 1990 and the Pentagon was asked to present the military options, they were able to roll out a plan that had been prepared in the event of a southward Soviet thrust.

The Gulf War provided a model for what can be described as casualty-free war—that is to say the use of high technology either to attack an enemy directly or to support a proxy, say the KLA in Kosovo or the Northern Alliance in Afghanistan. The idea now is that this high-tech warfare can be used against "rogue states" sponsoring terrorists. The same techniques were used against Iraq in December 1998, in Yugoslavia in 1999, and now in Afghanistan. They satisfy a confluence of interests. They fulfill the needs of the scientists, engineers, and companies that provide an infrastructure for the American military effort. They allow for a continuation of the imaginary war of the Cold War period from the point of view of Americans. They do not involve American casualties, and they can be watched on television and demonstrate the determination and power of the United States government—the "spectacles" as James Der Derian has put it, that "serve to deny imperial decline."[4] It is this imaginary character from an American perspective that explains Jean Baudrillard's famous remark that the Gulf War did not happen.

The program for national missile defense (NMD) has to be understood in the same vein. Even if the system cannot work, it provides imaginary protection for the United States, allowing the United States to engage in casualty-free war without fear of retaliation. This notion is evident from the way in which Donald Rumsfeld, the U.S. defense secretary, talks about how NMD will enhance deterrence through a combination of defensive and offensive measures. The weakness of deterrence was always the problem of credibility; a problem that leads to more and more useable nuclear weapons. With casualty-free war, the credibility of U.S. action is more convincing; after all, it is said that the attack on the World Trade Center was equivalent to the use of a substrategic nuclear weapon. NMD, at least psychologically, extends the possibilities for casualty-free war.

However, from the point of view of the victims, these wars are very real and not so different from new wars. However precise the strikes, it is impossible to avoid "mistakes" or "collateral damage." It does not make civilian casualties any more palatable to be told they were not intended. Moreover, the destruction of physical infrastructure and the support for one side in the conflict, as in the case of proxies, results in many more indirect casualties. In the case of the Gulf War, direct Iraqi casualties can probably be numbered in the tens of thousands, but the destruction of physical infrastructure and the ensuing wars with the Kurds and the Shi'ites caused hundreds of thousands of further casualties and seem to have entrenched the vicious and dangerous rule of Saddam Hussein. In the current war in Afghanistan, there have probably been thousands of casualties, both civilian and military, as well as thousands of people fleeing their homes and a humanitarian disaster because aid agencies have not been able to enter the country. The help provided to the hated Northern Alliance reduces the prospects of a broad-based Afghan government that might begin a process of stabilization. Far from extending support for democratic values, casualty-free war shows that American lives are privileged over the lives of others and contributes to a perception of the United States as a global bully.

Terms like imperialism are, however, misleading. The United States is best characterized not as an imperial power but as the "last nation-state." It is the only state, in this globalized world, that still has the capacity to act unilaterally. Its behavior is determined less by imperial considerations than by concerns about its own domestic public opinion. Casualty-free war is also a form of political mobilization. It is about satisfying various domestic constituencies, not about influencing the rest of the world, even though such actions have a profound impact on the rest of the world. . . .

What happened on September 11 was a crime against humanity. It was interpreted, however, in the U.S. as an attack on the U.S., and a parallel has been repeatedly drawn with Pearl Harbor. Bush talks about a "war on terrorism" and has said that "you are either with us or with the terrorists." The approach of casualty-free war was adopted, using high-tech strikes and a proxy, the Northern Alliance, to destroy the state sponsoring terrorism, the Taliban, and to destroy the Al Qaeda network. (At the time of writing, some U.S. Special Forces and Marines have been deployed on the ground.) We do not know how many people have died as a result of the strikes or have fled their homes, but it undoubtedly numbers in hundreds if not thousands. The chances of stabilizing Afghanistan exist but are reduced by the dominant role played by the Northern Alliance. Most importantly, perhaps, the approach contributes to a political polarization between the West and the rest, both because of the privileging of American lives and because of the language in which the war is conducted. While the Taliban has been overthrown and, hopefully, bin Laden may be caught, there is not likely to be any clear military victory. As I have argued, the political narrative, in this case of jihad against America, is central to the functioning of the network. Casualty-free war confirms the political narrative and sets up exactly the kind of war envisaged by the Al Qaeda network.

A humanitarian approach would have defined September 11 as a crime against humanity. It would have sought United Nations authorization for any action, and it would have adopted tactics aimed at increasing trust and confidence on the ground, for example through the establishment of safe havens in the north as well as humanitarian corridors. It would have established an International Court to try terrorists. It would have adopted some of the means already adopted to put pressure on terrorist networks through squeezing financial assets, for example, as well as efforts to catch the criminals. Such an approach would also have to eschew double standards. Catching Mladic and Karadzic, the perpetrators of the Srebrenica massacre, is just as important as catching bin Laden. Human rights violations in Palestine and Chechnya are no less serious than in Kosovo or Afghanistan.

A humanitarian approach, of course, has to be part of a wider political approach. In wars in which no military victory is possible, political approaches are key. An alternative political narrative, based on the idea of global justice, is the only way to minimize the exclusive political appeal of the networks.

I am aware that all this sounds impossibly utopian. Unfortunately, the humanitarian approach may be seen in retrospect as a brief expression of the interregnum between the end of the Cold War and September 11, 2001. We are, I fear, on the brink of a global new war, something like the wars in the Balkans or the Israel–Palestine war, on a global scale with no outsiders to constrain its course. Sooner or later, the impossibility of winning such a war must become evident, and that is why we need to keep the humanitarian approach alive. Even if it cannot solve these conflicts, it can offer some hope to those caught in the middle.

Notes

1. Stockholm International Peace Research Institute, *SIPRI Yearbook 2001: Armaments. Disarmament and International Security* (Oxford: Oxford University Press, 2001).
2. Freedman, "The Revolution in Strategic Affairs" *Adelphi Paper 318* (London: International Institute of Strategic Affairs, 1998).
3. Freedman, ibid., p. 70.
4. James Der Derian, M. Shapiro, eds., *International/Intertextual Relations: Postmodern Readings of World Politics* (Lexington, MA: Lexington Books, 1989). . . .

ARTICLE 8.5

Colossus *The Price of America's Empire*

Niall Ferguson

Historian Niall Ferguson believes that although the United States is an empire, it is a peculiar one. At the same time that it possesses enormous power, it cannot impose its will on other countries and mold them as it wishes. Recent examples of failed U.S. interventions include Haiti, Somalia, Afghanistan, Iraq, and Liberia. His argument is that although the United States can achieve military victory, it lacks sufficient economic clout, military manpower, and political will to achieve its goals following successful military intervention. According to Ferguson, the problem can be described as "inadequate resources for nonmilitary purposes and a truncated time horizon." Ferguson also describes the problem as attention deficit—the inability to stay the course following an armed intervention. Others might describe this same situation as a product of popular opposition to the aggressive exercise of U.S. power over other countries. Otherwise put, because the United States is a democracy, it is possible for movements opposing sustained military and political intervention to mobilize and recruit support.

Ferguson suggests that one reason why the United States is unable to impose its will is that globalization has diffused power and economic resources in the world. (One might consider this another aspect of the flatter world described by Friedman in Chapter 3.) The result is a relative decline in U.S. power, that is, diminished ability to coerce or persuade others.

Compare Ferguson's account with other selections in this chapter. What are the points of convergence and divergence? How can one most accurately characterize the relationship between the United States and other countries and regions?

Conclusion: Looking Homeward

La comperai
per novecentonovantanove anni,
on facoltà, ogni mese,
di rescindere i patti.
Sono in questo paese
elastici de, par, case e contratti.

[I've bought it
for nine hundred ninety-nine years,
but I can cancel the arrangement at a month's notice.
It seems that in this country
both houses and contracts are elastic.]

— GIACOMO PUCCINI, *Madama Butterfly*, Act I

Each of us is all the sums he has not counted: subtract us into nakedness and night again, and you shall see begin in Crete four thousand years ago the love that ended yesterday in Texas. The seed of our destruction will blossom in the desert. . . .

— THOMAS WOLFE, *Look Homeward, Angel*[1]

The United States today is an empire—but a peculiar kind of empire. It is vastly wealthy. It is militarily peerless. It has astonishing cultural reach. Yet by comparison with other empires it often struggles to impose its will beyond its shores. Its successes in exporting American institutions to foreign lands have been outnumbered by its failures.

In many respects, this American empire shares the same aspirations and ambitions as the last great Anglophone hegemon. Despite originating in a revolt against British imperialism, the United States inherited many of its begetter's defining characteristics. Styling itself, in good Whig terminology, an "empire of liberty," the fledgling Republic embarked on an astonishingly rapid colonization of the central belt of the North American continent. If anything, the independent Americans were even more ruthless in the way they expropriated indigenous peoples than they had been as British subjects.[2] However, the differences between the British and American empires became more apparent as the United States sought to extend its influence overseas.[3] Its experiment with overt imperialism after 1898 had distinctly mixed results, ending unhappily in both the Pacific and the Caribbean, with the notable exceptions of Hawaii and Puerto Rico. Like the fickle Lieutenant Pinkerton in Puccini's *Madama Butterfly*, American overseas interventions went through three phases: ardent in Act I, absent in Act II, anguished in Act III.

Only when the United States could cast itself in an anti-imperialist role—first against the British Empire during the Second World War and then (more wisely) against the Soviet Union during the cold war—were Americans able to perform their own cryptoimperial role with self-confidence. Even then, there were clear limits to American stamina. The doctrine of limited war led to a draw in Korea and a defeat in Vietnam. Contradictory commitments undermined U.S. predominance in the Middle East too. It took a succession of humanitarian disasters abroad in the 1990s and terrorist attacks at home in 2001 to rekindle public enthusiasm for a more assertive American foreign policy, though even this had to be cloaked in euphemism, its imperial character repeatedly denied.

The United States has invaded and occupied many countries over the past two centuries. Yet in terms of their economic and political institutions relatively few of these have evolved into anything remotely resembling miniature Americas. Will things go any better in Kosovo, Afghanistan and Iraq? And can President Bush live up to his implied threats to deal sooner or later with the other members of the "axis of evil," Iran and North Korea—to say nothing of Cuba, Libya and Syria, added to the list of rogue states in May 2002, as well as Burma and Zimbabwe, also singled out for presidential opprobrium in November last year?[4]

At the time of writing, simply imposing order in Iraq was proving difficult enough, even with British and Polish assistance. After all the bravado of the Three-Week War, the Bush administration felt constrained to request assistance from the United Nations for its Coalition Provisional Authority. To have any hope of securing this, the United States had to promise to expedite the transfer of power from the Anglo-American coalition to an elected Iraqi government. American power also looked circumscribed in the Middle East. When George W. Bush visited the region in June 2003, some expressed the hope that the overthrow of Saddam would help break the deadlock in the Middle Eastern peace process, sending a signal to Syria and Iran that their support for terrorist organizations bent on the destruction of Israel would no longer be tolerated, bolstering the moderates among the Palestinian leadership and encouraging a skeptical Israeli government to take the route marked on the American "road map." By the fall, however, Yasser Arafat had reasserted his control over the Palestinian administration, Ariel Sharon was building a replica of the Berlin Wall around the Palestinians and for the first time Americans were being targeted by terrorists in the occupied territories. At the same time, al Qa'eda began to attack the one Arab autocracy that the United States had pledged itself to preserve, the house of Saud.

The Bush administration had meanwhile made equally little headway in dealing with what was surely the most dangerous of all the world's rogue regimes, North Korea. Pyongyang's development of long-range missiles and its research into nuclear, chemical and biological weapons—to say nothing of its huge conventional armed forces—plainly posed a huge threat to the stability of East Asia. In December 2002 the North Koreans had repudiated a 1994 agreement shutting down its nuclear reactors and had expelled UN monitors; in October 2003 a North Korean Foreign Ministry spokesman threatened, somewhat opaquely, to "open [North Korea's] nuclear deterrent to the public as a physical force." Could the United States do anything about this? Apparently not—despite the fact that the country continued to depend on American aid to feed its half-starved population. Insisting that it be given not just handouts but a fully fledged nonaggression treaty with the United States, this repulsive little dictatorship defied the American hyperpower with impunity.

The United States even hesitated before sending a tiny force to the one basket case country in Africa for which it can be said to have any historical responsibility, Liberia. In August three ships, carrying around 4,500 sailors and marines, were sent to Liberia after repeated requests for American intervention. In all 225 U.S. personnel went ashore, of whom 50 succumbed to malaria. Two months later the Americans were gone.

This halfhearted African adventure seemed to exemplify the limits of American power. But how are we to explain these limits? As we have seen, by most conventional measures of power—economic, military and cultural—there has never been an empire mightier than the United States today. Its recent difficulties in achieving its foreign policy goals cannot simply be blamed on the Bush administration's alleged diplomatic ineptitude. Rather, we need fundamentally to rethink what we mean by power, for all too often we confuse that concept with other, quite different things—wealth, weaponry and a winning way with "soft power." It is in fact perfectly possible to have a great deal of all these things, yet to have only limited power. Indeed, that is precisely the American predicament. . . .

Three Deficits

. . . [T]here are three fundamental deficits that together explain why the United States has been a less effective empire than its British predecessor. They are its economic deficit, its manpower deficit and—the most serious of the three—its attention deficit.

In the space of four years Americans have intervened militarily against three rogue states in the Balkans, Central Asia and the Middle East. As I write, American troops patrol the streets of Kosovo, Kabul and Kirkuk. Whatever the rationale, each U.S. incursion has led to a change of political regime, of military occupation and an attempt at institutional transformation euphemistically described as nation building. But where will the money come from to make these undertakings successful? How many Americans will be willing to go to these places to oversee how that money is spent? And how long will the American public at home be prepared to support a policy that costs not only money but also lives—even if the quantities in both cases are comparatively modest?

There may be ways of bridging two of these three deficits, at least for a time. Since 1985, the United States has gone from being a net international creditor to being the world's biggest debtor; its net international liabilities are now equivalent to around a quarter of the gross domestic product. However, that is far from being the maximum ever run up by a developed economy. In the 1990s Australia's net foreign debt touched 60 percent of GDP, while New Zealand's came close to 90 percent.[5] It may therefore be possible to carry on borrowing from abroad since there seems to be an insatiable appetite on the part of foreign investors for dollar-denominated securities, no matter how low the return on them.[6] Unlike Australia and New Zealand, after all, the United States gets to issue debt denominated in the global reserve currency.

Admittedly, America's reliance on foreign capital is a balancing act on a very high wire. One conceivable and troubling scenario is that foreign expectations could shift, leading to simultaneous pressure on the exchange rate and bond prices, with higher interest rates threatening American growth more than a weak dollar boosts it.[7] No one should rule out the possibility that American fiscal profligacy, even with the most accommodating monetary policy in the history of the Fed, could still coincide with a Japanese-style deflation rather than a return to inflation, especially if American consumers began to save more and attempt to reduce their indebtedness. Two generations with no experience of sustained declines in prices would struggle to adjust their behavior in appropriate ways. In particular, people with large accumulations of mortgage and consumer debt would find apparently low nominal interest rates becoming painfully high in real terms if prices fell by more than 1 or 2 percent a year.

Yet the costs of such a crisis would be heavier outside the United States than inside. Even a modest reduction in the growth of American consumer demand in the years ahead would have serious consequences for the rest of the global economy, given that nearly 60 percent of the total growth in world output since 1995 has come from the United States.[8] And if the United States were to press for a devaluation of the dollar and some measure of protection against Chinese imports, there could be a deflationary chain reaction throughout the world economy.[9] A deflationary world would not necessarily be a disastrously depressed world; it might be more like the 1880s than the 1930s. The original Great Depression that began in the aftermath of the 1873 crash and lasted until 1895 saw prices depressed much more than output (which more than doubled in the United States), and although the period was associated with increases in tariffs, these were not so large as to choke off global trade. If such a Great Deflation were to happen again, America's latent fiscal crisis would not go away, of course; indeed, it might get even worse if real interest rates rose above the real growth rate or if the costs of Medicare continued to rise at a time when other prices were declining. As in the depression of the 1880s, the deflation losers might well turn to radical forms of politics to express their disgruntlement. Populism and socialism thrived as falling prices squeezed farmers and workers, while white-collar workers and small-business owners often turned to new strains of xenophobic nationalism. These were the first harbingers of the "end of globalization" in the mid-twentieth century. On the other hand, the British Empire's strategic position was positively enhanced by the late Victorian slowdown, not least because it discouraged the strategic ambitions of potential rivals. It was only after the deflation was over that the Germans began to build their navy and to pursue their "world policy." A Great Deflation would be likely to hurt Europe and China more than it hurt America.

Nor is America's manpower deficit insuperable. There is undoubtedly something perplexing about the apparent lack of American combat-effective troops at a time when the U.S. population is growing at 1.25 percent per annum, unemployment is proving stubbornly resistant to economic recovery (by one estimate there are 4 million victims of the current "job gap")[10] and the American prison population exceeds 2 million—1 in every 142 American residents.[11] If one adds together the illegal immigrants, the jobless and the convicts, there is surely ample raw material for a larger American army. One of the keys to the expansion of the Roman Empire was, after all, the opportunity offered to non-Romans to earn citizenship through military service. One of the mainsprings of British colonization was the policy of transportation that emptied the prison hulks of eighteenth-century England into ships bound for Australia. Reviving the draft would not necessarily be unpopular, so long as it was appropriately targeted.

The only alternative is to rely on foreign armies to provide auxiliary forces. There are precedents for this too. Without the Indian Army, Britain's empire would have suffered from a chronic manpower deficit. India was, as Lord Salisbury memorably remarked, "an English barrack in the Oriental Seas from which we may draw any number of troops without paying for them."[12] The British Empire relied heavily on its colonies to provide manpower in wartime: roughly a third and just under a half of total British forces during World War I and World War II, respectively. Having rashly dissolved the Iraqi Army, L. Paul Bremer belatedly came to see that resurrecting it might be his best hope of establishing order and reducing unemployment. The alternative, as we have seen, is to go begging to the UN or NATO for reinforcements. If Americans themselves are reluctant peace-keepers, they must be the peacekeepers' paymasters, and strike such bargains as the mercenaries of the "international community" may demand.

Of the three deficits, however, it is the third that may prove the most difficult to overcome—namely, the attention deficit that seems to be inherent in the American political system and that already threatens to call a premature halt to reconstruction in both Iraq and Afghanistan.[13] This is not intended as a term of abuse. The problem is systemic; it is the way the political process militates against farsighted leadership. In the words of retired General Anthony Zinni:

> There is a fundamental question that goes beyond the military. It's, "What is our obligation to the world?" We preach about values, democracy, human rights, but we haven't convinced the American people to pony up. . . . There's no leadership that steps up and says, "This is the right thing to do." . . . That's the basic problem. . . . There's got to be the political will and support for these things. We should believe that a stable world is a better place for us. If you had a policy and a forward-leaning engagement strategy, the

> U.S. would make a much greater difference to the world. It would intervene earlier and pick fights better.[14]

But a "forward-leaning engagement strategy" is much easier for a soldier to imagine than for an elected politician. It is not just that first-term American presidents have only two and a half years in office before the issue of securing reelection begins to loom. It is the fact that even sooner, midterm congressional elections can have the effect of emasculating their legislative program. It is the fact that American politics operates on three tiers simultaneously: the national, the state and the local. How could Californians be expected to pay full attention to the problems of nation building in Baghdad in the summer of 2003, when a self-selected mob of amateur politicians was noisily bidding to recall their incumbent governor? It is the fact that the federal executive itself is anything but a homogeneous entity. Interdepartmental rivalry is of course the norm in most human institutions of any size. But there were times in 2003 when the complete absence of coordination among the Defense Department, the State Department and the Treasury—to say nothing of the Commerce Department, the trade representative, the U.S. Agency for International Development and the host of institutions now notionally concerned with "homeland security"—recalled the worst "polycracy" of Wihelmine Germany.[15] The presidency is of course an elected rather than a hereditary office, but its recent incumbents have sometimes appeared to conduct business in the style of the last German kaiser, allowing policy to be determined by interagency competition rather than forging a sense of collective responsibility. Small wonder so many American interventions abroad have the spasmodic, undiplomatic quality of Wilhelm II's *Weltpolitik*. Imperial Germany too practiced what Michael Ignatieff has called imperialism in a hurry. It too was "impatient for quick results."[16]

Unlike the kaiser's Germany, however, the United States disclaims any interest in acquiring new "places in the sun." Its conquests are not merely temporary; they are not even regarded as conquests. The Victorian historian J. R. Seeley famously joked that the British had built their empire "in a fit of absence of mind." Americans, however, have gone one better; here absent-mindedness has become full-blown myopia. Few people outside the United States today doubt the existence of an American empire; that America is imperialistic is a truism in the eyes of most educated Europeans.[17] But as the theologian Reinhold Niebuhr noted as long ago as 1960, Americans persist in "frantically avoiding recognition of the imperialism [they] in fact exercise."[18]

Does imperial denial matter? The answer is that it does. Successful empire is seldom solely based on coercion; there must be some economic dividends for the ruled as well as the rulers, if only to buy the loyalty of indigenous elites, and these dividends need to be sustained for a significant length of time. The trouble with an empire in denial is that it tends to make two mistakes when it chooses to intervene in the affairs of lesser states. The first may be to allocate insufficient resources to the nonmilitary aspects of the project.[19] The second, and the more serious, is to attempt economic and political transformation in an unrealistically short time frame. As I write, the United States would seem to be making the second of these mistakes in both Iraq and Afghanistan. By insisting—and apparently intending—that they will remain in Iraq only until a democratic government can be established "and not a day longer," American spokespeople have unintentionally created a further disincentive for local people to cooperate with them. Who in these countries can feel confident that if he lends support to American initiatives, he will not lay himself open to the charge of collaboration as soon as the Americans go? "If the people of the Balkans realized America would be there," General John Shalikashvili remarked in the late 1990s, "it would be great. . . . Why is it such a crime to suggest a similar longevity [to the occupations of West Germany and Japan] in Bosnia and Kosovo?"[20] The answer is a political one. Today's GIs must be brought home, and soon.

These two points help explain why this vastly powerful economy, with its extraordinary military capability, has had such a very disappointing record when it has sought to bring about changes of political regime abroad. The worst failures—in Haiti, Cuba and Vietnam—were due, above all, to this fatal combination of inadequate resources for nonmilitary purposes and a truncated time horizon. It would be a tragedy if the same process were to repeat itself in the Balkans, Afghanistan and Iraq. But not a surprise. . .

The Terminator

The paradox of globalization is that as the world becomes more integrated, so power becomes more diffuse. Thanks to the dynamism of international capitalism, all but the poorest people in the world have significantly more purchasing power than their grandfathers dared dream of. The means of production were never more productive or—as China and India achieve their belated economic takeoffs—more widely shared. Thanks to the spread of democracy, a majority of people in the world now have markedly more political power than their grandfathers. The democratic means of election were never more widely accepted as the optimal form of government. The means of education too are accessible in most countries to much larger shares of the population than was the case two or three generations ago; more people than ever can harness their own brainpower. All these changes mean that the old monopolies on which power was traditionally based—monopolies on wealth, political office and knowledge—have in large measure been broken up. Unfortunately, thanks to the proliferation of modern means of destruction, the power to inflict violence has also become more evenly distributed. Firepower has also been shared out as never before.

Power, let us not forget, is not just about being able to buy whatever you want; that is mere wealth. Power is about being able to get whatever you want at below the market price. It is about being able to get people to perform services or part with goods that they would not ordinarily offer to sell at any price. For empires, those ambitious states that seek to exert power beyond their own borders, power depends on both the resolve of the masters and the consent of the subjects. Yet power diminishes as it is shared. One country with one nuclear bomb is more powerful, if the rest of the world has none, than a country with a thousand nuclear bombs, if everyone else has one.

Notes

1. Thomas Wolfe, *Look Homeward, Angel*, p. 5.
2. See Johnson, "America's New Empire for Liberty."
3. For a different account of the differences, see O'Brien, "Governance of Globalization."
4. For a skeptical answer, see Jowitt, "Rage, Hubris and Regime Change." See also Simes, "Reluctant Empire."
5. "The Price of Profligacy," *Economist*, September 20, 2003.
6. At the time of writing, foreign central banks' holdings of U.S. Treasury and "quasi-governmental agency" bonds for the first time exceeded $1 trillion: Päivi Munter and Jenny Wiggins, "Treasury Holdings Top $1,000bn," *Financial Times*, November 11, 2003.
7. The interest rate on a fixed-rate fifteen-year mortgage rose from 4.5 percent to 6.4 percent between the spring and summer of 2003: "Stormy Summer," *Economist*, August 9, 2003.
8. "Flying on One Engine," *Economist*, September 20, 2003.
9. In the words of Nouriel Roubini, "Either you want the dollar to depreciate against Asian currencies or you want to maintain low interest rates. You can't have it both ways. It just doesn't add up": quoted in "Gambling with the Dollar," *Washington Post*, September 24, 2003. See also Graham Turner, "The Fed Has Not Avoided Danger," *Financial Times*, June 30, 2003; John Plender, "On a Wing and a Prayer," *Financial Times*, July 3, 2003.
10. Stephen Cecchetti, "America's Job Gap Difficult to Close," *Financial Times*, October 1, 2003.
11. Robert Longley, "U.S. Prison Population Tops 2 Million," http://usgovinfo.about.com/cs/censusstatistic/a/aaprisonpop.htm. One in twenty American men has now spent some time behind bars; for black men the ratio is one in six. If penal policy continues unchanged, more than one in ten of boys born in 2001 will go to jail at some point in their lives: "In the Can," *Economist*, August 23, 2003.
12. Andrew and Kanya-Forstner, *France Overseas*, p. 13.
13. In the very apt words of Tom Friedman, "America is in an imperial role here, now. Our security and standing in the world ride on our getting Iraq right. If the Bush team has something more important to do, I'd like to know about it. Iraq can still go wrong for a hundred Iraqi reasons, but let's make sure it's not because America got bored, tired or distracted:" "Bored with Baghdad Already," *New York Times*, May 18, 2003.
14. Priest, *Mission*, p. 117.
15. Forman et al. *United States in a Global Age*, p. 16f.
16. Ignatieff, *Empire Lite*, p. 115. In Ignatieff's words (p. 90): "Effective imperial power also requires controlling the subject people's sense of time, convincing them that they will be ruled forever. The illusion of permanence was one secret of the British Empire's long survival. Empires cannot be maintained and national interests cannot be secured over the long term by a people always looking for the exit." This is precisely right. See also ibid., p. 113f.
17. See, e.g., Pierre Hassner, *The United States: The Empire of Force or the Force of Empire*, Institute for Security Studies of the European Union Chaillot Paper, 54, September 2002.
18. Quoted in Bacevich, *American Empire*, p. 243.
19. Matthews, "Hard Part," p. 51.
20. Priest, *Mission*, p. 57.

Bibliography

Andrew, Christopher M., and A. S. Kanya-Forstner, *France Overseas: The Great War and the Climax of French Imperial Expansion* (London, 1981).

Bacevich, Andrew J., *American Empire: The Realities and Consequences of U.S. Diplomacy* (Cambridge, Mass./London, 2002).

Forman, Shepard; Princeton Lyman and Stewart Patrick, *The United States in a Global Age: The Case for Multilateral Engagement* (New York, 2002).

Ignatieff, Michael, *Empire Lite: Nation-building in Bosnia, Kosovo and Afghanistan* (London, 2003).

Johnson, Paul, "America's New Empire for Liberty," *Hoover Digest*, 4 (2003), pp. 8– 13.

Jowitt, Ken, "Rage, Hubris and Regime Change," *Policy Review*, 118 (April and May 2003), pp. 33– 43.

Matthews, Jessica Tuchman, "Now for the Hard Part," *Foreign Policy* (July 2003), p. 51.

O'Brien, Patrick Karl, "The Governance of Globalization: The Political Economy of Anglo-American Hegemony," *CESifo Working Paper*, 1023 (September 2003).

Priest, Dana, *The Mission: Waging War and Keeping Peace with America's Military* (New York, 2003).

Simes, Dimitri K., "America's Imperial Dilemma," *Foreign Affairs*, 82, 6 (November– December 2003), pp. 91– 102.

Wolfe, Thomas, *Look Homeward, Angel: A Story of the Buried Life* (New York, 1970 [1929]).

ARTICLE 8.6

Incoherent Empire

Michael Mann

Political sociologist Michael Mann does not believe that the world is dominated by the United States. He argues that power is not unified but divided into different *dimensions,* notably military, economic, and political. Thought about in this way, a more complex picture emerges. Although the United States indisputably ranks at the top in terms of military power, it is much lower in the league tables when it comes to economic and political power. Hence, in Mann's view, American dominance rests on relatively weak foundations, for military dominance cannot be substituted for other sources of power.

Critically analyze and evaluate Mann's argument. Are the different forms of power completely unrelated? Are there ever instances where it makes sense to regard military, economic, and political power as reinforcing each other? How might one arbitrate among conflicting approaches, such as those developed with other selections in this chapter?

The Economic Back-Seat Driver

> Economic strength at home and abroad is the foundation of America's hard and soft power. Earlier enemies learned that America is the arsenal of democracy; today's enemies will learn that America is the economic engine for freedom, opportunity and development.

So declared U.S. Trade Representative Robert Zoellick, nine days after 9-11. But is it true?

The American economy is indeed formidable. World War II left it with half the world's production capacity and its reserve currency. The U.S. was able to appoint the director-generals of the World Bank and was given the only bloc vote in the IMF big enough to veto any policy initiative. American multinational corporations marched over the world.

But then the European and Japanese economies revived, and other East Asian economies developed. The U.S. economy remains the main engine of global growth, though nowadays this owes more to the massive consumption of its citizens than to leadership in productive industries. There is a slight leadership in high-tech communications and bio-technology, but not in manufacturing technology as a whole. In its overall volume of production and trade the U.S. is only one of three roughly equal economic blocs, level with the European Union, somewhat ahead of Japan/East Asia. Nor can the U.S. act unilaterally in bodies like the WTO, the G8, and other global organizations of economic coordination.

The decline of communism strengthened rival regional blocs more than it did the U.S. Russia's economic links with Europe are stronger than with the U.S. In 2002 37 percent of Russian trade was with the European Union, compared to only 5 percent with the U.S. In fact, the U.S. ranked below two individual EU countries, Germany and the Netherlands. The U.S. has 16 percent of foreign investment in Russia, slightly below Germany's and well below the combined EU total. China's main partners are Chinese expatriate business in the rest of Asia, and then Japan, with the U.S. and the EU level in third place. The former communist powers have tighter links with their neighbors than with the U.S. So any hegemony in production and trade would be more accurately called "Northern." It is the three Northern blocs which collectively dominate the world economy, providing over 80 percent of world production, trade and finance, and over 95 percent of its R&D. On the basis of its own productive engine, the U.S. could afford perhaps twice the military effort of Britain and France combined, but less than the combined EU. The U.S. presently spends much more than that.

It is finance which keeps the U.S. in a league of its own. Though the U.S. came off the gold standard in 1973, the dollar remains the world's reserve currency,

---

Michael Mann, *Incoherent Empire* (London: Verso, 2003): 49–51, 74–76. Reprinted by permission of Verso Books.

while the value of Wall Street trading is almost two-thirds that of the whole world's stock markets. Peter Gowan appropriately calls the international monetary system the "Dollar/Wall Street Regime." Since values are ultimately denominated in dollars, much of other nations' reserves and savings are held in dollars, for this is the safest currency. This security means it offers only low interest rates. The world invests through Wall Street in the U.S. economy, allowing American consumers to amass large debts and American governments to finance their massive trade and budget deficits. This means that the poorer countries subsidize the American economy far more than they ever receive in U.S. development aid. The U.S. is the biggest debtor nation, a sign not of weakness but of strength, giving it a unique degree of financial freedom. Finance, seemingly so transnational as it races around the world, actually carries an American passport.[1] Foreign investors provide most of the cash behind military strike-power. What could be more convenient for Americans?

But it would not last if the rest of world got so unhappy with the U.S. that its investors withdrew their savings. And they are largely held in securities, bonds and equities which can be easily liquidated. Japanese holders of American government bonds are crucial; so are the OPEC oil producers who denominate their sales in dollars. Foreign investors would only move out of the dollar and the U.S. if they lost confidence in the U.S. economy or U.S. ability to guarantee global economic and geopolitical stability. But as Robert Brenner has shown, neither the U.S. nor the global economy has been in very good health recently. For decades there has been an excess of global manufacturing capacity and production, reducing real profit levels. During the 1990s this was masked by financial dealings which generated the hi-tech stock-market bubble. When that bubble burst, crisis resulted. This was strongest in the U.S., which was also rocked by revelations that some of its major corporations, like Enron and WorldCom, had routinely falsified their book values, assisted by major accountancy firms like Arthur Andersen. U.S. corporations no longer seemed quite as predictable investments. U.S. equity values are falling, and this also had a knock-on effect on U.S. bond markets. This is a structural problem, not just a problem of a few criminals, since it results from the dominance of finance over productive capitalism in the U.S.[2] Indeed, the first signs of loss of confidence came as equity flows into the U.S. sharply declined from 2000 onward. The dollar weakened against the euro by about 20 percent, tax revenues declined, and fiscal deficits grew.

This is a problem for the entire global economy. As Brenner notes, solutions would have to be multilateral, involving coordination among the U.S., Europe and Japan. Obviously, American unilateral militarism cannot help this, especially if it is costly. Add a major war and American overstretch might begin. In the first 15 months of the Bush administration $150 billion went on new military spending, over and above the inherited annual budget of $329 billion. Later wars against terrorism and in Afghanistan cost about $2.5 billion per month. The 1991 Gulf War cost $80 billion in today's dollars, but the allies picked up 80 percent of the tab.[3]

The U.S. and Britain have to pick up the tab for the 2003 invasion of Iraq. Official estimates of its cost began at around $50 billion, then rose closer to $100 billion. Lawrence Lindsey, then chief economic advisor to the President, said it might cost up to $200 billion. He was fired, but he was probably right if we include the aftermath as well as the invasion itself. Iraq might be a second Vietnam in its impact on the American economy. The economic engine was not designed for this. Markets run on confidence and the U.S. does not control them, for this is capitalism . . .

Conclusion: A Greater Danger?

The U.S. productive engine remains formidable, the global financial system providing its fuel. But the U.S. is only a Back-seat driver since it cannot directly control either foreign investors or foreign economies. It has very limited powers over the economies of the North or other big economies, like Russia, China and India. Elsewhere in the South structural adjustment programs and trade agreements pressure though they do not actually drive their economies. Occasionally, the driver jumps into the front seat. The African Growth and Opportunity Act of 2000 contained a clause requiring participating African countries not to oppose U.S. foreign policy. This was used in late 2002 to get African support within the UN for an invasion of Iraq—though Mauritius had to dismiss its ambassador who still refused to sign on! The dollar also exacts indirect imperial tribute. In principle, the world is free to withdraw its subsidies to the U.S., but unless the U.S. really alienates the world *and* over-stretches its economy, this is unlikely. For the moment, the U.S. can finance substantial imperial activity. It does so carefully, spending billions on its strategic allies, however unworthy and oppressive they may be.

These are substantial imperial powers. Most states go along with American instructions most of the time. But they dug in and resisted over the invasion of Iraq. In February and March 2003 the U.S. tried all its economic carrots and sticks to win a majority of the Security Council members to its side, but failed. Chile, Mexico, Pakistan, Guinea, Angola and Cameroon all seemed to refuse to vote for the invasion. Perhaps some did not trust the U.S. to keep its promises either. Many promises of aid made to countries at the time of the 1991 UN vote over Iraq were not kept. Indeed, the first small tranche of aid promised 18 months ago to Pakistan (for support over Afghanistan) was only handed over in early March 2003 just as the U.S. was trying to win all their votes. An administration which is trying to cut taxes while waging war will not be able to hand out much cash around the world. This back-seat driver will not pay for the gas. It is difficult to build an Empire without spending money.

Other Northern countries are complicit in the exploitation of the South. They give more aid and criticize the U.S. at the margins. They are skeptical of neoliberalism and run their own economies on more social democratic or corporatist lines. But their business classes are happy to hide behind the U.S. and let it take the blowback. Yet the U.S. must be wary of alienating the other wealthy and big countries, for their investments in the U.S. ultimately subsidize its more direct imperial powers. The Back-seat driver would then see the automobile being steered in a direction it did not like.

This is all hypothetical, of course. But the idea that this is *benevolent* economic imperialism is not correct. Intentions may often be benevolent, and Americans may believe the rhetoric that neo-liberalism works—indeed that free trade and free capital flows are a part of freedom itself. But reality differs. The U.S. aid program is negligible and subordinated to strategic military goals. Neo-liberalism does not bring development to the poorest parts of the world, and it is biased toward the interests of the U.S., the North and the world's wealthy classes. To describe this as benevolent would be self-delusion or hypocrisy. This is not good against evil. On balance it tilts the other way according to most views of morality.

It could be more benevolent. The Millennium Challenge Fund seems the most promising initiative introduced by the administration of Bush the Younger. It could potentially offer the basis for an ambitious, benevolent policy of world development. Increase it tenfold, add more social programs and labor codes into it, and also into IMF and World Bank structural adjustment programs. Then compromise more sympathetically toward poor countries on protection and free trade. This would bring more economic growth to the world, and so would indirectly benefit the U.S. economy itself. But if the U.S. continues as at present, it creates a greater potential danger. If it remains the protector of rich and oppressive states, landlords and corporations, if it subordinates its aid program to bribes for oppressive allies, then it will incur increasing global hostility.

The *only* delegate to get jeered, slow handclapped and heckled at the Johannesburg Earth Summit Conference in September 2002 was not some oppressive dictator, nor even some stony-hearted corporate CEO. It was Colin Powell, representing the United States of America. President Bush had not dared attend, but imagine what they would have done to Donald Rumsfeld! Since the poor lack power resources, the U.S. might ride roughshod over them. But it should expect most of them to drag their heels on matters which benefit the U.S. alone, like Security Council votes. And it should expect some of them to hit back, a few of them armed with the weapons of the weak in the name of the poor and the oppressed of the world. To a degree, the U.S. would have deserved it. Poverty does not create terrorism, though oppression does. But poverty is the swamp in which oppression, ideologies of resistance, and mass support for terrorism breed.

Notes

1. Peter Gowan, *The Global Gamble. Washington's Faustian Bid for World Dominance*, London: Verso, 1999.
2. Robert Brenner, *The Boom and the Bubble. The U.S. in the World Economy*, London: Verso, 2002. Such American fragility is also emphasized by Emmanuel Todd in *Après l'Empire*, Paris: Gallimard, 2002, ch. 4.
3. Figures from *Arms Trade Resources Group*, *www.tompaine.com/feature.cfm/ID/6504/*.

ARTICLE 8.7

The Soft Underbelly of American Primacy

Tactical Advantages of Terror

Richard K. Betts

Military analyst Richard Betts argues that terrorism is not simply blind and purposeless; instead, it is a rational—if evil—response to "American global primacy. . . . To groups like al Qaeda, the United States is the enemy because American military power dominates their world, supports corrupt governments in their countries, and backs Israelis against Muslims; American cultural power insults their religion and pollutes their societies; and American economic power makes all these intrusions and desecrations possible."

Contrary to assertions in the selections by Panitch and Gindin, and Roy, in this chapter, Betts claims that U.S. primacy is relatively recent: it originated only following the implosion of the Soviet Union in the late 1980s. At that point, a bipolar world, in which the United States was one of the two leading players, was replaced by a unipolar world dominated by the United States. However, cautions Betts, the attacks of September 11 demonstrate that primacy is not equivalent to invulnerability.

What is the relationship between Betts's analysis, focusing on the issue of U.S. military dominance, and those of selections in this chapter that analyze economic and political aspects of the U.S. position in the world?

> In given conditions, action and reaction can be ridiculously out of proportion. . . . One can obtain results monstrously in excess of the effort. . . . Let's consider this auto smash-up. . . . The driver lost control at high speed while swiping at a wasp which had flown in through a window and was buzzing around his face. . . . The weight of a wasp is under half an ounce. Compared with a human being, the wasp's size is minute, its strength negligible. Its sole armament is a tiny syringe holding a drop of irritant, formic acid. . . . Nevertheless, that wasp killed four big men and converted a large, powerful car into a heap of scrap.
>
> —Eric Frank Russell[1]

To grasp some implications of the new first priority in U.S. foreign policy, it is necessary to understand the connections among three things: the imbalance of power between terrorist groups and counterterrorist governments; the reasons that groups choose terror tactics; and the operational advantage of attack over defense in the interactions of terrorists and their opponents. On

September 11, 2001, Americans were reminded that the overweening power that they had taken for granted over the past dozen years is not the same as omnipotence. What is less obvious but equally important is that the power is itself part of the cause of terrorist enmity and even a source of U.S. vulnerability.

There is no consensus on a definition of "terrorism," mainly because the term is so intensely pejorative.[2] When defined in terms of tactics, consistency falters, because most people can think of some "good" political cause that has used the tactics and whose purposes excuse them or at least warrant the group's designation as freedom fighters rather than terrorists. Israelis who call the Khobar Towers bombers of 1996 terrorists might reject that characterization for the Irgun, which did the same thing to the King David Hotel in 1946, or some Irish Americans would bridle at equating IRA bombings in Britain with Tamil Tiger bombings in Sri Lanka. Anticommunists labeled the Vietcong terrorists (because they engaged in combat out of uniform and assassinated local officials), but opponents of the Saigon government did not. Nevertheless, a functional definition is more sensible than one conditioned on the identity of the perpetrators. For this article, terrorism refers to the illegitimate, deliberate killing of civilians for purposes of punishment or coercion. This holds in abeyance the questions of whether deliberate killing of civilians can ever be legitimate or killing soldiers can be terrorism.

In any case, for all but the rare nihilistic psychopath, terror is a means, not an end in itself. Terror tactics are usually meant to serve a strategy of coercion.[3] They are a use of force designed to further some substantive aim. This is not always evident in the heat of rage felt by the victims of terror. Normal people find it hard to see instrumental reasoning behind an atrocity, especially when recognizing the political motives behind terrorism might seem to make its illegitimacy less extreme. Stripped of rhetoric, however, a war against terrorism must mean a war against political groups who choose terror as a tactic.

American global primacy is one of the causes of this war. It animates both the terrorists' purposes and their choice of tactics. To groups like al Qaeda, the United States is the enemy because American military power dominates their world, supports corrupt governments in their countries, and backs Israelis against Muslims; American cultural power insults their religion and pollutes their societies; and American economic power makes all these intrusions and desecrations possible. Japan, in contrast, is not high on al Qaeda's list of targets, because Japan's economic power does not make it a political, military, and cultural behemoth that penetrates their societies.

Political and cultural power makes the United States a target for those who blame it for their problems. At the same time, American economic and military

---

Richard K. Betts, "The Soft Underbelly of American Primacy: Tactical Advantages of Terror," *Political Science Quarterly* 117, no. 1 (Spring 2002); excerpts. Present version reprinted from Richard K. Betts, ed., *Conflict after the Cold War: Arguments on Causes of War and Peace,* second ed. (New York: Pearson, 2005), pp. 530–527, 533–536.

power prevents them from resisting or retaliating against the United States on its own terms. To smite the only superpower requires unconventional modes of force and tactics that make the combat cost exchange ratio favorable to the attacker. This offers hope to the weak that they can work their will despite their overall deficit in power.

Primacy on the Cheap

The United States has enjoyed military and political primacy (or hegemony, unipolarity, or whatever term best connotes international dominance) for barely a dozen years. Those who focus on the economic dimension of international relations spoke of American hegemony much earlier, but observers of the strategic landscape never did. For those who focus on national security, the world before 1945 was multipolar, and the world of the Cold War was bipolar. After 1945 the United States had exerted hegemony within the First World and for a while over the international economy. The strategic competition against the Second World, however, was seen as a titanic struggle between equal politicomilitary coalitions and a close-run thing until very near the end. Only the collapse of the Soviet pole, which coincided fortuitously with renewed relative strength of the American economy, marked the real arrival of U.S. global dominance.

The novelty of complete primacy may account for the thoughtless, indeed innocently arrogant way in which many Americans took its benefits for granted. Most who gave any thought to foreign policy came implicitly to regard the entire world after 1989 as they had regarded Western Europe and Japan during the past half-century: partners in principle but vassals in practice. The United States would lead the civilized community of nations in the expansion and consolidation of a liberal world order. Overwhelming military dominance was assumed to be secure and important across most of the domestic political spectrum.

Liberal multilateralists conflated U.S. primacy with political globalization, indeed, conflated ideological American nationalism with internationalist altruism.[4] They assumed that U.S. military power should be used to stabilize benighted countries and police international violence, albeit preferably camouflaged under the banner of institutions such as the United Nations, or at least NATO. They rejected the idea that illiberal impulses or movements represented more than a retreating challenge to the West's mission and its capacity to extend its values worldwide.

Conservative unilateralists assumed that unrivaled power relieved the United States of the need to cater to the demands of others. When America acted strategically abroad, others would have to join on its terms or be left out of the action. The United States should choose battles, avoid entanglements in incompetent polities, and let unfortunates stew in their own juice. For both multilateralists and nationalists, the issue was whether the United States would decide to make an effort for world welfare, not whether a strategic challenge could threaten its truly vital interests. (Colloquial depreciation of the adjective notwithstanding, literally vital U.S. interests are those necessary to life.)

For many, primacy was confused with invulnerability. American experts warned regularly of the danger of catastrophic terrorism—and Osama bin Laden explicitly declared war on the United States in his *fatwa* of February 1998. But the warnings did not register seriously in the consciousness of most people. Even some national security experts felt stunned when the attacks occurred on September 11. Before then, the American military wanted nothing to do with the mission of "homeland defense," cited the Posse Comitatus act to suggest that military operations within U.S. borders would be improper, and argued that homeland defense should be the responsibility of civilian agencies or the National Guard. The services preferred to define the active forces' mission as fighting and winning the nation's wars—as if wars were naturally something that happened abroad—and homeland defense involved no more than law enforcement, managing relief operations in natural disasters, or intercepting ballistic missiles outside U.S. airspace. Only in America could the nation's armed forces think of direct defense of national territory as a distraction.

Being Number One seemed cheap. The United States could cut the military burden on the economy by half after the Cold War (from 6 percent to 3 percent of GNP) yet still spend almost five times more than the combined military budgets of all potential enemy states. And this did not count the contributions of rich U.S. allies.[5] Of course the margin in dollar terms does not translate into a comparable quantitative margin in manpower or equipment, but that does not mean that a purchasing power parity estimate would reduce the implied gap in combat capability. The overwhelming qualitative superiority of U.S. conventional forces cuts in the other direction. Washington was also able to plan, organize, and fight a major war in 1991 at negligible cost in blood or treasure. Financially, nearly 90 percent of the bills for the war against Iraq were paid by allies. With fewer than 200 American battle deaths, the cost in blood was far lower than almost anyone had imagined it could be. Less than a decade later, Washington waged another war, over Kosovo, that cost no U.S. combat casualties at all.

In the one case where costs in casualties exceeded the apparent interests at stake—Somalia in 1993—Washington quickly stood down from the fight. This became the reference point for vulnerability: the failure of an operation that was small, far from home, and elective. Where material interests required strategic engagement, as in the oil-rich Persian Gulf, U.S. strategy could avoid costs by exploiting its huge advantage in conventional capability. Where conventional dominance proved less exploitable, as in Somalia, material interests did not require strategic engagement. Where the United States could not operate militarily with impunity, it could choose not to operate.

Finally, power made it possible to let moral interests override material interests where some Americans felt an intense moral concern, even if in doing so they claimed, dubiously, that the moral and material stakes coincided. To some extent this happened in Kosovo, although the decision to launch that war apparently flowed from overoptimism about how quickly a little bombing would lead Belgrade to capitulate. Most notably, it happened in the Arab-Israeli conflict. For more than three decades after the 1967 Six Day War, the United States supported Israel diplomatically, economically, and militarily against the Arabs, despite the fact that doing so put it on the side of a tiny country of a few million people with no oil, against more than ten times as many Arabs who controlled over a third of the world's oil reserves.

This policy was not just an effect of primacy, since the U.S.–Israel alignment began in the Cold War. The salience of the moral motive was indicated by the fact that U.S. policy proceeded despite the fact that it helped give Moscow a purchase in major Arab capitals such as Cairo, Damascus, and Baghdad. Luckily for the United States, however, the largest amounts of oil remained under the control of the conservative Arab states of the Gulf. In this sense the hegemony of the United States within the anticommunist world helped account for the policy. That margin of power also relieved Washington of the need to make hard choices about disciplining its client. For decades the United States opposed Israeli settlement of the West Bank, terming the settlements illegal; yet in all that time the United States never demanded that Israel refrain from colonizing the West Bank as a condition for receiving U.S. economic and military aid.[6] Washington continued to bankroll Israel at a higher per capita rate than any other country in the world, a level that has been indispensable to Israel, providing aid over the years that now totals well over $100 billion in today's dollars.[7] Although this policy enraged some Arabs and irritated the rest, U.S. power was great enough that such international political costs did not outweigh the domestic political costs of insisting on Israeli compliance with U.S. policy.

Of course, far more than subsidizing Israeli occupation of Palestinian land was involved in the enmity of Islamist terrorists toward the United States. Many of the other explanations, however, presuppose U.S. global primacy. When American power becomes the arbiter of conflicts around the world, it makes itself the target for groups who come out on the short end of those conflicts.

Primacy and Asymmetric Warfare

The irrational evil of terrorism seems most obvious to the powerful. They are accustomed to getting their way with conventional applications of force and are not as accustomed as the powerless to thinking of terror as the only form of force that might make their enemies do their will. This is why terrorism is the premier form of "asymmetric warfare," the Pentagon buzzword for the type of threats likely to confront the United States in the post–Cold War world.[8] Murderous tactics may become instrumentally appealing by default—when one party in a conflict lacks other military options.

Resort to terror is not necessarily limited to those facing far more powerful enemies. It can happen in a conventional war between great powers that becomes a total war, when the process of escalation pits whole societies against each other and shears away civilized restraints. That is something seldom seen, and last seen over a half-century ago. One does not need to accept the tendentious position that allied strategic bombing in World War II constituted terrorism to recognize that the British and Americans did systematically assault the urban population centers of Germany and Japan. They did so in large part because precision bombing of industrial facilities proved ineffective.[9] During the early phase of the Cold War, in turn, U.S. nuclear strategy relied on plans to counter Soviet conventional attack on Western Europe with a comprehensive nuclear attack on communist countries that would have killed hundreds of millions. In the 1950s, Strategic Air Command targeteers even went out of their way to plan "bonus" damage by moving aim points for military targets so that blasts would destroy adjacent towns as well.[10] In both World War II and planning for World War III, the rationale was less to kill civilians per se than to wreck the enemy economies—although that was also one of Osama bin Laden's rationales for the attacks on the World Trade Center.[11] In short, the instrumental appeal of strategic attacks on noncombatants may be easier to understand when one considers that states with legitimate purposes have sometimes resorted to such a strategy. Such a double standard, relaxing prohibitions against targeting noncombatants for the side with legitimate purposes (one's own side), occurs most readily when the enemy is at least a peer competitor threatening vital interests. When one's own primacy is taken for granted, it is easier to revert to a single standard that puts all deliberate attacks against civilians beyond the pale.

In contrast to World War II, most wars are limited—or at least limited for the stronger side when power is grossly imbalanced. In such cases, using terror to coerce is likely to seem the only potentially effective use of force for the weaker side, which faces a choice between surrender or savagery. Radical Muslim zealots cannot expel American power with conventional military means, so they substitute clandestine means of delivery against military targets (such as the Khobar Towers barracks in Saudi Arabia) or high-profile political targets (embassies in Kenya and Tanzania). More than once the line has been attributed to terrorists, "If you will let us lease one of your B-52s, we will use that instead of a truck bomb." The hijacking and conversion of U.S. airliners into kamikazes was the most dramatic means of asymmetric attack.

Kamikaze hijacking also reflects an impressive capacity for strategic judo, the turning of the West's strength against itself.[12] The flip-side of a primacy that diffuses its power throughout the world is that advanced elements of that power become more accessible to its enemies. Nineteen men from technologically backward societies did not have to rely on home-grown instruments to devastate the Pentagon and World Trade Center. They used computers and modern financial procedures with facility, and they forcibly appropriated the aviation technology of the West and used it as a weapon. They not only rebelled against the "soft power" of the United States, they trumped it by hijacking the country's hard power.[13] They also exploited the characteristics of U.S. society associated with soft power—the liberalism, openness, and respect for privacy that allowed them to go freely about the business of preparing the attacks without observation by the state security apparatus. When soft power met the clash of civilizations, it proved too soft.

Strategic judo is also apparent in the way in which U.S. retaliation may compromise its own purpose. The counter offensive after September 11 was necessary, if only to demonstrate to marginally motivated terrorists that they could not hope to strike the United States for free. The war in Afghanistan, however, does contribute to polarization in the Muslim world and to mobilization of potential terrorist recruits. U.S. leaders can say that they are not waging a war against Islam until they are blue in the face, but this will not convince Muslims who already distrust the United States. Success in deposing the Taliban may help U.S. policy by encouraging a bandwagon effect that rallies governments and moderates among the Muslim populace, but there will probably be as many who see the U.S. retaliation as confirming al Qaeda's diagnosis of American evil. Victory in Afghanistan and follow-up operations to prevent al Qaeda from relocating bases of operation to other countries will hurt that organization's capacity to act. The number of young zealots willing to emulate the "martyrdom operation" of the nineteen on September 11, however, is not likely to decline. . . .

Primacy and Policy

September 11 reminded those Americans with a rosy view that not all the world sees U.S. primacy as benign, that primacy does not guarantee security, and that security may now entail some retreats from the economic globalization that some had identified with American leadership. Primacy has two edges—dominance and provocation. Americans can enjoy the dominance but must recognize the risks it evokes. For terrorists who want to bring the United States down, U.S. strategic primacy is a formidable challenge, but one that can be overcome. On balance, Americans have overestimated the benefits of primacy, and terrorists have underestimated them.

For those who see a connection between American interventionism, cultural expansiveness, and support of Israel on one hand, and the rage of groups that turn to terrorism on the other, primacy may seem more trouble than it's worth, and the need to revise policies may seem more pressing. But most Americans have so far preferred the complacent and gluttonous form of primacy to the ascetic, blithely accepting steadily growing dependence on Persian Gulf oil that could be limited by compromises in lifestyle and unconventional energy policies. There have been no groundswells to get rid of SUVs, support the Palestinians, or refrain from promoting Western standards of democracy and human rights in societies where some elements see them as aggression.

There is little evidence that any appreciable number of Americans, elite or mass, see our primacy as provoking terrorism. Rather, most see it as a condition we can choose at will to exploit or not. So U.S. foreign policy has exercised primacy in a muscular way in byways of the post–Cold War world when intervention seemed cheap, but not when doing good deeds threatened to be costly. Power has allowed Washington to play simultaneously the roles of mediator and partisan supporter in the Arab-Israeli conflict. For a dozen years nothing, with the near exception of the Kosovo War, suggested that primacy could not get us out of whatever problems it generated.

How far the United States goes to adapt to the second edge of primacy probably depends on whether stunning damage is inflicted by terrorists again, or September 11 gradually fades into history. If al Qaeda and its ilk are crippled, and some years pass without more catastrophic attacks on U.S. home territory, scar tissue will harden on the soft underbelly, and the positive view of primacy will be reinforced. If the war against terrorism falters, however, and the exercise of power fails to prevent more big incidents, the consensus will crack. Then more extreme policy options will get more attention. Retrenchment and retreat will look more appealing to some, who may believe the words of Sheik Salman al-Awdah, a dissident Saudi religious scholar, who said, "If America just let well enough alone, and got out of their obligations overseas . . . no one would bother them."[14]

More likely, however, would be a more violent reaction. There is no reason to assume that terrorist enemies would let America off the hook if it retreated and would not remain as implacable as ever. Facing inability to suppress the threat through normal combat, covert action, and diplomatic pressure, many Americans would consider escalation to more ferocious strategies. In recent decades, the march of liberal legalism has delegitimized tactics and brutalities that once were accepted, but this delegitimation has occurred only in the context of fundamental security and dominance of the Western powers, not in a situation where they felt under supreme threat. In a situation of that sort, it is foolhardy to assume that American strategy would never turn to tactics like those used against Japanese and German civilians, or by the civilized French in the *sale guerre* in Algeria, or by the Russians in Chechnya in hopes of effectively eradicating terrorists despite astronomical damage to the civilian societies within which they lurk.

This possibility would highlight how terrorists have underestimated American primacy. There is much evidence that even in the age of unipolarity, opponents have mistakenly seen the United States as a paper tiger. For some reason—perhaps wishfully selective perception—they tend to see retreats from Vietnam, Beirut, and Somalia as typical weakness of American will, instead of considering decisive exercises of power in Panama, Kuwait, Kosovo, and now, Afghanistan.[15] As Osama bin Laden said in 1997, the United States left Somalia "after claiming that they were the largest power on earth. They left after some resistance from powerless, poor, unarmed people whose only weapon is the belief in Allah. . . . The Americans ran away."[16]

This apparently common view among those with an interest in pinning America's ears back ignores the difference between elective uses of force and desperate ones. The United States retreated where it ran into trouble helping others, not where it was saving itself. Unlike interventions of the 1990s in Africa, the Balkans, or Haiti, counterterrorism is not charity. With vital material interests involved, primacy unleashed may prove fearsomely potent.

Most likely America will see neither absolute victory nor abject failure in the war against terror. Then how long will a campaign of attrition last and stay popular? If the United States wants a strategy to cut the roots of terrorism, rather than just the branches, will American power be used effectively against the roots? Perhaps, but probably not. This depends of course on which of many possible root causes are at issue. Ironically, one problem is that American primacy itself is one of those roots.

A common assertion is that Third World poverty generates terrorism. While this must certainly be a contributing cause in many cases, there is little evidence that it is either a necessary or sufficient condition. Fundamentalist madrassas might not be full to overflowing if young Muslims had ample opportunities to make money, but the fifteen Saudis who hijacked the flights on September 11 were from one of the most affluent of Muslim countries. No U.S. policy could ever hope to make most incubators of terrorism less poor than Saudi Arabia. Iran, the biggest state sponsor of anti-American terrorism, is also better off than most Muslim countries. Poverty is endemic in the Third World, but terrorism is not.

Even if endemic poverty were the cause, the solution would not be obvious. Globalization generates stratification, creating winners and losers, as efficient societies with capitalist cultures move ahead and others fall behind, or as elite enclaves in some societies prosper while the masses stagnate. Moreover, even vastly increased U.S. development assistance would be spread thin if all poor countries are assumed to be incubators of terrorism. And what are the odds that U.S. intervention with economic aid would significantly reduce poverty? Successes in prompting dramatic economic development by outside assistance in the Third World have occurred, but they are the exception more than the rule.

The most virulent anti-American terrorist threats, however, do not emerge randomly in poor societies. They grow out of a few regions and are concentrated overwhelmingly in a few religiously motivated groups. These reflect political causes—ideological, nationalist, or transnational cultural impulses to militant mobilization—more than economic causes. Economic development in an area where the political and religious impulses remain unresolved could serve to improve the resource base for terrorism rather than undercut it.

A strategy of terrorism is most likely to flow from the coincidence of two conditions: intense political grievance and gross imbalance of power. Either one without the other is likely to produce either peace or conventional war. Peace is probable if power is imbalanced but grievance is modest; the weaker party is likely to live with the grievance. In that situation, conventional use of force appears to offer no hope of victory, while the righteous indignation is not great enough to overcome normal inhibitions against murderous tactics. Conventional war is probable if grievance is intense but power is more evenly balanced, since successful use of respectable forms of force appears possible.[17] Under American primacy, candidates for terrorism suffer from grossly inferior power by definition. This should focus attention on the political causes of their grievance.

How are political root causes addressed? At other times in history we have succeeded in fostering congenial revolutions—especially in the end of the Cold War, as the collapse of the Second World heralded an End of History of sorts.[18] The problem now, however, is the rebellion of anti-Western zealots against the secularist end of history. Remaking the world in the Western image is what Americans assume to be just, natural, and desirable, indeed only a matter of time. But that presumption is precisely what energizes many terrorists' hatred. Secular Western liberalism is not their salvation, but their scourge. Primacy could, paradoxically, remain both the solution and the problem for a long time.[19]

Notes

1. William Wolf in Eric Frank Russell, *Wasp* (London: Victor Gollancz, 2000, originally published 1957), 7.
2. "The word has become a political label rather than an analytical concept." Martha Crenshaw, *Terrorism and International Cooperation* (New York: Institute for East-West Security Studies, 1989); 5.
3. For a survey of types, see Christopher C. Harmon, "Five Strategies of Terrorism," *Small Wars and Insurgencies* 12 (Autumn 2001).
4. Rationalization of national power as altruism resembles the thinking about benign Pax Britannica in the Crowe Memorandum: ". . . the national policy of the insular and naval State is so directed as to harmonize with the general desires and ideals common to all mankind, and more particularly . . . is closely identified with the primary and vital interests of a majority, or as many as possible, of the other nations. . . . England, more than any other non-insular Power, has a direct and positive interest in the maintenance of the independence of nations, and therefore must be the natural enemy of any country threatening the independence of others, and the natural protector of the weaker communities." Eyre Crowe, "Memorandum on the Present State of British Relations with France and Germany," 1 January 1907, in G. P. Gooch and Harold Temperley, eds., *British Documents on the Origins of the War, 1898–1914*, vol. 3: *The Testing of the Entente, 1904–6* (London: His Majesty's Stationery Office, 1928), 402–403.
5. At the end of the twentieth century, the combined military budgets of China, Russia, Iraq, Yugoslavia (Serbia), North Korea, Iran, Libya, Cuba, Afghanistan, and Sudan added up to no more than $60 billion. *The Military Balance, 1999–2000* (London: International Institute for Strategic Studies, 1999), 102, 112, 132, 133, 159, 186, 275.
6. Washington certainly did exert pressure on Israel at some times. The administration of Bush the Elder, for example, threatened to withhold loans for housing construction, but this was a marginal portion of total U.S. aid. There was never a threat to cut off the basic annual maintenance payment of several billion dollars to which Israel became accustomed decades ago.
7. The United States has also given aid to friendly Arab governments—huge amounts to Egypt and some to Jordan. This does not counterbalance the aid to Israel, however, in terms of effects on opinions of strongly anti-Israeli Arabs. Islamists see the regimes in Cairo and Amman as American toadies, complicit in betrayal of the Palestinians.
8. Theoretically, this was anticipated by Samuel P. Huntington in his 1962 analysis of the differences between symmetrical intergovernmental war and asymmetrical antigovernmental war. "Patterns of Violence in World Politics" in Huntington, ed., *Changing Patterns of Military Politics* (New York: Free Press of Glencoe, 1962), 19–21. Some of Huntington's analysis of insurrectionary warfare within states applies as well to transnational terrorism.
9. The Royal Air Force gave up on precision bombing early and focused deliberately on night bombing of German cities, while the Americans continued to try precision daylight bombing. Firestorms in Hamburg, Darmstadt, and Dresden, and less incendiary attacks on other cities, killed several hundred thousand German civilians. Over Japan, the United States quickly gave up attempts at precision bombing when weather made it impractical and deliberately resorted to an incendiary campaign that burned most Japanese cities to the ground and killed at least 300,000 civilians (and perhaps more than

half a million) well before the nuclear attacks on Hiroshima and Nagasaki, which killed another 200,000. Michael S. Sherry, *The Rise of American Air Power. The Creation of Armageddon* (New Haven: Yale University Press, 1987), 260, 413–43.

10. The threat of deliberate nuclear escalation remained the bedrock of NATO doctrine throughout the Cold War, but after the Kennedy administration, the flexible response doctrine made it conditional and included options for nuclear first-use that did not involve deliberate targeting of population centers. In the Eisenhower administration, however, all-out attack on the Soviet bloc's cities was integral to plans for defense of Western Europe against Soviet armored divisions.
11. In a videotape months after the attacks, bin Laden said, "These blessed strikes showed clearly that this arrogant power, America, rests on a powerful but precarious economy, which rapidly crumbled . . . the global economy based on usury, which America uses along with its military might to impose infidelity and humiliation on oppressed people, can easily crumble. . . . Hit the economy, which is the basis of military might. If their economy is finished, they will become too busy to enslave oppressed people. . . . America is in decline; the economic drain is continuing but more strikes are required and the youths must strike the key sectors of the American economy." Videotape excerpts quoted in "Bin Laden's Words: 'America Is in Decline,' the Leader of Al Qaeda Says," *New York Times*, 28 December 2001.
12. This is similar to the concept of political judo discussed in Samuel L. Popkin, "Pacification: Politics and the Village," *Asian Survey* 10 (August 1970); and Popkin, "Internal Conflicts—South Vietnam" in Kenneth N. Waltz and Steven Spiegel, eds., *Conflict in World Politics* (Cambridge, MA: Winthrop, 1971).
13. Soft power is "indirect or cooptive" and "can rest on the attraction of one's ideas or on the ability to set the political agenda in a way that shapes the preferences that others express." It "tends to be associated with intangible power resources such as culture, ideology, and institutions." Joseph S. Nye, Jr., "The Changing Nature of World Power," *Political Science Quarterly* 105 (Summer 1990): 181. See also Nye, *Bound to Lead: The Changing Nature of American Power* (New York: Basic Books, 1990).
14. Quoted in Douglas Jehl, "After Prison, a Saudi Sheik Tempers His Words," *New York Times*, 27 December 2001.
15. See data in the study by Barry M. Blechman and Tamara Cofman Wittes, "Defining Moment: The Threat and Use of Force in American Foreign Policy," *Political Science Quarterly* 114 (Spring 1999).
16. Quoted in Steven Simon and Daniel Benjamin, "America and the New Terrorism," *Survival* 42 (Spring 2000), 69.
17. On why power imbalance is conducive to peace and parity to war, see Geoffrey Blainey, *The Causes of War*, 3rd. ed. (New York: Free Press, 1988), chap. 8.
18. Francis Fukuyama's thesis was widely misunderstood and caricatured. He noted that the Third World remained mired in history and that some developments could lead to restarting history. For the First World, the defeated Second World, and even some parts of the Third World, however, the triumph of Western liberalism could reasonably be seen by those who believe in its worth (as should Americans) as the final stage of evolution through fundamentally different forms of political and economic organization of societies. See Fukuyama, "The End of History?" *National Interest* no. 16 (Summer 1989); and Fukuyama, *The End of History and the Last Man* (New York: Free Press, 1992).
19. The author thanks Robert Jervis for comments on the first draft.

PART FOUR

Globalization from Below

CHAPTER 9

Transnational Contentious Politics, Terrorism, and the Movement for Global Justice

With the exception of Chapter 5, which analyzed work and workers in the global economy, most selections thus far have focused on what might be termed globalization from above, that is, the construction and operation of globalization by political and economic officials in top authoritative positions in the world's power structure. This focus is appropriate, for the decisions of key political officials in national and international governmental agencies, as well as those of executives who direct transnational corporations (TNCs), heavily influence the shape of globalization and deeply affect the lives of billions of people throughout the world. However, a full understanding of globalization requires widening our analysis from a focus on globalization from above to include what might be termed globalization from below. We cannot fully understand history by confining attention to kings, queens, rajahs, sultans, and their courtiers; we need to understand the role of ordinary folk—peasants, serfs, urban dwellers, and the like. Likewise for globalization today.

There is another reason to study globalization from below, and the analogy with studying history can again be instructive. The course of European and world history was changed forever when on July 14, 1789, a crowd stormed the Bastille, a prison in the heart of Paris. Historian Lynn Hunt has observed, "The French Revolution may be said to represent the transition to political and social modernity, the first occasion when the people entered upon the historical stage to remake the political community."[1] In a similar way, "the people" may be said to have burst upon

[1]Lynn Hunt, *Politics, Culture, and Class in the French Revolution* (Berkeley and Los Angeles: University of California Press, 1984), p. 56.

the historical stage of globalization in November 1999. Until that point, globalization was generally regarded as the affair of modern-day kings and queens: that is, governmental leaders, directors of IFIs, and members of the TNC corporate elite. Or at least, this was the general understanding. In November 1999, the World Trade Organization (WTO) convened a meeting in Seattle of economic and financial ministers from member states. The purpose was to ratify agreement on measures to further liberalize international trade. However, two major developments caused the summit to end in stalemate. First, governments of less developed countries balked at the demand that they open their borders to industrialized products from the North unless Northern governments agreed to phase out subsidies to their domestic farmers, the result of which has been to enable Northern farmers to keep the prices of farm produce low and thereby outcompete Southern farmers. The other reason that the WTO's Seattle summit failed was massive demonstrations that immobilized the city: over 50,000 people traveled to Seattle to protest WTO decisions made behind closed doors for the entire world without democratic consultation.

The WTO ministerial meeting at Seattle might be considered the first time that the antiglobalization movement crashed onto the world stage. On the one hand, this impression is misleading, since there had been numerous challenges to neoliberal globalization in the years before Seattle. But, because they occurred in places like Jakarta, Indonesia; Caracas, Venezuela; and Accra, Ghana, their importance (or even existence) was barely reported by media in the United States. Protests against globalization in many less developed countries dated back well over a decade before 1999—provoked by IMF demands that, as a condition for its granting loans, governments in these countries adopt structural adjustment policies including privatizing vital resources like water, cutting social spending, and raising taxes.

After Seattle, however, the Western media were quick to cover antiglobalization protests. Further, such protests occurred aplenty. At virtually every major economic international forum in the following years—Davos, Switzerland; Quebec, Canada; Washington, D.C.; Genoa, Italy—to name a few—there was a repeat performance of Seattle '99. So powerful was this tide of transnational contention that, following worldwide demonstrations on February 15, 2003, protesting the imminent attack on Iraq by a coalition led by the United States, the *New York Times* commented in an editorial, "There are now two superpowers in the world: the U.S. and global public opinion."[2]

The *Times* may have been carried away by the size of the demonstrations to overestimate the power of public opinion. After all, the protests neither deterred the U.S.-led coalition from attacking Iraq in 2003 nor prevented coalition forces from remaining in Iraq years after Saddam's regime was toppled. But the editorial does highlight that ordinary people, and not only those in high positions, can shape globalization.

The chapter in Part Four, as well as the Conclusion, put this issue front and center. They highlight the utility of focusing not simply on globalization from above or globalization from below but on their interaction at local, national, and global levels.

---

[2] *The New York Times*, February 17, 2003.

Consider some theoretical and methodological issues as you read these selections. First, what is the scope of globalization from below? Are all popular struggles in the current era linked to globalization? Or, might one try to construct a continuum in which some struggles are more closely linked than others to globalization? Consider two examples of popular movements that apparently have little to do with globalization: struggles involving violence against women and ethnonationalist struggles, that is, movements—such as the Kurds in Turkey and Iraq or the Basques in Spain—seeking a separate state on the basis of shared ethnic identity. Yet, on closer inspection, even these movements may have links to globalization. Locally based movements protesting violence against women may be influenced by a transnational network of movements focusing on women's rights.

Ethnonationalist movements may also be influenced by the diffusion of ideas across national borders. The idea that ethnic groups are "entitled" to their own state is relatively recent—and ethnonationalist movements may gain support by appealing to the fear that globalization is destroying distinctive national cultures. Yet beware of the danger of finding the influence of globalization wherever one looks. There is a risk of regarding all of current history as a manifestation or production of globalization—or a reaction against it! If everything is globalization, the term becomes so all-encompassing as to lose analytical utility. Thus, it might be preferable to distinguish the extent to which popular struggles are linked to globalization. This procedure thereby treats the influence of globalization as variable and suggests trying to assess the extent of its impact.

What is the normative valence of movements protesting globalization? The mere fact of protesting against globalization is no guarantee of moral excellence—or moral weakness. As you read the selections in these last chapters, evaluate what you think are the strengths and weaknesses of their claims and strategies.

A final methodological issue concerns how to define the boundaries of what to include as movements in this chapter. Not all protests qualify as social movements. It is preferable to reserve the term for movements that have an enduring character, which would exclude a one-time protest, however important that protest might be. A broader term that has been suggested is "contentious politics."[3] This term has the merit of breadth, in that it invites us to distinguish among various kinds of contention. Yet that strength is also problematic, for the concept is so vast as to include unorganized resistance, labor struggles, social movements, and revolutions. In reading the selections in this chapter, think about what are the alternative conceptual boundaries that can be drawn and what term(s) you think best describes the phenomenon or phenomena being studied.

---

[3]For an approach that analyzes a variety of forms of contention, such as strikes, social protest, and revolution, see Doug McAdam, Sidney Tarrow, and Charles Tilly, *Dynamics of Contention* (New York: Cambridge University Press, 2001).

ARTICLE 9.1

Activists Beyond Borders *Advocacy Networks in International Politics*

Margaret E. Keck and Kathryn Sikkink

This selection analyzes a particular form of organizing across national borders: what Margaret Keck and Kathryn Sikkink designate as transnational advocacy networks (TANs). They claim that these networks have arisen to challenge abuses that shock our moral sensibilities and thereby invite advocacy on principled, moral grounds. Examples include issues involving human rights, women's subordinate position, and environmental damage. TANs are effective because the information they disseminate about abuses widens the network of supporters and shames authorities into action. Contrast this with the consumer boycotts described by Naomi Klein in this chapter. Like TANs, these movements also publicize abuses, but the boycotts they organize seek to pressure corporations where it hurts: in their public image and balance sheet (profits).

Which kinds of issues lend themselves to mobilization by TANs? Why do you think one or another form of transnational contention is adopted? How effective have transnational advocacy networks been?

World politics at the end of the twentieth century involves, alongside states, many nonstate actors that interact with each other, with states, and with international organizations. These interactions are structured in terms of networks, and transnational networks are increasingly visible in international politics. Some involve economic actors and firms. Some are networks of scientists and experts whose professional ties and shared causal ideas underpin their efforts to influence policy.[1] Others are networks of activists, distinguishable largely by the centrality of principled ideas or values in motivating their formation.[2] We will call these *transnational advocacy networks*.

Advocacy networks are significant transnationally and domestically. By building new links among actors in civil societies, states, and international organizations, they multiply the channels of access to the international system. In such issue areas as the environment and human rights, they also make international

---

resources available to new actors in domestic political and social struggles. By thus blurring the boundaries between a state's relations with its own nationals and the recourse both citizens and states have to the international system, advocacy networks are helping to transform the practice of national sovereignty. . . .

Scholars have been slow to recognize either the rationality or the significance of activist networks. Motivated by values rather than by material concerns or professional norms, these networks fall outside our accustomed categories. More than other kinds of transnational actors, advocacy networks often reach beyond policy change to advocate and instigate changes in the institutional and principled basis of international interactions. When they succeed, they are an important part of an explanation for changes in world politics. A transnational advocacy network includes those relevant actors working internationally on an issue, who are bound together by shared values, a common discourse, and dense exchanges of information and services.[3] Such networks are most prevalent in issue areas characterized by high value content and informational uncertainty. At the core of the relationship is information exchange. What is novel in these networks is the ability of nontraditional international actors to mobilize information strategically to help create new issues and categories and to persuade, pressure, and gain leverage over much more powerful organizations and governments. Activists in networks try not only to influence policy outcomes, but to transform the terms and nature of the debate. They are not always successful in their efforts, but they are increasingly relevant players in policy debates.

Transnational advocacy networks are proliferating, and their goal is to change the behavior of states and of international organizations. Simultaneously principled and strategic actors, they "frame" issues to make them comprehensible to target audiences, to attract attention and encourage action, and to "fit" with favorable institutional venues.[4] Network actors bring new ideas, norms, and discourses into policy debates, and serve as sources of information and testimony. . .

How Do Transnational Advocacy Networks Work?

Transnational advocacy networks seek influence in many of the same ways that other political groups or social movements do. Since they are not powerful in a traditional sense of the word, they must use the power of their information, ideas, and strategies to alter the information and value contexts within which states make policies. The bulk of what networks do might be termed persuasion or socialization, but neither process is devoid of conflict. Persuasion and socialization often involve not just reasoning with opponents, but also bringing pressure, arm-twisting, encouraging sanctions, and shaming. Audie Klotz's work on norms and apartheid discusses coercion, incentive, and legitimation effects that are often part of a socialization process.[5]

Our typology of tactics that networks use in their efforts at persuasion, socialization, and pressure includes (1) *information politics*, or the ability to quickly and credibly generate politically usable information and move it to where it will have the most impact; (2) *symbolic politics*, or the ability to call upon symbols, actions, or stories that make sense of a situation for an audience that is frequently far away;[6] (3) *leverage politics*, or the ability to call upon powerful actors to affect a situation where weaker members of a network are unlikely to have influence; and (4) *accountability politics*, or the effort to hold powerful actors to their previously stated policies or principles.

A single campaign may contain many of these elements simultaneously. For example, the human rights network disseminated information about human rights abuses in Argentina in the period 1976–83. The Mothers of the Plaza de Mayo marched in circles in the central square in Buenos Aires wearing white handkerchiefs to draw symbolic attention to the plight of their missing children. The network also tried to use both material and moral leverage against the Argentine regime, by pressuring the United States and other governments to cut off military and economic aid, and by efforts to get the UN and the Inter-American Commission on Human Rights to condemn Argentina's human rights practices. Monitoring is a variation on information politics, in which activists use information strategically to ensure accountability with public statements, existing legislation and international standards.

The construction of cognitive frames is an essential component of networks' political strategies. David Snow has called this strategic activity "frame alignment": "by rendering events or occurrences meaningful, frames function to organize experience and guide action, whether individual or collective."[7] "Frame resonance" concerns the relationship between a movement organization's interpretive work and its ability to influence broader public understandings. The latter involve both the frame's internal coherence and its experiential fit with a broader political culture.[8] In recent work, Snow and his colleagues and Sidney Tarrow, in turn, have given frame resonance a historical dimension by joining it to Tarrow's notion of protest cycles.[9] Struggles over meaning and the creation of new frames of meaning occur early in a protest cycle, but over time "a given collective action frame becomes part of the political culture—which is to say, part of the reservoir of symbols from which future movement entrepreneurs can choose."[10]

Network members actively seek ways to bring issues to the public agenda by framing them in innovative ways and by seeking hospitable venues. Sometimes they create issues by framing old problems in new ways; occasionally they help transform other actors' understandings of their identities and their interests. Land use rights in the Amazon, for example, took on an entirely different character and gained quite different allies viewed in a deforestation frame than they did in either social justice or regional development frames. In the 1970s and 1980s many states decided for the first time that promotion of human rights in other countries was a legitimate foreign policy goal and an authentic expression of national interest. This decision came in part from interaction with an emerging global human rights network. We argue that this represents not the victory of morality over self-interest, but a transformed understanding of national interest, possible in part because of structured interactions between state components and networks. This changed understanding cannot be derived solely from changing global and economic conditions, although these are relevant.

Transnational networks normally involve a small number of activists from the organizations and institutions involved in a given campaign or advocacy role. The kinds of pressure and agenda politics in which advocacy networks engage rarely involve mass mobilization, except at key moments, although the peoples whose cause they espouse may engage in mass protest (for example, those ousted from their land in the Narmada dam case).[11] Boycott strategies are a partial exception. Instead of mass mobilization, network activists engage in what Baumgartner and Jones, borrowing from law, call "venue shopping," which relies "more on the dual strategy of the presentation of an image and the search for a more receptive political venue."[12] The recent coupling of indigenous rights and environmental issues is a good example of a strategic venue shift by indigenous activists, who found the environmental arena more receptive to their claims than human rights venues had been.

Information Politics

Information binds network members together and is essential for network effectiveness. Many information exchanges are informal—telephone calls, E-mail and fax communications, and the circulation of newsletters, pamphlets and bulletins. They provide information that would not otherwise be available, from sources that might not otherwise be heard, and they must make this information comprehensible and useful to activists and publics who may be geographically and/or socially distant.[13]

Nonstate actors gain influence by serving as alternate sources of information. Information flows in advocacy networks provide not only facts but testimony—stories told by people whose lives have been affected. Moreover, activists interpret facts and testimony, usually framing issues simply, in terms of right and wrong, because their purpose is to persuade people and stimulate them to act. How does this process of persuasion occur? An effective frame must show that a given state of affairs is neither natural nor accidental, identify the responsible party or parties, and propose credible solutions. These aims require clear, powerful messages that appeal to shared principles, which often have more impact on state policy than advice of technical experts. An important part of the political struggle over information is precisely whether an issue is defined primarily as technical—and thus subject to consideration by "qualified" experts—or as something that concerns a broader global constituency.

Even as we highlight the importance of testimony, however, we have to recognize the mediations involved. The process by which testimony is discovered and presented normally involves several layers of prior translation. Transnational actors may identify what kinds of testimony would be valuable, then ask an NGO in the area to seek out people who could tell those stories. They may filter the testimony through expatriates, through traveling scholars like ourselves, or through the media. There is frequently a huge gap between the story's original telling and the retellings—in its sociocultural context, its instrumental meaning, and even in its language. Local people, in other words, sometimes lose control over their stories in a transnational campaign. How this process of mediation/translation occurs is a particularly interesting facet of network politics.[14]

Networks strive to uncover and investigate problems, and alert the press and policymakers. One activist described this as the "human rights methodology"—"promoting change by reporting facts."[15] To be credible, the information produced by networks must be reliable and well documented. To gain attention, the information must be timely and dramatic. Sometimes these multiple goals of information politics conflict, but both credibility and drama seem to be essential components of a strategy aimed at persuading publics and policymakers to change their minds.

The notion of "reporting facts" does not fully express the way networks strategically use information to frame issues. Networks call attention to issues, or even create issues by using language that dramatizes and draws attention to their concerns. A good example is the recent campaign against the practice of female genital mutilation. Before 1976 the widespread practice of female circumcision in many African and a few Asian and Middle Eastern countries was known outside these regions mainly among medical experts and anthropologists.[16] A controversial campaign, initiated in 1974 by a network of women's and human rights organizations, began to draw wider attention to the issues by renaming the problem. Previously the practice was referred to by technically "neutral" terms such as female circumcision, clitoridectomy, or infibulation. The campaign around female genital "mutilation" raised its salience, literally creating the issue as a matter of public international concern. By renaming the practice the network broke the linkage with male circumcision (seen as a personal medical or cultural decision), implied a linkage with the more feared procedure of castration, and reframed the issue as one of violence against women. It thus resituated the practice as a human rights violation. The campaign generated action in many countries, including France and the United Kingdom, and the UN studied the problem and made a series of recommendations for eradicating certain traditional practices.[17]

Uncertainty is one of the most frequently cited dimensions of environmental issues. Not only is hard information scarce (although this is changing), but any given data may be open to a variety of interpretations. The tropical forest issue is fraught with scientific uncertainty about the role of forests in climate regulation, their regenerative capacity, and the value of undiscovered or untapped biological resources. Environmentalists are unlikely to resolve these questions, and what they have done in some recent campaigns is reframe the issue, calling attention to the impact of deforestation on particular human populations. By doing so, they called for action independent of the scientific data. Human rights activists, baby food campaigners, and women's groups play similar roles, dramatizing the situations of the victims and turning the cold facts into human stories, intended to move people to action. The baby food campaign, for example, relied heavily on public health studies that proved that improper bottle feeding contributed to infant malnutrition and mortality, and that corporate sales promotion was leading to a decline in breast feeding.[18] Network activists repackaged and interpreted this information in dramatic ways designed to promote action: the British development organization War on Want published a pamphlet entitled "The Baby Killers," which the Swiss Third World Action Group translated into German and retitled "Nestlé Kills Babies." Nestlé inadvertently gave activists a prominent public forum when it sued the Third World Action Group for defamation and libel.

Nongovernmental networks have helped legitimize the use of testimonial information along with technical and statistical information. Linkage of the two is crucial, for without the individual cases activists cannot motivate people to seek changed policies. Increasingly, international campaigns by networks take this two-level approach to information. In the 1980s even Greenpeace, which initially had eschewed rigorous research in favor of splashy media events, began to pay more attention to getting the facts right. Both technical information and dramatic testimony help to make the need for action more real for ordinary citizens.

A dense web of north-south exchange, aided by computer and fax communication, means that governments can no longer monopolize information flows as they could a mere half-decade ago. These technologies have had an enormous impact on moving information to and from third world countries, where mail service has often been slow and precarious; they also give special advantages of course, to organizations that have access to them. A good example of the new informational role of networks occurred when U.S. environmentalists pressured President George Bush to raise the issue of gold miners' ongoing invasions of the Yanomami indigenous reserve when Brazilian president Fernando Collor de Mello was in Washington in 1991. Collor believed that he had squelched protest over the Yanomami question by creating major media events out of the dynamiting of airstrips used by gold miners, but network members had current information faxed from Brazil, and they countered his claims with evidence that miners had rebuilt the airstrips and were still invading the Yanomami area.

The central role of information in these issues helps explain the drive to create networks. Information in these issue areas is both essential and dispersed. Nongovernmental actors depend on their access to information to help make them legitimate players. Contact with like-minded groups at home and abroad provides access to information necessary to their work, broadens their legitimacy, and helps to mobilize information around particular policy targets. Most nongovernmental organizations cannot afford to maintain staff people in a variety of countries. In exceptional cases they send staff members on investigation missions, but this is not practical for keeping informed on routine developments. Forging links with local organizations allows groups to receive and monitor information from many countries at a low cost. Local groups, in turn, depend on international contacts to get their information out and to help protect them in their work.

The media is an essential partner in network information politics. To reach a broader audience, networks strive to attract press attention. Sympathetic journalists may become part of the network, but more often network activists cultivate a reputation for credibility with the press, and package their information in a timely and dramatic way to draw press attention.[19]

Symbolic Politics

Activists frame issues by identifying and providing convincing explanations for powerful symbolic events, which in turn become catalysts for the growth of networks. Symbolic interpretation is part of the process of persuasion by which networks create awareness and expand their constituencies. Awarding the 1992 Nobel Peace Prize to Maya activist Rigoberta Menchú and the UN's designation of 1993 as the Year of Indigenous Peoples heightened public awareness of the situation of indigenous peoples in the Americas. Indigenous people's use of 1992, the 500th anniversary of the voyage of Columbus to the Americas, to raise a host of issues well illustrates the use of symbolic events to reshape understandings.[20]

The 1973 coup in Chile played this kind of catalytic role for the human rights community. Because Chile was the symbol of democracy in Latin America, the fact that such a brutal coup could happen there suggested that it could happen anywhere. For activists in the United States, the role of their government in undermining the Allende government intensified the need to take action. Often it is not one event but the juxtaposition of disparate events that makes people change their minds and act. For many people in the United States it was the juxtaposition of the coup in Chile, the war in Vietnam, Watergate, and the Civil Rights Movement that gave birth to the human rights movement. Likewise, dramatic footage of the Brazilian rainforest burning during the hot summer of 1988 in the United States may have convinced many people that global warming and tropical deforestation were serious and linked issues. The assassination of Brazilian rubber tapper leader Chico Mendes at the end of that year crystallized the belief that something was profoundly wrong in the Amazon.

Leverage Politics

Activists in advocacy networks are concerned with political effectiveness. Their definition of effectiveness often includes some policy change by "target actors" such as governments, international financial institutions like the World Bank, or private actors like transnational corporations. In order to bring about policy change, networks need to pressure and persuade more powerful actors. To gain influence the networks seek leverage (the word appears often in the discourse of advocacy organizations) over more powerful actors. By leveraging more powerful institutions, weak groups gain influence far beyond their ability to influence state practices directly. The identification of material or moral leverage is a crucial strategic step in network campaigns.

Material leverage usually links the issue to money or goods (but potentially also to votes in international organizations, prestigious offices, or other benefits). The human rights issue became negotiable because governments or financial institutions connected human rights practices to military and economic aid, or to bilateral diplomatic relations. In the United States, human rights groups got leverage by providing policy-makers with information that convinced them to cut off military and economic aid. To make the issue negotiable, NGOs first had to raise its profile or salience, using information and symbolic politics. Then more powerful members of the network had to link cooperation to something else of value: money, trade, or prestige. Similarly, in the environmentalists' multilateral development bank campaign, linkage of environmental protection with access to loans was very powerful.

Although NGO influence often depends on securing powerful allies, their credibility still depends in part on their ability to mobilize their own members and affect public opinion via the media. In democracies the potential to influence votes gives large membership organizations an advantage over nonmembership organizations in lobbying for policy change; environmental organizations, several of whose memberships number in the millions, are more likely to have this added clout than are human rights organizations.

Moral leverage involves what some commentators have called the "mobilization of shame," where the behavior of target actors is held up to the light of international scrutiny. Network activists exert moral leverage on the assumption that governments value the good opinion of others; insofar as networks can demonstrate that a state is violating international obligations or is not living up to its own claims, they hope to jeopardize its credit enough to motivate a change in policy or behavior. The degree to which states are vulnerable to this kind of pressure varies, and will be discussed further below.

Accountability Politics

Networks devote considerable energy to convincing governments and other actors to publicly change their positions on issues. This is often dismissed as inconsequential change, since talk is cheap and governments sometimes change discursive positions hoping to divert network and public attention. Network activists, however, try to make such statements into opportunities for accountability politics. Once a government has publicly committed itself to a principle—for example, in favor of human rights or democracy—networks can use those positions, and their command of information, to expose the distance between discourse and practice. This is embarrassing to many governments, which may try to save face by closing that distance.

Perhaps the best example of network accountability politics was the ability of the human rights network to use the human rights provisions of the 1975 Helsinki

Accords to pressure the Soviet Union and the governments of Eastern Europe for change. The Helsinki Accords helped revive the human rights movement in the Soviet Union, spawned new organizations like the Moscow Helsinki Group and the Helsinki Watch Committee in the United States, and helped protect activists from repression.[21] The human rights network refered to Moscow's obligations under the Helsinki Final Act and juxtaposed these with examples of abuses. In an illustration of the boomerang effect, human rights activist Yuri Orlov said, "We do not have the means to reach our government. My appeal to Brezhnev probably got as far as the regional KGB office. . . . The crucial question is what means are there for a Soviet citizen to approach his own government, other than indirectly through the governments of other countries."[22]

Domestic structures through which states and private actors can be held accountable to their pronouncements, to the law, or to contracts vary considerably from one nation to another, even among democracies. The centrality of the courts in U.S. politics creates a venue for the representation of diffuse interests that is not available in most European democracies.[23] It also explains the large number of U.S. advocacy organizations that specialize in litigation. The existence of legal mechanisms does not necessarily make them feasible instruments, however; Brazil has had a diffuse interests law granting standing to environmental and consumer advocacy organizations since 1985, but the sluggishness of Brazil's judiciary makes it largely ineffective.

Under What Conditions Do Advocacy Networks Have Influence?

To assess the influence of advocacy networks we must look at goal achievement at several different levels. We identify the following types or stages of network influence: (1) issue creation and agenda setting; (2) influence on discursive positions of states and international organizations; (3) influence on institutional procedures; (4) influence on policy change in "target actors" which may be states, international organizations like the World Bank, or private actors like the Nestlé Corporation; and (5) influence on state behavior.

Networks generate attention to new issues and help set agendas when they provoke media attention, debates, hearings, and meetings on issues that previously had not been a matter of public debate. Because values are the essence of advocacy networks, this stage of influence may require a modification of the "value context" in which policy debates takes place. The UN's theme years and decades, such as International Women's Decade and the Year of Indigenous Peoples, were international events promoted by networks that heightened awareness of issues.

Networks influence discursive positions when they help persuade states and international organizations to support international declarations or to change stated domestic policy positions. The role environmental networks played in shaping state positions and conference declarations at the 1992 "Earth Summit" in Rio de Janeiro is an example of this kind of impact. They may also pressure states to make more binding commitments by signing conventions and codes of conduct.

The targets of network campaigns frequently respond to demands for policy change with changes in procedures (which may affect policies in the future). . . Procedural changes can greatly increase the opportunity for advocacy organizations to develop regular contact with other key players on an issue, and they sometimes offer the opportunity to move from outside to inside pressure strategies.

A network's activities may produce changes in policies, not only of the target states, but also of other states and/or international institutions. Explicit policy shifts seem to denote success, but even here both their causes and meanings may be elusive. We can point with some confidence to network impact where human rights network pressures have achieved cut-offs of military aid to repressive regimes, or a curtailment of repressive practices. Sometimes human rights activity even affects regime stability. But we must take care to distinguish between policy change and change in behavior; official policies regarding timber extraction in Sarawak, Malaysia, for example, may say little about how timber companies behave on the ground in the absence of enforcement . . .

Notes

1. Peter Haas has called these "knowledge-based" or "epistemic communities." See Peter Haas, "Introduction: Epistemic Communities and International Policy Coordination," *Knowledge, Power and International Policy Coordination*, special issue, *International Organization* 46 (Winter 1992), pp. 1–36.
2. Ideas that specify criteria for determining whether actions are right and wrong and whether outcomes are just or unjust are shared principled beliefs or values. Beliefs about cause-effect relationships are shared casual beliefs. Judith Goldstein and Robert Keohane, eds., *Ideas and Foreign Policy: Beliefs, Institutions, and Political Change* (Ithaca: Cornell University Press, 1993), pp. 8–10.
3. See also J. Clyde Mitchell, "Networks, Norms, and Institutions," in *Network Analysis*, ed. Jeremy Boissevain and J. Clyde Mitchell (The Hague: Mouton, 1973), p. 23. A "common discourse" was suggested by Stewart Lawrence in "The Role of International 'Issue Networks' in Refugee Repatriation: The Case of El Salvador" (Columbia University, mimeo).
4. David Snow and his colleagues have adapted Erving Goffman's concept of framing. We use it to mean "conscious strategic efforts by groups of people to fashion shared understandings of the world and of themselves that legitimate and motivate collective action." Definition from Doug McAdam, John D. McCarthy, and Mayer N. Zald, "Introduction," *Comparative Perspectives on Social Movements: Political Opportunities, Mobilizing Structures, and Cultural Framings*, ed. McAdam, McCarthy, and Zald (New York: Cambridge University Press, 1996), p. 6. See also Frank Baumgartner and Bryan Jones, "Agenda Dynamics and Policy Subsystems," *Journal of Politics* 53:4 (1991): 1044–74.
5. Audie Klotz, *Norms in International Relations: The Struggle against Apartheid* (Ithaca: Cornell University Press, 1995), pp. 152–64.
6. Alison Brysk uses the categories "information politics" and "symbolic politics" to discuss strategies of transnational actors, especially networks around Indian rights. See "Acting Globally: Indian Rights and International Politics in Latin America," in *Indigenous Peoples and Democracy in Latin America*, ed. Donna Lee Van Cott (New York: St. Martin's Press/Inter-American Dialogue, 1994), pp. 29–51; and "Hearts and Minds: Bringing Symbolic Politics Back In," *Polity* 27 (Summer 1995): 559–85.
7. David A. Snow et al., "Frame Alignment Processes, Micromobilization, and Movement Participation," *American Sociological Review* 51 (1986): 464.
8. David A. Snow and Robert D. Benford, "Ideology, Frame Resonance, and Participant Mobilization," in *From Structure to Action: Comparing Social Movement Research across Cultures*, ed. Bert Klandermans, Hanspeter Kriesi, and Sidney Tarrow (Greenwich, Conn.: JAI Press, 1988), pp. 197–217.

9. David A. Snow and Robert D. Benford, "Master Frames and Cycles of Protest," in *Frontiers in Social Movement Theory*, eds. Aldon D. Morris and Carol McClurg Mueller (New Haven: Yale University Press) pp. 133–55.
10. Sidney Tarrow, "Mentalities, Political Cultures, and Collective Action Frames: Constructing Meanings through Action," in *Frontiers in Social Movement Theory*, p. 197.
11. Jürgen Gerhards and Dieter Rucht, "Mesomobilization: Organizing and Framing in Two Protest Campaigns in West Germany," *American Journal of Sociology* 98:3 (November 1992), details the organizational efforts to prepare demonstrations and parallel meetings to coincide with the 1988 meeting of the World Bank and International Monetary Fund in Berlin. This was by far the largest mass action in conjunction with the multilateral development bank campaign, which began holding meetings and demonstrations parallel to the banks' annual meetings in 1986. Interestingly, the authors seem not to have been aware of the existence of a transnational campaign of which this action was a part. On Narmada, see Medha Patkar, "The Struggle for Participation and Justice: A Historical Narrative," pp. 157–78; Anil Patel, "What Do the Narmada Tribals Want?," pp. 179–200; and Lori Udall, "The International Narmada Campaign: A Case of Sustained Advocacy," William F. Fisher, ed., *Toward Sustainable Development? Struggling over India's Narmada River* (Armonk, N.Y.: M. E.; Sharpe, 1995) pp. 201–30.
12. Frank Baumgartner and Bryan Jones, "Agenda Dynamics and Policy Subsystems," *Journal of Politics* 53:4 (1991): 1050.
13. James Rosenau, *Turbulence in World Politics* (Princeton: Princeton University Press, 1990), p. 199, argues that "as the adequacy of information and the very nature of knowledge have emerged as central issues, what were once regarded as the petty quarrels of scholars over the adequacy of evidence and the metaphysics of proof have become prominent activities in international relations."
14. We are grateful to Anna Lowenhaupt Tsing for this point.
15. Dorothy Q. Thomas, "Holding Governments Accountable by Public Pressure," in *Ours by Right: Women's Rights as Human Rights*, ed. Joanna Kerr (London: Zed Books, 1993), p. 83. This methodology is not new. See, for example, David H. Lumsdaine, *Moral Vision in International Politics: The Foreign Aid Regime, 1949–1989* (Princeton: Princeton University Press, 1993), pp. 187–88, 211–13.
16. Female genital mutilation is most widely practiced in Africa, where it is reported to occur in at least twenty-six countries. Between 85 and 114 million women in the world today are estimated to have experienced genital mutilation. *World Bank Development Report 1993: Investing in Health* (New York: Oxford University Press, 1993), p. 50.
17. See Leonard J. Kouba and Judith Muasher, "Female Circumcision in Africa: An Overview," *African Studies Review* 28:1 (March 1985): 95–110; Alison T. Slack, "Female Circumcision: A Critical Appraisal," *Human Rights Quarterly* 10:4 (November 1988): 437–86; and Elise A. Sochart, "Agenda Setting, the Role of Groups and the Legislative Process: The Prohibition of Female Circumcision in Britain," *Parliamentary Affairs* 41:4 (October 1988): 508–26. On France, see Marlise Simons, "Mutilation of Girls' Genitals: Ethnic Gulf in French Court," *New York Times*, 23 November 1993, p. 13. For UN recommendations, see the "Report of the Working Group on Traditional Practices Affecting the Health of Women and Children," UN Document E/CN.4/1986/42 at 26 (1986).
18. See D. B. Jellife and E. F. P. Jellife, *Human Milk in the Modern World* (Oxford: Oxford University Press, 1978).
19. See on social movements and media, see Todd Gitlin, *The Whole World Is Watching* (Berkeley: University of California Press, 1980). For a report on recent research, see William A. Gamson and Gadi Wolfsfeld, "Movements and Media as Interacting Systems," *Annals of the American Association of Political and Social Science* 528 (July 1993): 114–25.
20. Brysk, "Acting Globally."
21. Discussion of the Helsinki Accords is based on Daniel Thomas, "Norms and Change in World Politics: Human Rights, the Helsinki Accords, and the Demise of Communism, 1975–1990," Ph.D. diss., Cornell University, 1997.
22. Walter Parchomenko, *Soviet Images of Dissidents and Nonconformists* (New York: Praeger, 1986), p. 156, as cited in Thomas, p. 219.

23. On access to the courts and citizen oversight of environmental policy in the U.S. and Germany, see Susan Rose Ackerman, *Controlling Environmental Policy: The Limits of Public Law in Germany and the United States* (New Haven: Yale University Press, 1995).

No Logo: Taking Aim at the Brand Bullies

Naomi Klein

Journalist Naomi Klein analyzes and celebrates the global movement that has developed to target corporate wrongdoing. A principal aim of the movement is to increase awareness in wealthy countries of the backstage dirty secrets that underpin the way that clothing and other familiar products are produced. Movements that organize consumer boycotts can be effective because they affect transnational corporations where it hurts—at the bottom line of profit and loss.

Critics charge that consumer boycotts wrongly single out a particular corporation when an entire industry may be guilty; moreover, the particular corporation targeted for a boycott may not be the worst offender. Another criticism of consumer boycotts is that they ignore the responsibility of governments in wealthy and poor countries, and fail to advocate stiffer public regulation of labor conditions. Further, recall the argument of Kristof and WuDunn, in the selection in Chapter 5, that a boycott may hurt those who are least guilty and most vulnerable: workers in poor countries employed by TNCs or their subcontractors.

Consider the effectiveness and ethics of consumer boycotts. Compare the campaign targeting Nike that Klein describes with the transnational advocacy networks that Keck and Sikkink describe in the previous selection. What are the similarities and differences between the two forms of organizing? Which form do you think is more effective? Why? Or are different forms especially suited to particular kinds of issues? If so, which?

A Tale of Three Logos: The Swoosh, the Shell and the Arches

Dozens of brand-based campaigns have succeeded in rattling their corporate targets, in several cases pushing them to substantially alter their policies. But three campaigns stand out for having reached well beyond activist circles and deep into public consciousness. The tactics they have developed—among them the use of the courts to force transparency on corporations, and the Internet to bypass traditional media—are revolutionizing the future of political engagement. By now it should come as no surprise that the targets of these influential campaigns are three of the most familiar and best-tended logos on the brandscape: the Swoosh, the Shell and the Arches.

The Swoosh: The Fight for Good Jobs

Nike CEO Phil Knight has long been a hero of the business schools. Prestigious academic publications such as *The Harvard Business Review* have lauded his pioneering marketing techniques, his understanding of branding and his early use of outsourcing. Countless MBA candidates and other students of marketing and communications have studied the Nike formula of "brands, not products." So when Phil Knight was invited to be a guest speaker at the Stanford University Business School—Knight's own alma mater—in May 1997, the visit was expected to be one in a long line of Nike love-ins. Instead, Knight was greeted by a crowd of picketing students, and when he approached the microphone he was taunted with chants of "Hey Phil, off the stage. Pay your workers a living wage." The Nike honeymoon had come to a grinding halt.

No story illustrates the growing distrust of the culture of corporate branding more than the international anti-Nike movement—the most publicized and tenacious of the brand-based campaigns. Nike's sweatshop scandals have been the subject of over 1,500 news articles and opinion columns. Its Asian factories have been probed by cameras from nearly every major media organization, from CBS to Disney's sports station, ESPN. On top of all that, it has been the subject of a series of Doonesbury cartoon strips and the butt of Michael Moore's documentary *The Big One*. As a result, several people in Nike's PR department work full time dealing with the sweatshop controversy—fielding complaints, meeting with local groups and developing Nike's response—and the company has created a new executive position: vice president for corporate responsibility. Nike has received hundreds and thousands of letters of protest, faced hundreds of both small and large groups of demonstrators, and is the target of a dozen critical Web sites.

For the last two years, anti-Nike forces in North America and Europe have attempted to focus all the scattered swoosh bashing on a single day. Every six months they have declared an International Nike Day of Action, and brought their demands for fair wages and independent monitoring directly to Nike's customers, shoppers at flagship Nike Towns in urban centers or the less glamorous Foot Locker outlets in suburban malls. According to Campaign for Labor Rights, the largest anti-Nike event so far took place on October 18, 1997: eighty-five cities in thirteen countries participated. Not all the protests have attracted large crowds, but since the movement is so decentralized, the sheer number of individual anti-Nike events has left the company's public-relations department scrambling to get its spin onto dozens of local newscasts. Though you'd never know it from its branding ubiquity, even Nike can't be everywhere at once.

Since so many of the stores that sell Nike products are located in malls, protests often end with a security guard escorting participants into the parking lot. Jeff Smith, an activist from Grand Rapids, Michigan, reported that "when we asked if private property rights ruled over free speech rights, the [security] officer hesitated and then emphatically said YES!" (Though in the economically depressed city of St. John's, Newfoundland, anti-Nike campaigners reported that after being thrown out of a mall, "they were approached by a security guard who asked to sign their petition."[1]) But there's plenty that can be done on the sidewalk or in the mall parking lot. Campaigners have dramatized Nike's labor practices through what they call "sweatshop fashion shows," and "The Transnational Capital Auction: A Game of Survival" (the lowest bidder wins), and a global economy treadmill (run fast, stay in the same place). In Australia, anti-Nike protestors have been known to parade around in calico bags painted with the slogan "Rather wear a bag than Nike." Students at the University of Colorado in Boulder dramatized the difference between the legal minimum wage and a living wage by holding a fundraising run in which "participants pay an entrance fee of $1.60 (daily wages for a Nike worker in Vietnam) and the winner will receive $2.10 (the price of three square meals in Vietnam)."[2] Meanwhile, activists in Austin, Texas, made a giant papier-mâché Nike sneaker piñata, and a protest outside a Regina, Saskatchewan, shopping center featured a deface-the-swoosh booth. The last stunt is something of a running theme in all the anti-Nike actions: Nike's logo and slogan have been jammed so many times—on T-shirts, stickers, placards, banners and pins—that the semiotic bruises have turned them black and blue . . .

Tellingly, the anti-Nike movement is at its strongest inside the company's home state of Oregon, even though the area has reaped substantial economic benefits from Nike's success (Nike is the largest employer in Portland and a significant local philanthropist). Phil Knight's neighbors, nonetheless, have not all rushed to his defense in his hour of need. In fact, since the *Life* magazine soccer-ball story broke, many Oregonians have been out for blood. The demonstrations outside the Portland Nike Town are among the largest and most militant in the country, sometimes sporting a menacing giant Phil Knight puppet with dollar signs for eyes or a twelve-foot Nike swoosh dragged by small children (to dramatize child labor). And in contravention of the principles of nonviolence that govern the anti-Nike movement, one protest in Eugene, Oregon, led to acts of vandalism including the tearing-down of a fence surrounding the construction of a new Nike Town, gear pulled off shelves at an existing Nike store and, according to one eyewitness, "an entire rack of clothes . . . dumped off a balcony into a fountain below."[3]

Local papers in Oregon have aggressively (sometimes gleefully) followed Knight's sweatshop scandals, and the daily paper *The Oregonian* sent a reporter to Southeast Asia to do its own lengthy investigation of the factories. Mark Zusman, editor of the Oregon newspaper *The Willamette Week*, publicly admonished Knight in a 1996 "memo": "Frankly, Phil, it's time to get a little more sophisticated about this media orgy . . . Oregonians already have suffered through the shame of Tonya Harding, Bob Packwood and Wes Cooley. Spare us the added humiliation of being known as the home of the most exploitative capitalist in the free world."[4]

Even Nike's charitable donations have become controversial. In the midst of a critical fundraising drive to try to address a $15 million shortfall, the Portland School Board was torn apart by debate about whether to accept Nike's gift of $500,000 in cash and swooshed athletic gear. The board ended up accepting the donation, but not before looking their gift horse publicly in the mouth. "I asked myself," school board trustee Joseph Tam told *The Oregonian*, "Nike contributed this money so my children can have a better education, but at whose expense? At the expense of children who work for six cents an hour? . . . As an immigrant and as an Asian I have to face this moral and ethical dilemma."[5]

Nike's sponsorship scandals have reached far beyond the company's home state. In Edmonton, Alberta, teachers, parents and some students tried to block Nike from sponsoring a children's street hockey program because "a company which profits from child labor in Pakistan ought not to be held up as a hero to Edmonton children."[6] At least one school involved in the city-wide program sent back its swooshed equipment to Nike headquarters. And when Nike approached the City of Ottawa Council in March 1998 to suggest building one of its swooshed gymnasium floors in a local community center, it faced questions about "blood money." Nike withdrew its offer and gave the court to a more grateful center, run by the Boys and Girls Clubs. The dilemma of accepting Nike sponsorship money has also exploded on university campuses. . . .

At first, much of the outrage stemmed from the fact that when the sweatshop scandal hit the papers, Nike wasn't really acting all that sorry about it. While Kathie Lee Gifford and the Gap had at least displayed contrition when they got caught with their sweatshops showing, Phil Knight had practically stonewalled: denying responsibility, attacking journalists, blaming rogue contractors and sending out flacks to speak for the company. While Kathie Lee was crying on TV, Michael Jordan was shrugging his shoulders and saying that his job was to shoot hoop, not play politics. And while the Gap agreed to allow a particularly controversial factory in El Salvador to be monitored by local human-rights groups, Nike was paying lip service to a code of conduct that its Asian workers, when interviewed, had never even heard of.

But there was a critical difference between Nike and the Gap at this stage. Nike didn't panic when its scandals hit the middle-American mall, because the mall, while it is indeed where most Nike products are sold, is not where Nike's image was made. Unlike the Gap, Nike has drawn on the inner cities, merging, as we've seen, with the styles of poor black and Latino youth to load up on imagery and attitude. Nike's branding power is thoroughly intertwined with the African-American heroes who have endorsed its products since the mid-eighties: Michael Jordan, Charles Barkley, Scottie Pippen, Michael Johnson, Spike Lee, Tiger Woods, Bo Jackson—not to mention the rappers who wear Nike gear on stage. While hip-hop style was the major influence at the mall, Phil Knight must have known that as long as Nike was King Brand with Jordan fans in Compton and the Bronx, he could be stirred but not shaken. Sure, their parents, teachers and church leaders might be tut-tutting over sweatshops, but as far as Nike's core demographic of thirteen- to seventeen-year-old kids was concerned, the swoosh was still made of Teflon.

By 1997, it had become clear to Nike's critics that if they were serious about taking on the swoosh in an image war, they would have to get at the source of the brand's cachet—and as Nick Alexander of the multicultural *Third Force* magazine wrote in the summer of that year, they weren't even close. "Nobody has figured out how to make Nike break down and cry. The reason is that nobody has engaged African Americans in the fight. . . . To gain significant support from communities of color, corporate campaigns need to make connections between Nike's overseas operations and conditions here at home."[7]

The connections were there to be made. It is the cruelest irony of Nike's "brands, not products" formula that the people who have done the most to infuse the swoosh with cutting-edge meaning are the very people most hurt by the company's pumped-up prices and nonexistent manufacturing base. It is inner-city youth who have most directly felt the impact of Nike's decision to manufacture its products outside the U.S., both in high unemployment rates and in the erosion of the community tax base (which sets the stage for the deterioration of local public schools).

Instead of jobs for their parents, what the inner-city kids get from Nike is the occasional visit from its marketers and designers on "bro-ing" pilgrimages. "Hey, bro, what do you think of these new Jordans—are they fresh or what?" The effect of high-priced cool hunters whipping up brand frenzy on the cracked asphalt basketball courts of Harlem, the Bronx and Compton has already been discussed: kids incorporate the brands into gang-wear uniforms; some want the gear so badly they are willing to sell drugs, steal, mug, even kill for it. Jessie Collins, executive director of the Edenwald–Gun Hill Neighborhood Center in the northeast Bronx, tells me that it's sometimes drug or gang money, but more often it's the mothers' minimum-wage salaries or welfare checks that are spent on disposable status wear. When I asked her about the media reports of kids stabbing each other for their $150 Air Jordans she said dryly, "It's enough to beat up on your mother for . . . $150 is a hell of a lot of money."[8]

Shoe-store owners like Steven Roth of Essex House of Fashion are often uncomfortable with the way so-called street fashions play out for real on the postindustrial streets of Newark, New Jersey, where his store is located.

> I do get weary and worn down from it all. I'm always forced to face the fact that I make my money from poor people. A lot of them are on welfare. Sometimes a mother will come in here with a kid, and the kid is dirty and poorly dressed. But the kid wants a hundred-twenty-buck pair of shoes and that stupid mother buys them for him. I can feel that kid's inner need—this desire to own these things and have the feelings that go with them—but it hurts me that this is the way things are.[9]

It's easy to blame the parents for giving in, but that "deep inner need" for designer gear has grown so intense that it has confounded everyone from community leaders to the police. Everyone pretty much agrees that brands like Nike are playing a powerful surrogate role in the ghetto, subbing for everything from self-esteem to African-American cultural history to political power. What they are far less sure about is how to fill that need with empowerment and a sense of self-worth that does not necessarily come with a logo attached. Even broaching the subject of brand fetishism to these kids is risky. With so much emotion invested in celebrity consumer goods, many kids take criticism of Nike or Tommy as a personal attack, as grave a transgression as insulting someone's mother to his face.

Not surprisingly, Nike sees its appeal among disadvantaged kids differently. By supporting sports programs in Boys and Girls Clubs, by paying to repave urban basketball courts and by turning high-performance sports gear into street fashions, the company claims it is sending out the inspirational message that even poor kids can "Just Do It." In its press material and ads, there is an almost messianic quality to Nike's portrayal of its role in the inner cities: troubled kids will have higher self-esteem, fewer unwanted pregnancies and more ambition—all because at Nike "We see them as athletes." For Nike, its $150 Air Jordans are not a shoe but a kind of talisman with which poor kids can run out of the ghetto and better their lives. Nike's magic slippers will help them fly—just as they made Michael Jordan fly.

A remarkable, subversive accomplishment? Maybe. But one can't help thinking that one of the main reasons black urban youth can get out of the ghetto only by rapping or shooting hoops is that Nike and the other multinationals are reinforcing stereotypical images of black youth and simultaneously taking all the jobs away. As U.S. Congressman Bernie Sanders and Congresswoman Marcy Kaptur stated in a letter to the company, Nike has played a pivotal part in the industrial exodus from urban centers. "Nike has led the way in abandoning the manufacturing workers of the United States and their families. . . . Apparently, Nike believes that workers in the United States are good enough to purchase your shoe products, but are no longer worthy enough to manufacture them."[10]

And when the company's urban branding strategy is taken in conjunction with this employment record, Nike ceases to be the savior of the inner city and turns into the guy who steals your job, then sells you a pair of overpriced sneakers and yells, "Run like hell!" Hey, it's the only way out of the ghetto, kid. Just do it.

That's what Mike Gitelson thought, anyway. A social worker at the Bronx's Edenwald–Gun Hill Neighborhood Center, he was unimpressed with the swoosh's powers as a self-help guru in the projects and "sick of seeing kids wearing sneakers they couldn't afford and which their parents couldn't afford."[11] Nike's critics on college campuses and in the labor movement may be fueled largely by moral outrage, but Mike Gitelson and his colleagues simply feel ripped off. So rather than lecturing the kids on the virtues of frugality, they began telling them about how Nike made the shoes that they wanted so badly. Gitelson told them about the workers in Indonesia who earned $2 a day, he told them that it cost Nike only $5 to make the shoes they bought for between $100 and $180, and he told them about how Nike didn't make any of its shoes in the U.S.—which was part of the reason their parents had such a tough time finding work. "We got really angry," says Gitelson, "because they were taking so much money from us here and then going to other countries and exploiting people even worse. . . . We want our kids to see how it affects them here on the streets, but also how here on the streets affects people in Southeast Asia." His colleague at the center, youth worker Leo Johnson, lays out the issue using the kids' own lingo. "Yo, dude," he tells his preteen audiences, "you're being suckered if you pay $100 for a sneaker that costs $5 to make. If somebody did that to you on the block, you know where it's going."[12]

The kids at the center were upset to learn about the sweatshops but they were clearly most pissed off that Phil Knight and Michael Jordan were playing them for chumps. They sent Phil Knight a hundred letters about how much money they had spent on Nike gear over the years—and how, the way they figured it, Nike owed them big time. "I just bought a pair of Nikes for $100," one kid wrote. "It's not right what you're doing. A fair price would have been $30. Could you please send me back $70?" When the company answered the kids with a form letter, "That's when we got really angry and started putting together the protest," Gitelson says.

They decided the protest would take the form of a "shoe-in" at the Nike Town at Fifth Avenue and Fifty-seventh Street. Since most of the kids at the center are full-fledged swooshaholics, their closets are jam-packed with old Air Jordans and Air Carnivores that they would no longer even consider wearing. To put the obsolete shoes to practical use, they decided to gather them together in garbage bags and dump them on the doorstep of Nike Town.

When Nike executives got wind that a bunch of black and Latino kids from the Bronx were planning to publicly diss their company, the form letters came to an abrupt halt. Up to that point, Nike had met most criticism by attacking its critics as members of "fringe groups," but this was different: if a backlash took root in the inner cities, it could sink the brand at the mall. As Gitelson puts it, "Our kids are exactly who Nike depends upon to set the trends for them so that the rest of the country buys their sneakers. White middle-class adults who are fighting them, well, it's almost okay. But when youth of color start speaking out against Nike, they start getting scared."[13]

The executives in Oregon also knew, no doubt, that Edenwald was only the tip of the iceberg. For the past couple of years, debates have been raging in hip-hop scenes about rappers "label whoring for Nike and Tommy" instead of supporting black-owned clothing companies like FUBU (For Us By Us). And rapper KRS-One planned to launch the Temple of Hip Hop, a project that promised to wrest the culture of African-American youth away from white record and clothing labels and return it to the communities that built it. It was against this backdrop that, on September 10, 1997—two weeks before the shoe-in protest was scheduled to take place—Nike's chief of public relations, Vada Manager, made the unprecedented move of flying in from Oregon with a colleague to try to convince the center that the swoosh was a friend of the projects.

"He was working overtime to put the spins on us," says Gitelson. It didn't work. At the meeting, the center laid out three very concrete demands:

1. Those who work for Nike overseas should be paid a living wage, with independent monitoring to ensure that it is occurring.
2. Nike sneakers should be sold less expensively here in America with no concessions to American workforce (i.e. no downsizing, or loss of benefits)
3. Nike should seriously re-invest in the inner city in America, especially New York City since we have been the subject of much of their advertising.[14]

Gitelson may have recognized that Nike was scared—but not *that* scared. Once it became clear that the two parties were at an impasse, the meeting turned into a scolding session as the two Nike executives were required to listen to Edenwald director Jessie Collins comparing the company's Asian sweatshops with her experience as a young girl picking cotton in the share-cropping South. Back in Alabama, she told Manager, she earned $2 a day, just like the Indonesians. "And maybe a lot of Americans can't identify with those workers' situation, but I certainly can."[15]

Vada Manager returned to Oregon defeated and the protest went off as planned, with two hundred participants from eleven community centers around New York. The kids—most of whom were between eleven and thirteen years old—hooted and hollered and dumped several clear garbage bags of smelly old Nikes at the feet of a line of security guards who had been brought in on special assignment to protect the sacred Nike premises. Vada Manager again flew to New York to run damage control, but there was little he could do. Local TV crews covered the event, as did an ABC news team and *The New York Times*.

In a harsh bit of bad timing for the company, the *Times* piece ran on a page facing another story about Nike. Graphically underlining the urgency of the protest, this story reported that a fourteen-year-old boy from Crown Heights had just been murdered by a fifteen-year-old boy who beat him and left him on the subway tracks with a train approaching. "Police Say Teenager Died for His Sneakers and Beeper," the headline read. And the brand of his sneakers? Air Jordans. The article quoted the killer's mother saying that her son had got mixed up with gangs because he wanted to "have nice things." A friend of the victim explained that wearing designer clothes and carrying a beeper had become a way for poor kids to "feel important."

The African-American and Latino kids outside Nike Town on Fifth Avenue—the ones swarmed by cameras and surrounded by curious onlookers—were feeling pretty important, too. Taking on Nike "toe to toe," as they said, turned out to be even more fun than wearing Nikes. With the Fox News camera pointed in his face, one of the young activists—a thirteen-year-old boy from the Bronx—stared into the lens and delivered a message to Phil Knight: "Nike, we made you. We can break you."

What is perhaps most remarkable about the Nike backlash is its durability. After four solid years in the public eye, the Nike story still has legs (so too, of course, does the Nike brand). Still, most corporate scandals are successfully faced down with a statement of "regret" and a few glossy ads of children playing happily under the offending logo. Not with Nike. The news reports, labor studies and academic research documenting the sweat behind the swoosh have yet to slow down, and Nike critics remain tireless at dissecting the steady stream of materials churned out by Nike's PR machine. They were unmoved by Phil Knight's presence on the White House Task Force on Sweatshops—despite his priceless photo op standing beside President Clinton at the Rose Garden press conference. They sliced and diced the report Nike commissioned from civil-rights leader Andrew Young, pointing out that Young completely dodged the question of whether Nike's factory wages are inhumanely exploitative, and attacking him for relying on translators provided by Nike itself when he visited the factories in Indonesia and Vietnam. As for Nike's other study-for-hire—this one by a group of Dartmouth business students who concluded that workers in Vietnam were living the good life on less than $2 a day—well, everyone pretty much ignored that one altogether.

Finally, in May 1998, Phil Knight stepped out from behind the curtain of spin doctors and called a press conference in Washington to address his critics directly. Knight began by saying that he had been painted as a "corporate crook, the perfect corporate villain for these times." He acknowledged that his shoes "have become synonymous with slave wages, forced overtime and arbitrary abuse." Then, to much fanfare, he unveiled a plan to improve working conditions in Asia. It contained some tough new regulations on factory air quality and the use of petroleum-based chemicals. It promised to provide classes inside some Indonesian factories and promised not to hire anyone under eighteen years old in the shoe factories. But there was still nothing substantial in the plan about allowing independent outside monitors to inspect the factories, and there were no wage raises for the workers. Knight did promise, however, that Nike's contractors would no longer be permitted to appeal to the Indonesian government for a waiver on the minimum wage.

It wasn't enough. That September the San Francisco human-rights group Global Exchange, one of the company's harshest critics, released an alarming report on the status of Nike's Indonesian workers in the midst of the country's economic and political crisis. "While workers producing Nike shoes were low paid before their currency, the rupiah, began plummeting in late 1997, the dollar value of their wages has dropped from $2.47/day in 1997 to 80 cents/day in 1998." Meanwhile, the report noted that with soaring commodity prices, workers "estimated that their cost of living had gone up anywhere from 100 to 300 per cent."[16] Global Exchange called on Nike to double the wages of its Indonesian workforce, an exercise that would cost it $20 million a year—exactly what Michael Jordan is paid annually to endorse the company.

Not surprisingly, Nike did not double the wages, but it did, three weeks later, give 30 percent of the Indonesian workforce a 25 percent raise.[17] That, too, failed to silence the crowds outside the superstores, and five months later Nike came forward again, this time with what vice president of corporate responsibility Maria Eitel called "an aggressive corporate responsibility agenda at Nike."[18] As of April 1, 1999, workers would get another 6 percent raise. The company had also opened up a Vietnamese factory near Ho Chi Minh City to outside health and safety monitors, who found conditions much improved. Dara O'Rourke of the University of California at Berkeley reported that the factory had "implemented important changes over the past 18 months which appear to have significantly reduced worker exposures to toxic solvents, adhesives and other chemicals." What made the report all the more remarkable was that O'Rourke's inspection was a genuinely independent one: in fact, less than two years earlier, he had enraged the company by leaking a report conducted by Ernst & Young that showed that Nike was ignoring widespread violations at that same factory.

O'Rourke's findings weren't all glowing. There were still persistent problems with air quality, factory overheating and safety gear—and he had visited only the one factory.[19] As well, Nike's much-heralded 6 percent pay raise for Indonesian workers still left much to be desired; it amounted to an increase of one cent an hour and, with inflation and currency fluctuation, only brought wages to about half of what Nike paychecks were worth before the economic crisis. Even so, these were significant gestures coming from a company that two years earlier was playing the role of the powerless global shopper, claiming that contractors alone had the authority to set wages and make the rules.

The resilience of the Nike campaign in the face of the public-relations onslaught is persuasive evidence that invasive marketing, coupled with worker abandonment, strikes a wide range of people from different walks of life as grossly unfair and unsustainable. Moreover, many of those people are not interested in letting Nike off the hook simply because this formula has become the standard one for capitalism-as-usual. On the contrary, there seems to be a part of the public psyche that likes kicking the most macho and extreme of all the sporting-goods companies in the shins—I mean *really* likes it. Nike's critics have shown that they don't want this story to be brushed under the rug with a reassuring bit of corporate PR; they want it out in the open, where they can keep a close eye on it.

In large part, this is because Nike's critics know that the company's sweatshop scandals are not the result of a series of freak accidents: they know that the criticisms leveled at Nike apply to all the brand-based shoe companies contracting out to a global maze of firms. But rather than this serving as a justification, Nike—as the market leader—has become a lightning rod for this broader resentment. It has been latched on to as the essential story of the extremes of the current global economy: the disparities between those who profit from Nike's success and those who are exploited by it are so gaping that a child could understand what is wrong with this picture and indeed . . . it is children and teenagers who most readily do.

So, when does the total boycott of Nike products begin? Not soon, apparently. A cursory glance around any city in the world shows that the swoosh is still ubiquitous; some athletes still tattoo it on their navels, and plenty of high-school students still deck themselves out in the coveted gear. But at the same time, there can be little doubt that the millions of dollars that Nike has saved in labor costs over the years are beginning to bite back, and take a toll on its bottom line. "We didn't think that the Nike situation would be as bad as it seems to be," said Nikko stock analyst Tim Finucane in *The Wall Street Journal* in March 1998.[20] Wall Street really had no choice but to turn on the company that had been its darling for so many years. Despite the fact that Asia's plummeting currencies meant that Nike's labor costs in Indonesia, for instance, were a quarter of what they were before the crash, the company was still suffering. Nike's profits were down, orders were down, stock prices were *way* down, and after an average annual growth of 34 percent since 1995, quarterly earnings were suddenly down 70 percent. By the third quarter, which ended in February 1999, Nike's profits were once again up 70 percent—but by the company's own account, the recovery was not the result of rebounding sales but rather of Nike's decision to cut jobs and contracts. In fact, Nike's revenues and future orders were down in 1999 for the second year in a row.[21]

Nike has blamed its financial problems on everything *but* the human-rights campaign. The Asian currency crisis was the reason Nikes weren't selling well in Japan and South Korea; or it was because Americans were buying "brown shoes" (walking shoes and hiking boots) as opposed to big white sneakers. But the brown-shoe excuse rang hollow. Nike makes plenty of brown shoes—it has a line of hiking boots, and it owns Cole Haan (and recently saved millions by closing down the Cole Haan factory in Portand, Maine, and moving production to Mexico and Brazil).[22] More to the point, Adidas staged a massive comeback during the very year that Nike was free-falling. In the quarter when Nike nose-dived, Adidas sales were up 42 percent, its net income was up 48 percent, to $255 million, and its stock price had tripled in two years. The German company, as we have seen, turned its fortunes around by copying Nike's production structure and all but Xeroxing its approach to marketing and sponsorships. . . . In 1997–98, Adidas even redesigned its basketball shoes so they looked just like Nikes: big, white and ultra high tech. But unlike Nikes, they sold briskly. So much for the brown-shoe theory.

Over the years Nike has tried dozens of tactics to silence the cries of its critics, but the most ironic by far has been the company's desperate attempt to hide behind its product. "We're not political activists. We are a footwear manufacturer," said Nike spokeswoman Donna Gibbs, when the sweatshop scandal first began to erupt.[23] A footwear manufacturer? This from the company that made a concerted decision in the mid-eighties not to be about boring corporeal stuff like footwear—and certainly nothing as crass as manufacturing. Nike wanted to be about sports, Knight told us, it wanted to be about the idea of sports, then the idea of transcendence through sports; then it wanted to be about self-empowerment, women's rights, racial equality. It wanted its stores to be temples, its ads a religion, its customers a nation, its workers a tribe. After taking us all on such a branded ride, to turn around and say "Don't look at us, we just make shoes" rings laughably hollow.

Nike was the most inflated of all the balloon brands, and the bigger it grew, the louder it popped . . .

Notes

1. Memo, 4 May 1998, from the Maquila Solidarity Network, "Nike Day of Action Canada Report & Task Force Update."
2. "Nike protest update," *Labor Alerts*, 18 October 1997.
3. "Nike Mobilization: Local Reports," *Labor Alerts*, Campaign for Labor Rights, 26 October 1998.
4. Mark L. Zusman, "Editor's Notebook," *Willamette Week*, 12 June 1996.
5. *Oregonian*, 16 June 1996.
6. Campaign for Labor Rights Web site, regional reports.
7. Nick Alexander, "Sweatshop Activism: Missing Pieces," *Z Magazine*, September 1997, 14–17.
8. Personal interview, 6 October 1997.
9. Katz, *Just Do It*, 271.
10. Letter dated 24 October 1997.
11. Personal interview.
12. David Gonzalez, "Youthful Foes Go Toe to Toe with Nike," *New York Times*, 27 September 1997, B1.
13. Personal interview.
14. Minutes from 10 September meeting between Nike executives and the Edenwald–Gun Hill Neighborhood Center.
15. Personal interview.
16. "Wages and Living Expense for Nike Workers in Indonesia," report released by Global Exchange, 23 September 1998.
17. "Nike Raises Wages for Indonesian Workers," *Oregonian*, 16 October 1998.
18. "Nike to Improve Minimum Monthly Wage Package for Indonesian Workers," Nike press release, 19 March 1999.
19. Steven Greenhouse, "Nike Critic Praises Gains in Air Quality at Vietnam Factory," *New York Times*, 12 March 1999.
20. Shanthi Kalathil, "Being Tied to Nike Affects Share Price of Yue Yuen," *Wall Street Journal*, 25 March 1998.
21. "Third quarter brings 70 percent increase in net income for sneaker giant," Associated Press, 19 March 1999.
22. "Cole Haan Joins Ranks of Shoe Companies Leaving Maine," Associated Press, 23 April 1999.
23. Zusman, "Editor's Notebook."

ARTICLE 9.3

Still Poor, Latin Americans Protest Push for Open Markets

Juan Forero

New York Times journalist Juan Forero describes the outpouring of anger across Latin America provoked by the pursuit of neoliberal policies to promote economic globalization. A key element in neoliberal globalization is the privatization of state-owned utilities and services, such as the sale of water, telecommunications, and electricity production and distribution to private—often foreign—investors. Opposition to the policy mounted when the initial wave of privatizations did not produce the promised results of more efficient and cheaper service. Although privatization of some sectors resulted in improved service and broader access, in other cases the results were job layoffs and steep price increases that put basic necessities out of reach for many.

This selection recalls Shiva's discussion, in Chapter 3, which describes how TNCs in India engage in practices similar to those highlighted by Forero that have generated protest in Latin America. Imagine what advocates of globalization, such as Bhagwati, Friedman, and Rogoff (in their selections in PG) might reply to opponents of the privatizations described by Forero. Is there a way for poor countries to obtain the benefits from TNC operations, including capital investments and technological know-how—without incurring the costs described by Forero?

The protest that shook this colonial city [Arequipa, Peru] last month was very much like others in Latin America recently. There were Marxists shouting 60's-era slogans, and hard-bitten unionists. But there was also Fanny Puntaca, 64, a shopkeeper and grandmother of six.

Though she had never before protested, Ms. Puntaca said, she could not bear to see a Belgian company buy what she called "our wealth"—the region's two state-owned electrical generators. So armed with a metal pot to bang, she joined neighbors in a demonstration so unyielding that it forced President Alejandro Toledo to declare a state of emergency here, suspend the $167 million sale and eventually shake up his cabinet.

"I had to fight," Ms. Puntaca said proudly. "The government was going to sell our companies and enrich another country. This was my voice, my protest."

Across Latin America, millions of others are also letting their voices be heard. A popular and political ground swell is building from the Andes to Argentina against the decade-old experiment with free-market capitalism. The reforms that have shrunk the state and opened markets to foreign competition, many believe, have enriched corrupt officials and faceless multinationals, and failed to better their lives.

Sometimes-violent protests in recent weeks have derailed the sale of state-owned companies worth hundreds of millions of dollars. The unrest has made potential investors jittery, and whipsawed governments already weakened by recession.

The backlash has given rise to leftist politicians who have combined pocketbook issues and economic nationalism to explosive effect. Today the market reforms ushered in by American-trained economists after the global collapse of Communism are facing their greatest challenge in the upheavals sweeping the region.

"The most worrying reading is that perhaps we have come to the end of an era," said Rafael de la Fuente, chief Latin American economist for BNP Paribas in New York. "That we are closing the door on what was an unsuccessful attempt at orthodox economic reforms at the end of the 90's."

For a time the policies worked, and many economists and politicians say they still do. The reforms increased competition and fueled growth. Stratospheric inflation rates fell back to earth. Bloated bureaucracies were replaced with efficient companies that created jobs.

The formula helped give Chile the most robust economy in Latin America. In Mexico exports quintupled in a dozen years. In Bolivia, poverty fell from 86 percent of the population in the 70's to 58.6 percent today.

Still, the broad prosperity that was promised remains a dream for many Latin Americans. Today those same reforms are equated with unemployment and layoffs from both public and private companies, as well as recessions that have hamstrung economies.

"We privatized and we do not have less poverty, less unemployment," said Juan Manuel Guillen, the mayor of Arequipa and a leader in the antiprivatization movement here. "On the contrary. We have more poverty and unemployment. We are not debating theoretically here. We are looking at reality."

Indeed, 44 percent of Latin Americans still live in poverty, and the number of unemployed workers has more than doubled in a decade. Tens of millions of others—in some countries up to 70 percent of all workers—toil in the region's vast informal economy, as street vendors, for instance, barely making ends meet. Economic growth has been essentially flat for the last five years.

Popular perceptions—revealed in street protests, opinion polls and ballot boxes—are clearly shifting against the economic prescriptions for open markets, less government and tighter budgets that American officials and international financial institutions have preferred.

A regional survey supported by the Inter-American Development Bank found last year that 63 percent of respondents across 17 countries in the region said that privatization had not been beneficial.

"It's an emotional populist attitude people have," said Larry Birns, director of the Council on Hemispheric Affairs, a Washington-based policy analysis group. "It may not be reasoned, but it's real, and it's explosive and it's not going to be easily contained by coming up with arguments that free trade is the wave of the future."

In Brazil, South America's largest country and its economic engine, revulsion with American-led market orthodoxy has fueled strong support for the labor leader Luiz Inacio da Silva, known as Lula, who is now the front-runner in the October presidential election, to the chagrin of worried financial markets.

In Paraguay protests last month blocked the $400 million sale of the state phone company by President Luis Gonzalez Macchi, whose government has been dogged by a dismal economy and corruption charges. This week deadly demonstrations led the president to declare a state of emergency.

In Bolivia the country's political landscape was redrawn this month when Evo Morales, an indigenous leader who promised to nationalize industries, finished second among 11 candidates for president.

This spring, the sale of 17 electricity distributors in Ecuador fell through in the face of political resistance, a blow to a country that has adopted the dollar as its currency and is heavily dependent on foreign investment.

Meanwhile, in Venezuela, President Hugo Chavez's left-leaning government has been intent on scaling back reforms, exacerbating the divisions that led to his brief ouster in April.

The backlash in many of these countries gathered momentum with the economic meltdown in Argentina, which forced a change of presidents after widespread rioting in December.

While the causes are multifold, many Argentines blame the debacle on a combination of corrupt politicians and the government's adherence to economic prescriptions from abroad that have left the country with $141 billion in public debt, the banking system in ruins and one in five people unemployed.

Argentines now look for possible salvation from Elisa Carrio, a corruption fighter in Congress who has been scathing in her criticism of the International Monetary Fund. She is now the early favorite in the upcoming presidential election.

"This has created the backlash because now there's a debate all around Latin America," said Pedro Pablo Kuczynski, Peru's former economy minister and a favorite of Wall Street who resigned under pressure last week. "Everywhere you look, people say, 'The guys followed the model and they're in the soup. So obviously the model does not work.'"

The backlash comes as foreign direct investment in Latin America has fallen steeply, dropping from $105 billion in 1999 to $80 billion in 2001. A big reason for the decline is that many big-ticket sales of state companies to private investors have already been completed. But economists like Mr. Kuczynski, who say market reforms must continue for capital-poor Latin economies to progress, are worried.

Bolivia, for instance, was an early convert along with Chile in the 1990's to what is called the neoliberal model. It reined in loose monetary policies and shrank the government by unloading dozens of state-owned companies to private international investors. The results, particularly in taming inflation and reducing poverty, were impressive.

But in one of Latin America's poorest nations, it is hard for Bolivian officials to talk about progress to the wide portion of the population that continues to live in grinding poverty and feels that entitlements the government once provided in the form of subsidized rates for water and electricity have been stripped away.

The better services that have accompanied the sale of state enterprises have left many indifferent, particularly in impoverished areas where residents had invested their own money and sweat to string up electrical lines or put in water pipes and drainage.

"Clearly if you're poor and have no water, sewage and live in a rural area, having three long distance telephone companies when you have no phone lines doesn't make a bean of difference," Bolivia's president, Jorge Quiroga, acknowledged in an interview.

In Peru the resistance to privatization and market reforms is especially pronounced and, for its government, puzzling.

Unlike most of Latin America, the economy here has steadily grown since Mr. Toledo's election in June 2001 as the government has continued sales of assets begun during the decade-long rule of Alberto K. Fujimori.

Government officials say the program has been successful. Phone installation, which used to take years and cost $1,500 or more, now costs $50 and takes a day or two. Electrical service, once shoddy and limited, has spread across the country.

The privatization of mines, which is nearly complete, has improved efficiency and output so much that employment in that sector and related activities has increased to more than 60,000 today from 42,000 in 1993.

But government belt-tightening also led to widespread layoffs. Mr. Toledo's government has been hit hard by protests and popular discontent, much of it fueled by its inability to alleviate poverty. Many have blamed the privatizations, seeing them as a vestige of the corruption-riddled presidency of Mr. Fujimori, who is now in exile in Japan.

Here in Arequipa, where the economy was already limping, when word came that the government was about to sell the two state-owned electric companies, Egasa and Egesur, people recalled that Mr. Toledo had campaigned on a pledge never to sell the companies to private owners.

It did not matter that the government promised Arequipa half the sale price, and that the investor, the Brussels-based Tractebel S.A., would invest tens of millions of dollars more to improve services.

The promises were not believed. Soon the workers federation, neighborhood organizations and university students organized protests, suspecting that higher electricity costs and layoffs were on the way.

"Thanks to our fight, our perseverance, the government backed down," Alejandro Pacheco, a leader in the protests here, told a roomful of supporters this week. "Now we need to do this in the rest of Peru."

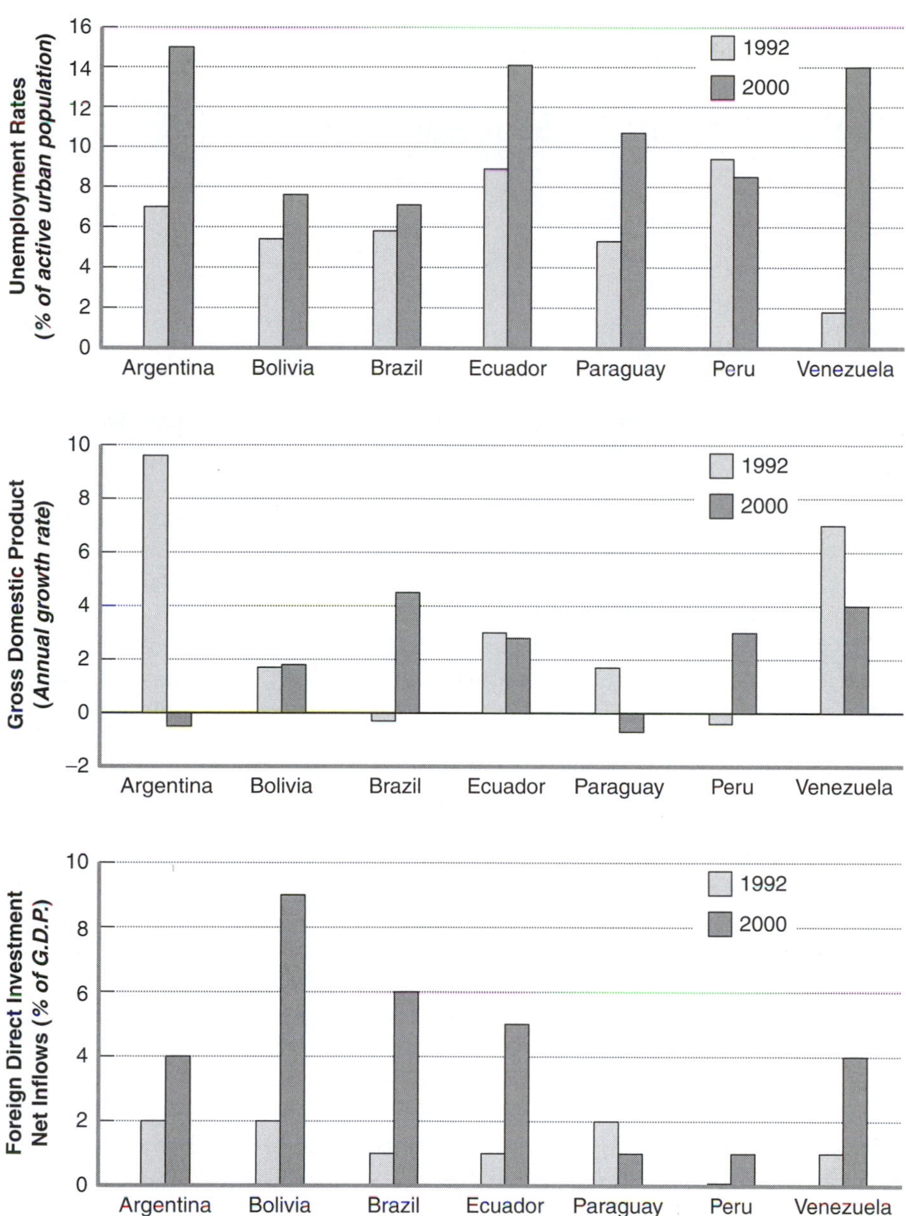

Chart: "FOR THE RECORD: Troubled Economies"

Unemployment has been rising while growth is uneven across Latin America, where reforms have opened local markets to foreign competition.

(SOURCES: World Bank, U.N. Economic Commission for Latin America and the Caribbean) (pg. A8)
LOAD-DATE: July 19, 2002

ARTICLE 9.4

The Ecology of the Movements

Notes from Nowhere

We Are Everywhere: The Irresistible Rise of Global Anticapitalism, the book from which this selection is taken, is a collection of articles describing movements protesting the "great transformation" of neoliberal globalization (see Polanyi, 2–2). The authors, including the editors (who wrote the article included here), participated in many of the protests and movements described in the book. This selection analyzes the organizational features that unite the many movements protesting globalization—movements that are radically decentralized yet not aimless. The authors claim that the movements resemble a swarm of ants, in that the many individuals and local movements who are participants, while highly diverse and acting in very different ways, are integrated into a relatively unified whole that is greater than the sum of the parts.

Do you think that this description is what actually exists, that what the authors recommend is a desirable organizational form, or both? What are the advantages of this organizational form? What might be the divisions and dilemmas of a swarm? Compare the movement in this selection with those described by Keck and Sikkink, (9–3), Klein (9–4), and Wapner (10–1). Do the diverse movements have similar goals and organizational structure? If there are differences, what might account for them?

> "In the age of global flows and networks . . . the small scale and the local are the places of greatest intensity."
>
> —*Jean Franco*, "What's Left of the Intelligensia?," North American Congress on Latin America's Report on the Americas, vol. 28, no. 2, 1994

A black balloon drifts across the dusty cement floor, pushed by an invisible draught. Printed on it in small, neat, white letters are the words, "Everything is connected to everything else." It's late September of 2000, and I'm in an enormous factory hangar on the outskirts of Prague. The machines have all gone, and in their place are thousands of bustling human beings. Some of them rush around, occasionally bumping into one another, exchanging a few words and then continuing on their way; a few stand alone, cell phone in hand,

Notes from Nowhere, *We are Everywhere: The Irresistible Rise of Global Anticapitalism*, pp. 19–29. Reprinted by permission of Verso, London, 2003.

engaged in distant dialogues, while still others sit in intimate circles on the floor, talking, plotting. I'm inside the convergence centre, a space where activists are preparing the actions against the World Bank and International Monetary Fund (IMF) meetings due to begin in a couple of days.

There are Catalonians building large yellow skeleton puppets, friendly-looking Polish punks with scary dogs, haggard protest veterans huddled over detailed maps of the city, and fresh-faced newcomers trying to work out how to put on gas masks. There is a German squatter building a police radio scrambler, a Maori activist being interviewed by an Indymedia camerawoman, and an Italian from a squatted social centre trying on his makeshift armour of inner-tube-and-cardboard. In one corner, British Earth Firstlers are planning a street communications team, in another Colombian peasants hold a workshop about the U.S. funding of Plan Colombia and Czech anarchists learn street first aid. Outside, the sound of a marching band from Seattle practicing its driving rhythms bounces off the building, while a few desultory Marxists attempt to sell their books and newspapers. Amidst the chaos, Dutch cooks prepare a massive meal to feed the rabble. And then there's me and my companion—an Indian activist from Narmada Bachao Andolan, the struggle against the Narmada dam project. He is wrapped in a brown wool cardigan and shivering slightly.

"What do you make of this?" I ask. "These people!" he says fiercely, throwing out his hand to encompass the entire chaotic scene, in which hundreds of people are taking part in a mass meeting to collectively agree on the plan to disrupt the summit, arguing over endless points of principle, in five different languages, "These people have NO LEADERS!" He pauses, waggling his head sternly. "It's very, very, very good."

The Strength of Stories

> "Act in assembly when together, act in network when apart."
>
> —*Mexican National Indigenous Congress*

How does this seemingly chaotic movement of movements—without leaders, with overflowing diversity and contradictions, without clear organizational structures, without a shared programme or manifesto, without a command and control centre—manage to bring thousands of activists from around the world to cities, such as Prague, Genoa or Seattle to protest a summit? How did swirling affinity groups besieging the IMF/World Bank meetings in Prague manage to force them to close a day earlier than scheduled? How was the agenda, according to one World Bank delegate, "effectively seized" by the protesters? And how did this movement coordinate a simultaneous global day of action in over 110 cities across the world in solidarity with the Prague mobilization? Surely this high level of organization is only possible with some form of leadership?

"Take me to your leader," is the first demand of aliens to earthlings, police to protesters, journalists to revolutionaries. But it's a demand that falls on deaf ears whenever directed to participants in this global uprising. Ask the neighbourhood assemblies of Argentina, the indigenous Zapatistas of Mexico, the autonomous island-dwellers of Kunayala off the coast of Panama or participants in the spokescouncils of the U.S. Direct Action Network who shut down the WTO in Seattle. All will speak of horizontal, as opposed to pyramidal structures of power, dispersed networks rather than united fronts.

Movements of the past are laden with charismatic leaders—Che Guevara, Rosa Luxemburg, Huey Newton, Karl Marx, Emma Goldman, Lenin, Mao Tse-Tung. But whose face can be found in the foreground of today's movement? Ironically, the first face that comes to mind is masked and bears the pseudonym "Subcomandante Marcos." This is the spokesperson for the Zapatistas, whose words have profoundly influenced the spirit of the movement. But he, like so much of this movement, thrives on the power and creativity of paradox, for he speaks of leading by obeying, carrying out the policies of a committee of indigenous campesinos. Note the "sub" commander, and the anonymity of the mask. He warns that the name Marcos is interchangeable—anyone can put on a ski mask and say "I am Marcos." In fact he says that Marcos does not exist, but is simply a window, a bridge, a mediator between worlds. He says that we are all Marcos. Not what one expects from a traditional leader.

It follows that a movement with no leaders organizes horizontally, through networks. And it was the poetic communiqués and powerful stories that trickled from the Zapatista autonomous zones in the Chiapas jungle onto the relatively new medium of the internet which told of their suffering, their struggles, their mythologies, that began to weave an electronic fabric of struggle in the mid-nineties. This web of connections between diverse groups gave birth to a series of face-to-face international gatherings—the Zapatista Encuentros—which soon grew to become the roaring, unstoppable torrent of movements for life and dignity and against capital that are emerging across the world. "We are the network," declared the Zapatistas, "all of us who resist."

Like a virus, uncontrollable and untameable, this inspiration flowed from city to city, country to country, spreading at the same speed as the trillions of dollars involved in the reckless unsustainable money game of transnational capital. Like the financial markets, the inspiration fed on rumour and myth. Unlike the markets, it thrived on the rejection of ownership and enclosure.

Capital's dream of super fast networks that will spread consumerism across the planet was turned on its head. For while the networked money markets were tearing the planet apart, our grassroots networks were bringing us together. People were using the global communications infrastructure for something completely different—to become more autonomous, to get the state and corporations off their backs, to live in a more healthy way. To talk to one another.

As the links grew, more stories were added to the flow, accounts of audacity and courage, moments of magic and hope. The tale of the Indian farmers demolishing the first Kentucky Fried Chicken in the country, or the news of five million French workers bringing the country to a standstill and reversing their government's neoliberal policies—layer upon layer of stories travelled along the thin copper threads of the internet, strengthening the global network and developing relationships between diverse groups and individuals. People found strength in the stories, which expressed a sense of identity and belonging, communicated a shared sense of purpose and mission. The movement was learning that it was as important to capture imaginations as to command actions.

Perhaps the first victim to be defeated by this nascent network of subversive information-sharing was the Multilateral Agreement on Investment (MAI), a treaty whose text was cooked up in the sweaty boiler rooms of the most powerful corporate lobby group on earth, the International Chamber of Commerce. If it had been implemented, the MAI would have enabled corporations to sue governments—it was a veritable charter for corporate rule. The network was galvanized when U.S. campaigners Public Citizen circulated the secret text on the internet in 1997. "If a negotiator says something to someone over a glass of wine, we'll have it on the internet within an hour," the campaigners claimed.

Against a total media blackout, the email inboxes of activists began bristling with life, with information, with strategy, with education. List-serves bulged as the nascent global network took shape with messages from Canadian truckers, Maori groups, Harvard trade lawyers, French cultural activists. Their defeat of the MAI in 1998 was the first real success story of the movement, sending a shiver down the spine of its next target: the World Trade Organization, which would meet the following year in Seattle. A rich blend of past political forms (especially from feminist, ecological, and peace movements) of the global North and various indigenous forms of organizing from the global South, these new hybrid networks didn't quite fit any previous models of political practice. Police forces, journalists, academics, politicians, and traditional leftist parties were at a loss to understand them. "Who ARE these guys?" wondered the *Financial Times* after the defeat of the MAI. Something important was stirring as the way of doing and thinking about politics was changing radically—yet still it remained below the radar screen.

The Logic of the Swarm

> "Those who dance are considered insane by those that cannot hear the music."
> — *George Carlin*

"We don't consider them terrorists. . . . We're not yet sure how to even label them," says a spokesman for Europol, Europe's transnational police agency, struggling to describe the new breed of protesters. British political commentator Hugo Young attacked the "herbivores" behind anticapitalist protests for making "a virtue out of being disorganized," while the head of the World Wildlife Fund referred to us in Genoa, as a "formless howling mob." It was the RAND Corporation, a U.S. military think tank, who actually came up with most accurate description. In their 2002 book, *Networks and Netwars*, they describe the Zapatista uprising, the web of interconnected activists' groups and NGOs, the affinity groups of Seattle, and the tactics of the Black Bloc as *swarms*, and predicted that swarming would be the main form of conflict in the future. While for most commentators, a bottom-up system that functioned so effectively was totally outside their conceptual framework, the RAND Institute, steeped in the latest developments of systems theory and complexity, turned to the natural world for the best metaphor. They realized what others failed to see—that there is enormous power and intelligence in the swarm.

Since the seventeenth century scientists have made enormous technical discoveries through taking the world apart, piece by piece, to try and understand how it works. Their mechanical model of reality saw life as a giant machine made up of separate parts. Linear processes of cause and effect, command and control dominated their thinking.

These mechanistic perceptions have been central to our patriarchal, Western "scientific" worldview. But this formulation of reality involves an enormous blind spot, one which science has only relatively recently started to uncover. As a result they have failed to recognize complex, interdependent systems. This is one of the root causes of our current ecological crises. Problems as different as global warming, homelessness, and mental illness are all seen in the context of single cause and effect processes. But these cannot be cured like a clock's workings can be mended. They require a different way of looking at the world—in other words, they require whole-systems thinking.

Witness how recent tests studying the effects of genetically modified organisms (GMOs) on the environment have taken place in so-called controlled field settings, ignoring the fact that such control does not exist in nature. GMO flowers produce pollen, as does any ordinary flower, and bees will take the pollen to other fields, thus contaminating other plants. There is nothing isolated in nature. Mechanistic thinking develops a world view which is unable to see the interconnection and interdependence of life, unable to see the world for what it is—a huge, complex, dynamic system where everything is connected to everything else, as the balloon in Prague so eloquently suggested.

But over the last few decades there has been a paradigm shift in scientific understandings of living systems. Scientists are now discovering what indigenous knowledge has long taught—everything is connected. Ecologists, biologists, physicists, and mathematicians have begun to be able to describe vastly complex connected webs of life, which are made up of networks within networks. They have gradually realized that life has the ability to self-organize and mutually adapt, without anyone in control. Their descriptions of living systems are perhaps the best model yet for how the movement functions.

Imagine watching thousands of birds take off one by one. As they begin to rise into the air, a pattern emerges. They group together and then, if a predator approaches, the flock rapidly turns direction, swooping up, down, left, right; all the birds stay together, and none of them bump into each other. The whole flock moves as one, as if it's one organism. Yet no one is in charge; it seems to happen as if magically. High-speed film reveals that the movement spreads across a flock in less than one-seventieth of a second. Yet this should be impossible, as it is much faster than a single bird's reaction time. The flock is clearly more than the sum of its parts. But how is this possible?

Observing the movement of affinity groups from police helicopters during many of the mass mobilizations of the past few years, or trying to map the daily flow of information between the forever-transforming activist groups on the internet must create a similar sense of bafflement for the authorities. Even participants in the movements are often confused as to how everything seems to somehow fit together so well. The logic of the swarm is an eerie thing, especially when you don't understand its simple rules. Those who are unable to learn from these observations will remain frozen in mechanistic logic, which thinks the whole is never greater than the sum of its parts.

The swarm phenomena can be observed everywhere. Think of the billions of neurons in your brain. A neuron on its own cannot have thought, cannot write poetry, move a muscle, or dream, but working with other neurons it can produce extraordinary things. Now think of a dense mass of bees swarming across a landscape in search of the perfect location for a new hive; all this happens without anyone in charge, without any single command centre.

It wasn't until the advent of high speed computers that scientists were able to begin to unravel this mystery. Prior to that, they had observed the phenomena, but because they were attached to their clockwork view of the world, they literally couldn't believe their eyes. For years after the idea had first been posited in the 1950s by Alan Turing, inventor of the computer, scientists couldn't believe it, and kept looking for a head bird, a leading cell. Only computers could model these hugely complex self-organized, and interconnected systems. What scientists saw was astounding—each element, seemed to be following simple rules, and yet when the multitude was working together they were forming a highly intelligent sophisticated self-organized system. Nowadays software designers, urban planners and ecologists all use these concepts in their day-to-day work; the realm of politics has yet [to] catch up.

For this is truly organizing from below. The process of simple local units generating complicated global or group behaviour, a process not directed by a conscious entity, but rather emerging through the interrelationships of the system's parts is known in scientific circles as *emergence*.

If numbers, neurons, crowds, computer programmes, cells, city dwellers, birds behave like this, why not a networked movement of movements?

Learning to Self-Organize

> "Chaos is a name for any order that produces confusion in our minds."
>
> — *George Santayana*

Emergence may seem to "just happen" but it's actually the result of clear sets of mathematical principles and processes that govern a highly connected network. Through these, we can learn how to organize creative actions and build sustainable movements in our local communities. There is a tendency within some aspects of anticapitalist movements to think that actions happen spontaneously, without planning or structure. An email from Australia inaccurately suggested that the Reclaim the Streets street parties in London resulted from pure spontaneity. The email's author bemoaned the fact that Australians somehow did not possess this magical ability to just turn up and create a street party from nothing. As any organizer can confirm, creating situations in which spontaneity can occur is a lot of hard, and mostly not magical work.

Spontaneity is a vital tool of resistance, but it occurs only under certain conditions. The most successful movements are those that are able to adapt to situations rapidly and spontaneously, much like the flock of birds avoiding the predator, precisely because of a stunning amount of preparation, interconnection, and flow of communication that is already in place.

What are the ingredients of successful mass actions? Incredible structures are developed beforehand: we find large buildings and transform them into convergence centres; we organize workshops, trainings, and coordinating meetings; we form affinity groups which meet each other and form clusters; we work out communication channels via mobile phones, pagers and so forth; we set up independent media centres and pirate radio stations, ready to compile information from multiple street reporters and feed it back to the streets; we develop beautiful and enticing printed propaganda; the list is endless. It takes months of planning to set up the networks from which can emerge the intelligence of a magically moving, thinking swarm, a shape-shifting organism that can survive the chaos of the streets or the disruption and repression of the state.

The Pentagon think-tank RAND, in its highly informative analysis of the successful swarming strategies of the Zapatistas' civil society networks and the Direct Action Network's WTO shut down in Seattle, suggests that this movement is ahead of state authorities in its mastery of swarming. But it also suggests that the police learned a lot from their failures, and that activist groups have learned little from our victories. Although mass mobilizations have grown steadily since then, there has been a tendency in the latest mobilizations to repeat ourselves, to attempt to reproduce Seattle, or even worse, to return to familiar forms of struggle, the mass marches instead of decentralized actions, rallies and speeches instead of assemblies and spokescouncils—forms which squander our new-found advantages, and do not reflect the new worlds we want to build. The new is always more daunting than the familiar, but if we don't want to repeat the failures of great rebellions of the past, we need to continue to develop ways of working that learn from our victories, which build on the past and yet are always reaching into the unmapped and unknown future.

Sustainability comes to those who can adapt and change the quickest, a concept that is alien to many older forms of political organizing. Many of the groups in these new networks call themselves "(dis)organizations," implying that they are loose networks rather than formal organizations.

Yet in order to give up control and allow the system to govern itself, we need to develop structures that will enable us to lose control with dignity and thus be able to overwhelm the dry and brittle forces of state repression with our invincible fluidity. Authoritarian systems are good at changing laws but not habits, and it seems that in the race for true network mastery in the political arena, we are already in the lead. By learning some of the principles of swarm logic and emergence, we can develop creative tactics and strategies that will put us even further ahead, not just for mass street actions, but for all forms of organization and mobilization in our networks, whether through the global reach of the internet, or within the local spaces of our communities. The future of the planet and society may well depend on who builds the most successful network of networks.

Watching the Ants

> "We need to work like the Zapatistas do, like ants who go everywhere no matter which political party the other belongs to. Zapatistas proved people can work together in spite of differences."
>
> —*Anna Esther Cecena* of the FZLN (Mexican support committee of the Zapatistas)

Systems theorists know there is no better way to learn about emergence than by looking at the extraordinary behaviour of ant colonies—one of nature's most successful examples of bottom-up intelligence. Ants are found virtually everywhere, from the tropics to the desert to the tundra, and account for over 18 per cent of the earth's biomass (the combined weight of every living thing on the planet). They grow fungi in farms, raise aphids as livestock, and have extraordinary engineering skills and city planning, building recycling dumps, lavatories, and graveyards situated away from the main body of the colony.

Ant colonies are perfectly self-managed without any single ant in charge. They can switch rapidly between roles of foraging, nest-building, and raising pupae; they can work out the shortest route to food, and prioritize food sources based on quality, ease of access, and distance from the nest; and the entire colony seems to know exactly how many ants are needed where and for what jobs at any given time. The best way to think of a colony is as a self-regulating organism, with its millions of cells and all its bio-chemical feedback loops constantly adjusting itself to reach homeostasis—regular heart beat, body temperature and so on.

Our cultural images of ants evoke military columns, with proud soldier ants marching in a straight line, one column going towards the food and the other back to the colony (just like a motorway), with isolated individuals tirelessly working for the queen. But if you really observe what is happening, you will see something quite different—the ants are actually all weaving in and out of line, and touching each other! Every single ant greets each ant coming from the other direction, heads and antennae stroke one another, communicating with pheromones, then going on its way and meeting the next ant. In any line of ants, virtually every ant will meet and briefly exchange information with every other ant. Somehow, these simple interactions multiplied enable the colony as a whole to adjust the tasks allotted to each ant, allowing the colony to run efficiently. In this cooperative conversation between separate local parts can be found the extraordinary phenomenon of emergence, where the sum of all the parts becomes greater than the whole.

Clearly, ants are very different from people. But the way the ant colony as a whole works, its process, is comparable to that of the movement of movements—the numerous email lists, the autonomous local groups networking globally, the face-to-face gatherings, the convergence centres, the ebb and flow of crowds in the occupied streets. This not only how our local actions produce global behaviour; but shows us how important the quality and amount of communication is in the maintenance of effective networks.

Most of the anticapitalist global days of action happened not because of central commands, but simply because a small group sent out a proposal. If the proposal captured other groups' imaginations, they disseminated it on email lists, discussed it at meetings, mentioned it in publications, web pages and so on. It multiplied exponentially in every direction, a kind of ricochet rebellion, and in the end, no one takes responsibility and yet everyone takes the credit. In emergent systems, you influence your neighbours and your neighbours influence you. All relationships are mutual feedback loops.

Paying attention to the lessons of the ants, and their emergent systems can help teach us how to build efficient trickle-up systems, networks where the local becomes global, where the top-down chains of command are broken and replaced by a multitude of individual, communicative links acting simultaneously.

Four Ways to Act Like an Ant and Dream Like a Giant

> "Our enemies did not cross our borders, they crept through our weaknesses like ants."
>
> —*Nizar Qabbani*

If we want to build networks that behave like a swarm, these four rules from the ant world can guide us:

More is different: A few ants roaming across your kitchen floor might find the bread crumb hiding under the table, a lone affinity group might find the breach in the fence around the summit, a few independent researchers might manage to find the link between the Enron scandal and their local council.

But increase their numbers and interconnect them and you'll have something which behaves quite differently—you'll get systematic change—a movement that can cause an entire summit to be cancelled, or the entire corporate accounting system to come crumbling down. Many interacting smaller pieces create the exponential magic of emergence: swarm logic.

Our movements are multiplying at an incredible rate. Every day new connections are developing both face to face and virtually as the internet grows to connect more sentient beings than any other technology before it. New webpages, email lists and Indymedia centres are springing up like grass after a downpour, leading to more networking, more co-ordination, and more actions. The crowd has always terrified those in authority, but a crowd where each individual is able to think and act autonomously, a crowd where everyone is connected to everyone else, will cause more than a shiver down their spine, because it behaves in ways that no one will ever be able to predict.

Stay small: The greatest feature of the ant colony is the simplicity of each ant; if one ant began to somehow assess the overall state of the whole colony, the sophisticated behaviour would stop trickling up from below, and swarm logic would collapse. Emergence teaches us that not to know everything is a strength and that local knowledge is sovereign. The magic is in densely interconnected systems made up of small simple elements.

As soon as our groups become too big, communication tends to break down and hierarchies develop. We must learn to divide like cells before this happens; big is unwieldy, small and connected is what we should aim for.

A network of a million small interconnected groups cannot be stopped by any of the world's police agencies, no leaders can be singled out for assassination or corruption, no single headquarters raided, no central party committee infiltrated. But that doesn't mean our movement is small—for we are all networked into a whole that is larger than anyone can possibly imagine.

Encourage randomness: Haphazard encounters are key to network-building—they are where creativity lies. Without the lone ant exploring new territory, no one would find new sources of food or develop ways to adapt to environmental conditions.

Decentralized systems thrive on the creativity of random encounters. How often have you been in a huge swirling crowd on the streets during a festival or an action and bumped into exactly the right person, or found out a key piece of information you were seeking? How often have you received a seemingly randomly forwarded e-mail from someone that happens to point you to someone else who will enable your new project to get off the ground?

Some may think that with perfect unity the revolution begins, but without randomness, evolution ends. While some toe the party line, others are drifting and dancing into new ways of changing the world. What may look like chaos to some is actually brimming with creativity.

Listen to your neighbours: "Local" turns out to be the key term in understanding swarm logic. Emergent behaviour happens because the ants are paying attention to their neighbours, rather than waiting for orders from a distant authority. The more ants do so, the more quickly their colony will solve problems. Local information leads to global wisdom; this is the secret of the intelligent swarm.

The ants teach us that by working locally and continually sharing our local stories globally, by connecting everything and creating a plethora of feedback loops, we don't need to—indeed cannot—"organize" the global network, it will regulate itself, swarm-like, life-like, if we develop the right structures and conditions.

The (r)Evolution Will Be Improvised

> "I saw everyone and saw no one, for every individual was subsumed into the same, countless, meandering crowd: I spoke to everybody but could remember neither my own words nor others, for my attention was at every step held by new events and objects, by unforeseen developments." —*Mikhail Bakunin*

When Bakunin wrote of his experience on the streets of Paris during the 1848 revolution, he was unknowingly describing emergence. Thinking and technology [have] evolved exponentially since he wrote, yet our thinking around political change has not evolved to the same degree. Although a revolution has occurred in our perception of the world, many of our perceptions of political change remain stuck and fixed in centuries old models—centralized parties, uniformity, manifestoes, taking control of power, hierarchical leadership.

Now that we better understand the workings of decentralized, diverse interconnected networks within networks, where everything is in flux—there is no excuse for our political forms to remain stuck in ways of seeing and thinking from the past, it's time to evolve.

One thing that has not changed since 1848 is the fact that revolutionary moments always open up the social space for people to begin to connect in new and manifold ways, spontaneous convergences occur, and a multitude of unaccustomed conversations arise. If we look at any revolutionary situation we see human interactions multiplying as the streets and squares are filled, groups and networks coalescing, as the human desire for conviviality swamps the alienation of capital. The town hall meetings of the American Revolution of 1776, for example, or the sections of the 1789 French revolution; the clubhouses of the 1871 Paris Commune or the numerous syndicates during the Spanish Civil War of 1936; the *Räte* in Hungary during the uprising of 1956 or the workers' councils of May 1968; the popular assemblies that appeared spontaneously across Argentina after the uprising of 19 December 2001.

What is emerging now is a dialogue of a million voices, which is building the first truly interconnected global uprising, an unprecedented transnational social evolution, a revolution made up of thousands of revolutions, not just one. A revolution that is not predetermined, or predictable: not going around in circles but moving in every direction simultaneously. What we are witnessing now is actually a lot more like evolution, a work in progress that makes itself up as it goes along, constantly adapting to each others' needs. An unprecedented global (r)Evolution, is taking place and many of us don't even recognize it.

Activist Hazel Wolf lived through a Russian Revolution, a Chinese Revolution, and the fall of the Berlin Wall. "The thing about all of them is, nobody knew they were going to happen," she says. A revolution, by its nature, hardly seems possible before it takes place; but it may seem obvious, even inevitable, in hindsight.

As the networks grow more connected, by webs and actions, wires and stories, many things will emerge that we, as mere neurons in the network, don't expect, don't understand, can't control, and may not even perceive. The only way to understand an emergent system is to let it run, because no individual agent will ever be able to reveal the whole. The global movement of movements for life against money, for autonomy and dignity, for the dream of distributed direct democracy, are following an irresistible logic. It is a logic as old as the hills and the forests, an eco-logic, a bio-logic, the profound logic of life.

ARTICLE 9.5

The Global Dimensions of Religious Terrorism

Mark Juergensmeyer

The transnational movements described in this selection are very different from those analyzed in other selections in this chapter. Mark Juergensmeyer focuses on what he calls *religious terrorism.* He argues that religious commitment often provides participants in transnational terrorist movements with the fierce certainty necessary to develop extraordinary motivation and to engage in violent actions that, paradoxically, appear to violate ethical precepts. (Juergensmeyer's observation recalls a remark by George Bernard Shaw, a British playwright, that the path to hell is paved with good intentions.) Juergensmeyer also stresses the importance of the transnational element in the movements he studies: religious terrorism often involves holy war on a global scale. This selection highlights the diversity of transnational social movements and networks, and the fact that some may be ugly and violent.

During the Cold War, America's prime enemy was the vast Soviet empire. Ten years after the fall of that empire, America's most wanted enemy was a single person—Osama bin Laden—a man without a state. Shunned by his native Saudi Arabia, bin Laden encamped in various places, most often in Afghanistan, where even the Taliban have found him to be a difficult guest. But he did not represent them or any other state, not even a rogue regime.

Bin Laden is not, however, a complete anomaly. He symbolizes a variety of movements of religious activism that despise the symbols of secular power in a global age, and he is a significant authority figure within a transnational network that encompasses a certain segment of these disgruntled activists. In America's anguish after the savage aerial assaults on the World Trade Center and the Pentagon on 11 September 2001, a critical question was how to retaliate: who or what should be attacked? Clearly bin Laden was implicated, as he was in the previous assault on the World Trade Center in 1993 and the bombing of American

Mark Juergensmeyer, "The Global Dimensions of Religious Terrorism," ch. 7 in Rodney Bruce Hall and Thomas J. Biersteker, eds., *The Emergence of Private Authority in Global Governance* (Cambridge: Cambridge University Press, 2002): 141–157.

embassies in Africa in 1998, but an appropriate response to these attacks was the subject of a great deal of debate both within and outside American diplomatic circles. In attempting to defeat bin Laden, no one in the U.S. administration was under the illusion that they could defeat terrorism everywhere, nor banish all of bin Laden's own brand of Islamic extremism. Though the United States wanted to punish those states that harbored terrorists, its policy-makers were keenly aware that they were confronting a new kind of enemy: one that was not a nation-state but an emerging transnational force.

The maddening thing about this new enemy was that it could not easily be located: it did not operate under a single command. For one thing, the religious activists who targeted the United States represented different strands of religion—various branches within the Hindu, Sikh, Buddhist, Christian, Jewish, and Muslim faiths—and their goals are diverse. Some aim to create a specific religious state. Others, like bin Laden, have no interest in establishing a single alternative government, but operate on a broader, transnational scale. They oppose what they believe to be sinister forces at work in an American-led transnational economy, one allied with the satellite transmission of secular popular culture.

The spectacular assault on the twin towers of the World Trade Center and the Pentagon, therefore, was the work of guerilla antiglobalists. These targets were symbols of globalization as well as of American strength. The paradox, however, is that to accomplish this assault they had to create their own transnational network. They formed a kind of shadow alternative globalism of their own.

What both religious nationalism and guerilla antiglobalism have in common is their reliance on bases of authority that in secular societies are not perceived as public. These new movements of transnational private authority, such as bin Laden's al Qaeda network, are based on pillars of power that are in fact quite old: religion and extra-legal violence. Indeed, the two are related. Religious ideology provides ethical justifications for violence, thereby providing a moral base for assaulting what Max Weber described as essential for the public authority of the state—a monopoly on the moral sanction for killing. At the same time, violence—especially violence performed in unpredictable and frightening acts of terrorism—empowers religion. In the wake of the World Trade Center assault, bin Laden basked in the stature suddenly attributed to him as America's greatest enemy. Acts of violence have given religious activists a credibility they otherwise would not have had.

Terrorism and Religion

Around the world religious terrorism at the turn of the twenty-first century became a way of life. The French dealt with subway bombs planted by Algerian Islamic activists; the British with exploding trucks and buses ignited by groups on both sides in the dispute in Northern Ireland; the Japanese with nerve gas placed in Tokyo subways by members of a Hindu-Buddhist sect. In India, residents of Delhi experienced car bombings by both Sikh and Kashmiri Muslim separatists;

in Sri Lanka whole sections of the city of Colombo were destroyed both by Tamil Hindu and Sinhalese Buddhist militants; Egyptians lived with militant Islamic attacks in coffee-houses and on river boats; Algerians lost whole villages to savage attacks perpetrated allegedly by supporters of the Islamic Salvation Front; and Israelis and Palestinians confronted the deadly deeds of extremists from both the Jewish and Muslim sides.

Religious violence has appeared in virtually every part of the world, and in association with every major religious tradition. In the United States most acts of terrorism have been related to Christian militia and racist religious movements: the 1999 attacks on a Jewish day-care center in Los Angeles and ethnic assaults in Illinois and Indiana, abortion clinic bombings in Alabama and Georgia in 1997, the bomb blast at the Olympics in Atlanta in 1996, and the tragic destruction of the federal building at Oklahoma City in 1995. These incidents, the 1993 assault on the World Trade Center, and the spectacular attacks on 11 September 2001 have brought Americans into the same uneasy location occupied by many in the rest of the world: confronting religious violence as a political reality. But what is the political point of such violent demonstrations of power?

To search for answers to this and other questions relating to the emergence of religious terrorism at this moment of history, I have gone to the sources. In a series of case studies, including Hamas suicide bombings, Jewish militancy in Israel, the Tokyo subway nerve gas attack, and abortion clinic bombings in the United States, I interviewed a number of religious activists and their supporters.[1] The point was to try to penetrate into their view of the world, and to look for commonalities in the thinking of violent religious activists across cultural boundaries.

One of these conversations was with Mahmud Abouhalima, convicted for his role in the 1993 bombing of the World Trade Center. When I talked with him he was serving a life sentence at the Federal Penitentiary at Lompoc, California. He was open to discussing a wide range of topics regarding the relationship between religion and politics but, since he was hoping to appeal his conviction, he was wary about getting into the specifics of his own case. He did, however, discuss the bombing of the Oklahoma City federal building and the trials of Terry Nichols and Timothy McVeigh. In trying to help me understand why someone would choose a government building—and hundreds of innocent workers and bystanders who happened to be at the wrong place at the wrong time—Abouhalima told me that it was done "for a very, very specific reason." Abouhalima added that "they wanted to reach the government with the message that we are not tolerating the way that you are dealing with our citizens."[2] It was a message, he said, that normal life was intolerable, and that someone other than the government had the power to act in a dramatic public way.

Was the bombing an act of terrorism, I asked him? Abouhalima thought for a moment, then explained that the whole concept was "messed up." The term seemed to be used only for incidents of violence that people didn't like or, rather, Abouhalima explained, for incidents that the media have labeled terrorist. "What about the United States government?," Abouhalima asked me. "How do they justify their acts of bombings, of killing innocent people, directly or indirectly, openly or secretly? They're killing people everywhere in the world: before, today, and tomorrow." "How do you define that?," he asked. Then he described what he regarded as America's terrorist attitude toward the world. According to Abouhalima, the United States tries to "terrorize nations," to "obliterate their power," and to tell them that they "are nothing" and that they "have to follow" America's lead. Abouhalima implied that any form of international political or economic control was a form of terrorism. With these assertions Abouhalima indicated that he did not regard U.S. power as legitimate. It is, in his mind, non-authoritative. He sought to challenge U.S. authority transnationally.

Abouhalima also gave specific examples of where he felt the United States had used its power to kill people indiscriminately. "In Japan, for instance," Abouhalima said, referring to the atomic bomb blasts, "through the bombs . . . that killed more than 200,000 people." Perhaps it was just a coincidence, but the number that Abouhalima cited as having been killed in Hiroshima and Nagasaki was exactly the number that is estimated would have been killed in the 2001 World Trade Center collapse if both towers had toppled immediately and fallen into adjacent buildings rather than imploded into themselves.

Was the Oklahoma City blast a terrorist response to the government's terrorism? "That's what I'm saying," Abouhalima replied. "If they believe, if these guys, whoever they are, did whatever bombing they say they did in Oklahoma City, if they believe that the government unjustifiably killed the people in Waco, then they have their own way to respond." "They absolutely have their own way to respond," Abouhalima added for emphasis, indicating that the Oklahoma City bombing "response" was morally justified. "Yet," I said, in an effort to put the event in context, "it killed a lot of innocent people, and ultimately it did not seem to change anything."

"But it's as I said," Abouhalima responded, "at least the government got the message." Moreover, Abouhalima told me, the only thing that humans can do in response to great injustice is to send a message. Stressing the point that all human efforts are futile, and that those who bomb buildings should not expect any immediate, tangible change in the government's policies as a result, Abouhalima said that real change—effective change—"is not in our hands," only "in God's hands."

This led to a general discussion about what he regarded as the natural connection between Islam and political order. Abouhalima said this relationship had been weakened by modern leaders of Islamic countries, such as those in his native Egypt, as a result of the influence of the West in general and the United States in particular. The president of Egypt, for example, was not really Muslim, Abouhalima implied, since he "watered down" Islamic law. Leaders such as President Hosni Mubarak "said yes" to Islamic law and principles, Abouhalima explained, but then turned around and "said yes" to secular ideas as well, especially regarding such matters as family law, education, and financial institutions (Muslim law prohibits usury).[3] He offered these examples of the deceitful character of many contemporary politicians: they pretended to be Muslim, but in practice followed secular—implicitly Western—codes of conduct.

Anti-America, Anti-Globalization

The enemy, in Abouhalima's view, was a kind of shadowy force of secularism out to destroy Islam. He and his colleagues, such as Osama bin Laden, thought that the United States was not only the prime example of anti-religion but also its chief supporter. Long before the bombing of the World Trade Center, Abouhalima's spiritual leader, Sheik Omar Abdul Rahman, expressed his disdain over America's role in propping up the Mubarak regime in Egypt. "America is behind all these un-Islamic governments," the sheik explained, arguing that the purpose of American political and economic support was "to keep them strong" and to try to "defeat the Islamic movements."[4] The Ayatollah Khomeini saw the shah and the American government linked together as evil twins: America was tarred by its association with the shah, and the shah, in turn, was corrupted by being a "companion" of "satanic forces"—i.e., America.[5] When Khomeini prayed to his "noble God for protection from the evil of every wicked traitor" and asked Him to "destroy the enemies," the primary traitor he had in mind was the shah, and the main enemy America.[6]

During a lengthy speech given in the courtroom at the end of the trial that convicted him of conspiracy in the 1993 bombing of the World Trade Center, Sheik Omar Abdul Rahman predicted that a "revengeful" God would "scratch" America from the face of the earth.[7] He was not alone, however, in his strident anti-Americanism. According to the RAND Chronicle of International Terrorism, each year since 1968 the United States has headed the list of countries whose citizens and property were most frequently attacked.[8] The U.S. State Department's counter-terrorism unit reported that, during the 1990s, 40 percent of all acts of terrorism worldwide were against American citizens and facilities.[9]

One of the world's best-known critics of America, Osama bin Laden, who was implicated not only in the 11 September 2001 attacks in New York City and Washington, D.C., but also in the attack on the USS *Cole* in Yemen in 1999, and in the bombing of American embassies in Kenya and Tanzania in 1998, explained in an interview in 1997 that America deserved to be targeted because it was "the biggest terrorist in the world."[10] It was an insult returned to bin Laden after the embassy bombings when U.S. National Security Advisor Samuel Berger labeled bin Laden "the most dangerous non-state terrorist in the world."[11] President George W. Bush, after the 11 September 2001 attacks, dubbed him "evil incarnate." The reason bin Laden gave for targeting America was its list of "crimes," which included "occupying the lands of Islam in the holiest of places, the Arabian Peninsula, plundering its riches, dictating to its rulers, humiliating its people, terrorizing its neighbors, and turning its bases in the peninsula into a spearhead through which to fight the neighboring Muslim peoples."[12] In response to what bin Laden regarded as a declaration of war on Muslims by America, he issued a *fatwa* calling on "every Muslim" as "an individual duty" to join him in what he felt was a righteous war "to kill the Americans and their allies." Their obligation was not only "to kill the Americans" but also to "plunder their money wherever and whenever they find it." He sealed his *fatwa* with the reassurance that "this is in accordance with the words of Almighty God," and that "every Muslim who believes in God and wishes to be rewarded" should "comply with God's order."[13] In these statements bin Laden was drawing upon what he regarded as the transcendent moral authority of Islam and his own convictions about God's will to justify his attack on the public authority of the most powerful Western secular state and its agents. In bin Laden's reasoning, a citizen of such a state is *de facto* an agent of this state.

It is not difficult to discern in these assertions an explicit appeal to the moral authority of the transcendent. Bin Laden claims, in essence, to know the mind of God, the ultimate moral authority, and to argue that this moral authority not only opposes America and its secular, Western popular and political culture, but commands Muslims to kill Americans and their allies, and plunder their property, wherever they are found. The authority of the secular state is not simply challenged by bin Laden's ideas and actions. It is so thoroughly obliterated by a transcendent moral authority that the agency on part of the secular Western state implied, somehow, by citizenship within it is judged by the moral authority of the transcendent to be punishable by death.

According to bin Laden's line of reasoning, even moderate Muslim leaders in Arab nations are manipulated by the United States in what amounts to a virtually global conspiracy to assert an American control—one that is perceived as having cultural and economic dimensions as well as military ones. The cultural argument is persuasive in a world where, increasingly, villagers in remote corners of the globe have access to MTV, Hollywood movies, and the internet. They are assaulted with images and values that are both secular and American. In Israel both conservative Jewish rabbis and Muslim mullahs have agreed that the United States was the "capital of the devil."[14] In a similar vein, Mahmud Abouhalima told me that he was bitter that Islam did not have influence over the global media the way that secular America did. America, he believed, was using its power of information to promote the immoral values of secular society.[15]

When Abouhalima linked America's control of the media with its economic power—thought to be in Jewish hands—he was echoing a sentiment earlier articulated by the Ayatollah Khomeini. When he identified the "satanic" forces that were out to destroy Islam, he included not only Israelis but also "more satanic" Westerners: corporate leaders with "no religious belief" who saw Islam as "the major obstacle in the path of their materialistic ambitions and the chief threat to their political power."[16] The ayatollah went on to claim that "all the problems of Iran" were due to the treachery of "foreign colonialists."[17] On another occasion, the ayatollah blended political, personal, and spiritual issues together in generalizing about the cosmic foe—Western colonialism—and about "the black and dreadful future" which "the agents of colonialism, may God Almighty abandon them all," have in mind for Islam and the Muslim people.[18]

What the ayatollah was thinking of when he prophesized a "black and dreadful future" for Islam was the global domination of American economy and culture. This fear of globalization is linked with the fear of America as a dominant military, economic, and cultural force. These apprehensions about globalization have been felt even within certain right-wing quarters of the United States where militias have been convinced that the "new world order" proclaimed by President George Bush was more than a mood of global cooperation: it was a conspiratorial plot to control the world. Accepting this paranoid vision of American leaders' global designs, the Aum Shinrikyo master, Shoko Asahara, linked the United States Army with the Japanese government, Freemasons, and Jews in the image of a global conspiratorial band.

Conspiracy theories aside, there is a certain amount of truth to the notion that globalization and American dominance are related. U.S. culture and economy have influenced societies around the world in ways that have caused concern to protectors of local societies. The vast financial and media networks of American-backed corporations and information systems have affected the whole of the globe. There has indeed been a great conflict between secular and religious life throughout the world, and America does inevitably support the secular side of the fight. Financial aid provided to leaders such as Egypt's Hosni Mubarak has shored up the political power of politicians opposed to religious nationalism. Moreover, after the fall of the Soviet Union, the United States has been virtually the only coherent military power in the world. Hence it has been easy for it to be blamed when people have felt that their lives were going askew or were being controlled by forces that they could not easily see. The extreme form of this anti-Americanism is satanization: imagining America as a demonic entity. This gives its critics the license to strike American people and property as if they were cosmic foes.

New Religious Nationalism

By describing America as a great foe, religious activists like Osama bin Laden have implicitly placed themselves on an international playing field. Their scenario of cosmic war is designed not only to lower the United States, but also to elevate themselves to a level of national—or even transnational—importance. For this reason, some activist groups have gone to some effort to make themselves credible in the eyes of their opponents. Acts of violence, including the U.S. Embassy bombings in Africa, have been perpetrated in part in order to fulfill threats made against their enemies. The Kashmiri rebels who killed their American and European hostages were said to have found themselves in a dilemma: not necessarily wanting to murder the young men, but feeling that they had an obligation to be true to their word when they threatened to kill them if their demands were not met.

Although it may appear as if these acts were meant as signs of respect to their opponents, they also showed something else: that the movements acted as if they were their opponent's equals. Kashmiri rebels thought themselves to be as important as the Indian government; Osama bin Laden's network imagined itself to be equal to the greatest superpower on earth. In a display of what René Girard has described as mimesis, they were not only imitating their rivals, but also showing their superiority in terms that they believed that their rivals would understand.[19] In doing so, they make an implicit claim to represent a form of authority that is morally superior to, and that competes with, the public authority of the secular Western state. Many activists used their courtroom trials as arenas to get across the notion that through their acts they were sparring with the government and taunting it by accusing it of abandoning the very values it professed. Timothy McVeigh, for example, cited Justice Brandeis in implying that the U.S. government had set a bad example.[20] Defendants in the trials for the 1993 World Trade Center attack called the U.S. Department of Justice the department of "injustice," and Paul Hill, during his trial in Miami for the murder of a provider of abortions on 4 October 1994 accused the U.S. government that was convicting him of murder of being "unjust."[21]

In the same vein, the suicide bombings perpetrated by the Hamas movement in residential neighborhoods of Tel Aviv and Jerusalem were, as one Hamas leader described them, "letters to Israel." They were invasions of the most domestic of their rival's quarters, with messages intended to show that "Hamas cannot be ignored," and that "the security for Israel's people is zero."[22] In that sense the message was the medium in which it was sent: the bombing provided a moment of chaos, warfare, and victimage that the Hamas movement wanted Israeli society to experience. It made the point that war was at hand by providing a bloody scene of battle in Israel's own quiet neighborhoods.

What was buttressed in these acts of symbolic empowerment was not just the credibility of the leadership of the Hamas movement and their equality with government officials, but also the legitimacy of religious social order as an ideology of nationalism and as an alternative source of authority. Through the currency of violence they were drawing attention to what they thought was significant and true about the social arena around them. In the language of Bourdieu, they were creating a perverse "habitus," a dark world of social reality, and forcing everyone—Israelis and Palestinians alike—to take stock of their perception of the world.[23] Their acts of terror were aimed at displaying power that not only elevated them personally, but also forwarded the sociopolitical agenda of their groups. The very act of performing violence in public is a political act: it announces that the power of the group is equal or superior to that of the state. In most cases this is exactly the message that the group wants to convey. These are clearly authority claims, assertions regarding the legitimacy of a social order that is based upon a notion of moral truth that these actors hold.

Thus at the same time that acts of religious violence announce that their religious authority is in competition with that of the secular order, they also highlight chinks in the armor of the secular state. They explicitly attack the claim of the state to provide what John Herz has called a "hard shell of territoriality" to protect its citizens. To the extent that these actors demonstrate the inability of the secular state to provide this protection, they implicitly delegitimate the state and diminish its authority.

In Israel, for instance, the Jewish right has long accused the secular government of using its devotion to democracy as an excuse for not fully embracing the idea that Israel is a Jewish religious entity rather than a secular state. Years before his attack on innocent Muslims at the Shrine of the Patriarchs in Hebron, Dr. Baruch Goldstein, in a letter to the editor of the *New York Times*, wrote that "Israelis will soon have to choose between a Jewish state and a democratic one."[24] Goldstein's massacre, I was told by one of his followers, displayed how serious he was about that choice. The supporter went on to tell me that now "Jews will have to learn to worship in a national way."[25] One of Goldstein's colleagues, Yoel Lerner, agreed with this position, telling me that in his opinion Israel should not be a democracy but a "Tohracracy"—a society based on the principle of Jewish law.[26]

This idea of a nation based on religious law was on the minds of American religious activists as well. Several associated with the ideology of Christian Identity advocated the creation of a Christian Republic.[27] White supremacists from throughout the United States and Canada met in Idaho allegedly to plot the forcible overthrow of the federal government and to create a separate Aryan nation within the United States. A government indictment based on information gleaned from this meeting stated that they planned to "carry out assassinations of federal officials, politicians, and Jews, as well as bombings and polluting of municipal water supplies."[28]

The establishment of a rule based on religious law has been the primary aim of many Muslim groups. Members of Hamas regarded this as the main difference between their organization and the secular ideology of Fateh and other groups associated with Yasir Arafat's Palestinian Authority. A similar argument was made by activists associated with Egyptian groups. Mahmud Abouhalima told me that President Hosni Mubarak could not be a true Muslim because he did not make *shari'a*—Islamic law—the law of the land, and that their movement's goal was to purify Arab nations.[29] A cleric in Cairo's conservative Al-Azhar theological school told me he resented his government's preference for Western law. "Why should we obey Western laws when Muslim laws are better?," he asked me.[30] It was this position that was assumed by many Muslim activists: that Western political institutions and the ideology on which they were based should be banished from their territories. They wanted to rebuild their societies on Islamic foundations.

In some cases activist groups carried this critique to an extreme. They not only rejected secular political authority but also created alternatives to it. Aum Shinrikyo, for instance, designated the leaders in its organization with government administrative titles such as minister of defense, minister of intelligence, minister of internal affairs, and minister of science and technology. The idea was not only to show that their organization could do government's job, but also to prepare the movement for indeed doing that job after the arrival of the global catastrophe predicted by Shoko Asahara. When that dark day came, the government of Aum Shinrikyo would be the only entity remaining to administer civil order.

In India, during the height of the Sikh rebellion in the 1980s, militants were treated as if they possessed an authority rivaling that of police and other government officials. Villagers in terrorist zones around the Punjab cities of Batala and Tarn Taran were unwilling to report violent incidents to officials, and radical youth set up their own courts and governmental offices. "Politics can be beautiful," I was told by a former head priest of Sikhism's central shrine.[31] "But it must be the right kind of politics." By this he meant a politics fused with religion, where "religion dominated politics," rather than the other way around.[32] When the country of Khalistan was created and Sikh rule was established, one of the leaders of the movement told me, it would be a rule of law that would bring justice to all, not just Sikhs, in a regime that lauded the tenets of the Sikh scriptures, the Guru Granth Sahib, as supreme.[33] Exactly how this differed from the current form of political organization in India remained obscure. It was clear, however, that this new Sikh authority would be a form of public authority, albeit public authority with a "divine" source and sanction. Thus the claim, and goal, is an alternative conception of a moral public order.

One of the reasons why these activists wanted to create religious nations was to restore the ideological and organizational dominance of religion—a role that religion enjoyed before the Enlightenment concept of secular nationalism took hold around the world. By its nature, the secular state has been opposed to the idea that religion should have a role in public life. From the time that modern secular nationalism emerged in the eighteenth century as a product of the European Enlightenment's political values it did so with a distinctly anti-religious, or at least anti-clerical, posture. The ideas of John Locke about the origins of a civil community, and the social contract theories of Jean Jacques Rousseau required very little commitment to religious belief. Although they allowed for a divine order that made the rights of humans possible, their ideas had the effect of taking religion—at least institutional religion—out of public life.

At the time, religious "enemies of the Enlightenment"—as the historian, Darrin McMahon, described them—protested religion's public demise.[34] But their views were submerged in a wave of approval for a new view of social order in which secular nationalism was thought to be virtually a natural law, universally applicable and morally right. The result of religion's devaluation has been "a general crisis of religious belief," as Pierre Bourdieu has put it.[35] This causes a problem not just for believers but for society as a whole, for it has undercut the public's ability to rely on public symbols. Bourdieu describes this as "the collapse of a world of representations" and "the disintegration of an entire universe of social relations."[36]

In countering this disintegration, resurgent religious activists have proclaimed the death of secularism and reasserted the primacy of religious values in the public sphere. They have experienced what I once described as a "loss of faith" in secular politics.[37] They have dismissed the efforts of secular culture and its forms of nationalism to replace religion. They have challenged the notion that secular society and the modern nation-state are able to provide the moral fiber that unites national communities, or give it the ideological strength to sustain states buffeted by ethical, economic, and military failures. Their message has been easy to believe, and has been widely received because the failures of the secular state have been so real.

Acts of religious terrorism, therefore, have been more than hollow gestures. The very act of killing on behalf of a moral code is a political statement. Such acts break the state's monopoly on morally sanctioned killing. By taking the right to take life into their own hands, the perpetrators of religious violence make a daring claim of power on behalf of the powerless, a basis of legitimacy for public order other than that upon which the secular state relies. In doing so, they demonstrate to everyone how fragile public order actually is, and how fickle can be the populace's assent to the moral authority of the secular national public order.

Yet after over a decade of religious violence, the outlines of most attempts at asserting religious nationalism are still quite sketchy. Curiously, the goals are the most obscure among groups that are the most violent. In fact, no religious regime has ever been established through the means of terrorism: not in Afghanistan, Sudan, or Iran; not when Muslim activists were briefly in control in Turkey and Tajikistan; and not when they almost came to power in Algeria. These religious regimes rode into power on the vehicles of peaceful democratic elections or through well-organized military takeovers. It was not through the sporadic and extreme performances of power that characterize terrorist acts.

In fact, despite their bravado, groups associated with terrorism have largely shied from politics. They have eschewed elections. When given the opportunity to run for office they have rejected it, as Hamas did in Palestine in 1996 and radical Sikhs did in Punjab in 1992. Or if they did attempt to win at the polls, as Aum Shinrikyo did in 1990, they failed miserably. Nor have they attempted to develop effective fighting forces other than those needed for a hit-and-run style of terrorist bombing. The al Qaeda network of Osama bin Laden, for example, has no state, no political ideology, no army, and no military strategy.

While their claims that their goals are sanctioned by the moral authority of the transcendent have been quite clear, the images of political order that they yearned to create have been fuzzy—perhaps deliberately so. Sometimes they have been democratic, sometimes socialist, sometimes a sort of religious oligarchy. Although it was clear who the religious activists hated, nowhere in their program was a design for a political entity—Islamic or otherwise—that could actually administer the results of a victory over American and secular rule and the emergence of a religious revolution, should they have achieved it. My conclusion is that, despite their political potency, acts of religious terrorism are largely devices for symbolic empowerment in wars that cannot be won and for goals that cannot be achieved. For many, the notion of ideal political authority that fuels their imagination is not a national one, but one that is transnational and utopian: a righteous global political order, one slightly beyond the frame for mortal history.

Transnational Networks

Islamic movements especially have held the illusion of waging a global struggle. The assemblage of al Qaeda activists coordinated by Osama bin Laden is profoundly multinational in membership: Egyptian, Palestinian, Jordanian, Saudi

Arabian, Afghan, Algerian, Sudanese, Yemeni, and Pakistani. Their groups have been transnational in part because of the multicultural background of expatriate Muslims who have congregated in their movements. Similarly, the Hamas leader, Abdul Aziz Rantisi, told me that what distinguished his organization from Yasir Arafat's was that the Palestinian Authority was waging a "national struggle" whereas Hamas was "transnational."[38] It is supported by Muslims everywhere.

Compatriots from different parts of the world also make up the militant backing of movements such as Sinhalese and Tamil rebels in Sri Lanka and Sikh separatists in India. Although expatriate Tamils and Sikhs may find themselves on the periphery of society in Britain, Canada, the United States, and the many other parts of the world to which they migrated, militant movements provided them with the opportunity to display their commitment and prove their importance to the community in a powerful way. This phenomenon has been called "e-mail ethnicities": transnational networks of people tied together culturally despite the diversities of their places of residence and the limitations of national borders.[39] These ethnicities, united by web sites and the internet, have been not only extensions of traditional societies whose adherents and cultures are dispersed around the world, but harbingers of global cultures as well.[40] Among these expatriate groups have been some notoriously politically active ones.

Osama bin Laden and his lieutenants have trooped from Saudi Arabia to Sudan to Afghanistan. Sheik Omar Abdul Rahman, for instance, lived variously in Egypt, Sudan, and New Jersey, and other members of his network originated from diverse locations in the Muslim world. Among them was Mohammed Salameh, whose story was paradigmatic of the religious radical expatriate experience. Salameh lived virtually from hand to mouth, sharing addresses with several other people in Jersey City, in a busy working-class neighborhood that teemed with new immigrants from Haiti and the Middle East. The setting was in some ways not unlike the social situation and economic conditions in the crowded Palestinian refugee camps on the West Bank and in Jordan where Salameh was born and raised, and from which he departed in 1987 for America in order to improve his educational and financial situation. In the United States, where his limited English continued to be a social barrier, Salameh associated primarily with other Arabs. His life became focused around the local mosque, located above a Chinese restaurant, led by the charismatic Sheik Omar Abdul Rahman. The trajectory of his life led ultimately to his participation in the 1993 bombing of the World Trade Center, when the world came to know him as the terrorist who foolishly returned to the Ryder rental agency to retrieve his U.S.$ 200 deposit for the van he had rented and had subsequently blown up, and was immediately caught by waiting agents of the FBI.[41]

The socially uprooted and dislocated Salameh found a new identity in a transnational community of radical Muslims. Appropriately, perhaps, they identified their miseries as global as well: the emerging transnational economy and the global culture seemingly promoted by the United States. It was a perception shared especially by those who were geographically dislocated, but their attitude of suspicion and cynicism was one that was widely experienced throughout the post–Cold War world. Even the United States saw a remarkable degree of disaffection with its political leaders and witnessed the rise of right-wing religious movements that fed on the public's perception of the inherent immorality of government. But the global shifts that have given rise to antimodernist movements have also affected less developed nations. Religious activists such as the Algerian leaders of the Islamic Salvation Front, the Ayatollah Khomeini in Iran, Sheik Ahmed Yassin in Palestine, Sayyid Qutb and his disciple, Sheik Omar Abdul Rahman in Egypt, L. K. Advani in India, and Sant Jarnail Singh Bhindranwale in India's Punjab have asserted the legitimacy of a postcolonial political identity based on traditional culture.[42]

In some cases these voices have been stridently nationalist; in others they hint at transnational political solutions. The al Qaeda network of Osama bin Laden sought no specific political goal but imagined itself embroiled in a global war. This uncertainty about what constitutes a valid basis for social order is on the one hand a kind of guerilla antiglobalism; on the other hand it is a political form of postmodernism.[43] In Iran it has resulted in the rejection of a modern Western political regime and the creation of a successful religious state. Yet, what lies beyond modernity is not necessarily a new form of political order, be it national or religious. In regions formerly under Soviet control, for example, the specter of the future beyond the socialist form of modernity has been one of cultural anarchism. The fear that there will be a spiritual as well as a political collapse at modernity's center has, in many areas of the world, led to terror. Hence the rise of religious violence across geographic boundaries has been a sigh of distress. In the horrific destruction of the World Trade Center and other assaults on modern secular public life, it is a sign of vicious desperation. For at least some who perpetrate these actions, however, it has also been a tragic longing: a cry for social coherence and moral community in a time of global change.

Notes

1. Mark Juergensmeyer, *Terror in the Mind of God: The Global Rise of Religious Violence* (Berkeley: University of California Press, 2000). This essay includes revised excerpts from this book.
2. Interview with Mahmud Abouhalima, Federal Penitentiary, Lompoc, California, 30 September 1997.
3. Interview with Abouhalima, 19 August 1997. The topic of the relationship between Islam and public order was discussed in both interviews.
4. Sheik Omar Abdul Rahman, recorded on audiotape cassettes made in the United States and quoted in Kim Murphy, "Have the Islamic Militants Turned to a New Battlefront in the U.S.?," *Los Angeles Times*, 3 March 1993, A20.
5. Imam [Ayatollah] Khomeini, *Collection of Speeches, Position Statements* (Arlington, Va.: Joint Publications Research Service, 1979), p. 24.
6. Ibid., p. 30.
7. John J. Goldman, "Defendants Given 25 Years to Life in New York Terror Plot," *Los Angeles Times*, 18 January 1996, A1.
8. RAND, "Chronicle of International Terrorism," reported in Bruce Hoffman, *Terrorism Targeting: Tactics, Trends, and Potentialities* (Santa Monica, Cal.: RAND Corporation Papers, 1992), p. 17.

9. State Department statistics cited by Robin Wright, "Prophetic 'Terror 2000' Mapped Evolving Threat," *Los Angeles Times*, 9 August 1998, A16.
10. Osama bin Laden, interviewed on an ABC News report, rebroadcast on 9 August 1998.
11. Samuel Berger, quoted in Osama bin Laden, *fatwa* issued February 1998, "Jihad Is an Individual Duty," *Los Angeles Times*, 13 August 1998, B9.
12. Excerpts from ibid.
13. Ibid.
14. Interview with Rabbi Manachem Fruman, Tuqua settlement, West Bank, Israel, 14 August 1995.
15. Interview with Abouhalima, 30 September 1997.
16. Khomeini, *Islam and Revolution: Writings and Declarations*, trans. and annotated by Hamid Algar (London: Routledge and Kegan Paul, 1985), pp. 27–28.
17. Khomeini, *Collection of Speeches, Position Statements*, p. 3.
18. Ibid., p. 25.
19. See René Girard, *Violence and the Sacred*, trans. by Patrick Gregory (Baltimore, Md.: Johns Hopkins University Press, 1977); and Girard, *The Scapegoat*, trans. by Yvonne Freccero (Baltimore, Md.: Johns Hopkins University Press, 1986); Walter Burkhert, René Girard, and Jonathan Z. Smith, *Violent Origins: Ritual Killing and Cultural Formation*, edited by Robert G. Hamerton-Kelly (Stanford: Stanford University Press, 1987).
20. Timothy McVeigh, quoted in Richard A. Serrano, "McVeigh Speaks Out, Receives Death Sentence," *Los Angeles Times*, 15 August 1997, A1.
21. Paul Hill, quoted in Mike Clary, "Suspect in Abortion Slayings Acts as Own Attorney at Trial," *Los Angeles Times*, 5 October 1994, A5.
22. Interview with Imad Faluji, journalist and member of the political wing of Hamas, in Gaza, 19 August 1995.
23. Pierre Bourdieu and Loic J. D. Wacquant, *An Invitation to Reflexive Sociology* (Chicago: University of Chicago Press, 1992), p. 131.
24. Dr. Baruch Goldstein, Letter to the Editor, *New York Times*, 30 June 1981.
25. Interview with Yochay Ron, Kiryat Arba, Israel, 18 August 1995.
26. Interview with Yoel Lerner, director of the Sannhedrin Institute, Jerusalem, 17 August 1995.
27. Leonard Zeskind, *The "Christian Identity" Movement: Analyzing Its Theological Rationalization for Racist and Anti-Semitic Violence* (New York: Division of Church and Society of the National Council of the Churches of Christ in the USA, 1986), pp. 35–42.
28. Reported in *Arkansas Gazette* (Little Rock, Ark.), 27 April 1987, quoted in Bruce Hoffman, *"Holy Terror": The Implications of Terrorism Motivated by a Religious Imperative* (Santa Monica, Cal.: RAND Corporation Papers, 1993), p. 8.
29. Interview with Abouhalima, 19 August 1997.
30. Interview with Dr. Muhammad Ibraheem el-Geyoushi, dean of the Faculty of Dawah, Al-Azhar University, Cairo, 30 May 1990.
31. Interview with Darshan Singh Ragi, former Jatedar, Akal Takhat, at Bhai Vir Singh Sadan, New Delhi, 13 January 1991.
32. Ibid.
33. Interview with Sohan Singh, leader of the Sohan Singh faction, Khalistan Liberation Force, Mohalli, Punjab, 3 August 1996.
34. Darrin McMahon, *Enemies of the Enlightenment: The French Counter-Enlightenment and the Making of Modernity* (New York: Oxford University Press, 2001).
35. Pierre Bourdieu, *Language and Symbolic Power* (Cambridge, Mass.: Harvard University Press, 1991), p. 116.
36. Ibid.
37. Mark Juergensmeyer, *The New Cold War? Religious Nationalism Confronts the Secular State* (Berkeley: University of California Press, 1993), p. 11.
38. Interview with Abdul Aziz Rantisi, cofounder and political leader of Hamas, in Khan Yunis, Gaza, 1 March 1998.

39. I do not know who coined the term "e-mail ethnicities." I first heard it used by the anthropologist Benedict Anderson, in comments made at a conference on nationalism held by the Center for German and European Studies, University of California, Berkeley, 15 March 1992.
40. I discuss further this notion of the global diaspora of religious cultures in my essay, "Thinking Globally About Religion," in Juergensmeyer (ed.), *Global Religion: A Handbook* (New York: Oxford University Press, forthcoming).
41. The story of Salameh's capture is told in Jim Dwyer, David Kocieniewski, Deidre Murphy, and Peg Tyre, *Two Seconds Under the Bomb. Terror Comes to America: The Conspiracy Behind the World Trade Center Bombing* (New York: Crown Publishers, 1994), pp. 89–101.
42. For a forceful statement of this thesis, see Partha Chatterjee; *The Nation and Its Fragments: Colonial and Postcolonial Histories* (Princeton, N.J.: Princeton University Press, 1993).
43. For the distinction between postmodernity as a social phenomenon and as a mode of analysis, see David Lyon, *Postmodernity* (Minneapolis: University of Minnesota Press, 1994).

CHAPTER 10

Culture and Migration

For many anthropologists, globalization involves changes in the way that people view the world as well as altered patterns of social interaction. Globalization can promote what Benedict Anderson calls "imagined communities," in which people at great physical distance imagine that they are part of the same community because they read the same newspapers, share a common political identity, and seek some of the same political goals.[1] (The fact that Anderson describes imagined communities developing in nineteenth-century Latin America suggests that this aspect of globalization did not originate yesterday, although recent technological innovations certainly facilitate the process!)

A key issue in regard to the connection between globalization and cultural change is whether globalization is promoting a common world culture, that is, whether it is flattening and homogenizing formerly distinctive cultures around the world. If it is, what are the elements of the new world culture and the mechanisms for its diffusion?

Those who defend this claim may differ on the particular features that are coming to constitute the world's cultural stock. Among the candidates are human rights, liberal democracy, the English language, free enterprise, Westernization, hedonism and consumerism, and world music. As one can see, the list is long, varied, and, therefore possibly not very helpful! For every element on the list, one can identify movements either challenging the development or simply untouched by it.

Consider the issue of human rights. Within the past few decades, human rights have become diffused on a global level and can now be considered part of the world's political heritage, as evidenced by near-unanimous ratification of United Nations treaties on human rights, women's rights, and so on. There has been the rapid growth of organizations of national and transnational human rights advocates seeking to ensure compliance with these standards by states and private

[1]See Benedict Anderson, *Imagined Communities: Reflections on the Origins and Spread of Nationalism* (New York: Verso, 1991).

groups. Yet, a skeptic might counter, "Not so fast!" In all too many cases, adhering to human rights is honored in the breach as much or more than in actual practice. The barbaric genocides that have claimed millions of innocent victims in Rwanda, Bosnia, and the Sudan within the recent past (and, as we write this, in the present in Darfur, Sudan) tragically challenge the claim that human rights have become fully accepted and practiced. Although governments universally proclaim their attachment to human rights, they often defend practices as necessary and permissible that reputable observers judge as grave violations of those rights.

The phenomenon of terrorism has recently complicated the comforting and comfortable view that adherence to human rights is on the rise. Those who engage in suicide bombing of civilians or fly fuel-laden civilian airliners into the World Trade Center make a mockery of human rights. But the "war on terrorism" has also been invoked to justify human rights abuses by governments that claim to set the gold standard for protecting human rights. Take the case of the United States. Thanks to the infamous photographs beamed around the world in 2004 (an example of how communications is now instantaneously global), it is painfully clear that U.S. military and intelligence personnel at Abu Ghraib prison in Iraq repeatedly engaged in abuses that violated the human rights of prisoners. According to the widely respected and independent nongovernmental organization (NGO) Amnesty International USA, in its 2005 Annual Report, the very highest U.S. government officials are responsible for violating prisoners' human rights, for example, when regulations are issued to incarcerate those designated as enemy combatants without benefit of judicial review, when prisoners are held for indefinite periods (without reporting their identity to the International Red Cross, as required by international law), and when they are tortured (the antiseptic phrase often used is "harsh interrogation techniques"). Since Amnesty International's report was issued in 2005, other questionable practices by the United States government came to light, including the technique of "extraordinary rendition," in which the government secretly transferred prisoners to regimes that routinely practice torture; as well as secret surveillance of U.S. citizens without judicial warrant, in violation of congressional legislation. When a government that proclaims itself a foremost champion of human rights engages in such activities, this casts considerable doubt on the claim that human rights are on the march in the world.

What about less overtly political aspects of culture, such as music and leisure activities? Has world music replaced local and national musical idioms? Does everyone in the world now march and dance to the beat of MTV, Disney, and Fox Entertainment? Here again, there is some evidence for the diffusion of cultural patterns across the world—as well as counterevidence that suggests one should not jump too quickly to the conclusion that territory, space, and the local have become irrelevant in our brave new virtual e-world. Anthropologists have found that, if people throughout the world may be increasingly aware of salient symbols—sports heroes, pop music stars, television programs beamed around the world—this cultural stock is refracted through the lens of distinctive cultures and thereby experienced differently. Nor is all of the new transnational or world culture produced and directed from Hollywood and New York. The largest number of new films produced these days—which attract the largest audiences in countries around the world—originate in Bollywood, as film studios in the former city of Bombay, India (now renamed Mumbai) are known.

Further, a continual ferment results in the preservation, reworking, and creation of locally based cultures, rather than simply their obliteration under the tsunami of one (Western-based) culture. The selection by Pieterse below claims that, rather than globalization's promoting a homogenized culture that represents an extension of Western values, there is a process of cultural diffusion that produces local varieties of hybrid cultures.

This chapter also includes a selection on immigration, in order to underline that it is not simply disembodied ideas that travel. Immigrants are a key vehicle for diffusing culture; they bring with them their own cultural stock, which is both changed when they emigrate, and which in turn influences the culture that they encounter. And immigrants who remain in contact with their homelands have an important impact on the cultures and communities they leave behind. As the selection by Sassen makes clear, immigration is partly the result of voluntary choice, but it is also strongly influenced by structural factors, notably poverty and political repression. At the same time, she suggests in her discussion of the trafficking of women and children, immigrants may be the target of harsh abuse. (For example, one estimate is that four fifths of the 5,500 prostitutes in London are foreign-born; half are recruited by trafficking and are virtual sex slaves.)[2]

The selections in this chapter provide yet another facet of the complicated mosaic of globalization. In reading them, think about the interconnections between culture and immigration, as well as between these two topics and others surveyed in PG, including economic globalization, transnational political institutions, and transnational social movements. Try to sort out the causal connections: What is causing what? What difference does it make whether the causal connections run in one direction or another?

---

[2]Michael Goldfarb, special report on trafficking of women and children, WBUR, Boston, June 17, 2005.

Horizontal Politics *Transnational Environmental Activism and Global Cultural Change*

Paul Wapner

Paul Wapner claims that nongovernmental organization (NGOs), that is, private nonprofit organizations, often use culture as a lever to promote changes in policies and practices. A frequent focus of NGO activity is thus to shape "the way vast numbers of people understand themselves and the world around them." Wapner urges us to study the interconnections between cultural beliefs and political institutions and policies. The article analyzes the diverse strategies of environmental NGOs that aim to "persuade ordinary citizens throughout the world to adopt environmentalist values." But, he stresses, changing values is insufficient if the process ends there: it must also produce changes in the policies and practices of influential public and private actors, notably, governments and corporations.

Which is more important: broad cultural beliefs and values, or public policies? The conventional view is that, in the final analysis, what really counts is the "hard power" of institutions and laws, whereas values exist in the realm of "soft power." Wapner invites us to consider the opposite position: "Governmental decrees, from this perspective, are not the source of change but are merely reflections of it." Is this argument persuasive? In reading this and other selections in PG, consider the relation between values, policies, and political change, not only in the realm of environmental protection but in relation to other aspects of globalization. The issue is complex, fascinating, and important, both in terms of social theory and political activism.

. . . NGOs are not simply political organizations, but they are also cultural agents that shape the way vast numbers of people understand themselves and the world around them. As is well-known, notions of right and wrong, good and bad, hip or unhip, and other valuations change under various socio-historical contexts. NGOs try to identify and manipulate the ideational codes underpinning such valuations. In this capacity, they work to shape per-

Paul Wapner, *Horizontal Politics: Transnational Environmental Activism and Global Cultural Change,* GLOBAL ENVIROMENTAL POLITICS, 2:2 (May, 2002), pp. 37–62.

sonal identity and the broader "moral-intellectual universe"[1] within which societies operate. Amnesty International, for example, both pressures states and other actors to respect human rights and attempts to influence the way people throughout the world fundamentally conceptualize human beings and the moral status of regimes within which many people live. Likewise, Sisterhood is Global seeks legislative change throughout the world on behalf of women but also works to change the way people in all walks of life think about and act toward women and themselves. One can make similar observations about almost all NGOs.

Most scholars ignore the cultural dimension of NGO work either because it seemingly lacks political significance or because alterations in cultural life are difficult to gauge. This article addresses both these concerns in an effort to develop analysis that can more fully appreciate NGO cultural efforts. With regard to the first issue, the article demonstrates that, from the perspective of long-term change, NGO cultural challenges may have *more* political significance than direct and obvious forms of political activism and engagement. With regard to the second, notwithstanding formidable methodological challenges, there are ways to measure shifts in broad ideational frameworks—even across borders—and scholars can adopt these in productive ways. The article advances both of these points in an effort to appreciate both the political dimensions of culture and the cultural dimensions of NGO politics. . . .

. . . [T]he article focuses specifically on environmental NGOs. Environmental issues now capture the attention of people in all walks of life the world over. Vast numbers of people in both the developed and developing worlds know about environmental problems and the discourse of environmentalism has spread across the globe. Environmental NGOs are central to these phenomena. Environmental NGOs have been advocating on behalf of environmental well-being for over a century and have been part and parcel with the dissemination of widespread ecological concern. Over the past twenty-five years, these organizations have increased in number and power such that they represent a formidable sector of agency in world environmental politics. The article describes and explains the cultural dimension of their politics.

Environmental NGOs

Let me start by briefly defining the term NGO and specifying how I use it in the article. In the broadest sense, NGOs are groups whose members come together to share interests, cultural affinities, professional vocations, political goals and other sources of solidarity outside the formal organs of the state. NGOs, as such, arise to advance cultural and religious values, promote economic interests, enjoy recreational activities, share educational experiences or undertake public service. In this article I use the term in a more restricted sense. I use it to refer to groups that form on a voluntary basis with the aim of addressing a given problem in the world or advancing a particular cause.[2] NGOs, in other words, are groups that work to alleviate what they perceive to be hardships or misfortunes, or to change the way people think and act with regard to public issues. NGOs, as I use the term, are equivalent to transnational activist or advocacy groups . . .

Environmental NGOs are distinguished insofar as they arise to protect some dimension of the non-human world. Their members share a sense of concern about the degradation of air, land, water and diversity of species across the earth, and the interaction between human beings and the natural environment. Environmental NGOs come in countless varieties in terms of geographical focus, level of political engagement, ideological orientation and relationship to other actors and issues. This article studies those environmental NGOs that focus on regional or global dimensions of environmental harm and that use multiple means of political engagement, without any litmus test in terms of ideological commitment. Many of these—such as the Sierra Club in the United States, the Center for Science and Environment in India, or the Australian Conservation Foundation—are national in terms of their organizational home but nonetheless concentrate on transboundary environmental issues. Others—such as Greenpeace, World Wide Fund for Nature (WWF) and Conservation International—are genuinely transnational in the sense that they have offices in more than one country and concern themselves primarily with transboundary environmental issues. The article focuses on these types of NGOs in an effort to understand transnational cultural changes induced by environmental NGOs.

Environmental NGOs and Policy Politics

While this article concentrates on the cultural dimension of environmental NGO politics, one cannot ignore the more obvious and conventional NGO efforts to change the policies and procedures of specific organizations. NGOs act mostly as pressure groups trying to get states, corporations and other actors to adopt more environmentally friendly programs and policies. Thus, this article would be woefully inadequate without some mention of these kinds of efforts. Additionally, the article would be inadequate if it ignored NGO lobbying insofar as such work is, ironically, part and parcel of their cultural politics. States, firms, IGOs and other actors that NGOs target are not simply executors of policies but also, themselves, cultural agents. Through their influence on social mores and broad practices, they have an enormous influence on the ideational institutions that inform contemporary life. As such, they play an important role, along with NGOs, in fomenting transnational cultural changes. For both these reasons, the article first addresses NGO policy politics.

Changing State Behavior

States are the most obvious and arguably most important actors in world politics due to their ability to shape the behavior of their citizens through a combination of persuasion and coercion. Their governing capacity is so impressive that the international system itself is often equated with the state-system. Environmental NGOs recognize this and focus much of their efforts on pressuring government officials to support environmental protection.

NGO state-oriented politics take many forms. One of the most important . . . is the attempt to intervene in the formation, maintenance and modification of international environmental regimes. International regimes are rules, codes of conduct, principles and decision-making procedures that govern state behavior in specific issue areas.[3] Environmental regimes are rules, principles and so forth that guide inter-state behavior with regard to environmental issues. NGOs try to shape the quality of these regimes.

One way NGOs do this is by actually participating in international conferences that address environmental issues. Since the 1972 United Nations Conference on the Human Environment (UNCHE), NGOs have increasingly gained greater access to multilateral environmental negotiations and decision-making meetings.[4] Today, much of this participation is formalized through official UN accreditation. The UN Economic and Social Council (ECOSOC) accredited 1400 NGOs with "observer status" at the 1992 United Nations Conference on Environment and Development (UNCED).[5] This enabled NGOs to participate in working and expert groups, introduce documentation, and win invitations to speak at plenary and other sessions. This had, and continues to have, an enormous effect on NGO influence. NGOs have used formal access to shape directly and sometimes even author international agreements. For example, according to Simmons and Oudrat, NGOs were the principal authors, along with states, of the 1992 Framework Convention on Climate Change and NGOs continue to provide much of the structure and content of on-going climate change negotiations.[6]

NGOs enjoy even greater insider status when they become official members of national negotiating teams. For example, New Zealand placed a member of Greenpeace on its delegation to the London Dumping Convention;[7] members of the Centre for Science and Environment helped represent India at UNCED; and, in the post-Rio negotiations over climate change, the small state of Vanuatu invited NGOs to take over its entire delegation.[8] In these cases, NGOs are able to become actual negotiators. Through their respective delegations, they are able to table proposals, develop allies and directly participate in the formulation of international environmental treaties.[9]

As outsiders, NGOs lobby government officials directly or organize their members to do so. This has had a significant effect in terms of prodding states to international action. Key to their lobbying efforts is their ability to work both domestically and internationally and they are able to do this through extensive NGO networking across state borders.[10] An early sign of lobbying influence came when NGOs transformed the International Whaling Commission (IWC) from an international club of whaling states to a governing mechanism to protect whales throughout the globe. Established in 1946, the IWC allowed non-whaling states representation and NGOs exploited this by lobbying such states, encouraging them to push for tight restrictions on whaling. Many of these states complied and it is clear that NGOs were indispensable to them doing so and to establishing the broad restrictions that today protect whales.[11]

A similar story can be told with regard to stratospheric ozone protection. Domestic NGOs operating within the U.S., such as the Natural Resources Defense Council and Environmental Defense Fund, successfully pressured the federal government to propose legislation that would ban chlorofluorocarbon (CFC) production within the U.S.[12] Moreover, a coterie of transnational NGOs, including, most prominently, Friends of the Earth, organized actions around the world to pressure state representatives to support ozone protection measures at international fora. This included active participation in international negotiations which culminated in the 1987 Montreal Protocol on Substances that Deplete the Ozone Layer.[13] The real strength of NGOs was demonstrated in the follow-up meetings to Montreal where they pushed for more stringent measures.[14] As part of this, NGOs influenced the 1988 World Conference on the Changing Atmosphere in Toronto, where they called for complete elimination of CFC emissions by the year 2000. States adopted this recommendation and made it part of the conference action plan. According to Stephen Lewis, the Canadian Ambassador to the UN at the time, this action plan was essentially "pilfered" from NGO recommendations.[15] All of this is not to suggest that NGOs were single-handedly responsible for international regulation of ozone-depleting substances. It claims only that NGOs were an important player in the negotiations and eventual outcome.

Environmental NGOs participate not only in the creation and revision of international regimes. They also play an important maintenance role through their compliance efforts. NGOs monitor and verify state conformity with international treaties. They track compliance through unofficial investigative reporting and through serving as secretariat partners for certain treaties such as the Convention on International Trade in Endangered Species (CITES).[16] . . .

One of the key factors to NGOs' compliance efforts is the ability of NGOs to work together and exploit judicial and executive systems throughout the world. For example, in the U.S., American constitutional separation of powers enables NGOs to litigate on behalf of environmental well-being and thus to sue the government for lack of compliance with international agreements. This has led some to see NGOs as "extensions of [U.S.] government regulators."[17] In Europe, the European Union relies almost exclusively on citizens and NGOs to report noncompliance.[18] NGOs have mostly registered complaints against government infringements of EU environmental directives, and some of these have successfully triggered legal action by the European Commission.[19] Finally, many NGOs attempt to monitor compliance in the developing world often by publicly exposing government failures at treaty conformity[20] or legally challenging government compliance in domestic courts. This latter strategy was used successfully, for instance, in 1993 with regard to India's noncompliance with the Ramsar Convention.[21]

These examples illustrate some of the many state-oriented strategies NGOs undertake to change state behavior. As mentioned, states are arguably the most important actors in world affairs. Thus, NGO efforts to pressure them represent a significant form of their politics.

Changing Economic Activity

The production, distribution and consumption of products throughout the world takes a heavy toll on environmental well-being. Most economic output entails extracting resources from the earth and releasing wastes into the earth's ecosystem. The world economy continues to grow at an accelerating rate, fueling greater resource use and waste production. From 1950 to 1995, the world economy expanded from U.S. $4 trillion to $20 trillion. Between 1985 and 1995 alone, it grew by $4 trillion.[22] In 1999, the world economy stood at $29 trillion.[23] Part of this increasingly rapid economic expansion has to do with the ability of newly industrializing countries to take advantage of technological innovations already practiced by developed countries. Part of this also has to do with the sustained economic power of the U.S. which, throughout the 1990s, experienced its longest peacetime economic expansion in decades. Whatever the causes, the expansion presses the biophysical constraints of the earth. And, it is for this reason that NGOs focus on changing economic practices in an effort to protect the environment.

Economic activity courses through all aspects of human life and operates across state boundaries, and this makes it difficult to engage economic forces in an efficient and effective manner. NGOs meet this challenge by "unpacking" the world economy and identifying certain nodes of power within it. They then target and try to change the character of those nodes that most effectively relate to environmental issues. NGOs adopt a number of strategies to do this. One of the most successful involves pressuring specific corporations to modify their conduct.

In the spring of 1995, Shell Oil announced plans and *received governmental approval* to dispose of one of its oil installations, the Brent Spar, by dumping it into the North Sea. There are over 400 gas/oil rigs in the North Sea and for decades companies have been able to dispose of them in the water without much restriction. Since the 1970s, Greenpeace and other environmental NGOs have worked to prevent and ultimately ban ocean dumping because they see the practice as environmentally dangerous. This campaign found significant momentum in the spring of 1995 when Greenpeace targeted Shell's plans for the Brent Spar. Greenpeace maintained that the 4,000-ton installation was loaded with toxic and radioactive sludge, and discarding it at sea would release this into a relatively fragile marine environment.[24] In May 1995, Greenpeace organized an intensive campaign against Shell. Over two dozen activists from six North Sea countries staged an on-site protest with Greenpeace offices around the world publicizing the event from their respective home countries. Among its many activities, Greenpeace landed a helicopter on the oil platform and brought activists by sea to occupy the installation. This action included unfurling a banner that read, "Save the North Sea," to publicize the issue. Additionally, two Greenpeace ships circled the rig with photographers producing images of the occupation that were sent out electronically to media sources throughout the world. Furthermore, Greenpeace organized a boycott of Shell products that led, according to the London *Times*, to a 30 percent reduction in sales throughout Europe.[25] Greenpeace's efforts paid off. In June 1995, after constant pressure, Shell reversed its decision and announced that it would tow the installation to land and dismantle it on shore.[26] Shell did this even though it was not required to do so by governments.[27] Moreover, in 1998, Shell publicly announced a new attitude toward its business practices in which it would assume social responsibility for its corporate activities.[28] Activist pressure was key to these actions. . . .

Environmental NGOs and Cultural Change

States and firms greatly influence behavior throughout the world and this is the reason why NGOs pressure them to adopt environmentally-friendly policies or procedures. But NGOs direct their efforts at other actors as well. It is in this latter sense that one begins to appreciate the cultural dimension of their work. In addition to states and firms, NGOs try to persuade ordinary citizens throughout the world to care about, and take action to protect, environmental well-being. Such action involves not only educating people about given problems but also engaging widespread value systems and cultivating new understandings of personal identity. NGOs attempt, in other words, to disseminate an "ecological sensibility" among all people in the hope that this will inspire many to act more responsibly toward the environment.[29] This type of action forms the bulk of their cultural politics . . .[30]

The lynchpin behind NGO cultural politics is that social institutions are dynamic and change over time. Moreover, they change not simply as a matter of course, but through the concerted efforts of people seeking new understandings and different social conditions. Finally, they change not only by altering material conditions—as if social institutions were mere superstructural reflections—but also by directly engaging the cultural attributes that constitute them. This entails reformatting, as it were, the ideational codes of conduct, systems of understanding, or ruling discourses of people throughout the world with regard to environmental issues. To be sure, there is nothing straightforward or easy about such a politics. It involves an ability to identify the ideational structures that inform widespread practices and to find ways to manipulate them. Environmental NGOs have found creative ways of doing this.

In parts of Asia, there is a tradition of ingesting wild plants and animals to boost one's health. Because of increasing demand, this tradition threatens particular species and biological diversity more generally. For example, many East Asians believe that the bile from bear gall bladders acts as a health restorative, working as an antidote to liver cancer, hemorrhoids and conjunctivitis. According to the Hong Kong office of the World Wide Fund for Nature, people collect the bile by holding bears in captivity and slowly draining their bile intravenously in a way that keeps the bears alive while still producing enough bile to sell.[31] The widely-held belief that ingesting bear bile provides health benefits threatens bears throughout the world . . . Similar belief systems threaten tigers, rhinoceros and other living things thought to have health benefits.

Environmental NGOs work to reduce demand for bears, tigers and rhinos by engaging in a host of activities. Many of these involve lobbying states and intervening in international regimes . . . Nonetheless, NGOs recognize that this work has its limitations. No matter how stringent international regimes are, if cultural understandings still support the exploitation of endangered species, bears, tigers and other living entities will always be at risk. As a result, NGOs try directly to change cultural practices.

The World Wide Fund for Nature, for instance, has been engaged in an ongoing dialogue with consumers and medical practitioners throughout East Asia to alter the way they understand endangered species and the necessity of using such species for medicinal purposes. This has involved a dual strategy of, on the one hand, trying to re-acculturate people to different understandings of health and the use of plants and animals, and, on the other, convincing medical practitioners and consumers of the benefits of synthetic substitutes. The first involves changing the ideational context within which some traditional Eastern medicine operates. It aims to persuade people to disbelieve existing medical promises. In this capacity, WWF publicizes medical evidence that contradicts longstanding local ideas. (It also, by the way, publicizes ecological information explaining the biophysical role certain animals play within their environments and their endangered status.) The second entails accommodating that tradition through technological intervention. It tries to assure medical practitioners that synthetic substitutes are functionally equivalent to the original source.[32] The purpose of both strategies is to change the way people understand their own health and the ruling discourses that inform local medicinal practices. As such, both represent attempts to engage the cultural dimension of collective life.

One need not go to the East to discover the impact of cultural forces on environmental affairs. Particular understandings of nature animate all societies and, in an increasingly interdependent world, do so across borders. NGOs try to change or modify such understandings in support of environmental well-being . . . Environmentalists have worked for years to instill . . . compassion in people for whales, wolves, harp seals, elephants, tigers and so on.

Modern environmentalism cut its teeth on campaigning on behalf of whales. Whales are still, arguably, the flagship symbol of the movement itself. For more than two decades, organizations such as the Sea Shepherds Conservation Society, Friends of the Earth, Greenpeace, WWF and others have tried to change the way people think about and act toward whales. This has involved educating the public about the anthropomorphic qualities of whales and using this link as a way to generate respect and win protection for whales. Activists have done this by, for example, using photographs, films and audio recordings to advertise whales' evident intelligence, gentleness and unique vocalizations now known as whale "songs." Additionally, NGOs have undertaken direct actions to stop the killing of whales in the oceans and have projected images of such actions through the media to the world's publics at large. Recent innovations in communication technologies enable NGOs to carry out direct actions not simply as a form of confrontation but also as media events that can change the way people understand the natural world and the human relationship to it. NGOs create dramatic images that get picked up by the media and which symbolize new ways of thinking about the environment and the efforts by activists to protect it. Due in large measure to NGO efforts, many people throughout the world no longer view whales merely as resources. Indeed, many now see whales in an almost mystical light, deserving a privileged status among large animals.[33] This shift began taking place in the late 1970s and early 1980s, and led to widespread, transnational public support for things such as "Operation Rescue," an international effort costing U.S. $5 million to save three whales trapped in ice off the coast of Alaska.[34] At the heart of this shift was a new ethical sensibility. Indeed, according to Sand, the entire effort to change thinking and action about whales has been based on ethical rather than scientific grounds.[35]

Environmental NGOs undertake direct action and work to shift cultural understandings in all environmental issue areas. Groups like RAN, Greenpeace, EarthFirst! and Friends of the Earth have been known to parachute from the top of smokestacks, block trains carrying CFCs, float hot-air balloons into nuclear test sites, and scale and unfurl banners on skyscrapers in an effort to bring greater awareness and instill greater concern about environmental issues. Organizations such as Centre for Science and Environment, National Wildlife Federation and the Green Belt Movement publish magazines, support films and host educational enterprises to heighten environmental awareness. Through all these efforts, NGOs work the cultural dimension of global collective life. They manipulate cultural frames of reference to sway public thought and action.

Environmental NGOs, States, Economic Actors and Social Mores: Cultural Politics Revisited

NGOs identify and manipulate cultural frames of reference in an effort to persuade ordinary citizens throughout the world to adopt environmentalist values. They do so, in other words, to disseminate widely an ecological sensibility. This type of politics takes on additional meaning, however, insofar as states and economic actors are themselves embedded in broad cultural institutions and are thus vulnerable to widespread cultural change. States and economic actors, like individuals, are not static entities with given interests. Rather, they develop identities and concerns over time and in different socio-historical contexts.[36] Put differently, they are constructed and motivated by cultural frames of reference. As a result, their nature, purposes, behavior and self-understanding get redefined as cultural frames themselves change.[37] When NGOs try to shift the terms of cultural reference, then, they are not merely targeting ordinary citizens but are influencing the ideational structure within which states and corporations also operate. NGOs target widely-shared orientations in an attempt to disseminate an ecological sensibility in the broadest and most politically expansive sense of this phrase. They hope that, in so doing, they will manipulate states, economic actors and ordinary people to adopt more ecologically sound practices . . .

One can gain a fuller understanding of the cultural dimension of NGO politics by taking seriously the multifaceted character of states, economic actors and individual citizen practices. That each of these engender cultural institutions speaks to the overlaps that exist between different spheres of collective life. Governmental or state activity, for example, at both the domestic and international levels, is neither separate nor immune from economic and cultural dynamics. Rather, in many ways it mirrors the qualities and patterns of economic and cultural activity. One can say the same thing about economic processes and cultural institutions: they are infused with qualities and patterns that animate states and the international state-system. Another way to say this is that the cultural, governmental and economic dimensions of collective life, while analytically distinguishable, cannot be empirically separated.

Indeed, the NGO actions mentioned above suggest as much. For example, when Greenpeace occupied the Brent Spar it targeted Shell Oil directly and forced the company to dismantle its installation on land. But the campaign had an impact that went far beyond Shell and its immediate decision about Brent Spar. In the aftermath of Greenpeace's campaign, oil and gas companies operating in the region voluntarily dismantled 12 installations on shore even in the absence of governmental regulation and even though 3 of these were in deep enough water to justify easily leaving them *in situ*.[38] Moreover, in response to Greenpeace's Brent Spar campaign, all parties to the Oslo and Paris Commission (OSPARCOM), an intergovernmental body that regulates pollution in the north-east Atlantic, agreed to a moratorium on ocean dumping of oil and gas installations and this was eventually turned into a formal ban when OSPARCOM met in July 1998.[39] Both sets of action point to the tight relationship between non-compulsory economic practice and governmental directives. Additionally, if one considers the role of public opinion and the governing character of widespread understandings, it is clear that Brent Spar was also about cultural change. The campaign set a new precedent for dismantling oil/gas installations that finds codification not only in governmental directives and sensitive corporations worried about customers, but also in the broad notion of what constitutes appropriate action. While earlier it was acceptable to dump oil/gas rigs in the sea, now good conduct warrants land disposal. In general, the campaign demonstrates the permeable lines between governmental, economic and cultural practices and how actions in one sphere influence dynamics in the other spheres . . .

This interconnectedness helps explain why one can say that NGO cultural politics may be more politically significant than NGO policy efforts. Students of politics have long had what could be called a "cash register" notion of political significance. They notice much political activity though they measure its ultimate meaning in terms of changing state behavior. States are, by most counts, the most important governors of widespread thought and behavior, and the state-system remains the most obvious and effective form of political organization at the international level. As a result, political action becomes effective ultimately when it moves such organizations. The state and the state-system sit at the end of the line like a cash register does in a store, gauging the political value of all that goes before them. Without the register, political action loses importance; without the register, action may be sociologically interesting but politically insignificant. This view greatly skews political analysis.

Scholars nonetheless justify this view by identifying state action with "hard," in contrast to "soft," law and privileging it as a form of effective governance. State directives, policies and programs enjoy the designation of hard law because they possess legal status and can thus be backed up with coercion. Customs, norms, values, principles and the like, that make up cultural life, embody no such status and thus have, theoretically, less of a pull on people's minds and actions. With this distinction in mind, many scholars claim that state laws are not only more powerful than norms but more primary in the sense of generating norms themselves. That is, laws serve as the "base" while values, codes of conduct and shared principles constitute the "superstructure." This orientation clearly privileges state action, regarding it as the *sine qua non* of politics.

An appreciation for cultural politics turns this view on its head, arguing that social mores are more fundamental to social change. Governmental decrees, from this perspective, are not the source of change but are merely reflections of it. Laws and policies arise out of, or give authoritative expression to, norms that already enjoy widespread acceptance. Social mores are primary political agents. This view, in contrast to the one above, sees norms constituting the base of political life with laws being the superstructure.

Obviously, neither of these positions is completely accurate. It thus makes sense to consider at least both factors in political analysis . . .

Assessing Transnational Cultural Change

Scholars have difficulty appreciating the political effectiveness of NGO cultural efforts because cultural changes are difficult to assess. This is especially the case with broad, historically significant types of change. How, in fact, can one notice and measure cultural change? Where does one look for it? Against what criteria does one gauge alteration or novelty? These questions are compounded by the difficulty of attributing causation. How can one draw neat causal lines between NGO efforts and broad cultural shifts? How can one determine the causal mechanisms that mediate the connection? Given that day-to-day practices generate, maintain and modify cultural structures, and that countless social interactions are at work, can one really claim that NGOs play a role in cultural change? . . .

Conclusion

This article explores the cultural dimension of environmental NGO politics. It describes those NGO activities that target the constitutive quality of norms, values and predispositions in an effort to use cultural attributes as levers for political change. NGOs assume that, while cultural life is tightly woven into all aspects of collective life, it can also be manipulated in the sense of political change. This article is centrally concerned with bringing this aspect of NGO politics into high relief.

The article goes further than this, however, in noticing that cultural politics does not take place in a vacuum. Rather, it inter-relates with more obvious kinds of lobbying and pressuring that attempt to change directly the behavior of organizations. For this reason, the article describes NGO efforts to alter the actions of states and economic actors. It explains how such efforts have a broader cultural element to them and thus argues for including them when assessing NGO cultural politics.

Furthermore, the article tries to gauge the political significance of such a politics. It does so by arguing that, in the long run, the governing power of cultural attributes has a deep and enduring imprint on human thought and behavior. Using constitutive notions of power, it explains how cultural attributes work to construct identities and how this more effectively has a long-standing pull on widespread thought and action. Finally, the article steps back from environmental NGO efforts and, by relating NGOs to the environmental movement more generally, charts the kinds of broad cultural changes brought about partly by environmental NGOs.

Protecting the global environment is an immense challenge that calls for discovering and enlisting multiple mechanisms of governance. NGOs work for global environmental protection by lobbying states, pressuring corporations and engaging social mores. Scholars have long dismissed this last element because it is too difficult to address analytically and to work with methodologically. This article attempts to alleviate some of those problems. Normatively, the hope is that by clarifying this type of politics, scholars will devote more effort to understanding it and practitioners will more self-consciously undertake it.

Notes

1. Gamson 1998, 57.
2. Weiss and Gordenker 1996, 19.
3. Krasner 1983; Hasenclever, Mayer, and Rittberger 1997.
4. Elliot 1998.
5. Conca 1996, 107.
6. Simmons and Oudrat 2001, 5.
7. Stairs and Taylor 1992, 133.
8. Mathews 1997, 55.
9. See generally, Tamiotti and Finger 2001.
10. Keck and Sikkink 1998.
11. Sand 2001, 288. See also Keck and Sikkink 1998; and Stoett 1995.

12. Bramble and Porter 1992.
13. Benedick 1998.
14. Tamiotti and Finger 2001, 36; and see generally, Agarwal, Narain, and Sharma 1999.
15. Bramble and Porter 1992, 339.
16. Weiss 1998, 111; and Peterson 1997, 128.
17. Vogel and Kessler 1998, 34.
18. Vogel and Kessler 1998.
19. Sand 2001, 295.
20. For example Agarwal, Narain, and Sharma 1999.
21. Sand 2001, 295.
22. Brown 1996, 3.
23. World Bank 2000, 274.
24. Greenpeace's estimates about the amounts of toxic and radioactive sludge turned out to be inaccurate. Greenpeace acknowledged this but such acknowledgment did not stop the campaign. Greenpeace claimed that, even at much lower levels, dumping the Brent Spar at sea posed harmful ecological risks. See Wapner 2000.
25. P. Millar, "Green Pressure, Plain Blackmail," *The Times of London*, 22 June 1995, 19.
26. T. Radford, and M. White, "Shell Gives Up Battle for Oil Rig," *The Guardian*, 21 June 1995, 1.
27. N. Nutall, and A. Leathley, "Shell Abandons: Ministers Furious Over Capitulation to Greens," *The Times of London*, 21 June 1995, 1; and Wapner 2000, 99.
28. Giddens 1998, 49.
29. Wapner 1996.
30. To be sure, NGOs are so diverse that it is inaccurate to say that they work to disseminate a single ecological sensibility. There are significant disagreements among NGOs about, for example, which environmental issues are worthy of attention, how one should understand responsibilities toward such issues and even the meaning of environmental protection itself . . .
31. Private interview 1998; and TRAFFIC 1995.
32. TRAFFIC 1997a; and TRAFFIC 1997b.
33. For a sense of this shift in the late 1980s, see Day 1989, 52ff.
34. Rose 1989.
35. Sand 2001, 288.
36. Wendt 1999; and Finnemore 1996.
37. Boli and Thomas 1999, 14.
38. Greenpeace 1998.
39. Greenpeace 1998.

References

Agarwal, Anil, Sunita Narain, and Anju Sharma, eds. 1999. *Green Politics: Global Environmental Negotiations*. New Delhi: Centre for Science and Environment.

Benedick, Richard. 1998. *Ozone Diplomacy: New Directions in Safeguarding the Planet*. Cambridge, MA: Harvard University Press.

Boli, John, and George Thomas. 1999. Introduction. In *Constructing World Culture: International Nongovernmental Organizations Since 1875*, edited by John Boli and George Thomas. Stanford, CA: Stanford University Press.

Bramble, Barbara, and Gareth Porter. 1992. Non-Governmental Organizations and the Making of U.S. International Environmental Policy. In *The International Politics of the Environment*, edited by Andrew Hurrell and Benedict Kingsbury. New York: Oxford University Press.

Brown, Lester. 1996. The Acceleration of History. In *State of the World 1996*, edited by Lester Brown et al. New York: W.W. Norton.

Conca, Kenneth. 1996. Greening the UN: Environmental Organizations and the UN System. In *NGOs, the UN and Global Governance*, edited by Thomas Weiss and Leon Gordenker. Boulder, CO: Lynne Rienner.

Day, David, 1989. *The Environmental Wars*. New York: Ballantine Books.

Elliot, Lorraine. 1998. *Global Politics of the Environment*. New York: New York University Press.

Finnemore, Martha. 1996. *National Interests in International Society*. Ithaca, NY: Cornell University Press.

Gamson, William. 1998. Social Movements and Cultural Change. In *From Contention to Democracy*, edited by Marco Giugni, Doug McAdam and Charles Tilly. Lanham, MD: Rowman and Littlefield.

Giddens, Anthony. 1998. *The Third Way: The Renewal of Social Democracy*. Cambridge, UK: Polity Press.

Greenpeace 1998. Greenpeace Applauds Norwegian Government Decision on Esso Rig. Available at http:www.greenpeace.org/~comms/brent/odinpro01.html (visited 25 January 2002).

Hasenclever, Andreas, Peter Mayer, and Volker Rittberger. 1997. *Theories of International Regimes*. New York: Cambridge University Press.

Keck, Margaret, and Kathryn Sikkink. 1998. *Activists Across Borders: Advocacy Networks in World Politics*. Ithaca, NY: Cornell University Press.

Krasner, Stephen. 1983. Structural Causes and Regime Consequences: Regimes as Intervening Variables. In *International Regimes*, edited by Stephen Krasner. Ithaca, NY: Cornell University Press.

Mathews, Jessica. 1997. Power Shift. *Foreign Affairs* 76 (1) January/February.

Peterson, M. J. 1997. International Organizations and the Implementation of Environmental Regimes. In *Global Governance: Drawing Insights from the Environmental Experience*, edited by Oran Young. Cambridge, MA: MIT.

Rose, Tom. 1989. *Freeing the Whales: How the Media Created the World's Greatest Non-Event*, New York: Birch Lane Press.

Sand, Peter. 2001. Environment: Nature Conservation. In *Managing Global Issues*, edited by P. J. Simmons and Chantal de Jonge Oudraat. Washington DC: Carnegie Endowment for International Peace.

Simmons, P. J., and Chantal de Jonge Oudraat. 2001. Managing Global Issues: An Introduction. In *Managing Global Issues*, edited by P. J. Simmons and Chantal de Jonge Oudraat. Washington DC: Carnegie Endowment for International Peace.

Stairs, Kevin, and Peter Taylor. 1992. Non-Governmental Organizations and the Legal Protection of the Oceans: A Case Study. In *The International Politics of the Environment*, edited by Andrew Hurrell and Benedict Kingsbury. New York: Oxford University Press.

Stoett, Peter. 1995. *Atoms, Whales, and Rivers: Global Environmental Security and International Organization*. Commack, New York: Nova Science.

Tamiotti, Ludivine, and Matthias Finger. 2001. Environmental Organizations: Changing Roles and Functions in Global Politics. *Global Environmental Politics* 1 (1) February: 56–76.

TRAFFIC. 1995. *The Bear Facts: The East Asian Market for Bear Gall Bladder:* TRAFFIC Network Report.

———. 1997a. *Traffic Dispatches*. February.

———. 1997b. *Traffic Bulletin* 16 (3) March.

Vogel, David, and Timothy Kessler. 1998. How Compliance Happens and Doesn't Happen Domestically. In *Engaging Countries: Strengthening Compliance with International Environmental Accords*, edited by Edith Brown Weiss and Harold Jacobson. Cambridge, MA: MIT.

Wapner, Paul. 1996. *Environmental Activism and World Civic Politics*. Albany: State University of New York.

———. 2000. Transnational Politics of Environmental NGOs: Governmental, Economic and Social Activism. In *The Global Environment in the Twenty-First Century: Prospects for International Cooperation*, edited by Pamela Chase. New York: United Nations University.

Weiss, Edith Brown. 1998. The Five International Treaties: A Living History. In *Engaging Countries: Strengthening Compliance with International Accords*, edited by Edith Brown Weiss and Harold Jacobson. Cambridge, MA: MIT.

Weiss, Thomas, and Leon Gordenker. 1996. Pluralizing Global Governance: Analytic Approaches and Dimensions. In *NGOs, the UN and Global Governance*, edited by Thomas Weiss and Leon Gordenker. Boulder, CO: Lynne Rienner.

Wendt, Alexander. 1999. *Social Theory of International Politics*. New York: Cambridge University Press.

World Bank. 2000. *World Development Report 2000/2001: Attacking Poverty*. New York Oxford University Press.

Globalization and Culture *Global Mélange*

Jan Nederveen Pieterse

Jan Nederveen Pieterse claims that globalization is not producing a homogenization of culture so much as diverse and complex cultural mixtures or hybrids. "Cultural hybridization refers to the mixing of Asian, African, American, [and] European cultures. . . ." Although this has always been the case, he suggests that the extent or the tempo of cultural mixing varies historically. Confusing as it may appear, "contemporary accelerated globalization means the hybridization of hybrid cultures."

Can you think of concrete examples of what Nederveen Pieterse means by hybridity or cultural mixing? How can this approach be reconciled with the argument that there is a "culture industry" controlled by a handful of influential media giants, global in scope and headquartered in rich countries (especially the United States)? More generally, how can Nederveen Pieterse's understanding of culture be enriched by analyzing local, national, and international inequalities in the ability to shape culture?

Global Mélange

How do we come to terms with phenomena such as Thai boxing by Moroccan girls in Amsterdam, Asian rap in London, Irish bagels, Chinese tacos, and Mardi Gras Indians in the United States, or "Mexican school-girls dressed in Greek togas dancing in the style of Isadora Duncan" (Rowe and Schelling 1991: 161)? How do we interpret Peter Brook directing the Mahabharata, or Ariane Mnouchkine staging a Shakespeare play in Japanese Kabuki style for a Paris audience in the Théâtre Soleil? Cultural experiences, past or present, have not been simply moving in the direction of cultural uniformity and standardization. This is not to say that the notion of global cultural synchronization (Schiller 1989) is irrelevant, on the contrary, but it is fundamentally incomplete. It overlooks the countercurrents—the impact nonwestern cultures have been making on the West. It downplays the ambivalence of the globalizing momentum and ignores the role of local reception of western culture—for example, the indigenization of western elements. It fails to see the influence nonwestern cultures have been exercising on one another. It has no room for crossover culture, as in the development of

Jan Nederveen Pieterse, *Globalization and Culture: Global Mélange* (Lanham, MD: Rowman & Littlefield, 2004): 69–83. Reprinted by permission.

"third cultures" such as world music. It overrates the homogeneity of western culture and overlooks the fact that many of the standards exported by the West and its cultural industries themselves turn out to be of culturally mixed character if we examine their cultural lineages. Centuries of South-North cultural osmosis have resulted in intercontinental crossover culture. European and western culture are *part* of this global mélange. This is an obvious case if we reckon that Europe until the fourteenth century was invariably the recipient of cultural influences from the "Orient." The hegemony of the West dates only from very recent time, from 1800 and, arguably, from industrialization . . .

. . . In the United States, *crossover* culture denotes the adoption of black cultural characteristics by European Americans and of white elements by African Americans. As a general notion, crossover culture may aptly describe long-term global intercultural osmosis and global mélange. Still what are not clarified are the *terms* under which cultural interplay and crossover take place. In terms such as global mélange, what is missing is acknowledgment of the actual unevenness, asymmetry, and inequality in global relations.

Theorizing Hybridity

Given the backdrop of nineteenth-century discourse, it's no wonder that those arguments that acknowledge hybridity often do so on a note of regret and loss—loss of purity, wholeness, authenticity. Thus according to the sociologist Hisham Sharabi, neopatriarchical society in the contemporary Arab world is "a new, hybrid sort of society/culture," "neither modern nor traditional" (1988: 4). The "neopatriarchal petty bourgeoisie" is likewise characterized as a "hybrid class" (1988: 6). This argument is based on an analysis of "the political and economic conditions of distorted, dependent capitalism" in the Arab world (1988: 5), in other words, it is derived from the framework of dependency theory.

In arguments such as these hybridity functions as a negative trope, in line with the nineteenth-century paradigm according to which hybridity, mixture, mutation are negative developments that detract from prelapsarian purity—in society and culture as in biology. Since the development of Mendelian genetics in the 1870s and subsequently in early twentieth-century biology, however, a revaluation has taken place according to which crossbreeding and polygenic inheritance have come to be positively valued as enrichments of gene pools. Gradually this has been seeping through in wider circles; the work of the anthropologist Gregory Bateson (1972), as one of the few to connect the natural sciences and the social sciences, has been influential in this regard . . .

A theory of hybridity would be attractive. We are so used to theories that are concerned with establishing boundaries and demarcations among phenomena—units or processes that are as neatly as possible set apart from other units or processes—that a theory that instead would focus on fuzziness and mélange, cut'n'mix, crisscross and crossover, might well be a relief in itself. Yet, ironically, of course, it would have to prove itself by giving as neat as possible a version of messiness, or an unhybrid categorization of hybridities.

By what yardstick would we differentiate hybridities? One consideration is in what context hybridity functions. At a general level, hybridity concerns the mixture of phenomena that are held to be different, separate; hybridization then refers to a *cross-category* process. Thus with the linguist Bakhtin (1968) hybridization refers to sites, such as fairs, that bring together the exotic and the familiar, villagers and townspeople, performers and observers. The categories can also be cultures, nations, ethnicities, status groups, classes, genres, and hybridity by its very existence blurs the distinctions among them. Hybridity functions, next, as part of a power relationship between center and margin, hegemony and minority, and indicates a blurring, destabilization or subversion of that hierarchical relationship.

One of the original notions of hybridity is *syncretism*, the fusion of religious forms. Here we can distinguish syncretism as *mimicry*—as in Santería, Candomblé, Vodûn, in which Catholic saints serve as masks behind which non-Christian forms of worship are practiced (Thompson 1984). The Virgin of Guadeloupe as a mask for Pacha Mama is another example. On the other hand, we find syncretism as a mélange not only of forms but also of beliefs, a merger in which both religions, Christian and native, have changed and a "third religion" has developed (as in Kimbangism in the Congo).

Another phenomenon is hybridity as migration mélange. A common observation is that second generation immigrants, in the West and elsewhere, display mixed cultural traits—a separation between and, next, a mix of a home culture and language (matching the culture of origin) and an outdoor culture (matching the culture of residence), as in the combination "Muslim in the daytime, disco in the evening" (Feddema 1992).

In postcolonial literature, hybridity is a familiar and ambivalent trope. Homi Bhabha (1990) refers to hybrids as intercultural brokers in the interstices between nation and empire, producing counternarratives from the nation's margins to the "totalizing boundaries" of the nation. At the same time, refusing nostalgic models of precolonial purity, hybrids, by way of mimicry, may conform to the "hegemonized rewriting of the Eurocentre." Hybridity, in this perspective, can be a condition tantamount to alienation, a state of homelessness. Smadar Lavie comments: "This is a response-oriented model of hybridity. It lacks agency, by not empowering the hybrid. The result is a fragmented Otherness in the hybrid" (1992: 92). In the work of Gloria Anzaldúa and others, she recognizes, on the other hand, a community-oriented mode of hybridity, and notes that "reworking the past exposes its hybridity, and to recognize and acknowledge this hybrid past in terms of the present empowers the community and gives it agency" (ibid.).

An ironical case of hybridity as intercultural crossover is mentioned by Michael Bérubé, interviewing the African American literary critic Houston Baker, Jr.: "That reminds me of your article in *Technoculture*, where you write that when a bunch of Columbia-graduate white boys known as Third Bass attack Hammer for not being black enough or strong enough . . . *that's* the moment of hybridity" (1992: 551).

Taking in these lines of thought, we can construct a *continuum of hybridities*: on one end, an assimilationist hybridity that leans over towards the center, adopts the canon and mimics hegemony and, at the other end, a destabilizing hybridity that blurs the canon, reverses the current, subverts the center. Hybridities, then, may be differentiated according to the components in the mélange: an assimilationist hybridity in which the center predominates—as in V.S. Naipaul, known for his trenchant observations such as there's no decent cup of coffee to be had in Trinidad; a posture that has given rise to the term Naipaulitis—and on the other hand, a hybridity that blurs (passive) or destabilizes (active) the canon and its categories. Perhaps this spectrum of hybridities can be summed up as ranging from Naipaul to Salman Rushdie (cf. Brennan 1989), Edward Said, and Subaltern Studies. Still what does it mean to destabilize the canon? It is worth reflecting on the politics of hybridity.

Politics of Hybridity

Relations of power and hegemony are inscribed and reproduced *within* hybridity for wherever we look closely enough we find the traces of asymmetry in culture, place, descent. Hence, hybridity raises the question of the *terms* of mixture, the conditions of mixing. At the same time, it's important to note the ways in which hegemony is not merely reproduced but *refigured* in the process of hybridization. Generally, what is the bearing of hybridity in relation to political engagement?

> At times, the anti-essentialist emphasis on hybrid identities comes dangerously close to dismissing all searches for communitarian origins as an archaeological excavation of an idealized, irretrievable past. Yet, on another level, while avoiding any nostalgia for a prelapsarian community, or for any unitary and transparent identity predating the "fall," we must also ask whether it is possible to forge a collective resistance without inscribing a communal past. (Shohat 1992: 109)

Isn't there a close relationship between political mobilization and collective memory? Isn't the remembrance of deeds past, the commemoration of collective itineraries, victories and defeats—such as the Matanza for the FMLN in El Salvador, Katipunan for the NPA in the Philippines, Heroes Day for the ANC—fundamental to the symbolism of resistance and the moral economy of mobilization? Still, this line of argument involves several problems. While there may be a link, there is no necessary symmetry between communal past/collective resistance. What is the basis of bonding in collective action—past or future, memory or project? While communal symbolism may be important, collective symbolism and discourse merging a heterogeneous collectivity in a common project may be more important. Thus while Heroes Day is significant to the ANC (December 16 is the founding day of Umkhonto we Sizwe), the Freedom Charter and, specifically, the project of nonracial democracy (nonsexism has been added later) has been of much greater importance. These projects are not of a communal nature: their strength is precisely that they transcend communal boundaries. Generally, emancipations may be thought of in the plural, as an ensemble of projects that in itself is diverse, heterogeneous, multivocal.[1] The argument linking communal past/collective resistance imposes a unity and transparency which in effect reduces the space for critical engagement, for plurality *within* the movement, diversity within the process of emancipation. It privileges a communal view of collective action, a primordial view of identity, and ignores or downplays the importance of *intra*-group differences and conflicts over group representation, demands, and tactics, including reconstructions of the past. It argues as if the questions of whether demands should be for autonomy or inclusion, whether the group should be inward or outward looking, have already been settled, while in reality these are political dilemmas. The nexus between communal past/collective engagement is one strand in political mobilization, but so are the hybrid past/plural projects, and in everyday politics the point is how to negotiate these strands in roundtable politics. This involves going beyond a past to a future orientation—for what is the point of collective action without a future? The lure of community, powerful and prevalent in left as well as right politics, has been questioned often enough. In contrast, hybridity when thought through as a politics may be subversive of essentialism and homogeneity, disruptive of static spatial and political categories of center and periphery, high and low, class and ethnos, and in recognizing multiple identities, widen the space for critical engagement. Thus, the nostalgia paradigm of community politics has been contrasted to the landscape of the city, along with a reading of "politics as relations among strangers" (Young 1990).

What is the significance of this outlook in the context of global inequities and politics? Political theory on a global scale is relatively undeveloped. Traditionally political theory is concerned with the relations between sovereign and people, state and society. It's of little help to turn to the "great political theorists" from Locke to Mill for they are all essentially concerned with the state-society framework. International relations theory extrapolates from this core preoccupation with concepts such as national interest and balance of power. Strictly speaking, international relations theory, at any rate neorealist theory, precludes global political theory. In the absence of a "world society," how can there be a worldwide social contract or global democracy? This frontier has opened up through ideas such as global civil society and the transnational networks of nongovernmental organizations: "The growth of global civil society represents an ongoing project of civil society to reconstruct, re-imagine, or re-map world politics" (Lipschutz 1992: 391). While global society and postinternational politics are relevant, a limitation to these reconceptualizations remains the absence of legal provisions that are globally binding rather than merely in interstate relations. Hence new initiatives such as the International Criminal Court and the Kyoto Protocol are particularly significant.

The question remains what kind of conceptual tools we can develop to address questions such as the double standards prevailing in global politics: perennial issues such as western countries practicing democracy at home and imperialism abroad: the edifying use of terms such as self-determination and sovereignty while the United States invades Panama, Grenada, or Iraq. The term *imperialism* may no longer be adequate to address the present situation. It may be adequate in relation to U.S. actions in Panama or Grenada, but less so to describe the Gulf War. Empire is the control exercised by a state over the domestic and foreign policy of another political society (Doyle 1986: 45), which is not an adequate terminology to characterize the Gulf War episode. If we consider that major actors in today's global circumstance are the IMF, World Bank, and World Trade Organization, transnational corporations, and regional investment banks, it is easy to acknowledge their influence on the domestic policies of countries from Brazil to the Philippines: but the situation differs from imperialism in two ways: the actors are not states and the foreign policy of the countries involved is not necessarily affected. The casual use of terms such as recolonization or neocolonialism to describe the impact of IMF conditionalities on African countries remains just that, casual. The situation has changed also since the emergence of regional blocs which can potentially exercise joint foreign policy (e.g., the European Union) or which within themselves contain two or more "worlds" (e.g., NAFTA, APEC). Both these situations differ from imperialism in the old sense. Literature in international political economy shows a shift from "imperialism" to "globalization." According to Tomlinson,

> the distribution of global power that we know as "imperialism". . . characterised the modern period up to, say, the 1960s. What replaces "imperialism" is "globalisation." Globalisation may be distinguished from imperialism in that it is a far less coherent or culturally directed process. . . . The idea of "globalisation" suggests interconnection and interdependency of all global areas which happens in a less purposeful way. (1991: 175)

This is a particularly narrow interpretation in which globalization matches the epoch of late capitalism; still what is interesting is the observation that the present phase of globalization is less coherent and less purposeful than imperialism. Domination may be more dispersed, less orchestrated, more heterogeneous. To address global inequalities and develop global political theory a different kind of conceptualization is needed. We are not without points of reference but we lack a theory of global political action. The sociologist Alberto Melucci has discussed the "planetarization" of collective action (1989). Some of the implications of globalization for democracy have been examined by Held (1992). As regards the basics of a global political consensus, the UN Declaration of Human Rights, and its amendments by the Movement of Nonaligned Countries, may be a point of reference (Parekh 1992).[2]

Post-hybridity?

Cultural hybridization refers to the mixing of Asian, African, American, European cultures: hybridization is the making of global culture as a global mélange. As a category, hybridity serves a purpose based on the assumption of *difference* between the categories, forms, beliefs that go into the mixture. Yet the very process of hybridization shows the difference to be relative and, with a slight shift of perspective, the relationship can also be described in terms of an affirmation of *similarity*. Thus, the Catholic saints can be taken as icons of Christianity but can also be viewed as holdovers of pre-Christian paganism inscribed in the Christian canon. In that light, their use as masks for non-Christian gods is less quaint and rather intimates transcultural pagan affinities.

Ariane Mnouchkine's use of Kabuki style to stage a Shakespeare play leads to the question which Shakespeare play? The play is *Henry IV*, which is set in a context of European high feudalism. In that light, the use of Japanese feudal Samurai style to portray European feudalism (Kreidt 1987: 255) makes a point about transcultural historical affinities. "Mexican schoolgirls dressed in Greek togas dancing in the style of Isadora Duncan," mentioned before, reflects transnational bourgeois class affinities, mirroring themselves in classical European culture. Chinese tacos and Irish bagels reflect ethnic crossover in employment patterns in the American fast food sector. Asian rap refers to cross-cultural stylistic convergence in popular youth culture . . .

What makes it difficult to discuss these issues is that two quite distinct concepts of *culture* are generally being used indiscriminately. The first concept of culture (culture 1) views culture as essentially territorial; it assumes that culture stems from a learning process that is, in the main, localized. This is culture in the sense of *a culture*, that is, the culture of a society or social group: a notion that goes back to nineteenth-century romanticism and that has been elaborated in twentieth-century anthropology, in particular cultural relativism—with the notion of cultures as a whole, a Gestalt, configuration. A related idea is the organic or "tree" model of culture.

A wider understanding of culture (culture 2) views culture as a general human "software" (Banuri 1990: 77), as in nature/culture arguments. This notion has been implicit in theories of evolution and diffusion, in which culture is viewed as, in the main, a *translocal* learning process. These understandings are not incompatible: culture 2 finds expression in culture 1; cultures are the vehicles of culture. But they do reflect different emphases in relation to historical processes of culture formation and hence generate markedly different assessments of cultural relations. Divergent meta-assumptions about culture underlie the varied vocabularies in which cultural relations are discussed (table 1).

Culture 2 or translocal culture is not without place (there is no culture without place), but it involves an *outward looking* sense of place, whereas culture 1 is based on an *inward looking* sense of place. Culture 2 involves what the geographer Doreen Massey calls "a global sense of place": "the specificity of place which derives from the fact that each place is the focus of a distinct *mixture* of wider and more local social relations" (1993: 240).

The general terminology of cultural pluralism, multicultural society, intercultural relations, and so on, does not clarify whether it refers to culture 1 or culture 2. Thus, relations among cultures can be viewed in a static fashion (in which cultures retain their separateness in interaction) or a fluid fashion (in which cultures interpenetrate) (table 2).

Table 1
Assumptions about Culture

Territorial Culture	*Translocal Culture*
endogenous	exogenous
orthogenetic	heterogenetic
societies, nations, empires	diasporas, migrations
locales, regions	crossroads, borders, interstices
community-based	networks, brokers, strangers
organic, unitary	diffusion, heterogeneity
authenticity	translation
inward looking	outward looking
community linguistics	contact linguistics
race	half-caste, half-breed, métis
ethnicity	new ethnicity
identity	identification, new identity

Hybridization as a perspective belongs to the fluid end of relations between cultures: the mixing of cultures and not their separateness is emphasized. At the same time, the underlying assumption about culture is that of culture/place. Cultural forms are called hybrid/syncretic/mixed/creolized because the elements in the mix derive from different cultural contexts. Thus, Hannerz defines Creole cultures as follows: "Creole cultures like creole languages are those which draw in some way on two or more historical sources, often originally widely different. They have had some time to develop and integrate, and to become elaborate and pervasive" (1987: 552). But in this sense would not every culture be a Creole culture? Can we identify any culture that is *not* Creole in the sense of drawing on one or more different historical sources?[3] A scholar of music makes a similar point about world music: "All music is essentially world music" (Bor 1994: 2).

A further question is: Are cultural elements different merely because they originate from different cultures? More often, what may be at issue, as argued above, is the *similarity* of cultural elements when viewed from the point of class, status

Table 2
Cultural Relations

Static	*Fluid*
plural society (Furnivall)	pluralism, melting pot
multiculturalism (static)	multiculturalism (fluid), interculturalism
global mosaic	cultural flows in space (Hannerz)
clash of civilizations	third cultures

Table 3
Homogenization versus Diversification

Globalization/homogenization	*Globalization/diversification*
cultural imperialism	cultural planetarization
cultural dependence	cultural interdependence
cultural hegemony	cultural interpenetration
autonomy	syncretism, synthesis, hybridity
modernity	modernities
westernization	global mélange
cultural convergence	creolization, crossover
world civilization	global ecumene

group, life style, or function. Hence, at some stage, toward the end of the story, the notion of cultural hybridity itself unravels or, at least, needs reworking. To explore what this means in the context of globalization, we can contrast the vocabularies and connotations of globalization-as-homogenization and globalization-as-hybridization (table 3).

What is common to some perspectives on both sides of the globalization/homogenization/heterogenization axis is a territorial view of culture. The territoriality of culture, however, itself is not constant over time. For some time we have entered a period of accelerated globalization and cultural mixing. This also involves an overall tendency towards the deterritorialization of culture, or an overall shift in orientation from culture 1 to culture 2. Introverted cultures, which have been prominent over a long stretch of history and overshadowed translocal culture, are gradually receding into the background, while translocal culture made up of diverse elements is coming to the foreground. This transition and the hybridization processes themselves unleash intense and dramatic nostalgia politics, of which ethnic upsurges, ethnicization of nations, and religious revivalism form part.

Hybridization refers not only to the crisscrossing of cultures (culture 1) but also and by the same token to a transition from the provenance of culture 1 to culture 2. Another aspect of this transition is that due to advancing information technology and biotechnology different *modes* of hybridity emerge on the horizon: in the light of hybrid forms such as cyborgs, virtual reality and electronic simulation, intercultural differences may begin to pale to relative insignificance—although of great local intensity. Biotechnology opens up the perspective of "merged evolution," in the sense of the merger of the evolutionary streams of genetics, cultural evolution, and information technology, and the near prospect of humans intervening in genetic evolution, through the matrix of cultural evolution and information technologies (Goonatilake 1991).

Forward Moves

Globalization/hybridization makes, first, an empirical case: that processes of globalization, past and present, can be adequately described as processes of hybridization. Secondly, it is a critical argument: against viewing globalization in terms of homogenization, or of modernization/westernization, as empirically narrow and historically flat . . .

Structural hybridization, or the increase in the range of organizational options, and cultural hybridization, or the doors of erstwhile imagined communities opening up, are signs of an age of boundary crossing, not, surely, of the erasure of boundaries. Thus, state power remains strategic, but it is no longer the only game in town. The tide of globalization reduces the room of maneuver of states, while international institutions, transnational transactions, regional cooperation, subnational dynamics, and non-governmental organizations expand in impact and scope (Cooperrider and Dutton 1999).

In historical terms, writing diaspora histories of global culture may deepen this perspective. Due to nationalism as the dominant paradigm since the nineteenth century, cultural achievements have been routinely claimed for nations and culture has been "nationalized," territorialized. A different historical record can be constructed based on the contributions to culture formation and diffusion by diasporas, migrations, strangers, brokers . . . A related project would be histories of the hybridization of metropolitan cultures, that is, a counterhistory to the narrative of imperial history. Such historical inquiries may show that hybridization has been taking place all along but has been concealed by religious, national, imperial, and civilizational chauvinisms. Moreover, they may deepen our understanding of the temporalities of hybridization: how certain junctures witness downturns or upswings of hybridization, slowdowns or speedups. At the same time it follows that, if we accept that cultures have been hybrid *all along,* hybridization is in effect a tautology: contemporary accelerated globalization means the hybridization of hybrid cultures.

As such, the hybridization perspective remains meaningful only as a critique of essentialism. Essentialism will remain strategic as a mobilizational device as long as the units of nation, state, region, civilization, ethnicity remain strategic: and for just as long hybridization remains a relevant approach. Hybridity unsettles the introverted concept of culture that underlies romantic nationalism, racism, ethnicism, religious revivalism, civilizational chauvinism, and cultural essentialism. Hybridization, then, is a perspective that is meaningful as a counterweight to introverted notions of culture; at the same time, the very process of hybridization unsettles the introverted gaze, and accordingly, hybridization eventually ushers in post-hybridity, or transcultural cut-and-paste.

Hybridization is a factor in the reorganization of social spaces. Structural hybridization, or the emergence of new practices of social cooperation and competition, and cultural hybridization, or new translocal cultural expressions, are interdependent: new forms of cooperation require and evoke new cultural imaginaries . . .

In relation to the global human condition of inequality, the hybridization perspective releases reflection and engagement from the bounds of nation, community, ethnicity, or class. Fixities have become fragments as the kaleidoscope of collective experience is in motion. It has been in motion all along, and the fixities of nation, community, ethnicity, and class have been grids superimposed upon experiences more complex and subtle than reflexivity and organization could accommodate.

Notes

1. In *Pour Rushdie,* a collection of essays by Arab and Islamic intellectuals in support of freedom of expression, Paris is referred to as a "capitale Arabe." This evokes another notion of hybridity, one that claims a collective ground based on multiple subjectivities in the name of a universal value.
2. I use critical globalism as an approach to current configurations (Nederveen Pieterse 2001). This discussion of imperialism versus globalization is dated since in the wake of 9/11 has come a new imperial turn; this is taken up in a forthcoming book on *Globalization or Empire?* (Routledge, 2004).
3. Some of the "primitive isolates," the traditional study objects of anthropology, might be exceptions, although even this may be questioned in the long stretch of time.

Bibliography

Bakhtin, Mikhail, *Rabelais and His World.* Cambridge: MIT Press, 1968.

Banuri, Tariq. "Modernization and Its Discontents: A Cultural Perspective on Theories of Development." Pp. 73–101 in *Dominating Knowledge,* edited by F. Appfel-Marglin and S. A. Marglin. Oxford: Clarendon Press, 1990.

Bateson, Gregory. *Steps to an Ecology of Mind.* San Francisco: Chandler, 1972.

Bérubé, Michael. "Hybridity in the Center: An Interview with Houston A. Baker, Jr." *African American Review* 26, no. 4 (1992); 547–64.

Bhabha, Homi K. "Dissemination: Time, Narrative and the Margins of the Modern Nation." In *Nation and Narration,* edited by idem. London: Routledge, 1990.

Bor, Joep. "Studying World Music: The Next Phase." Unpublished paper, 1994.

Brennan, Timothy. *Salman Rushdie and the Third World: Myths of the Nation.* New York: St. Martin's Press, 1989.

Cooperrider, David L., and Jane E. Dutton, eds. *Organizational Dimensions of Global Change: No Limits to Cooperation.* London: Sage, 1999.

Doyle, Michael W. *Empires.* Ithaca, NY: Cornell University Press, 1986.

Feddema, R. "Op Weg tussen Hoop en Vrees: De levensoriëntatie van jonge Turken en Marokkanen in Nederland." Utrecht University, Ph.D. diss., 1992.

Goonatilake, Susantha. *The Evolution of Information: Lineages in Gene, Culture and Artifact.* London: Pinter, 1991.

Hannerz, Ulf. "The World in Creolisation." *Africa* 57, no. 4 (1987): 546–59.

Held, David. "Democracy: From City-States to a Cosmopolitan Order?" Pp. 13–52 in *Prospects for Democracy,* edited by D. Held. Cambridge: Polity, 1992.

Kreidt, D. "Kann Uns Zum Vaterland die Fremde Werden? Exotismus im Schauspieltheater." Pp. 248–55 in *Exotische Welten, Europäische Phantasien.* Wurttemberg: Cantz, 1987.

Lavie, Smadar. "Blow-ups in the Borderzones: Third World Israeli Authors' Gropings for Home." *New Formations* 18 (1992): 84–106.

Lipschutz, Ronald D. "Reconstructing World Politics: The Emergence of Global Civil Society." *Millennium* 21, no. 3 (1992): 389–420.
Massey, Doreen. "A Global Sense of Place." Pp. 232–40 in *Studying Culture*, edited by A. Gray and J. McGuigan. London: Edward Arnold, 1993.
Melucci, Alberto. *Nomads of the Present*. London: Hutchinson Radius, 1989.
Nederveen Pieterse, Jan P. *Empire and Emancipation: Power and Liberation on a World Scale*. New York: Praeger, 1989.
———. "Unpacking the West: How European Is Europe?" Pp. 129–49 in *Racism, Modernity, Identity*, edited by A. Rattansi and S. Westwood. Cambridge: Polity Press, 1994.
———. *Development Theory: Deconstructions/Reconstructions*. London: Sage, 2001.
Parekh, Bhikhu. The Cultural Particularity of Liberal Democracy." Pp. 156–75 in *Prospects for Democracy*, edited by Held, 1992.
Pour Rushdie. Paris: Ed. La Découverte/Carrefour des Littératures/Colibri, 1993.
Rowe, William, and Vivian Schelling. *Memory and Modernity: Popular Culture in Latin America*. London: Verso, 1991.
Schiller, Herbert I. *Culture Inc*. New York: Oxford University Press, 1989.
Sharabi, Hisham. *Neopatriarchy: A Theory of Distorted Change in Arab Society*. New York: Oxford University Press, 1988.
Shohat, Ella. "Notes on the 'Post-Colonial.'" *Social Text* 31/32, (1992): 99–113.
Thompson, Robert Faris. *Flash of the Spirit: African and Afro-American Art and Philosophy*. New York: Vintage, 1984.
Tomlinson, John. *Cultural Imperialism*. Baltimore, MD: Johns Hopkins University Press, 1991.
Young, Iris Marion. *Justice and the Politics of Difference*. Princeton, NJ: Princeton University Press, 1990.

Immigration in a Global Era

Saskia Sassen

Saskia Sassen highlights that immigration in the global era is closely connected to processes and policies surveyed in previous selections in this book, including gender inequality, the impact of economic globalization on poverty and inequality, and policies of international organizations like the IMF. As she puts it, "The same infrastructure, both technical and institutional, that has enabled global flows of capital and goods, services and the new transnational managerial and professional class, also enables migrations and illegal trafficking." However, whereas affluent states and influential international organizations generally support free trade and the free movement of capital across national borders, they oppose the mobility of labor, that is, temporary or permanent migration. Can you suggest why this should be so?

Sassen also highlights the impact of migration on both sending and receiving countries. She notes the importance of remittances sent back home by immigrants:

the volume of remittances ranks among the largest sources of revenue for countries like the Philippines and Bangladesh, which have large emigrant populations. And she also stresses the close connections between immigration, the international tourism and entertainment industry, and the trafficking of women and children for the international sex industry. Finally, Sassen points to the impact of the various forms of immigration on receiving countries. Immigrants can provide important benefits to affluent countries, whose birth rates have declined sharply. By contrast, a large criminal industry has arisen in response to restrictions on immigration, especially in the post-9/11 era, when there has been an increase in governmental repression to secure borders. Desperate people in poor countries or those with repressive governments are willing to pay large sums to "coyotes" to help them evade immigration restrictions; clandestine trips across borders often tragically end in injury and death.

Sassen's article invites us to think about the theoretical, political, and human aspects of immigration. Can you think of ways to resolve the problems produced by the present patterns and policies involving immigration?

Over the last decade we have seen a sharp increase in the estimated numbers of would-be immigrants who have died trying to get into the United States and into Europe. Who is it we are determined to keep out to the point that they risk their lives to get in? An equally determined but tiny minority of men, women and children from mostly poor countries, who will come no matter what in search of work or refuge. They are not criminals. But the result of our determination is that we are feeding a criminal trade. There has been a sharp growth in illegal trafficking of people as receiving countries have clamped down on entries and semi-militarized more and more borders.

These developments raise two issues. One concerns the old trade-off between policies that criminalize what may not intrinsically be a criminal act and do so in the name of controlling a somewhat untenable situation; this in turn raises the incentives for genuinely criminal actors to promote the forbidden activity. A familiar instance of this trade-off concerns marijuana control policy. Does the criminalizing of marijuana in the U.S.—and the UK—really work better as a policy to control its use than the controlled legality of marijuana in the Netherlands, which leaves very little room for profit making by drug dealers and hence no incentive to expand its use?

The second policy issue raised by these developments is that the deaths of these thousands of people attempting to enter affect us all, not only those directly concerned. The fact that these people lack the proper documents for entry is easily represented in policy and media circles as exempting us from any

---

Saskia Sassen, *Immigration in a Global Era,* New Politics IX, no. 4 (Winter 2004): 35–42. Reprinted by permission.

responsibility as societies for these deaths. The lack of proper documents somehow seems to make these deaths less human and reduce whatever might be our responsibility contributing to these deaths.

The trend toward greater police and military control and growing disregard for international human rights codes as well as our civil liberties laws is promoting illegal trafficking and weakening our rule of law and thereby our democracies. These policies are adding to an already growing mix of what I would describe as negative incentives, or incentives with negative outcomes for significant sectors of our societies.

Illegal trafficking and the deaths of men, women and children who are not criminals, and who die on our "soil" eventually touches the fabric of *our* societies and distorts or weakens the rule of law. In the long run it will affect us all. Yes, the central victims are the men and women who are trafficked and especially those who die. But we would be foolish to think that we can allow these abuses and deaths to happen in the name of maintaining control, and remain untouched. The growth in illegal trafficking and the sharpening of extreme anti-immigrant politics willing to sacrifice some civil liberties in the name of control are indications of this broader negative effect.

The Interconnectedness of Violence

Part of the challenge is to recognize the interconnectedness of forms of violence that we do not always recognize as being connected or for that matter, as being forms of violence. The sharp growth of government debt, poverty, unemployment and the closing of traditional economic sectors in the global south, partly due to neoliberal economic globalization, has created whole new migrations as well as fed an exploding illegal trade in people. We now have growing evidence that International Monetary Fund (IMF) policy has sharpened these conditions, even as it has brought great prosperity to about 20 percent of residents in many countries in the global south.

By supporting IMF policies, our governments are contributing to those conditions that are going to stimulate emigration and illegal trafficking in people. Further, as the rich economies become richer partly because of these same IMF policies, they also become more desirable destinations. This in turn creates a source for hard currency for the governments of the sending countries in a context where they face mounting debt and declines in national revenues as neoliberal globalization weakens and often destroys many of the national economic sectors in these countries. Thus these governments are not interested particularly in regulating emigration either. Finally, as these same policies have also raised inequality and unemployment inside the rich economies, the disadvantaged have become radicalized, often taking on extreme right wing politics, a growing trend in Western Europe.

The tragedy is that those most affected negatively, those to whom violence has been done both in the global south and in the rich economies, the victims of it all, now confront each other as enemies inside our countries. Anti-immigrant sentiment probably runs highest among those who have hurt from the same policies that have hurt the poor and the middle classes (though not the upper 20 percent) from where come the immigrants and would-be immigrants. And as the rich countries raise their walls to keep immigrants and refugees out, they feed the illegal trade in people and raise the profits to be made as despair rises in the global south and fear in the global north. This is not sound policy. This is a vicious policy cycle.

The same infrastructure, both technical and institutional, that has enabled global flows of capital and goods, services and the new transnational managerial and professional class, also enables migrations and illegal trafficking. And it facilitates the flow of remittances back to sending countries, a major incentive for not doing anything on the part of these governments. These various entanglements raise the complexity of the challenge of how to regulate immigration. But these entanglements and this type of complexity are going in the wrong direction. We need to reverse this dynamic.

When globalization policies go wrong, they really go very wrong for countries in the global south. Thereby these policies sharpen the incentives for both emigration and trafficking for emigrants, traffickers and governments in the global south, given growing government indebtedness and lack of opportunity for workers and would be entrepreneurs in much of the global south.

Emigrants enter the macro-level of development strategies for sending countries through their remittances. In many countries these represent a major source of foreign exchange reserves for the government. While the flows of remittances may be minor compared to the massive daily capital flows in various financial markets, they are often very significant for developing or struggling economies.

In 1998—the last year for which comprehensive data are available—global remittances sent by immigrants to their home countries reached over seventy billion dollars. To understand the significance of this figure, it should be related to the GDP (gross domestic product) and foreign currency reserves in the specific countries involved, rather than compared to the global flow of capital. For instance, in the Philippines, a key sender of migrants generally and of women for the entertainment industry in several countries, remittances were the third largest source of foreign exchange over the last several years. In Bangladesh, another country with significant numbers of its workers in the Middle East, Japan and several European countries, remittances represent about a third of foreign exchange. Exporting workers and remittances are means for governments of coping with unemployment and foreign debt.

This would also seem to be the case given the growing interdependencies brought on by globalization, which also enables illegal trafficking. Cross-border business travel, global tourism, the Internet and other conditions integral to globalization enable multiple global flows not foreseen by the framers and developers of economic globalization. This creates a difficult trade-off in a context where September 11th has further sharpened the will to control immigration and resident immigrants. Increased illegal trafficking and the reduction in civil liberties will not facilitate the need to learn how to accommodate more immigration to respond to the future demographic turn.

Let me focus next with some detail on one specific flow, which brings many of these issues together.

Illegal Trafficking

Trafficking in workers for both licit and illegal work (e.g. unauthorized sex work) illuminates a number of intersections between the negative conditions in the global south and some of the tensions in the immigration regime.[1] Trafficking is a violation of several distinct types of rights: human, civil, political. Trafficking in people appears to be mainly related to the sex market, to labor markets, to illegal migration. Much legislative work has been done to address trafficking: international treaties and charters, United Nations resolutions and various bodies and commissions. Trafficking was also addressed in the G8 meeting in Birmingham in May 1998. The heads of the eight major industrialized countries stressed the importance of cooperation against international organized crime and trafficking in persons. President Clinton issued a set of directives to his administration to strengthen and increase efforts against trafficking in women and girls, and Paul Wellstone introduced a senate bill that addressed the issue in 1999.

NGOs are also playing an increasingly important role. For instance, the Coalition Against Trafficking in Women has centers and representatives in Australia, Bangladesh, Europe, Latin America, North America, Africa and Asia Pacific. The Women's Rights Advocacy Program has established the Initiative Against Trafficking in Persons to combat the global trade in persons.

This type of trafficking shows us one of the meanings of interdependence in the current global system. There are two distinct issues here: one is that globalization has produced new conditions and dynamics, especially the growing demand for these types of workers by the expanding high income professional workforce associated largely, though not exclusively, with globalization.[2] The second issue is that globalization has enabled older trafficking networks and practices which used to be national or regional to become global.

Here I want to focus on some of the data on the trafficking of women, especially for the sex industries and the growing weight of this trafficking as a profit making option for the traffickers, especially it would seem from the global south. This, then, adds to the role of emigrants' remittances generally, whether from lawful, unauthorized or trafficked immigrants in the account balance of many of the impoverished governments of sending countries. Profits and revenues are, clearly, a disincentive to attack this trade. Insofar as the countries of the global north are one of the key destinations, they do not escape the consequences of this illegal trade either.

Trafficking in migrants is a profitable business. According to a United Nations report, criminal organizations in the 1990s generated an estimated $3.5 billion per year in profits from trafficking migrants (excluding most of the women trafficked for the sex industry). The entry of organized crime is a recent development in the case of migrant trafficking; in the past it was mostly petty criminals who engaged in this type of trafficking.

The Central Intelligence Agency reports that organized crime groups are creating intercontinental strategic alliances through networks of co-ethnics throughout several countries; this facilitates transport, local contact and distribution, provision of false documents and so on. The Global Survival Network in 1997 reported on these practices after a two-year investigation using the establishment of a dummy company to enter the illegal trade. Such networks also facilitate the organized circulation of trafficked women among third countries—not only from sending to receiving countries. Traffickers may move women from Burma, Laos, Vietnam and China to Thailand, while Thai women may have been moved to Japan and the United States.[3]

Although there is no exhaustive data, the available information suggests that trafficking in women, including minors, for the sex industry is highly profitable for those running the trade. The UN estimates that four million women were trafficked in 1998, producing a profit of $7 billion for criminal groups. These funds include remittances from prostitutes' earnings and payments to organizers and facilitators in these countries.

In Japan, where the so-called entertainment industry is legal, profits are about 4.2 trillion yen per year over the last few years; there is growing evidence that illegally trafficked women are a growing share of sex workers. In Poland, police estimate that for each Polish woman delivered, the trafficker receives about $700. In Australia, the federal police estimate that the cash flow from 200 prostitutes is up to $900,000 a week. Ukrainian and Russian women, in high demand in the sex market, earn the criminal gangs involved about $500 to $1000 per woman delivered. These women can be expected to service on average 15 clients a day, and each can be expected to make about $215,000 per month for the gang.[4]

It is estimated that in recent years several million women and girls are trafficked within and out of Asia and the former Soviet Union, two major trafficking areas. Increases in trafficking in both these areas can be linked to women being pushed into poverty or sold to brokers due to the poverty of their households or parents. High unemployment in the former Soviet republics has been one factor promoting growth of criminal gangs as well as growth of trafficking in women. Unemployment rates among women in Armenia, Russia, Bulgaria and Croatia reached 70 percent and in Ukraine 80 percent with the implementation of market policies. There is some research indicating that economic need is the bottom line for entry into prostitution.[5]

Some of the features of immigration policy and enforcement may well contribute to make women who are victims of trafficking even more vulnerable and to give them little recourse to the law. If they are undocumented, which they are likely to be, they will not be treated as victims of abuse but as violators of the law insofar as they have violated entry, residence and work laws. Efforts to address undocumented immigration and trafficking through greater border controls over entry raise the likelihood that women will use traffickers to cross the border, and some of these may turn out to belong to criminal organizations linked to the sex industry.

Further, in many countries prostitution is forbidden for foreign women, which enhances the role of criminal gangs in prostitution. It also diminishes one of the survival options of foreign women who may have limited access to jobs generally. Prostitution is tolerated for foreign women in many countries while regular labor market jobs are less so—this is the case for instance in the Netherlands and in Switzerland. According to International Organization for Migration data, the number of migrant women prostitutes in many European Union countries is far higher than that for nationals: 75 percent in Germany, 80 percent in the case of Milan in Italy, etc.

While some women know that they are being trafficked for prostitution, for many the conditions of their recruitment and the extent of abuse and bondage only become evident after they arrive in the receiving country. The conditions of confinement are often extreme, akin to slavery, and so are the conditions of abuse, including rape and other forms of sexual violence and physical punishments. They are severely underpaid, and wages are often withheld. They are prevented from using protection methods against AIDS, and typically have no right to medical treatment. If they seek police help they may be taken into detention because they are in violation of immigration laws; if they have been provided with false documents there are criminal charges.[6]

Entertainment and Poverty

As tourism has grown sharply over the last decade and become a major development strategy for cities, regions and whole countries, the entertainment sector has seen a parallel growth and recognition as a key development strategy. In many places, the sex trade is part of the entertainment industry and has similarly grown. At some point it becomes clear that the sex trade itself can become a development strategy in areas with high unemployment and poverty and governments desperate for revenue and foreign exchange reserves. When local manufacturing and agriculture can no longer function as sources of employment, of profits and of government revenue, what was once a marginal source of earnings, profits and revenues, now becomes a far more important one.

The increased importance of these sectors in development generates growing tie-ins. For instance, when the IMF and the World Bank see tourism as a solution to some of the growth challenges in many poor countries and provide loans for its development or expansion, they may well be contributing to develop a broader institutional setting for the expansion of the entertainment industry and indirectly of the sex trade.

This tie-in with development strategies signals that trafficking in women may well see further expansion. It is a worrisome possibility, especially in the context of growing numbers of women with few if any employment options. And such growing numbers are to be expected given high unemployment and poverty, the shrinking of a world of work opportunities that were embedded in the more traditional sectors of these economies, and the growing debt burden of governments rendering them incapable of providing social services and support to the poor. Under these conditions, women in the sex industry also can become a source of government revenue. These tie-ins are structural, not a function of conspiracies. Their weight in an economy will be raised by the absence or limitations of other sources for securing a livelihood, profits and revenues for respectively workers, enterprises and governments.

Even as the rich countries try harder and harder to keep would-be immigrants and refugees out, they face a growing demographic deficit and rapidly aging populations. According to a major study, at the end of the current century and under current fertility and immigration patterns, population size in Western Europe will have shrunk by 75 million and almost 50 percent of the population will be over 60 years old—a first in its history.[7] Europe, perhaps more so than the U.S. given its relatively larger intake of immigrants, faces some difficult decisions. Where will they find the new young workers needed to support the growing elderly population and to do jobs considered unattractive by the native born, particularly in a context of rising educational attainment? The numbers of these jobs are not declining, even if the incidence of some of them is; one sector that is likely to add jobs is home and institutional care for the growing numbers of elderly people. Export of older people and of economic activities is one option being considered now. But there is a limit to how many elderly people and low wage jobs an economy can export and a society can tolerate. Immigration is expected to be part of the solution.

In the United States the evidence suggests a slightly different pattern. By century's end the forecasted fall for the U.S. is 34 million people, though this represents a point in the upward slope, which will not be completed until after the end of this century. The evidence is fairly clear that a significant component of population growth in the U.S. over the last two decades as well as labor force growth is accounted for by immigrants, both second generation and foreign born. In both cases, immigrants account for a larger component of growth than their share in respectively the general population and the total labor force.

Yet the way the countries in the global north are proceeding is not preparing them to handle this scenario. They are building walls to keep would-be immigrants out. At a time of growing refugee flows, the UN High Commissioner for Refugees faces an even greater shortage of funds than usual. Given an effective demand for immigrant workers, and indeed families for demographic purposes, both of these policy preferences are likely to have negative repercussions for Europe. They construct the immigrant and the refugee as a negative and undesirable subject, thereby encumbering integration. Further, given firms and households interested in hiring immigrants or determined to do so, for whatever reasons, restrictive policies and racialized representations of the immigrant and the refugee, can be expected to feed the already growing illegal trafficking of people.

Immigration Policy

The large and looming issue confronting societies under the rule of law is whether policies that brutalize people—no matter what their nationality—and promote criminalized profit-making through the trade in people, are desirable and indeed sustainable if we are to keep up our systems based on the rule of law for which our forebears fought so hard and spilled so much blood. Allowing this sort of brutalization and criminality is a very high price to pay for maintaining border control, and sooner or later it begins to tear at the fabric of the lawful state and of civil society.

The risks to fully documented citizens are illustrated by what is happening today in the U.S. The events of September 11th and the subsequent restrictions on the civil liberties of particular immigration groups in the U.S. are tearing at, and some would say weakening the rule of law as it affects all U.S. residents. The government is granting itself more and more authority to deal directly, in an extrajudicial way, with matters that used to run through judiciaries or that would not be considered a matter for the government to get involved with. In so doing, the federal government is violating basic rights not only of those it has profiled as possibly dangerous, but also of its citizens, all citizens, not just those who might be suspect.

Are there ways of regulating the flow of people into our societies that could strengthen, rather than weaken, the civic fabric? The repeated incidents of would-be immigrants dying at the hands of illegal traffickers do not. They risk producing indifference when it happens over and over again. And they risk promoting acceptance of these deaths by ourselves and our children—all in the name of maintaining control over entry.

We are not only paying a price for those who die on our soil; we are also paying a price for those who are smuggled into our countries alive. The price we pay for allowing the abuse that is human smuggling is much higher than the "price" we pay for accommodating these people who just want a chance to work—and work they do. Indeed, much research suggests that we actually gain from the presence of these immigrants. For instance, seventeen percent of entrepreneurs in London belong to ethnic communities, a far higher share than their population share.

Continuing to use policies that make possible the brutalization of would-be migrants and the profit making of criminal smugglers is a cancer deep inside *our* states and societies. It is the price we pay for criminalizing undocumented immigrants and, more generally, for resorting to policing and militarization as the way of regulating immigration. The U.S. illustrates this to some extent. In the name of effective control, the 1996 Immigration Act strengthened policing by reducing judiciary review of immigration police actions. A crucial issue here is the object of the expanded policing: It is not known criminals or firms suspected of violating environmental regulations or drug dealers. It is a population sector, not even select individuals, but a fairly broad spectrum of men, women and children.

There are consequences to this tension between, on the one hand, the strengthening of police approaches to immigrant regulation and, on the other, the strengthening of civil and human rights and the civic empowerment associated with a stronger sense of civil society. Sooner or later this policing will get caught in the expanding web of civil and human rights. And these rights will include those of citizens. Policing, when unchecked by civil review, can easily violate such rights and interfere with the functioning of civil society.

If my son decided to go write the great American novel by spending time with farm workers or in garment sweatshops, and there were an Immigration and Naturalization Service (INS) raid he could well be part of the suspects—because I know he would not be carrying his passport with him. Or worse, if he were among the farm workers in California running away from the INS police and pushed towards jumping in one of the water levies, as has happened a number of times over the last few years, he might have been one of those who drowned.

As a result of the 1996 law, the actions of INS agents can escape review and accountability in front of a judge if the persecuted were merely suspected of being undocumented. Sooner or later abusive or excess policing and the weakening of judicial review of such police actions will interfere with the aspiration towards the rule of law that is such a deep part of our inheritance and our lived reality. We need to find another way of regulating entry: now we are strengthening modes of regulation that carry a high cost not only in immigrant deaths but also to the rule of law.

Bibliography

Diana Alarcon-Gonzalez and Terry McKinley, "The adverse effects of structural adjustment on working women in Mexico," *Latin American Perspectives*, Vol. 26, no. 3 (1999).

Sietske Altink, *Stolen Lives: Trading Women into Sex and Slavery*. New York: Harrington Park Press, 1995.

Asoka Bandarage, *Women, Population and Crisis*. London: Zed, 1997.

Walden Bello, *A Siamese Tragedy: Development and Disintegration in Modern Thailand*. London: Zed, 1998.

William Booth, "Thirteen charged in gang importing prostitutes," *Washington Post*, August 21, 1999.

York Bradshaw, Rita Noonan, Laura Gash and Claudia Buchmann, "Borrowing against the future: Children and third world indebtness," *Social Forces* Vol. 71, no. 3 (1993).

"Brides from the Phillippines?" www.geocites.co.jp/Milkyway-Kaigan/5501/ph7.html.

Claudia Buchmann, "The debt crisis, structural adjustment and women's education," *International Journal of Comparative Studies*, Vol. 37, nos. 1–2 (1996).

Nilufer Cagatay and Sule Ozler, "Feminization of the labor force: The effects of long-term development and structural adjustment." *World Development*, Vol. 23, no. 11 (1995).

Stephen Castles and Mark J. Miller, *The Age of Migration: International Population Movements in the Modern World*, New York: Macmillan, 1998.

Grace Chang, "Undocumented Latinas: The new employable mothers," in M. Andersen and Patricia Hill Collins, eds., *Race, Class, and Gender*. London: Wadsworth, 1998.

Micel Chossudovsky, *The Globalisation of Poverty*. London: Zed, 1997.

Christine Chin, "Walls of silence and late 20th century representations of foreign female domestic workers: The case of Filipina and Indonesian houseservants in Malaysia," *International Migration Review*, Vol. 31, no. 1 (1997).

Janie Chuang, "Redirecting the Debate over Trafficking in Women: Definitions, Paradigms, and Contexts," *Harvard Human Rights Journal*, no. 10 (Winter 1998).

CIA, "International Trafficking in Women to the United States: A Contemporary Manifestation of Slavery and Organized Crime." Prepared by Amy O'Neill Richard. Washington, D.C.: Center for the Study of Intelligence, 2000. www.cia.gov/csi/monograph/women/trafficking.pdf.

Coalition to Abolish Slavery and Trafficking, *Factsheet*. www.traffickedwomen.org/fact.html.

Coalition Against Trafficking in Women. (Annual). *Reports*.

David Natacha, "Migrants made the scapegoats of the crisis," *ICFTU Online*, 1999. International Confederation of Free Trade Unions: www.hartford-hwp.com/archives/50/012.html.

Barbara Ehrenreich and Arlie Hochschild, eds., *Global Woman*. New York: Metropolitan Books, 2002.

Stephanie Farrior, "The International Law on Trafficking in Women and Children for Prostitution: Making it Live up to its Potential," *Harvard Human Rights Journal*, 10 (Winter 1997).

Global Survival Network, "Crime and Servitude: An Expose of the Traffic in Women for Prostitution from the Newly Independent States." *www.globalsurvival.net/femaletrade.html* (November 1997).

Noeleen Heyzer, *The Trade in Domestic Workers*. London: Zed, 1994.

International Institute for Applied Systems Analysis, *Special Report: Global Population*. Vienna: IIASA, 2001.

International Organization for Migration, *Trafficking in Migrants* (Quarterly Bulletin). Geneva: IOM. wwww.iom.int

Erika Jones, "The gendered toll of global debt crisis," *Sojourner*, Vol. 25, no. 3 (1999).

Kamala Kempadoo and Jo Doezema, *Global Sex Workers: Rights, Resistance, and Redefinition*. London: Routledge, 1998.

Lap-Chew Lin and Wijers Marjan, *Trafficking in women, forced labour and slavery-like practices in marriage, domestic labour and prostitution*. Utrecht: Foundation Against Trafficking in Women, and Bangkok: Global Alliance Against Traffic in Women, 1997.

Lin Lim, *The Sex Sector: The Economic and Social Bases of Prostitution in Southeast Asia*. Geneva: International Labor Office, 1998.

Richard Longworth, *Global Squeeze. The coming crisis for firstworld nations*. Chicago: Contemporary Books, 1998.

Rekha Mehra, "Women, empowerment and economic development," *Annals of the American Academy of Political and Social Science* (November 1997).

Eddy Meng, "Mail Order Brides: Gilded Prostitution and the Legal Responses," *University of Michigan Journal of Law Reform* (Fall 1998).

Aihwa Ong, "Globalization and Women's Rights: The Asian Debate on Citizenship and Communitarianism," *Indiana Journal of Global Legal Studies*, Vol. 4, no. 1 (Fall 1996).

OXFAM, *International submission to the HIPC debt review*, (April 1999). www.caa.org/au/oxfam/advocacy/debt/hipcreview.html.

Philippines Information Service, "Filipina Brides," 1999. www.pis.or.jp/data/tothug.htm.

Saskia Sassen, "The Participation of States and Citizens in Global Governance," in *Indiana Journal of Global Legal Studies*, Vol. 10, no. 1 (2003).

Saskia Sassen, "Globalization or Denationalization?" *Review of International Political Economy*, Vol. 10, no. 1 (February 2003).

Saskia Sassen, "The Repositioning of Citizenship: Emergent Subjects and Spaces for Politics," *Berkeley Journal of Sociology*, Vol. 46 (2002).

Saskia Sassen, *Guests and Aliens*. New York: New Press, 1999.

Susan Shannon, "The Global Sex Trade: Humans as the Ultimate Commodity," *Crime and Justice International* (May 1999).

James Tyner, "The global context of gendered labor emigration from the Philippines to the United States," *American Behavioral Scientist*, Vol. 42, no. 40 (1999).

Kathryn Ward and Jean Pyle, "Gender, Industrialization and Development," in Christine E. Bose and Edna Acosta-Belen, eds., *Women in the Latin American Development Process: From Structural Subordination to Empowerment*. Philadelphia: Temple University Press, 1995.

Brenda Yeoh, Shirlena Huang, and Joaquin Gonzalez III, "Migrant Female Domestic Workers: debating the economic, social and political impacts in Singapore," *International Migration Review*, Vol. 33, no. 1 (1999).

Notes

1. Trafficking involves the forced recruitment and/or transportation of people within and across states for work or services through a variety of forms all involving coercion.
2. One process that captures this specific type of interdependence is the global migration of maids, nannies and nurses. *See* Barbara Ehrenreich and Arlie Hochschild (2002).
3. There are various reports on the particular cross-border movements in trafficking. Malay brokers sell Malay women into prostitution in Australia. East European women from Albania and Kosovo have been trafficked by gangs into prostitution in London. European teens from Paris and other cities have been sold to Arab and African customers. In the U.S., the police broke up an international Asian ring that imported women from China, Thailand, Korea, Malaysia and Vietnam. The women were charged between $30,000 and $40,000 in contracts to be paid through their work in the sex trade or needle trade. The women in the sex trade were shuttled around several states in the U.S. to bring "continuing variety to the clients." *See* Martin Booth (1999).
4. For more detailed information, see Marjan Wijers and Marieke van Doorninck, *Only Rights Can Stop Wrongs: A Critical Assessment of the Anti-Trafficking Strategies, from the Conference on Preventing and Combating Trafficking in Human Beings (2002).*
5. There is also a growing trade in children for the sex industry—this has long been the case in Thailand but now is also present in several other Asian countries, in Eastern Europe and Latin America.
6. A fact sheet by the Coalition to Abolish Slavery and Trafficking reports that one survey of Asian sex workers found that rape often preceded their being sold into prostitution and that about one third had been falsely led to becoming sold into prostitution.
7. IIAS (2001) As is well known, several large European countries are now below reproduction levels, notably Italy and France.

CHAPTER 11

Conclusion: What Is to Be Done: Fix It or Nix It?

The title of the concluding chapter of PG is borrowed from two sources. The phrase "What Is to Be Done?" is the title of a pamphlet written by the Russian revolutionary Vladimir Illich Lenin, mastermind of the Russian Revolution in 1917. Lenin published this pamphlet in 1902 when the Communist movement was at a low point. What did the fiercely dedicated revolutionary propose for the movement to succeed? The answer may surprise you. Lenin claimed that the movement needed to give priority to promoting the newspaper *Iskra,* which means "The Spark," on whose editorial board Lenin served. He claimed that the newspaper could be the spark that could ignite revolution—and history proved him right.

A superficial understanding of the writings of Karl Marx, the revolutionary thinker who was the principal inspiration for Lenin's theory and actions, would not prepare one to guess Lenin's answer. Marx is known as an economic reductionist—that is, a doctrine that ideas don't matter and that what counts is the economic base of a society. (We hasten to add that this view represents a fundamental misunderstanding of Marx's thought. If he didn't believe that ideas were terribly important, he wouldn't have devoted decades trying to understand the mysterious character of capitalism!)

In "What Is to Be Done?" Lenin asserted that the communist movement needed a clear set of ideas to provide it with coherence and help it win new recruits. The title of the pamphlet has inspired political activists for generations, including many who do not share Lenin's political commitments. We borrow it here, since authors of the selections in this chapter seek to answer the same question that Lenin posed.

The subtitle of this concluding chapter has summarized a strategic debate dividing antiglobalization activists for years: should the movement give priority to seeking improvements in existing international financial institutions (IFIs) and regulations (that is, to "fix" globalization)? Or are these institutions and rules for international trade and investment irredeemable—unfixable? If so, the appropriate goal for activists is to seek to "nix it," that is, dismantle the existing nexus of IFIs.

The debate has historic roots among radical activists: it parallels the debate between those advocating reform versus revolution that divided radical movements of the nineteenth and twentieth centuries. What are the arguments in favor of one or the other position? Reformists claim that it is better to achieve a half loaf, that is, reforms, rather than holding out for a whole loaf and failing to even obtain crumbs. Double or nothing risks achieving . . . nothing. Applying this debate to the present situation, many reformers claim that the existing system of globalization is deeply flawed but not irredeemable. Some share the position, to paraphrase Winston Churchill, Britain's World War II prime minister, in his comment about democracy, that it is the worst of all possible forms—except for all the others! Some reformers believe that international trade and investment can be mutually beneficial to countries—on condition that the framework that regulates such exchanges is equitable and democratic. The principal problem, in their view, is that the present system is neither equitable nor democratic. For example, Joseph Stiglitz, in several selections included in PG, describes why he believes that the International Monetary Fund (IMF) is selected by undemocratic procedures, is responsible to bankers and ministries of finance rather than to broad constituencies, and pursues flawed policies. Stiglitz contends that these flaws have caused great hardships and that they are responsible for widespread opposition to globalization. But he ardently defends globalization—on condition that drastic surgery produces reforms in the structure and policies of IFIs like the IMF.

IFIs have been responsive to criticisms voiced by reformers and have adopted important changes in procedures and policies. For example, the IMF and World Bank have created advisory panels composed of NGOs that are consulted before major policy decisions are made. After years of protests by movements of environmentalists and indigenous peoples, the World Bank decided to end funding for large dam projects, since they displace many people and cause important environmental changes. Are these reforms sufficient? Don't expect a consensus on a response to this question!

Revolutionaries in the early years of the socialist and communist movements argued that reforms of the existing system of capitalism would inevitably fail because of fundamental design flaws in capitalism. Rather than repaired, capitalism should be nixed and replaced with a wholly different system of production and exchange. Those critics of globalization who support the "nix it" position adopt a similar posture toward economic globalization. Walden Bello, in the selection in this chapter, claims that the basic problem is the very concept of globalization. No amount of tinkering can resolve problems associated with globalization, including the economic costs and environmental damage resulting from transporting goods across long distances, assaults on local autonomy, and North-South inequalities inherent in global exchanges.

One hears the slogan "fix it or nix it" less often these days. In part, this is because the antiglobalization movement has itself been transformed. Those opposing neoliberal globalization are now more likely to use the term "movement for global justice" to describe their movement. The change occurred a few years after the 1999 demonstrations at Seattle, when activists decided that they were not simply trying to stop neoliberal globalization but to achieve a more ambitious and positive goal. The content of what should be included in the concept of global justice is, of course, highly complex and contentious. It is one of the major issues considered by the World Social Forum (WSF), an annual meeting of activists around the world that since 2001 has convened (most years) at Porto Alegro, Brazil, and by regional social forums modeled on the WSF held on continents around the world.

The stark opposition between fixing and nixing globalization, between reform and revolution, is useful as an analytical point of departure in distinguishing between different positions critical of globalization. But the opposition may not accurately map the actual positions of critics of existing globalization. As Martin Khor suggests in the selection in Cavanagh and Mander below, opponents of globalization are often internally divided in their own beliefs and, in their programmatic stance and actions, may alternate between the two poles. Moreover, those in one camp may not agree with others in the same camp—beyond the fact of shared opposition to those in the other camp! For example, radical opponents of globalization differ on the principal target of opposition. Should it be IFIs and other "summit" meetings of the elite? Should activists target national political institutions? TNCs? Or should they "think globally but act locally," in the famous phrase—which directs activists to mount protests around local or national manifestations of globalization, such as privatization of public services or large dam projects?

Finally, as the selection by Mike Moore, former director of the WTO, illustrates, even the most passionate advocates of globalization may place themselves in the camp of reformers. Moore's proposals illustrate a famous observation by Edmund Burke, a distinguished conservative political thinker, that "A state without the means of some change is without the means of its conservation."[1]

When you read the following selections, (re)think your own position on globalization, in light of the proposals developed in this chapter and the varied discussions of globalization in previous chapters. Where do you locate yourself? Are you in one camp or the other? Or do you believe, as does Mike Moore, that the way to fix the problems associated with globalization is more globalization?

---

[1]That is, Moore believes that changes are needed for neoliberal globalization to gain wider support and function more effectively.

Edmund Burke, *Reflections on the French Revolution* (London: J. M. Dent & Sons, 1955) pp. 19–20.

Alternatives to Economic Globalization

A Better World Is Possible

John Cavanagh and Jerry Mander

This selection is part of a larger study by activists and scholars who have helped sponsor the World Social Forum, an international assembly that has met annually since 2001, usually in Porto Alegro, Brazil, to critique neoliberal globalization and share ideas on how to promote global social justice. The major goal that the authors identify here is economic democracy on a global scale, that is, a system in which all those involved in the production of goods and services would participate in making decisions about production.

Economic democracy is often criticized for being both utopian—that is, unrealistic—and undesirable, since, its critics allege, it is less efficient than the present, typically hierarchical, organization of production. The activists in the World Social Forum disagree on both counts. How convincing is their argument? Also see the selection by Bello in this chapter, who argues that promoting more humane systems of production requires replacing the present pattern of globalization by more locally based patterns of production and consumption.

Conflicting Worldviews

The millions of people who have taken to the streets in India, the Philippines, Indonesia, Brazil, Bolivia, the United States, Canada, Mexico, Argentina, Venezuela, France, Germany, Italy, the Czech Republic, Spain, Sweden, the United Kingdom, New Zealand, Australia, Kenya, South Africa, Thailand, Malaysia, and elsewhere in massive demonstrations against the institutions and policies of corporate globalization have often been met by skepticism or even hostility from the media. Rarely have mainstream media attempted seriously to inform the public on the issues behind the protests, usually preferring to characterize demonstrators as "ignorant protectionists" who offer no alternatives and do not merit serious attention. Many in the media have tried to reduce the complex issues involved to a simplistic contest between "protectionism" and "openness,"

---

or between "anarchy" and "an orderly democratic process." In North America and Europe, those involved in the protests are dismissed as spoiled children of privilege—selfish, ill-informed malcontents who would end trade and international cooperation.

Anyone who makes even the smallest effort to find out why millions of people from virtually every nation and walk of life have taken to the streets finds these simplistic characterizations to be untrue. As for the charge of being antipoor, the largest protests are in low-income countries, and most of those involved are themselves poor. The charges of isolation and xenophobia are equally uninformed; the resistance against corporate globalization is global in scope and is dedicated to international cooperation to achieve economic justice for every person on the planet. As for the charge of being antitrade, many of the movement's leaders are actively involved in the promotion of *fair* trade—in contrast to the often exploitative *free* trade they oppose—as a means of improving the economic conditions of poor people and their communities.

In fact, the resistance is grounded in a sophisticated, well-developed critique set forth in countless publications and public presentations, including, among many others, documents available from the International Forum on Globalization (IFG) and numerous books and articles by IFG associates. The critique is also available in the publications of a thriving independent media that tells the stories and communicates the opinions that the mainstream media so often ignores or dismisses. These independent information sources are gradually expanding public awareness and enlarging the constituency for transformational change, but they have not yet reached sufficient critical mass to force a reframing of the terms of the political debate still dominated by corporate media and interests.

The claim that the protestors offer no alternatives is as false as the other claims. In addition to the alternatives described in books, periodicals, conferences, and individual articles and presentations, numerous consensus statements have been carefully crafted by civil society groups over the past two decades that set forth a wealth of alternatives with a striking convergence in their beliefs about the underlying values human society should serve. Since 2001, tens of thousands have gathered annually in Porto Alegre, Brazil, or Mumbai, India, for the World Social Forum titled "Another World Is Possible" to carry forward this process of popular consensus building toward a world that works for all.

Perhaps the most obvious and straightforward alternative advocated by civil society is simply to place a moratorium on the negotiation of new trade agreements. More ambitious proposals . . . center on redirecting global, national, and local priorities toward the task of creating healthy, sustainable human societies that work for all.

Although many of the protests have centered on opposition to trade agreements, global civil society does not oppose trade. Humans have engaged in trade since the beginning of time and as long as two or more members of the species survive will surely continue to do so. What the protesters reject is the use by corporate interests of international trade *agreements* to circumvent democracy in their global campaign to strip away social and environmental protections that ordinary people have struggled for decades—even centuries—to put in place.

The issue is governance. Will ordinary people have a democratic voice in deciding what rules are in the best interests of society? Or will a small ruling elite, meeting in secret and far from public view, be allowed to continue to set the rules that shape humanity's future? If the concern of the decision makers is only for next quarter's corporate profits, who will care for the health and well-being of people and the planet?

These are increasingly serious questions for a great many people who live with the violence and insecurity that spreads through the world in tandem with growing inequality, an unraveling social fabric, and the collapse of critical environmental systems. It is this reality of social and environmental disintegration that has brought millions of people together in a loose global alliance that spans national borders to forge what may be considered the most truly global and inclusive social movement in human history.

Different Worlds

The corporate globalists who meet in posh gatherings to chart the course of corporate globalization in the name of private profits, and the citizen movements that organize to thwart them in the name of democracy, are separated by deep differences in values, worldview, and definitions of progress. At times it seems they must be living in wholly different worlds—which, in fact, in many respects they do. Understanding their differences is key to understanding the implications of the profound choices humanity currently faces.

Corporate globalists inhabit a world of power and privilege. They see progress at hand everywhere, because from their vantage point the drive to privatize public assets and free the market from governmental interference spreads freedom and prosperity around the world, improving the lives of people everywhere and creating the financial and material wealth necessary to end poverty and protect the environment. They see themselves as champions of an inexorable and beneficial historical process toward erasing the economic and political borders that hinder corporate expansion, eliminating the tyranny of inefficient and meddlesome public bureaucracies, and unleashing the enormous innovation and wealth-creating power of competition and private enterprise.

Corporate globalists undertake to accelerate these trends as a great mission. They seek public policies and international agreements that provide greater safeguards for investors and private property while removing restraints to the free movement of goods, money, and corporations in search of economic opportunity wherever it may be found. They embrace global corporations as the greatest and most efficient human institutions, powerful engines of innovation and wealth creation that are peeling away the barriers to human progress and accomplishment everywhere. They celebrate the World Bank, the International Monetary Fund, and the World Trade Organization as essential and beneficial institutions for global governance engaged in the great work of rewriting the rules of commerce to free the market and create conditions essential to economic growth.

Corporate globalists subscribe to this worldview like a catechism. They differ among themselves mainly in their views of the extent to which it is appropriate for government to subsidize private corporations or provide safety nets to cushion the fall of the losers in the market's relentless competition.

Citizen movements, on the other hand, see a very different reality. Focused on people and the environment, they see a world in a crisis of such magnitude that it threatens the fabric of civilization and the survival of the species—a world of rapidly growing inequality, erosion of relationships of trust and caring, and failing planetary life-support systems. Where corporate globalists promote the spread of market economies, citizen movements see the power to govern shifting away from people and communities to financial speculators and to global corporations dedicated to the pursuit of short-term profit in disregard of all human and natural concerns. They see corporations replacing democracies of people with autocracies of money, replacing self-organizing markets with centrally planned corporate economies, and replacing diverse cultures with cultures of greed and materialism.

In the eyes of citizen movements, these trends are not the result of some inexorable historical force but rather of the intentional actions of a corrupted political system awash in corporate money. They see the World Bank, the IMF, and the World Trade Organization as leading instruments of this assault against people and the environment.

Ironically, the citizen movements seek many of the things the corporate globalists claim to offer but in fact fail to deliver: democratic participation, economies comprising enterprises that provide good jobs and respond to the real needs and preferences of their customers, a healthy environment, an end to poverty. However, where the corporate globalists seek a competitive global economy ruled by megacorporations that owe no loyalty to place or person, citizen movements seek a planetary system of economies made up of locally owned enterprises accountable to all their stakeholders. Citizen movements work for economic justice for all, international cooperation, vibrant cultural diversity, and healthy, sustainable societies that value life more than money.

Citizen movements recognize that corporate globalists *cannot* deliver on their promises because the narrow and shortsighted financial imperatives that drive their institutions are antithetical to them. Many corporate globalists may act with the best intentions, but they are blinded by their own financial success to the costs of this success for those who have no place at the table, including future generations.

Corporate globalists generally measure progress by indicators of their own financial wealth, such as rising stock prices and indicators of the total output of goods and services available to those who have the money to pay. With the exception of occasional cyclical setbacks in Latin America and elsewhere and declining per capita incomes in the poorest African countries, these indicators generally perform well, confirming in the eyes of corporate globalists their premise that their program is enriching the world.

In contrast, citizen movements measure progress by indicators of the well-being of people and nature, with particular concern for the lives of those most in need. With the exception of the highly visible pockets of privilege enjoyed by corporate globalists, these indicators show deterioration at a frightening pace, suggesting that in terms of what really matters, the world is rapidly growing poorer.

The U.N. Food and Agricultural Organization (FAO) reports that the number of chronically hungry people in the world declined steadily during the 1970s and 1980s but has been increasing since the early 1990s. The U.S. Department of Agriculture estimates that by 2008 two-thirds of the people of sub-Saharan Africa will be undernourished, and 40 percent will be undernourished in Asia.

In a world in which a few enjoy unimaginable wealth, two hundred million children under age five are underweight because of a lack of food. Some fourteen million children die each year from hunger-related diseases. A hundred million children are living or working on the streets. Three hundred thousand children were conscripted as soldiers during the 1990s, and six million were injured in armed conflicts. Eight hundred million people go to bed hungry each night.

This human tragedy is not confined to poor countries. Even in a country as wealthy as the United States, 6.1 million adults and 3.3 million children experience outright hunger. Some 10 percent of U.S. households, accounting for 31 million people, do not have access to enough food to meet their basic needs. These are some of the many indicators of a deepening global social crisis.

On the environmental side, a joint study released in September 2000 by the United Nations Development Program (UNDP), the United Nations Environment Program (UNEP), the World Bank, and the World Resources Institute assessed five ecosystem types—agricultural, coastal, forest, freshwater, and grassland—in relation to five ecosystem services—food and fiber production, water quantity, air quality, biodiversity, and carbon storage. It found that of these twenty-five ecosystem-service combinations, sixteen had declining trends. The only positive trend was in food and fiber production by forest ecosystems, which has been achieved by an expansion of industrial forest monocropping at the expense of species diversity.

Human activity—in particular, fossil fuel combustion—is estimated to have increased atmospheric concentrations of carbon dioxide to their highest levels in twenty million years. According to the Worldwatch Institute, an environmental think tank, natural disasters, including weather-related disasters such as storms, floods, and fires, affected more than two billion people and caused in excess of $608 billion in economic losses worldwide during the decade of the 1990s—more than the previous four decades combined. Three hundred million people were displaced from their homes or forced to resettle because of extreme weather events in 1998 alone.

It becomes more imperative to rethink human priorities and institutions by the day. Yet most corporate globalists, in deep denial, reiterate their mantra that with time and patience corporate globalization will create the wealth needed to end poverty and protect the environment.

Citizen movements counter that the policies and processes of corporate globalization are destroying the real wealth of the planet while advancing a primitive winner-takes-all competition that inexorably widens the gap between rich and poor. They reject as absurd the argument that the poor must be exploited and the environment destroyed to make the money necessary to end poverty and save the planet.

Many citizen movements embrace the present imperative for transformational change as an opportunity to lift humanity to a new level of possibility—the greatest creative challenge in the history of the species. Yet experience leads them to conclude that the institutions with the power to provide the leadership are neither inclined nor suited to doing so. Nor is there realistic cause for hope that leaders who are lavishly rewarded by the status quo and hold steadfastly to the view that there is no alternative will suddenly experience an epiphany.

The challenge of providing leadership to create a just and sustainable world thus falls by default to the hundreds of millions of extraordinary people in an emerging global civil society who believe a better world is possible—and who are forging global alliances that seek to shift the powers of governance to democratic, locally rooted, human-scale institutions that value life more than money. Although the most visible among them are those who have taken to the streets in protest, equally important and even more numerous are those struggling to rebuild their local communities and economies in the face of the institutional forces aligned against them.

Economic Democracy

The current and future well-being of humanity depends on transforming the relationships of power within and between societies toward more democratic and mutually accountable modes of managing human affairs that are self-organizing, power-sharing, and minimize the need for coercive central authority. *Economic* democracy, which involves the equitable participation of all people in the ownership of the productive assets on which their livelihood depends, is essential to such a transformation because the concentration of economic power is the Achilles heel of *political* democracy, as the experience of corporate globalization demonstrates.

The defining political struggles of the twentieth century centered on a choice between socialism and capitalism. Both centralized the power of ownership in institutions that could not be held accountable: the state in the case of socialism and the corporation in the case of capitalism. Both worked against the classic liberal economic ideal of self-organizing markets, markets in which communities organize themselves to respond to local needs within a framework of democratically determined rules.

Although rarely noted, economic democracy is as essential to the efficient functioning of economies as sound public regulation. Because today's markets respond only to money, they are overly attentive to the wants of the rich and neglect the most basic needs of the poor. Economic democracy is also a necessary foundation of individual, community, and national economic self-determination—the ability to determine one's own economic priorities and the rules of one's economic life—because it helps secure a political voice for each person.

At the same time, there are real and often difficult trade-offs to be considered in the choice between local, national, and global rule making. For example, civil society has a strong commitment to raising social and environmental standards everywhere. To this end, some activists call for setting universal labor, health and safety, and environmental standards, possibly enforced with trade sanctions. They correctly point out that allowing different standards in an open, competitive global economy inevitably puts competitive pressure on everyone to lower their standards.

But others note that it is invariably the strong nations who advocate for uniform standards because they hold the power to impose self-serving rules of their own choosing on weaker nations. Furthermore, uniform international standards not only violate the democratic right to self-determination but also fail to take into account differing local conditions and preferences. Those on this side of the argument call for measures to secure the right of nations and even localities to adopt standards of their choosing appropriate to their circumstances, as long as they do not shift the burden of their decisions onto others.

Both positions are based on valid concerns. The differences relate in part to the extent of the priority given to economic self-reliance. The less the self-reliance of a community or nation, the greater its external dependence and the greater the need for globally uniform rules to avoid a downward pressure on standards everywhere. By the same token, the greater the self-reliance of a community or nation, the greater the scope for local flexibility and adaptation to local circumstances. Dialogue on these trade-offs in the IFG has led to a consensus tilt in favor of self-reliance and local self-determination.

Concerns about local self-reliance and self-determination have important implications for global governance. For example, in a self-reliant and localized system, the primary authority to set and enforce rules rests with the national and local governments of the jurisdictions to which they apply. The proper role of international institutions is to facilitate the coordination of national policies on matters where the interests of nations are inherently intertwined—global warming, for example.

Of course, a democratic commitment to self-determination means that ultimately it is left up to the people of every nation—if not every indigenous group or local community—to decide the extent to which they will integrate their own economy with the economies of other nations. The people of different countries will likely reach different decisions. The international interest is properly confined to ensuring that these decisions are made democratically, that economic relationships among countries are just and balanced, that no country builds up unpayable debts to the rest of the system, and that each national economy is secure against predatory interventions from foreign nations and corporations.

There is certainly a need for international institutions to facilitate cooperative exchange and the working through of inevitable competing national interests toward solutions to global problems. These institutions must, however, be transparent and democratic and support the rights of people, communities, and nations to self-determination. The World Bank, the IMF, and the World Trade Organization violate each of these conditions to such an extent that the authors of this [article] recommend that they be decommissioned and new institutions be built under the authority of a strengthened and reformed United Nations. These new institutions would be responsible for freeing Third World nations from the burden of unpayable international debts, helping all nations bring their international trade and investment accounts into balance with the global system, and working with national governments to establish the public accountability of corporations with operations that span national borders.

Momentum for Change

Less than a decade ago, the claims of corporate globalists of the inevitability of their cause seemed credible to many. Talk of economic alternatives seemed little more than bravado. Today, although corporate globalization remains a formidable force, it no longer seems quite as invincible, nor discussion of alternatives quite as fanciful. Public consciousness of the pervasive abuse of corporate power has fueled the growth of a powerful opposition movement.

For example, secret negotiations during the 1990s toward a multilateral agreement on investment (MAI) under the Organization for Economic Cooperation and Development (OECD) were exposed and ultimately ended. U.S. President Clinton was twice denied the "fast track" authority he sought, which would have allowed him a free hand in negotiating trade agreements with minimal congressional debate and no amendment. (A Republican Congress finally did grant this authority to President George W. Bush in 2002, by three votes.) Efforts to launch a new round of trade negotiations at the 1999 WTO ministerial meeting in Seattle were disrupted, and the WTO was forced to expose its undemocratic nature by moving its 2001 ministerial meeting to Qatar, a remote monarchy where public protest is ruthlessly suppressed. In April 2000, police shut down much of Washington, D.C., to secure a World Bank–IMF meeting from protestors demanding the decommissioning of these institutions and the cancellation of Third World debt. A subsequent meeting of IMF and World Bank directors in Prague closed a day early, and a planned meeting in Barcelona was canceled. In 2001, pharmaceutical corporations were forced to make concessions allowing greater use of low-cost generic drugs in poor countries. And . . . in fall 2003 protesters joined some poor country governments in Cancun, Mexico, and in Miami to derail global and regional trade negotiations.

The evolving alliance of civil society organizations brings together union members, farmers, landless peasants, people of faith, women's organizations, youth organizations, small business owners, artisanal producers, economic justice organizers, prison reform advocates, environmentalists, AIDS and other health activists, politicians, independent media organizations, civil servants, the homeless, peace and human rights organizations, gay and lesbian groups, intellectuals, consumer advocates, and even a few corporate CEOs of every age, religion, race, and nationality. It is the product of a largely spontaneous awakening of millions of people to the reality that their future and the future of their children depends on exercising their democratic right to participate in the decisions that shape their future.

Unified by a deep commitment to universal values of democracy, justice, and respect for life, this alliance functions with growing effectiveness without a central organization, leadership, or defining ideology. It also takes different forms in different settings.

In India, activists seek to empower local people through the democratic community control of resources under the banner of a millions-strong Living Democracy movement. In Canada, hundreds of organizations have joined together to articulate a citizens' agenda that seeks to wrest control of governmental institutions back from corporations. In Chile, coalitions of environmental groups have created a powerful Sustainable Chile proposal that seeks to reverse that country's drift toward free markets and reassert popular democratic control over national priorities and resources. The focus in Brazil is on the rights of workers, the poor, and the landless. In Bolivia, a mass movement of peasants and workers has successfully blocked the privatization of water. In Mexico, the Mayan people have reignited the spirit of Zapata in a movement to confirm the rights of indigenous people to land and resources. French farmers have risen up in revolt against trade rules that threaten to destroy small farms. The construction of new highways in the United Kingdom has brought out hundreds of thousands of people who oppose this desecration of the countryside to meet globalization's relentless demand for ever more high-speed transport.

These are only a few examples of the initiatives and actions in defense of democratic rights that are occurring around the world. Some are purely local; others are national or international. Some seek major reforms to the current structures; others seek complete transformation. Some are short-term and address the debates of the moment; others are long-term and spell out new rules and institutions to advance sustainable societies. (See Box by Martin Khor of the Malaysia-based Third World Network for further discussion of these different approaches to alternatives work.) But all are linked together in common rejection of the illegitimate power and false promises of global corporations and in a proactive commitment to revitalize democracy at local, regional, national, and global levels. Each contributes to an emerging vision of the healthy, just, and sustainable society that humanity has the means to create. Each adds its voice to a growing global chorus proclaiming the right of "We the people of planet earth" to create such a society.

Box: Commentary—Conflicting Paradigms

By Martin Khor, Third World Network

Let me put forward two conflicting paradigms that civil society is now facing and which require that we make some difficult choices about how we advance our work. The first paradigm involves the choice to work in the system of globalization, in which we feel we are trapped. If we do work within that system, we begin by asking: "Are the rules of the game fair, particularly to the weaker partners, or are they being twisted and manipulated by the strong partners in order to keep the weaker countries down?" If the latter, then we should fight for the reform of the rules of the game so that they can be more fair. We should monitor and be aware where the rules of the game go against the weak and the poor. In this first paradigm, we will be working and arguing within the parameters of the system and trying to tinker with it, because we may conclude that there is no choice, at least in the short run. And this may be an approach pragmatic people will take who are involved in, say, survival for the next five years or ten years.

But we realize that even as we work in that system and make it more fair for all the participants, that system may not last very long because of ecological limits. In other words, if we continue to emphasize high growth, but the growth is more equitably shared and the poor are made to come out better, still the whole system of industrialism goes on. So the debate is whether the textile mills should continue to be in London and provide jobs for British workers with high standards of living and security or whether they should be transferred to Bangladesh where child labor is exploited. But maybe it's better for the child laborer to be exploited than to be out of a job, and dead. It's that kind of debate that we may be entering into within this first paradigm. Is it fair for the Bangladeshi to be exploited in a factory or should he remain unexploited; should his labor standard go up? If his labor standard goes up he may lose his job because the factory may move back to London and the London worker will have the job.

So then the issue becomes this: maybe the factory shouldn't exist in London or Bangladesh either because industrialism is bad; perhaps industrialism is incompatible with the long-term survival of the world. This is the basis of the second paradigm—that this debate over North-South is irrelevant because in twenty or thirty years the whole system will blow up anyway. So, in the second paradigm, we work for Gandhi-style, community-based, self-reliant family units of production, trading mainly within the community and the region and only making occasional exchanges with the rest of the world, as needed.

Now if you are working within this second paradigm, you might say, "I don't want transnational corporations. I will use any methods to kick them out, and I will go back to emphasizing local production." So, if we are working from this second paradigm we would certainly come out with different policy conclusions than if we were working from the first paradigm, which is for fairer trade, fairer economic relations.

The debate on whether worker rights and environmental rights should be addressed in trade agreements is really contained in that first paradigm, while at the same time we must remember there is that second paradigm. But sometimes we borrow ideas from that second paradigm to buttress our arguments for the first paradigm, and vice versa, and we get confused. So as we work and debate which initiatives make sense, we should be explicit as to whether we are arguing from the first or the second paradigm.

Let us be clear that the real world is moving ahead in the first paradigm. Some of us may be fighting from within that paradigm to point out where there are inequities, where there are double standards, and where there must be fairer terms of exchange, and so forth. I personally often work in the context of the first paradigm, whereas emotionally I really belong to the second one. So if we ask if we should trade with the rest of the world, we must make it very clear what our assumptions are and which paradigm we are proceeding from. Because at the end of the day, it is better if we can infuse the second paradigm into the first paradigm as a kind of transition.

For example, as we grapple with trade and environment under the first paradigm, we would do well to ask how we make the globalized system more environmentally sustainable as a transition toward the second paradigm. And to do it in such a way that the poor do not suffer and the costs of adjusting are borne by the rich.

I believe that for now we must always try to work in both paradigms. In this sense, we can devise a system that moves toward environmental sustainability in a socially equitable manner that will reduce income inequalities; resolve the poverty problem, but at the same time solve the environmental problem. Can trade mechanisms, systems of prices and products, and other things be devised so that we have this transition toward Paradigm Two? This is one of our greatest challenges.

Source: Martin Khor, "Commentary." In John Cavanagh, ed., *South-North: Citizen Strategies to Transform a Divided World.* San Francisco: International Forum on Globalization, November 1995.

The End of Poverty *Economic Possibilities for Our Time*

Jeffrey D. Sachs

Economist Jeffrey Sachs argues that it is eminently feasible to provide villages in poor regions of the world with adequate resources to escape traps associated with poverty, disease, and economic stagnation. He claims that doing so would cost only a tiny fraction of the income of affluent countries. Further, quite aside from the ethical obligation to promote a global development program, such an investment would more than pay for itself because of the savings reaped from improved health, longer life expectancy, and a more productive population. As he describes it, the cost of this effort—about $70 a person annually for several years—should be regarded "not as a welfare handout, but as an investment in sustained economic growth." He suggests that adequate economic development theories already exist to guide how funds should be allocated to launch poverty-reduction programs. What has been lacking thus far is not knowledge but political will among states and citizens in rich countries. Do you agree with his analysis? Is his proposal desirable and feasible? It has been claimed that, even if the experiment failed, no great loss would be incurred, so it is worth trying even if victory in the fight against global poverty is not assured. Do you agree?

On-the-Ground Solutions for Ending Poverty

The end of poverty will require a global network of cooperation among people who have never met and who do not necessarily trust each other. One part of the puzzle is relatively easy. Most people in the world, with a little bit of prodding, would accept the fact that schools, clinics, roads, electricity, ports, soil nutrients, clean drinking water, and the like are the basic necessities not only for a life of dignity and health, but also for economic productivity. They would also accept the fact that the poor may need help to meet their basic needs, but they might be skeptical that the world could pull off any effective way to give that help.

If the poor are poor because they are lazy or their governments are corrupt, how could global cooperation help? Fortunately, these common beliefs are misconceptions, only a small part of the explanation, if at all, of why the poor are poor. I have noted repeatedly that in all corners of the world, the poor face structural challenges that keep them from getting even their first foot on the ladder of development. Most societies with good harbors, close contacts with the rich world, favorable climates, adequate energy sources, and freedom from epidemic disease have escaped from poverty. The world's remaining challenge is not mainly to overcome laziness and corruption, but rather to take on geographic isolation, disease, vulnerability to climate shocks, and so on, with new systems of political responsibility that can get the job done.

. . . [My] strategy for ending extreme poverty by 2025 . . . focuses on the key investments—in people and in infrastructure—that can give impoverished communities around the world, both rural and urban, the tools for sustainable development. We need plans, systems, mutual accountability, and financing mechanisms. But even before we have all of that apparatus—or economic plumb-

---

ing—in place, we must first understand more concretely what such a strategy means to the one billion-plus people who can be helped. It is the bravery, fortitude, realism, and sense of responsibility of the impoverished and disempowered, for themselves and especially for their children, that give us hope, and spur us on to end extreme poverty in our time.

Meeting with the Rural Poor: Sauri, Kenya

Together with colleagues from the UN Millennium Project and the Earth Institute, I spent several days in July 2004 in a group of eight Kenyan villages known as the Sauri sublocation in the Siaya district of Nyanza Province, about forty-four kilometers from Kisumu, in western Kenya. We visited farms, clinics, a subdistrict and district hospital, and schools in Sauri and the environs. We met with international organizations working in the region, including ICRAF (the World Agroforestry Center), the UN Development Program, and the U.S. Centers for Disease Control and Prevention. The visit made vivid both why extreme poverty persists in rural areas and how it can be ended.

We found a region beset by hunger, AIDS, and malaria. The situation is far more grim than is described in official documents. The situation is also salvageable, but the international community requires a much better understanding of its severity, dynamics, and solutions if the crisis in Sauri and the rest of rural Africa is to be solved.

The situation is best understood through the voices of Sauri's struggling residents. In response to an invitation from our group, more than two hundred members of the community came to meet with us one afternoon. . . . Hungry, thin, and ill, they stayed for three and a half hours, speaking with dignity, eloquence, and clarity about their predicament. They are impoverished, but they are capable and resourceful. Though struggling to survive at present, they are not dispirited but determined to improve their situation. They know well how they could get back to high ground.

The meeting took place on the grounds of a school called the Bar Sauri Primary School, under the auspices of a remarkable school headmistress, Ms. Anne Marcelline Omolo, who shepherds hundreds of hungry and impoverished schoolchildren, many of them orphans, through primary education and the travails of daily life. Despite disease, orphanhood, and hunger, all thirty-three of last year's eighth-grade class passed the Kenyan national secondary school exams. On a Sunday in July, we saw why. On their "day off" from school, this year's class of eighth graders sat at their desks from 6:30 A.M. until 6:00 P.M. preparing months in advance for this year's national examinations in November. Unfortunately, many who will pass the exams will be unable to take a position in a secondary school because of lack of funds for tuition, uniforms, and supplies. Nonetheless, to boost the fortitude of the eighth graders during the critical examination year, the community provides them with a cooked midday meal, with the fuel wood and water brought from home by the students. . . . Alas, the community is currently unable to provide midday meals for the younger children, who must fend for themselves. Many go hungry the entire school day.

The village meeting got underway on a Monday afternoon, with the villagers arriving on foot from several kilometers away. I introduced my colleagues and told the community of the Millennium Project's assignment from UN Secretary-General Kofi Annan to understand the situation of communities like Sauri, and to work with villagers to identify ways to help such communities to achieve the worldwide Millennium Development Goals of reducing extreme poverty, hunger, disease, and lack of access to safe water and sanitation. I also announced that thanks to a remarkable grant from the Lenfest Foundation in the United States, the Earth Institute at Columbia University would be able to put some of the ideas to work in Sauri and help the international community learn from the experience in Sauri for the benefit of villages in other parts of Africa and beyond. Several hours later, around 5:30 P.M., we all rose from a discussion that was distressing, uplifting, and profoundly challenging—challenging, most of all, for the rich world.

Whatever the official data may show about "stagnant" rural incomes in places like Sauri, stagnation is a euphemism for decline and early death. Food output per person is falling; malaria is pervasive and increasing; AIDS stalks the community and the region, with adult prevalence on the order of 30 percent, if not higher. Rudimentary springs for collecting water for household use are often dirty, especially later in the day after extensive morning use. An NGO from the UK helped install a few protected water points, but they are too few in number, far from many homesteads, and heavily congested, sometimes yielding little more than a trickle and therefore requiring several minutes to fill a jug. Rapid population growth in the past has made farm sizes small. Fertility rates are around six children per woman, and the villagers have no access whatsoever to family planning and reproductive health services or to modern contraceptives.

I canvased the group on the material conditions of the community, and received very perceptive accounts of the grim situation. Only two of the two hundred or so farmers at the meeting reported using fertilizer at present. Around 25 percent are using improved fallows with nitrogen-fixing trees, a scientific farming approach developed and introduced into Sauri by ICRAF. With this novel technique, villagers grow trees that naturally fix nitrogen, meaning that the trees convert atmospheric nitrogen, which most food crops cannot use directly, into a nitrogen compound that food crops can use as a nutrient. The leguminous (nitrogen-fixing) trees can be planted alongside maize or other food crops. By choosing the right timing for planting and the right combination of trees and crops, the farmer gets a natural substitute for chemical nitrogen fertilizer.

So far, just one fourth of Sauri farmers use the new method. It costs money to introduce the technique and one planting season is lost. Farmers may also need to add some nonnitrogen fertilizers, especially potassium, which is also costly, too costly for the impoverished farmers. All of these additional complications could easily be addressed, and the ICRAF technique could be scaled up throughout the village, if only there were additional financial resources available to ICRAF and the village to jump-start the process.

The rest of the community is farming on tiny plots, often no more than 0.1 hectares, with soils that are utterly exhausted of nutrients, and therefore biologically unable to produce an adequate crop. The soils are so depleted of nutrients and organic matter that even if the rains are good, with yields of around one ton of maize per hectare, the households still go hungry. If the rains fail, the households face the risk of death from immunosuppression because of severe undernutrition. Stunting, meaning low height for one's age, is widespread, a sign of the pervasive and chronic undernutrition of the children.

The real shocker came with my follow-up question. How many farmers had used fertilizers in the past? Every hand in the room went up. Farmer after farmer described how the price of fertilizer was now out of reach, and how their current impoverishment left them unable to purchase what they had used in the past. A fifty-kilo bag of diammonium phosphate (DAP) fertilizer sells for around 2,000 Ksh (Kenyan shillings) (US$25). At $500 a ton, that is at least twice the world market price. A proper application might require two to four bags per hectare, or $50 to $100 per hectare, a cost vastly beyond what the household can afford. Credits to buy fertilizer are neither available nor prudent for these farmers: a single failed crop season, an untimely episode of malaria, or some other calamity can push a household that has taken on debt into a spiral of unending indebtedness and destitution.

In my mind I started the calculations as the conversation progressed. Scaling up an appropriate combination of agroforestry and chemical fertilizer inputs would cost some tens of thousands of dollars. Yes, the amount was out of reach of the villagers themselves, but would represent a low cost per person in villages like Sauri if donors would rise to the occasion. Fortunately, on this occasion, the Earth Institute was able to respond.

As the afternoon discussion unfolded, the gravity of the community's predicament became more and more apparent. AIDS is ravaging the village, and nobody has yet had access to antiretroviral therapy. I asked how many households were home to one or more orphaned children left behind by the pandemic. Virtually every hand in the room shot up. I asked how many households were receiving remittances from family members living in Nairobi and other cities. The response was that the only things coming back from the cities were coffins and orphans, not remittances.

I asked how many households had somebody currently suffering from malaria. Around three fourths of the hands shot up. How many used antimalarial bed nets? Two out of two hundred hands went up. How many knew about bed nets? All hands. And how many would like to use bed nets? All hands remained up. The problem, many of the women explained, is that they cannot afford the bed nets, which sell for a few dollars per net, and are too expensive even when partially subsidized (socially marketed) by international donor agencies. How many in the community were using medicine to treat a bout of malaria? A few hands went up, but the vast majority remained down. A woman launched into an explanation that the medicines sell at prices well beyond what the villagers can afford.

A year or so ago, Sauri had a small clinic. . . . The doctor has since left and the clinic is now padlocked. The villagers explained that they could not afford to pay the doctor and buy the medicines, so the doctor departed. Now they fend for themselves without health care or medicines. When malaria gets bad, and their children fall into anemia-induced tachycardia (rapid heartbeat), gasping for breath in small, ravaged bodies deprived of oxygen-carrying hemoglobin, they rush the child to the subdistrict hospital in nearby Yala. The mothers may carry the children on their backs or push them in wheelbarrows for several kilometers over dirt paths. Yet when we visited the Yala subdistrict hospital on our way from the village, we found a hospital with patients lying on cots in the halls—without running water, an in-house doctor (one visits only two afternoons per week), or even one complete surgical kit.

A few years back, Sauri's residents cooked with locally collected fuel wood, but the decline in the number of trees has left the sublocation bereft of sufficient fuel wood. The quarter or so households who are using the ICRAF system of improved fallows, based on leguminous trees, have a dedicated supply of fuel wood. Other farmer households do not. Villagers said that they now buy pieces of fuel wood in Yala or Muhanda (both a few kilometers away), a bundle of seven sticks costing around twenty-five shillings (thirty cents). These seven sticks are barely sufficient for cooking one meal. In our meeting with the villagers, I conveyed astonishment at the price, thirty cents per meal, for a community that earns almost no money at all. A woman responded that many villagers had in fact reverted to cooking with cow dung or to eating uncooked meals.

As this village dies of hunger, AIDS, and malaria, its isolation is stunning. There are no cars or trucks owned or even used within Sauri, and only a handful of villagers said they had ridden in any kind of motorized transport during the past year. Only three or four of the two hundred or so said that they get to the regional city of Kisumu each month, and about the same number said that they had been to Nairobi, Kenya's commercial and political capital, four hundred kilometers away, once during the past year. There are virtually no remittances reaching the village. Indeed, there is virtually no cash income of any kind reaching the village. Given the farmers' meager production, farm output must be used almost entirely for the household's own consumption, rather than for sales in the market. The community has no money for fertilizers, medicines, school fees, or other basic needs that must be purchased from outside of the villages. Around half of the individuals at the meeting said that they had never made a phone call in their entire lives. (Ironically, and promisingly, our own mobile phones worked fine in the village, relying on a cell tower in Yala. Extending low-cost telephony to the village, for example based on a mobile phone shared by the community, would therefore pose no infrastructure problems.)

This year the rains are failing again, another disaster in an increasingly erratic climate, quite possibly a climate showing the increasing effects of long-term manmade climate change emanating from the rich world. The two roof-water harvesting cisterns at the school are now empty, and the farmers fear disaster in the harvest next month. The Kenyan government has already put out a worldwide appeal for emergency aid to fight imminent starvation in several provinces, including Nyanza.

This village could be rescued, and could achieve the Millennium Development Goals, but not by itself. Survival depends on addressing a series of specific challenges: nutrient-depleted soils, erratic rainfall, holoendemic malaria, pandemic HIV/AIDS, lack of adequate education opportunities, lack of access to safe drinking water and latrines, and the unmet need for basic transport, electricity, cooking fuels, and communications. All of these challenges can be met, with *known, proven, reliable, and appropriate* technologies and interventions.

The crux of the matter for Sauri sublocation can be stated simply and directly:

Sauri's villages, and impoverished villages like them all over the world, can be saved and set on a path of development at a cost that is tiny for the world but too high for the villages themselves and for the Kenyan government on its own.

African safari guides speak of the Big Five animals to watch for on the savannah. The international development community should speak of the Big Five development interventions that would spell the difference between hunger, disease, and death and health and economic development. Sauri's Big Five, identified by the villagers as well as by the UN Millennium Project, are

- *Agricultural inputs.* With fertilizers, improved fallows (with ICRAF's proven technologies), green manures and cover crops, water harvesting and small-scale irrigation, and improved seeds, Sauri's farmers could triple the food yields per hectare and quickly end chronic hunger. In addition, storage facilities would allow the village to sell the grain over the course of months, rather than all at once, thereby getting more favorable prices. Grain could be protected in locally made storage bins using leaves from the improved fallow species tephrosia, which has insecticide properties. These improvements would be of particular advantage for the women, who do the lion's share of African farm and household work.
- *Investments in basic health.* A village clinic with one doctor and nurse for the five thousand residents would provide free antimalarial bed nets; effective antimalarial medicines; treatments for HIV/AIDS opportunistic infections (including highly effective and low-cost Bactrim); antiretroviral therapy for late-stage AIDS; and a range of other essential health services, including skilled birth attendants and sexual and reproductive health services.
- *Investments in education.* Meals for all the children at the primary school could improve the health of the schoolchildren, the quality of education, and the attendance at school. Expanded vocational training for the students could teach them the skills of modern farming (for example, using improved fallows and fertilizer), computer literacy, basic infrastructure maintenance (electrical wiring, use and maintenance of a diesel generator, water harvesting, borewell construction and maintenance), carpentry, and the like. With a mere thousand households in Sauri, villagewide classes once a month could train adults in

hygiene, HIV/AIDS, malaria control, computer and mobile phone use, and a myriad of other technical and enormously pressing topics. Without doubt, the village is ready and eager to be empowered by increased information and technical knowledge.

- *Power, transport, and communications services.* Electricity could be made available to the villages either via a power line (from Yala or Nyanminia) or an off-grid diesel generator. The electricity would power lights and perhaps a computer for the school; pumps for safe well water; power for milling grain and other food processing, refrigeration, carpentry; charges for household batteries (which could be used for household illumination); and other needs. The villagers emphasized that the students would like to study after sunset but cannot do so without electric lighting. A village truck could bring in fertilizers, other farm inputs, and modern cooking fuels (for example, canisters of liquid petroleum gas [LPG], familiar from American backyard barbecues), and take out harvests to the market, transport perishable goods and milk for sale in Kisumu, and increase opportunities for off-farm employment for youth. The truck could rush women with childbirth complications and children with acute complications of anemia to the hospital. One or more shared mobile phones for the village could be used for emergencies, market information, and generally to connect Sauri with the outside world.
- *Safe drinking water and sanitation.* With enough water points and latrines for the safety and convenience of the entire village, women and children of the village would save countless hours of toil each day fetching water. The water could be provided through a combination of protected springs, borewells, rainwater harvesting, and other basic technologies. There is even the possibility of establishing links with an existing large-scale storage tank and pumping station a few kilometers away.

The irony is that the costs of these services for Sauri's five thousand residents would be very low. Here are some quick guesses, which colleagues at the Earth Institute are refining:

Fertilizers and improved fallows for the five hundred or so arable hectares would be roughly $100 per hectare per year, or $50,000 per year for the community.

A clinic, staffed by a doctor and nurse, providing free malaria prevention and care and additional free basic services other than antiretrovirals, would cost around $50,000 per year. (Antiretrovirals would be provided by the Global Fund to Fight AIDS, TB, and Malaria, the U.S. Emergency Plan, and other programs.) School meals could be paid for communally out of just a small part of the incremental grain yields achieved through the application of fertilizers.

A village truck would be an annual inclusive running cost of perhaps $15,000 per year if amortized over several years (or leased from a manufacturer). Modern cooking fuel for the primary and secondary school students (numbering about a thousand) in the entire sublocation would cost an additional $5,000 per year. A few village cell phones and a grain storage facility would add perhaps $5,000 per year, for a total of $25,000 per year.

A combination of protected springs (with improved access), borewells (with pumps), and community taps connected to the large-scale storage system would provide access to water at ten convenient locations and cost around $25,000.

Electricity could be provided to the school, the nearby clinic, and five water points by a dedicated off-grid generator or by a power line from Yala or Nyanminia for an initial cost of about $35,000. For another $40,000 in initial costs and recurring costs of $10,000, every household could be provided with a battery/bulb assembly to light a small bulb for a few hours every night with the battery charging station connected to the village generator. The annualized costs would be $25,000 per year.

Additional expenses would include scaling up educational activities, various costs of local management, technical advice from agricultural extension officers, and other related delivery services.

My Earth Institute colleagues and I estimated that the combined costs of these improvements would total around $350,000 per year, or roughly $70 per person per year in Sauri, for at least the next few years. The benefits would be astounding: decisive malaria control (with transmission reduced by perhaps 90 percent, judging from recent CDC bed-net trials in a neighboring area), a doubling or tripling of food yields per hectare with a drastic reduction of chronic hunger and undernutrition, improved school attendance, a reduction of waterborne disease, a rise in incomes through the sale of surplus grains and cash crops, the growth of cash incomes via food processing, carpentry, small-scale clothing manufacturing, horticulture, aquaculture, animal husbandry, and a myriad of other benefits. With anti-AIDS drugs added to the clinic's services, the mass deaths from AIDS, as well as the deluge of newly orphaned children, could also be stanched.

Sooner rather than later, these investments would repay themselves not only in lives saved, children educated, and communities preserved, but also in direct commercial returns. Consider the case of fertilizers, which are currently unused, since households lack access to storage, transport, credit, and a financial cushion against the risk of crop failures even if credit is made available. A fertilizer application of $100 per hectare (such as two hundred kilos of DAP), combined with or substituted by improved fallows (as appropriate), could raise crop yields in a normal season from one ton per hectare to three tons per hectare, with a marketable value of the increment of roughly $200 to $400 per hectare, assuming that transport is available and there is a stable price for the maize crop. In a drought year, fertilizer and/or improved fallows would mean the difference between harvesting one ton and a failed crop (with attendant acute hunger, if not starvation). In the first few years, *fertilizers and improved fallows should be given largely for free to the villagers* to boost their own nutrition and health, and to build a small financial cushion. Later on it will be possible to share the costs with the community and, eventually, perhaps in a decade, to provide the fertilizer and improved fallows on a full commercial basis.

International Donors and Villages Like Sauri

The international donor community should be thinking round the clock about one question: *how can the Big Five interventions be scaled up in rural areas like Sauri?* With a population of some thirty-three million people, of whom two thirds are in rural areas, Kenya would require annual investments on the order of $1.5 billion per year for its Sauris, with donors filling most of that financing gap, since the national government is already stretched beyond its means. (More precise estimates of cost would have to be worked out in the context of detailed development plans. . . .) Instead, donor support to Kenya is around $100 million, or a mere one fifteenth of what is needed. Kenya's debt servicing to the rich world is around $600 million per year, so its budget is still being drained by the international community, not bolstered by it.

This is all the more remarkable since Kenya is a new and fragile democracy that should be receiving considerable help from its development partners. Kenya, ironically, is also a victim of global terrorism, caught in a war not of its own making. U.S. and Israeli targets on Kenyan soil have been hit in recent years, sending Kenya's tourist industry into a downward spiral and causing hundreds of deaths of Kenyans and massive property damage.

The UN Millennium Project is working with the government of Kenya to ensure that its poverty reduction efforts are bold enough to achieve the Millennium Development Goals. This strategy will require much greater development assistance and deeper debt cancellation from the rich world to enable Kenya to invest in the Big Five—agriculture, health and education, electricity, transport and communications, and safe drinking water—not only in Sauri villages, but across impoverished rural Kenya. Yet when the Kenyan government recently proposed a national social health insurance fund, the very thing needed to scale up access to basic health care, donors quickly objected rather than jumped at the opportunity to examine how it could actually be accomplished.

The issue of corruption overshadows donor relations with the Kenyan government. Much of the corruption reflects holdouts from the earlier regime of more than two decades, corrupt officials who have not yet been weeded out. Part of the corruption is new and completely avoidable, but only if donors help Kenya to improve the functioning of the public administration, not by moralizing and finger pointing but by the installation of computer systems, published accounts, job training and upgrading, higher pay for senior managers so that they do not have to live off bribes and side payments, continued support for the government's already major efforts to improve the judicial system, empowerment of local villages to oversee the provision of public services, and some humility on the part of donors. Most donor governments have corruption inside their own governments and even in the provision of foreign aid (which is often linked to powerful political interests within the donor countries). The affliction is widespread, and needs to be attacked systematically and cleverly, but without useless and false moralizing.

Donors should sit down with the government leadership and say, "We'd like to help you scale up the Big Five in Kenya's villages to enable you to ensure that all of Kenya's rural poor have access to agricultural inputs, health, education, electricity, communications and transport, and safe water and sanitation. Together, let's design a budgetary and management system that will reach the villages and ensure a monitorable, governable, and scalable set of interventions across the country. We're prepared to pay if you are prepared to ensure good governance on such a historic project." Private international consulting firms could be brought in to help design these systems and to lend credibility to their implementation and performance.

With a little more forethought, donors and governments could take advantage of the crucial fact that villages like Sauri have a group monitoring and enforcement mechanism automatically built into village life that can help to ensure that aid to the village is well used. Just as experience with group lending in microfinance has been highly successful, projects that empower village-based community organizations to oversee village services have also been highly successful. Recent experiences with village governance in India, based on the *panchayats* (local councils), are but one notable example. In Sauri, the villagers jumped with eagerness at the invitation to form various committees (schooling, clinics, transport and electricity, farming) to help prepare for the actual investments and to ensure proper governance as they are put into place. Headmistress Omolo, who oversaw the formation of the committees, also ensured that the village women, with their special needs and burdens and even legal obstacles, would be well represented in each of the committees.

If donor officials would join the government of Kenya in meeting with the villagers and brainstorming with government officials, they could come up with dozens of fruitful approaches to ensure that aid actually reaches the villages. We need to be more creative in order to save the lives of millions of people now struggling to survive—and often failing—in the impoverished villages around the world. The donors and the government of Kenya can and should agree on a suitable and bold strategy. Kenya's new democracy, from the national government down to the villages, is prepared to govern the use of international help with transparency, efficiency, and equity if we can get the delivery mechanisms right and invest in the supporting information and reporting technologies . . .

The Problem of Scale

The end of poverty must start in the villages of Sauri . . . and millions of places like them. The key to ending poverty is to create a global network of connections that reach from impoverished communities to the very centers of world power and wealth and back again. Looking at the conditions in Sauri, we can see how far $70 per person can go in changing lives—not as a welfare handout, but as an investment in sustained economic growth. . . .

The starting points . . . are the poor themselves. They are ready to act, both individually and collectively. They are already hard working, prepared to struggle to stay afloat and to get ahead. They have a very realistic idea about their conditions and how to improve them, not a mystical acceptance of their fate. They are also ready to govern themselves responsibly, ensuring that any help that they receive is used for the benefits of the group rather than pocketed by powerful individuals. But they are too poor to solve their problems on their own. So, too, are their own governments. The rich world, which could readily provide the missing finances, wonders how to ensure that money made available would actually reach the poor and be an investment in ending poverty rather than an endless provision of emergency rations. This question can be answered by showing how networks of mutual accountability can run alongside the networks of financing.

In short, we need a strategy for scaling up the investments that will end poverty, including a system of governance that empowers the poor while holding them accountable. In each low-income country, it is time to design a poverty reduction strategy that can meet this challenge.

ARTICLE 11.3

Globalization and Its Discontents

Joseph E. Stiglitz

Previous selections by Joseph Stiglitz (Chapters 3 and 7) identified what he regarded as major shortcomings in the structure and policies of the International Monetary Fund and other international financial institutions. In this selection, he proposes some solutions, centering on the need to change what he terms the "mind-set" of international financial institutions, the IMF in particular. He charges that the IMF's mistaken policies are directed to serving the interests of private bankers, who are the major constituency of the finance ministers and central bank governors who govern the IMF, while the interests of broader publics are not represented at the table where IMF decisions are made. (The situation is only marginally different at the World Trade Organization—WTO.) In order to change this situation, the structure of governance must be changed by broadening the interests represented in the governing structure of IFIs. In particular, voting rights need to be redistributed to strengthen the rights of poor countries as well as workers and consumers in affluent countries. A first step, easier to implement, is to require greater transparency in the way that decisions are reached. How valid are Stiglitz's criticisms and the proposals he suggests? How might the kinds of reforms that he proposes be achieved? What are the prospects for their adoption?

Globalization today is not working for many of the world's poor. It is not working for much of the environment. It is not working for the stability of the global economy. The transition from communism to a market economy has been so badly managed that, with the exception of China, Vietnam, and a few Eastern European countries, poverty has soared as incomes have plummeted.

To some, there is an easy answer: Abandon globalization. That is neither feasible nor desirable. . . . [G]lobalization has also brought huge benefits—East Asia's success was based on globalization, especially on the opportunities for trade, and increased access to markets and technology. Globalization has brought better health, as well as an active global civil society fighting for more democracy and greater social justice. The problem is not with globalization, but with how it has been managed. Part of the problem lies with the international economic institutions, with the IMF, World Bank, and WTO, which help set the rules of the game. They have done so in ways that, all too often, have served the interests of the more advanced industrialized countries—and particular interests within those countries—rather than those of the developing world. But it is not just that they have served those interests; too often, they have approached globalization from particular narrow mind-sets, shaped by a particular vision of the economy and society.

The demand for reform is palpable—from congressionally appointed commissions and foundation-supported groups of eminent economists writing reports on changes in the global financial architecture to the protests that mark almost every international meeting. In response, there has already been some change. The new round of trade negotiations that was agreed to in November 2001 at Doha, Qatar, has been characterized as the "development round," intended not just to open up markets further but to rectify some of the imbalances of the past, and the debate at Doha was far more open than in the past. The IMF and the World Bank have changed their rhetoric—there is much more talk about poverty, and at least at the World Bank, there is a sincere attempt to live up to its commitment to "put the country in the driver's seat" in its programs in many countries. But many of the critics of the international institutions are skeptical. They see the changes as simply the institutions facing the political reality that they *must* change their rhetoric if they are to survive. These critics doubt that there is real commitment.

They were not reassured when, in 2000, the IMF appointed to its number two position someone who had been chief economist at the World Bank during the period when it took on market fundamentalist ideology. Some critics are so doubtful about these reforms that they continue to call for more drastic actions such as the abolition of the IMF, but I believe this is pointless. Were the Fund to be abolished, it would most likely be recreated in some other form. In times of international crises, government leaders like to feel there is someone in charge, that an international agency is doing something. Today, the IMF fills that role.

I believe that globalization can be reshaped to realize its potential for good and I believe that the international economic institutions can be reshaped in ways that will help ensure that this is accomplished. But to understand how these institutions should be reshaped, we need to understand better why they have failed, and failed so miserably . . .

The Need for International Public Institutions

We cannot go back on globalization; it is here to stay. The issue is how can we make it work. And if it is to work, there have to be global public institutions to help set the rules.

These international institutions should, of course, focus on issues where global collective action is desirable, or even necessary. Over the past three decades there has been an increased understanding of the circumstances under which collective action, at whatever level, is required. Earlier, I discussed how collective action is required when markets by themselves do not result in efficient outcomes. When there are externalities—when the actions of individuals have effects on others for which they neither pay nor are compensated—the market will typically result in the overproduction of some goods and the underproduction of others. Markets cannot be relied upon to produce goods that are essentially public in nature, like defense.[1] In some areas, markets fail to exist;[2] governments have provided student loans, for instance, because the market, on its own, failed to provide funding for investments in human capital. And for a variety of reasons, markets are often not self-regulating—there are booms and busts—so the government has an important role in promoting economic stability.

Over the past decade, there has been an increased understanding of the appropriate level—local, national, or global—at which collective action is desirable. Actions the benefits of which accrue largely locally (such as actions related to local pollution) should be conducted at the local level; while those that benefit the citizens of an entire country should be undertaken at the national level. Globalization has meant that there is increasing recognition of arenas where impacts are global. It is in these arenas where global collective action is required—and systems of global governance are essential. The recognition of these areas has been paralleled by the creation of global institutions to address such concerns. The United Nations can be thought of as focusing upon issues of global political security, while the international financial institutions, and in particular the IMF, are supposed to focus on global economic stability. Both can be thought of as dealing with externalities that can take on global dimensions. Local wars, unless contained and defused, can draw in others, until they become global conflagrations. An economic downturn in one country can lead to slowdowns elsewhere. In 1998 the great concern was that a crisis in emerging markets might lead to a global economic meltdown.

But these are not the only arenas in which global collective action is essential. There are global environmental issues, especially those that concern the oceans and atmosphere. Global warming caused by the industrial countries' use of fossil fuels, leading to concentrations of greenhouse gasses (CO_2), affects those living in preindustrial economies, whether in a South Sea island or in the heart of Africa. The hole in the ozone layer caused by the use of chlorofluorocarbons (CFCs) similarly affects everyone—not just those who made use of these chemicals. As the importance of these international environmental issues has grown, international conventions have been signed. Some have worked remarkably well, such as the one directed at the ozone problem (the Montreal Protocol of 1987); while others, such as those that address global warming, have yet to make a significant dent in the problem.

There are also global health issues like the spread of highly contagious diseases such as AIDS, which respect no boundaries. The World Health Organization has succeeded in eradicating a few diseases, notably river blindness and smallpox, but in many areas of global public health the challenges ahead are enormous. Knowledge itself is an important global public good: the fruits of research can be of benefit to anyone, anywhere, at essentially no additional cost.

International humanitarian assistance is a form of collective action that springs from a shared compassion for others. As efficient as markets may be, they do not ensure that individuals have enough food, clothes to wear, or shelter. The World Bank's main mission is to eradicate poverty, not so much by providing humanitarian assistance at the time of crisis as by enabling countries to grow, to stand on their own.

Although specialized institutions in most of these areas have evolved in response to specific needs, the problems they face are often interrelated. Poverty can lead to environmental degradation, and environmental degradation can contribute to poverty. People in poor countries like Nepal with little in the way of heat and energy resources are reduced to deforestation, stripping the land of trees and brush to obtain fuel for heating and cooking, which leads to soil erosion, and thus to further impoverishment.

Globalization, by increasing the interdependence among the people of the world, has enhanced the need for global collective action and the importance of global public goods. That the global institutions which have been created in response have not worked perfectly is not a surprise: the problems are complex and collective action at any level is difficult. But . . . complaints . . . go well beyond the charge that they have not worked perfectly. In some cases their failures have been grave; in other cases they have pursued an agenda that is unbalanced—with some benefiting from globalization much more than others, and some actually being hurt.

Governance

So far, we have traced the failures of globalization to the fact that in setting the rules of the game, commercial and financial interests and mind-sets have seemingly prevailed within the international economic institutions. A particular view of the role of government and markets has come to prevail—a view which is not universally accepted within the developed countries, but which is being forced upon the developing countries and the economies in transition.

The question is, why has this come about? And the answer is not hard to find: It is the finance ministers and central bank governors who sit around the table at the IMF making decisions, the trade ministers at the WTO. Even when they stretch, to push policies that are in their countries' broader national interests (or occasionally, stretching further, to push policies that are in a broader global interest), they see the world through particular, inevitably more parochial, perspectives.

I have argued that there needs to be a change in mind-set. But the mind-set of an institution is inevitably linked to whom it is *directly* accountable. Voting rights matter, and who has a seat at the table—even with limited voting rights—matters. It determines whose voices get heard. The IMF is not just concerned with technical arrangements among bankers, such as how to make bank check-clearing systems more efficient. The IMF's actions affect the lives and livelihoods of billions throughout the developing world; yet they have little say in its actions. The workers who are thrown out of jobs as a result of the IMF programs have no seat at the table; while the bankers, who insist on getting repaid, are well represented through the finance ministers and central bank governors. The consequences for policy have been predictable: bailout packages which pay more attention to getting creditors repaid than to maintaining the economy at full employment. The consequences for the choice of the institution's management have equally been predictable: there has been more of a concern with finding a leader whose views are congruent with the dominant "shareholders" than with finding one that has expertise in the problems of the developing countries, the mainstay of the Fund's business today.

Governance at the WTO is more complicated. As at the IMF, it is the voices of trade ministers that are heard. No wonder, then, that little attention is often paid to concerns about the environment. Yet while the voting arrangements at the IMF ensure that the rich countries predominate, at the WTO each country has a single vote, and decisions are largely by consensus. But in practice, the United States, Europe, and Japan have dominated in the past. This may now be changing. At the last meeting at Doha, the developing countries insisted that if another round of trade negotiations was to be initiated, their concerns had to be heard—and they achieved some notable concessions. With China's joining the WTO, the developing countries have a powerful voice on their side—though the interests of China and those of many of the other developing countries do not fully coincide.

The most fundamental change that is required to make globalization work in the way that it should is a change in governance. This entails, at the IMF and the World Bank, a change in voting rights, and in all of the international economic institutions changes to ensure that it is not just the voices of trade ministers that are heard in the WTO or the voices of the finance ministries and treasuries that are heard at the IMF and World Bank.

Such changes are not going to be easy. The United States is unlikely to give up its effective veto at the IMF. The advanced industrial countries are not likely to give up their votes so that the developing countries can have more votes. They will even put up specious arguments: voting rights, as in any corporation, are assigned on the basis of capital contributions. China would long ago have been willing to increase its capital contribution, if that was required to give it more voting rights. U.S. Treasury Secretary Paul O'Neill has tried to give the impression that it is the American taxpayers, its plumbers and carpenters, who pay for the multi-billion-dollar bailouts—and because they pay the costs, they ought to have the vote. But that is wrong. The money comes ultimately from the workers and other taxpayers in the developing countries, for the IMF almost always gets repaid.

But although change is not easy, it is possible. The changes that the developing countries wrenched from the developed countries in November 2001 as the price for beginning another round of trade negotiations show that, at least in the WTO, there has been a change in bargaining power.

Still, I am not sanguine that fundamental reforms in the *formal* governance of the IMF and World Bank will come soon. Yet in the short run, there are changes in *practices* and *procedures* that can have significant effects. At the World Bank and the IMF there are twenty-four seats at the table. Each seat speaks for several countries. In the present configuration, Africa has very few seats simply because it has so few votes, and it has so few votes because, as we noted, votes are allocated on the basis of economic power. Even without changing the voting arrangements, one could have more African seats; their voice would be heard even if their votes were not counted.

Effective participation requires that the representatives of the developing countries be well informed. Because the countries are poor, they simply cannot afford the kinds of staff that the United States, for instance, can muster to support its positions at all the international economic institutions. If the developed countries were serious about paying more attention to the voices of the developing countries, they could help fund a think tank—independent from the international economic organizations—that would help them formulate strategies and positions.

Transparency

Short of a fundamental change in their governance, the most important way to ensure that the international economic institutions are more responsive to the poor, to the environment, to the broader political and social concerns that I have emphasized is to increase openness and transparency. We have come to take for granted the important role that an informed and free press has in reining in even our democratically elected governments: any mischief, any minor indiscretion, any favoritism, is subject to scrutiny, and public pressure works powerfully. Transparency is even more important in public institutions like the IMF, the World Bank, and the WTO, because their leaders are not elected directly. Though they are public, there is no *direct* accountability to the public. But while this should imply that these institutions be even more open, in fact, they are even less transparent.

The problem of lack of transparency affects each of the international institutions, though in slightly different ways. At the WTO, the negotiations that lead up to agreements are all done behind closed doors, making it difficult—until it is too late—to see the influence of corporate and other special interests. The deliberations of the WTO panels that rule on whether there has been a violation of the WTO agreements occur in secret. It is perhaps not surprising that the trade lawyers and ex-trade officials who often comprise such panels pay, for instance, little attention to the environment; but by bringing the deliberations more out into the open, public scrutiny would either make the panels more sensitive to public concerns or force a reform in the adjudication process.

The IMF comes by its penchant for secrecy naturally: central banks, though public institutions, have traditionally been secretive. Within the financial community, secrecy is viewed as natural—in contrast to academia, where openness is the accepted norm. Before September 11, 2001, the secretary of treasury even defended the secrecy of the offshore banking centers. The billions of dollars in the Cayman Islands and other such centers are not there because those islands provide better banking services than Wall Street, London, or Frankfurt; they are there because the secrecy allows them to engage in tax evasion, money laundering, and other nefarious activities. Only after September 11 was it recognized that among those other nefarious activities was the financing of terrorism.

But the IMF is not a private bank; it is a public institution.

The absence of open discourse means that models and policies are not subjected to timely criticism. Had the actions and policies of the IMF during the 1997 crisis been subject to conventional democratic processes, and there had been a full and open debate in the crisis countries about the proffered IMF policies, it is possible that they would never have been adopted, and that far saner policies would have emerged. That discourse might not only have exposed the faulty economic assumptions on which the policy prescriptions were based but also revealed that the interests of the creditors were being placed ahead of those of workers and small businesses. There were alternative courses of actions, where less of the risk was borne by these less powerful parties, and these alternative courses of actions might have been given the serious consideration that they deserved.

Earlier, in my days at the Council of Economic Advisers, I had seen and come to understand the strong forces that drove secrecy. Secrecy allows government officials the kind of discretion that they would not have if their actions were subject to public scrutiny. Secrecy not only makes their life easy but allows special interests full sway. Secrecy also serves to hide the mistakes, whether innocent or not, whether the result of a failure to think matters through or not. As it is sometimes put, "Sunshine is the strongest antiseptic."

Even when policies are not driven by special interests, secrecy engenders suspicions—whose interests are really being served?—and such suspicions, even when groundless, undermine the political sustainability of the policies. It is this secrecy, and the suspicions it gives rise to, that has helped sustain the protest movement. One of the demands of the protestors has been for greater openness and transparency.

These demands had a special resonance because the IMF itself emphasized the importance of transparency during the East Asia crisis. One of the clearly *unintended* consequences of the IMF's rhetorical emphasis on transparency was that eventually, when the transparency spotlight was turned around to shine on the IMF itself, it was found wanting.[3]

Secrecy also undermines democracy. There can be democratic accountability only if those to whom these public institutions are supposed to be accountable are well informed about what they are doing—including what choices they confronted and how those decisions were made . . .

Notes

1. Economists have analyzed what are the attributes of such goods; they are goods for which the marginal costs of supplying the goods to an additional individual are small or zero, and for which the costs of excluding them from the benefits are large.
2. Economists have analyzed deeply why such markets may not exist, e.g., as a result of problems of information imperfections (information asymmetries), called *adverse selection* and *moral hazard*.
3. It was ironic that the calls for transparency were coming from the IMF, long criticized for its own lack of openness, and the U.S. Treasury, the most secretive agency of the U.S. government (where I saw that even the White House often had trouble extracting information about what they were up to).

Deglobalization *Ideas for a New World Economy*

Walden Bello

Walden Bello is the founding director of Focus on the Global South, an institute in Bangkok, Thailand, devoted to policy research involving the poor countries in the South. He is a leading advocate of the "nix it" position regarding globalization. In his view, the present system of globalization promotes free trade and investment in order to create a homogenized and unified world economy. He proposes an alternative vision: deglobalization, which defends decentralized, distinctive, local economies and communities throughout the world. For starters, he suggests, the IMF, WB, and WTO should be "decommissioned," that is, eliminated, because they are so deeply flawed. After this process of deconstruction has been completed, globalization should be reconstructed by building democratic regional economic institutions from the ground up.

Bello published his account shortly before the WTO's Fifth Ministerial Meeting at Cancun, Mexico, in 2003. He advocated blocking a proposal among governments represented at Cancun to further liberalize trade and investment. Following publication of this selection, an alliance of popular movements and the governments of India, Brazil, and other developing nations did succeed in blocking the plan, and the meeting ended in stalemate.

What are Bello's reasons for proposing deglobalization? What are the costs and benefits of his plan? What is your evaluation of its feasibility and merits?

The Alternative: Deglobalization

The crisis that is wrenching the current system of global economic governance is a systemic one. It is not one that can be addressed by mere adjustments within the system, for these would be merely marginal in their impact or they might merely postpone a bigger crisis. To borrow the insights of Thomas Kuhn's classic *Structure of Scientific Revolutions*, when a paradigm is in crisis, there are two responses. One is that followed by the adherents of the old Ptolemaic paradigm, which was to make more and more complicated adjustments to their system of explanation until

---

Walden Bello, *Deglobalization: Ideas for a New World Economy* (London: Zed, 2002), ch. 7: 107–118. Reprinted by permission of Zed Books.

it became too complex and virtually useless in promoting scientific advance. This is the approach taken by most of the proposals for reform. . . .

The other path was that taken by the partisans of the new Copernican system, which was to break away completely from the old paradigm and work within the parameters of the competing paradigm, which could not only accommodate dissonant data in a far more simple fashion but also point to new exciting problems.[1] This is the direction proposed [here].

In contrast to science, however, breaking with the past is a far more complicated affair when it comes to global economic governance. In social change, new systems cannot really be effectively constructed without weakening the hold of old systems, which do not take fundamental challenges to their hegemony lightly. A crisis of legitimacy is critical in weakening current structures, but it is not enough. A vision of a new world may be entrancing, but it will remain a vision without a hard strategy for realizing it, and part of that strategy is the deliberate dismantling of the old.

Thus a strategy of *deconstruction* must necessarily proceed alongside one of *reconstruction*.

Deconstruction

The big anti-corporate globalization demonstrations of the last few years have been right in bringing up the strategic demand of dismantling the WTO and the Bretton Woods institutions. Advancing this demand and getting more and more people behind it has been central in creating the crisis of legitimacy of these institutions.

Tactically, however, it would be important to try to bring coalitions together on more broadly acceptable goals, the achievement of which can nevertheless have a big impact in terms of drastically reducing the power of these institutions or effectively neutering them. In the case of the IMF, for instance, a demand that has potential to unite a broad front of people is that of converting it into a research agency with no policy powers but one tasked with the job of monitoring global capital and exchange rate movements—in other words turning it into an advisory and research institution along the lines of the Organisation for Economic Co-operation and Development (OECD).

In the case of the World Bank, uniting with the demand to end its loan-making capacity and devolving its grant activities to appropriate regional institutions marked by participatory processes (which would eliminate the Asian Development and other existing regional development banks as alternatives) could serve as a point of unity for diverse political forces and be a major step to effectively disempowering it. These initiatives could be coordinated with campaigns to boycott World Bank bonds, deny new appropriations for the International Development Association (IDA), and oppose calls for quota increases for the IMF. Unlike the Soros approach, the thrust of this multi-dimensional effort would be not one of reforming but drastically shrinking the power and jurisdiction of the Bretton Woods institutions.

Given its centrality and unique characteristics as a global institution, however, it is the WTO that must be the main target of the deconstruction enterprise . . .

The strategy of the deconstruction enterprise must respond to the needs of the moment in the struggle against corporate-driven globalization. This can be derived only by identifying the strategic objective, accurately assessing the global context or conjuncture, and elaborating an effective strategy and tactical repertoire that responds to the particularities of the conjuncture.

For the movement against corporate-driven globalization, it seems fairly clear that the strategic goal must be halting or reversing WTO-mandated liberalization in trade and trade-related areas. The context or "conjuncture" is characterized by a fragile victory on the part of the free trade globalizers at the Fourth Ministerial at Doha, where they bludgeoned developing countries into agreeing to a limited round of trade talks for more liberalization on agriculture, services and industrial tariffs. The conjuncture is marked by the globalizers' effort to build momentum so as to have the Fifth Ministerial in Mexico launch negotiations for liberalization in the so-called trade-related areas of investment, competition policy, government procurement and trade facilitation. *Their aim is to have the Fifth Ministerial expand the limited set of negotiations they extracted at Doha into a comprehensive round of negotiations that would rival the Uruguay Round.*

This expansion of the free trade mandate and the expansion of the power and jurisdiction of the WTO, which is now the most powerful multilateral instrument of the global corporations, is a mortal threat to development, social justice and equity, and the environment. And it is the goal that we must thwart at all costs, for we might as well kiss goodbye to sustainable development, social justice, equity and the environment if the big trading powers and their corporate elites have their way and launch another global round for liberalization during the WTO's Fifth Ministerial Assembly in Mexico in 2003.

Given the strategic goal of stopping and reversing trade liberalization, the campaign objective on which the movement against corporate-driven globalization must focus its efforts and energies is simple and stark: derailing the drive for free trade at the Fifth Ministerial, which will serve as the key global mechanism for advancing free trade.

. . . [T]he free trade partisan C. Fred Bergsten, head of the Institute of International Economics (IIE), has compared free trade and the WTO to a bicycle: they collapse if they do not move forward. Which is why Seattle was such a mortal threat to the WTO and why the globalizers were so determined to extract a mandate for liberalization at Doha. Had they failed at Doha, the likely prospect was not simply a stalemate but a retreat from free trade. For the movement against corporate-driven globalization, derailing the Fifth Ministerial or preventing agreement on the launching of a new comprehensive round would mean not only fighting the WTO and free trade to a standstill. It would mean creating momentum for a rollback of free trade and a reduction of the power of the WTO. This is well understood by, among others, *The Economist,* which warned its corporate readers that "globalization is reversible."

If derailing the drive for free trade at the 5th Ministerial is indeed the goal, then the main tactical focus of the strategy becomes clear: *consensus decision-making is the Achilles' heel of the WTO, and it is the emergence of consensus that we must prevent at all costs from emerging.*

Before the Fifth Ministerial, the anti-corporate globalization movement must focus its energy on ensuring that countries do not come into agreement in any of the areas now being negotiated or about to be negotiated, that is, agriculture, services and industrial tariffs; and at the Ministerial itself, preventing any consensus from emerging on negotiating the new issues of government procurement, competition policy, investment and trade facilitation. The aim must be, as in Seattle, to have the delegates go to the Ministerial with a "heavily bracketed" declaration—that is, one where there is no consensus on the key issues—and at the Ministerial itself, to prevent consensus via last-minute horse-trading. *As in Seattle, the end goal must be to have the Ministerial end in disagreement and lack of consensus . . .*

Deglobalizing in a Pluralist World

Hand in hand with the deconstruction campaign must unfold the reconstruction process or the enterprise to set up an alternative system of global governance.

There is a crying need for an alternative system of global governance. The idea is floating around that thinking about an alternative system of global governance is a task that for the most part is still in a primeval state. In fact, many or most of the basic or broad principles for an alternative order have already been articulated, *and it is really a question of specifying these broad principles to concrete societies in ways that respect the diversity of societies.*

Work on alternatives has been a collective past and present effort, one to which many in the North and South have contributed. The key points of this collective effort might be synthesized as a double movement of "deglobalization" of the national economy and the construction of a "pluralist system of global economic governance."

The context for the discussion of deglobalization is the increasing evidence not only of the poverty, inequality and stagnation that have accompanied the spread of globalized systems of production but also of their unsustainability and fragility. The International Forum on Globalization (IFG) points out, for instance, that

> the average plate of food eaten in western industrial food-importing nations is likely to have travelled 2,000 miles from source to plate. Each one of those miles contributes to the environmental and social crises of our times. Shortening the distance between producer and consumer has to be one of the crucial reform goals of any transition away from industrial agriculture.[2]

Or as Barry Lynn has asserted, so much industrial production has been outsourced to a few areas such as Taiwan, that, had the earthquake of September 21, 1999 experienced by that island been "a few tenths of a point stronger, or centered a few miles closer to the vital Hsinchu industrial park, great swaths of the world economy could have been paralyzed for months."[3]

What is deglobalization? While the following proposal is derived principally from the experience of societies in the South, it has relevance as well to the economies of the North.

Deglobalization is not about withdrawing from the international economy. It is about reorienting economies from the emphasis on production for export to production for the local market.

- drawing most of a country's financial resources for development from within rather than becoming dependent on foreign investment and foreign financial markets;
- carrying out the long-postponed measures of income redistribution and land redistribution to create a vibrant internal market that would be the anchor of the economy and create the financial resources for investment;
- de-emphasizing growth and maximizing equity in order radically to reduce environmental disequilibrium;
- not leaving strategic economic decisions to the market but making them subject to democratic choice;
- subjecting the private sector and the state to constant monitoring by civil society;
- creating a new production and exchange complex that includes community cooperatives, private enterprises and state enterprises, and excludes TNCs;
- enshrining the principle of subsidiarity in economic life by encouraging production of goods to take place at the community and national level if it can be done at reasonable cost in order to preserve community.

This is, moreover, about an approach that consciously subordinates the logic of the market, the pursuit of cost efficiency, to the values of security, equity and social solidarity. This is, to use the language of the great social democratic scholar Karl Polanyi, about re-embedding the economy in society, rather than having society driven by the economy.[4]

True, efficiency in the narrow terms of constant reduction of unit costs may well suffer, but what will be gained—or perhaps the most appropriate term is regained—are the conditions for the development of integrity, solidarity, community, greater and more democracy, and sustainability.

It is these principles that today drive many bold enterprises that have achieved some success, mainly at a local, community level. As Kevin Danaher of Global Exchange has pointed out, the list includes fair trade arrangements between Southern farmers and Northern consumers in coffee and other commodities, microcredit schemes such as the Grameen Bank, community currency systems delinking exchange from global and national monetary systems and linking it to local production and consumption, participatory budgeting as in Porto Alegre, and sustainable eco-communities such as Gaviotas in Colombia.[5]

The reigning god, however, is a jealous one that will not take lightly challenges to its hegemony. Even the smallest experiment must either be smashed or emasculated, as the imperious Bank of Thailand did when it told several villages in the Kud Chum district in Thailand's Northeast region to abandon their local currency system. Peaceful co-existence between different systems is, unfortunately, ultimately not an option.

Thus deglobalization or the re-empowerment of the local and national, however, can only succeed if it takes place within an alternative system of global economic governance. The emergence of such a system is, of course, dependent on greatly reducing the power of the Western corporations that are the main drivers of globalization and the political and military hegemony of the states—particularly the United States—that protect them. But even as we devise strategies to erode the power of the corporations and the dominant states, we need to envision and already lay the groundwork for an alternative system of global economic governance.

What are the contours of such a world economic order? The answer to this is suggested by our critique of the Bretton Woods-cum-WTO system as a monolithic system of universal rules imposed by highly centralized institutions to further the interests of corporations—and, in particular, U.S. corporations. To try to supplant this with another centralized global system of rules and institutions, although these may be premised on different principles, is likely to reproduce the same Jurassic trap that ensnared organizations as different as IBM, the IMF and the Soviet state, and this is the inability to tolerate and profit from diversity. Incidentally, the idea that the need for one central set of global rules is unquestionable and that the challenge is to replace the neoliberal rules with social democratic ones is a remnant of a techno-optimist variant of Marxism that infuses both the Social Democratic and Leninist visions of the world, producing what Indian author Arundhati Roy calls the predilection for "gigantism."

Today's need is not another centralized global institution but the deconcentration and decentralization of institutional power and the creation of a pluralistic system of institutions and organizations interacting with one another, guided by broad and flexible agreements and understandings.

This is not something completely new. For it was under such a more pluralistic system of global economic governance, where hegemonic power was still far from institutionalized in a set of all-encompassing and powerful multilateral organizations and institutions, that a number of Latin American and Asian countries were able to achieve a modicum of industrial development in the period from 1950 to 1970. It was under such a pluralistic system, under a General Agreement on Tariffs and Trade (GATT) that was limited in its power, flexible and more sympathetic to the special status of developing countries, that the East and Southeast Asian countries were able to become newly industrializing countries through activist state trade and industrial policies that departed significantly from the free market biases enshrined in the WTO.

Of course, economic relations among countries prior to the attempt to institutionalize one global free market system beginning in the early 1980s were not ideal, nor were the Third World economies that resulted ideal. They failed to address a number of needs illuminated by recent advances in feminist, ecological and post-post-development economics. What is simply being pointed out is that the pre-1994 situation underlines the fact that the alternative to an economic Pax Romana built around the World Bank–IMF–WTO system is not a Hobbesian state of nature. The reality of international relations in a world marked by a multiplicity of international and regional institutions that check one another is a far cry from the propaganda image of a "nasty" and "brutish" world the partisans of the WTO evoked in order to stampede the developing country governments to ratify the WTO in 1994.

Of course, the threat of unilateral action by the powerful is ever present in such a system, but it is one that even the most powerful hesitate to take for fear of its consequences on their legitimacy as well as the reaction it would provoke in the form of opposing coalitions.

In other words, what developing countries and international civil society should aim at is not to reform the TNC-driven WTO and Bretton Woods institutions, but, through a combination of passive and active measures, to either a) decommission them; b) neuter them (e.g., converting the IMF into a pure research institution monitoring exchange rates of global capital flows); or c) radically reduce their powers and turn them into just another set of actors co-existing with and being checked by other international organizations, agreements and regional groupings. This strategy would include strengthening diverse actors and institutions such as UNCTAD, multilateral environmental agreements, the International Labor Organization and regional economic blocs.

Regional economic blocs in the South would be important actors in this process of economic devolution. But they would have to be developed beyond their current manifestations in the European Union, Mercosur in Latin America and ASEAN (Association of Southeast Asian Nations) in Southeast Asia.

A key aspect of "strengthening," of course, is making sure these formations evolve in a people-oriented direction and cease to remain regional elite projects. Trade efficiency in neoclassical economic terms should be supplanted as the key criterion of union by "capacity building." That is, trade would have to be reoriented from its present dynamics of locking communities and countries into a division of labour that diminishes their capabilities in the name of "comparative advantage" and "interdependence." It must be transformed into a process that enhances the capacities of communities, that ensures that initial cleavages that develop owing to initial division-of-labour agreements do not congeal into permanent cleavages, and which has mechanisms, including income, capital, and technology-sharing arrangements that prevent exploitative arrangements from developing among trading communities.

Needless to say, the formation of such regional blocs must actively involve not only government and business but also NGOs and people's organizations. Indeed, the agenda of people-oriented sustainable development can succeed only if it is evolved democratically rather than imposed from above by regional elites, as was the case with the European Union, Mercosur and ASEAN. Regional integration has increasingly become an essential condition for national development, but it can be effective only if it is carried out as a project of economic union from below.

Many of the elements of a pluralist system of global economic governance already exist, but there are undoubtedly others that need to be established. Here the emphasis must be on the formation of international and regional institutions that would be dedicated to creating and protecting the space for devolving the greater part of production, trade and economic decision-making to the regional, national and community level. One such institution is the establishment of an effective international organization for the preservation and strengthening of the economies of the hundreds of thousands of indigenous economies throughout the world.

Indeed, a central role of international organizations in a world where toleration of diversity is a central principle of economic organization would be, as the British philosopher John Gray puts it, "to express and protect local and national cultures by embodying and sheltering their distinctive practices."[6]

More space, more flexibility, more compromise—these should be the goals of the Southern agenda and the international civil society effort to build a new system of global economic governance. It is in such a more fluid, less structured, more pluralistic world, with multiple checks and balances, that the nations and communities of the South—and the North—will be able to carve out the space to develop based on their values, their rhythms, and the strategies of their choice.

Notes

1. See Thomas Kuhn, *The Structure of Scientific Revolutions* (Chicago: University of Chicago Press, 1971).
2. John Cavanagh et al., "Alternatives to Economic Globalization," International Forum on Globalization, San Francisco.
3. Barry Lynn, "Unmade in America: The True Cost of a Global Assembly Line," *Harper's*, June 2002, p. 36.
4. See Karl Polanyi, *The Great Transformation* (Boston: Beacon, 1957).
5. Speech at the University of Montana, Missoula, Montana, June 16, 2002.
6. John Gray, *Enlightenment's Wake* (London: Routledge, 1995), p. 181.

A World Without Walls *Freedom, Development, Free Trade and Global Governance*

Mike Moore

Mike Moore directed the World Trade Organization (WTO) when he wrote this selection. He defends here the goal of broadening the WTO's mandate to eliminate barriers to transnational investment beyond its initial responsibility of promoting free trade. Opponents of such a multilateral agreement on investment (MAI) claim that depriving countries of the ability to regulate inflows and outflows of capital makes them vulnerable to sudden shifts in international movements of capital and thus promotes instability. The result is especially harmful to poor countries. Moore counters that creating such a system would make poor countries more attractive sites for foreign investment and would actually reduce sudden outflows of capital (what is called capital flight). He also defends other measures to promote international economic integration, for example, opening government procurement (purchases of goods and services) to international competition. The result would be to lower procurement costs and thereby help consumers and taxpayers. Opponents claim that the major benefits would go to major transnational corporations, who would outbid domestic firms in landing contracts, and that governments would become less able to regulate their economies. Moore further argues that the WTO is the logical international agency to enforce the rules of a more liberalized world economy.

What criticisms of Moore's position have been made in other selections in this and other chapters? What is your evaluation of the debate?

Trade and Investment

. . . Attracting more FDI [foreign direct investment] has become a key economic policy objective for many WTO Members, particularly developing countries, to help them integrate further and faster into the world economy. It brings an attractive foreign capital inflow, one that is comparatively stable, that has no fixed interest payments attached to it, and that contributes directly to productive in-

Mike Moore, *A World Without Walls: Freedom, Development, Free Trade and Global Governance* (Cambridge: Cambridge University Press, 2003): 155–160.

vestment. It also brings entrepreneurship, technology, managerial skills and marketing know-how—assets that are in short supply in many countries and difficult for them to acquire, yet which are vital to helping them raise productivity and accelerate their growth and development.

Broadening the multilateral system to cover foreign investment will help in achieving the WTO's core objectives—improving the allocation and use of resources worldwide and deepening the international division of labour. Foreign investment and trade are complementary. Host countries with open trade policies can hope to attract FDI that is highly competitive and that will help them develop export capacity. A liberal investment regime, that is transparent, non-discriminatory and relies on market forces, reinforces the benefits of a liberal trade regime. It will attract high-quality FDI, with state-of-the-art technology and know-how, which can make a crucial difference to the growth prospects of many WTO Member countries. Which country suffers from too much efficiently directed investment?

FDI has been growing much faster than trade, reaching a record flow of $1.3 trillion in 2000. Yet the bulk of this is still concentrated in the developed countries and a handful of the largest and most advanced developing countries. Others are failing to attract FDI in significant quantities to help supplement their domestic savings and meet their investment needs, despite having adopted in many cases more liberal investment regimes. Part of the explanation is that business still perceives the commercial risk involved to be too high, even in those countries that are actively pursuing bilateral investment treaties with their main partners.

The WTO can help correct this. A multilateral framework that brings greater transparency, stability and predictability to investment policymaking, underwritten by WTO rules, surveillance and dispute settlement arrangements, will help close the current gap between perceived and actual policy risk in the eyes of foreign investors, as it has done in the area of international trade. Lower policy risk means lower commercial risk, which means new, profitable investment opportunities and more investment overall. Further liberalisation of investment policies will reinforce this effect. The WTO cannot influence how FDI is distributed, any more than it can do so for trade flows. But the more FDI there is to go around, the more opportunity each country will have to attract a share of it.

Foreign investment should not only flow along bilateral channels; it should be encouraged to flow internationally, and be made more accessible to those developing and least developed countries most in need of it. However clean rules and transparency would cut out or limit the scope for corruption, which some politicians are reluctant to forgo.

Two groups seem to oppose an agreement on investment: rich country NGOs who talk of investment being a race to the bottom, and some in poor countries who cling to the notion that investment equals colonialism equals exploitation and the "it's all an American plot" theorists. Unfortunately, this view is held strongest by some self-appointed spokespeople for the poor who live in rich countries. The truth is the opposite. Some 80 per cent of FDI by U.S. manufacturing firms in 1998 went to other high wage countries like Britain, Canada, the Netherlands, Germany and Singapore. And the U.S.A. has itself over the last decade been the world's largest recipient of foreign investment.[1]

A better investment climate also increases domestic investment and reduces capital flight, observes Peter Watson, CEO of the Overseas Private Investment Corporation, who quotes former ABB Chairman Percy Barnevik's comments that, while there are masses of potentially profitable projects in the developing countries, only a fraction of the available capital ends up there, and it is also extremely unevenly distributed. "Indeed 12 major developing countries take 75 per cent, while 140 developing countries (including the poorest ones) share 5 per cent." Barnevik asks: "Why do various Arab funds invest in property in London and New York instead of in Egypt, Syria and the Gaza Strip? It is the investment climate."[2]

In reality, U.S. negotiators are at best lukewarm over an investment agreement. The strongest promoters are the EU, Japan and Switzerland. The U.S. economic magnet doesn't need investment rules; the U.S. attracts one-third of the world's FDI.[3] Meanwhile, FDI outflows from the U.S.A. in 1998 to the rest of the world were $133 billion, an increase of 500 per cent over a decade. The rate of outward bound FDI is greater than the rate of increase in trade and is greater than the rate of increase in world output.[4] Ironically, it is the investment-starved nations that need the very rules that many of them oppose for nationalistic political purposes. I've seen developing country ministers oppose even discussing the issue, and then leave to lead inward investment missions to New York and London. Again, we should look at the coherence the Doha Development Agenda offers in addressing these issues.

The mindset of developing countries against FDI has its origins in the fact that so much of it involves mineral and resource extraction, and as such is a bitter reminder of imperialist times. Their anger and fear can be better understood against this historic background. They also see richer countries operating by double standards—wanting to invest in their forests, but then putting tariff escalator clauses on to penalise local added value and local jobs. Equally bewildering is pressure from foreign investors who, once in a protected market, then seek protection from competition while they graze on the "rents" such protection provides. The battle in Mexico between IBM, Hewlett Packard and Apple to enjoy the profits of protection is played out in many countries where "first-in best-served" companies organise disparate coalitions of businesses, unions and local politicians, who band together in the name of sovereignty to prevent future liberalisation or competition. This was also true of small developed countries like New Zealand in the 1980s.

Negotiating a WTO investment agreement is not synonymous with surrendering national economic sovereignty to global capitalism. It's the opposite; it can preserve integrity and transparency, level the playing field, and could set acceptable rules of conduct for multinationals. The Ministerial mandate from Doha provides ample scope for provisions to be included in the eventual agreement that will respect host governments' right to regulate in the public interest and to pursue national development policies and objectives. The special development, trade and financial needs of developing and least developed countries are to be taken fully into account, and obligations and commitments are to be commensurate with these countries' individual needs and circumstances. However, it is one of the most confrontational of issues. Deeply felt views about sovereignty and commercial and political interests make it a minefield. But political appeasement to vested interests is surrender and economic death by instalment.

Transparency in Government Procurement

Governments, inter-governmental organisations and regional groupings around the world recognise the importance of promoting the basic principles of transparency and competition in this area. In the last two decades, many countries have set up or improved their domestic legal framework, often using the UN Commission on International Trade Law (UNCITRAL) Model Law. The World Bank and the regional development banks have not only been promoting the use of their guidelines for procurements related to projects funded by these agencies but have also been participating actively in legislative reform and institution-building efforts in a large number of developing countries. The Asia-Pacific Economic Cooperation (APEC) and the Free Trade Area of the Americas (FTAA) have been developing disciplines reflecting the core principles of transparency. The recognition of the economic importance of government procurement in trade relations also manifests itself in the recent surge of commitments related to government procurement in regional or bilateral agreements.

Governments have been aware of the importance of maintaining principles and disciplines in this area because of the substantial share of procurement in GDP. According to a recent OECD report, government procurement (excluding defence) is estimated to represent 7.6 per cent of the 1998 GDP (US$1,795 billion) for the OECD countries and 5.1 per cent (US$288 billion) for non-OECD countries—equivalent to 30 per cent of the world merchandise and commercial services exports in 1998. Other estimates made for the EC by the Commission (which include the procurement of public utilities) are rather higher, at some 14 per cent. Whatever is the correct figure, it is clear that, since more open and competitive government procurement procedures can often lead to savings of 20 per cent or more, there is very considerable benefit to be further reaped, especially in developing countries where government resources are scarce.

Government procurement is not new to the WTO. A plurilateral agreement, the Agreement on Government Procurement, in effect since 1981, contains rules on market access as well as transparency which are currently binding on twenty-seven WTO Members, with some fifteen others in the process of acceding to that Agreement. Moreover, the General Agreement on Trade in Services (GATS) incorporates provisions mandating multilateral negotiations in services.

The Doha Declaration reflects WTO Members' acceptance that there is a case for a multilateral agreement on transparency in government procurement because of the trade implications of government procurement practices, and the benefits of enhanced international cooperation in this area. The development dimension of procurement will be an important consideration in the negotiations, as they will take into account participants' development priorities, especially those of least developed country participants, and will be limited to the transparency aspects and therefore will not restrict the scope for countries to give preferences to domestic supplies and suppliers.

A WTO agreement laying down principles and disciplines in this area will underpin the domestic reforms that have been undertaken and would help guarantee the effective implementation of national legislation that has been drawn up recently in many developing countries and economies in transition. Many countries are not ready for serious negotiations. With some political parties raising their funds through "friends" who seek government contracts, this area is a goldmine for the corrupt and is another good governance and development issue that needs to be faced.

Trade Facilitation

In the area of trade facilitation, the Doha Ministerial introduced a new stage for WTO work. While the initial mandate restricted the Secretariat to undertaking "exploratory and analytical work," the Doha declaration calls for the preparation of negotiations on this issue. The new mandate bears witness to Members' recognition that trade facilitation efforts need to be reinforced.

Increasing levels of trade liberalisation have become a worldwide reality. Successive GATT rounds significantly reduced traditional trade barriers, but serious practical obstacles in international trade remain. Traders from both the developed and the developing world have repeatedly pointed to the significant red tape that still exists in moving goods across borders. Documentation requirements frequently lack transparency, they are vastly duplicative and vary between countries.

Differing product standards, restrictive and non-transparent administrative regulations and border delays accounting for up to 20 per cent of the overall transport time hamper the integration into the global economy and threaten to undo some of the benefits of recent liberalisation efforts. Experience shows that the cost of complying with administrative procedures often exceeds the cost of duties to be paid. Recent studies indicate that the overall deadweight welfare loss caused by those inefficiencies amounts to $70 billion.

An Inter-American Bank study showed that a truck travelling through three South American countries spent 200 hours on the road, 100 hours of which were delays due to bureaucracy. It costs three times as much to move a container from some African countries to New York than from Hong Kong. APEC studies suggest facilitation gains would add 0.25 per cent to GNP. The small or new businessperson doesn't have the "correct" contacts to push their case. The moral hazard created is dangerous to political life. Removing these hurdles is therefore a must to ensure the full realisation of negotiated trade benefits. In some countries, the richest civil servant in town is the customs officer. One ambassador told me the story in his country of a person who was offered a job in Customs and, on being told of the conditions and pay, asked, "What? I get paid as well?"

Cutting the red tape will benefit both developing and developed countries by encouraging inward investment and trade growth. Facilitating trade means cheaper goods for producers, lower prices for consumers and a more cost-effective recovery of revenue. Experience shows that trade facilitation is not only compatible with revenue collection and enforcement, but even increases the achievement of those objectives. Simplified procedures lower trade transaction costs, improve the investment climate, foster competition and reduce corruption. They further help governments improve their administration, reduce operating costs and detect illicit transactions. Improved rules also help harness private sector support. Gains will be especially high for small and medium-sized enterprises and traders from developing countries, where difficulties created by opaque and cumbersome administrative burdens often keep them from engaging in trade at all.

Many countries have already recognised the numerous benefits of facilitating trade and are actively pursuing steps to facilitate import and export transactions. They see trade facilitation as a competitive advantage and are aware that the costs of non-participation will become increasingly burdensome in terms of lost investment and economic isolation.

As a key organisation for international trade, the WTO has a natural role in setting rules in this field. A rules-based approach will guarantee transparency and predictability for traders, ensure political commitment and steer reform in a consistent direction. A WTO framework would also ensure that regional initiatives develop in the same direction.

WTO rules are therefore necessary to secure many of the key benefits of trade facilitation. Only the WTO can assure the top-down approach required for thorough and lasting reform. At a time of economic turbulence, which has the potential to arouse protectionist sentiments, this is all the more important. If administrative and procedural obstacles risk subverting trade liberalisation, which we have worked so hard for in the WTO over the last fifty years, then the WTO should be part of any solution. Resolving this issue will be good for the taxpayer, consumer and honest businessperson, and bad for corrupt officials and politicians. This is a key development issue. . . .

Notes

1. Daniel T. Griswold. *WTO Report Card: America's Economic Stake in Open Trade*. 2000.
2. Peter S. Watson. *The Economic Arsenal Against Terrorism*. 2002.
3. Stephen Brooks and William Wohlforth. American primacy in perspective. *Foreign Affairs*. July/August 2002.
4. *Report of the President 2000*. 2000.

In Defense of Globalization

Jagdish Bhagwati

Economist Jagdish Bhagwati is a prominent advocate for free trade. In this selection, he argues that, rather than limiting international trade when it produces dislocations such as job displacement, assistance should be provided to workers who, through no fault of their own, are injured by free trade. He argues that this is a win-win situation, since the costs involved in compensating the victims of trade are far less than the overall gains from increased efficiency. The alternative of blocking international trade, on the other hand, is lose-lose, since it results in a loss of efficiency gains for all concerned.

Evaluate the pros and cons of Bhagwati's proposal. Is it an adequate response to criticisms by Cavanagh and Mander, Stiglitz, and Bello in this chapter? Why or why not?

Adjustment Assistance

The idea that we should provide adjustment assistance to workers and industries affected by import competition is not new. Economics itself tells us that free trade (like each policy) can be unambiguously declared to be welfare-enhancing only if those who lose from it can be compensated by taking income from the winners while leaving the winners still better off. Most economists will not be satisfied with this potential-compensation criterion; they will want the compensation to be actually made. To see this clearly, imagine a strongly conservative administration saying, "Free trade is fine because the poor, who have gotten poorer, can be compensated by the rich, who have gotten richer," and then leaving the poor poorer. Not too many people would buy that!

Of course, one cannot do this compensation policy by policy; that would leave lots of policies captive to compensation schemes that actually cut into the policies' beneficial effects through taxes and transfers. Since it is also politically unlikely that such compensation can be attached to every policy change in practice, it is surely more sensible, generally speaking, to go for more general and com-

---

prehensive schemes such as unemployment insurance and retraining programs for all workers who are laid off, for instance.

But then politics kicks in also. In a world where "us" and "them" distinctions between domestic and foreign communities and nations had disappeared and total cosmopolitanism in a borderless world had taken its place, one could settle for fully general unemployment relief and adjustment assistance programs aimed at relief regardless of the source of the distress. Then one would agree with President Ronald Reagan, who complained that the Trade Adjustment Assistance program introduced by President Kennedy in 1962 was in error "because these benefits are paid out on top of normal unemployment benefits, [and therefore] we wind up paying greater benefits to those who lose their jobs because of foreign competition. Anyone must agree that this is unfair."[1]

But, as it happens, workers and citizens generally do not seem to believe that they should be allowed to go to the wall if they lose their jobs to foreign competition, though they are generally less outraged when the job loss is to domestic competition. If a steel mill closes down in Pennsylvania because steel in California has become cheaper, workers tend to accept that as something that happens, and the general unemployment insurance seems to be an adequate way to deal with the bad hand that an unpredictable fate has dealt one. But the same workers get indignant when the loss is to a steel producer in Korea or Brazil, and they go off agitating for anti-dumping action (which has happened often in the past) or a safeguards tariff (as happened recently, under the George W. Bush administration). Or they ask for special relief in the form of additional unemployment compensation, with or without retraining benefits and requirements. With import competition hitting you, the reaction is like that to a natural disaster: the government must intervene with special support. This quasi-xenophobia is just a fact of life. If trade liberalization is to occur and be sustained, one or more of these special programs and policies have to be considered, and working with adjustment assistance rather than protection is the better way to go, since the latter is more expensive.[2]

In fact, President Kennedy introduced the Trade Adjustment Assistance program precisely to ensure union support for congressional approval for launching the Kennedy Round of multilateral trade negotiations. The program helped the president to get the critical AFL-CIO support. As the union's president, George Meany, said: "There is no question whatever that adjustment assistance is essential to the success of trade expansion. And as we have said many times, it is indispensable to our support of the trade program as a whole."[3]

So if the rich countries have these programs, we surely need them in the poor countries as well, and even more so, as the workers who might be laid off are more likely to be close to malnourishment and are often unable to manage and finance transitions to new jobs. Trade liberalization occurs typically without systematic adjustment assistance, and this creates both economic and political risks to its success.

But how is one to finance such adjustment assistance, whatever form it takes? Poor countries typically can ill afford adjustment programs. Many argue that these countries should start by eliminating the defense expenditures that can absorb scarce resources to excess, but hardly any country follows this precept to the degree required.

So we need to think of institutional programs of adjustment assistance that can be domestically implemented but financed externally. The obvious candidate for this task is the World Bank, which should put its money where its proglobalization mouth is. In some cases, it may even be possible to get such financing from the corporate sector: exporting firms may well be willing to buy out opposition from import-competing workers by providing adjustment assistance to the poor governments whose markets they seek to export to. Then again, we know that industries such as the shoe industry in the United States often adjusted to imports by being bought out by the exporting firms, which then offered to use their sales network to turn them into distributive outlets. Such accommodation, which reduces the pain of adjusting to import competition, may also be encouraged by governments where appropriate.

Dispute Settlement Mechanism at the WTO

In 1999, small Caribbean countries that had been enjoying preferential entry into the European markets found themselves facing the prospect of a major loss of markets and export earnings to South American nations. The WTO Dispute Settlement Mechanism had little choice except to find against these preferential schemes, as they violated, without legitimate foundation in WTO law, the MFN principle, which requires that imports from all WTO members must enjoy the most favorable tariff extended to other members.[4]

But while such a finding was absolutely correct in law, its impact was to leave these small and poor Caribbean nations with an estimated loss in their national incomes of up to 15 percent! When oil prices went up almost fourfold in 1973, the effect was a near macroeconomic disaster in the rich countries for almost a decade (and these countries have highly developed institutions and labor markets to facilitate flexible response). But small Caribbean nations are not so blessed. So I telephoned my contacts at the World Bank to see if the Bank was creating a program of special aid to compensate and otherwise assist these countries facing huge losses. While the aid sums would be large for these small countries, they would be negligible as a fraction of what the World Bank spends and disburses. I found that nothing was in the works.

In my view, the Bank should automatically trigger support when the WTO's Dispute Settlement Mechanism brings a significant loss of income and attending adjustment problem for producers in poor countries who have lost market access. Regrettably, the World Bank, which is crippled now by overreach into everything under its so-called comprehensive development strategy, appears to suffer from a lack of appropriate prioritization.

Handling Volatility in Agriculture

The focus of the preceding arguments was on adjustment problems, regardless of which activity they related to. But agriculture (and dependence on one or two primary products for the bulk of exports and often of national income as well), poses special problems related to volatility of prices and earnings, especially in the poor countries of Africa.

These concerns are long-standing and, if anything, have somewhat faded from view. Because they were the principal focus of attention almost a quarter of a century ago, when many poor countries happened to be dependent on a few agricultural and primary exports, there had indeed been some institutional response at the international level. Unfortunately, much international effort went into thinking up so-called commodity schemes aimed at stabilizing prices. But these did not get anywhere in the end because the producing countries were interested in them when prices were down while consuming countries were interested in them when prices were up, the two sets of countries rarely working together. Besides, it is not even clear that prices should be stabilized. If there is a supply disturbance such as a harvest failure, the rise in prices offsets the fall in production and hence is good, not bad, for the farmers in the producing countries.

The international effort to develop commodity schemes, whether to stabilize prices or incomes, was therefore soon seen to be not an optimal or even feasible way to set about the business of handling commodity problems. The result was that the central corrective effort was addressed not to eliminating the volatility of export earnings but to coping with its consequences. Hence, the IMF developed "facilities" in the 1960s and 1970s to extend special loans to the poor countries when their export earnings declined, to be repaid when they went up. The IMF set up its Extended Fund Facility in 1974 to assist countries suffering from balance-of-payments imbalances, whereas the Compensatory Financing Facility, established in the 1960s, was meant to assist countries experiencing an export shortfall or excess import cost that was of a short-term nature and attributable to factors beyond the country's control.[5] It would therefore be incorrect to argue that institutions do not exist today to assist the poor countries to cope with volatility and the economic insecurity that can follow from it.

The question of volatility must be distinguished, however, from the fear that the terms of trade of poor countries' exports are declining over time—that is, that the prices of their primary exports, relative to the prices of their imports of manufactures, are in free fall and therefore these countries face in the world economy a tightening noose round their emaciated necks. The assertion of a historic downward trend was not warranted by the facts, nor was the inference that this non-existing decline would continue! The alleged decline was a product of fallacious comparisons, among them a specious choice of periods such as taking the peak prices of primary products during the Korean War and then looking at their decline in the years thereafter. It is unworthy of attention, leave aside remedial action.

Economic Insecurity and Domestic Institutional Support

But there is a different problem of economic security, most acutely applicable to farmers in the poor countries, where institutional support is necessary but lacking. It arises from the intensification of competition today and the thinning of competitive advantage so that . . . we have knife-edge situations where sudden loss of a market to foreign rivals can occur. A number of potential and actual competitors are in the market today; and small changes in conditions abroad can make them more deadly rivals. I say therefore that comparative advantage today has become kaleidoscopic: a small turn of the instrument and you get a different image, a configuration of costs and prices that suddenly and swiftly turns you from a winner into a loser.

We sometimes hear stories from the field about how farmers turned to commercial crops for sale in world markets, borrowing and investing, only to find themselves suddenly overcome by competitors and pushed into starvation. Similar stories are told, unrelated to globalization, where investments in raising production have led to gluts that ruin the farmers, leading in turn to reduced plantings, which produce shortages and even famines. Economists have for over a century called this particular phenomenon a "cobweb cycle," where increased production leads to lower prices, which trigger lower production, which then leads to higher prices, which then cause more production, and the wheels of the cycle keep turning. The cobweb metaphor is unwittingly apt and ghastly because the cobweb draws into itself the hapless farmers in these countries.

Consider the recent experience in Ethiopia, reported in the *Wall Street Journal*, where farmers responded to market incentives, reinforced by governmental exhortations, to boost production to the point where grain harvests in the latter half of the 1990s averaged 11 million tons annually, about 4 million tons more than in the 1980s. In the bumper years of 2000 and 2001, harvests hit more than 13 million tons.[6] Because the emphasis was on "let's just produce," according to one observer, and there was no thought given to the possibility of a glut, the result was an economic disaster for the farmers. As the *Wall Street Journal* commented:

> In more-developed farming markets, meshing aspects of both the free market and government support, storage facilities would allow grain to be held until prices improved, and crops could be sold on a futures market. Loans might be guaranteed by the government, and farmers protected by crop insurance. Ethiopia's farmers had none of this.[7]

The astonishing and tragic fact is that none of this should have happened since countless numbers of people warned against this risk and highlighted the need to contain it with appropriate policies at the time of the green revolution in India three decades earlier. The Indian government put price support schemes in place, heeding the argument that if the green revolution was allowed to occur without supporting mechanisms to maintain prices as output increased, the price fall could devastate all, and would certainly ruin those who had not been able to produce more, and that an untended green revolution could then usher in a red revolution! One wonders therefore why these obvious caveats were forgotten thirty years later, when the World Bank had a resident mission in Ethiopia. Indeed, one may ask in anger why several million dollars are being spent on lucrative salaries for an immense professional staff when even elementary lessons can be forgotten at great cost to the poor countries.

But to return to the theme of globalization, we need to keep in view the possibility that a shift to internationally traded crops can put farmers at risk. Farmers in the poor countries are often small peasants and are unaware that the shift to global markets carries risks as well. They cannot therefore be expected to ensure that they are sufficiently hedged against such possibilities. It is really up to the governments to provide the required institutional support to handle the downside if and when it arises. As before, given the potentially large scale of assistance involved and given that it must span both import and export commodities, this will require several policy measures: some to provide temporary protection (as in the case of GATT Article 19, often called the Safeguards Clause, which permits countries that run into unanticipated difficulties with negotiated trade tariff reductions to withdraw these concessions) and adjustment assistance instead for export industries that lose external markets and which therefore cannot be helped by temporary import restrictions. Insofar as adjustment assistance requires financial resources, again, the role of aid agencies such as the World Bank becomes relevant to the provision of such appropriate governance.

To conclude: Appropriate handling of the downsides that will undoubtedly occur with integration into the world economy, and in the course of transition to such integration as well, requires a complex set of new policies and institutions. While many of the rich countries, which have gone through a substantial shift to openness in the postwar decades, have already made much of the institutional transition to handle the downside of openness, the poor countries typically have not developed the necessary institutions to handle the intensified challenges of increasing openness to the world economy. But the design and financing of these new institutions and policies cannot be left simply to the governments in these nations. International developmental agencies and rich-country donors also have a role to play, particularly in financing cash-strapped governments when these policies require disbursements of funds and in ensuring that institutional support to manage the downside of openness is rapidly created in the poor countries as well.

Notes

1. Quoted in Steve Charnowitz, "Worker Adjustment: The Missing Ingredient in Trade Policy," *California Management Review* 28, 2 (1986): 163. This excellent article has a most useful history of American efforts at providing adjustment assistance. There have, of course, been changes and yet newer measures since the article was written.

2. This view is developed by me in *Protectionism* (Cambridge: MIT Press, 1988).
3. Quoted in Charnowitz, "Worker Adjustment," 158.
4. All articles related to the case can be found on the Web site of the United States mission to the European Union: http://www.useu.be/issues/bananadossier.html.
5. See *Financial Organization and Operations of the IMF,* Treasurer's Department, International Monetary Fund: Washington D.C., 2001, 42–45.
6. See Roger Thurow, "Behind the Famine in Ethiopia: Glut and Aid Policies Gone Bad," *Wall Street Journal*, July 1, 2003, A1, A4.
7. Ibid., A4.